RONALD GLENN

*The work of science is to substitute facts for appearances
and demonstrations for impressions.*—Ruskin.

# ACTUARIAL MATHEMATICS

*By*

NEWTON L. BOWERS, JR.

HANS U. GERBER

JAMES C. HICKMAN

DONALD A. JONES

CECIL J. NESBITT

*Published by*
THE SOCIETY OF ACTUARIES
1986

**Library of Congress Cataloging-in-Publication Data**

Actuarial mathematics.

Bibliography
Includes index.
1. Insurance—Mathematics.  I. Bowers, Newton
L., 1933–      .  II. Society of Actuaries.
HG8781.A26  1986    368'.01        86-61747
ISBN 0-938959-10-7

First Edition

Printed in the United States of America
97  96  95  94  93  92  91  90  89  5  4  3  2

Edited by Millicent M. Treloar

Art figures and cover design by Knut Einarsen Design
Typesetting by Edwards Brothers, Inc.
Printed by Edwards Brothers, Inc.

# CONTENTS

# CONTENTS

CONTENTS

**Chapter 9
Multiple
Decrement
Models**

**Chapter 10
Valuation Theory
for Pension Plans**

**Chapter 17
Advanced
Multiple Life
Theory**

**Chapter 18
Population
Theory**

**Chapter 19
Theory of
Pension Funding**

**Appendices**

In the years that have passed since the first publication of *Life Contingencies* by C. Wallace Jordan, significant changes have occurred in the mathematical foundations underlying actuarial science. This new textbook on actuarial mathematics, written by five distinguished members of the Society, presents these modern foundations and develops some powerful tools for the actuary of the future.

The stochastic approach used in the text produces functions with the same properties exhibited in the earlier deterministic approaches. But, the work goes considerably beyond this by integrating contingency theory into a structure combining risk theory, economics and population theory.

In its educational approach, the text discussions emphasize basic building blocks and methods. The exercises require students to use those basics to build new structures. The overall result is a text providing skills as well as methods that allow for the calculation of both expected (mean) values and their variances—recognizing the inherent random nature of the underlying information.

The Education and Examination Committee of the Society has directed the project. Warren R. Adams, Director of Education at the start of the project, helped to define the specifications, arranged for the selection of authors and established the needed funding. John W. Paddon, Michael J. Cowell and James J. Murphy, all past General Chairpersons, Judy Faucett, to be General Chairperson in 1987, and Linden N. Cole, Director of Professional Education, have all made major contributions to the project.

Robert J. McKay organized the extensive review process that was undertaken. He was ably assisted by Gylles Binet, John M. Boermeester, Roy Goldman, David L. E. Bates, David A. Hilbrink, Alastair G. Longley-Cook and James M. Robinson.

William A. Halvorson, Past President, and Anna M. Rappaport, past Chairperson of the Education Policy Committee, both helped to support and nurture the project through to completion.

The Board of Governors of the Society of Actuaries is most appreciative of the efforts of Professors Bowers, Gerber, Hickman, Jones and Nesbitt in producing this seminal textbook that helps advance the foundations of our profession into the twenty-first century.

HAROLD G. INGRAHAM, JR.
President

CURTIS E. HUNTINGTON
General Chairperson
Education and Examination
Committee

M. DAVID R. BROWN
Chairperson
Education Policy Committee

November 1986

NEWTON L. BOWERS, JR., Ph.D., FSA, MAAA studied at Yale University, 1954, BS, and the University of Minnesota, 1965, Ph.D. From 1954 to 1959, he was at the New York Life Insurance Company. After graduate work at the University of Minnesota and the University of California, San Diego, he joined the faculty at the University of Michigan, 1965 to 1969. Since 1969, he has been at Drake University's College of Business Administration where he is Centennial Professor of Actuarial Science. Professor Bowers' research activities are in pension funding and risk theory. In 1981, he shared the David Garrett Halmstad Memorial Prize with Professors Hickman and Nesbitt for the article "Notes on the Dynamics of Pension Funding."

HANS U. GERBER, Ph.D., ASA was born in Switzerland in 1943. He studied mathematics at the Swiss Federal Institute of Technology in Zurich under Hans Bühlmann, receiving his Ph.D. in 1969. From 1970 to 1971 and from 1972 to 1981, he was on the faculty of the University of Michigan. He was at the University of Rochester from 1969 to 1970, and at the Swiss Life Insurance and Pension Company from 1971 to 1972. Since 1981, he has been on the faculty of the École des H.E.C. (Business School) of the University of Lausanne, Switzerland. Professor Gerber's research activities are in risk theory and applied probability. He is coeditor of the journal *Insurance: Mathematics and Economics*. His monograph, "An Introduction to Mathematical Risk Theory," was published by the Huebner Foundation in 1980.

JAMES C. HICKMAN, Ph.D., FSA, ACAS, EA, MAAA, was born in Indianola, Iowa. Following service in the U.S. Army Air Force, he studied at Simpson College, 1950, BA, and the University of Iowa, MS, 1952. From 1952 to 1957, he was on the actuarial staff of Bankers Life Company. In 1961, he receivied a Ph.D. from the University of Iowa. From 1961 to 1972, he was a member of the faculty, Department of Statistics, University of Iowa. Since 1972, he has been Professor, Business and Statistics, University of Wisconsin, Madison where he is Dean, School of Business. He has served the Society of Actuaries as a member of the Board of Governors, 1971 to 1974, and as a Vice President, 1975 to 1977. In addition, he has contributed papers on a number of different topics to the *Transactions* of the Society of Actuaries.

DONALD A. JONES, Ph.D., ASA, EA, MAAA received a BS from Iowa State College in 1952 and an MS, 1956, and Ph.D. in Mathematical Statistics, 1959, from the State University of Iowa. Since 1959, he has been on the actuarial faculty at the University of Michigan. He has also taught in the summer program at Northwestern Mutual Life Insurance Company. In addition, since 1967 he has been a consulting actuary, currently Vice President of Ann Arbor Actuaries, Incorporated. He has served as a consultant to the Michigan Insurance Bureau and the Employees Retirement System of Puerto Rico among other assignments. His research interests are in the actuarial applications of statistics.

CECIL J. NESBITT, Ph.D., FSA, MAAA, received his mathematical education at the University of Toronto and at the Institute for Advanced Study in Princeton. He taught actuarial mathematics at the University of Michigan from 1938 to 1980 and in summer programs at John Hancock and Northwestern Mutual Life Insurance Companies. Since 1981, he has been Research Director for the Actuarial Education and Research Fund. He became a Fellow of the Society of Actuaries in 1946, was Chairman of the Committee on Research, 1971 to 1973, was a member of the Board of Governors, 1974 to 1977, and is now Vice President for Research and Studies. His activities at the American Academy of Actuaries have included social insurance issues. He also serves on the International Actuarial Association's Permanent Committee on Notation. He is coauthor, with Marjorie V. Butcher, of the 1971 textbook, *Mathematics of Compound Interest*.

## Introduction

This text represents a first step in communicating the revolution in the actuarial profession that is taking place in this age of high-speed computers. During the short period of time since the invention of the microchip, actuaries have been freed from numerous constraints of primitive computing devices in designing and managing insurance systems. They are now able to focus more of their attention on creative solutions to society's demands for financial security.

To provide an educational basis for this focus, the major objectives of this work are to integrate life contingencies into a full risk theory framework and to demonstrate the wide variety of constructs which are then possible to build from basic models at the foundation of actuarial science. Actuarial science is ever evolving and the procedures for model building in risk theory are at its forefront. Therefore, we examine the nature of models before proceeding with a more detailed discussion of the text.

Intellectual and physical models are constructed either to organize observations into a comprehensive and coherent theory or to enable us to simulate, in a laboratory or a computer system, the operation of the corresponding full scale entity. Models are absolutely essential in science, engineering, and the management of large organizations. One must, however, always keep in mind the sharp distinction between a model and the reality it represents. A satisfactory model captures enough of reality to give insights into the successful operation of the system it represents.

The insurance models developed in this text have proved useful and have deepened our insights about insurance systems. Nevertheless, we need to always keep before us the idea that real insurance systems operate in an environment that is more complex and dynamic than the models studied here. Because models are only approximations of reality, the work of model building is never done; approximations can be improved and reality may shift. It is a continuing endeavor of any scientific discipline to revise and update its basic models. Actuarial science is no exception.

Actuarial science developed at a time when mathematical tools (probability and calculus, in particular), the necessary data (especially mortality data in the form of life tables), and the socially perceived need (to protect families and businesses from the financial consequences of untimely death) coexisted. The models constructed at the genesis of actuarial science are still useful. However, the general environment in which actuarial science exists continues to change and it is necessary to periodically restate the fundamentals of actuarial science in response to these changes.

We illustrate this with three examples:

1. The insurance needs of modern societies are evolving and, in response, new systems of employee benefits and social insurance have developed. New models for these systems have been needed and constructed.

2. Mathematics has also evolved, and some concepts that were not available for use in building the original foundations of actuarial science are now part of a general mathematics education. If actuarial science is to remain in the mainstream of the applied sciences, it is necessary to recast basic models in the language of contemporary mathematics.

3. Finally, as previously stated, the development of high-speed computing equipment has greatly increased the ability to manipulate complex models. This has far reaching consequences for the degree of completeness that can be incorporated into actuarial models.

This work features models that are fundamental to the current practice of actuarial science. They are explored with tools acquired in the study of mathematics, in particular, undergraduate level calculus and probability. The proposition guiding Chapters 1–13 is that there is a set of basic models at the heart of actuarial science that should be studied by all students aspiring to practice within any of the various actuarial specialities. These models are constructed using only a limited number of ideas. We will find many relationships among those models that lead to a unity in the foundations of actuarial science. These basic models are followed, in Chapters 14–19, by some more elaborate models particularly appropriate to life insurance and pensions.

While this treatise is intended to be comprehensive, it is not meant to be exhaustive. In order to avoid any misunderstanding, we will indicate the limitations of the text:

• Mathematical ideas that could unify and, in some cases, simplify the ideas presented, but which are not included in typical undergraduate courses, are not used. For example, moment generating functions, but not characteristic functions, are used in developments regarding probability distributions. Stieltjes integrals, which could be used in some cases to unify the presentation of discrete and continuous cases, are not used because of this basic decision on mathematical prerequisites.

• The chapters devoted to life insurance stress the randomness of the time at which a claim payment must be made. In the same chapters, the interest rates used to convert future payments to a present value are considered deterministic and are usually taken as constants. In view of the high volatility possible in interest rates, it is natural to ask why probability models for interest rates were not incorporated. Our answer is that the mathematics of life contingencies on a probabilistic foundation (except for interest) does not involve ideas beyond those covered in an undergraduate program. On the other hand, the modeling of interest rates requires ideas from economics and statistics that are not included in the prerequisites of this volume. In addition, there are some technical problems in building models to combine random interest and random time of claim that are only in the process of being solved at the time of this publication.

- Methods for estimating the parameters of basic actuarial models from observations are not covered. For example, the construction of life tables is not discussed.
- This is not a text on computing. The issues involved in optimizing the organization of input data and computation in actuarial models are not discussed. This is a rapidly changing area, seemingly best left for readers to resolve as they choose in light of their own resources. Simulation, which is a useful method for studying models with random components, also is not included. Computation in terms of classical commutation functions is indicated briefly after the main development of a topic has been presented in terms of basic functions. This provides one choice of computing method for the reader.
- Many important actuarial problems created by long-term practice and insurance regulation are not discussed. This is true in sections treating topics such as premiums actually charged for life insurance policies, costs reported for pensions, restrictions on benefit provisions, and financial reporting as required by regulators.
- Ideas that lead to interesting puzzles, but which do not appear in basic actuarial models, are avoided. Average age at death problems for a stationary population do not appear for this reason.

This text has a number of features that distinguish it from previous fine textbooks on life contingencies. A number of these features represent decisions by the authors on material to be included and will be discussed under headings suggestive of the topics involved.

**Probability Approach:**

As indicated earlier, the sharpest break between the approach taken here and that taken in earlier English language textbooks on actuarial mathematics is the much fuller use of a probabilistic approach in the treatment of the mathematics of life contingencies. Actuaries have usually written and spoken of applying probabilities in their models but their results could be, and often were, obtained by a deterministic rate approach. In this work, the treatment of life contingencies is based on the assumption that time-until-death is a continuous type random variable. This admits a rich field of random variable concepts such as distribution function, probability density function, expected value, variance and moment generating function. This approach is timely, based on the availability of high-speed computers, and is called for, based on the observation that the economic role of life insurance and pensions can be best seen when the random value of time-until-death is stressed. Also, these probability ideas are now part of general education in mathematics, and a fuller realization thereof relates life contingencies to other fields of applied probability, for example, reliability theory in engineering.

Additionally, the deterministic rate approach is described for completeness and is a tool in some developments. However, the results obtained from using a deterministic model usually can be obtained as expected values in a probabilistic model.

### Integration with Risk Theory:

Risk theory is defined as the study of deviations of financial results from those expected and methods of avoiding inconvenient consequences from such deviations. The probabilistic approach to life contingencies makes it easy to incorporate long-term contracts into risk theory models and, in fact, makes life contingencies only a part, but a very important one, of risk theory. Ruin theory, another important part of risk theory, is included as it provides insight into one source, the insurance claims, of adverse long-term financial deviations. This source is the most unique aspect of models for insurance enterprises.

### Utility Theory:

This text contains topics on the economics of insurance. The goal is to provide a motivation, based on a normative theory of individual behavior in the face of uncertainty, for the study of insurance models. Although the models used are highly simplified, they lead to insights into the economic role of insurance, and to an appreciation of some of the issues that arise in making insurance decisions.

### Consistent Assumptions:

The assumption of a uniform distribution of deaths in each year of age is consistently used to evaluate actuarial functions at nonintegral ages. This eliminates some of the anomalies that have been observed when inconsistent assumptions are applied in situations involving high interest rates.

## Guide to Study

The reader could consider this text as covering the two branches of risk theory. Individual risk theory views each policy as a unit and allows construction of a model for a group of policies by adding the financial results for the separate policies in the group. Collective risk theory uses a probabilistic model for total claims that avoids the step of adding the results for individual policies. This distinction is sometimes difficult to maintain in practice. However, the chapters can be classified as illustrated below.

**Classification of Chapters by Branch of Risk Theory**

| Individual Risk Theory | Collective Risk Theory |
|---|---|
| 1,2,3,4,5,6,7,8,9,10, 14,15,16,17 | 1,11,12,13,18,19 |

It is also possible to divide insurance models into those appropriate for short-term insurance, where investment income is not a significant factor, and long-term insurance, where investment income is important. The following classification scheme provides this division of chapters along with an additional division of long-term models between those for life insurance and those for pensions.

**Chapters Classified by Term of Insurance and Field of Application**

| Short-Term Insurance | Long-Term Insurance | |
| | Life Insurance | Pensions |
|---|---|---|
| 1,2,11,12,13 | 3,4,5,6,7,8,9 14,15,16,17 | 3,5,8,9,10 18,19 |

The selection of topics, and their organization, does not follow a traditional pattern. As stated previously, the new organization arose from the goal to first cover material considered basic for all actuarial students (Chapters 1–13) and then to include a more in-depth treatment of selected topics for students specializing in life insurance and pensions (Chapters 14–19).

The discussion in Chapter 1 is devoted to the ideas that random events can disrupt the plans of decision makers and that insurance systems are designed to reduce the adverse financial effects of these events. To illustrate the latter idea, single insurance policies are discussed and convenient, if not necessarily realistic, distributions of the loss random variable are used. In subsequent chapters, more detailed models are constructed for use with insurance systems.

In Chapter 2 the individual risk model is developed, first in regard to single policies, then in regard to a portfolio of policies. In this model, a random variable $S$, the total claims in a single period, is the sum of a fixed number of independent random variables each of which is associated with a single policy. Each component of the sum $S$ can take either the value 0 or a random claim amount in the course of a single period.

From the viewpoint of risk theory, the ideas developed in Chapters 3 through 10 can be seen as extending the ideas of Chapter 2. Instead of considering the potential claims in a short period from an individual policy, we consider loss variables which take into account the financial results of several periods. Since such random variables are no longer restricted to a short time period, they reflect the time value of money. For groups of individuals, one can then proceed, as in Chapter 2, to use an approximation such as the normal approximation, to make probability statements about the sum of the random variables in respect to the individual members.

In Chapter 3 the time-of-death is treated as a continuous random variable and, after defining the probability density function, several features of the probability distribution are introduced and explored. In Chapters 4 and 5 life insurances and annuities are introduced and the present value of the benefits is expressed as a function of the time of death. From this, expected values and variances of the financial random variables are calculated. In Chapter 6 the principle of equivalence is introduced and used to define and evaluate periodic net premiums. In Chapter 7, the prospective future loss on a contract already in force is investigated and the reserve is defined as the expected value of this loss. In Chapter 8, annuity and insurance contracts involving two lives are studied. (The discussion of more advanced multiple life theory is deferred until Chapter 17.) The discussion in Chapters 9 and 10 investigates a more realistic model in which several causes of decrement are possible. In Chapter 9 basic theory is examined while in Chapter 10 the theory is applied to calculating actuarial present values for pension plans.

In Chapter 11, the collective risk model is developed in regard to single period considerations of a portfolio of policies. The distribution of total claims for the period is developed by postulating the characteristics of the portfolio in the aggregate rather than as a sum of individual policies. In Chapter 12 these ideas are extended to a continuous time model that can be used to study solvency requirements over a long time period. Applications of risk theory to insurance models are overviewed in Chapter 13.

Elaboration of the individual model to incorporate operational constraints such as acquisition and administrative expenses, accounting requirements and the effects of contract terminations are treated in Chapters 14 and 15. In Chapter 16, individual risk theory models are used to obtain actuarial present values, net and gross premiums, and net premium reserves for selected special plans including life annuities with certain periods, variable and flexible products, and disability insurance. In Chapter 17, the elementary models for plans involving two lives are extended to incorporate contingencies based on a larger number of lives and more complicated benefits.

In Chapter 18, concepts of population theory are introduced. These concepts are then applied to tracing the progress of life insurance benefits provided on a group, or population, basis. In Chapter 19 the tools from population theory are applied to tracing the progress of retirement income benefits provided on a group basis.

The following diagram indicates the prerequisite structure of chapters within the text.

**Interrelationships of Chapters**

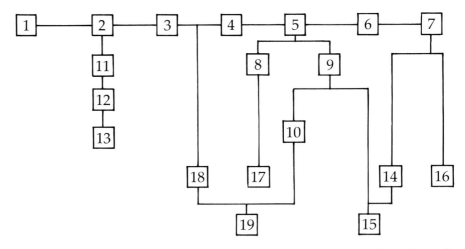

We have a couple of hints for the reader, particularly for those for whom the material is new. The exercises are an important part of the text and include material not covered in the main discussion. In some cases, hints will be offered to aid in the solution. Answers to all exercises are provided except where the answer is given in the formulation of the problem. Writing computer programs and using electronic spreadsheets for the evaluation of basic formulas are excellent ways of determining the level of understanding of the material. The student is encouraged to use these tools even though no specific exercises of this nature are set out in this work.

We conclude these introductory comments with some miscellaneous information on the format of the text. First, each chapter concludes with a reference section providing guidance to those who wish to pursue further study of the topics covered in the chapter. These sections also contain comments relating the ideas used in insurance models to those used in other areas.

Second, Chapters 1, 11, 12, 13 and 17 contain some theorems with their proofs included as chapter appendices. These proofs are included for completeness, but are not essential to an understanding of the material. They may be excluded from study at the discretion of the student. Exercises associated with these appendices should also be considered optional.

Third, general appendices appear at the end of the text. Included here are numerical tables for computations for examples and exercises, an index to notation, a discussion of general rules for writing actuarial symbols, reference citations, answers to exercises, a subject index, and supplemental mathematical formulas that are not assumed to be a part of the mathematical prerequisites.

Fourth, we observe two notational conventions. A referenced random variable, $X$ for example, is designated with a capital letter. This notational convention is not used in older texts on probability theory. We will use the general abbreviation, log, to refer to natural (base e) logarithms, as a distinction between natural and common logarithms is unnecessary in the examples and exercises. We assume the natural logarithm in our computations.

Fifth, currencies such as dollar, pound, lira, yen and so on are not specified in the examples and exercises due to the international character of the required computations.

Finally, as prerequisites to this work have been discussed, some major theorems from undergraduate calculus and probability theory will be used without review or restatement in the discussions and exercises.

# Chapter 1
## THE ECONOMICS OF INSURANCE

## 1.1
## Introduction

Each of us makes plans and has expectations about the path his or her life will follow. However, experience teaches that plans will not unfold with certainty and sometimes expectations will not be realized. Occasionally plans are frustrated because they are built on unrealistic assumptions. In other situations, fortuitous circumstances interfere. Insurance is designed to protect against serious financial reversals that may result from random events intruding on the plans of individuals.

We should understand certain basic limitations on insurance protection. First, it is restricted to reducing those consequences of random events that can be measured in monetary terms. Other types of losses may be important, but not amenable to reduction through insurance.

For example, pain and suffering may be caused by a random event. However, insurance coverages designed to compensate for pain and suffering often have been troubled by the difficulty of measuring the loss in monetary units. On the other hand, economic losses may be caused by events such as property set on fire by its owner. While the monetary terms of such losses may be easy to define, the events are not insurable because of the nonrandom nature of creating the losses.

A second basic limitation is that insurance does not directly reduce the probability of loss. The existence of windstorm insurance will not alter the probability of a destructive storm. However, a well-designed insurance system often will provide financial incentives for loss prevention activities. An insurance product that encouraged the destruction of property or the withdrawal of a productive person from the labor force would affect the probability of these economically adverse events. Such insurance would not be in the public interest.

Several examples of situations where random events may cause financial losses are the following:
- The destruction of property by fire or storm is usually considered a random event in which the loss can be measured in monetary terms.
- A damage award imposed by a court as a result of a negligent act is often considered a random event with resulting monetary loss.
- Prolonged illness may strike at an unexpected time and result in financial losses. These losses will be due to extra health care expenses and reduced earned income.
- The death of a young adult may occur while long-term commitments to family or business remain unfulfilled. Or, if the individual survives to an advanced age, resources for meeting the costs of living may be depleted.

These examples are designed to illustrate the definition:

An *insurance system* is a mechanism for reducing the adverse financial impact of random events that prevent the fulfillment of reasonable expectations.

It is helpful to make certain distinctions between insurance and related systems. Banking institutions were developed for the purpose of receiving, investing and dispensing the savings of individuals and corporations. The cash flows in and out of a savings institution do not follow deterministic paths. However, unlike insurance systems, savings institutions do not make payments based on the size of a financial loss occurring from an event outside the control of the person suffering the loss.

Another system that does make payments based on the occurrence of random events is gambling. Gambling or wagering, however, stands in contrast to an insurance system in that an insurance system is designed to protect against the economic impact of risks that exist independently of, and are largely beyond the control of, the insured. The typical gambling arrangement is established by defining payoff rules about the occurrence of a contrived event and the risk is voluntarily sought by the participants. Like insurance, a gambling arrangement typically redistributes wealth, but it is there that the similarity ends.

Our definition of an insurance system is purposefully broad. It encompasses systems that cover losses in both property and human-life values. It is intended to cover insurance systems based on individual decisions to participate as well as systems where participation is a condition of employment or residence.

The economic justification for an insurance system is that it contributes to general welfare by improving the prospect that plans will not be frustrated by random events. Such systems may also increase total production by encouraging individuals and corporations to embark on ventures where the possibility of large losses would inhibit such projects in the absence of insurance. The development of marine insurance, for reducing the financial impact of the perils of the sea, is an example of this point. Foreign trade permitted specialization and more efficient production, yet mutually advantageous trading activity might be too hazardous for some potential trading partners without an insurance system to cover possible losses at sea.

## 1.2
## Utility Theory

If people could foretell the consequences of their decisions, their lives would be simpler but less interesting. We would all make decisions on the basis of preferences for certain consequences. However, we do not possess perfect foresight. At best we can select an action that will lead to one set of uncertainties rather than another. An elaborate theory has been developed that provides insights into decision making in the face of uncertainty. This body of knowledge is called *utility theory*. Because of its relevance to insurance systems, its main points will be outlined here.

One solution to the problem of decision making in the face of uncertainty is to define the value of an economic project with a random outcome to be its expected value. By this *expected value principle* the distribution of possible outcomes may be replaced for decision pur-

# THE ECONOMICS OF INSURANCE

poses by a single number, the expected value of the random monetary outcomes. By this principle, a decision maker would be indifferent between assuming the random loss $X$ and paying amount $E[X]$ in order to be relieved of the possible loss. Similarly, a decision maker would be willing to pay up to $E[Y]$ to participate in a gamble with random payoff $Y$. In economics the expected value of random prospects with monetary payments is frequently called the *fair* or *actuarial value* of the prospect.

Many decision makers do not adopt the expected value principle. For them, their wealth level and other aspects of the distribution of outcomes influence their decisions.

Below is an illustration designed to show the inadequacy of the expected value principle for a decision maker considering the value of accident insurance. In all cases, it is assumed that the probability of an accident is 0.1 and the probability of no accident is 0.9. Three cases are considered according to the amount of loss arising from an accident; the expected loss is tabulated for each.

| Case | Possible Losses | | Expected Loss |
|------|-----|------|------|
| 1 | 0 | 1 | 0.1 |
| 2 | 0 | 1 000 | 100.0 |
| 3 | 0 | 100 000 | 10 000.0 |

A loss of 1 might be of little concern to the decision maker who then might be unwilling to pay more than the expected loss to obtain insurance. However, the loss of 100,000, which may exceed his net worth, could be catastrophic. In this case, the decision maker might well be willing to pay more than the expected loss of 10,000 in order to obtain insurance. The fact that the amount a decision maker would pay for protection against a random loss may differ from the expected value suggests that the expected value principle is inadequate to model behavior.

We will now study another approach to explain why a decision maker may be willing to pay more than the expected value. At first we shall simply assume that the value or utility that a particular decision maker attaches to wealth of amount $w$, measured in dollars, can be specified in the form of a function $u(w)$, to be called a *utility function*. We shall demonstrate a procedure by which a few values of such a function can be determined. For this we will assume that our decision maker has wealth equal to 20,000. As we shall see, a linear transformation,

$$u^*(w) = a\,u(w) + b \quad a > 0,$$

yields a function $u^*(w)$, which is essentially equivalent to $u(w)$. It then follows by choice of $a$ and $b$ that we can determine arbitrarily the 0 point and one additional point of an individual's utility function. Therefore, we will fix $u(0) = -1$ and $u(20,000) = 0$. These values are plotted on the solid line in Figure 1.1.

**Figure 1.1
Determination of a
Utility Function**

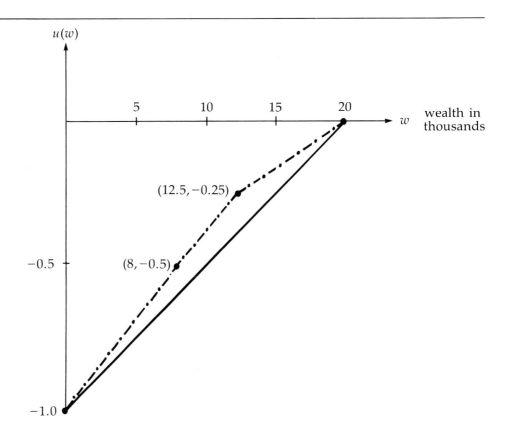

We now ask a question of our decision maker: Suppose you face a loss of 20,000 with probability 0.5, and will remain at your current level of wealth with probability 0.5. What is the maximum amount* G you would be willing to pay for complete insurance protection against this random loss? We can express this question in the following way: For what value of G does

$$u(20{,}000 - G) = 0.5\,u(20{,}000) + 0.5\,u(0)$$
$$= (0.5)(0) + (0.5)(-1) = -0.5?$$

If he pays amount G, his wealth will certainly remain at $20{,}000 - G$. The equal sign indicates that the decision maker is indifferent between paying G with certainty and accepting the expected utility of wealth expressed on the right-hand side.

---

*Premium quantities, by convention in insurance literature, are capitalized although they are not random variables.

# THE ECONOMICS OF INSURANCE

Suppose the decision maker's answer is $G = 12{,}000$. Therefore,

$$u(20{,}000 - 12{,}000) = u(8000) = -0.5.$$

This result is plotted on the dashed line in Figure 1.1. Perhaps the most important aspect of the decision maker's response is that he is willing to pay an amount for insurance that is greater than

$$(0.5)(0) + (0.5)(20{,}000) = 10{,}000,$$

the expected value of the loss.

This procedure can be used to add as many points $[w, u(w)]$, for $0 \leq w \leq 20{,}000$, as needed to obtain a satisfactory approximation to the utility of wealth function. Once a utility value has been assigned to wealth levels $w_1$ and $w_2$, where $0 \leq w_1 < w_2 \leq 20{,}000$, we can determine an additional point by asking the decision maker the following question: What is the maximum amount you would pay for complete insurance against a situation that could leave you with wealth $w_2$ with specified probability $p$, or at reduced wealth level $w_1$ with probability $1 - p$? We are asking the decision maker to fix a value $G$ such that

$$u(w_2 - G) = (1 - p)u(w_1) + pu(w_2). \qquad (1.2.1)$$

Once the value $w_2 - G = w_3$ is available, the point $[w_3, (1-p)u(w_1) + pu(w_2)]$ is determined as another point of the utility function. Such a process has been used to assign a fourth point $(12{,}500, -0.25)$ in Figure 1.1.

After a decision maker has determined his utility of wealth function by the method outlined, the function can be used to compare two random economic prospects. The prospects will be denoted by the random variables $X$ and $Y$. We seek a decision rule that will be consistent with the preferences already elicited in the determination of the utility of wealth function. Thus if the decision maker has wealth $w$, and must compare the random prospects $X$ and $Y$, the decision maker will select $X$ if

$$E[u(w + X)] > E[u(w + Y)],$$

and the decision maker will be indifferent between $X$ and $Y$ if

$$E[u(w + X)] = E[u(w + Y)].$$

Although the method of eliciting and using a utility function may seem plausible, it is clear that our informal development must be augmented by a more rigorous chain of reasoning if utility theory is to provide a coherent and comprehensive framework for decision making in the face of uncertainty. If we are to understand the economic role of insurance, such a framework is needed. An outline of this more rigorous theory follows.

The theory starts with the assumption that a rational decision maker, when faced with two distributions of outcomes affecting wealth, will be able to express a preference for one of the distributions or indifference between them. Furthermore, the preferences must satisfy certain consistency requirements. The theory culminates in a theorem stating that if preferences satisfy the consistency requirements, there is a utility function $u(w)$ such that if the distribution of $X$ is preferred to the distribution of $Y$, $E[u(X)] > E[u(Y)]$, and if the decision maker is indifferent between the two distributions, $E[u(X)] = E[u(Y)]$. That is, the qualitative preference or indifference relation may be replaced by a consistent numerical comparison. In Section 1.6, references are given for the detailed development of this theory.

Before turning to applications of utility theory for insights into insurance, we shall record some observations about utility.

**Observation:**

1. Utility theory is built on the assumed existence and consistency of preferences for probability distributions of outcomes. A utility function should reveal no surprises. It is a numerical description of existing preferences.

2. A utility function need not, in fact cannot, be determined uniquely. For example, if

$$u^*(w) = a\,u(w) + b \qquad a > 0,$$

then

$$E[u(X)] > E[u(Y)]$$

is equivalent to

$$E[u^*(X)] > E[u^*(Y)].$$

That is, preferences are preserved when the utility function is an increasing linear transformation of the original form. This fact was used in the Figure 1.1 illustration where two points were chosen arbitrarily.

3. Suppose the utility function is linear; that is,

$$u(w) = a\,w + b \qquad a > 0.$$

Then, if $E[X] = \mu_X$ and $E[Y] = \mu_Y$, we have

$$E[u(X)] = a\,\mu_X + b > E[u(Y)] = a\,\mu_Y + b$$

if and only if $\mu_X > \mu_Y$. That is, for increasing linear utility functions, preferences for distributions of outcomes are in the same order as the expected values of the distributions being compared. Therefore, the expected value principle for rational economic behavior in the face of uncertainty is consistent with the expected utility rule when the utility function is an increasing linear one.

## 1.3
## Insurance and Utility

In Section 1.2 we outlined utility theory for the purpose of gaining insights into the economic role of insurance. To examine this role we start with an illustration. Suppose a decision maker owns a property that may be damaged or destroyed in the next accounting period. The amount of the loss, which may be 0, is a random variable to be denoted by $X$. We shall assume that the distribution of $X$ is known. Then $E[X]$, the expected loss in the next period, may be interpreted as the long-term average loss if the experiment of exposing the property to damage may be observed under identical conditions a great many times. It is clear that this long-term set of trials could not be performed by an individual decision maker.

Suppose that an insurance organization (*insurer*) was established to help reduce the financial consequences of the damage or destruction of property. The insurer would issue contracts (*policies*) that would promise to pay the owner of a property a defined amount equal to or less than the financial loss if the property were damaged or destroyed during the period of the policy. The contingent payment linked to the amount of the loss is called a *claim* payment. In return for the promise contained in the policy, the owner of the property (*insured*) pays a consideration (*premium*).

The amount of the premium payment is determined following the adoption of an economic decision principle by each of the insurer and insured. An opportunity exists for a mutually advantageous insurance policy when the premium for the policy set by the insurer is less than the maximum amount that the property owner is willing to pay for insurance.

Within the range of financial outcomes for an individual insurance policy, the insurer's utility function might be approximated by a straight line. In this case, the insurer would adopt the expected value principle in setting its premium, as indicated in Section 1.2, Observation 3. That is, the insurer would set its basic price for full insurance coverage as the expected loss, $E[X] = \mu$. In this context $\mu$ is called the *pure* or *net premium* for the 1-period insurance policy. To provide for expenses, taxes, profit, and for some security against adverse loss experience, the insurance system would decide to set the premium for the policy by *loading*, adding to, the pure premium. For instance, the loaded premium, denoted by $H$, might be given by

$$H = \mu(1 + \theta) + c \qquad \theta > 0, c > 0.$$

In this expression the quantity $\mu\theta$ can be viewed as being associated with expenses that vary with expected losses and with the risk that claims experience will deviate from expected. The constant $c$ provides for expected expenses that do not vary with losses. Later we will illustrate other economic principles for determining premiums that might be adopted by the insurer.

We now apply utility theory to the decision problems faced by the owner of the property subject to loss. The property owner has a utility of wealth function $u(w)$ where wealth $w$ is measured in monetary terms. The owner faces a possible loss due to random events that may damage the property. The distribution of the random loss $X$ is assumed known. Much as in (1.2.1), the owner will be indifferent between paying an amount $G$ to the insurer, having the insurer assume the random financial loss, and assuming the risk himself. This situation can be stated as

$$u(w - G) = E[u(w - X)]. \qquad (1.3.1)$$

The right-hand side of (1.3.1) represents the expected utility of not buying insurance when the owner's current wealth is $w$. The left-hand side of (1.3.1) represents the expected value of paying $G$ for complete financial protection.

If the owner has an increasing linear utility function,

$$u(w) = bw + d,$$

the owner will be adopting the expected value principle. In this case (1.3.1) becomes

$$u(w - G) = b(w - G) + d = E[u(w - X)] = E[b(w - X) + d]$$
$$b(w - G) + d = b(w - \mu) + d$$
$$G = \mu.$$

That is, if the owner has an increasing linear utility function, the premium payment that will make the owner indifferent between complete insurance and no insurance is equal to the expected loss. In the absence of a subsidy an insurer, over the long term, must charge more than its expected losses. Therefore in this case, there seems to be little opportunity for a mutually advantageous insurance contract. If an insurance contract is to result, the insurer must charge a premium in excess of expected losses to avoid a bias toward insufficient income. The property owner then cannot have a linear utility function.

In Section 1.2 it was mentioned that the preferences of a decision maker must satisfy certain consistency requirements to assure the existence of a utility function. Although these requirements were not listed, they do not include any specifications that would force a utility function to be linear, quadratic, exponential, logarithmic or any other particular form. In fact, each of these named functions might serve as a utility function for some decision maker or they might be spliced together to reflect some other decision maker's preferences.

Nevertheless, it seems natural to assume that $u(w)$ is an increasing function, more is better. In addition, it has been observed that for many decision makers, each additional equal increment of wealth results in a smaller increment of associated utility. This is the idea of decreasing marginal utility in economics.

The approximate utility function of Figure 1.1 consists of straight line segments with positive slopes. It is such that $\Delta^2 u(w) \leq 0$. If these

# THE ECONOMICS OF INSURANCE

ideas are extended to smoother functions, the two properties suggested by observation are $u'(w) > 0$ and $u''(w) < 0$. The second inequality indicates that $u(w)$ is a strictly concave downward function.

In discussing insurance decisions using strictly concave downward utility functions, we will make use of *Jensen's inequality.* This inequality states that if $u''(w) < 0$ and $X$ is a random variable, then

$$E[u(X)] \leq u(E[X]). \quad * \qquad (1.3.2)$$

Jensen's inequality requires the existence of the two expected values. One proof of the inequality is required by Exercise 1.3. A second proof is almost immediate from a consideration of Figure 1.2.

**Figure 1.2**
**Proof of Jensen's**
**Inequality**
**Assuming $u'(w) > 0$**
**and $u''(w) < 0$**

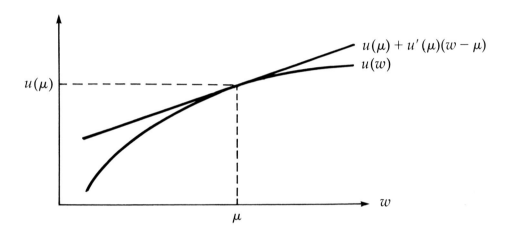

If $E[X] = \mu$ exists, one considers the tangent line,

$$y = u(\mu) + u'(\mu)(w - \mu),$$

at the point $[\mu, u(\mu)]$. Because of the strictly concave characteristic of $u(w)$, the graph of $u(w)$ will be below the tangent line. That is,

$$u(w) \leq u(\mu) + u'(\mu)(w - \mu) \qquad (1.3.3)$$

for all values of $w$. If $w$ is replaced by the random variable $X$, and the expectation is taken on each side of the inequality (1.3.3), we have $E[u(X)] \leq u(\mu)$. This basic inequality has several applications in actuarial mathematics.

Let us apply Jensen's inequality to the decision maker's insurance problem as formulated in (1.3.1). We will assume that the decision maker's preferences are such that $u'(w) > 0$ and $u''(w) < 0$. Applying Jensen's inequality to (1.3.1) we have

$$u(w - G) = E[u(w - X)] \leq u(w - \mu). \qquad (1.3.4)$$

Because $u'(w) > 0$, $u(w)$ is an increasing function. Therefore, (1.3.4)

---

*The inequality is strict except when $X$ is a constant.

implies that $w - G \leq w - \mu$, or $G \geq \mu$ with $G > \mu$ unless $X$ is a constant. In economic terms, we have found that if $u'(w) > 0$ and $u''(w) < 0$, the decision maker will pay an amount greater than the expected loss for insurance. Such a decision maker will be said to be *risk averse.* If $G$ is at least equal to the premium set by the insurer, there is an opportunity for a mutually advantageous insurance policy.

Earlier in this section the utility of wealth function of the insurer was approximated by a straight line in the range of outcomes associated with a single policy. We now employ a general utility function for the insurer. We let $u_I(w)$ denote the utility of wealth function of the insurer and $w_I$ denote the current wealth of the insurer measured in monetary terms. Then the minimum acceptable premium $H$ for assuming random loss $X$, from the viewpoint of the insurer, may be determined from (1.3.5):

$$u_I(w_I) = E[u_I(w_I + H - X)]. \tag{1.3.5}$$

The left-hand side of (1.3.5) is the utility attached to the insurer's current position. The right-hand side is the expected utility associated with collecting premium $H$ and paying random loss $X$. In other words, the insurer is indifferent between the current position and providing insurance for $X$ at premium $H$. If the insurer is risk averse, $u_I'(w) > 0$, $u_I''(w) < 0$, we can use Jensen's inequality along with (1.3.5) to obtain

$$u_I(w_I) = E[u_I(w_I + H - X)] \leq u_I(w_I + H - \mu).$$

Following the same line of reasoning displayed in connection with (1.3.4), we can conclude that $H \geq \mu$. If $G$, as determined by the decision maker by solving (1.3.4), is such that $G \geq H \geq \mu$, an insurance policy is *feasible.* That is, the expected utility of neither party to the contract is decreased.

A utility function is based on the decision maker's preferences for various distributions of outcomes. An insurer need not be an individual. It may be a partnership, corporation or government agency. In this situation the determination of $u_I(w)$, the insurer's utility function, may be a rather complicated matter. For example, if the insurer is a corporation, one of management's responsibilities is the formulation of a coherent set of preferences for various risky insurance ventures. These preferences may involve compromises between conflicting attitudes toward risk among the groups of stockholders.

Several elementary functions are used to illustrate properties of utility functions. Here we will examine exponential, fractional power and quadratic forms. Exercises 1.6, 1.8, 1.9, 1.10 and 1.13 cover the logarithmic utility function.

An *exponential utility function* is of the form

$$u(w) = -e^{-\alpha w} \qquad \alpha > 0$$

# THE ECONOMICS OF INSURANCE

and has several attractive features. First

$$u'(w) = \alpha e^{-\alpha w} > 0$$

and

$$u''(w) = -\alpha^2 e^{-\alpha w} < 0.$$

Therefore, $u(w)$ may serve as the utility function of a risk-averse individual. Second, finding

$$E[-e^{-\alpha X}] = -E[e^{-\alpha X}] = -M_X(-\alpha)$$

is essentially the same as finding the moment generating function (m.g.f.) of $X$. In this expression,

$$M_X(t) = E[e^{tX}]$$

denotes the m.g.f. of $X$. Third, insurance premiums do not depend on the wealth of the decision maker. This statement is verified for the insured by substituting the exponential utility function into (1.3.1). That is,

$$-e^{-\alpha(w-G)} = E[-e^{-\alpha(w-X)}]$$
$$e^{\alpha G} = M_X(\alpha)$$
$$G = \frac{\log M_X(\alpha)}{\alpha},$$

and does not depend on $w$.

The verification for the insurer is done by substituting the exponential utility function with parameter $\alpha_I$ into (1.3.5):

$$-e^{-\alpha_I w_I} = E[-e^{-\alpha_I(w_I+H-X)}]$$
$$-e^{-\alpha_I w_I} = -e^{-\alpha_I(w_I+H)} M_X(\alpha_I)$$
$$H = \frac{\log M_X(\alpha_I)}{\alpha_I}.$$

**Example 1.1:**

A decision maker's utility function is given by $u(w) = -e^{-5w}$. The decision maker has two random economic prospects available. The outcome of the first, denoted by $X$, has a normal distribution with mean 5 and variance 2. Henceforth, a statement about a normal distribution with mean $\mu$ and variance $\sigma^2$ will be abbreviated as $N(\mu, \sigma^2)$. The second prospect, denoted by $Y$, is distributed as $N(6, 2.5)$. Which prospect will be preferred?

**Solution:**
We have

$$E[u(X)] = E[-e^{-5X}]$$
$$= -M_X(-5) = -e^{[-5(5)+(5^2)(2)/2]}$$
$$= -1,$$

and

$$E[u(Y)] = E[-e^{-5Y}]$$
$$= -M_Y(-5) = -e^{[-5(6)+(5^2)(2.5)/2]}$$
$$= -e^{1.25}.$$

Therefore,

$$E[u(X)] = -1 > E[u(Y)] = -e^{1.25}$$

and the distribution of $X$ is preferred to the distribution of $Y$.  ▼

In Example 1.1 prospect $X$ is preferred to $Y$ despite the fact that $\mu_X = 5 < \mu_Y = 6$. Since the decision maker is risk averse, the fact that the distribution of $Y$ is more diffuse than the distribution of $X$ is weighted heavily against the distribution of $Y$ in assessing its desirability. If $Y$ had a $N(6,2.4)$ distribution, $E[u(Y)] = -1$ and the decision maker would be indifferent between the distributions of $X$ and $Y$.

The family of fractional power utility functions is given by

$$u(w) = w^\gamma \quad w > 0, 0 < \gamma < 1.$$

A member of this family might represent the preferences of a risk-averse decision maker since

$$u'(w) = \gamma w^{\gamma-1} > 0$$

and

$$u''(w) = \gamma(\gamma - 1)w^{\gamma-2} < 0.$$

In this family, premiums depend on the wealth of the decision maker in a manner that may be sufficiently realistic in many situations.

**Example 1.2:**

A decision maker's utility function is given by $u(w) = \sqrt{w}$. The decision maker has wealth of $w = 10$ and faces a random loss $X$ with a uniform distribution on $(0,10)$. What is the maximum amount this decision maker will pay for complete insurance against the random loss?

**Solution:**
Substituting into (1.3.1) we have

$$\sqrt{10 - G} = E[\sqrt{10 - X}]$$
$$= \int_0^{10} \sqrt{10 - x}\ 10^{-1}\, dx$$
$$= \frac{-2\,(10 - x)^{3/2}}{3\,(10)} \Bigg|_0^{10}$$
$$= \frac{2}{3}\sqrt{10}$$

$$G = 5.5556.$$

# THE ECONOMICS OF INSURANCE

The decision maker is risk averse. Following the discussion of (1.3.4), we would expect $G > E[X]$, and in this example $G = 5.5556 > E[X] = 5$. ▼

The family of *quadratic utility functions* is given by

$$u(w) = w - \alpha w^2 \quad w < (2\alpha)^{-1}, \alpha > 0.$$

A member of this family might represent the preferences of a risk-averse decision maker since $u'(w) = 1 - 2\alpha w > 0$, when $w < (2\alpha)^{-1}$ and $u''(w) = -2\alpha$. While a quadratic utility function is convenient because decisions will depend only on the first two moments of the distributions of outcomes under consideration, there are certain consequences of its use that strike some people as being unreasonable. Example 1.3 will illustrate one of these consequences.

**Example 1.3:**

A decision maker's utility of wealth function is given by

$$u(w) = w - 0.01 w^2 \quad w < 50.$$

The decision maker will retain wealth of amount $w$ with probability $p$ and suffer a financial loss of amount $c$ with probability $1 - p$. For the values of $w$, $c$ and $p$ exhibited in the table below, find the maximum insurance premium that the decision maker will pay for complete insurance.

**Solution:**
For the facts stated, (1.3.1) becomes

$$u(w - G) = p\,u(w) + (1 - p)\,u(w - c)$$

$$(w - G) - 0.01\,(w - G)^2 = p\,[w - 0.01\,w^2]$$
$$+ (1 - p)\,[(w - c) - 0.01\,(w - c)^2].$$

For given values of $w$, $p$ and $c$ this expression becomes a quadratic equation. Two solutions are shown.

| Wealth $w$ | Loss $c$ | Probability $p$ | Insurance Premium $G$ |
|---|---|---|---|
| 10 | 10 | 0.5 | 5.28 |
| 20 | 10 | 0.5 | 5.37 |

▼

In Example 1.3, as anticipated, $G$ is greater than the expected loss of 5. However, the maximum insurance premium for exactly the same loss distribution increases with the wealth of the decision maker. This result seems unreasonable to some who anticipate that more typical behavior would be a decrease in the amount a decision maker would pay for insurance when an increase in wealth would permit the decision maker to absorb more of a random loss. Unfortunately, a maximum insurance premium that increases with wealth is a property of quadratic utility functions. Consequently, these utility functions should not be selected by a decision maker who perceives that his ability to absorb random losses goes up with increases in wealth.

If we rework Example 1.3 using an exponential utility function, we know that the premium $G$ will not depend on $w$, the amount of wealth. In fact, if $u(w) = -e^{-0.01w}$, it can be shown that $G = 5.12$ for both $w = 10$ and $w = 20$.

**Example 1.4:**   The probability that a property will not be damaged in the next period is 0.75. The probability density function (p.d.f.) of a positive loss is given by

$$f(x) = 0.25\,[0.01\,e^{-0.01x}] \quad x > 0.$$

The owner of the property has a utility function given by

$$u(w) = -e^{-0.005w}.$$

Calculate the expected loss and the maximum insurance premium the property owner will pay.

**Solution:**
The expected loss is given by

$$E[X] = 0.75\,(0) + 0.25 \int_0^\infty x\,(0.01\,e^{-0.01x})\,dx$$

$$= 25.$$

We apply (1.3.1) to determine the maximum premium that the owner will pay for complete insurance. This premium will be consistent with the property owner's preferences as summarized in the utility function:

$$u(w - G) = 0.75\,u(w) + \int_0^\infty u(w - x)f(x)\,dx$$

$$-e^{-0.005(w-G)} = -0.75\,e^{-0.005w} - 0.25 \int_0^\infty e^{-0.005(w-x)}\,(0.01\,e^{-0.01x})\,dx$$

$$e^{0.005G} = 0.75 + (0.25)\,(2)$$

$$= 1.25$$

$$G = 200\log 1.25$$

$$= 44.63.$$

Therefore, in accord with the property owner's preferences, he will pay up to $44.63 - 25 = 19.63$ in excess of the expected loss to purchase insurance covering all losses in the next period.   ▼

In Example 1.5 the notion of insurance that covers something less than the complete loss will be introduced. A modification will be made in (1.3.1) to accommodate the fact that losses will be shared by the decision maker and the insurance system.

**Example 1.5:**

The property owner in Example 1.4 is offered an insurance policy that will pay 1/2 of any loss during the next period. The expected value of the partial loss payment is $E[X/2] = 12.50$. Calculate the maximum premium that the property owner will pay for this insurance.

**Solution:**

Consistent with his attitude toward risk, as summarized in his utility function, the premium will be determined from

$$0.75\, u(w - G) + \int_0^\infty u\left(w - G - \frac{x}{2}\right) f(x)\, dx$$

$$= 0.75\, u(w) + \int_0^\infty u(w - x)\, f(x)\, dx.$$

The left-hand side of this equation represents the expected utility with the partial insurance coverage. The right-hand side represents the expected utility with no insurance. For the exponential utility function and p.d.f. of losses specified in Example 1.4, it can be shown that $G = 28.62$. The property owner is willing to pay up to $G - \mu = 28.62 - 12.50 = 16.12$ more than the expected partial loss for the partial insurance coverage. ▼

**1.4 Elements of Insurance**

Individuals and organizations face the threat of financial loss due to random events. In Section 1.3 we saw how insurance can increase the expected utility of a decision maker facing such random losses. Insurance systems are unique in that the alleviation of financial losses in which the number, size or time of occurrence is random is the primary reason for their existence. In this section we shall review some of the factors influencing the organization and management of an insurance system.

An insurance system may be organized only after the identification of a class of situations where random losses may occur. The word random is taken to mean, along with other attributes, that the frequency, size or time of loss is not under the control of the prospective insured. If such control exists, or if a claim payment exceeds the actual financial loss, an incentive to incur a loss will exist. In such a situation, the assumptions under which the insurance system was organized will become invalid. The actual conditions under which premiums are collected and claims paid will be different from those assumed in organizing the system. The system will not achieve its intended objective of not decreasing the expected utilities of both the insured and the insurer.

Once a class of insurable situations is identified, information on the expected utilities and the loss-generating process can be obtained. Market research in insurance can be viewed as an effort to learn about the utility functions, that is, the risk preferences of consumers.

The processes generating size and time of loss may be sufficiently stable over time so that past information can be used to plan the system. When a new insurance system is organized, directly relevant statistics are not often available. However, enough ancillary information from similar risk situations may be obtained to identify the risks and to provide preliminary estimates of the probability distributions needed to determine premiums. Because most insurance systems operate under dynamic conditions, it is important that a plan exist for collecting and analyzing insurance operating data so that the insurance system can adapt. Adaptation in this case may mean changing premiums, paying an experience-based dividend or premium refund, or modifying future policies.

In a competitive economy, market forces will encourage insurers to price short-term policies so that deviations of experience from expected value will behave as independent random variables. Deviations should exhibit no pattern that might be exploited by the insured or insurer to produce consistent gains. Such consistent deviations would indicate inefficiencies in the insurance market.

As a result, the classification of risks into homogeneous groups is an important function within a market-based insurance system. Experience deviations that are random indicate efficiency or equity in classification. In a competitive insurance market, the continual interaction of numerous buyers and sellers forces experimentation with classification systems as the market participants attempt to take advantage of perceived patterns of deviations. Because insurance losses may be relatively rare events, it is often difficult to identify nonrandom patterns. The cost of classification information for a refined classification system also places a bound on experimentation in this area.

For insurance systems organized to serve groups rather than individuals, the issue is no longer whether deviations in insurance experience are random for each individual. Instead, the question is whether deviations in group experience are random. Consistent deviations in experience from that expected would indicate the need for a revision in the system.

Group insurance decisions do not rest on individual expected utility comparisons. Instead, group insurance plans are based on a collective decision as to whether the system increases the total welfare of the group. Group health insurance providing benefits for the employees of a firm is an example.

## 1.5 Optimal Insurance

The ideas outlined in Sections 1.2, 1.3 and 1.4 have been used as the foundation of an elaborate theory for guiding insurance decision makers to actions consistent with their preferences. In this section we will present one of the main results from this theory, and review many of the ideas introduced so far.

A decision maker has wealth of amount $w$ and faces a loss in the next period. This loss is a random variable and is denoted by $X$. The decision maker can buy an insurance policy that will pay $I(x)$ of the loss. In order to avoid an incentive to incur the loss, we will assume that all feasible insurance policies are such that $0 \leq I(x) \leq x$. We make

# THE ECONOMICS OF INSURANCE

the simplifying assumption that any feasible insurance policy can be purchased for the amount of the expected claim payment. That is, the premium for a policy paying $I(x)$ is $E[I(X)] \leq E[X]$.

The decision maker has formulated a utility function $u(w)$ that is consistent with his preferences for distributions of outcomes. We will assume that the decision maker is risk averse, that is $u'(w) > 0$ and $u''(w) < 0$. We further assume that the decision maker has decided on the amount, denoted by $P$, to be paid for insurance. The question is, which of the insurance policies from the class of feasible policies should be purchased to maximize the expected utility of the decision maker?

One subclass of the class of feasible insurance policies is defined as follows:

$$I_d(x) = \begin{cases} 0 & x < d \\ x - d & x \geq d. \end{cases} \tag{1.5.1}$$

This class of policies is characterized by the fact that claim payments do not start until the loss exceeds the deductible amount $d$. For losses above the deductible amount, the excess is paid under the terms of the policy. This type of policy is sometimes called **stop-loss** or **excess-of-loss insurance.**

In the problem discussed in this section the premium $P$ is equal to the expected claims. In (1.5.2) the symbol $f(x)$ denotes the p.d.f. and the symbol $F(x)$ denotes the distribution function (d.f.) associated with the random variable $X$:

$$P = \int_d^\infty (x - d) f(x) \, dx \tag{1.5.2A}$$

or

$$P = \int_d^\infty [1 - F(x)] \, dx. \tag{1.5.2B}$$

Equation (1.5.2B) is obtained by integration by parts. In the following, the amount of premium $P$ is given. Then (1.5.2) provides explicit equations for the corresponding deductible, denoted by $d^*$. In Exercise 1.15, it is shown that $d^*$ exists and is unique.

The main result of this section will be stated as a theorem.

**Theorem 1.1:**

If a decision maker
- has wealth of amount $w$,
- is risk averse, in other words, has utility of wealth function $u(w)$ such that $u'(w) > 0$ and $u''(w) < 0$,
- faces a random loss $X$,
- will spend amount $P$ on insurance where $0 < P \leq E[X] = \mu$, and

the insurance market

- offers all feasible insurance policies of the form $I(x)$, $0 \leq I(x) \leq x$, and
- offers purchase of an insurance policy for its expected loss payment, $E[I(X)]$,

then the decision maker's expected utility will be maximized by purchasing an insurance policy

$$I_{d^*}(x) = \begin{cases} 0 & x < d^* \\ x - d^* & x \geq d^* \end{cases}$$

where $d^*$ is the solution of

$$P - \int_d^\infty (x - d) f(x)\, dx = 0.$$

The theorem is proved in the Appendix to this chapter.

Theorem 1.1 is an important result and illustrates many of the ideas developed in this chapter. However, it is instructive to consider certain limitations on its applicability. First, insurance cannot be purchased for its expected claims, although the additional considerations for expenses, profit and security are small relative to the basic cost so that the theorem is valid for more risk averse individuals. Also, while the theorem indicates the form of insurance, it does not help to determine the amount $P$ to spend. In the theorem, $P$ is fixed.

## 1.6 Notes and References

The role of risk in business was developed in a pioneering thesis by Willett (1951). Borch (1974) has published a series of papers applying utility theory to insurance questions. DeGroot (1970) gives a complete development of utility theory starting from basic axioms for consistency among preferences for various distributions of outcomes. DeGroot and Borch both discuss the historically important St. Petersburg paradox, outlined in Exercise 1.2. A paper by Friedman and Savage (1948) provides many insights into utility theory and human behavior.

Pratt (1964) has studied (1.3.1) and derived several theorems about premiums and utility functions. Exercise 1.10, which uses two rough approximations, is related to one of Pratt's results.

Theorem 1.1 on optimal insurance was proved by Arrow (1963) in the context of health insurance. The theorem in Exercise 1.20, in which the goal of insurance is to minimize the variance of retained losses, was the subject of papers by Borch (1960) and Kahn (1961).

## Appendix

**Lemma:**

If $u''(y) < 0$ for all $y$ in $(z, w)$, then

$$u(w) - u(z) \leq (w - z)u'(z). \tag{1.A.1}$$

**Proof:**
The lemma may be established with the aid of Figure 1.2. Using the point slope form, a line tangent to $u(w)$ at the point $[w_0, u(w_0)]$ has the equation $y - u(w_0) = u'(w_0)(w - w_0)$ and will be above the

graph of the function $u(w)$ except at the point $[w_0, u(w_0)]$. Therefore

$$u(w) - u(w_0) \leq u'(w_0)(w - w_0).$$

The same argument may be repeated for any number $z$. ■

In Exercise 1.18 an alternative proof is required.

**Proof of Theorem 1.1:**
Let $I(x)$ be associated with an insurance policy satisfying the hypothesis of the theorem. Then from the lemma

$$u(w - x + I(x) - P) - u(w - x + I_{d^*}(x) - P)$$

$$\leq [I(x) - I_{d^*}(x)]\,u'(w - x + I_{d^*}(x) - P). \qquad (1.A.2)$$

In addition we claim

$$[I(x) - I_{d^*}(x)]\,u'(w - x + I_{d^*}(x) - P)$$

$$\leq [I(x) - I_{d^*}(x)]\,u'(w - d^* - P). \qquad (1.A.3)$$

To establish inequality (1.A.3), we must consider three cases:

Case I.  $I_{d^*}(x) = I(x)$
In this case equality holds, (1.A.3) is 0 on both sides.

Case II.  $I_{d^*}(x) > I(x)$
In this case $I_{d^*}(x) > 0$ and from (1.5.1), $x - I_{d^*}(x) = d^*$. Therefore, equality holds with each side of (1.A.3) equal to $[I(x) - I_{d^*}(x)]\,u'(w - d^* - P)$.

Case III.  $I_{d^*}(x) < I(x)$
In this case $I(x) - I_{d^*}(x) > 0$. From (1.5.1) we obtain $I_{d^*}(x) - x \geq -d^*$ and $I_{d^*}(x) - x - P \geq -d^* - P$. Therefore

$$u'(w - x + I_{d^*}(x) - P) \leq u'(w - d^* - P)$$

since the second derivative of $u(x)$ is negative and $u'(x)$ is a decreasing function.

Therefore, in each case

$$[I(x) - I_{d^*}(x)]\,u'(w - x + I_{d^*}(x) - P) \leq [I(x) - I_{d^*}(x)]\,u'(w - P - d^*)$$

establishing inequality (1.A.3).

Now combining inequalities (1.A.2) and (1.A.3) and taking expectations we have

$$E[u(w - X + I(X) - P)] - E[u(w - X + I_{d^*}(X) - P)]$$

$$\leq E[I(X) - I_{d^*}(X)]\,u'(w - d^* - P) = (P - P)\,u'(w - d^* - P) = 0.$$

Therefore,

$$E[u(w - X + I(X) - P)] \leq E[u(w - X + I_{d^*}(X) - P]$$

and the expected utility will be maximized by selecting $I_{d^*}(x)$, the stop-loss policy. ■

## Exercises

*Section 1.2*

1.1. Assume that a decision maker's current wealth is 10,000. Assign $u(0) = -1$ and $u(10,000) = 0$.
   a. When facing a loss of $X$ with probability 0.5, and remaining at current wealth with probability 0.5, the decision maker would be willing to pay up to $G$ for complete insurance. The values for $X$ and $G$ in three situations are given below.

| $X$ | $G$ |
|---|---|
| 10 000 | 6 000 |
| 6 000 | 3 300 |
| 3 300 | 1 700 |

   Determine three values on the decision maker's utility of wealth function $u$.
   b. Compute first and second divided differences on the given values of $u(0)$, $u(10,000)$ and the three intermediate values of $u$ determined in part (a).
   c. Put yourself in the role of a decision maker with wealth 10,000. In addition to the given values of $u(0)$ and $u(10,000)$, elicit three additional values on your utility of wealth function $u$.
   d. On the basis of the five values of your utility function, calculate first and second divided differences.

1.2. **St. Petersburg paradox:** Consider a game of chance that consists of tossing a coin until a head appears. The probability of a head is 0.5 and the repeated trials are independent. Let the random variable $N$ be the number of the trial on which the first head occurs.
   a. Show that the probability function (p.f.) of $N$ is given by
   $$f(n) = (1/2)^n \quad n = 1, 2, 3, \ldots.$$
   b. Find $E[N]$ and $Var[N]$.
   c. If a reward of $X = 2^N$ is paid, prove that the expectation of the reward does not exist.
   d. If this reward has utility $u(w) = \log w$, find $E[u(X)]$.

*Section 1.3*

1.3. **Jensen's inequality:** a. Assume $u''(w) < 0$, $E[X] = \mu$ and $E[u(X)]$ exists; prove that $E[u(X)] \leq u(\mu)$. [Hint: Express $u(w)$ as a series around the point $w = \mu$ and terminate the expansion with an error term involving the second derivative. Note that Jensen's inequality does not require that $u'(w) > 0$.]
   b. If $u''(w) > 0$, prove that $E[u(X)] \geq u(\mu)$.
   c. Discuss Jensen's inequality for the special case $u(w) = w^2$. What is $E[u(X)] - u(E[X])$?

1.4. If a utility function is such that $u'(w) > 0$ and $u''(w) > 0$, use (1.3.1) to show $G \leq \mu$. A decision maker with preferences consistent with such a utility function is a *risk lover*.

# Chapter 1

## THE ECONOMICS OF INSURANCE

1.5. Construct a geometric argument, based on a graph like that displayed in Figure 1.2, that if $u'(w) < 0$ and $u''(w) < 0$, then (1.3.3) follows.

1.6. Confirm that the utility function $u(w) = \log w$, $w > 0$, is the utility function of a decision maker who is risk averse for $w > 0$.

1.7. A utility function is given by

$$u(w) = \begin{cases} e^{-(w-100)^2/200} & w < 100 \\ 2 - e^{-(w-100)^2/200} & w \geq 100. \end{cases}$$

a. Is $u'(w) \geq 0$?
b. For what range of $w$ is $u''(w) < 0$?

1.8. If one assumes, as did J. Bernoulli in his comments on the St. Petersburg paradox, that utility of wealth satisfies the differential equation

$$\frac{du(w)}{dw} = \frac{k}{w} \qquad w > 0, k > 0,$$

confirm that $u(w) = k \log w + c$.

1.9. A decision maker has utility function $u(w) = k \log w$. The decision maker has wealth $w$, $w > 1$, and faces a random loss $X$ which has a uniform distribution on the interval $(0,1)$. Use (1.3.1) to show that the maximum insurance premium that the decision maker will pay is

$$G = w - \frac{w^w}{e(w-1)^{w-1}}.$$

1.10. a. In (1.3.1) use the approximations

$$u(w - G) \cong u(w - \mu) + (\mu - G) u'(w - \mu)$$

$$u(w - x) \cong u(w - \mu) + (\mu - x) u'(w - \mu) + \frac{1}{2}(\mu - x)^2 u''(w - \mu)$$

and derive the following approximation for $G$:

$$G \cong \mu - \frac{1}{2} \frac{u''(w - \mu)}{u'(w - \mu)} \sigma^2.$$

b. If $u(w) = k \log w$, use the approximation developed in part (a) to obtain

$$G \cong \mu + \frac{1}{2} \frac{\sigma^2}{(w - \mu)}.$$

1.11. The decision maker has a utility function $u(w) = -e^{-\alpha w}$ and is faced with a random loss that has a chi-square distribution with $n$ degrees of freedom. If $0 < \alpha < 1/2$, use (1.3.1) to obtain an expression for $G$, the maximum insurance premium the decision maker will pay, and prove that $G > n = \mu$.

1.12. Rework Example 1.4 for
   a. $u(w) = -e^{-w/400}$
   b. $u(w) = -e^{-w/150}$.

1.13. a. A small insurer with net worth 100 has accepted (and col-
        lected the premium for) a risk $X$ with the following proba-
        bility distribution:

$$\Pr(X = 0) = \Pr(X = 51) = \frac{1}{2}.$$

     What is the maximum amount $G$ it should pay a reinsurer
     to accept 100% of this loss? Assume the insurer's utility
     function of wealth is $u(w) = \log w$.
   b. A large reinsurer, with wealth 650 and the same utility func-
      tion, $u(w) = \log w$, is considering accepting the above risk.
      What is the minimum amount $H$ it would accept as a pre-
      mium to reinsure 100% of the loss?

*Section 1.4*

1.14. A hospital expense policy is issued to a group consisting of $n$
      individuals. The policy pays $B$ dollars each time a member of
      the group enters a hospital. The group is not homogeneous
      with respect to the expected number of hospital admissions each
      year. The group may be divided into $r$ subgroups. There are $n_i$
      individuals in subgroup $i$ and $\sum_1^r n_i = n$. For subgroup $i$ the
      number of annual hospital admissions for each member has a
      Poisson distribution with parameter $\lambda_i$, $i = 1, 2, \ldots, r$. The
      number of annual hospital admissions for members of the group
      are mutually independent.
   a. Show that the expected claims payment in 1 year is

$$B \sum_1^r n_i \lambda_i = B n \bar{\lambda}$$

   where

$$\bar{\lambda} = \frac{\sum_1^r n_i \lambda_i}{n}.$$

   b. Show that the number of hospital admissions in 1 year for
      the group has a Poisson distribution with parameter $n \bar{\lambda}$.

*Section 1.5*

1.15. a. Differentiate the right-hand side of (1.5.2A) with respect
        to $d$.
   b. Let $P$ be a number such that $0 < P < E[X]$. Show that (1.5.2)
      has a unique solution $d^*$.

1.16. Perform the integration by parts indicated in (1.5.2B). Use the
      fact that if $E[X]$ exists, then $\lim_{x \to \infty} x[1 - F(x)] = 0$.

1.17. Let the loss random variable $X$ have a p.d.f. given by

$$f(x) = 0.1 e^{-0.1x} \quad x > 0.$$

a. Calculate $E[X]$ and $\operatorname{Var}[X]$.
b. If $P = 5$ is to be spent for insurance to be purchased by the payment of the pure premium, show that

$$I(x) = \frac{x}{2}$$

and

$$I_d(x) = \begin{cases} 0 & x < 10 \log 2 \\ x - 10 \log 2 & x \ge 10 \log 2 \end{cases}$$

both represent feasible insurance policies with pure premium $P = 5$. $I(x)$ is called *proportional insurance.*

1.18. The loss random variable $X$ has a p.d.f. given by

$$f(x) = \frac{1}{100} \quad 0 < x < 100.$$

a. Calculate $E[X]$ and $\operatorname{Var}[X]$.
b. Consider a proportional policy where

$$I_1(x) = kx \quad 0 < k < 1,$$

and a stop-loss policy where

$$I_2(x) = \begin{cases} 0 & x < d \\ x - d & x \ge d. \end{cases}$$

Determine $k$ and $d$ such that the pure premium in each case is $P = 12.5$.
c. Show that $\operatorname{Var}[X - I_1(X)] > \operatorname{Var}[X - I_2(X)]$.

*Appendix*

1.19. Establish the lemma by using an analytic rather than a geometric argument. [Hint: Expand $u(w)$ in a series as far as a second derivative remainder around the point $w_0$ and subtract $u(w_0)$.]

1.20. Adopt the hypotheses of Theorem 1.1 with respect to the premium $P$ and insurance policies $I(x)$. Prove that

$$\operatorname{Var}[X - I(X)] = E[(X - I(X) - \mu + P)^2]$$

is a minimum when $I(x) = I_{d^*}(x)$. You will be proving that for a fixed pure premium, a stop-loss insurance policy will minimize the variance of retained claims. [Hint: one may follow the proof of Theorem 1.1 by first proving that $x^2 - z^2 \ge (x - z)(2z)$ and then establishing that

$$[x - I(x)]^2 - [x - I_{d^*}(x)]^2 \ge [I_{d^*}(x) - I(x)][2x - 2I_{d^*}(x)]$$

$$\ge 2[I_{d^*}(x) - I(x)]d^*.$$

The final inequality may be established by breaking the proof into three cases. Alternatively, by proper choice of wealth level and utility function, the result of this exercise is a special case of Theorem 1.1.]

Chapter 2

# INDIVIDUAL RISK MODELS
# FOR A SHORT TERM

## 2.1
## Introduction

In Chapter 1 we examined how a decision maker can use insurance to reduce the adverse financial impact of some types of random events. That examination was quite general. The decision maker could have been an individual seeking protection against the loss of property, savings or income. The decision maker could have been an organization seeking protection against those same types of losses. In fact, the organization could have been an insurance company seeking protection against the loss of funds due to too many claims either by an individual or by its portfolio of insureds. Such protection is called reinsurance and will be introduced in this chapter.

As you recall, the theory in Chapter 1 requires a probabilistic model for the potential losses. Here we will examine one of two models commonly used in insurance pricing, reserve and reinsurance applications.

For an insuring organization, let the random loss on a segment of its risks be denoted by $S$. Then $S$ is the random variable for which we seek a probability distribution. Historically, there have been two sets of postulates for distributions of $S$. The **individual risk model** defines

$$S = X_1 + X_2 + \cdots + X_n \qquad (2.1.1)$$

where $X_i$ is the loss on insured unit $i$ and $n$ is the number of risk units insured. Usually the $X_i$'s are postulated to be independent random variables, because the mathematics is easier and no historical data on the dependence relationship are needed. The other model is the collective risk model described in Chapter 11.

The individual risk model discussed in this chapter will not recognize the time value of money. This is for simplicity, and is why the title refers to short terms. Chapters 4–10 cover models for long terms.

In this chapter we will discuss only **closed models,** that is, the number of insured units $n$ in (2.1.1) is known and fixed at the beginning of the period. If we postulate about migration in and out of the insurance system, we have an **open model.**

## 2.2
## Models for
## Individual Claim
## Random
## Variables

First, we will review basic concepts with a life insurance product. In a **1-year term life insurance** the insurer agrees to pay an amount $b$ if the insured dies within a year of policy issue and to pay nothing if the insured survives the year. The probability of a claim during the year is denoted by $q$. The claim random variable, $X$, has a distribution that can be described by either its p.f. or its distribution function, d.f. The p.f. is

$$f(x) = \Pr(X = x) = \begin{cases} 1 - q & x = 0 \\ q & x = b \\ 0 & \text{elsewhere,} \end{cases} \qquad (2.2.1)$$

and the d.f. is

$$F(x) = \Pr(X \le x) = \begin{cases} 0 & x < 0 \\ 1 - q & 0 \le x < b \\ 1 & x \ge b. \end{cases} \quad (2.2.2)$$

From the p.f. and the definition of moments

$$E[X] = bq \quad (2.2.3)$$

$$E[X^2] = b^2 q,$$

and

$$\text{Var}[X] = b^2 q (1 - q). \quad (2.2.4)$$

These formulas can also be obtained by writing

$$X = Ib \quad (2.2.5)$$

where $b$ is the constant amount payable in the event of death and $I$ is the random variable that is 1 for the event of death and 0 otherwise. Thus $\Pr(I = 0) = 1 - q$ and $\Pr(I = 1) = q$, the mean and variance of $I$ are $q$ and $q(1 - q)$ respectively, and the mean and variance of $X$ are $bq$ and $b^2 q (1 - q)$ as above.

The random variable $I$ with its $\{0,1\}$ range is widely applicable in actuarial models. In probability textbooks it is called an *indicator, Bernoulli random variable,* or a *binomial random variable* for a single trial. We shall refer to it as an indicator for the sake of brevity and because it does indicate the occurrence, $I = 1$, or nonoccurrence, $I = 0$, of a given event.

We now seek more general models in which the amount of claim is also a random variable and several claims can occur in a period. Health, automobile, and other property and liability coverages provide immediate examples. Extending (2.2.5) we postulate that

$$X = IB \quad (2.2.6)$$

where $X$ is the claim random variable for the period, $B$ gives the total claim amount incurred during the period, and $I$ is the indicator for the event that at least 1 claim has occurred. As the indicator for this event, $I$ reports the occurrence ($I = 1$) or nonoccurrence ($I = 0$) of claims in this period and not the number of claims in the period. $\Pr(I = 1)$ will still be denoted by $q$.

Let us look at several situations and determine the distributions of $I$ and $B$ for a model. First consider a 1-year term life insurance paying an extra benefit in case of accidental death. To be specific, if death is accidental, the benefit amount is 50,000. For other causes of death, the benefit amount is 25,000. Let's assume that for the age, health and occupation of a specific individual, the probability of an accidental death within the year is 0.0005 while the probability of a non-

## INDIVIDUAL RISK MODELS
## FOR A SHORT TERM

accidental death is 0.0020. More succinctly,

$$\Pr(I = 1 \text{ and } B = 50{,}000) = 0.0005$$

and

$$\Pr(I = 1 \text{ and } B = 25{,}000) = 0.0020.$$

Summing over the possible values of $B$, we have

$$\Pr(I = 1) = 0.0025,$$

and then

$$\Pr(I = 0) = 1 - \Pr(I = 1) = 0.9975.$$

The conditional distribution of $B$, given $I = 1$, is

$$\Pr(B = 25{,}000 | I = 1) = \frac{\Pr(B = 25{,}000 \text{ and } I = 1)}{\Pr(I = 1)} = \frac{0.0020}{0.0025} = 0.8$$

$$\Pr(B = 50{,}000 | I = 1) = \frac{\Pr(B = 50{,}000 \text{ and } I = 1)}{\Pr(I = 1)} = \frac{0.0005}{0.0025} = 0.2.$$

Let us now consider an automobile insurance providing collision coverage (indemnifies the owner for collision damage to his car) above a 250 deductible up to a maximum claim of 2000. For illustrative purposes, assume that for a particular individual the probability of 1 claim in a period is 0.15 and the chance of more than 1 claim is 0:

$$\Pr(I = 0) = 0.85$$

$$\Pr(I = 1) = 0.15.$$

(The unrealistic assumption of no more than 1 claim per period is made to simplify the distribution of $B$. We will remove that assumption in a later section after we discuss the distribution of the sum of a number of claims.) Since $B$ is the claim incurred by the insurer, rather than the amount of damage to the car, we can infer two characteristics of $I$ and $B$. First, the event $I = 0$ includes those collisions in which the damage is less than the 250 deductible. The other inference is that $B$'s distribution will have a probability mass at the maximum claim size of 2000. Let's assume this probability mass is 0.1. Furthermore, let's assume that claim amounts between 0 and 2000 can be modeled by a continuous distribution with a p.d.f. proportional to $1 - x/2000$ for $0 < x < 2000$. (In practice the continuous curve chosen to represent the distribution of claims would be the result of a study of claims by size over a recent period.) Summarizing these assumptions about the conditional distribution of $B$, given $I = 1$, we have a mixed distribution with positive density from 0 to 2000 and a mass at 2000. This is illustrated in Figure 2.1.

# INDIVIDUAL RISK MODELS
# FOR A SHORT TERM

**Figure 2.1
Density and Mass
Function for $B$, given
$I = 1$**

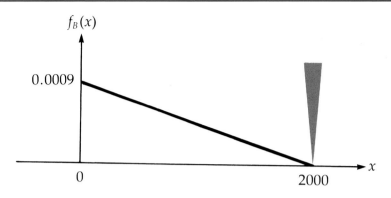

In the figure, the area of the unshaded triangular region is 0.9 and the mass at 2000 is 0.1. The d.f. of this conditional distribution is

$$\Pr(B \le x | I = 1) = \begin{cases} 0 & x \le 0 \\ 0.9\left[1 - \left(1 - \dfrac{x}{2000}\right)^2\right] & 0 < x < 2000 \\ 1 & x \ge 2000. \end{cases}$$

We shall see in Section 2.4 that the moments of the claim random variable, $X$, in particular the mean and variance, are extensively used. For this automobile insurance, we shall calculate the mean and the variance by two methods.

First we shall derive the distribution of $X$ and use it to calculate $\mathrm{E}[X]$ and $\mathrm{Var}[X]$. Letting $F(x)$ be the d.f. of $X$, we have

$$\begin{aligned} F(x) = \Pr(X \le x) &= \Pr(IB \le x) \\ &= \Pr(IB \le x | I = 0)\Pr(I = 0) \qquad (2.2.7) \\ &\quad + \Pr(IB \le x | I = 1)\Pr(I = 1). \end{aligned}$$

For $x < 0$,

$$F(x) = 0\,(0.85) + 0\,(0.15) = 0.$$

For $0 \le x < 2000$,

$$F(x) = 1\,(0.85) + 0.9\left[1 - \left(1 - \dfrac{x}{2000}\right)^2\right](0.15).$$

For $x \ge 2000$,

$$F(x) = 1\,(0.85) + 1\,(0.15) = 1.$$

This is a mixed distribution. It has both probability masses and a continuous part as can be seen in its graph in Figure 2.2.

Corresponding to this d.f. is a combination p.f. and p.d.f. given by

$$f(0) = \Pr(X = 0) = 0.85$$
$$f(2000) = \Pr(X = 2000) = 0.015 \qquad (2.2.8)$$

# INDIVIDUAL RISK MODELS
# FOR A SHORT TERM

**Figure 2.2**
**Distribution Function**
**of** $X = IB$

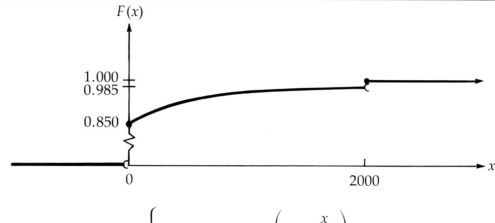

$$f(x) = \begin{cases} F'(x) = 0.000135 \left(1 - \dfrac{x}{2000}\right) & 0 < x < 2000 \\ 0 & \text{elsewhere.} \end{cases}$$

Moments of $X$ can then be calculated by

$$E(X^k) = 0f(0) + (2000)^k f(2000) + \int_0^{2000} x^k f(x)\, dx, \qquad (2.2.9)$$

specifically,

$$E[X] = 120$$

and

$$E[X^2] = 150,000.$$

Thus,

$$Var[X] = 135,600.$$

There are some general formulas relating the moments of random variables by conditional expectation. For the mean and variance these are

$$E[W] = E[E[W|V]] \qquad (2.2.10)$$

and

$$Var[W] = Var[E[W|V]] + E[Var[W|V]]. \qquad (2.2.11)$$

In these equations we think of calculating the terms on the left-hand sides by direct use of $W$'s distribution. In the terms on the right-hand sides, the $E[W|V]$ and $Var[W|V]$ are calculated by use of $W$'s conditional distribution for a given value of $V$. These components are then functions of the random variable $V$, and we can calculate their moments by use of $V$'s distribution.

In many actuarial models conditional distributions are used. This makes the formulas above directly applicable. In our model, $X = IB$, we can substitute $X$ for $W$ and $I$ for $V$ to obtain

$$E[X] = E[E[X|I]] \tag{2.2.12}$$

and

$$\text{Var}[X] = \text{Var}[E[X|I]] + E[\text{Var}[X|I]]. \tag{2.2.13}$$

Now let's write

$$\mu = E[B|I = 1] \tag{2.2.14}$$

$$\sigma^2 = \text{Var}[B|I = 1] \tag{2.2.15}$$

and look at the conditional means

$$E[X|I = 0] = 0 \tag{2.2.16}$$

and

$$E[X|I = 1] = E[B|I = 1] = \mu. \tag{2.2.17}$$

Formulas (2.2.16) and (2.2.17) define $E[X|I]$ as a function of $I$, which can be written by the formula

$$E[X|I] = \mu I. \tag{2.2.18}$$

Hence,

$$E[E[X|I]] = \mu E[I] = \mu q \tag{2.2.19}$$

and

$$\text{Var}[E[X|I]] = \mu^2 \text{Var}[I] = \mu^2 q (1 - q). \tag{2.2.20}$$

Since $X = 0$ for $I = 0$, we have

$$\text{Var}[X|I = 0] = 0. \tag{2.2.21}$$

For $I = 1$ we have $X = B$ and

$$\text{Var}[X|I = 1] = \text{Var}[B|I = 1] = \sigma^2. \tag{2.2.22}$$

Formulas (2.2.21) and (2.2.22) can be combined as

$$\text{Var}[X|I] = \sigma^2 I. \tag{2.2.23}$$

Then

$$E[\text{Var}[X|I]] = \sigma^2 E[I] = \sigma^2 q. \tag{2.2.24}$$

Substituting (2.2.19), (2.2.20) and (2.2.24) into (2.2.12) and (2.2.13) we have

$$E[X] = \mu q \tag{2.2.25}$$

and

$$\text{Var}[X] = \mu^2 q (1 - q) + \sigma^2 q. \tag{2.2.26}$$

Let us now apply these formulas to calculate $E[X]$ and $\text{Var}[X]$ for the automobile insurance modeled in (2.2.9). Since the p.d.f. for $B$, given $I = 1$, is

$$f_{B|I}(x|1) = \begin{cases} 0.0009\left(1 - \dfrac{x}{2000}\right) & 0 < x < 2000 \\ 0 & \text{elsewhere,} \end{cases}$$

with $\Pr(B = 2000|I = 1) = 0.1$ we have

$$\mu = \int_0^{2000} 0.0009\, x\left(1 - \frac{x}{2000}\right) dx + (0.1)(2000) = 800$$

$$E[B^2|I = 1] = \int_0^{2000} 0.0009\, x^2\left(1 - \frac{x}{2000}\right) dx + (0.1)(2000)^2 = 1{,}000{,}000$$

and

$$\sigma^2 = 1{,}000{,}000 - (800)^2 = 360{,}000.$$

Finally, with $q = 0.15$ we obtain the following from (2.2.25) and (2.2.26):

$$E[X] = 800\,(0.15) = 120$$

and

$$\text{Var}[X] = (800)^2\,(0.15)\,(0.85) + (360{,}000)\,(0.15)$$
$$= 135{,}600.$$

There are other possible models for $B$ in different insurance situations. As an example, let us consider a model for the number of deaths due to crashes during an airline's year of operation. We can start with a random variable for the number of deaths, $X$, on a single flight and then add up a set of such random variables over the set of flights for the year. For a single flight, the event $I = 1$ will be the event of an accident during the flight. The number of deaths in the accident, $B$, will be modeled as the product of two random variables, $L$ and $Q$, where $L$ is the load factor, the number of persons on board at the time of the crash, and $Q$ is the fraction of deaths among persons on board. The number of deaths $B$ is modeled in this way since separate statistical data for the distributions of $L$ and $Q$ may be more readily available than is total data for $B$. We have $X = ILQ$. While the fraction of passengers killed in a crash and the fraction of seats occupied are probably related, $L$ and $Q$ might be assumed to be independent as a first approximation.

## 2.3 Sums of Independent Random Variables

In the individual risk model, claims of an insuring organization are modeled as the sum of the claims of many insured individuals.

The claims for the individuals are assumed to be independent in most applications. In this section we shall review two methods for determining the distribution of the sum of independent random variables. First let us consider the sum of two random variables, $S = X + Y$, with the sample space shown in Figure 2.3.

**Figure 2.3**
**Event $[X + Y \le s]$**

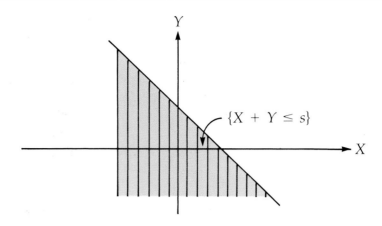

The line $X + Y = s$ and the region below the line represent the event $[S = X + Y \le s]$. Hence the d.f. of $S$ is

$$F_S(s) = \Pr(S \le s) = \Pr(X + Y \le s). \qquad (2.3.1)$$

For two discrete, nonnegative random variables, we can use the law of total probability to write (2.3.1) as

$$F_S(s) = \sum_{\text{all } y \le s} \Pr(X + Y \le s | Y = y) \Pr(Y = y)$$

$$= \sum_{\text{all } y \le s} \Pr(X \le s - y | Y = y) \Pr(Y = y). \qquad (2.3.2)$$

When $X$ and $Y$ are independent, this last sum can be written

$$F_S(s) = \sum_{\text{all } y \le s} F_X(s - y) f_Y(y). \qquad (2.3.3)$$

The p.f. corresponding to this d.f. can be calculated by

$$f_S(s) = \sum_{\text{all } y \le s} f_X(s - y) f_Y(y). \qquad (2.3.4)$$

For continuous, nonnegative random variables the formulas corresponding to (2.3.2), (2.3.3), and (2.3.4) are

$$F_S(s) = \int_0^s \Pr(X \le s - y | Y = y) f_Y(y) \, dy \qquad (2.3.5)$$

$$F_S(s) = \int_0^s F_X(s - y) f_Y(y) \, dy \qquad (2.3.6)$$

$$f_S(s) = \int_0^s f_X(s - y) f_Y(y) \, dy. \qquad (2.3.7)$$

When either one, or both, of $X$ and $Y$ have a mixed-type distribution (typical in individual risk model applications), the formulas are analogous but more complex. For random variables that may also take

## INDIVIDUAL RISK MODELS
## FOR A SHORT TERM

on negative values, the sums and integrals in the formulas above are over all $y$ values from $-\infty$ to $+\infty$.

In mathematical analysis the operation in (2.3.3) and (2.3.6) is called the ***convolution*** of the pair of distribution functions $F_X(x)$ and $F_Y(y)$ and is denoted by $F_X*F_Y$. The convolution process is simple in concept, however, it can be tedious to calculate in even simple examples.

**Example 2.1:**

Let $X$ have a uniform distribution on $(0,2)$ and let $Y$ be independent of $X$ with a uniform distribution over $(0,3)$. Determine the d.f. of $S = X + Y$.

**Solution:**
Since $X$ and $Y$ are continuous, we will use (2.3.6):

$$F_X(x) = \begin{cases} 0 & x < 0 \\ \dfrac{x}{2} & 0 \le x < 2 \\ 1 & x \ge 2 \end{cases}$$

and

$$f_Y(y) = \begin{cases} \dfrac{1}{3} & 0 < y < 3 \\ 0 & \text{elsewhere.} \end{cases}$$

Then

$$F_S(s) = \int_0^s F_X(s - y) f_Y(y)\,dy.$$

The $X$, $Y$ sample space is illustrated in Figure 2.4. The rectangular region contains all of the probability for $X$ and $Y$. The event of interest, $X + Y \le s$, has been illustrated in the figure for five values of $s$. For each value, the line intersects the $y$-axis at $s$ and the line

**Figure 2.4
Convolution of Two
Uniform
Distributions**

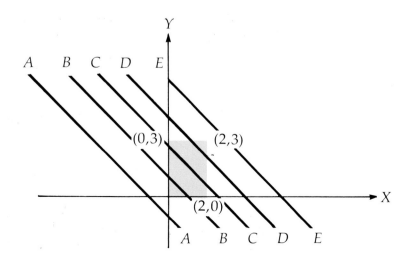

$x = 2$ at $s - 2$. The values of $F_S$ for these five cases are

$$F_S(s) = \begin{cases} 0 & s < 0 & \text{line } A \\[2ex] \displaystyle\int_0^s \frac{1}{3}\frac{s-y}{2}\,dy = \frac{s^2}{12} & 0 \le s < 2 & \text{line } B \\[2ex] \displaystyle\int_0^{s-2}\frac{1}{3}1\,dy + \int_{s-2}^s \frac{1}{3}\frac{s-y}{2}\,dy = \frac{s-1}{3} & 2 \le s < 3 & \text{line } C \\[2ex] \displaystyle\int_0^{s-2}\frac{1}{3}1\,dy + \int_{s-2}^3 \frac{1}{3}\frac{s-y}{2}\,dy = 1 - \frac{(5-s)^2}{12} & 3 \le s < 5 & \text{line } D \\[2ex] 1 & s \ge 5 & \text{line } E. \end{cases}$$

▼

To determine the distribution of the sum of more than two random variables, we can use the convolution process iteratively. For $S = X_1 + X_2 + \cdots + X_n$ where the $X_i$'s are independent random variables, $F_i$ is the d.f. of $X_i$, and $F^{(k)}$ is the d.f. of $X_1 + X_2 + \cdots + X_k$, we would have

$$F^{(2)} = F_2 * F^{(1)} = F_2 * F_1$$

$$F^{(3)} = F_3 * F^{(2)}$$

$$F^{(4)} = F_4 * F^{(3)}$$

$$\vdots$$

$$F_S = F^{(n)} = F_n * F^{(n-1)}.$$

Example 2.2 illustrates this procedure for three discrete random variables. When we have identically distributed random variables ($F_i = F$, $i = 1, 2, \ldots, n$) this distribution is called the $n$th convolution of $F$ and is denoted by $F^{*n}$.

**Example 2.2:** The random variables $X_1$, $X_2$ and $X_3$ are independent with distributions defined by Columns (1), (2), and (3) of the table. Derive the d.f. and p.f. of $S = X_1 + X_2 + X_3$.

**Solution:**
The notation of the previous paragraph is used in the table:

- Columns (1)–(3) are given information.
- Column (4) is the d.f. for Column (1).
- Column (5) is derived from Columns (2) and (4) by use of (2.3.3).
- Column (6) is derived from Columns (3) and (5) by use of (2.3.3).

The derivation of Column (6) completes the determination of the distribution of $S$, and its p.f. could be derived by differencing

# Chapter 2

## INDIVIDUAL RISK MODELS
## FOR A SHORT TERM

| $x$ | (1) $f_1(x)$ | (2) $f_2(x)$ | (3) $f_3(x)$ | (4) $F_1(x)$ | (5) $F^{(2)}(x)$ | (6) $F^{(3)}(x)$ | (7) $f^{(2)}(x)$ | (8) $f^{(3)}(x)$ |
|---|---|---|---|---|---|---|---|---|
| 0 | 0.4 | 0.5 | 0.6 | 0.4 | 0.20 | 0.120 | 0.20 | 0.120 |
| 1 | 0.3 | 0.2 | 0.0 | 0.7 | 0.43 | 0.258 | 0.23 | 0.138 |
| 2 | 0.2 | 0.1 | 0.1 | 0.9 | 0.63 | 0.398 | 0.20 | 0.140 |
| 3 | 0.1 | 0.1 | 0.1 | 1.0 | 0.79 | 0.537 | 0.16 | 0.139 |
| 4 | 0.0 | 0.1 | 0.1 | 1.0 | 0.90 | 0.666 | 0.11 | 0.129 |
| 5 | 0.0 | 0.0 | 0.1 | 1.0 | 0.96 | 0.781 | 0.06 | 0.115 |
| 6 | 0.0 | 0.0 | 0.0 | 1.0 | 0.99 | 0.869 | 0.03 | 0.088 |
| 7 | 0.0 | 0.0 | 0.0 | 1.0 | 1.00 | 0.928 | 0.01 | 0.059 |
| 8 | 0.0 | 0.0 | 0.0 | 1.0 | 1.00 | 0.964 | 0.00 | 0.036 |
| 9 | 0.0 | 0.0 | 0.0 | 1.0 | 1.00 | 0.985 | 0.00 | 0.021 |
| 10 | 0.0 | 0.0 | 0.0 | 1.0 | 1.00 | 0.995 | 0.00 | 0.010 |
| 11 | 0.0 | 0.0 | 0.0 | 1.0 | 1.00 | 0.999 | 0.00 | 0.004 |
| 12 | 0.0 | 0.0 | 0.0 | 1.0 | 1.00 | 1.000 | 0.00 | 0.001 |

Column (6). For illustrative purposes we have included Column (7), which can be derived from Columns (1) and (2) by use of (2.3.4). Then Columns (3) and (7) can be used in (2.3.4) to obtain Column (8). ▼

Several iterations of the convolution process can be very complex and involve numerous calculations. In many cases the result cannot be represented by any simpler formula than the convolution formulas given above. These formulas are suitable for use on programmable calculators and computers.

Another method to determine the distribution of the sum of independent random variables is based on the uniqueness of the *moment generating function* (m.g.f.), which, for the random variable $X$, is defined by $M_X(t) = \mathrm{E}[e^{tX}]$. If this expectation is finite for all $t$ in an open interval, then $M_X(t)$ is the only m.g.f. of the distribution of $X$ and it is not the m.g.f. of any other distribution. This uniqueness can be used as follows: For the sum $S = X_1 + X_2 + \cdots + X_n$, we have

$$
\begin{aligned}
M_S(t) = \mathrm{E}[e^{tS}] &= \mathrm{E}[e^{t(X_1 + X_2 + \cdots + X_n)}] \\
&= \mathrm{E}[e^{tX_1} e^{tX_2} \cdots e^{tX_n}].
\end{aligned}
\tag{2.3.8}
$$

If $X_1, X_2, \ldots, X_n$ are independent, then the expectation of the product in (2.3.8) is equal to

$$ \mathrm{E}[e^{tX_1}] \, \mathrm{E}[e^{tX_2}] \cdots \mathrm{E}[e^{tX_n}] $$

so that

$$ M_S(t) = M_{X_1}(t) \, M_{X_2}(t) \cdots M_{X_n}(t). \tag{2.3.9} $$

Recognition of the unique distribution corresponding to (2.3.9) would complete the determination of $S$'s distribution. If identification by recognition is not possible, then a process based on mathematics beyond the scope of this book must be used. (See Section 2.6.)

## 2.4 Approximations for the Distribution of the Sum

The *central limit theorem* suggests a method to obtain numerical values for the distribution of the sum of independent random variables. The usual statement of the theorem is for a sequence of independent and identically distributed random variables, $X_1, X_2, \ldots$, with $E[X_i] = \mu$ and $\text{Var}[X_i] = \sigma^2$. For each $n$, the distribution of $\sqrt{n}\,(\bar{X}_n - \mu)/\sigma$, where $\bar{X}_n = (X_1 + X_2 + \cdots + X_n)/n$, has mean 0 and variance 1. The sequence of distributions ($n = 1, 2, \ldots$) is known to approach the standard normal distribution. When $n$ is large the theorem is applied to approximate the distribution of $\bar{X}_n$ by a normal distribution with mean $\mu$ and variance $\sigma^2/n$. Equivalently the distribution of the sum of the $n$ random variables is approximated by a normal distribution with mean $n\mu$ and variance $n\sigma^2$. The effectiveness of these approximations depends not only on the number of variables but also on the departure of the distribution of the summands from normality. Many elementary statistics textbooks recommend that $n$ be at least 30 for the approximations to be reasonable. One routine used to generate normally distributed random variables for simulation is based on the average of only 12 independent random variables uniformly distributed over $(0,1)$.

In many individual risk models the random variables in the sum are not identically distributed. This will be illustrated by examples in the next section. The central limit theorem does extend to sequences of nonidentically distributed random variables.

To illustrate some applications of the individual risk model, we will use a normal approximation to the distribution of the sum of independent random variables to obtain numerical answers. If

$$S = X_1 + X_2 + \cdots + X_n,$$

then

$$E[S] = \sum_{k=1}^{n} E[X_k],$$

and further, under the assumption of independence,

$$\text{Var}[S] = \sum_{k=1}^{n} \text{Var}[X_k].$$

For an application we need only
• evaluate the means and variances of the individual loss random variables,
• sum them to obtain the mean and variance for the loss of the insuring organization as a whole,
• apply the normal approximation.

Illustrations of this process are in the following section.

# Chapter 2
## INDIVIDUAL RISK MODELS FOR A SHORT TERM

**2.5
Applications
to Insurance**

**Example 2.3:**

In this section three examples illustrate the results of Section 2.2 and use of the normal approximation.

A life insurance company issues 1-year term life contracts for benefit amounts of 1 and 2 units to individuals with probabilities of death of 0.02 or 0.10. The following table gives the number of individuals $n_k$ in each of the four classes created by a benefit amount $b_k$ and a probability of claim $q_k$.

| $k$ | $q_k$ | $b_k$ | $n_k$ |
|---|---|---|---|
| 1 | 0.02 | 1 | 500 |
| 2 | 0.02 | 2 | 500 |
| 3 | 0.10 | 1 | 300 |
| 4 | 0.10 | 2 | 500 |

The company wants to collect, from this population of 1800 individuals, an amount equal to the 95th percentile of the distribution of total claims. Moreover, it wants each individual's share of this amount to be proportional to that individual's expected claim. The share for individual $j$ with mean $E[X_j]$ would be $(1 + \theta)E[X_j]$. The 95th percentile requirement suggests that $\theta > 0$. This extra amount, $\theta E[X_j]$, is the *security loading* and $\theta$ is the *relative security loading*. Calculate $\theta$.

**Solution:**
The criterion for $\theta$ is $\Pr(S \le (1 + \theta)E[S]) = 0.95$ where $S = X_1 + X_2 + \cdots + X_{1800}$. This probability statement is equivalent to

$$\Pr\left(\frac{S - E[S]}{\sqrt{\mathrm{Var}[S]}} \le \frac{\theta E[S]}{\sqrt{\mathrm{Var}[S]}}\right) = 0.95.$$

Following the discussion of the central limit theorem in Section 2.4, we will approximate the distribution of $(S - E[S])/\sqrt{\mathrm{Var}[S]}$ by the standard normal distribution and use its 95th percentile to obtain

$$\frac{\theta E[S]}{\sqrt{\mathrm{Var}[S]}} = 1.645.$$

It remains to calculate the mean and variance of $S$ and to calculate $\theta$ by this equation.

For the four classes of insured individuals, we have the results given below.

| $k$ | $q_k$ | $b_k$ | Mean $b_k q_k$ | Variance $b_k^2 q_k (1 - q_k)$ | $n_k$ |
|---|---|---|---|---|---|
| 1 | 0.02 | 1 | 0.02 | 0.0196 | 500 |
| 2 | 0.02 | 2 | 0.04 | 0.0784 | 500 |
| 3 | 0.10 | 1 | 0.10 | 0.0900 | 300 |
| 4 | 0.10 | 2 | 0.20 | 0.3600 | 500 |

Then

$$E[S] = \sum_{j=1}^{1800} E[X_j] = \sum_{k=1}^{4} n_k \mu_k = 160$$

and

$$\text{Var}[S] = \sum_{j=1}^{1800} \text{Var}[X_j] = \sum_{k=1}^{4} n_k \sigma_k^2 = 256.$$

Thus, the relative security loading is

$$\theta = 1.645 \frac{\sqrt{\text{Var}[S]}}{E[S]} = 1.645 \frac{16}{160} = 0.1645.$$ ▼

**Example 2.4:**

The policyholders of an automobile insurance company fall into two classes.

| Class $k$ | Number in Class $n_k$ | Claim Probability $q_k$ | Distribution of Claim Amount, $B_k$, Parameters of Truncated Exponential | |
|---|---|---|---|---|
| | | | $\lambda$ | $L$ |
| 1 | 500 | 0.10 | 1 | 2.5 |
| 2 | 2 000 | 0.05 | 2 | 5.0 |

A truncated exponential distribution is defined by the d.f.

$$F(x) = \begin{cases} 0 & x < 0 \\ 1 - e^{-\lambda x} & 0 \le x < L \\ 1 & x \ge L. \end{cases}$$

This is a mixed distribution with p.d.f. $f(x) = \lambda e^{-\lambda x}$, $0 < x < L$, and a probability mass $e^{-\lambda L}$ at $L$. A graph of the p.d.f. and probability mass appears in Figure 2.5.

**Figure 2.5
Truncated
Exponential
Distribution**

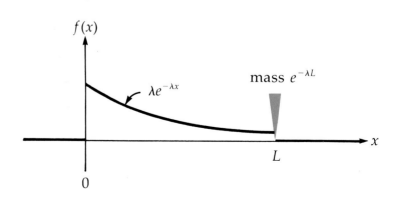

# INDIVIDUAL RISK MODELS FOR A SHORT TERM

Again, the probability that total claims exceed the amount collected from policyholders is to be 0.05. We assume that the relative security loading, $\theta$, is to be the same for the two classes. Calculate $\theta$.

**Solution:**
This example is much like the previous one. It differs in that the claim amounts are random variables. First we obtain formulas for the moments of the truncated exponential distribution in preparation for applying (2.2.25) and (2.2.26):

$$\mu = E[B|I = 1] = \int_0^L x\lambda e^{-\lambda x}\,dx + Le^{-\lambda L} = \frac{1 - e^{-\lambda L}}{\lambda}$$

$$E[B^2|I = 1] = \int_0^L x^2\lambda e^{-\lambda x}\,dx + L^2 e^{-\lambda L} = \frac{2}{\lambda^2}(1 - e^{-\lambda L}) - \frac{2L}{\lambda}e^{-\lambda L}$$

$$\sigma^2 = E[B^2|I = 1] - (E[B|I = 1])^2 = \frac{1 - 2\lambda Le^{-\lambda L} - e^{-2\lambda L}}{\lambda^2}.$$

Using the parameter values given and applying formulas (2.2.25) and (2.2.26) we obtain the following results.

| $k$ | $q_k$ | $\mu_k$ | $\sigma_k^2$ | Mean $q_k\mu_k$ | Variance $\mu_k^2 q_k(1 - q_k) + \sigma_k^2 q_k$ | $n_k$ |
|---|---|---|---|---|---|---|
| 1 | 0.10 | 0.9179 | 0.5828 | 0.09179 | 0.13411 | 500 |
| 2 | 0.05 | 0.5000 | 0.2498 | 0.02500 | 0.02436 | 2 000 |

Then $S$, the sum of the claims, has moments

$$E[S] = 500(0.09179) + 2000(0.02500) = 95.89$$

$$\text{Var}[S] = 500(0.13411) + 2000(0.02436) = 115.78.$$

The criterion for $\theta$ is the same as in Example 2.3,

$$\Pr(S \le (1 + \theta)E[S]) = 0.95.$$

Again by the normal approximation,

$$\frac{\theta E[S]}{\sqrt{\text{Var}[S]}} = 1.645$$

and

$$\theta = \frac{1.645\sqrt{115.78}}{95.89} = 0.1846.$$

▼

**Example 2.5:**

A life insurance company covers 16,000 lives for 1-year term life insurance in amounts shown below.

# INDIVIDUAL RISK MODELS
# FOR A SHORT TERM

| Benefit Amount $b_k$ | Number Covered $n_k$ |
|---|---|
| 10 000 | 8 000 |
| 20 000 | 3 500 |
| 30 000 | 2 500 |
| 50 000 | 1 500 |
| 100 000 | 500 |

The probability of a claim $q_k$ for each of the 16,000 lives, assumed to be mutually independent, is 0.02. The company wants to set a *retention limit.* For each life, the retention limit is the amount below which this (the *ceding*) company will retain the insurance and above which it will purchase *reinsurance* coverage from another (the *reinsuring*) company. For example, if the retention limit is 20,000, the company retains up to 20,000 on each life and purchases reinsurance for the excess over 20,000 of the benefit amount for each of the 4500 individuals with benefit amounts over 20,000. As a decision criterion, the company wants to minimize the probability that retained claims plus the amount that it pays for reinsurance will exceed 8,250,000. Reinsurance is available at a cost of 0.025 per unit of coverage (at 125% of the expected claim amount per unit, 0.02). We will consider the block of business as closed. New policies sold during the year are not to enter this decision process. Calculate the retention limit that minimizes the probability the company's retained claims plus cost of reinsurance will exceed 8,250,000.

**Partial Solution:**
First, let's do all calculations in benefit units of 10,000. As an illustrative step let $S$ be the amount of retained claims paid when the retention limit is 2 (20,000). Our portfolio of retained business is given by

| Retained Amount $b_k$ | Number Covered $n_k$ |
|---|---|
| 1 | 8 000 |
| 2 | 8 000 |

$$E[S] = \sum_{k=1}^{2} n_k b_k q_k = 8000\,(1)\,(0.02) + 8000\,(2)\,(0.02) = 480$$

and

$$\text{Var}\,[S] = \sum_{k=1}^{2} n_k b_k^2 q_k (1 - q_k)$$

$$= 8000\,(1)\,(0.02)\,(0.98) + 8000\,(4)\,(0.02)\,(0.98) = 784.$$

In addition to the retained claims, $S$, there is the cost of reinsurance premiums. The total coverage in the plan is

$$8000\,(1) + 3500\,(2) + 2500\,(3) + 1500\,(5) + 500\,(10) = 35,000.$$

## INDIVIDUAL RISK MODELS
## FOR A SHORT TERM

The retained amount is

$$8000\,(1) + 8000\,(2) = 24{,}000.$$

Therefore, the total amount reinsured is $35{,}000 - 24{,}000 = 11{,}000$ and the reinsurance cost is $11{,}000\,(0.025) = 275$. Thus, at retention limit 2, the retained claims plus reinsurance cost is $S + 275$. The decision criterion is based on the probability that this total cost will exceed 825,

$$\Pr\,(S + 275 > 825) = \Pr\,(S > 550)$$

$$= \Pr\left(\frac{S - \mathrm{E}[S]}{\sqrt{\mathrm{Var}\,[S]}} > \frac{550 - \mathrm{E}[S]}{\sqrt{\mathrm{Var}\,[S]}}\right)$$

$$= \Pr\left(\frac{S - \mathrm{E}[S]}{\sqrt{\mathrm{Var}\,[S]}} > 2.5\right).$$

Using the normal distribution we have this to be approximately 0.0062. The solution is completed in Exercises 2.13 and 2.14.    ▼

## 2.6
## Notes and
## References

The basis of the material in Sections 2.2, 2.3 and 2.4 can be found in a number of post-calculus probability and statistics texts. Mood et al. (1974) prove the theorems given in formulas (2.2.10) and (2.2.11). They also provide an extensive discussion of properties of the moment generating function. For a discussion of the advanced mathematical methods for deriving the distribution function that corresponds to a given moment generating function, see Bellman et al. (1966).

DeGroot (1986) provides a discussion of several conditions under which the central limit theorem holds. Kendall and Stuart (1977) provide material on **normal power expansions** that may be viewed as modifications of the normal approximation to improve numerical results. Bowers (1967) also describes the use of normal power expansions and gives an application to approximate the distribution of present values for an annuity portfolio.

## Exercises

*Section 2.2*

2.1. Use (2.2.3) and (2.2.4) to obtain the mean and variance of the claim random variable $X$ where $q = 0.05$ and the claim amount is fixed at 10.

2.2. Obtain the mean and variance of the claim random variable $X$ where $q = 0.05$ and the claim amount random variable $B$ is uniformly distributed between 0 and 20.

2.3. Let $X$ be the number of heads observed in 5 tosses of a true coin. Then, $X$ true dice are thrown. Let $Y$ be the sum of the numbers showing on the dice. Determine the mean and variance of $Y$. [Hint: Apply (2.2.10) and (2.2.11).]

2.4. Let $X$ be the number showing when 1 true die is thrown. Let $Y$ be the number of heads obtained when $X$ true coins are then tossed. Calculate $E[Y]$ and $\text{Var}[Y]$.

2.5. Let $X$ be the number obtained when 1 true die is tossed. Let $Y$ be the sum of the numbers obtained when $X$ true dice are then thrown. Calculate $E[Y]$ and $\text{Var}[Y]$.

2.6. The probability of a fire in a certain structure in a given time period is 0.02. If a fire occurs, the damage to the structure is uniformly distributed over the interval from 0 to its total value, $a$. Calculate the mean and variance of fire damage to the structure within the time period.

*Section 2.3*

2.7. Independent random variables $X_k$ for 4 lives have the discrete probability functions given below.

| $x$ | $\Pr(X_1 = x)$ | $\Pr(X_2 = x)$ | $\Pr(X_3 = x)$ | $\Pr(X_4 = x)$ |
|---|---|---|---|---|
| 0 | 0.6 | 0.7 | 0.6 | 0.9 |
| 1 | 0.0 | 0.2 | 0.0 | 0.0 |
| 2 | 0.3 | 0.1 | 0.0 | 0.0 |
| 3 | 0.0 | 0.0 | 0.4 | 0.0 |
| 4 | 0.1 | 0.0 | 0.0 | 0.1 |

Use a convolution process on the nonnegative integer values of $x$ to obtain $F_S(x)$ for $x = 0$, 1, 2, ..., 13 where $S = X_1 + X_2 + X_3 + X_4$.

2.8. Let $X_i$ for $i = 1, 2, 3$ be independent and identically distributed with the d.f.

$$F(x) = \begin{cases} 0 & x < 0 \\ x & 0 \le x < 1 \\ 1 & x \ge 1 \end{cases}$$

Let $S = X_1 + X_2 + X_3$.
a. Show that $F_S(x)$ is given by

$$F_S(x) = \begin{cases} 0 & x < 0 \\ x^3/6 & 0 \le x < 1 \\ [x^3 - 3(x-1)^3]/6 & 1 \le x < 2 \\ [x^3 - 3(x-1)^3 + 3(x-2)^3]/6 & 2 \le x < 3 \\ 1 & x \ge 3. \end{cases}$$

b. Show that $E[S] = 1.5$ and $\text{Var}[S] = 0.25$.
c. Evaluate the following probabilities using the d.f. of part (a).

(i)     $\Pr(S \le 0.5)$

(ii)    $\Pr(S \le 1.0)$

(iii)   $\Pr(S \le 1.5)$

# Chapter 2

## INDIVIDUAL RISK MODELS
## FOR A SHORT TERM

2.9. Consider three independent random variables $X_1$, $X_2$, $X_3$. Each has an exponential distribution with $E[X_i] = i$, $i = 1, 2, 3$. Derive the p.d.f. of $S = X_1 + X_2 + X_3$
   a. by the convolution process
   b. from the m.g.f. of $S$ using partial fractions.

*Section 2.4*

2.10. Calculate the mean and variance of $X$ and $Y$ in Example 2.1. Use a normal distribution to approximate $\Pr(X + Y > 4)$. Compare this with the exact answer.

2.11. a. Use the central limit theorem to calculate $b$, $c$ and $d$, for given $a$, in the statement

$$\Pr\left[\sum_1^n X_i \geq n\mu + a\sqrt{n}\,\sigma\right] \cong c + b\,\Phi(d)$$

   where the $X_i$'s are independent and identically distributed with mean $\mu$ and variance $\sigma^2$ and $\Phi(z)$ is the d.f. of the standard normal distribution.
   b. Evaluate the probabilities in (2.8.c) by use of the normal approximation developed in part (a).

2.12. A random variable $U$ has m.g.f.

$$M_U(t) = (1 - 2t)^{-9} \qquad t < \frac{1}{2}.$$

   a. Use the m.g.f. to calculate the mean and variance of $U$.
   b. Use a normal approximation to calculate points $y_{0.05}$ and $y_{0.01}$ such that $\Pr(U > y_\epsilon) = \epsilon$.

   Note that the random variable $U$ has a gamma distribution with parameters $\alpha = 9$ and $\beta = 1/2$. Gamma distributions with $\alpha = n/2$ and $\beta = 1/2$ are chi-square distributions with $n$ degrees of freedom. Thus $U$ has a chi-square distribution with 18 degrees of freedom. From tables of d.f.'s of chi-square distributions, we obtain $y_{0.05} = 28.869$ and $y_{0.01} = 34.805$.

*Section 2.5*

2.13. Calculate the probability that the total cost in Example 2.5 will exceed 8,250,000 if the retention limit is
   a. 30,000     b. 50,000.

2.14. Calculate the retention limit that minimizes the probability of the total cost in Example 2.5 exceeding 8,250,000. Assume that the limit is between 30,000 and 50,000.

2.15. A fire insurance company covers 160 structures against fire damage up to an amount stated in the contract. The numbers of contracts at the different contract amounts are given below.

| Contract Amount | Number of Contracts |
| --- | --- |
| 10 000 | 80 |
| 20 000 | 35 |
| 30 000 | 25 |
| 50 000 | 15 |
| 100 000 | 5 |

Assume, that for each of the structures, the probability of 1 claim within a year is 0.04 and the probability of more than 1 claim is 0. Assume that fires in the structures are mutually independent events. Furthermore, assume that the conditional distribution of the claim size, given that a claim has occurred, is uniformly distributed over the interval from 0 to the contract amount. Let $N$ be the number of claims and let $S$ be the amount of claims in a 1-year period.

a. Calculate the mean and variance of $N$.

b. Calculate the mean and variance of $S$.

c. What relative security loading, $\theta$, should be used so the company can collect an amount equal to the 99th percentile of the distribution of total claims? (Use a normal approximation.)

2.16. Consider a portfolio of 32 policies. For each policy, the probability $q$ of a claim is $1/6$ and $B$, the benefit amount given that there is a claim, has p.d.f.

$$f(y) = \begin{cases} 2(1 - y) & 0 < y < 1 \\ 0 & \text{elsewhere.} \end{cases}$$

Let $S$ be the total claims for the portfolio. Using a normal approximation, estimate $\Pr(S > 4)$.

# Chapter 3
## SURVIVAL DISTRIBUTIONS AND LIFE TABLES

**3**

## 3.1 Introduction

Chapter 1 was dedicated to showing how insurance can increase the expected utility of individuals facing random losses. In Chapter 2 simple models for single-period insurance policies were developed. The foundations of these models were Bernoulli random variables associated with the occurrence or nonoccurrence of a loss. The occurrence of a loss, in some examples, resulted in a second random process generating the amount of the loss. Chapters 4 through 7 will deal primarily with models for insurance systems designed to manage random losses where the randomness is related to how long an individual will survive. In these chapters the *time-until-death* random variable, $T(x)$, will be the basic building block. This chapter will develop a set of ideas for describing and using the distribution of time-until-death, and the distribution of the corresponding age-at-death, $X$.

We will show how a distribution of the age-at-death random variable can be summarized by a *life table*. Such tables are useful in many fields of science. Consequently a profusion of notation and nomenclature has developed among the various professions using life tables. For example, engineers use life tables to study the reliability of complex mechanical and electronic systems. Biostatisticians use life tables to compare the effectiveness of alternative treatments of serious diseases. Demographers use life tables as tools in population projections. In this text, life tables will be used to build models for insurance systems designed to assist individuals facing uncertainty about the times of their deaths. This application will determine the viewpoint adopted. However, when it will provide a bridge to other disciplines, notes relating to alternative applications of life tables will be added.

A life table is an indispensable component of many models in actuarial science. In fact, some scholars fix the date of the beginning of actuarial science as 1693. In that year, Edmund Halley published "An Estimate of the Degrees of the Mortality of Mankind, Drawn from Various Tables of Births and Funerals at the City of Breslau." The life table, called the Breslau Table, contained in Halley's paper remains of interest because of its surprisingly modern notation and ideas.

## 3.2 Probability for the Age-at-Death

In this section we formulate the uncertainty of age-at-death in probability concepts.

## 3.2.1 The Survival Function

Let us consider a newborn child. This newborn's age-at-death, $X$, is a continuous type random variable. Let $F(x)$ denote the d.f. of $X$,

$$F(x) = \Pr(X \le x) \qquad x \ge 0, \qquad (3.2.1)$$

and set

$$s(x) = 1 - F(x) = \Pr(X > x) \qquad x \ge 0. \qquad (3.2.2)$$

We shall always assume that $F(0) = 0$, which implies $s(0) = 1$. The function $s(x)$ is called the **survival function.** For any positive $x$, $s(x)$ is the probability a newborn will attain age $x$. The distribution of $X$ can be defined by specifying either the function $F(x)$ or the function $s(x)$. Within actuarial science and demography, the survival function has traditionally been used as a starting point for developments. Within probability and statistics, the d.f. usually plays this role. However, from the properties of the d.f., one can deduce corresponding properties of the survival function.

Using the laws of probability, one can make probability statements about the age-at-death in terms of either the survival function or the distribution function. For instance, the probability a newborn dies between ages $x$ and $z$ $(x < z)$ is

$$\Pr(x < X \le z) = F(z) - F(x)$$
$$= s(x) - s(z).$$

### 3.2.2 Time-Until-Death for a Person Aged $x$

The conditional probability that a newborn will die between the ages $x$ and $z$, given survival to age $x$, is

$$\Pr(x < X \le z | X > x) = \frac{F(z) - F(x)}{1 - F(x)}$$
$$= \frac{s(x) - s(z)}{s(x)}. \qquad (3.2.3)$$

The symbol $(x)$ will be used to denote a **life-aged-x.** The future life-time of $(x)$, $X - x$, will also be denoted by $T(x)$.

Within actuarial science, it is frequently necessary to make probability statements about $T(x)$. For this purpose, and in order to promote research and communication, a set of symbols, part of the International Actuarial Notation, was originally adopted by the 1898 International Actuarial Congress. Symbols for common actuarial functions, and principles to guide the adoption of new symbols, were established. Since then this system has been subject to constant review and is revised or extended as necessary by the International Actuarial Association's Permanent Committee on Notation. Insofar as possible, these notational conventions will be followed.

These symbols differ from those used for probability notation, and the reader may be unfamiliar with them. For example, a single-variate function that would be written $q(x)$ in probability notation is written $q_x$ in this system. Likewise, a multi-variate function is written in actuarial notation using combinations of subscripts, superscripts and other symbols. The general rules for defining a function in actuarial notation are given in Appendix 4. The reader may want to study these forms before continuing the text discussions of the future-lifetime random variable.

# Chapter 3

## SURVIVAL DISTRIBUTIONS AND LIFE TABLES

To make probability statements about $T(x)$, we have the notations

$$_tq_x = \Pr[T(x) \le t] \qquad t \ge 0 \qquad (3.2.4)$$

$$_tp_x = 1 - {_tq_x} = \Pr[T(x) > t] \qquad t \ge 0. \qquad (3.2.5)$$

The symbol $_tq_x$ can be interpreted as the probability $(x)$ will die within $t$ years; that is, $_tq_x$ is the distribution function of $T(x)$. On the other hand, $_tp_x$ can be interpreted as the probability $(x)$ will attain age $x + t$; that is, $_tp_x$ is the survival function for $(x)$. In the special case of a life-aged-0, we have $T(0) = X$ and

$$_xp_0 = s(x) \qquad x \ge 0. \qquad (3.2.6)$$

If $t = 1$, convention permits us to omit the prefix in the symbols defined in (3.2.4) and (3.2.5), and we have

$$q_x = \Pr[(x) \text{ will die within 1 year}]$$

$$p_x = \Pr[(x) \text{ will attain age } x + 1].$$

There is a special symbol for the more general event that $(x)$ will survive $t$ years and die within the following $u$ years; that is, $(x)$ will die between ages $x + t$ and $x + t + u$. This special symbol is given by

$$_{t|u}q_x = \Pr[t < T(x) \le t + u]$$

$$= {_{t+u}q_x} - {_tq_x}$$

$$= {_tp_x} - {_{t+u}p_x}. \qquad (3.2.7)$$

As before if $u = 1$, the prefix is deleted in $_{t|u}q_x$ and we have $_{t|}q_x$.

At this point it appears there are two expressions for the probability that $(x)$ will die between ages $x$ and $x + u$. Formula (3.2.7) with $t = 0$ is one such expression, (3.2.3) with $z = x + u$ is a second expression. Are these two probabilities different? Formula (3.2.3) can be interpreted as the conditional probability that a newborn will die between ages $x$ and $z = x + u$, given survival to age $x$. The only information on the newborn, now at age $x$, is its survival to that age. Hence, the probability statement is based on a conditional distribution of survival for newborns.

On the other hand, (3.2.7) with $t = 0$ defines a probability that a **life observed** at age $x$ will die between ages $x$ and $x + u$. The observation on the life at age $x$ might include information other than simply survival. Such information might be that the life has just passed a physical examination for insurance, or it might be that the life had commenced treatment for a serious illness. Life tables for situations where the observation of a life at age $x$ implies more than simply survival of a newborn to age $x$ will be discussed in Section 3.8. In this section, we will continue the development of the theory without further reference to the distinction between (3.2.3) and (3.2.7). Observation of survival at age $x$ will yield the same conditional distribution of survival as the hypothesis that a newborn has survived to age $x$; that is,

$$_tp_x = \frac{_{x+t}p_0}{_xp_0} = \frac{s(x + t)}{s(x)} \tag{3.2.8}$$

$$_tq_x = 1 - \frac{s(x + t)}{s(x)}. \tag{3.2.9}$$

Under this approach, (3.2.7), and its many special cases, can be expressed as

$$\begin{aligned}
_{t|u}q_x &= \frac{s(x + t) - s(x + t + u)}{s(x)} \\
&= \frac{s(x + t)}{s(x)} \frac{s(x + t) - s(x + t + u)}{s(x + t)} \\
&= {_tp_x}\,{_uq_{x+t}}.
\end{aligned} \tag{3.2.10}$$

### 3.2.3 Curtate-Future-Lifetime

A discrete random variable associated with the future lifetime is the number of future years completed by $(x)$ prior to death, or the curtate-future-lifetime of $(x)$. This random variable, $K(x)$, has the p.f.

$$\begin{aligned}
\Pr[K(x) = k] &= \Pr[k \le T(x) < k + 1] \\
&= \Pr[k < T(x) \le k + 1] \\
&= {_kp_x} - {_{k+1}p_x} \tag{3.2.11} \\
&= {_kp_x}\,q_{x+k} = {_{k|}q_x} \qquad k = 0,1,2,\ldots
\end{aligned}$$

The switching of inequalities is possible since, under our assumption that $T(x)$ is a continuous type random variable, $\Pr[T(x) = k] = \Pr[T(x) = k + 1] = 0$. Expression (3.2.11) is a special case of (3.2.7) where $u=1$ and $k$ is a nonnegative integer. From (3.2.11) we can see that the d.f. of $K(x)$ is the step function

$$\sum_{h=0}^{k} {_{h|}q_x} = {_{k+1}q_x},\ k = 0, 1, 2,\ldots$$

It often follows from context that $T(x)$ is the future lifetime of $(x)$, in which case we may write $T$ instead of $T(x)$. Likewise, we may write $K$ instead of $K(x)$.

### 3.2.4 Force of Mortality

Formula (3.2.3) expresses, in terms of the d.f. and in terms of the survival function, the conditional probability that (0) will die between ages $x$ and $z$, given survival to $x$. With $z - x$ held constant, say at $c$, then considered as a function of $x$, this conditional probability describes the distribution of the probability of death in the near future (between time 0 and $c$) for a life of attained age $x$. An analogue of this function for instantaneous death can be obtained by using the density of probability of death at attained age $x$, that is, using (3.2.3) with $z = x + \Delta x$,

# SURVIVAL DISTRIBUTIONS AND LIFE TABLES

$$\Pr[x < X \le x + \Delta x | X > x] = \frac{F(x + \Delta x) - F(x)}{1 - F(x)}$$

$$\cong \frac{f(x)\Delta x}{1 - F(x)}. \qquad (3.2.12)$$

In this expression $F'(x) = f(x)$ is the p.d.f. of the continuous age-at-death random variable. The function

$$\frac{f(x)}{1 - F(x)}$$

in (3.2.12) has a conditional probability density interpretation. For each age $x$, it gives the value of the conditional p.d.f. of $X$ at exact age $x$, given survival to that age. It is denoted by $\mu_x$. We have

$$\mu_x = \frac{f(x)}{1 - F(x)}$$

$$= \frac{-s'(x)}{s(x)}. \qquad (3.2.13)$$

The properties of $f(x)$ and of $1 - F(x)$ imply that $\mu_x \ge 0$.

In actuarial science and demography $\mu_x$ is called the **force of mortality.** In reliability theory, the study of the survival probabilities of manufactured parts and systems, $\mu_x$ is called the **failure rate** or **hazard rate** or, more fully, the **hazard rate function.**

As is true for the survival function, the force of mortality can be used to specify the distribution of $X$. To obtain this result, we start with (3.2.13), change $x$ to $y$ and rearrange to obtain

$$-\mu_y \, dy = d \log s(y).$$

Integrating this expression from $x$ to $x + n$, we have

$$-\int_x^{x+n} \mu_y \, dy = \log\left[\frac{s(x + n)}{s(x)}\right]$$

$$= \log {}_n p_x$$

and on taking exponentials obtain

$${}_n p_x = \exp(-\int_x^{x+n} \mu_y \, dy). \qquad (3.2.14)$$

Sometimes it is convenient to rewrite (3.2.14), with $s = y - x$, as

$${}_n p_x = \exp(-\int_0^n \mu_{x+s} \, ds). \qquad (3.2.15)$$

In particular, we will change the notation to conform with that used in (3.2.6) by setting the age already lived to 0 and denoting the time of survival by $x$. We then have

$${}_x p_0 = s(x) = \exp(-\int_0^x \mu_s \, ds). \qquad (3.2.16)$$

In addition

$$F(x) = 1 - s(x) = 1 - \exp(-\int_0^x \mu_s\, ds) \qquad (3.2.17)$$

and

$$F'(x) = f(x) = \exp(-\int_0^x \mu_s\, ds)\, \mu_x$$

$$= {}_x p_0\, \mu_x. \qquad (3.2.18)$$

Let $G(t)$ and $g(t)$ denote, respectively, the d.f. and p.d.f. of $T(x)$, the future lifetime of $(x)$. From (3.2.4) we note that $G(t) = {}_t q_x$. Therefore,

$$g(t) = \frac{d}{dt}\, {}_t q_x$$

$$= \frac{d}{dt}\left[1 - \frac{s(x+t)}{s(x)}\right]$$

$$= \frac{s(x+t)}{s(x)}\left[-\frac{s'(x+t)}{s(x+t)}\right]$$

$$= {}_t p_x\, \mu_{x+t} \qquad t \geq 0. \qquad (3.2.19)$$

Thus ${}_t p_x\, \mu_{x+t}\, dt$ is the probability that $(x)$ dies between $t$ and $t + dt$, and

$$\int_0^\infty {}_t p_x\, \mu_{x+t}\, dt = 1$$

where the upper limit on the integral is written as positive infinity (an abbreviation for integrating over all positive probability density).

It follows from (3.2.19) that

$$\frac{d}{dt}(1 - {}_t p_x) = -\frac{d}{dt}\, {}_t p_x = {}_t p_x\, \mu_{x+t}. \qquad (3.2.20)$$

This equivalent form is useful in several developments in actuarial mathematics.

Since

$$\lim_{n \to \infty} {}_n p_x = 0,$$

we have

$$\lim_{n \to \infty}(-\log {}_n p_x) = \infty;$$

that is,

$$\lim_{n \to \infty} \int_x^{x+n} \mu_y\, dy = \infty.$$

# Chapter 3

## SURVIVAL DISTRIBUTIONS AND LIFE TABLES

**Table 3.1.1**
**Definitions**

| Name of Concept | Symbol |
|---|---|
| Age-at-death random variable | $X$ |
| a life-aged-$x$ | $(x)$ |
| time-until-death random variable future-lifetime-of-$(x)$ random variable remaining-lifetime-of-$(x)$ random variable | $T(x)$ or $T$ |

The developments of this section are summarized in Tables 3.1.1 and 3.1.2.

**Table 3.1.2**
**Probability Theory Functions for Age-at-Death, $X$**

| | d.f $F(x)$ | p.d.f. $f(x)$ | Survival Function $s(x)$ | Force of Mortality $\mu_x$ |
|---|---|---|---|---|
| **Requirements** | | | | |
| For $x < 0$ | $F(x) = 0$ | $f(x) = 0$ | $s(x) = 1$ | $\mu_x = 0$ |
| For $x = 0$ | $F(x) = 0$ | $f(x) \geq 0$ | $s(x) = 1$ | $\mu_x \geq 0$ |
| For $x \geq 0$ | non-decreasing | $f(x) \geq 0$ | non-increasing | $\mu_x \geq 0$ |
| $\lim_{x \to \infty}$ | $F(\infty) = 1$ | $\int_0^\infty f(x)\,dx = 1$ | $s(\infty) = 0$ | $\int_0^\infty \mu_x\,dx = \infty$ |
| **Relationships** | | | | |
| Function in terms of | | | | |
| $F(x)$ | $F(x)$ | $F'(x)$ | $1 - F$ | $F'(x)/[1 - F(x)]$ |
| $f(x)$ | $\int_0^\infty f(s)\,ds$ | $f(x)$ | $1 - \int_0^\infty f(s)\,ds$ | $f(x)/\int_x^\infty f(s)\,ds$ |
| $s(x) = {}_x p_0$ | $1 - s(x)$ | $-s'(x)$ | $s(x)$ | $-s'(x)/s(x)$ |
| $\mu_x$ | $1 - e^{(-\int_0^x \mu_s ds)}$ | $e^{(-\int_0^x \mu_s ds)}\mu_x$ | $e^{(-\int_0^x \mu_s ds)}$ | $\mu_x$ |

The lower half of Table 3.1.2 summarizes some of the relationships among functions of general probability theory and those specific to age-at-death applications. There are many other examples where age-at-death questions can be formed in the more general probability setting. The following will illustrate this point.

**Example 3.1:**

If $\bar{A}$ refers to the complement of the event $A$ within the sample space and $\Pr(\bar{A}) \neq 0$, the following expresses an identity in probability theory:

$$\Pr(A \cup B) = \Pr(A) + \Pr(\bar{A}) \Pr(B|\bar{A}).$$

Rewrite this identity in actuarial notation for the events $A = [T(x) \leq t]$ and $B = [t < T(x) \leq 1]$, $0 < t < 1$.

**Solution:**
$\Pr(A \cup B)$ becomes $\Pr[T(x) \leq 1] = q_x$, $\Pr(A)$ is ${}_t q_x$ and $\Pr(B|\bar{A})$ is ${}_{1-t}q_{x+t}$, hence

$$q_x = {}_t q_x + {}_t p_x \, {}_{1-t}q_{x+t}.$$

▼

## 3.3
## Life Tables

A published life table usually contains tabulations, by individual ages, of the basic functions $q_x$, $l_x$, $d_x$, and, possibly, additional derived functions. Before presenting such a table, we consider an interpretation of these functions that is directly related to the probability functions discussed in the preceding section.

## 3.3.1
## Relation of Life Table Functions to the Survival Function

In (3.2.9) we expressed the conditional probability that $(x)$ will die within $t$ years by

$$_tq_x = 1 - \frac{s(x + t)}{s(x)}$$

and, in particular, we have

$$q_x = 1 - \frac{s(x + 1)}{s(x)}.$$

We now consider a group of $l_0$ newborns, $l_0 = 100{,}000$ for instance. Each newborn's age-at-death has a distribution specified by the survival function $s(x)$. In addition, we let $\mathscr{L}(x)$ denote the cohort's number of survivors to age $x$. We index these lives by $j = 1,2,\ldots,l_0$ and observe that

$$\mathscr{L}(x) = \sum_{j=1}^{l_0} I_j$$

where $I_j$ is an indicator for the survival of life $j$; that is,

$$I_j = \begin{cases} 1 & \text{if life } j \text{ survives to age } x \\ 0 & \text{otherwise.} \end{cases}$$

Since $\mathrm{E}[I_j] = s(x)$,

$$\mathrm{E}[\mathscr{L}(x)] = \sum_{j=1}^{l_0} \mathrm{E}[I_j] = l_0\, s(x).$$

We denote $\mathrm{E}[\mathscr{L}(x)]$ by $l_x$; that is, $l_x$ represents the expected number of survivors to age $x$ from the $l_0$ newborns, and we have

$$l_x = l_0\, s(x). \tag{3.3.1}$$

Moreover, under the assumption that the indicators $I_j$ are mutually independent, $\mathscr{L}(x)$ has a binomial distribution with parameters $n = l_0$ and $p = s(x)$. Note, however, that (3.3.1) does not require the independence assumption.

In a similar fashion, $_n\mathscr{D}_x$ will denote the number of deaths between ages $x$ and $x + n$ from among the initial $l_0$ lives. We will denote $\mathrm{E}[_n\mathscr{D}_x]$ by $_nd_x$. Since a newborn has probability $s(x) - s(x + n)$ of death between ages $x$ and $x + n$ we can, by an argument similar to that for $l_x$, express

# Chapter 3
## SURVIVAL DISTRIBUTIONS AND LIFE TABLES

$$
\begin{aligned}
{}_nd_x = \mathrm{E}[{}_n\mathscr{D}_x] &= l_0\,[s(x) - s(x + n)] \\
&= l_x - l_{x+n}.
\end{aligned}
\tag{3.3.2}
$$

When $n = 1$, we omit the prefixes on ${}_n\mathscr{D}_x$ and ${}_nd_x$.

From (3.3.1), we see that

$$
-\frac{1}{l_x}\frac{dl_x}{dx} = -\frac{1}{s(x)}\frac{ds(x)}{dx} = \mu_x
\tag{3.3.3}
$$

and

$$
-dl_x = l_x\,\mu_x\,dx.
\tag{3.3.4}
$$

Since

$$
l_x\,\mu_x = l_0\,{}_xp_0\,\mu_x = l_0\,f(x),
$$

the factor $l_x\,\mu_x$ in (3.3.4) can be interpreted as the expected density of deaths in the age interval $(x,\ x + dx)$. We note further that

$$
l_x = l_0 \exp\left(-\int_0^x \mu_y\,dy\right)
\tag{3.3.5}
$$

$$
l_{x+n} = l_x \exp\left(-\int_x^{x+n} \mu_y\,dy\right)
\tag{3.3.6}
$$

$$
l_x - l_{x+n} = \int_x^{x+n} l_y\,\mu_y\,dy.
\tag{3.3.7}
$$

For human lives, there have been few observations of age-at-death beyond 110. Consequently, it is often assumed that there is an age $\omega$ such that $s(x) > 0$ for $x < \omega$, and $s(x) = 0$ for $x \geq \omega$. The age $\omega$, if assumed, is called the *limiting age.*

For convenience of reference, we shall call this concept of $l_0$ newborns, each with survival function $s(x)$, a *random survivorship group.*

**3.3.2**
**Life Table**
**Example**

In "Life Table for the Total Population: United States, 1979–81" (Table 3.2), the functions ${}_tq_x$, $l_x$ and ${}_td_x$ are presented with $l_0 = 100{,}000$. Except for the first year of life, the value of $t$ in the tabulated functions ${}_tq_x$ and ${}_td_x$ is 1. The other functions appearing in the table are discussed in Section 3.5.

The 1979–81 U.S. Life Table was not constructed by observing 100,000 newborns until the last survivor died. Instead, it was based on estimates of probabilities of death, given survival to various ages, derived from the experience of the entire U.S. population in the years around the 1980 census. In using the random survivorship group concept with this table, we must make the assumption that the probabilities derived from the table will be appropriate for the lifetimes of those who belong to the survivorship group.

Several observations about the 1979–81 U.S. Life Table are instructive.

**Observation:**

1. Approximately 1% of a survivorship group of newborns would be expected to die in the first year of life.

2. It would be expected that about 77% of a group of newborns would survive to age 65.

3. The maximum number of deaths within a group would be expected to occur at age 83.

4. The limiting age is not defined. It is clear that there is a probability of survival to age 110, but the table does not indicate the age $\omega$ where $s(\omega) = 0$.

5. Local minimums in the expected number of deaths occur around ages 11 and 27.

6. Although the values of $l_x$ have been rounded to integers, there is no compelling reason, according to (3.3.1), to do so.

A display such as Table 3.2 is the conventional method for describing the distribution of age-at-death. Alternatively, a survival function could be described in analytic form such as $s(x) = e^{-cx}$, $c > 0$, $x \geq 0$. However, most studies of human mortality for insurance purposes use the representation $s(x) = l_x/l_0$, as illustrated in Table 3.2. Since 100,000 $s(x)$ is displayed for only integer values of $x$, there is a need to interpolate in evaluating $s(x)$ for noninteger values. This will be the subject of Section 3.6.

**Example 3.2:**

On the basis of Table 3.2, evaluate the probability that (20) will
  a. live to 100
  b. die before 70
  c. die in the tenth decade of life.

**Solution:**

a. $\dfrac{s(100)}{s(20)} = \dfrac{l_{100}}{l_{20}} = \dfrac{1150}{97{,}741} = 0.0118$

b. $\dfrac{[s(20) - s(70)]}{s(20)} = 1 - \dfrac{l_{70}}{l_{20}} = 1 - \dfrac{68{,}248}{97{,}741} = 0.3017$

c. $\dfrac{[s(90) - s(100)]}{s(20)} = \dfrac{(l_{90} - l_{100})}{l_{20}} = \dfrac{(14{,}154 - 1150)}{97{,}741} = 0.1330$      ▼

Insight into life table functions can be obtained by studying Figures 3.1, 3.2 and 3.3. These have been drawn to be representative of current human mortality and are not taken directly from Table 3.2.

In Figure 3.1 note that
• the force of mortality is positive and the requirement

$$\int_0^\infty \mu_x \, dx = \infty$$

appears satisfied. (See Table 3.1.2.)

# Chapter 3
# SURVIVAL DISTRIBUTIONS AND LIFE TABLES

**Table 3.2**
**Life Table for the Total Population: United States, 1979–81**

| Age Interval | Proportion Dying | Of 100,000 Born Alive | | Stationary Population* (Years Lived) | | Average Remaining Lifetime |
|---|---|---|---|---|---|---|
| Period of Life between Two Ages (1) $x$ to $x + t$ | Proportion of Persons Alive at Beginning of Age Interval Dying During Interval (2) $_tq_x$ | Number Living at Beginning of Age Interval (3) $l_x$ | Number Dying During Age Interval (4) $_td_x$ | In the Age Interval (5) $_tL_x$ | In This and All Subsequent Age Intervals (6) $T_x$ | Average Number of Years of Life Remaining at Beginning of Age Interval (7) $\overset{\circ}{e}_x$ |
| **Days** | | | | | | |
| 0–1 | 0.00463 | 100 000 | 463 | 273 | 7 387 758 | 73.88 |
| 1–7 | 0.00246 | 99 537 | 245 | 1 635 | 7 387 485 | 74.22 |
| 7–28 | 0.00139 | 99 292 | 138 | 5 708 | 7 385 850 | 74.38 |
| 28–365 | 0.00418 | 99 154 | 414 | 91 357 | 7 380 142 | 74.43 |
| **Years** | | | | | | |
| 0–1 | 0.01260 | 100 000 | 1 260 | 98 973 | 7 387 758 | 73.88 |
| 1–2 | 0.00093 | 98 740 | 92 | 98 694 | 7 288 785 | 73.82 |
| 2–3 | 0.00065 | 98 648 | 64 | 98 617 | 7 190 091 | 72.89 |
| 3–4 | 0.00050 | 98 584 | 49 | 98 560 | 7 091 474 | 71.93 |
| 4–5 | 0.00040 | 98 535 | 40 | 98 515 | 6 992 914 | 70.97 |
| 5–6 | 0.00037 | 98 495 | 36 | 98 477 | 6 894 399 | 70.00 |
| 6–7 | 0.00033 | 98 459 | 33 | 98 442 | 6 795 922 | 69.02 |
| 7–8 | 0.00030 | 98 426 | 30 | 98 412 | 6 697 480 | 68.05 |
| 8–9 | 0.00027 | 98 396 | 26 | 98 383 | 6 599 068 | 67.07 |
| 9–10 | 0.00023 | 98 370 | 23 | 98 358 | 6 500 685 | 66.08 |
| 10–11 | 0.00020 | 98 347 | 19 | 98 338 | 6 402 327 | 65.10 |
| 11–12 | 0.00019 | 98 328 | 19 | 98 319 | 6 303 989 | 64.11 |
| 12–13 | 0.00025 | 98 309 | 24 | 98 297 | 6 205 670 | 63.12 |
| 13–14 | 0.00037 | 98 285 | 37 | 98 266 | 6 107 373 | 62.14 |
| 14–15 | 0.00053 | 98 248 | 52 | 98 222 | 6 009 107 | 61.16 |
| 15–16 | 0.00069 | 98 196 | 67 | 98 163 | 5 910 885 | 60.19 |
| 16–17 | 0.00083 | 98 129 | 82 | 98 087 | 5 812 722 | 59.24 |
| 17–18 | 0.00095 | 98 047 | 94 | 98 000 | 5 714 635 | 58.28 |
| 18–19 | 0.00105 | 97 953 | 102 | 97 902 | 5 616 635 | 57.34 |
| 19–20 | 0.00112 | 97 851 | 110 | 97 796 | 5 518 733 | 56.40 |
| 20–21 | 0.00120 | 97 741 | 118 | 97 682 | 5 420 937 | 55.46 |
| 21–22 | 0.00127 | 97 623 | 124 | 97 561 | 5 323 255 | 54.53 |
| 22–23 | 0.00132 | 97 499 | 129 | 97 435 | 5 225 694 | 53.60 |
| 23–24 | 0.00134 | 97 370 | 130 | 97 306 | 5 128 259 | 52.67 |
| 24–25 | 0.00133 | 97 240 | 130 | 97 175 | 5 030 953 | 51.74 |
| 25–26 | 0.00132 | 97 110 | 128 | 97 046 | 4 933 778 | 50.81 |
| 26–27 | 0.00131 | 96 982 | 126 | 96 919 | 4 836 732 | 49.87 |
| 27–28 | 0.00130 | 96 856 | 126 | 96 793 | 4 739 813 | 48.94 |
| 28–29 | 0.00130 | 96 730 | 126 | 96 667 | 4 643 020 | 48.00 |
| 29–30 | 0.00131 | 96 604 | 127 | 96 541 | 4 546 353 | 47.06 |

*Stationary population is a demographic concept treated in Chapter 18.

# SURVIVAL DISTRIBUTIONS AND LIFE TABLES

**Table 3.2**
**Life Table for the Total Population: United States, 1979–81—Continued**

| Age Interval | Proportion Dying | Of 100,000 Born Alive | | Stationary Population* *(Years Lived)* | | Average Remaining Lifetime |
|---|---|---|---|---|---|---|
| Period of Life between Two Ages (1) $x$ to $x + t$ | Proportion of Persons Alive at Beginning of Age Interval Dying During Interval (2) $_tq_x$ | Number Living at Beginning of Age Interval (3) $l_x$ | Number Dying During Age Interval (4) $_td_x$ | In the Age Interval (5) $_tL_x$ | In This and All Subsequent Age Intervals (6) $T_x$ | Average Number of Years of Life Remaining at Beginning of Age Interval (7) $\overset{\circ}{e}_x$ |
| Years—continued | | | | | | |
| 30–31 | 0.00133 | 96 477 | 127 | 96 414 | 4 449 812 | 46.12 |
| 31–32 | 0.00134 | 96 350 | 130 | 96 284 | 4 353 398 | 45.18 |
| 32–33 | 0.00137 | 96 220 | 132 | 96 155 | 4 257 114 | 44.24 |
| 33–34 | 0.00142 | 96 088 | 137 | 96 019 | 4 160 959 | 43.30 |
| 34–35 | 0.00150 | 95 951 | 143 | 95 880 | 4 064 940 | 42.36 |
| 35–36 | 0.00159 | 95 808 | 153 | 95 731 | 3 969 060 | 41.43 |
| 36–37 | 0.00170 | 95 655 | 163 | 95 574 | 3 873 329 | 40.49 |
| 37–38 | 0.00183 | 95 492 | 175 | 95 404 | 3 777 755 | 39.56 |
| 38–39 | 0.00197 | 95 317 | 188 | 95 224 | 3 682 351 | 38.63 |
| 39–40 | 0.00213 | 95 129 | 203 | 95 027 | 3 587 127 | 37.71 |
| 40–41 | 0.00232 | 94 926 | 220 | 94 817 | 3 492 100 | 36.79 |
| 41–42 | 0.00254 | 94 706 | 241 | 94 585 | 3 397 283 | 35.87 |
| 42–43 | 0.00279 | 94 465 | 264 | 94 334 | 3 302 698 | 34.96 |
| 43–44 | 0.00306 | 94 201 | 288 | 94 057 | 3 208 364 | 34.06 |
| 44–45 | 0.00335 | 93 913 | 314 | 93 756 | 3 114 307 | 33.16 |
| 45–46 | 0.00366 | 93 599 | 343 | 93 427 | 3 020 551 | 32.27 |
| 46–47 | 0.00401 | 93 256 | 374 | 93 069 | 2 927 124 | 31.39 |
| 47–48 | 0.00442 | 92 882 | 410 | 92 677 | 2 834 055 | 30.51 |
| 48–49 | 0.00488 | 92 472 | 451 | 92 246 | 2 741 378 | 29.65 |
| 49–50 | 0.00538 | 92 021 | 495 | 91 773 | 2 649 132 | 28.79 |
| 50–51 | 0.00589 | 91 526 | 540 | 91 256 | 2 557 359 | 27.94 |
| 51–52 | 0.00642 | 90 986 | 584 | 90 695 | 2 466 103 | 27.10 |
| 52–53 | 0.00699 | 90 402 | 631 | 90 086 | 2 375 408 | 26.28 |
| 53–54 | 0.00761 | 89 771 | 684 | 89 430 | 2 285 322 | 25.46 |
| 54–55 | 0.00830 | 89 087 | 739 | 88 717 | 2 195 892 | 24.65 |
| 55–56 | 0.00902 | 88 348 | 797 | 87 950 | 2 107 175 | 23.85 |
| 56–57 | 0.00978 | 87 551 | 856 | 87 122 | 2 019 225 | 23.06 |
| 57–58 | 0.01059 | 86 695 | 919 | 86 236 | 1 932 103 | 22.29 |
| 58–59 | 0.01151 | 85 776 | 987 | 85 283 | 1 845 867 | 21.52 |
| 59–60 | 0.01254 | 84 789 | 1 063 | 84 258 | 1 760 584 | 20.76 |
| 60–61 | 0.01368 | 83 726 | 1 145 | 83 153 | 1 676 326 | 20.02 |
| 61–62 | 0.01493 | 82 581 | 1 233 | 81 965 | 1 593 173 | 19.29 |
| 62–63 | 0.01628 | 81 348 | 1 324 | 80 686 | 1 511 208 | 18.58 |
| 63–64 | 0.01767 | 80 024 | 1 415 | 79 316 | 1 430 522 | 17.88 |
| 64–65 | 0.01911 | 78 609 | 1 502 | 77 859 | 1 351 206 | 17.19 |

*Stationary population is a demographic concept treated in Chapter 18.

# SURVIVAL DISTRIBUTIONS AND LIFE TABLES

**Table 3.2**
**Life Table for the Total Population: United States, 1979–81—Continued**

| Age Interval | Proportion Dying | Of 100,000 Born Alive | | Stationary Population* (Years Lived) | | Average Remaining Lifetime |
|---|---|---|---|---|---|---|
| Period of Life between Two Ages (1) | Proportion of Persons Alive at Beginning of Age Interval Dying During Interval (2) | Number Living at Beginning of Age Interval (3) | Number Dying During Age Interval (4) | In the Age Interval (5) | In This and All Subsequent Age Intervals (6) | Average Number of Years of Life Remaining at Beginning of Age Interval (7) |
| $x$ to $x + t$ | $_tq_x$ | $l_x$ | $_td_x$ | $_tL_x$ | $T_x$ | $\overset{\circ}{e}_x$ |
| Years—continued | | | | | | |
| 65–66 | 0.02059 | 77 107 | 1 587 | 76 314 | 1 273 347 | 16.51 |
| 66–67 | 0.02216 | 75 520 | 1 674 | 74 683 | 1 197 033 | 15.85 |
| 67–68 | 0.02389 | 73 846 | 1 764 | 72 964 | 1 122 350 | 15.20 |
| 68–69 | 0.02585 | 72 082 | 1 864 | 71 150 | 1 049 386 | 14.56 |
| 69–70 | 0.02806 | 70 218 | 1 970 | 69 233 | 978 236 | 13.93 |
| 70–71 | 0.03052 | 68 248 | 2 083 | 67 206 | 909 003 | 13.32 |
| 71–72 | 0.03315 | 66 165 | 2 193 | 65 069 | 841 797 | 12.72 |
| 72–73 | 0.03593 | 63 972 | 2 299 | 62 823 | 776 728 | 12.14 |
| 73–74 | 0.03882 | 61 673 | 2 394 | 60 476 | 713 905 | 11.58 |
| 74–75 | 0.04184 | 59 279 | 2 480 | 58 039 | 653 429 | 11.02 |
| 75–76 | 0.04507 | 56 799 | 2 560 | 55 520 | 595 390 | 10.48 |
| 76–77 | 0.04867 | 54 239 | 2 640 | 52 919 | 539 870 | 9.95 |
| 77–78 | 0.05274 | 51 599 | 2 721 | 50 238 | 486 951 | 9.44 |
| 78–79 | 0.05742 | 48 878 | 2 807 | 47 475 | 436 713 | 8.93 |
| 79–80 | 0.06277 | 46 071 | 2 891 | 44 626 | 389 238 | 8.45 |
| 80–81 | 0.06882 | 43 180 | 2 972 | 41 694 | 344 612 | 7.98 |
| 81–82 | 0.07552 | 40 208 | 3 036 | 38 689 | 302 918 | 7.53 |
| 82–83 | 0.08278 | 37 172 | 3 077 | 35 634 | 264 229 | 7.11 |
| 83–84 | 0.09041 | 34 095 | 3 083 | 32 553 | 228 595 | 6.70 |
| 84–85 | 0.09842 | 31 012 | 3 052 | 29 486 | 196 042 | 6.32 |
| 85–86 | 0.10725 | 27 960 | 2 999 | 26 461 | 166 556 | 5.96 |
| 86–87 | 0.11712 | 24 961 | 2 923 | 23 500 | 140 095 | 5.61 |
| 87–88 | 0.12717 | 22 038 | 2 803 | 20 636 | 116 595 | 5.29 |
| 88–89 | 0.13708 | 19 235 | 2 637 | 17 917 | 95 959 | 4.99 |
| 89–90 | 0.14728 | 16 598 | 2 444 | 15 376 | 78 042 | 4.70 |
| 90–91 | 0.15868 | 14 154 | 2 246 | 13 031 | 62 666 | 4.43 |
| 91–92 | 0.17169 | 11 908 | 2 045 | 10 886 | 49 635 | 4.17 |
| 92–93 | 0.18570 | 9 863 | 1 831 | 8 948 | 38 749 | 3.93 |
| 93–94 | 0.20023 | 8 032 | 1 608 | 7 228 | 29 801 | 3.71 |
| 94–95 | 0.21495 | 6 424 | 1 381 | 5 733 | 22 573 | 3.51 |
| 95–96 | 0.22976 | 5 043 | 1 159 | 4 463 | 16 840 | 3.34 |
| 96–97 | 0.24338 | 3 884 | 945 | 3 412 | 12 377 | 3.19 |
| 97–98 | 0.25637 | 2 939 | 754 | 2 562 | 8 965 | 3.05 |
| 98–99 | 0.26868 | 2 185 | 587 | 1 892 | 6 403 | 2.93 |
| 99–100 | 0.28030 | 1 598 | 448 | 1 374 | 4 511 | 2.82 |

*Stationary population is a demographic concept treated in Chapter 18.

**Table 3.2**
**Life Table for the Total Population: United States, 1979–81—Continued**

| Age Interval | Proportion Dying | Of 100,000 Born Alive | | Stationary Population* _(Years Lived)_ | | Average Remaining Lifetime |
|---|---|---|---|---|---|---|
| Period of Life between Two Ages | Proportion of Persons Alive at Beginning of Age Interval Dying During Interval | Number Living at Beginning of Age Interval | Number Dying During Age Interval | In the Age Interval | In This and All Subsequent Age Intervals | Average Number of Years of Life Remaining at Beginning of Age Interval |
| (1) | (2) | (3) | (4) | (5) | (6) | (7) |
| $x$ to $x+t$ | $_t q_x$ | $l_x$ | $_t d_x$ | $_t L_x$ | $T_x$ | $\overset{\circ}{e}_x$ |
| Years—continued | | | | | | |
| 100–101 | 0.29120 | 1 150 | 335 | 983 | 3 137 | 2.73 |
| 101–102 | 0.30139 | 815 | 245 | 692 | 2 154 | 2.64 |
| 102–103 | 0.31089 | 570 | 177 | 481 | 1 462 | 2.57 |
| 103–104 | 0.31970 | 393 | 126 | 330 | 981 | 2.50 |
| 104–105 | 0.32786 | 267 | 88 | 223 | 651 | 2.44 |
| 105–106 | 0.33539 | 179 | 60 | 150 | 428 | 2.38 |
| 106–107 | 0.34233 | 119 | 41 | 99 | 278 | 2.33 |
| 107–108 | 0.34870 | 78 | 27 | 64 | 179 | 2.29 |
| 108–109 | 0.35453 | 51 | 18 | 42 | 115 | 2.24 |
| 109–110 | 0.35988 | 33 | 12 | 27 | 73 | 2.20 |

*Stationary population is a demographic concept treated in Chapter 18.

**Figure 3.1**
**Force of Mortality**

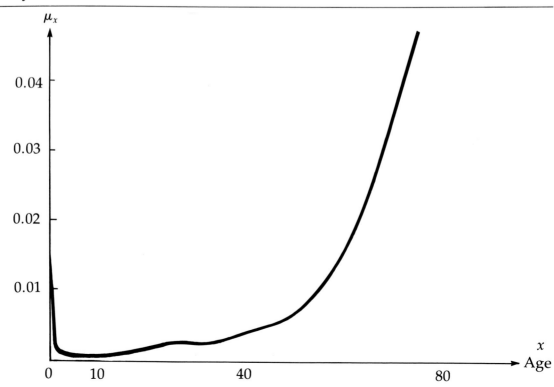

# SURVIVAL DISTRIBUTIONS
# AND LIFE TABLES

**Figure 3.2**
**Graph of $l_x\mu_x$**

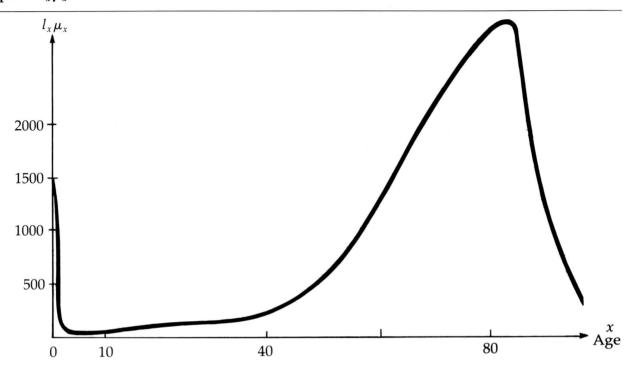

**Figure 3.3**
**Graph of $l_x$**

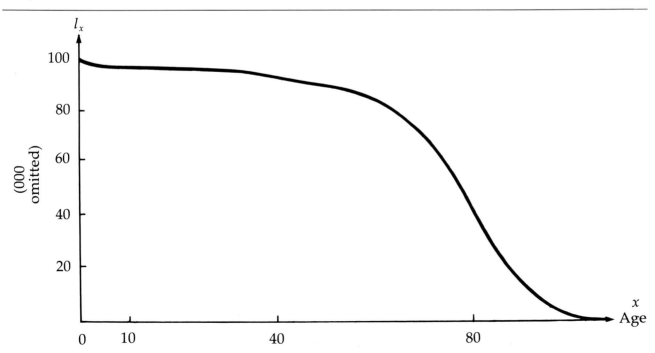

- the force of mortality starts out rather large and then drops to a minimum around age 10.

In Figures 3.2 and 3.3 note that
- the function $l_x \mu_x$ is proportional to the p.d.f. of the age-at-death of a newborn. Since $l_x \mu_x$ is the expected density of deaths at age $x$, under the random survivorship group idea, the graph of $l_x \mu_x$ is called *the curve of deaths.*
- there is a local minimum of $l_x \mu_x$ at about age 10. The mode of the distribution of deaths—the age at which the maximum of the curve of deaths occurs—is around age 80.
- the function $l_x$ is proportional to the survival function $s(x)$. It can also be interpreted as the expected number living at age $x$ out of an initial group of size $l_0$.
- local extreme points of $l_x \mu_x$ correspond to points of inflection of $l_x$ since

$$\frac{d}{dx} l_x \mu_x = \frac{d}{dx}\left(-\frac{d}{dx} l_x\right) = -\frac{d^2}{dx^2} l_x.$$

## 3.4 The Deterministic Survivorship Group

We proceed now to a second, and nonprobabilistic, interpretation of the life table. This is rooted mathematically in the concept of decrement (negative growth) rates. As such, it is related to growth-rate applications in biology and in economics. It is deterministic in nature and leads to the concept of a *deterministic survivorship group* or *cohort*.

A deterministic survivorship group, as represented by a life table, has the following characteristics:
- The group initially consists of $l_0$ lives aged 0.
- The members of the group are subject, at each age of their lives, to effective annual rates of mortality (decrement) specified by the values of $q_x$ in the life table.
- The group is closed. No further entrants are allowed beyond the initial $l_0$. The only decreases come as a result of the effective annual rates of mortality (decrement).

From these characteristics it follows that the progress of the group will be determined by

$$l_1 = l_0 (1 - q_0) = l_0 - d_0$$

$$l_2 = l_1 (1 - q_1) = l_1 - d_1 = l_0 - (d_0 + d_1)$$

$$\vdots \qquad \vdots \qquad\qquad \vdots \qquad\qquad \vdots \qquad\qquad\qquad (3.4.1)$$

$$l_x = l_{x-1}(1 - q_{x-1}) = l_{x-1} - d_{x-1} = l_0 - \sum_{y=0}^{x-1} d_y$$

$$= l_0 \left(1 - \frac{\sum_{y=0}^{x-1} d_y}{l_0}\right) = l_0 (1 - {}_x q_0)$$

# Chapter 3

## SURVIVAL DISTRIBUTIONS AND LIFE TABLES

where $l_x$ is the number of lives attaining age $x$ in the survivorship group. This chain of equalities, generated by a value $l_0$ called the **radix** and a set of $q_x$ values, can be rewritten as

$$l_1 = l_0 p_0$$

$$l_2 = l_1 p_1 = (l_0 p_0) p_1 \qquad (3.4.2)$$

$$\vdots \qquad \vdots \qquad \vdots$$

$$l_x = l_{x-1} p_{x-1} = l_0 \left( \prod_{y=0}^{x-1} p_y \right) = l_0 \, _x p_0.$$

There is an analogy between the deterministic survivorship group and the model for compound interest. Table 3.3 is designed to summarize some of this parallelism.

**Table 3.3**
**Related Concepts of the Mathematics of Compound Interest and of Deterministic Survivorship Groups**

| Compound Interest | Survivorship Group |
|---|---|
| $A(t)$ = Size of fund at time $t$, time measured in years | $l_x$ = Size of group at age $x$, age measured in years |
| Effective annual rate of interest (increment) $$i_t = \frac{A(t+1) - A(t)}{A(t)}$$ | Effective annual rate of mortality (decrement) $$q_x = \frac{l_x - l_{x+1}}{l_x}$$ |
| Effective $n$-year rate of interest, starting at time $t$ $$_n i_t = \frac{A(t+n) - A(t)}{A(t)} \quad *$$ | Effective $n$-year rate of mortality, starting at age $x$ $$_n q_x = \frac{l_x - l_{x+n}}{l_x}$$ |
| Force of interest at time $t$ $$\delta_t = \lim_{\Delta t \to 0} \left[ \frac{A(t + \Delta t) - A(t)}{A(t)\, \Delta t} \right]$$ $$= \frac{1}{A(t)} \frac{dA(t)}{dt}$$ | Force of mortality at age $x$ $$\mu_x = \lim_{\Delta x \to 0} \left[ \frac{l_x - l_{x+\Delta x}}{l_x\, \Delta x} \right]$$ $$= -\frac{1}{l_x} \frac{dl_x}{dx}$$ |

*There is no universally accepted symbol for an effective $n$-year rate of interest.

The headings of the $_t q_x$, $l_x$ and $_t d_x$ columns in Table 3.2 refer to the deterministic survivorship group interpretation. While the mathematical foundations of the random survivorship group and the deterministic survivorship group are different, the resulting functions $q_x$, $l_x$, $d_x$ have the same mathematical properties and subsequent analysis. The random survivorship group concept has the advantage of allowing for the full use of probability theory. The deterministic survivorship group is conceptually simple and easy to apply, but does not take account of random variation in the number of survivors.

## 3.5
## Other Life Table Functions

Before proceeding to derive expressions for the moments of the distribution of $T(x)$, we shall prove a theorem useful in computing expected values. Two versions of the theorem will be proved. One version, Theorem 3.1, will pertain to continuous random variables. The second version, Theorem 3.2, will pertain to discrete random variables.

**Theorem 3.1:**

If $T$ is a continuous type random variable with d.f. $G(t)$ such that $G(0) = 0$ and p.d.f. $G'(t) = g(t)$, and $z(t)$ is such that
• it is a nonnegative, monotonic, differentiable function and
• $E[z(T)]$ exists,

then

$$E[z(T)] = \int_0^\infty z(t)\, g(t)\, dt$$

$$= z(0) + \int_0^\infty z'(t)[1 - G(t)]\, dt.$$

**Proof:**
Integrating by parts we have

$$\int_0^t z(s)\, g(s)\, ds = -\int_0^t z(s)\, d[1 - G(s)]$$

$$= -z(s)\,[1 - G(s)]\big|_0^t + \int_0^t [1 - G(s)]\, z'(s)\, ds.$$

The theorem follows if $\lim_{t \to \infty} z(t)[1 - G(t)] = 0$. We consider two cases:

a. If the nonnegative function $z(t)$ is nonincreasing, then clearly $\lim_{t \to \infty} z(t)[1 - G(t)] = 0$.

b. If the nonnegative function $z(t)$ is nondecreasing, then

$$0 \le z(t)[1 - G(t)] = z(t) \int_t^\infty g(s)\, ds \le \int_t^\infty z(s)\, g(s)\, ds.$$

But if $E[z(T)]$ exists, then

$$\lim_{t \to \infty} \int_t^\infty z(s)\, g(s)\, ds = 0,$$

hence

$$\lim_{t \to \infty} z(t)[1 - G(t)] = 0,$$

and the theorem follows.                                          ■

Theorem 3.1 will be used to relate two formulas for $E[T(x)]$. This expected value is denoted by $\overset{\circ}{e}_x$ and is called the *complete-expectation-of-life*. By definition, we have

# SURVIVAL DISTRIBUTIONS
# AND LIFE TABLES

$$\overset{\circ}{e}_x = E[T(x)] = \int_0^\infty t \; {}_tp_x \; \mu_{x+t} dt. \tag{3.5.1}$$

Using Theorem 3.1, with $z(t) = t$ and $G(t) = 1 - {}_tp_x$, we have

$$\overset{\circ}{e}_x = \int_0^\infty {}_tp_x \, dt. \tag{3.5.2}$$

The complete-expectation-of-life at various ages is often used to compare levels of public health among different populations.

We can also use Theorem 3.1 with $z(t) = t^2$ to obtain equivalent expressions for $E[T(x)^2]$ by

$$E[T(x)^2] = \int_0^\infty t^2 \; {}_tp_x \; \mu_{x+t} \, dt$$

$$= 2 \int_0^\infty t \; {}_tp_x \, dt.$$

This result is useful in the calculation of $\text{Var}[T(x)]$ by

$$\text{Var}[T(x)] = E[T(x)^2] - E[T(x)]^2$$

$$= 2 \int_0^\infty t \; {}_tp_x \, dt - \overset{\circ}{e}_x^2.$$

In these applications of Theorem 3.1, we have assumed that $E[T(x)]$ and $E[T(x)^2]$ exist. One can construct survival functions such as $s(x) = (1+x)^{-1}$ where this would not be true.

Other characteristics of the distribution of $T(x)$ can be determined. The **median future lifetime** of $(x)$, to be denoted by $m(x)$, can be found by solving

$$\Pr[T(x) > m(x)] = \frac{1}{2},$$

or

$$\frac{s[x + m(x)]}{s(x)} = \frac{1}{2}, \tag{3.5.3}$$

for $m(x)$. In particular, $m(0)$ is given by solving $s[m(0)] = 1/2$. One can also find the mode of $T(x)$ by locating the value of $t$ that will yield a maximum value of ${}_tp_x \, \mu_{x+t}$.

For discrete random variables, we have a theorem analogous to Theorem 3.1 that can be established by a parallel proof.

**Theorem 3.2:**  If $K$ is a discrete random variable with probability only on the nonnegative integers, with d.f. $G(k)$ and p.f. $g(k) = \Delta G(k-1)$, and $z(k)$ is a nonnegative, monotonic function such that $E[z(K)]$ exists, then

$$E[z(K)] = \sum_{k=0}^{\infty} z(k)\, g(k)$$

$$= z(0) + \sum_{k=0}^{\infty} [1 - G(k)]\, \Delta z(k).$$

**Proof:**

Summing by parts we get

$$\sum_{j=0}^{k-1} z(j)\, g(j) = -\sum_{j=0}^{k-1} z(j)\, \Delta[1 - G(j-1)]$$

$$= -z(j)\,[1 - G(j-1)]\Big|_0^k + \sum_{j=0}^{k-1} [1 - G(j)]\, \Delta z(j).$$

The theorem follows if

$$\lim_{k \to \infty} z(k)\,[1 - G(k-1)] = 0.$$

We consider

• if the nonnegative function $z(k)$ is nonincreasing, then clearly

$$\lim_{k \to \infty} z(k)\,[1 - G(k-1)] = 0.$$

• if the nonnegative function $z(k)$ is nondecreasing, then

$$0 \le z(k)[1 - G(k-1)] = z(k) \sum_{j=k}^{\infty} g(j) \le \sum_{j=k}^{\infty} z(j)\, g(j).$$

But, if $E[z(K)]$ exists, then

$$\lim_{k \to \infty} \sum_{j=k}^{\infty} z(j)\, g(j) = 0,$$

hence

$$\lim_{k \to \infty} z(k)\,[1 - G(k-1)] = 0,$$

and the theorem follows.                                                    ∎

In the special case where $K$ is the curtate-future-lifetime of $(x)$, we can use Theorem 3.2 to state the conclusion

$$E[z(K)] = z(0) + \sum_{k=0}^{\infty} \Delta z(k)\, _{k+1}p_x. \tag{3.5.4}$$

This result can be used to calculate some of the properties of the distribution of $K$ in a fashion parallel to that of using Theorem 3.1 in connection with $T$. For example,

# Chapter 3

## SURVIVAL DISTRIBUTIONS AND LIFE TABLES

$$E[K] = \sum_{k=0}^{\infty} k \, {}_kp_x \, q_{x+k}$$

$$e_x = \sum_{k=0}^{\infty} {}_{k+1}p_x \qquad (3.5.5)$$

where, in applying Theorem 3.2, the role of $z(k)$ is played by $k$. The symbol for $E[K]$ is $e_x$ and is called the **curtate-expectation-of-life.**

Following the outline used for the continuous model, we have

$$E[K^2] = \sum_{k=0}^{\infty} k^2 \, {}_kp_x \, q_{x+k} \qquad (3.5.6)$$

$$= \sum_{k=0}^{\infty} (2k + 1) \, {}_{k+1}p_x.$$

In (3.5.6) Theorem 3.2 is used with the role of $z(k)$ played by $k^2$. Then

$$\text{Var}\,[K] = E[K^2] - E[K]^2$$

$$= \sum_{k=0}^{\infty} (2k + 1) \, {}_{k+1}p_x - e_x^2.$$

To complete the discussion of some of the entries in Table 3.2, we must define additional functions. The symbol $L_x$ will denote the total expected number of years lived between ages $x$ and $x + 1$ by survivors of the initial group of $l_0$ lives. We have

$$L_x = \int_0^1 t \, l_{x+t} \, \mu_{x+t} \, dt + l_{x+1} \qquad (3.5.7)$$

where the integral counts the years lived of those who die between ages $x$ and $x + 1$, and the term $l_{x+1}$ counts the years lived between ages $x$ and $x + 1$ by those who survive to age $x + 1$. Integration by parts yields

$$L_x = -\int_0^1 t \, dl_{x+t} + l_{x+1}$$

$$= -t \, l_{x+t}\Big|_0^1 + \int_0^1 l_{x+t} \, dt + l_{x+1}$$

$$= \int_0^1 l_{x+t} \, dt. \qquad (3.5.8)$$

The function $L_x$ is also used in defining the **central-death-rate at age $x$,** denoted by $m_x$ where

$$m_x = \frac{\displaystyle\int_0^1 l_{x+t} \, \mu_{x+t} \, dt}{\displaystyle\int_0^1 l_{x+t} \, dt} = \frac{l_x - l_{x+1}}{L_x}. \qquad (3.5.9)$$

# SURVIVAL DISTRIBUTIONS AND LIFE TABLES

An application of this function is found in Chapter 9.

The symbol $T_x$ will denote the total number of years lived beyond age $x$, by the survivorship group with $l_0$ initial members. We have

$$T_x = \int_0^\infty t\, l_{x+t}\, \mu_{x+t}\, dt$$

$$= -\int_0^\infty t\, dl_{x+t}$$

$$= \int_0^\infty l_{x+t}\, dt. \tag{3.5.10}$$

The final expression can be interpreted as the integral of the total time lived between ages $x + t$ and $x + t + dt$ by the $l_{x+t}$ lives who survive to that age interval. Also, the development of (3.5.10) can be obtained immediately from Theorem 3.1 by observing that

$$l_{x+t}\, \mu_{x+t} = l_x\, {}_tp_x\, \mu_{x+t}.$$

The average number of years of future lifetime of the $l_x$ survivors of the group at age $x$ is given by

$$\frac{T_x}{l_x} = \frac{\displaystyle\int_0^\infty l_{x+t}\, dt}{l_x}$$

$$= \int_0^\infty {}_tp_x\, dt$$

$$= \overset{\circ}{e}_x,$$

as determined previously in (3.5.1) and (3.5.2).

A final function, related to the interpretation of the life table developed in this section, is the average number of years lived between ages $x$ and $x + 1$ by those of the survivorship group who die between those ages. This function is denoted by $a(x)$ and is defined by

$$a(x) = \frac{\displaystyle\int_0^1 t\, l_{x+t}\, \mu_{x+t}\, dt}{\displaystyle\int_0^1 l_{x+t}\, \mu_{x+t}\, dt}. \tag{3.5.11}$$

For the probabilistic view of the life table, we would have

$$a(x) = \frac{\displaystyle\int_0^1 t\, {}_tp_x\, \mu_{x+t}\, dt}{\displaystyle\int_0^1 {}_tp_x\, \mu_{x+t}\, dt} = E[T|T < 1].$$

# Chapter 3
## SURVIVAL DISTRIBUTIONS AND LIFE TABLES

If we assume that

$$l_{x+t} \, \mu_{x+t} \, dt = d_x \, dt \qquad 0 \leq t \leq 1,$$

that is, if deaths are uniformly distributed in the year of age, we have

$$a(x) = \int_0^1 t \, dt = \frac{1}{2}.$$

This is the usual approximation for $a(x)$, except for young and old years of age where Figure 3.2 shows that the assumption may be inappropriate.

**Example 3.3:**  Show that

$$L_x = a(x) \, l_x + [1 - a(x)] \, l_{x+1}$$

and

$$L_x \cong \frac{l_x + l_{x+1}}{2}.$$

**Solution:**
From (3.5.7) and (3.5.11), we have

$$a(x) = \frac{L_x - l_{x+1}}{l_x - l_{x+1}}$$

or

$$L_x = a(x) \, l_x + [1 - a(x)] \, l_{x+1}.$$

The formula

$$L_x \cong \frac{l_x + l_{x+1}}{2}$$

can be justified by using the trapezoidal rule for approximate integration on (3.5.8).  ▼

Key life-table terminology, defined in Sections 3.3–3.5, is summarized in Table 3.4.

## 3.6
## Assumptions for Fractional Ages

In this chapter we have discussed the continuous random variable remaining lifetime, $T$, and the discrete random variable curtate-future-lifetime, $K$. The life table developed in Section 3.3 specifies the probability distribution of $K$ completely. To specify the distribution of $T$, we must postulate an analytic form or adopt a life table and an assumption about the distribution between integers.

We will examine three widely used assumptions in actuarial science. These will be stated in terms of the survival function. In each

**Table 3.4
Definitions**

| Name of Concept | Symbol |
|---|---|
| curtate-future-lifetime-of-$(x)$ random variable | $K(x) = K$ |
| curtate-expectation-of-life for $(x)$ | $e_x = E[K(x)] = E[K]$ |
| complete-expectation-of-life for $(x)$ | $\overset{\circ}{e}_x = E[T(x)] = E[T]$ |
| future-lifetime-of-$(x)$ random variable | $T(x)$ or $T$ |
| total number of years lived beyond age $x$, by the survivorship group (cohort) with $l_0$ initial members at age 0 | $T_x$ |
| cohort's number of survivors to age $x$, random variable | $\mathcal{L}(x)$ |
| cohort's expected number of survivors to age $x$ | $l_x$ |
| number of deaths between ages $x$ and $x+n$ random variable | $_n\mathcal{D}_x$ |
| expected number of deaths between ages $x$ and $x+n$ | $_nd_x = E[_n\mathcal{D}_x]$ |
| median-future-lifetime of $(x)$ | $m(x)$ |
| central-death-rate at age $x$ | $m_x$ |

statement, $x$ is an integer and $0 \le t \le 1$. The assumptions are the following:

- Uniform distribution of deaths $s(x+t) = (1-t)\,s(x) + t\,s(x+1)$.
- Constant force of mortality $s(x+t) = s(x)\,e^{-\mu t}$ where $\mu = -\log p_x$.
- Balducci assumption* $1/s(x+t) = (1-t)/s(x) + t/s(x+1)$.

We could have elected to propose equivalent definitions in terms of the p.d.f., the d.f. or the force of mortality.

**Table 3.5
Probability Theory
Functions for
Fractional Ages**

| Assumption / Function | (1) Uniform Distribution | (2) Constant Force | (3) Balducci |
|---|---|---|---|
| $_tq_x$ | $t\,q_x$ | $1 - e^{-\mu t}$ | $\dfrac{t\,q_x}{1 - (1-t)\,q_x}$ |
| $_tp_x$ | $1 - t\,q_x$ | $e^{-\mu t}$ | $\dfrac{p_x}{1 - (1-t)\,q_x}$ |
| $_yq_{x+t}$ | $\dfrac{y\,q_x}{1 - t\,q_x}$ | $1 - e^{-\mu y}$ | $\dfrac{y\,q_x}{1 - (1 - y - t)\,q_x}$ |
| $\mu_{x+t}$ | $\dfrac{q_x}{1 - t\,q_x}$ | $\mu$ | $\dfrac{q_x}{1 - (1-t)\,q_x}$ |
| $_tp_x\,\mu_{x+t}$ | $q_x$ | $e^{-\mu t}\,\mu$ | $\dfrac{p_x\,q_x}{[1 - (1-t)\,q_x]^2}$ |

Note that, in this table, $x$ is an integer, $0 < t < 1$, $0 \le y \le 1$, $y + t \le 1$ and $\mu = -\log p_x$. For the first three rows, the relationships also hold for t = 0 and t = 1.

*This assumption is named after Balducci, an Italian actuary, who pointed out its role in the traditional actuarial method of constructing life tables. However, it should be noted that all three methods had already been proposed by Wittstein in 1862.

# Chapter 3

## SURVIVAL DISTRIBUTIONS AND LIFE TABLES

With these basic definitions formulas can be derived for other standard probability functions in terms of life table probabilities. These results are presented in Table 3.5.

The derivations of the entries in Table 3.5 are exercises in substituting the stated assumption about $s(x + t)$ into the appropriate formulas of Sections 3.2 and 3.3. We will illustrate the process for the uniform distribution of deaths. This assumption will be used extensively throughout this text.

To derive the first entry in the uniform distribution column, one can start with

$$_t q_x = \frac{s(x) - s(x + t)}{s(x)} \qquad 0 \le t \le 1,$$

then substitute for $s(x + t)$,

$$_t q_x = \frac{s(x) - [(1 - t) s(x) + t s(x + 1)]}{s(x)} = \frac{t [s(x) - s(x + 1)]}{s(x)} = t q_x.$$

The second entry is the complement of the first.

For the third entry, we start with

$$_y q_{x+t} = \frac{s(x + t) - s(x + t + y)}{s(x + t)},$$

then substitute for $s(x + t)$ and $s(x + t + y)$ to obtain

$$_y q_{x+t} = \frac{[(1 - t) s(x) + t s(x + 1)] - [(1 - t - y) s(x) + (t + y) s(x + 1)]}{(1 - t) s(x) + t s(x + 1)}$$

$$= \frac{y [s(x) - s(x + 1)]/s(x)}{\{s(x) - t [s(x) - s(x + 1)]\}/s(x)}$$

$$= \frac{y q_x}{1 - t q_x}.$$

For the fourth entry, we use

$$\mu_{x+t} = -\frac{s'(x + t)}{s(x + t)},$$

then, substituting for $s(x + t)$, we have

$$\mu_{x+t} = \frac{[s(x) - s(x + 1)]}{[(1 - t) s(x) + t s(x + 1)]}.$$

Dividing both numerator and denominator of the right-hand side by $s(x)$ yields

$$\mu_{x+t} = \frac{q_x}{(1 - t q_x)}.$$

# SURVIVAL DISTRIBUTIONS AND LIFE TABLES

The final entry for the uniform distribution column is the product of the second and fourth entries.

If, as before, $x$ is an integer, insight can be obtained by defining a random variable $S = S(x)$ by

$$T = K + S \tag{3.6.1}$$

where $T$ is time-until-death, $K$ is the curtate-future-lifetime and $S$ is the random variable representing the fractional part of a year lived in the year of death. Then

$$\Pr\,[k < T \le k + s] = \Pr\,[(K = k) \cap (S \le s)]$$

$$= {}_{k|s}q_x$$

$$= {}_k p_x \, {}_s q_{x+k}.$$

To this point, the development has involved expressing the required probability in terms of special actuarial symbols. If we now use the uniform distribution assumption as shown in Table 3.5 for ${}_s q_{x+k}$, we have

$$\Pr\,[(K = k) \cap (S \le s)] = {}_k p_x \, s \, q_{x+k}$$

$$= {}_{k|}q_x \, s \tag{3.6.2}$$

$$= \Pr\,(K = k)\,\Pr\,(S \le s).$$

Therefore, the joint probability involving $K$ and $S$ can be factored into separate probabilities of $K$ and $S$. It follows that, under the uniform distribution of deaths assumption, the random variables $K$ and $S$ are independent. What is more, since $\Pr\,(S \le s) = s$ is the d.f. of a uniform distribution on $(0,1)$, $S$ has such a uniform distribution.

**Example 3.4:**

Under the constant force of mortality assumption, are the random variables $K$ and $S$ independent?

**Solution:**
Using entries from Table 3.5 for the constant force assumption, we obtain

$$\Pr\,[(K = k) \cap (S \le s)] = {}_k p_x \, {}_s q_{x+k}$$

$$= {}_k p_x \,[1 - (p_{x+k})^s].$$

To discuss this result, we distinguish two cases:
- If $p_{x+k}$ is not independent of $k$, we cannot factor the joint probability of $K$ and $S$ into separate probabilities. We conclude that $K$ and $S$ are not independent.
- In the special case where $p_{x+k} = p$, a constant,

$$\Pr\,[(K = k) \cap (S \le s)] = p^k(1 - p^s) = \frac{(1 - p)p^k(1 - p^s)}{(1 - p)}$$

$$= \Pr\,(K = k)\,\Pr\,(S \le s),$$

and we conclude that $K$ and $S$ are independent.  ▼

# Chapter 3
## SURVIVAL DISTRIBUTIONS AND LIFE TABLES

**Example 3.5:**

Under the assumption of uniform distribution of deaths, show that

$$\text{a. } \mathring{e}_x = e_x + \frac{1}{2}$$

$$\text{b. } \text{Var}[T] = \text{Var}[K] + \frac{1}{12}.$$

**Solution:**

a. $\mathring{e}_x = E[T] = E[K + S]$
   $= E[K] + E[S]$
   $= e_x + \frac{1}{2}$

b. $\text{Var}[T] = \text{Var}[K + S]$

From the independence of $K$ and $S$, under the uniform distribution assumption, it follows that

$$\text{Var}[T] = \text{Var}[K] + \text{Var}[S].$$

Further, since $S$ is uniformly distributed over $(0,1)$,

$$\text{Var}[T] = \text{Var}[K] + \frac{1}{12}. \qquad \blacktriangledown$$

## 3.7 Some Analytical Laws of Mortality

There are three principal justifications for postulating an analytic form for mortality or survival functions. The first is philosophic. Many phenomena studied in physics can be explained efficiently by simple formulas. Therefore, using biological arguments, some authors have suggested that human survival is governed by an equally simple law. The second justification is practical. It is easier to communicate a function with a few parameters than it is to communicate a life table with perhaps 100 parameters or mortality probabilities. In addition, some of the analytic forms have elegant properties that are convenient in evaluating probability statements involving more than one life. The third justification for a simple analytic survival function is the ease of estimating a few parameters of the function from mortality data.

The support for simple analytic survival functions has declined in recent years. Many feel that the belief in universal laws of mortality is naive. Also, with the advent of high-speed computers, the advantages of some analytic forms in computations involving more than

**Table 3.6 Mortality and Survival Functions under Various Laws**

| Originator | $\mu_x$ | $s(x)$ | Restrictions |
|---|---|---|---|
| de Moivre (1729) | $(\omega - x)^{-1}$ | $1 - \dfrac{x}{\omega}$ | $0 \le x < \omega$ |
| Gompertz (1825) | $B c^x$ | $\exp[-m(c^x - 1)]$ | $B > 0, \ c > 1, \ x \ge 0$ |
| Makeham (1860) | $A + B c^x$ | $\exp[-Ax - m(c^x - 1)]$ | $B > 0, \ A \ge -B, \ c > 1, \ x \ge 0$ |
| Weibull (1939) | $k x^n$ | $\exp(-u x^{n+1})$ | $k > 0, \ n > 0, \ x \ge 0$ |

one life are no longer of great importance. Nevertheless, some interesting research has recently reiterated the biological arguments for analytic laws of mortality.

In Table 3.6, several families of simple analytic mortality and survival functions, corresponding to various postulated laws, are displayed. The names of the originators of the laws and the dates of publication are included for identification purposes.

Note that
- the special symbols are defined as

$$m = \frac{B}{\log c}, \quad u = \frac{k}{(n+1)}.$$

- Gompertz's law is a special case of Makeham's law with $A = 0$.
- if $c = 1$ in Gompertz's and Makeham's laws, the exponential (constant force) distribution results.
- in connection with Makeham's law, the constant $A$ has been interpreted as capturing accident hazard, and the term $Bc^x$ as capturing the hazard of aging.

The entries in the $s(x)$ column of Table 3.6 were obtained by substituting into (3.2.16). For example, for Makeham's law, we have

$$s(x) = \exp[-\int_0^x (A + Bc^s)\,ds]$$

$$= \exp[-Ax - B(c^x - 1)/\log c]$$

$$= \exp[-Ax - m(c^x - 1)]$$

where $m = B/\log c$.

Two objectives governed the development of a mortality table for computational purposes in the examples and exercises. One objective was to have mortality rates in the middle of the range of variation for groups differentiated by such factors as residence, gender, insured status, annuity status, marital status and occupation. The second objective was to have a Makeham law at most ages to illustrate how calculations for multiple lives can be performed. The Illustrative Life Table in Appendix 2A is based on the Makeham law for ages 13–110,

$$1000\,\mu_x = 0.7 + 0.05\,(10^{0.04})^x. \tag{3.7.1}$$

The calculations of the basic functions $q_x$, $l_x$ and $d_x$ from (3.7.1) were all done directly from (3.7.1) instead of calculating $l_x$ and $d_x$ from the truncated values of $q_x$. It was found that the latter choice would make little difference in the applications. It should be kept in mind that the Illustrative Life Table, as its name implies, is for illustrative purposes only.

# Chapter 3

## SURVIVAL DISTRIBUTIONS AND LIFE TABLES

**3.8
Select and
Ultimate Tables**

In Section 3.2 we discussed how $_t p_x$ (the probability that $(x)$ will survive to age $x + t$) might be interpreted in two ways. The first interpretation was that the probability can be evaluated by a survival function appropriate for newborns, under the single hypothesis that the newborn has survived to age $x$. The second interpretation was that additional knowledge available about the life at age $x$ might make the original survival function inappropriate for evaluating probability statements about the future lifetime of $(x)$. To illustrate, the life might have been accepted for life insurance at age $x$. This information would lead us to believe that $(x)$'s future-lifetime distribution is different from what we might otherwise assume for lives aged $x$. For a second illustration, the life might have become disabled at age $x$. This information would lead us to believe that the future-lifetime distribution for $(x)$ is different from that of those not disabled at age $x$. In these two illustrations, a special survival function that incorporates the particular information available at age $x$ would be preferred. In other words, the complete model for such lives is a set of survival functions including one for each age at which information is available on issue of insurance, disability and so on. This set of survival functions can be thought of as a function of two variables. One variable is the age at policy issue or the onset of disability, $[x]$, and the second variable is the duration since policy issue or duration since disablement, $t$. Then each of the usual life table functions associated with this bivariate survival function is a two-dimensional array on $[x]$ and $t$.

The schematic diagram in Figure 3.4 illustrates these ideas. For instance, suppose some special information is available about a group of lives aged 30. Perhaps they have been accepted for life insurance or perhaps they have become disabled. A special life table could be built for these lives. The conditional probability of death in each year of duration would be denoted by $q_{[30]+i}$, $i = 0, 1, 2, \ldots$, and would be entered on the first row of Figure 3.4. The subscript reflects the bivariate nature of this function with the bracketed thirty, $[30]$, denoting that the survival function in the first row is conditional on special information available at age 30. The second row of Figure 3.4 would contain the probabilities of death for lives on which the special information became available at age 31. In actuarial science, such a life table is called a **select life** table.

The impact of selection on the distribution of time-until-death, $T$, may diminish following selection. Beyond this time period the $q$'s at equal attained ages would be essentially equal regardless of the ages at selection. More precisely, if there is a smallest integer $r$ such that $\left| q_{[x]+r} - q_{[x-j]+r+j} \right|$ is less than some small positive constant for all ages of selection $[x]$ and for all $j > 0$, it would be economical to construct a set of **select-and-ultimate** tables by truncation of the two-dimensional array after the $(r + 1)$ column. For durations beyond $r$ one would use

$$q_{[x-j]+r+j} \cong q_{[x]+r} \quad j > 0.$$

The first $r$ years of duration comprise the **select period.**

# SURVIVAL DISTRIBUTIONS AND LIFE TABLES

**Figure 3.4**
**Select, Ultimate and**
**Aggregate Mortality,**
**15-Year Select Period**

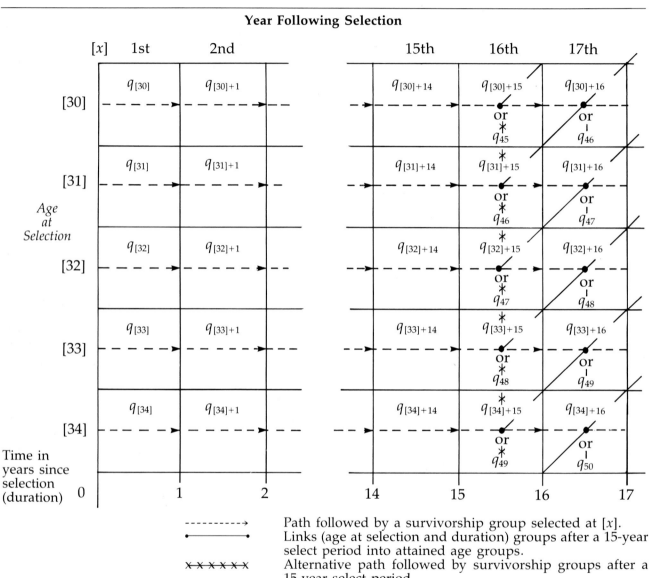

**Year Following Selection**

----------→   Path followed by a survivorship group selected at [x].
•———————•   Links (age at selection and duration) groups after a 15-year select period into attained age groups.
×-×-×-×-×-×   Alternative path followed by survivorship groups after a 15-year select period.

The Society of Actuaries mortality studies of lives who were issued individual life insurance on a standard basis use a 15-year select period. That is, it is accepted that

$$q_{[x-j]+15+j} \cong q_{[x]+15} \quad j > 0 .$$

Beyond the select period, the probabilities of death are subscripted by attained age only. That is, $q_{[x-j]+r+j}$ is written as $q_{x+r}$. For instance, with $r = 15$, $q_{[30]+15}$ and $q_{[25]+20}$ would be written as $q_{45}$.

# Chapter 3

## SURVIVAL DISTRIBUTIONS AND LIFE TABLES

A life table in which the functions are given only for attained ages is called an *aggregate table,* Table 3.2 for instance. The last column in a select-and-ultimate table is a special aggregate table that is usually referred to as an *ultimate table.*

Table 3.7 contains mortality probabilities and corresponding values of the $l_{[x]+k}$ function, as given in the British Life Assurance Table, A 1967–70, published by the Institute of Actuaries and the Faculty of Actuaries. This table has a 2-year select period and is easier to use for illustrative purposes than tables with a 15-year select period such as the Basic Tables, published by the Society of Actuaries.

**Table 3.7**
**Excerpt from the A 1967–70 Select-and-Ultimate Table**

| [x] | (1) 1000 $q_{[x]}$ | (2) 1000 $q_{[x]+1}$ | (3) 1000 $q_{x+2}$ | (4) $l_{[x]}$ | (5) $l_{[x]+1}$ | (6) $l_{x+2}$ | (7) x + 2 |
|-----|------|------|------|------|------|------|-----|
| 30 | 0.43767 | 0.57371 | 0.69882 | 33 829 | 33 814 | 33 795 | 32 |
| 31 | 0.45326 | 0.59924 | 0.73813 | 33 807 | 33 791 | 33 771 | 33 |
| 32 | 0.47711 | 0.63446 | 0.79004 | 33 784 | 33 767 | 33 746 | 34 |
| 33 | 0.50961 | 0.68001 | 0.85577 | 33 760 | 33 742 | 33 719 | 35 |
| 34 | 0.55117 | 0.73655 | 0.93663 | 33 734 | 33 715 | 33 690 | 36 |

In Table 3.7, we observe three mortality probabilities for age 32, namely,

$$q_{[32]} = 0.00047711 < q_{[31]+1} = 0.00059924 < q_{32} = 0.00069882.$$

The order among these probabilities is plausible since mortality should be lower for lives immediately after acceptance for life insurance. Column (3) can be viewed as providing ultimate mortality probabilities.

To construct a select-and-ultimate life table, one would construct the ultimate portion first. Formulas such as (3.4.1) might be used. This would yield a set of values of $l_{x+r} = l_{[x]+r}$ where $r$ is the length of the select period. One could then complete the select segments by using the relation

$$l_{[x]+r-k-1} = \frac{l_{[x]+r-k}}{p_{[x]+r-k-1}} \qquad k = 0,1,2, \ldots, r - 1.$$

**Example 3.6:**

Use Table 3.7 to evaluate

    a. $_2p_{[30]}$      b. $_5p_{[30]}$
    c. $_{1|}q_{[31]}$      d. $_3q_{[31]+1}.$

**Solution:**
Formulas developed in the earlier part of this chapter can be adapted to select-and-ultimate tables yielding

a. $_2p_{[30]} = \dfrac{l_{32}}{l_{[30]}} = \dfrac{33,795}{33,829} = 0.99899$

b. $_5p_{[30]} = \dfrac{l_{35}}{l_{[30]}} = \dfrac{33,719}{33,829} = 0.99675$

$$\text{c. } {}_{1|}q_{[31]} = \frac{l_{[31]+1} - l_{33}}{l_{[31]}} = \frac{33{,}791 - 33{,}771}{33{,}807} = 0.00059$$

$$\text{d. } {}_{3}q_{[31]+1} = \frac{l_{[31]+1} - l_{35}}{l_{[31]+1}} = \frac{33{,}791 - 33{,}719}{33{,}791} = 0.00213. \qquad \blacktriangledown$$

**3.9**
**Notes and**
**References**

Life tables are a cornerstone of actuarial science. Consequently, they are extensively discussed in several English language textbooks on life contingencies,

- King (1902)
- Spurgeon (1932)
- Jordan (1967)
- Hooker and Longley-Cook (1953)
- Neill (1977),

that have been used in actuarial education. In addition, life tables are used by biostatisticians. An exposition of this latter approach is given by Chiang (1968) and Elandt-Johnson and Johnson (1980). The deterministic rate function interpretation was discussed by Allen (1907).

The historically important analytic forms for survival functions are referred to in Table 3.6. Brillinger (1961) provides an argument for certain analytic forms from the viewpoint of statistical life testing. Tenenbein and Vanderhoof (1980) have restated the case for analytic laws of mortality and have developed formulas for select mortality. Some of the methods for evaluating probabilities for fractional ages are reviewed by Mereu (1961), and in Batten's textbook on mortality estimation (1978) (see also Seal's historical review (1977)). Discussions of the length of the select period for various types of insurance selection procedures have a long history, for example, Williamson (1942), Thompson (1934) and Jenkins (1943). The Society of Actuaries 1965–70 Basic Tables use a 15-year select period and were published in *TSA Reports 1973*. International Actuarial Notation is outlined in *TASA 48 (1947)*.

**Exercises**

*Section 3.2*

3.1. Using the ideas summarized in Table 3.1.2, complete the entries below.

| $s(x)$ | $F(x)$ | $f(x)$ | $\mu_x$ |
|---|---|---|---|
| | | | $\tan x, 0 \le x \le \dfrac{\pi}{2}$ |
| $e^{-x}, x \ge 0$ | | | |
| | $1 - \dfrac{1}{1+x}, x \ge 0$ | | |

3.2. Confirm that each of the following functions can serve as a force of mortality. Exhibit the corresponding survival function. In each case $x \ge 0$.

| a. $Bc^x$ | $B > 0$ | $c > 1$ | (Gompertz) |
| b. $kx^n$ | $n > 0$ | $k > 0$ | (Weibull) |
| c. $a(b+x)^{-1}$ | $a > 0$ | $b > 0$ | (Pareto) |

3.3. Confirm that the following can serve as a survival function. Exhibit the corresponding $\mu_x$, $f(x)$, and $F(x)$.

$$s(x) = e^{-x^3/12} \quad x \geq 0.$$

3.4. State why each of the following functions cannot serve in the role indicated by the symbol.

a. $\mu_x = (1 + x)^{-3}$, $x \geq 0$

b. $s(x) = 1 - \dfrac{22x}{12} + \dfrac{11x^2}{8} - \dfrac{7x^3}{24}$, $0 \leq x \leq 3$

c. $f(x) = x^{n-1} e^{-x/2}$, $x \geq 0$, $n \geq 1$

3.5. If $s(x) = 1 - \dfrac{x}{100}$, $0 \leq x \leq 100$, calculate

a. $\mu_x$             b. $F(x)$

c. $f(x)$            d. $\Pr(10 < X < 40)$.

3.6. Confirm that $_{k|}q_0 = -\Delta s(k)$, and that $\displaystyle\sum_{k=0}^{\infty} {_{k|}q_0} = 1$.

3.7. If $\mu_x = 0.001$ for $20 \leq x \leq 25$, evaluate $_{2|2}q_{20}$.

*Sections 3.3, 3.4*

3.8. If the survival times of 10 lives in a survivorship group are independent with survival defined by Table 3.2, exhibit the p.f. of $\mathcal{L}(65)$ and the mean and variance of $\mathcal{L}(65)$.

3.9. If $s(x) = 1 - \dfrac{x}{12}$, $0 \leq x \leq 12$, $l_0 = 9$, and the survival times are independent, then $(_3\mathcal{D}_0, {_3\mathcal{D}_3}, {_3\mathcal{D}_6}, {_3\mathcal{D}_9})$ is known to have a multinomial distribution. Calculate

a. the expected value of each random variable
b. the variance of each random variable
c. the coefficient of correlation between each pair of random variables.

3.10. On the basis of Table 3.2,

a. compare the values of $_5q_0$ and $_5q_5$
b. evaluate the probability that (25) will die between ages 80 and 85.

3.11. Given that $l_{x+t}$ is strictly decreasing in the interval $0 \leq t \leq 1$ show that

a. if $l_{x+t}$ is concave down, then $q_x > \mu_x$
b. if $l_{x+t}$ is concave up, then $q_x < \mu_x$.

3.12. Show that

a. $\dfrac{d}{dx} l_x \mu_x < 0$      when $\dfrac{d}{dx} \mu_x < \mu_x^2$

b. $\dfrac{d}{dx}\, l_x\, \mu_x = 0$     when $\dfrac{d}{dx}\, \mu_x = \mu_x^2$

c. $\dfrac{d}{dx}\, l_x\, \mu_x > 0$     when $\dfrac{d}{dx}\, \mu_x > \mu_x^2$.

3.13. Consider a random survivorship group consisting of two subgroups: (1) the survivors of 1600 births; (2) the survivors of 540 persons joining 10 years later at age 10. An excerpt from the appropriate mortality table for both subgroups follows:

| $x$ | $l_x$ |
| --- | --- |
| 0 | 40 |
| 10 | 39 |
| 70 | 26 |

If $Y_1$ and $Y_2$ are the numbers of survivors to age 70 out of subgroups (1) and (2) respectively, estimate a number $c$ such that $\Pr(Y_1 + Y_2 > c) = 0.05$. Assume the lives are independent and ignore half-unit corrections.

*Section 3.5*

3.14. Let $\overset{\circ}{e}_{x:\overline{n}|}$ denote the expected future lifetime of $(x)$ between ages $x$ and $x + n$. Show that

$$\overset{\circ}{e}_{x:\overline{n}|} = \int_0^n t \; {}_tp_x\, \mu_{x+t}\, dt + n \; {}_np_x$$

$$= \int_0^n {}_tp_x\, dt.$$

This is called a **partial life expectancy.**

3.15. If the random variable $T$ has p.d.f. given by $f(t) = ce^{-ct}$ for $t \geq 0$, $c > 0$, calculate
a. $\overset{\circ}{e}_x = E[T]$     b. $Var[T]$     c. median$[T]$.

3.16. If $\mu_{x+t} = t$, $t \geq 0$, calculate
a. ${}_tp_x\, \mu_{x+t}$     b. $\overset{\circ}{e}_x$.

[Hint: Recall, from the study of probability, that $\dfrac{1}{\sqrt{2\pi}} e^{-t^2/2}$ is the p.d.f. for the standard normal distribution].

3.17. If the random variable $T$ has d.f. given by

$$F(t) = \begin{cases} \dfrac{t}{(100 - x)} & 0 \leq t < 100 - x \\ 1 & t \geq 100 - x, \end{cases}$$

calculate
a. $\overset{\circ}{e}_x$     b. $Var[T]$     c. median$[T]$.

# Chapter 3
## SURVIVAL DISTRIBUTIONS AND LIFE TABLES

3.18. Show that

a. $\dfrac{\partial}{\partial x}\, {}_tp_x = {}_tp_x\,(\mu_x - \mu_{x+t})$

b. $\dfrac{d}{dx}\, \mathring{e}_x = \mathring{e}_x\,\mu_x - 1$

c. $\Delta e_x = q_x\, e_{x+1} - p_x$.

3.19. If $s(x) = \dfrac{\sqrt{100 - x}}{10},\ 0 \le x \le 100$, evaluate

a. ${}_{17}p_{19}$      b. ${}_{15}q_{36}$      c. ${}_{15|13}q_{36}$
d. $\mu_{36}$      e. $\mathring{e}_{36}$.

3.20. Confirm the following statements:
a. $a(x)\, d_x = L_x - l_{x+1}$
b. The approximation developed in Example 3.3 was not used to calculate $L_0$ in Table 3.2, but was used to calculate $L_1$.

c. $T_x = \displaystyle\sum_{k=0}^{\infty} L_{x+k}$

*Section 3.6*

3.21. Verify the entries for the constant force of mortality and the Balducci assumptions in Table 3.5.

3.22. Graph $\mu_{x+t}$, $0 < t < 1$, for each of the three assumptions in Table 3.5. Also graph the survival function for each assumption.

3.23. Using the $l_x$ column of Table 3.2, compute ${}_{1/2}p_{65}$ for each of the three assumptions in Table 3.5.

3.24. Use Table 3.2 and an assumption of uniform distribution of deaths in each year of age to find median $[T]$, where $T$ is the future lifetime of a person
a. age 0      b. age 50.

3.25. If $q_{70} = 0.04$ and $q_{71} = 0.05$, calculate the probability that (70) will die between ages $70^1/_2$ and $71^1/_2$ under
a. the assumption that deaths are uniformly distributed within each year of age
b. the Balducci assumption for each year of age.

3.26. Using the $l_x$ column in Table 3.2 and each of the assumptions in Table 3.5, compute
a. $\displaystyle\lim_{x \to 60^-} \mu_x$      b. $\displaystyle\lim_{x \to 60^+} \mu_x$      c. $\mu_{60^1/_2}$.

3.27. If the constant force assumption is adopted, show that

a. $a(x) = \dfrac{[(1 - e^{-\mu})/\mu] - e^{-\mu}}{1 - e^{-\mu}}$      b. $a(x) \cong \dfrac{1}{2} - \dfrac{q_x}{12}$.

3.28. If the Balducci assumption is adopted, show

a. $a(x) = -\dfrac{p_x}{q_x^2}\,[q_x + \log p_x]$      b. $a(x) \cong \dfrac{1}{2} - \dfrac{q_x}{6}$.

*Section 3.7*

3.29. Verify the entries in Table 3.6 for de Moivre's law and Weibull's law.

3.30. Consider a modification of de Moivre's law given by

$$s(x) = \left(1 - \frac{x}{\omega}\right)^{\alpha} \quad 0 \le x < \omega, \quad \alpha > 0.$$

Calculate
a. $\mu_x$  b. $\overset{\circ}{e}_x$.

*Section 3.8*

3.31. Using Table 3.7, calculate
a. $_2q_{[32]+1}$  b. $_2p_{[31]+1}$.

3.32. The quantity

$$1 - \frac{q_{[x]+k}}{q_{x+k}} = I(x,k)$$

has been called the **index of selection.** When it is close to 0 the indication is that selection has worn off. From Table 3.7, calculate the index for $x = 32$, $k = 0,1$.

*Miscellaneous*

3.33. A life aged 50 is subject to an extra hazard during the year of age 50 to 51. If the normal probability of death from age 50 to 51 is 0.006, and if the extra risk may be expressed by an addition to the normal force of mortality that decreases uniformly from 0.03 at the beginning of year to 0 at the end of the year, calculate the probability that the life will survive to age 51.

3.34. If the force of mortality $\mu_{x+t}$, $0 \le t \le 1$, changes to $\mu_{x+t} - c$ where $c$ is a positive constant, find the value of $c$ for which the probability that $(x)$ will die within a year will be halved. Express the answer in terms of $q_x$.

3.35. From a standard mortality table, a second table is prepared by doubling the force of mortality of the standard table. Is the rate of mortality, $q'_x$, at any given age under the new table, more than double, exactly double or less than double the mortality rate, $q_x$, of the standard table?

3.36. If $\mu_x = B\,c^x$, $c > 1$, show that the function $l_x\,\mu_x$ has its maximum at age $x_0$ where $\mu_{x_0} = \log c$. [Hint: This exercise makes use of Exercise 3.12].

3.37. Assume $\mu_x = \dfrac{A\,c^x}{1 + B\,c^x}$ for $x > 0$.
a. Calculate the survival function, $s(x)$.
b. Verify that the mode of the distribution of $X$, the age-at-death, is given by

$$x_0 = \frac{\log(\log c) - \log A}{\log c}.$$

# Chapter 3

## SURVIVAL DISTRIBUTIONS AND LIFE TABLES

3.38. If $\mu_x = \dfrac{3}{100 - x} - \dfrac{10}{250 - x}$ for $40 < x < 100$, calculate

    a. $_{40}p_{50}$
    b. the mode of the distribution of $X$, the age-at-death.

3.39. a. Show that, under the uniform distribution of deaths assumption,

$$m_x = \frac{q_x}{1 - (1/2)q_x} \quad \text{and} \quad q_x = \frac{m_x}{1 + (1/2)m_x}.$$

    b. Calculate $m_x$ in terms of $q_x$ under the constant force assumption.
    c. Calculate $m_x$ in terms of $q_x$ under the Balducci assumption.
    d. If $l_x = 100 - x$ for $0 \le x \le 100$, calculate $_{10}m_{50}$ where

$$_{n}m_x = \frac{\displaystyle\int_0^n l_{x+t}\,\mu_{x+t}\,dt}{\displaystyle\int_0^n l_{x+t}\,dt}.$$

3.40. Show that $K$ and $S$ are independent if and only if the expression

$$\frac{_{s}q_{x+k}}{q_{x+k}}$$

does not depend on $k$ for $0 \le s \le 1$.

# Chapter 4
# LIFE INSURANCE

## 4.1 Introduction

We have stated that insurance systems are established to reduce the adverse financial impact of some types of random events. Within these systems individuals and organizations adopt utility models to represent preferences, stochastic models to represent uncertain financial impact and economic principles to guide pricing. Agreements are reached after analyses of these models.

In Chapter 2 we developed an elementary model for the financial impact of random events in which the occurrence and the size of impact were both uncertain. In that model, the policy term was assumed to be sufficiently short so the uncertainty of investment income from a random payment time could be ignored.

In this chapter we shall develop models for life insurances designed to reduce the financial impact of the random event of untimely death. Due to the long-term nature of these insurances, the amount of investment earnings, up to the time of payment, provides a significant element of uncertainty. In fact, there will be insurances for which the occurrence and the size of claim are certain and the time of claim is the only uncertainty within the model. In the life insurances considered here, the size and time of payment will depend only on the time of death of the insured. In other words, our model will be built in terms of functions of $T$, the insured's future-lifetime random variable.

While everything in this chapter will be stated as insurances on human lives, the ideas would be the same for other objects such as equipment, machines, loans and business ventures. In fact, the general model is useful in any situation where the size and time of a financial impact can be expressed solely in terms of the time of the random event.

## 4.2 Insurances Payable at the Moment of Death

As covered in this chapter, the amount and the time of payment of a life insurance benefit will depend only on the length of the interval from the issue of the insurance to the death of the insured. Our model will be developed with a benefit function, $b_t$, and a discount function, $v_t$. In our model, $v_t$ is the interest discount factor from the time of payment back to the time of policy issue, $t$ is the length of the interval from issue to death. In the case of endowments, covered in this section, $t$ can be greater than or equal to the length of the interval from issue to payment.

For the discount function we shall assume that the underlying force of interest is deterministic; that is, the model will not include a probability distribution for the force of interest. Moreover, we shall usually show the simple formulas resulting from the assumption of a constant, as well as a deterministic, force of interest.

We shall define the present value function, $z_t$, by

$$z_t = b_t v_t. \tag{4.2.1}$$

Thus, $z_t$ is the present value, at policy issue, of the benefit payment.

The elapsed time from policy issue to the death of the insured is the insured's future-lifetime random variable, $T = T(x)$, defined in Section 3.2.2. Thus, the present value, at policy issue, of the benefit payment is the random variable $z_T$. Unless the context requires a more elaborate symbol, we shall denote this random variable by $Z$, and base the model for the insurance on the equation

$$Z = b_T \, v_T. \qquad (4.2.2)$$

The random variable $Z$ is an example of a claim random variable and, as such, of an $X_i$ term in the sum of the individual-risk model, as defined by (2.1.1). This model will be used in later sections when we consider applications involving portfolios. We now turn to the development of the probability model for $Z$.

The first step in our analysis of a life insurance will be to define $b_t$ and $v_t$. The next step will be to determine some characteristics of the probability distribution of $Z$ that are consequences of an assumed distribution for $T$. We shall work through these steps for several conventional insurances. A summary is provided in Table 4.1.

### 4.2.1 Level Benefit Insurance

An *n-year term life insurance* provides for a payment only if the insured dies within the $n$-year term of an insurance commencing at issue. If a unit is payable at the moment of death of $(x)$, then

$$b_t = \begin{cases} 1 & t \leq n \\ 0 & t > n \end{cases}$$

$$v_t = \quad v^t \quad\quad t \geq 0$$

$$Z = \begin{cases} v^T & T \leq n \\ 0 & T > n. \end{cases}$$

These definitions use two conventions. First, since the future lifetime is a nonnegative variable, we define $b_t$, $v_t$ and $Z$ only on nonnegative values. Second, for a $t$ value where $b_t$ is 0, the value of $v_t$ is irrelevant. Therefore, we shall adopt definitions of $v_t$ by convenience.

For a life insurance, the expectation of the present-value random variable, $Z$, is called the *net single premium.* It is net because it has not been loaded as discussed in Chapter 1. It is a single premium in contrast to annual, semiannual, quarterly, monthly or other premiums that are acceptable in life insurance practice.

The reader will find that the expectation of the present value of a set of payments contingent on the occurrence of a set of events is referred to by different terms in different contexts. In Chapter 1, the expected loss was called the pure premium. This vocabulary is commonly used in property-liability insurance. In Chapter 5, the expectation of the present value of a set of payments contingent on survival (a contingent annuity) is called the *actuarial present value.* This is consistent with retirement plan terminology. Here we shall use net single premium, although any of the three terms would be appropriate. A more exact statement, but more cumbersome, would be

# Chapter 4

## LIFE INSURANCE

*expectation of the present value of the payments.* We shall denote net single premiums by their symbols according to the International Actuarial Notation (see Appendix 4).

The net single premium for the $n$-year term insurance with a unit payable at the moment of death of $(x)$ is $E[Z]$, denoted by $\bar{A}^1_{x:\overline{n}|}$. This can be calculated by recognizing $Z$ as a function of $T$ so that $E[Z] = E[z_T]$. Then we use the p.d.f. of $T$ given in (3.2.19) to obtain

$$\bar{A}^1_{x:\overline{n}|} = E[Z] = E[z_T] = \int_0^\infty z_t\, g(t)\, dt = \int_0^n v^t\, {}_tp_x\, \mu_{x+t}\, dt. \quad (4.2.3)$$

The $j$th moment of the distribution of $Z$ can be found by

$$E[Z^j] = \int_0^n (v^t)^j\, {}_tp_x\, \mu_{x+t}\, dt$$

$$= \int_0^n e^{-(\delta j)t}\, {}_tp_x\, \mu_{x+t}\, dt.$$

The second integral shows that the $j$th moment of $Z$ is equal to the net single premium for an $n$-year term insurance for a unit amount payable at the moment of death of $(x)$, calculated at a force of interest equal to $j$ times the given force of interest, or $j\,\delta$.

This property of the higher moments holds generally for insurances paying a unit amount when the force of interest is deterministic, constant or not. We shall state sufficient conditions for this in the following theorem.

**Theorem 4.1:** For a life insurance on $(x)$, let the force of interest at time $t$ (since policy issue) be $\delta_t$ and let the benefit and discount functions be $b_t$ and $v_t$ respectively. If $b_t^j = b_t$ for all $t$, then $E[Z^j]$ calculated at force of interest $\delta_t$ equals $E[Z]$ calculated at the force of interest $j\,\delta_t$ for $j > 0$. That is, $E[Z^j] @ \delta_t = E[Z] @ j\,\delta_t$.

**Proof:**

$$E[Z^j] = E[(b_T\, v_T)^j]$$

$$= E[b_T^j\, v_T^j]$$

$$= E[b_T\, v_T^j]$$

In general,

$$v_t = \exp\left(-\int_0^t \delta_s\, ds\right) \quad (4.2.4)$$

where $t$ is the elapsed time from policy issue to death of the insured. Raising both sides of (4.2.4) to the $j$th power, we have

$$v_t^j = \exp\left(-\int_0^t j\,\delta_s\, ds\right),$$

that is, $v_t$ at the force of interest $j\,\delta_t$. ∎

It follows from Theorem 4.1 that

$$\text{Var}[Z] = {}^{2}\bar{A}^{1}_{x:\overline{n}|} - (\bar{A}^{1}_{x:\overline{n}|})^{2} \qquad (4.2.5)$$

where ${}^{2}\bar{A}^{1}_{x:\overline{n}|}$ is the net single premium for an $n$-year term insurance for a unit amount calculated at force of interest $2\,\delta$.

Theorem 4.1, as proved, is for an insurance paying the sum insured at the moment of death $t$. It can be extended to insurances where the sum is payable at a time that is a function of the moment of death. This is accomplished by replacing $t$, in the upper limit of the integral of (4.2.4), with the function of the moment of death.

*Whole life insurance* provides for a payment following the death of the insured at any time in the future. If the payment is to be a unit amount at the moment of death of $(x)$, then

$$b_t = 1 \qquad t \geq 0$$

$$v_t = v^t \qquad t \geq 0$$

$$Z = v^T \qquad T \geq 0.$$

The net single premium is

$$\bar{A}_x = E[Z] = \int_0^\infty v^t \, {}_tp_x \, \mu_{x+t} \, dt. \qquad (4.2.6)$$

Whole life insurance is the limiting case of $n$-year term insurance as $n \to \infty$.

**Example 4.1:**

The p.d.f. of the future lifetime, $T$, for $(x)$ is assumed to be

$$g(t) = \begin{cases} \dfrac{1}{80} & 0 < t < 80 \\ 0 & \text{elsewhere.} \end{cases}$$

At a force of interest, $\delta$, calculate for $Z$ (the present-value random variable for a whole life insurance of unit amount issued to $(x)$):

    a. the net single premium
    b. the variance
    c. the 90th percentile, $\xi_{0.9}$.

**Solution:**

a. $\bar{A}_x = E[Z] = \displaystyle\int_0^\infty v^t g(t)\, dt = \int_0^{80} e^{-\delta t} \frac{1}{80}\, dt = \frac{1 - e^{-80\delta}}{80\,\delta} \qquad \delta \neq 0$

b. By Theorem 4.1,

$$\text{Var}[Z] = \frac{1 - e^{-160\delta}}{160\,\delta} - \left( \frac{1 - e^{-80\delta}}{80\,\delta} \right)^2 \qquad \delta \neq 0.$$

c. For the continuous random variable, $Z$, we have

$$\Pr(Z \leq \xi_{0.9}) = 0.9.$$

Chapter 4

LIFE INSURANCE

**Figure 4.1**
**Determination of $\xi_{0.9}$**

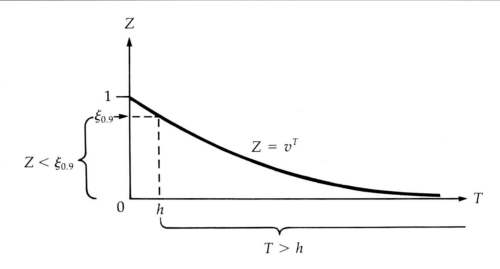

Since we have the p.d.f. for $T$ and not for $Z$, we proceed by finding the event for $T$ which corresponds to $Z \leq \xi_{0.9}$. Figure 4.1 shows the relationship between the sample space of $T$ (on the horizontal axis) and the sample space of $Z$ (on the vertical axis).

Here $h$ is such that

$$\Pr(T > h) = 0.9$$

$$\int_h^{80} \frac{1}{80} dt = 0.9,$$

thus

$$h = 8$$

and

$$\xi_{0.9} = v^8. \qquad \blacktriangledown$$

We now turn our attention to a common application involving portfolios of risks—determining an initial investment fund for a segment of insurances in the total portfolio. The individual risk model and the normal approximation (as discussed in Section 2.4) will be used.

**Example 4.2:**

Assume that each of 100 independent lives
- is age $x$,
- is subject to a constant force of mortality, $\mu = 0.04$, and
- is insured for a death benefit amount of 10 units, payable at the moment of death.

The benefit payments are to be withdrawn from an investment fund earning $\delta = 0.06$. Calculate the minimum amount at $t = 0$ so that the probability is approximately 0.95 that sufficient funds will be on hand to withdraw the benefit payment at the death of each individual.

# LIFE INSURANCE

**Solution:**
For each life,

$$b_t = 10 \qquad t \geq 0$$

$$v_t = v^t \qquad t \geq 0$$

$$Z = 10\,v^T \qquad T \geq 0.$$

If we think of the lives as numbered, perhaps by the order of issuing policies, then at $t = 0$ the present value of all payments to be made is

$$S = \sum_{1}^{100} Z_j$$

where $Z_j$ is the present value at $t = 0$ for the payment to be made at the death of the $j$th life.

We can use the fact that $Z$ is 10 times the present-value random variable for the unit amount whole life insurance to calculate the mean and variance. For constant forces of interest, $\delta$, and mortality, $\mu$, the net single premium for the unit amount whole life insurance is

$$\bar{A}_x = \int_0^\infty e^{-\delta t}\, e^{-\mu t}\, \mu\, dt = \frac{\mu}{\mu + \delta}.$$

Then, for this example

$$E[Z] = 10\,\bar{A}_x = 10\frac{0.04}{0.1} = 4$$

$$E[Z^2] = 10^2\; {}^2\bar{A}_x = 100\,\frac{0.04}{0.04 + 2\,(0.06)} = 25$$

and $\mathrm{Var}[Z] = 9$.

Using these values for the mean and the variance of each term in the sum for $S$, we have

$$E[S] = 100\,(4) = 400$$

$$\mathrm{Var}[S] = 100\,(9) = 900.$$

Analytically, the required minimum amount is a number, $h$, such that

$$\Pr(S \leq h) = 0.95,$$

or equivalently

$$\Pr\left(\frac{S - E[S]}{\sigma(S)} \leq \frac{h - 400}{30}\right) = 0.95.$$

By use of a normal approximation, we obtain

$$\frac{h - 400}{30} = 1.645$$

$$h = 449.35. \qquad \blacktriangledown$$

The 49.35 difference between this initial fund of 449.35 and the expectation of the present value of all payments, 400, is the risk loading of Chapter 1. The loading is 0.4935 per life, or 4.935% per unit payment, or 12.34% of the net single premium.

This example, like Examples 2.2 and 2.3, used the individual risk model and a normal approximation to the probability distribution of $S$. In the short-period examples, the collected income, equal to expected claims plus a risk loading, was determined to have a high probability of being in excess of claims. In this long-period life insurance example, the collected income plus interest income thereon at the assumed interest rate is determined to be sufficient to cover the benefit payments. The initial fund of 449.35 will cover less than 45% of the eventual certain payment of 1000. A graph of the amount in the fund during the first 2 years for a payout pattern when 1 death occurs at each of times 1/8, 7/8, 9/8, 13/8 and 15/8 and 2 deaths occur at time 10/8 is shown in Figure 4.2. Between the benefit payments, represented by the discontinuities, are exponential arcs representing the growth of the fund at $\delta = 0.06$.

There are infinitely many payout patterns, each with its own graph. Both the number of claims and the times of those claims affect the

**Figure 4.2**
**Graph of an Outcome**
**for the Fund**

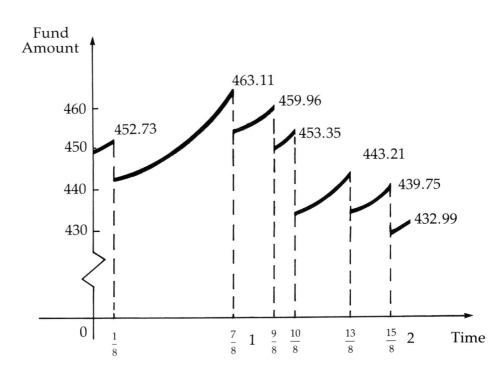

fund. For example, had the 7 claims all occurred within the first instant, instead of the payout pattern of Figure 4.2, the fund would have dropped immediately to 379.35 and then grown to 427.72 by the end of the second year.

These examples illustrate the different roles of the three random elements in risk model building, that is, whether or not a claim will occur, the size and the time of payment if one occurs. In Example 2.2 there was uncertainty about only the occurrence of the claim. In Example 4.2 there was uncertainty about only the time of claim payment. Other uncertainties have been ignored in these models. In Examples 4.1 and 4.2 we have ignored the possibility of the fund earning interest at rates different from the deterministic rates assumed.

## 4.2.2 Endowment Insurance

An **n-year pure endowment** provides for a payment at the end of the $n$ years if and only if the insured survives at least $n$ years from the time of policy issue. If the amount payable is a unit, then

$$b_t = \begin{cases} 0 & t \le n \\ 1 & t > n \end{cases}$$

$$v_t = v^n \qquad t \ge 0$$

$$Z = \begin{cases} 0 & T \le n \\ v^n & T > n. \end{cases}$$

The only element of uncertainty in the pure endowment is whether or not a claim will occur. The size and time of payment, if a claim occurs, are predetermined. The net single premium is denoted by $A_{x:\overline{n}|}^{\;1}$. In the expression, $Z = v^n Y$, $Y$ is the indicator of the event of survival to age $x + n$. This $Y$ has the value 1 if the insured survives to age $x + n$ and has the value 0 otherwise. The net single premium is

$$A_{x:\overline{n}|}^{\;1} = \mathrm{E}[Z] = v^n\, \mathrm{E}[Y] = v^n\, {}_{n}p_x,$$

and

$$\mathrm{Var}\,[Z] = v^{2n}\,\mathrm{Var}\,[Y] = v^{2n}\,{}_{n}p_x\,{}_{n}q_x \qquad (4.2.7)$$

$$= {}^{2}A_{x:\overline{n}|}^{\;1} - (A_{x:\overline{n}|}^{\;1})^2.$$

An **n-year endowment insurance** provides for an amount to be payable either following the death of the insured or upon the survival of the insured to the end of the $n$-year term, whichever occurs first. If the insurance is for a unit amount and the death benefit is payable at the moment of death, then

$$b_t = 1 \qquad t \ge 0$$

$$v_t = \begin{cases} v^t & t \le n \\ v^n & t > n \end{cases}$$

$$Z = \begin{cases} v^T & T \le n \\ v^n & T > n. \end{cases}$$

The net single premium is denoted by $\bar{A}_{x:\overline{n}|}$.

This insurance can be viewed as the combination of an $n$-year term insurance and an $n$-year pure endowment—each for a unit amount. Let $Z_1$, $Z_2$ and $Z_3$ denote the present-value random variables of the term, the pure endowment and the endowment insurances respectively, with death benefits payable at the moment of death of $(x)$. From the preceding definitions we have

$$Z_1 = \begin{cases} v^T & T \leq n \\ 0 & T > n \end{cases}$$

$$Z_2 = \begin{cases} 0 & T \leq n \\ v^n & T > n \end{cases}$$

$$Z_3 = \begin{cases} v^T & T \leq n \\ v^n & T > n. \end{cases}$$

It follows that

$$Z_3 = Z_1 + Z_2, \tag{4.2.8}$$

and by taking expectations of both sides

$$\bar{A}_{x:\overline{n}|} = \bar{A}^1_{x:\overline{n}|} + A_{x:\overline{n}|}^{\phantom{x}1}. \tag{4.2.9}$$

Since $b_t = 1$ for the endowment insurance, we have by Theorem 4.1,

$$E[Z_3^j] \text{ @ } \delta = E[Z_3] \text{ @ } j\delta.$$

Moreover,

$$\text{Var}[Z_3] = {}^2\bar{A}_{x:\overline{n}|} - (\bar{A}_{x:\overline{n}|})^2. \tag{4.2.10}$$

We can also find the $\text{Var}[Z_3]$ by using (4.2.8),

$$\text{Var}[Z_3] = \text{Var}[Z_1] + \text{Var}[Z_2] + 2\,\text{Cov}[Z_1,Z_2]. \tag{4.2.11}$$

By use of the formula

$$\text{Cov}[X,Y] = E[XY] - E[X]E[Y] \tag{4.2.12}$$

and the observation that

$$Z_1 Z_2 = 0$$

for all $T$, we have

$$\text{Cov}[Z_1,Z_2] = -E[Z_1]E[Z_2] = -\bar{A}^1_{x:\overline{n}|} A_{x:\overline{n}|}^{\phantom{x}1}. \tag{4.2.13}$$

Substituting (4.2.5), (4.2.7) and (4.2.13) into (4.2.11) produces a formula for $\text{Var}[Z_3]$ in terms of net single premiums for an $n$-year term insurance and a pure endowment.

Since the net single premiums are positive, the $\text{Cov}[Z_1,Z_2]$ is negative. This is to be anticipated since of the pair $Z_1$ and $Z_2$, one is always 0 and the other positive. On the other hand, the correlation coefficient of $Z_1$ and $Z_2$ is not $-1$ since they are not linear functions of each other.

## 4.2.3
## Deferred
## Insurance

An *m-year deferred insurance* provides for a benefit following the death of the insured only if the insured dies at least $m$ years following policy issue. The benefit payable and the term of the insurance may be any of those discussed above. For example, an $m$-year deferred whole life insurance with a unit amount payable at the moment of death has

$$b_t = \begin{cases} 1 & t > m \\ 0 & t \le m \end{cases}$$

$$v_t = v^t \qquad t > 0$$

$$Z = \begin{cases} v^T & T > m \\ 0 & T \le m. \end{cases}$$

The net single premium is denoted by $_{m|}\bar{A}_x$ and is equal to

$$\int_m^\infty v^t \; {}_tp_x \; \mu_{x+t} \; dt. \qquad (4.2.14)$$

**Example 4.3:**

Consider a 5-year deferred whole life insurance payable at the moment of the death of $(x)$. The individual is subject to a constant force of mortality $\mu = 0.04$. For the distribution of the present value of the benefit payment, at $\delta = 0.10$, calculate the

  a. expectation
  b. variance
  c. median $\xi_{0.5}$.

**Solution:**

a. For arbitrary forces $\mu$ and $\delta$,

$$_{5|}\bar{A}_x = \int_5^\infty e^{-\delta t} e^{-\mu t} \mu \, dt = \frac{\mu}{\mu + \delta} e^{-5(\mu+\delta)},$$

hence for $\mu = 0.04$ and $\delta = 0.10$,

$$_{5|}\bar{A}_x = \frac{2}{7} e^{-0.7} = 0.1419.$$

b. By Theorem 4.1

$$\text{Var}\,[Z] = \frac{0.04}{0.04 + 0.20} e^{-5(0.04+0.20)} - \frac{4}{49} e^{-1.4} = 0.0301.$$

c. As in Example 4.1, a graph of the relation between $Z$ and $T$ provides an outline for the solution. For the general $m$-year deferment period and the case when $\Pr\,(T \le m) < 0.5$, the graph is given in Figure 4.3.

While $T$ is a continuous random variable, $Z$ is mixed with a probability mass at 0 because $Z = 0$ corresponds to $T \le m$. If $\Pr\,(Z = 0) \ge 0.5$, then $\xi_{0.5} = 0$, otherwise $\xi_{0.5}$ is the solution of

$$\Pr\,(Z \le \xi_{0.5}) = 0.5. \qquad (4.2.15)$$

Chapter 4

# LIFE INSURANCE

**Figure 4.3
Determination of
Median**

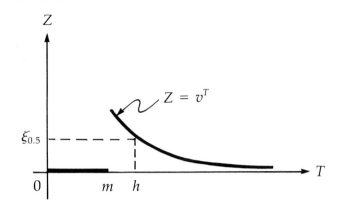

In this example

$$\Pr(Z = 0) = \Pr(T \leq 5) = \int_0^5 e^{-0.04t} 0.04\, dt = 1 - e^{-0.2} = 0.1813,$$

thus $\xi_{0.5}$ is not 0 and we can write (4.2.15) in the form

$$\Pr(Z = 0) + \Pr(0 < Z \leq \xi_{0.5}) = 0.5,$$

and then reduce it to

$$\Pr(0 < Z \leq \xi_{0.5}) = 0.3187.$$

This equation is equivalent to

$$\Pr(v^T < \xi_{0.5}) = 0.3187$$

and can be transformed to

$$\Pr\left(T > \frac{\log \xi_{0.5}}{\log v}\right) = 0.3187.$$

$Pr(T > h) = {}_hp_x$

Therefore we seek an $h$ such that

$$_hp_x = 0.3187$$

$$e^{-0.04h} = 0.3187,$$

$$h = \frac{\log(0.3187)}{-0.04}.$$

$\xi_{0.5} = (0.3187)^{\delta/\mu}$

Then

$$\frac{\log \xi_{0.5}}{\log v} = \frac{\log(0.3187)}{-0.04}$$

$\mu$

and thus

$$\xi_{0.5} = (0.3187)^{\delta/0.04} = 0.0573.$$

The largest value of $Z$ with nonzero probability density in this example is $e^{-0.1(5)} = 0.6065$, corresponding to $T = 5$. It can be shown, by a development similar to the one used to find the median, that

$$F(y) = \Pr(Z \leq y) = 0.1813 + y^{0.4}, \text{ for } 0 < y \leq 0.6065.$$

Then the probability density function is $0.4y^{-0.6}$, $0 < y \leq 0.6065$. A sketch of the distribution of Z is given in Figure 4.4. The shaded spike represents the probability mass at $Z = 0$, its value is 0.1813, and should not be read from the scale on the vertical axis as it applies only to the p.d.f. at $y > 0$.

The distribution of Z in this example is highly skewed to the right. While its total mass is in the interval [0,0.6065] and its mean is 0.1419, its median is only 0.0573. This skewness in the direction of large positive values is characteristic of many claim distributions in all fields of insurance.                                              ▼

**Figure 4.4**
**Distribution of Z**

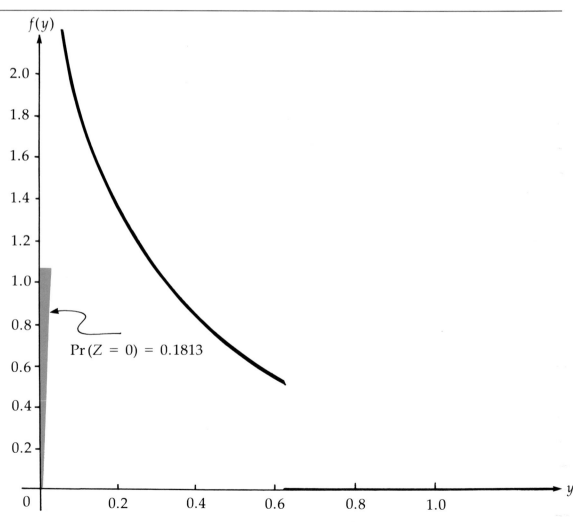

$\Pr(Z = 0) = 0.1813$

**4.2.4
Varying Benefit
Insurance**

The general model given by (4.2.1) can be used for analysis in most applications. We have used it with level benefit life insurances. It can also be applied to insurances where the level of the death benefit either increases or decreases in arithmetic progression over all or a part of the term of the insurance. Such insurances are often sold as an additional benefit when a basic insurance provides for the return of periodic premiums at death or when an annuity contract contains a guarantee of sufficient payments to match its initial premium.

An *increasing whole life insurance* providing 1 at the moment of death during the first year, 2 at the moment of death in the second year and so on is characterized by the following functions:

$$b_t = [t + 1] \qquad t \geq 0$$

$$v_t = v^t \qquad t \geq 0$$

$$Z = [T + 1] v^T \qquad T \geq 0.$$

The brackets denote the greatest integer function,

$$[t] = k \qquad k \leq t < k + 1, k = 0, \pm 1, \ldots.$$

The net single premium for such an insurance is

$$(I\bar{A})_x = E[Z] = \int_0^\infty [t + 1] \, v^t \, {}_tp_x \, \mu_{x+t} \, dt.$$

The higher order moments are not equal to the net single premium at an adjusted force of interest as was the case for insurances with level benefit payments. These moments can be calculated directly from their definitions.

The increases in the benefit of the insurance can occur more, or less, frequently than once per year. For an *m*thly increasing whole life insurance the benefit would be $1/m$ at the moment of death during the first *m*th of a year of the term of the insurance, $2/m$ at the moment of death during the second *m*th of a year during the term of the insurance and so on increasing by $1/m$ at *m*thly intervals throughout the term of the insurance. For such a whole life insurance the functions are

$$b_t = \frac{[t\,m + 1]}{m} \qquad t \geq 0$$

$$v_t = v^t \qquad t \geq 0$$

$$Z = \frac{v^T [T\,m + 1]}{m} \qquad T \geq 0.$$

The net single premium is

$$(I^{(m)}\bar{A})_x = E[Z].$$

The limiting case, as $m \to \infty$ in the *m*thly increasing whole life

# LIFE INSURANCE

insurance, is an insurance paying $t$ at the time of death, $t$. Its functions are

$$b_t = t \qquad t \geq 0$$

$$v_t = v^t \qquad t \geq 0$$

$$Z = T v^t \qquad T \geq 0.$$

Its net single premium symbol is $(\bar{I}\bar{A})_x$.

This continuously increasing whole life insurance is equivalent to a set of deferred level whole life insurances. This equivalence is shown graphically in Figure 4.5 where the region between the line $b_t = t$ and the $t$-axis represents the insurance over the future lifetime. If the infinitesimal regions are joined in the vertical direction for a fixed $t$, the total benefit payable at $t$ is obtained. If they are joined in the horizontal direction for a fixed $s$, an $s$-year deferred whole life insurance for the level amount $ds$ is obtained.

This equivalence implies that the net single premiums for the coverages are equal. The equality can be established as follows.

By definition,

$$(\bar{I}\bar{A})_x = \int_0^\infty t \, v^t \, {}_t p_x \, \mu_{x+t} \, dt,$$

and interpreting $t$ in the integrand as the integral from 0 to $t$ in Figure 4.5 we have

**Figure 4.5
Continuously
Increasing Insurance**

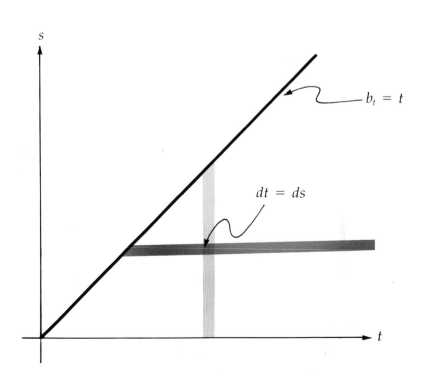

# LIFE INSURANCE

$$(\bar{I}\bar{A})_x = \int_0^\infty \left( \int_0^t ds \right) v^t \, _tp_x \, \mu_{x+t} \, dt.$$

If we reverse the order of integration and, for each $s$ value, integrate on $t$ from $s$ to $\infty$, we have

$$(\bar{I}\bar{A})_x = \int_0^\infty \int_s^\infty v^t \, _tp_x \, \mu_{x+t} \, dt \, ds,$$

$$= \int_0^\infty \, _{s|}\bar{A}_x \, ds$$

by (4.2.14).

If, for any of these $m$thly increasing life insurances, the benefit is payable only if death occurs within a term of $n$ years, the insurance is an increasing $n$-year term life insurance.

Complementary to the increasing $n$-year term life insurance is the *decreasing $n$-year term life insurance* providing $n$ at the moment of death during the first year, $n-1$ at the moment of death during the second year and so on with coverage terminating at the end of the $n$th year. Such an insurance has the following functions:

$$b_t = \begin{cases} n - [t] & t \le n \\ 0 & t > n \end{cases}$$

$$v_t = v^t \qquad\qquad\qquad t > 0$$

$$Z = \begin{cases} v^T (n - [T]) & T \le n \\ 0 & T > n. \end{cases}$$

The net single premium for this insurance is

$$(D\bar{A})^1_{x:\overline{n}|} = \int_0^n v^t \, (n - [t]) \, _tp_x \, \mu_{x+t} \, dt.$$

This insurance is complementary to the increasing $n$-year term insurance in the sense that the sum of their benefit functions is the constant $n+1$ for the $n$-year term.

Table 4.1 is a summary of the models in this section. The insurance plan name appears in the first column followed by the benefit and discount functions that define it in terms of the future lifetime of the insured at policy issue. The present value function, which is always derived as the product of the previous functions, is shown next. In the fifth column the International Actuarial Notation for the net single premium is shown. In the last column, a reference is given to a footnote stating whether or not Theorem 4.1 can be used in the calculation of higher order moments.

## Table 4.1
## Summary of Insurances Payable Immediately on Death

| (1)<br>Insurance<br>Name | (2)<br>Benefit<br>Function $b_t$ | | (3)<br>Discount<br>Function $v_t$ | (4)<br>Present Value<br>Function $z_t$ | | (5)<br>Net<br>Single<br>Premium | (6)<br>Higher<br>Moments |
|---|---|---|---|---|---|---|---|
| Whole Life | 1 | | $v^t$ | $v^t$ | | $\bar{A}_x$ | 1. |
| $n$-Year Term | 1<br>0 | $t \le n$<br>$t > n$ | $v^t$ | $v^t$<br>0 | $t \le n$<br>$t > n$ | $\bar{A}^1_{x:\overline{n}|}$ | 1. |
| $n$-Year Pure<br>Endowment | 0<br>1 | $t \le n$<br>$t > n$ | $v^n$ | 0<br>$v^n$ | $t \le n$<br>$t > n$ | $A_{x:\overline{n}|}^{\;\;1}$ | 1. |
| $n$-Year Endowment | 1 | | $v^t$ $\quad t \le n$<br>$v^n$ $\quad t > n$ | $v^t$<br>$v^n$ | $t \le n$<br>$t > n$ | $\bar{A}_{x:\overline{n}|}$ | 1. |
| $m$-Year Deferred<br>$n$-Year Term | 1<br>0 | $m < t \le n+m$<br>$t \le m,\ t > n+m$ | $v^t$ | $v^t$<br>0 | $m < t \le n+m$<br>$t \le m,\ t > n+m$ | ${}_{m|n}\bar{A}_x$ | 1. |
| $n$-Year Term<br>Increasing Annually | $[t+1]$<br>0 | $t \le n$<br>$t > n$ | $v^t$ | $[t+1]v^t$<br>0 | $t \le n$<br>$t > n$ | $(I\bar{A})^1_{x:\overline{n}|}$ | 2. |
| $n$-Year Term<br>Decreasing Annually | $n - [t]$<br>0 | $t \le n$<br>$t > n$ | $v^t$ | $(n - [t])v^t$<br>0 | $t \le n$<br>$t > n$ | $(D\bar{A})^1_{x:\overline{n}|}$ | 2. |
| Whole Life<br>Increasing $m$thly | $[tm+1]/m$ | | $v^t$ | $v^t[tm+1]/m$ | | $(I^{(m)}\bar{A})_x$ | 2. |

$b_t$, $v_t$ and $z_t$ are defined only for $t \ge 0$.
1. The $j$th moment is equal to the net single premium at $j$ times the given force of interest, denoted by $^jA$ for $j > 1$. Then the variance is $^2A - A^2$, symbolically.
2. Calculate directly from the definition, $E[Z^j]$.

## 4.3
## Insurances Payable at the End of the Year of Death

In the previous section we developed models for life insurances with death benefits payable at the moment of death. In practice, this is the time of payment for almost all insurances. The models were built in terms of $T$, the future lifetime of the insured at policy issue. In most life insurance applications, the best information available on the probability distribution of $T$ is in the form of a discrete life table; that is, the probability distribution of $K$, the curtate-future-lifetime of the insured at policy issue, a function of $T$. In this and the following section we shall bridge this gap by building models for life insurances in which the size and time of payment of the death benefits depend only on the number of complete years lived by the insured from policy issue up to the time of death. We shall simply refer to these insurances as *payable at the end of the year of death*.

Our model will be in terms of functions of the curtate-future-lifetime of the insured. The benefit function, $b_{k+1}$, and the discount function, $v_{k+1}$, will be respectively the benefit amount payable and the discount factor required for the period from the time of payment back to the time of policy issue when the insured's curtate-future-lifetime is $k$, that is, when the insured dies in year $k+1$ of insurance. The present value, at policy issue, of this benefit payment, denoted by $z_{k+1}$, is

$$z_{k+1} = b_{k+1} v_{k+1}. \tag{4.3.1}$$

At the time of policy issue, the insurance year of death is 1 plus the curtate-future-lifetime random variable, $K$, defined in Section 3.2.3.

# Chapter 4
## LIFE INSURANCE

As in the previous section, we shall denote the present-value random variable $z_{K+1}$, by $Z$.

For an $n$-year term insurance providing a unit amount at the end of the year of death, we have

$$b_{k+1} = \begin{cases} 1 & k = 0,1,\ldots,n-1 \\ 0 & \text{elsewhere} \end{cases}$$

$$v_{k+1} = v^{k+1}$$

$$Z = \begin{cases} v^{K+1} & K = 0,1,\ldots,n-1 \\ 0 & \text{elsewhere.} \end{cases}$$

The net single premium for this insurance is given by

$$A^1_{x:\overline{n}|} = \text{E}[Z] = \sum_{k=0}^{n-1} v^{k+1} \, {}_kp_x \, q_{x+k}. \tag{4.3.2}$$

Theorem 4.1, with the appropriate changes in notation, also holds for insurances payable at the end of the year of death.

For example, for the $n$-year term insurance above,

$$\text{Var}[Z] = {}^2A^1_{x:\overline{n}|} - (A^1_{x:\overline{n}|})^2$$

where

$$ {}^2A^1_{x:\overline{n}|} = \sum_{k=0}^{n-1} e^{-2\delta(k+1)} \, {}_kp_x \, q_{x+k}. $$

For a whole life insurance issued to $(x)$, the model may be obtained by letting $n \to \infty$ in the $n$-year term insurance model. For the net single premium we have

$$A_x = \sum_{k=0}^{\infty} v^{k+1} \, {}_kp_x \, q_{x+k}. \tag{4.3.3}$$

Multiplication of both sides of (4.3.3) by $l_x$ yields

$$l_x A_x = \sum_{k=0}^{\infty} v^{k+1} d_{x+k}. \tag{4.3.4}$$

Equation (4.3.4) shows the balance, at the time of policy issue, between the aggregate fund of net single premiums for $l_x$ lives insured at age $x$ and the outflow of funds in accordance with their expected deaths. It is a compound interest equation of value that is stated on an expected value basis.

The expression,

$$\sum_{k=r}^{\infty} v^{k+1} d_{x+k}, \tag{4.3.5}$$

is that part of the fund at issue which, together with interest at the assumed rate, will provide the payments for the expected deaths after the $r$th insurance year.

Accumulation of (4.3.5) at the assumed interest rate for $r$ years yields

$$\sum_{k=r}^{\infty} v^{k-r+1}\, d_{x+k}, \qquad\qquad (4.3.6)$$

the expected amount in the fund after $r$ insurance years. A comparison of expression (4.3.6) to (4.3.4) shows it to be $l_{x+r}\, A_{x+r}$. The difference between this amount and an actual fund is due to deviations of the actual deaths from the expected deaths (according to the life table adopted), and deviations of the actual interest income from the interest income at the assumed rate.

**Example 4.4:**

A group of 100 males aged 30 set up a fund to pay 1000 at the end of the year of death of each member to his designated survivor. Their mutual agreement is to pay into the fund an amount equal to the whole life insurance net single premium calculated on the basis of the Life Table for Total Males: U.S. 1979–1981 at 6% interest. The members, not selected by an insurance company, decided to use this population table for males as the basis of their plan. The actual experience of the fund is 1 death in each of the second and fifth years; interest income at 6% in the first year, $6\tfrac{1}{2}\%$ in the second and third years, 7% in the fourth and fifth years. What is the difference, at the end of the first 5-years, between the expected size of the fund as determined at the inception of the plan and the actual fund?

**Solution:**
On the agreed bases, $1000\, A_{30} = 115.18$, so, for the 100 lives, the fund starts at 11,518. Also, $A_{35} = 0.1445842$ and $l_{35}/l_{30} = 0.9902582$.

For 100 lives aged 30, the expected size of the fund after 5 years will be

$$(1000)\,(100)\,\frac{l_{35}}{l_{30}}\, A_{35} = 14{,}317.57.$$

The development of the actual fund would be as follows, where $F_k$ denotes its size at the end of insurance year $k$:

$$F_0 = 11{,}518$$

$$F_1 = (11{,}518.00)\,(1.06) = 12{,}209.08$$

$$F_2 = (12{,}209.08)\,(1.065) - 1000 = 12{,}002.67$$

$$F_3 = (12{,}002.67)\,(1.065) = 12{,}782.84$$

$$F_4 = (12{,}782.84)\,(1.07) = 13{,}677.64$$

$$F_5 = (13{,}677.64)\,(1.07) - 1000 = 13{,}635.07.$$

Thus the required difference is $14{,}317.57 - 13{,}635.07 = 682.50$. This is an aggregate result in the sense that it combines the investment experience and the mortality experience for the 5-year period. There were gains from the investment earnings in excess of the assumed rate of 6%. On the other hand, there were losses on the mortality experience of 2 deaths as compared to the expected number of 0.9742. The interpretation of such an aggregate result in terms of the various sources such as investment earnings, mortality and so on is one of the responsibilities of a practicing actuary.    ▼

The $n$-year endowment insurance with a unit amount payable at the end of the year of death is a combination of the $n$-year term insurance of this section and the $n$-year pure endowment for a unit amount that was discussed in the previous section. Hence the functions for it are

$$b_{k+1} = 1 \qquad k = 0,1,\ldots$$

$$v_{k+1} = \begin{cases} v^{k+1} & k = 0,1,\ldots,n-1 \\ v^n & k = n,n+1,\ldots \end{cases}$$

$$Z = \begin{cases} v^{K+1} & K = 0,1,\ldots,n-1 \\ v^n & K = n,n+1,\ldots . \end{cases}$$

The net single premium is

$$A_{x:\overline{n}|} = \sum_{k=0}^{n-1} v^{k+1}\, {}_kp_x\, q_{x+k} + v^n\, {}_np_x. \qquad (4.3.7)$$

The increasing whole life insurance, paying $k+1$ units at the end of insurance year $k+1$ provided the insured dies in that insurance year, has the benefit, discount and present-value random variables as follows:

$$b_{K+1} = K + 1 \qquad K = 0,1,2,\ldots$$
$$v_{K+1} = v^{K+1} \qquad K = 0,1,2,\ldots$$
$$Z = (K+1)v^{K+1} \qquad K = 0,1,2,\ldots .$$

The net single premium is denoted by $(IA)_x$.

The decreasing $n$-year term insurance, during the $n$-year period, provides a benefit at the end of the year of death in an amount equal to $n-k$ where $k$ is the number of complete years lived by the insured since issue. Its functions are

$$b_{k+1} = \begin{cases} n-k & k = 0,1,\ldots,n-1 \\ 0 & k = n,n+1,\ldots \end{cases}$$

$$v_{k+1} = v^{k+1} \qquad k = 0,1,\ldots$$

$$Z = \begin{cases} (n-K)v^{K+1} & K = 0,1,\ldots,n-1 \\ 0 & K = n,n+1,\ldots . \end{cases}$$

The net single premium symbol for this insurance is $(DA)^1_{x:\overline{n}|}$.

As illustrated by Figure 4.5 for insurances payable at the moment of death, increasing insurances payable at the end of the year of death are equivalent to a combination of deferred level insurances each for a unit amount. Similarly, decreasing term insurances are equivalent to a combination of level term insurances of various term lengths. Figure 4.6 illustrates this for a decreasing 8-year term insurance.

Figure 4.6 shows the graph of the benefit function $b_{k+1}$. Each unit square region between the horizontal steps and the $k$-axis represents a deferred 1-year term insurance. When these are summed vertically, the deferred 1-year term insurances for the decreasing amounts are obtained. When the squares are summed horizontally, the level amount term insurances of varying duration are obtained. These vertical and horizontal sums are also indicated in Figure 4.6.

The equality of the net single premiums for the combination of level term insurances and the combination of deferred term insurances can be demonstrated analytically. Thus, by definition

$$(DA)^1_{x:\overline{n}|} = \sum_{k=0}^{n-1} (n-k)\, v^{k+1} \,_k p_x \, q_{x+k}$$

$$= \sum_{k=0}^{n-1} (n-k)\, (v^k \,_k p_x)\, (v\, q_{x+k}) \qquad (4.3.8)$$

$$= \sum_{k=0}^{n-1} (n-k) \,_{k|}A^1_{x:\overline{1}|},$$

the total of the column sums.

In (4.3.8) we can substitute

$$n - k = \sum_{j=0}^{n-k-1} (1)$$

to obtain

$$(DA)^1_{x:\overline{n}|} = \sum_{k=0}^{n-1} \sum_{j=0}^{n-k-1} (1)\, v^{k+1} \,_k p_x \, q_{x+k}.$$

By changing the order of summation we obtain

$$\sum_{j=0}^{n-1} \sum_{k=0}^{n-j-1} (1)\, v^{k+1} \,_k p_x \, q_{x+k},$$

and then by comparing the inner summation to (4.3.2) we can write

$$(DA)^1_{x:\overline{n}|} = \sum_{j=0}^{n-1} A^1_{x:\overline{n-j}|}.$$

Table 4.2 provides a summary of functions and symbols for the elementary insurances payable at the end of the year of death that were discussed in this section.

# LIFE INSURANCE

**Figure 4.6
Decreasing 8-Year
Term Insurance**

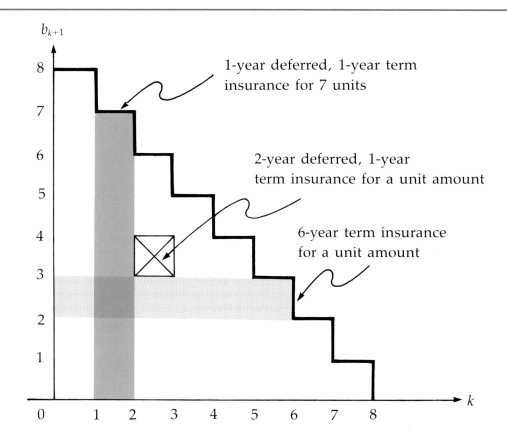

1-year deferred, 1-year term
insurance for 7 units

2-year deferred, 1-year
term insurance for a unit amount

6-year term insurance
for a unit amount

## Table 4.2
## Summary of Insurances Payable at End of Year of Death

| (1) Insurance Name | (2) Benefit Function $b_{k+1}$ | | (3) Discount Function $v_{k+1}$ | (4) Present Value Function $z_{k+1}$ | | (5) Net Single Premium | (6) Higher Moments |
|---|---|---|---|---|---|---|---|
| Whole Life | 1 | | $v^{k+1}$ | $v^{k+1}$ | | $A_x$ | 1. |
| $n$-Year Term | 1 0 | $k = 0,1,\dots,n-1$ $k = n,n+1,\dots$ | $v^{k+1}$ | $v^{k+1}$ 0 | $k = 0,1,\dots,n-1$ $k = n,n+1,\dots$ | $A^1_{x:\overline{n}|}$ | 1. |
| $n$-Year Endowment | 1 | | $v^{k+1}$ $v^n$ | $\begin{matrix}v^{k+1}\\v^n\end{matrix}$ | $k = 0,1,\dots,n-1$ $k = n,n+1,\dots$ | $A_{x:\overline{n}|}$ | 1. |
| $m$-Year Deferred $n$-Year Term | 1 0 | $k = m,m+1,\dots,m+n-1$ $k = 0,\dots,m-1$ $k = m+n,\dots$ | $v^{k+1}$ | $v^{k+1}$ 0 | $k = m,m+1,\dots,m+n-1$ $k = 0,\dots,m-1$ $k = m+n,\dots$ | $_{m|n}A_x$ | 1. |
| $n$-Year Term Increasing Annually | $k+1$ 0 | $k = 0,1,\dots,n-1$ $k = n,n+1,\dots$ | $v^{k+1}$ | $(k+1)v^{k+1}$ 0 | $k = 0,1,\dots,n-1$ $k = n,n+1,\dots$ | $(IA)^1_{x:\overline{n}|}$ | 2. |
| $n$-Year Term Decreasing Annually | $n-k$ 0 | $k = 0,1,\dots,n-1$ $k = n,n+1,\dots$ | $v^{k+1}$ | $(n-k)v^{k+1}$ 0 | $k = 0,1,\dots,n-1$ $k = n,n+1,\dots$ | $(DA)^1_{x:\overline{n}|}$ | 2. |
| Whole Life Increasing Annually | $k+1$ | $k = 0,1,\dots$ | $v^{k+1}$ | $(k+1)v^{k+1}$ | $k = 0,1,\dots$ | $(IA)_x$ | 2. |

$b_{k+1}$, $v_{k+1}$, and $z_{k+1}$ are defined only for nonnegative integral values of $k$.
1. Theorem 4.1 holds, thus $\text{Var}[Z] = {}^2A - A^2$ symbolically.
2. Theorem 4.1 does not hold.

## 4.4
## Relationships between Insurances Payable at the Moment of Death and the End of the Year of Death

We shall begin the study of these relationships with an analysis of the net single premium for whole life insurance paying a unit benefit at the moment of death. From (4.2.6) we have

$$
\begin{aligned}
\bar{A}_x &= \int_0^\infty v^t \, {}_t p_x \, \mu_{x+t} \, dt \\
&= \sum_{k=0}^\infty \int_k^{k+1} v^t \, {}_t p_x \, \mu_{x+t} \, dt \\
&= \sum_{k=0}^\infty \int_0^1 v^{k+s} \, {}_{k+s} p_x \, \mu_{x+k+s} \, ds \\
&= \sum_{k=0}^\infty v^{k+1} \, {}_k p_x \int_0^1 v^{s-1} \, {}_s p_{x+k} \, \mu_{x+k+s} \, ds.
\end{aligned}
\tag{4.4.1}
$$

The integral in (4.4.1) can be expressed in discrete life table functions by adopting one of the assumptions about the form of the mortality function between integers as discussed in Section 3.6.

Under the assumption of a uniform distribution of deaths over the year of age,

$$
{}_s p_{x+k} \, \mu_{x+k+s} = q_{x+k} \qquad 0 \le s \le 1,
$$

which can be placed in (4.4.1) to obtain

$$
\begin{aligned}
\bar{A}_x &= \sum_{k=0}^\infty v^{k+1} \, {}_k p_x \, q_{x+k} \int_0^1 (1+i)^{1-s} \, ds \\
&= \sum_{k=0}^\infty v^{k+1} \, {}_k p_x \, q_{x+k} \, \bar{s}_{\overline{1}|} = \frac{i}{\delta} A_x.
\end{aligned}
\tag{4.4.2}
$$

This equation might have been anticipated under the assumption of a uniform distribution of deaths between integral ages. The effect of the assumption is to make the unit payable at the moment of death equivalent to a unit payable continuously throughout the year of death. With respect to interest, a unit payable continuously over the year is equivalent to $i/\delta$ at the end of the year.

The identity in (4.4.2) can be reached using the properties of the future-lifetime random variable under the assumption of a uniform distribution of deaths, as developed in Section 3.6. From (3.6.1) we write $T = K + S$ where $S$ is the random variable *fractional-part-of-a-year-lived-in-the-year-of-death*. We observed that, under the assumption of a uniform distribution of deaths, $K$ and $S$ are independent and $S$ has a uniform distribution over the unit interval. As corollaries to these observations, $K + 1$ and $1 - S$ are also independent, and $1 - S$ has a uniform distribution over the unit interval. In the identity

$$
\bar{A}_x = \mathrm{E}[v^T] = \mathrm{E}[v^{K+1}(1+i)^{1-S}],
$$

we can use the independence of $K + 1$ and $1 - S$ to calculate the expectation of the product as the product of the expectations,

$$E[v^{K+1}(1+i)^{1-S}] = E[v^{K+1}]E[(1+i)^{1-S}]. \qquad (4.4.3)$$

The first factor on the right-hand side is $A_x$. Since $1-S$ has the uniform distribution over the unit interval, the second factor is

$$E[(1+i)^{1-S}] = \int_0^1 (1+i)^t \, 1 \, dt = \frac{i}{\delta}.$$

Hence, again we have $\bar{A}_x = (i/\delta) A_x$ under the assumption of uniform distribution of deaths.

In Section 3.6 we also discussed the assumption that the force of mortality is constant between integral ages. The relationship between the net single premiums for whole life insurances payable at the moment of death and at the end of the year of death under this assumption will be developed in Exercise 4.16. Since the Balducci Assumption implies that the force of mortality decreases over the year of age (see Exercise 3.22), it is not realistic for human lives. Moreover it leads to more complicated relationships that we will not develop here.

Next we turn to an analysis of the annually increasing $n$-year term insurance payable at the moment of death. For this insurance, the present-value random variable is

$$Z = \begin{cases} [T+1]v^T & T < n \\ 0 & T \ge n. \end{cases}$$

Since $[T+1] = K+1$, we can use the relation $T = K + S$ to obtain

$$Z = \begin{cases} (K+1)v^{K+1}v^{S-1} & T < n \\ 0 & T \ge n. \end{cases}$$

Now if we let $W$ be the present-value random variable for the annually increasing $n$-year term insurance payable at the end of the year of death,

$$W = \begin{cases} (K+1)v^{K+1} & K = 0,1,\ldots,n-1 \\ 0 & K = n,n+1,\ldots. \end{cases}$$

Then

$$Z = W(1+i)^{1-S}$$

and

$$E[Z] = E[W(1+i)^{1-S}].$$

Since $W$ is a function of $K+1$ alone and $K+1$ and $1-S$ are independent,

$$E[Z] = E[W]E[(1+i)^{1-S}]$$

$$= (IA)^1_{x:\overline{n}|} \frac{i}{\delta}.$$

# LIFE INSURANCE

These results for the whole life and the increasing term insurances, under the assumption of a uniform distribution of deaths over the year of age, are very similar,

$$\bar{A}_x = \frac{i}{\delta} A_x$$

and

$$(I\bar{A})^1_{x:\overline{n}|} = \frac{i}{\delta}(IA)^1_{x:\overline{n}|}.$$

Let us look at the general model to find the basis of the similarities. From (4.2.2),

$$Z = b_T v_T. \tag{4.4.4}$$

For the two insurances above, the conditions used were
- $v_T = v^T$, and
- $b_T$ was a function of only the integral part of $T$, the-curtate-future-lifetime, $K$.

Writing this latter property as $b_T = b^*_{K+1}$ we can write (4.4.4) as

$$Z = b^*_{K+1} v^T$$
$$= b^*_{K+1} v^{K+1}(1+i)^{1-S}$$

and

$$E[Z] = E[b^*_{K+1} v^{K+1}(1+i)^{1-S}]. \tag{4.4.5}$$

Under the assumption of a uniform distribution of deaths over the year of age, we can infer the independence of $K$ and $S$ and that $1-S$ also has a uniform distribution. Then we can write (4.4.5) as

$$E[Z] = E[b^*_{K+1} v^{K+1}] E[(1+i)^{1-S}]$$

$$= E[b^*_{K+1} v^{K+1}] \frac{i}{\delta}. \tag{4.4.6}$$

**Example 4.5:**

Calculate the net single premium and the variance for a 10,000, 30-year endowment insurance providing the death benefit at the moment of death for a male aged 35 at issue of the policy. Use the Illustrative Life Table, the uniform distribution of deaths assumption and $i = 0.06$. (Then $^2\bar{A}^1_{35:\overline{30}|} = 0.0309294$.)

**Solution:**
For endowment insurance, $v_T \neq v^T$. Therefore, we cannot apply (4.4.6) directly. Recalling (4.2.8), which showed the endowment insurance as the sum of a term insurance and pure endowment, we can apply (4.4.6) to the term insurance component and then calculate the pure endowment insurance part. Thus, using (4.2.9) and (4.2.10), we can calculate the net single premium as follows:

$$\bar{A}_{35:\overline{30|}} = \frac{i}{\delta} A^1_{35:\overline{30|}} + A_{35:\overset{1}{\overline{30|}}}$$

$$= (1.0297087)\left[A_{35} - (1.06)^{-30}\frac{l_{65}}{l_{35}} A_{65}\right] + (1.06)^{-30}\frac{l_{65}}{l_{35}}$$

$$= 0.208727,$$

and the variance as

$$\text{Var}[Z] = {}^2\bar{A}_{35:\overline{30|}} - (\bar{A}_{35:\overline{30|}})^2$$

$$= 0.0309294 + (1.1236)^{-30}\frac{l_{65}}{l_{35}} - (0.208727)^2$$

$$= 0.011606.$$

For the 10,000 sum insured, $10{,}000\,\bar{A}_{35:\overline{30|}} = 2{,}087.27$ and $(10{,}000)^2\,\text{Var}[Z] = 1{,}160{,}600.$   ▼

**Example 4.6:**      Calculate, for a male aged 50, the net single premium for an annually decreasing 5-year term insurance paying 5000 at the moment of death in the first year, 4000 in the second year, and so on. Use the Illustrative Life Table, uniform distribution of deaths assumption and $i = 0.06$.

**Solution:**
Referring to Table 4.1, we see that

$$b_t = \begin{cases} 5 - [t] & t \le 5 \\ 0 & t > 5 \end{cases}$$

is a function of only $k$, the integral part of $t$, and hence we may write it as

$$b_t = \begin{cases} 5 - k & k = 0,1,2,3,4 \\ 0 & k > 4. \end{cases}$$

The discount function is $v^t$, so we have

$$(D\bar{A})^1_{50:\overline{5|}} = \frac{i}{\delta}(DA)^1_{50:\overline{5|}}$$

$$= (1.0297087)\sum_{k=0}^{4}(5-k)\,v^{k+1}\,{}_kp_{50}\,q_{50+k}$$

$$= (1.0297087)\frac{\sum_{k=0}^{4}(5-k)\,v^{k+1}\,d_{50+k}}{l_{50}}$$

$$= 0.088307.$$

Then, $1000\,(D\bar{A})^1_{50:\overline{5|}} = 88.307.$   ▼

For an insurance providing a death benefit at the moment of death that is not a function of $K$, further analysis is required to express its values in terms of those for an insurance payable at the end of the year of death. For instance, let us consider the continuously increasing whole life insurance payable at the moment of death. This insurance was discussed extensively in Section 4.2 and its benefit function analyzed in Figure 4.5. Its functions are

$$b_t = t \qquad t > 0$$

$$v_t = v^t \qquad t > 0$$

$$z_t = t v^t \qquad t > 0.$$

To find $(\bar{I}\bar{A})_x$ we will rewrite

$$Z = (K + S) v^{K+S}$$

$$= (K + 1) v^{K+S} - (1 - S) v^{K+1} (1 + i)^{1-S}$$

$$= (K + 1) v^{K+1} (1 + i)^{1-S} - v^{K+1} (1 - S)(1 + i)^{1-S}.$$

Now taking expectations, under the assumption of a uniform distribution of deaths, we have

$$E[Z] = E[(K + 1) v^{K+1}] E[(1 + i)^{1-S}] - E[v^{K+1}] E[(1 - S)(1 + i)^{1-S}]$$

$$= (IA)_x \frac{i}{\delta} - A_x E[(1 - S)(1 + i)^{1-S}].$$

We can simplify the last factor directly since $1 - S$ has a uniform distribution,

$$E[(1 - S)(1 + i)^{1-S}] = \int_0^1 u (1 + i)^u \, du = (\bar{D}\bar{s})_{\overline{1}|} = \frac{1 + i}{\delta} - \frac{i}{\delta^2}.$$

Thus, we can write

$$(\bar{I}\bar{A})_x = \frac{i}{\delta}\left[ (IA)_x - \left(\frac{1}{d} - \frac{1}{\delta}\right) A_x \right].$$

## 4.5 Recursion Equations

Recursion equations for the values of the insurance models can be derived directly from the expressions in the previous sections. For example,

$$A_x = \sum_{k=0}^{\infty} v^{k+1} \, {}_k p_x \, q_{x+k}$$

$$= v q_x + \sum_{k=1}^{\infty} v^{k+1} \, {}_k p_x \, q_{x+k}$$

$$= v q_x + v p_x \sum_{k=1}^{\infty} v^k \, {}_{k-1} p_{x+1} \, q_{x+k}$$

## LIFE INSURANCE

$$= v q_x + v p_x \sum_{j=0}^{\infty} v^{j+1} \, {}_j p_{x+1} \, q_{x+1+j}$$

$$= v q_x + v p_x A_{x+1}.$$

This algebraic demonstration has the interpretation that, at the end of the first year, the net single premium for whole life insurance for $(x)$, $A_x$, must provide either a unit in the event of death within the year or the net single premium for a unit whole life insurance at the attained age in the case of survival.

These expressions can also be obtained from a probabilistic viewpoint. Let us consider $A_x$ again but this time from its definition $E[Z] = E[v^{K+1}]$. For emphasis we now write this as

$$A_x = E[Z] = E[v^{K+1}|K \geq 0],$$

which is redundant since all of $K$'s probability is on the nonnegative integers.

Now $E[Z]$ can be calculated by considering the event $(x)$ dies in the first year, that is, $K = 0$, and its complement, $(x)$ survives the first year, that is, $K \geq 1$. We can write

$$E[Z] = E[v^{K+1}|K = 0] \Pr(K = 0) + E[v^{K+1}|K \geq 1] \Pr(K \geq 1). \quad (4.5.1)$$

In this expression we can readily substitute

$$E[v^{K+1}|K = 0] = v$$

$$\Pr(K = 0) = q_x,$$

and

$$\Pr(K \geq 1) = p_x.$$

To find an expression for the remaining factor, we rewrite it as

$$E[v^{K+1}|K \geq 1] = v \, E[v^{(K-1)+1}|(K - 1) \geq 0].$$

Since $K$ is the curtate-future-lifetime of $(x)$, given $K \geq 1$, $K - 1$ must be the curtate-future-lifetime of $(x + 1)$.

If we are willing to use the same probabilities for the conditional distribution of $K - 1$ given $K \geq 1$, as we would for a newly considered life aged $x + 1$, then we may write

$$E[v^{(K-1)+1}|K - 1 \geq 0] = A_{x+1} \quad (4.5.2)$$

and substitute it into (4.5.1) to obtain

$$A_x = v q_x + v A_{x+1} p_x. \quad (4.5.3)$$

This assumed equality,

(the distribution of the future lifetime

of a newly insured life aged $x + 1$)

$\qquad$ = (the distribution of the future lifetime of a life

now aged $x + 1$ who was insured 1 year ago),

was discussed in Section 3.8. In terms of select tables, the right-hand side of (4.5.2) would be $A_{[x]+1}$. In (4.5.3), every $x$ would be $[x]$.

After replacement of $p_x$ by $1 - q_x$ and the multiplication of both sides by $(1 + i)\, l_x$, (4.5.3) can be rearranged as

$$l_x (1 + i)\, A_x = l_x A_{x+1} + d_x (1 - A_{x+1}).$$

For the random survivorship group, this equation has the following interpretation: Together with one year's interest, $A_x$ will provide $A_{x+1}$ for all and an additional $1 - A_{x+1}$ for those expected to die within the year.

Dividing by $l_x$ and then subtracting $A_x + q_x (1 - A_{x+1})$ from both sides of the previous equation we have

$$A_{x+1} - A_x = i A_x - q_x (1 - A_{x+1}). \tag{4.5.4}$$

This expression shows that the difference in the net single premiums between the issue age, $x$, and the age attained 1 year later, $x + 1$, is equal to the interest on the issue age net single premium less the cost of providing a unit of insurance for a year.

Another expression for $A_x$ can be obtained by subtracting $i A_x$ from both sides of (4.5.4) and then multiplying by $v^x$,

$$v^x A_{x+1} - v^{x-1} A_x = -v^x q_x (1 - A_{x+1}). \tag{4.5.5}$$

Now, summing from $x = y$ to $\infty$, we obtain

$$-v^{y-1} A_y = -\sum_{x=y}^{\infty} v^x q_x (1 - A_{x+1}),$$

and hence

$$A_y = \sum_{x=y}^{\infty} v^{x-y+1} q_x (1 - A_{x+1}).$$

This expression shows that the net single premium for $(y)$ is the present value of the annual costs of insurance over the lifetime of the insured.

Similar expressions can be established for insurances payable at the moment of death. These are developed using infinitesimal calculus and lead to differential equations.

For a whole life insurance for $(x)$,

$$\frac{d}{dx} \bar{A}_x = -\mu_x + \bar{A}_x (\delta + \mu_x) = \delta \bar{A}_x - \mu_x (1 - \bar{A}_x), \tag{4.5.6}$$

which are the continuous analogues of (4.5.4). Verification of these expressions have been left to Exercise 4.17.

On the other hand, (4.5.6) can be developed from the definition of $\bar{A}_x$ by using conditional expectation as we did for $A_x$,

$$\bar{A}_x = E[v^T]$$

$$= E[v^T | T \le h] \Pr(T \le h) + E[v^T | T > h] \Pr(T > h). \quad (4.5.7)$$

Now

$$\Pr(T \le h) = {}_h q_x \quad \text{and} \quad \Pr(T > h) = {}_h p_x, \quad (4.5.8)$$

and the conditional p.d.f. of $T$ given $T \le h$ is

$$f(t | T \le h) = \begin{cases} \dfrac{f(t)}{F(h)} = \dfrac{{}_t p_x \, \mu_{x+t}}{{}_h q_x} & 0 \le t \le h \\[2ex] 0 & \text{elsewhere.} \end{cases}$$

Thus,

$$E[v^T | T \le h] = \int_0^h v^t \frac{{}_t p_x \, \mu_{x+t}}{{}_h q_x} \, dt. \quad (4.5.9)$$

As we did in the expression for $A_x$, we will write

$$E[v^T | T > h] = v^h E[v^{T-h} | (T - h) > 0]$$
$$= v^h \bar{A}_{x+h}. \quad (4.5.10)$$

Substitution of (4.5.8), (4.5.9) and (4.5.10) into (4.5.7) yields

$$\bar{A}_x = \int_0^h v^t \frac{{}_t p_x \, \mu_{x+t}}{{}_h q_x} \, dt \, {}_h q_x + v^h \bar{A}_{x+h} \, {}_h p_x. \quad (4.5.11)$$

Then, on both sides of (4.5.11), we multiply by $-1$, add $\bar{A}_{x+h}$ and divide by $h$ to obtain

$$\frac{\bar{A}_{x+h} - \bar{A}_x}{h} = \frac{-1}{h} \int_0^h v^t \, {}_t p_x \, \mu_{x+t} \, dt + \bar{A}_{x+h} \frac{1 - v^h \, {}_h p_x}{h}. \quad (4.5.12)$$

Now

$$\lim_{h \to 0} \frac{1}{h} \int_0^h v^t \, {}_t p_x \, \mu_{x+t} \, dt = \frac{d}{ds} \int_0^s v^t \, {}_t p_x \, \mu_{x+t} \, dt \Big|_{s=0} = \mu_x$$

and

$$\lim_{h \to 0} \frac{1 - v^h \, {}_h p_x}{h} = -\frac{d}{dt} (v^t \, {}_t p_x) \Big|_{t=0} = \mu_x + \delta.$$

Using these two limits as $h \to 0$ in (4.5.12) we obtain (4.5.6)

$$\frac{d}{dx} \bar{A}_x = -\mu_x + \bar{A}_x (\mu_x + \delta).$$

## 4.6 Commutation Functions

Commutation functions have been developed to write net single premium formulas in terms of stored intermediate values. We note that in (4.3.4),

$$l_x A_x = \sum_{k=0}^{\infty} v^{k+1} d_{x+k},$$

each term in the sum is a function of both duration and attained age. When the force of interest is constant, we can multiply both sides of (4.3.4) by $v^x$, and then express each term as a function of only attained age. That is,

$$v^x l_x A_x = \sum_{k=0}^{\infty} v^{x+k+1} d_{x+k},$$

which motivates the definition of commutation functions:

$$D_x = v^x l_x$$

$$C_x = v^{x+1} d_x = D_x v q_x$$

$$M_x = \sum_{k=0}^{\infty} C_{x+k}$$

$$R_x = \sum_{k=0}^{\infty} M_{x+k} = \sum_{k=0}^{\infty} (k + 1) C_{x+k}.$$

With these definitions, the net single premium for a deferred term insurance paying a unit benefit at the end of the year of death of $(x)$, if death occurs between ages $y$ and $z$, can be expressed as

$$_{y-x|z-y} A_x = \frac{M_y - M_z}{D_x}.$$

From Table 4.2 we see that the net single premium for the $n$-year increasing term insurance payable at the end of the year of death of $(x)$ is

$$(IA)^1_{x:\overline{n}|} = \sum_{k=0}^{n-1} (k + 1) \, v^{k+1} \, _{k|}q_x$$

$$= \sum_{k=0}^{n-1} \frac{(k + 1) \, v^{x+k+1} \, d_{x+k}}{v^x l_x}$$

$$= \frac{\sum_{k=0}^{n-1} (k + 1) C_{x+k}}{D_x}$$

$$= \frac{\sum_{k=0}^{n-1} (M_{x+k} - M_{x+n})}{D_x} \qquad (4.6.1)$$

$$= \frac{R_x - R_{x+n} - n M_{x+n}}{D_x}.$$

The net single premium for the $n$-year pure endowment can be written as

$$A_{x:\overline{n}|}^{\ 1} = \frac{D_{x+n}}{D_x}.$$ (4.6.2)

For the net single premium for an $n$-year endowment insurance, we write

$$A_{x:\overline{n}|} = \frac{M_x - M_{x+n} + D_{x+n}}{D_x}.$$

Commutation functions have also been defined for use in formulas for net single premiums of insurances payable at the moment of death. For example,

$$\bar{C}_x = \int_0^1 v^{x+t} l_{x+t} \, \mu_{x+t} \, dt$$

$$= \int_0^1 D_{x+t} \, \mu_{x+t} \, dt.$$ (4.6.3)

$$\bar{M}_x = \sum_{y=x}^{\infty} \bar{C}_y = \int_x^{\infty} D_y \, \mu_y \, dy$$

$$\bar{R}_x = \sum_{y=x}^{\infty} \bar{M}_y.$$

**Example 4.7:** For a life aged 30 at policy issue, calculate the net single premium for a decreasing 10-year term insurance paying 10,000 at the moment of death in the first year, 9000 at the moment of death in the second year and so on
a. with the coverage terminating at the end of the tenth year.
b. with the coverage terminating at the end of the fifth year.

Use the Illustrative Life Table, the assumption of uniform distribution of deaths in each year of age and $i = 0.06$.

**Solution:**
a. Following the argument in Example 4.6, we have

$$1000\,(D\bar{A})^1_{30:\overline{10}|} = 1000\,\frac{i}{\delta}\,(DA)^1_{30:\overline{10}|}.$$

To express $(DA)^1_{30:\overline{10}|}$ in commutation functions we can think of it as the premium for 10 units of whole life insurance at age 30 less 1 unit of whole life insurance commencing at each of the ages from 31 through 40. (See Figure 4.6.) Thus

$$(DA)^1_{30:\overline{10}|} = \frac{10\,M_{30} - \displaystyle\sum_{y=31}^{40} M_y}{D_{30}}$$

$$= \frac{10\,M_{30} - R_{31} + R_{41}}{D_{30}}.$$

For the insurance described, we have

$$1000 \frac{i}{\delta} (DA)^1_{30:\overline{10}|} = 1000 \, (1.02971) \, (0.078164991)$$

$$= 80.49.$$

b. This insurance is a combination of 5 units of 5-year term insurance and a 5-year decreasing term insurance. Thus the net single premium is

$$1000 \, [5 \, \bar{A}^1_{30:\overline{5}|} + (D\bar{A})^1_{30:\overline{5}|}]$$

$$= 1000 \, (1.02971) \left[ \frac{5 \, (M_{30} - M_{35}) + 5 M_{30} - R_{31} + R_{36}}{D_{30}} \right]$$

$$= 1000 \, (1.02971) \left( \frac{10 M_{30} - 5 M_{35} - R_{31} + R_{36}}{D_{30}} \right)$$

$$= 58.69. \qquad \blacktriangledown$$

## 4.7
## Notes and
## References

The life contingencies textbooks listed in Appendix 6 give other developments of formulas for life insurance net single premiums. For example, with constant interest rates, commutation functions are employed extensively in Jordan (1967).

There is little material in these textbooks on the concept of the time-until-death of an insured as a random variable. Until recently, research and exposition on this concept has been called *individual risk theory.* Cramér (1930) gives a detailed exposition of the ideas up to that time. Kahn (1962) and Seal (1969) give concise bibliographical information on both research and expository papers over a 100-year span.

Since 1970 there has been interest in actuarial models that consider both the time-until-death and the investment-rate-of-return as random variables. Bellhouse and Panjer (1980), and some of the references therein, develop these stochastic models.

## Exercises

Assume, unless otherwise stated, that insurances are payable at the moment of death, and that the force of interest is a constant $\delta$ with $i$ and $d$ as the equivalent rates of interest and discount.

*Section 4.2*

4.1. If $\mu_x = \mu$, a positive constant, for all $x > 0$, show that $\bar{A}_x = \mu/(\mu + \delta)$.

4.2. Let $\mu_x = 1/(1 + x)$, for all $x > 0$.
   a. Integrate by parts to show that

$$\bar{A}_x = 1 - \delta \int_0^\infty e^{-\delta t} \frac{1 + x}{1 + x + t} \, dt.$$

   b. Use the expression in (a) to show that $d\bar{A}_x/dx < 0$ for all $x > 0$.

4.3. Show that $d\bar{A}_x/di = -v(\bar{I}\bar{A})_x$.

4.4. Show that the expressions for the variance of the present value of an $n$-year endowment insurance paying a unit benefit, as given by (4.2.10) and (4.2.11), are identical.

4.5. Let $Z_1$ and $Z_2$ be as defined in equation (4.2.8).
  a. Show that $\lim_{n\to 0} \text{Cov}[Z_1,Z_2] = \lim_{n\to\infty} \text{Cov}[Z_1,Z_2] = 0$.
  b. Develop an implicit equation for the term of the endowment for which $\text{Cov}[Z_1,Z_2]$ is minimized.
  c. Develop a formula for the minimum in (b).
  d. Simplify the formulas in (b) and (c) for the case when the force of mortality is a constant $\mu$.

4.6. Assume mortality is described by $l_x = 100 - x$ for $0 \le x \le 100$ and that the force of interest is $\delta = 0.05$.
  a. Calculate $\bar{A}^1_{40:\overline{25}|}$.
  b. Determine the net single premium for a 25-year term insurance with benefit amount for death at time $t$ equal to $e^{0.05t}$ for a person aged 40 at policy issue.

4.7. Assuming de Moivre's survival function with $\omega = 100$ and $i = 0.10$, calculate
  a. $\bar{A}^1_{30:\overline{10}|}$
  b. the variance of the present value, at policy issue, of the benefit of the insurance in (a).

4.8. If $\delta_t = 0.2/(1 + 0.05\,t)$ and $l_x = 100 - x$ for $0 \le x \le 100$, calculate
  a. for a whole life insurance issued at age $x$, the net single premium and the variance of the present value of the benefits
  b. $(\bar{I}\bar{A})_x$.

4.9. a. Show that $\bar{A}_x$ is the moment generating function of $T$, the future lifetime of $(x)$, evaluated at $-\delta$.
  b. Hence, show that if $T$ has a gamma distribution with parameters $\alpha$ and $\beta$, then $\bar{A}_x = (1 + \delta/\beta)^{-\alpha}$.

4.10. Given $b_t = t$, $\mu_{x+t} = \mu$ and $\delta_t = \delta$ for all $t > 0$, derive expressions for
  a. $(\bar{I}\bar{A})_x = E[b_T v^T]$  b. $\text{Var}[b_T v^T]$.

*Section 4.3*

4.11. If $l_x = 100 - x$ for $0 \le x \le 100$ and $i = 0.05$, evaluate
  a. $A_{40:\overline{25}|}$       b. $(IA)_{40}$.

4.12. Show $A_{x:\overline{n}|} = A^1_{x:\overline{m}|} + v^m\,{}_mp_x\,A_{x+m:\overline{n-m}|}$ for $m < n$ and verbally interpret the result.

4.13. If $A_x = 0.25$, $A_{x+20} = 0.40$ and $A_{x:\overline{20}|} = 0.55$, calculate
  a. $A_{x:\overline{20}|}^{\phantom{1}}$       b. $A^1_{x:\overline{20}|}$.

4.14. a. Describe the benefits of the insurance with net single premium given by the symbol $(IA)_{x:\overline{m}|}$.

# LIFE INSURANCE

b. Express the net single premium of (a) in terms of the symbols given in Tables 4.1 and 4.2.

*Section 4.4*

4.15. Consider the time scale measured in intervals of length $1/m$ where the unit is a year. Let a whole life insurance for a unit amount be payable at the end of the $m$thly interval in which death occurs. Let $k$ be the number of complete insurance years lived prior to death and let $j$ be the number of complete $m$ths of a year lived in the year of death.
   a. What is the present value function for this insurance?
   b. Set up a formula analogous to (4.4.1) for the net single premium, $A_x^{(m)}$, for this insurance.
   c. Show algebraically that, under the assumption of a uniform distribution of deaths over the insurance year of age,

$$A_x^{(m)} = \frac{i}{i^{(m)}} A_x.$$

4.16. Show, under the assumption of a constant force of mortality between integral ages, that (4.4.1) may be written

$$\bar{A}_x = \sum_{k=0}^{\infty} v^{k+1} \; {}_k p_x \; \mu_{x+k} \; \frac{i + q_{x+k}}{\delta + \mu_{x+k}}$$

where $\mu_{x+k} = -\log p_{x+k}$.

*Section 4.5*

4.17. a. Show that (4.2.6) can be rewritten as

$$\bar{A}_x = \frac{1}{{}_x p_0 \; v^x} \int_x^{\infty} v^y \; {}_y p_0 \; \mu_y \; dy \qquad x \geq 0.$$

b. Differentiate the formula of (a) to establish (4.5.6),

$$\frac{d\bar{A}_x}{dx} = \bar{A}_x (\mu_x + \delta) - \mu_x \qquad x \geq 0.$$

c. Use the same technique to show

$$\frac{d\bar{A}^1_{x:\overline{n}|}}{dx} = \bar{A}^1_{x:\overline{n}|} (\mu_x + \delta) + A_{x:\overline{n}|}^{\;\;1} \mu_{x+n} - \mu_x \qquad x \geq 0.$$

4.18. Solve the differential equation (4.5.6) as follows:
   a. Use the integrating factor

$$\exp\left[ -\int_y^x (\delta + \mu_z) \, dz \right]$$

   to obtain

$$\bar{A}_y = \int_y^{\infty} \mu_x \exp\left[ -\int_y^x (\delta + \mu_z) dz \right] dx.$$

# Chapter 4
## LIFE INSURANCE

b. Use the integrating factor $e^{-\delta x}$ to obtain

$$\bar{A}_y = \int_y^\infty \mu_x v^{x-y}(1 - \bar{A}_x)\,dx.$$

4.19. Show that

$$(IA)_x = v\,q_x + v\,[A_{x+1} + (IA)_{x+1}]\,p_x.$$

What assumptions did you use to establish the identity?

*Section 4.6*

4.20. Show algebraically and interpret

$$\frac{1}{D_x}\left[\sum_{k=0}^{n-1} C_{x+k}\,v^{n-k-1} + D_{x+n}\right] = v^n.$$

4.21. Verify the equivalence of the last three expressions in (4.6.1).

4.22. Express, in commutation functions, the net single premium for a Double Protection to Age 65 policy which provides a benefit of 2 in the event of death prior to age 65 and a benefit of 1 after age 65. Assume benefits are paid at the end of the year of death.

4.23. A policy is issued at age 0 with the following graded scale of death benefits payable at the moment of death.

| Age | Death Benefits |
|---|---|
| 0 | 1 000 |
| 1 | 2 000 |
| 2 | 4 000 |
| 3 | 6 000 |
| 4 | 8 000 |
| 5–20 | 10 000 |
| 21 and over | 50 000 |

Write the net single premium in terms of commutation functions.

4.24. Under the assumption of a uniform distribution of deaths, express the net single premiums below in terms of $D_x$, $C_x$, $M_x$ and $R_x$.

a. $(I\bar{A})_{30:\overline{35}|}$   b. $(\bar{I}\bar{A})_{30:\overline{35}|}$   c. $(\bar{I}_{\overline{10}|}\bar{A})_{30:\overline{35}|}$.

*Miscellaneous*

4.25. a. Determine whether or not a constant increase in the force of mortality has the same effect on $A_x$ as the same increase in the force of interest.

   b. Show that if the single probability of death $q_{x+n}$ is increased to $q_{x+n} + c$, then $A_x$ will be increased by

$$c\,v^{n+1}\,{}_np_x\,(1 - A_{x+n+1}).$$

4.26. The net single premium for a modified pure endowment of 1000 issued at age $x$ for $n$ years is 700 with return of the net single premium in event of death during the $n$-year period, and is 650 with no refund at death.

a. Calculate the net single premium for a modified pure endowment of 1000 issued at age $x$ for $n$ years if $100k\%$ of the net single premium is to be returned at death during the period.

b. For the modified pure endowment in (a), express the variance of the present value at policy issue in terms of net single premiums for pure endowments and term insurances.

4.27. An appliance manufacturer sells his product with a 5-year warranty promising the return of cash equal to the pro rata share of the initial purchase price for failure within 5 years. For example, if failure is reported 3-3/4 years following purchase, 25% of the purchase price will be returned. From statistical studies, the probability of failure of a new product during the first year is estimated to be 0.2, in each of the second, third and fourth years, 0.1, and in the fifth year, 0.2.

a. Assuming that failures are reported uniformly within each year since purchase, determine the fraction of the purchase price that serves as the net single premium for this warranty. Assume $i = 0.10$.

b. If the warranted return is the reduction on the purchase price of a new product with a 5-year warranty, would the answer to (a) change?

4.28. a. Show that

$$\mu_x \cong \frac{(i/\delta)\,(M_{x-1} - M_{x+1})}{2\,D_x}.$$

b. Approximate $\mu_{30}$ using the Illustrative Life Table with $i = 0.06$.

c. Using $i = 0$, redo part (b).

# Chapter 5
# LIFE ANNUITIES

## 5.1
## Introduction

In the preceding chapter we studied payments contingent on death, as provided by various forms of life insurances. In this chapter we shall study payments contingent on survival, as provided by various forms of life annuities. A *life annuity* is a series of payments made continuously or at equal intervals (such as months, quarters, years) while a given life survives. It may be temporary, that is, limited to a given term of years, or it may be payable for the whole of life. The payment intervals may commence immediately or, alternatively, the annuity may be deferred. Payments may be due at the beginnings of the payment intervals (*annuities-due*) or at the ends of such intervals (*annuities-immediate*).

Through the study of *annuities-certain* in the theory of interest, the student already has a knowledge of annuity terminology, notation and theory. Life annuity theory is analogous but brings in survival as a condition for payment. This condition has been encountered already in Chapter 4 in connection with pure endowments and the maturity payments under endowment insurances.

Life annuities play a major role in life insurance operations. As we shall see in the next chapter, life insurances are usually purchased by a life annuity of premiums rather than by a single premium. The amount payable at the time of claim may be converted through a settlement option into some form of life annuity for the beneficiary. Some types of life insurance carry this concept even further and, instead of featuring a lump sum payable on death, provide stated forms of income benefits. Thus, for example, there may be a monthly income of 1000 payable to a surviving spouse or to a retired insured.

Annuities are even more central in pension systems. In fact, a retirement plan can be regarded as a system for purchasing deferred life annuities (payable during retirement) by some form of temporary annuity of contributions during active service. The temporary annuity may consist of varying contributions, and valuation of it may take into account not only interest and mortality but other factors such as salary increases and the termination of participation for reasons other than death.

Life annuities also have a role in disability and workers' compensation insurances. In the case of disability insurance, termination of the annuity benefit by reason of recovery of the disabled insured may need to be considered. For surviving spouse benefits under workers' compensation, remarriage may terminate the annuity.

In preparation for applying what we shall call the *current payment technique* for valuing life annuities, we shall, in Section 5.2, consider a single payment contingent on survival. This is in analogy to compound interest theory where we start with the accumulated value and the present value of a single payment and then extend the valuation concepts to a series of payments by means of summation or integration. The current payment technique proceeds on similar lines for life annuities. Alternatively, we shall employ an *aggregate payment technique* that proceeds by consideration of the total value received by the time the annuity terminates by death or by expiration of its term. Each of these techniques has its special advantages and offers various insights. The equivalence of the formulas produced by the two techniques follows as an immediate consequence of Theorems 3.1 and 3.2.

As in the preceding chapter on life insurances, we shall, unless otherwise stated, assume a constant effective annual rate of interest $i$ (or the equivalent constant force of interest $\delta$).

In most applications of the theory developed in this chapter, annuity payments continue while a human life remains in a particular status. However, the possible applications of the theory are much wider. It may be applied to any set of periodic payments where the payments are not made with certainty. Examples of these applications will be seen in later chapters dealing with multiple lives or multiple causes of decrement.

## 5.2
## Single Payment Contingent on Survival

We now consider a unit payment due at the end of $n$ years provided that a life now aged $x$ survives the $n$ years. In Chapter 4, such a benefit was called an $n$-year pure endowment of 1 in respect to $(x)$. In connection with insurances, it was natural to use the term net single premium and the notation $A_{x:\overline{n}|}^{\phantom{x}1}$ for the expectation of the present value of the unit pure endowment. In connection with annuities and, in particular, for pension funding, the term actuarial present value and the notation $_nE_x$ are frequently used and we shall employ them here. The word actuarial here implies that an expectation or other factor besides interest has entered the calculation. Thus the actuarial present value of 1 due at the end of $n$ years provided that $(x)$ survives is

$$_nE_x = A_{x:\overline{n}|}^{\phantom{x}1} = v^n \, _np_x \qquad (5.2.1)$$

(see Table 4.1).

**Example 5.1:**

Find the actuarial present value of 10,000 due at the end of 40 years if a man aged 25 survives. For valuation basis, use the Illustrative Life Table with interest at the effective annual rate of 6%.

**Solution:**
Here we require

$$10,000 \, _{40}E_{25} = 10,000 \, v^{40} \, _{40}p_{25}$$

$$= 10,000 \, (0.09722219)(0.78765825)$$

$$= 765.78.$$

In this example, the interest discounting has much more effect than the survival factor. ▼

Formula (5.2.1) may be rewritten in the form

$$l_x \, _nE_x \, (1 + i)^n = l_{x+n}. \qquad (5.2.2)$$

# Chapter 5

# LIFE ANNUITIES

In terms of the deterministic survivorship group concept, this indicates that if the $l_x$ survivors at age $x$ each deposit $_nE_x$ into a fund to accumulate under the effective rate of interest $i$, there will be a sufficient amount at the end of $n$ years to pay 1 to each of the $l_{x+n}$ survivors at age $x + n$. We are here assuming that the size of the group at age $x$ will decrease exactly as indicated in the life table.

To illustrate by means of the data of Example 5.1, if 765.78 is contributed by the $l_{25} = 95,650.15$ survivors at age 25 (according to the Illustrative Life Table), and if this fund accumulates at an effective annual rate of interest of 6% for 40 years, we have the following results:

| | |
|---|---|
| Original fund | = 73,246,972 |
| Accumulation factor $(1.06)^{40}$ | = 10.285718 |
| Accumulated fund at end of 40 years | = 753,397,698 |
| Survivors at age 65 ($l_{65}$) | = 75,339.63 |
| Share per survivor | = 10,000. |

This calculation exhibits the actuarial present value

$$10,000 \; _{40}E_{25} = 765.78$$

as the amount which, if contributed by each survivor at age 25, would accumulate, under 6% interest, a sufficient fund to provide 10,000 per survivor at age 65. Only survivors at age 65 participate in the distribution of the fund; the contributions of the $l_{25} - l_{65}$ deaths accumulated with interest are applied to increase the share of each survivor. Because of the dual operation of interest in increasing the fund and of survivorship in decreasing the number of beneficiaries of the fund, this is often described by saying that the 765.78 has been accumulated in 40 years with benefit of interest and survivorship to 10,000. In this text, we shall refer to the 10,000 as the actuarial accumulated value at age 65 from 765.78 at age 25. For further insight into these concepts, see Exercise 5.3.

More generally, we shall define the **_actuarial accumulated value_** at the end of $n$ years of 1 contributed at age $x$ to be such an amount $S$ that its actuarial present value is 1. Thus $S \; _nE_x = 1$ or

$$S = \frac{1}{_nE_x} = \frac{1}{v^n \; _np_x} = (1 + i)^n \frac{l_x}{l_{x+n}}. \tag{5.2.3}$$

Formula (5.2.3) exhibits the actuarial accumulation factor $1/_nE_x$ as the product of the interest accumulation factor $(1 + i)^n$ and a survivorship accumulation factor $1/_np_x = l_x/l_{x+n}$.

**Example 5.2:**

Find the actuarial accumulated value at age 65 of 1000 contributed at age 25, on the basis of the Illustrative Life Table with interest at the effective annual rate of 6%.

**Solution:**

$$1000 \, \frac{1}{_{40}E_{25}} = 1000 \, (1.06)^{40} \, \frac{l_{25}}{l_{65}} = 13{,}058.60$$

In this example, the annual mortality rates range from 0.0012230 at age 25 to 0.0195231 at age 64 and have much less effect than interest at the 6% annual rate. ▼

**Example 5.3:**

Obtain formulas for

$$\text{a. } \frac{\partial}{\partial x} \, _{n}E_{x} \qquad \text{b. } \frac{\partial}{\partial n} \, _{n}E_{x}.$$

Observe how $_{n}E_{x}$ varies with $x$ for given $n$ and how it varies with $n$ for given $x$.

**Solution:**

a. $\dfrac{\partial}{\partial x} \, _{n}E_{x} = v^{n} \dfrac{\partial}{\partial x} \, _{n}p_{x} = v^{n} \, _{n}p_{x} \, (\mu_{x} - \mu_{x+n}) = \, _{n}E_{x} \, (\mu_{x} - \mu_{x+n})$

Note that if $\mu_{y}' > 0$, $x \le y \le x + n$, so that $\mu_{y}$ is an increasing function, then $\partial \, _{n}E_{x}/\partial x < 0$ and $_{n}E_{x}$ decreases with age. Also, if $\mu_{y} = c$, $x \le y \le x + n$, then $\partial \, _{n}E_{x}/\partial x = 0$ and $_{n}E_{x}$ does not change with age. Finally, if $\mu_{y}' < 0$, $x \le y \le x + n$, as can happen at the earliest ages, then $_{n}E_{x}$ increases with age.

b. $\dfrac{\partial}{\partial n} \, _{n}E_{x} = \dfrac{\partial}{\partial n} \exp\left[ -\int_{x}^{x+n} (\mu_{y} + \delta)\, dy \right]$

$\qquad = \, _{n}E_{x} \dfrac{\partial}{\partial n} \left[ -\int_{x}^{x+n} (\mu_{y} + \delta)\, dy \right]$

$\qquad = - \, _{n}E_{x} \, (\mu_{x+n} + \delta)$

Here one observes that $\partial \, _{n}E_{x}/\partial n < 0$, that is, $_{n}E_{x}$ is a decreasing function of $n$, as one would expect. ▼

**Example 5.4:**

Show and interpret the relations for $n > t$.

a. $_{n}E_{x} = \, _{t}E_{x} \, _{n-t}E_{x+t}$

b. $\dfrac{_{t}E_{x}}{_{n}E_{x}} = \dfrac{1}{_{n-t}E_{x+t}}$

**Solution:**

a. $_{n}E_{x} = v^{n} \, _{n}p_{x} = v^{t} \, v^{n-t} \, _{t}p_{x} \, _{n-t}p_{x+t} = \, _{t}E_{x} \, _{n-t}E_{x+t}$

The actuarial present value of 1 due at the end of $n$ years if $(x)$ survives can be found by taking the actuarial present value at age $x + t$ of the payment due at age $x + n$ and then taking the actuarial present value at age $x$ of the value found as of age $x + t$.

b. This formula follows by rearrangement of the formula in (a). The accumulated actuarial value at age $x + n$ of a unit contributed at age $x + t$ can be found by taking the actuarial present value at age $x$ of the unit and accumulating such value to age $x + n$.  ▼

## 5.3 Continuous Life Annuities

When we define the actuarial present values of life annuities, we can use either an aggregate payment technique or a current payment technique. The steps in the aggregate payment technique are

• record the interest only present value of all payments to be made by the annuity if death occurs at time $t$;
• multiply the present value, found above, by the probability or probability density of death at time $t$;
• add (integrate) over all times of death $t$.

For the current payment technique, the steps are

• record the amount of payment due at time $t$;
• determine the actuarial present value of the payment due at time $t$;
• add (integrate) these actuarial present values for all payment times $t$.

The first technique lends itself to interpretation in terms of the future-lifetime random variable. The steps are seen to yield an expectation. The current payment technique can be based on a probabilistic model also. A deterministic interpretation is possible for both techniques, but for deterministic models the current payment technique would normally be used.

These techniques are well illustrated by how we define the actuarial present value of a whole life annuity of 1 per annum payable continuously while $(x)$ survives. The notation for this value is $\bar{a}_x$.

With $T$ representing the future lifetime of $(x)$, the present value of the annuity payments made up until death is $Y = \bar{a}_{\overline{T}|}$, and by the aggregate payment technique we are led to define the actuarial present value of the annuity as

$$\bar{a}_x = \mathrm{E}[Y] = \mathrm{E}[\bar{a}_{\overline{T}|}]. \tag{5.3.1}$$

Since the p.d.f. of $T$ is $_t p_x \, \mu_{x+t}$, we have

$$\bar{a}_x = \int_0^\infty \bar{a}_{\overline{t}|} \, _t p_x \, \mu_{x+t} \, dt. \tag{5.3.2A}$$

Alternatively, in analogy with the compound interest formula

$$\bar{a}_{\overline{n}|} = \int_0^n v^t \, dt,$$

we consider (under the current payment technique) the actuarial present value $v^t \, _t p_x \, dt$ of the momentary payment $dt$ made at time $t$ and integrate all such momentary values to obtain the definition

$$\bar{a}_x = \int_0^{\infty} v^t \; {}_tp_x \; dt. \tag{5.3.2B}$$

By use of Theorem 3.1, with $z(t) = \bar{a}_{\overline{t}|}$, $g(t) = {}_tp_x \; \mu_{x+t}$, (5.3.2A) reduces to (5.3.2B), which demonstrates the equivalence of definitions (5.3.1) and (5.3.2B).

Further, by applying Theorem 3.1 with $z(t) = v^t$, $g(t) = {}_tp_x \; \mu_{x+t}$ to

$$\bar{A}_x = \int_0^{\infty} v^t \; {}_tp_x \; \mu_{x+t} \; dt,$$

we find

$$\bar{A}_x = 1 + \int_0^{\infty} {}_tp_x \; dv^t$$

$$= 1 - \delta\bar{a}_x \tag{5.3.3}$$

or

$$1 = \delta\bar{a}_x + \bar{A}_x. \tag{5.3.4}$$

Formula (5.3.4) is analogous to the relation

$$1 = \delta\bar{a}_{\overline{t}|} + v^t$$

in interest theory, and it indicates that a unit invested now will produce annual interest of $\delta$ payable continuously while $(x)$ survives plus the repayment of the unit upon the death of $(x)$.

The relations between $\bar{a}_x$ and $\bar{A}_x$ can be obtained by expressing

$$Y = \bar{a}_{\overline{T}|} = \frac{1 - v^T}{\delta} = \frac{1 - Z}{\delta} \tag{5.3.5}$$

where $Z = v^T$ is the present-value random variable for a whole life insurance. Then substituting in (5.3.1), we get

$$\bar{a}_x = E\left[\frac{1 - Z}{\delta}\right] = \frac{1 - \bar{A}_x}{\delta}, \tag{5.3.6}$$

which is equivalent to (5.3.3) and (5.3.4). Formula (5.3.6) can be written as

$$\bar{a}_x = \bar{a}_{\overline{\infty}|} - \bar{a}_{\overline{\infty}|}\bar{A}_x. \tag{5.3.7}$$

This last formula indicates that the whole life annuity is equivalent to a perpetuity payable continuously less a perpetuity commencing on the death of $(x)$ (which in effect, terminates the life annuity).

To measure, on the basis of the assumptions of our model, the mortality risk in a continuous life annuity, we are interested in $\mathrm{Var}[\bar{a}_{\overline{T}|}]$. We determine

# LIFE ANNUITIES

$$\text{Var}[\bar{a}_{\overline{T}|}] = \text{Var}\left[\frac{1 - v^T}{\delta}\right]$$

$$= \frac{1}{\delta^2}\text{Var}[v^T]$$

$$= \frac{1}{\delta^2}[{}^2\bar{A}_x - \bar{A}_x^2] \qquad (5.3.8)$$

where, as in Chapter 4, ${}^2\bar{A}_x$ is calculated at force of interest $2\delta$.

One can observe further that

$$\delta\bar{a}_{\overline{T}|} + v^T = 1 \qquad (5.3.9)$$

identically, from which follows

$$\text{E}[\delta\bar{a}_{\overline{T}|} + v^T] = \delta\bar{a}_x + \bar{A}_x = 1$$

[formula (5.3.4)], and

$$\text{Var}[\delta\bar{a}_{\overline{T}|} + v^T] = 0.$$

Formula (5.3.9) shows that there is no mortality risk for the combination of a continuous life annuity of $\delta$ per year and a life insurance of 1 payable on death.

**Example 5.5:**

Under the assumptions of a constant force of mortality, $\mu = 0.04$, and of a constant force of interest, $\delta = 0.06$, evaluate

a. $\bar{a}_x$
b. the standard deviation of $\bar{a}_{\overline{T}|}$
c. the probability that $\bar{a}_{\overline{T}|}$ will exceed $\bar{a}_x$.

**Solution:**

a. $\bar{a}_x = \displaystyle\int_0^\infty v^t \, {}_tp_x \, dt$

$= \displaystyle\int_0^\infty e^{-0.06t} \, e^{-0.04t} \, dt$

$= \displaystyle\int_0^\infty e^{-0.10t} \, dt = 10$

b. $\bar{A}_x = \text{E}[e^{-0.06T}] = \displaystyle\int_0^\infty e^{-0.06t} \, e^{-0.04t} \, (0.04) \, dt = 0.4$

$${}^2\bar{A}_x = \int_0^\infty e^{-0.12t} \, e^{-0.04t} \, (0.04) \, dt = 0.25$$

$$\text{Var}[\bar{a}_{\overline{T}|}] = \frac{1}{(0.06)^2}[0.25 - (0.4)^2] = 25$$

Thus the standard deviation of $\bar{a}_{\overline{T}|}$ equals 5.

c. $\Pr[\bar{a}_{\overline{T}|} > \bar{a}_x] = \Pr[\bar{a}_{\overline{T}|} > 10]$

$$= \Pr\left[\frac{1 - v^T}{0.06} > 10\right] = \Pr[0.4 > e^{-0.06T}]$$

$$= \Pr\left[T > \left(-\frac{\log 0.4}{0.06}\right)\right] = \Pr[T > 15.27]$$

$$= \int_{15.27}^{\infty} e^{-0.04t}\, 0.04\, dt = 0.54 \qquad \int_{15.27}^{\infty} {}_t p_x\, \mu_{x+t}\, dt$$

Thus, under the stated assumptions, there is a 54% chance that $\bar{a}_x$ will be insufficient to provide the unit life annuity. ▼

We now turn to temporary and deferred life annuities. The actuarial present value of an $n$-year temporary life annuity of 1 per annum, payable continuously while $(x)$ survives during the next $n$ years, is denoted by $\bar{a}_{x:\overline{n}|}$. By the current payment technique,

$$\bar{a}_{x:\overline{n}|} = \int_0^n v^t\, {}_t p_x\, dt. \qquad (5.3.10)$$

Now, by applying integration by parts to

$$\bar{A}^1_{x:\overline{n}|} = \int_0^n v^t\, {}_t p_x\, \mu_{x+t}\, dt = \int_0^n v^t\, (-d_t p_x),$$

we have

$$\bar{A}^1_{x:\overline{n}|} = 1 - v^n\, {}_n p_x - \delta\, \bar{a}_{x:\overline{n}|},$$

or

$$1 = \delta\, \bar{a}_{x:\overline{n}|} + \bar{A}_{x:\overline{n}|}. \qquad (5.3.11)$$

The student is left to compare formulas (5.3.4) and (5.3.11) and to interpret the latter.

The aggregate payment technique begins with the present-value random variable $Y$ where

$$Y = \begin{cases} \bar{a}_{\overline{T}|} & 0 \le T < n \\ \bar{a}_{\overline{n}|} & T \ge n \end{cases} \qquad (5.3.12)$$

and sets

$$\bar{a}_{x:\overline{n}|} = \mathrm{E}[Y]$$

$$= \int_0^n \bar{a}_{\overline{T}|}\, {}_t p_x\, \mu_{x+t}\, dt + \bar{a}_{\overline{n}|}\, {}_n p_x.$$

After integration by parts this becomes (5.3.10). On substituting $(1 - v^T)/\delta$ for $\bar{a}_{\overline{T}|}$ and $(1 - v^n)/\delta$ for $\bar{a}_{\overline{n}|}$, in (5.3.12), one sees that $Y = (1 - Z)/\delta$ where

$$Z = \begin{cases} v^T & 0 \le T < n \\ v^n & T \ge n \end{cases}$$

is the present-value random variable for an $n$-year endowment insurance [see Table 4.1 and compare with (5.3.5)].

Now

$$\bar{a}_{x:\overline{n}|} = \mathrm{E}[Y] = \frac{1}{\delta}(1 - \mathrm{E}[Z]) = \frac{1}{\delta}[1 - \bar{A}_{x:\overline{n}|}] \qquad (5.3.13)$$

and is equivalent to (5.3.11).

To calculate the variance we can use the relation $Y = (1 - Z)/\delta$ and (4.2.10) to obtain

$$\mathrm{Var}[Y] = \frac{1}{\delta^2}\mathrm{Var}[Z] = \frac{1}{\delta^2}[{}^2\bar{A}_{x:\overline{n}|} - \bar{A}^2_{x:\overline{n}|}]. \qquad (5.3.14)$$

In terms of annuity values, formula (5.3.14) becomes

$$\mathrm{Var}[Y] = \frac{1}{\delta^2}[1 - 2\delta\,{}^2\bar{a}_{x:\overline{n}|} - (1 - \delta\bar{a}_{x:\overline{n}|})^2]$$

$$= \frac{2}{\delta}[\bar{a}_{x:\overline{n}|} - {}^2\bar{a}_{x:\overline{n}|}] - \bar{a}^2_{x:\overline{n}|}. \qquad (5.3.15)$$

The actuarial present value of a deferred life annuity of 1 per annum payable continuously while $(x)$ survives beyond age $x + n$ is denoted by $_{n|}\bar{a}_x$. By the current payment technique, we have

$$_{n|}\bar{a}_x = \int_n^\infty v^t \,{}_tp_x \, dt \qquad (5.3.16)$$

and also the relations

$$_{n|}\bar{a}_x = \int_0^\infty v^t \,{}_tp_x \, dt - \int_0^n v^t \,{}_tp_x \, dt$$

$$= \bar{a}_x - \bar{a}_{x:\overline{n}|} \qquad (5.3.17)$$

$$= \frac{\bar{A}_{x:\overline{n}|} - \bar{A}_x}{\delta}. \qquad (5.3.18)$$

To apply the aggregate payment technique, one begins with the present-value random variable $Y$ where

$$Y = \begin{cases} 0 = \bar{a}_{\overline{T}|} - \bar{a}_{\overline{T}|} & 0 \le T < n \\ v^n \,\bar{a}_{\overline{T-n}|} = \bar{a}_{\overline{T}|} - \bar{a}_{\overline{n}|} & T \ge n. \end{cases}$$

Then

$$_{n|}\bar{a}_x = \mathrm{E}[Y] = \int_n^\infty v^n \,\bar{a}_{\overline{T-n}|} \,{}_tp_x \, \mu_{x+t} \, dt$$

$$= \int_0^\infty v^n \,\bar{a}_{\overline{s}|} \,{}_{n+s}p_x \, \mu_{x+n+s} \, ds$$

$$= v^n \; _np_x \int_0^\infty \bar{a}_{\overline{s}|} \; _sp_{x+n} \; \mu_{x+n+s} \; ds,$$

which shows

$$_{n|}\bar{a}_x = \; _nE_x \; \bar{a}_{x+n}. \tag{5.3.19}$$

This formula could have been obtained from (5.3.16) by substituting $t = n + s$. We see also, from the definitions of $Y$, that

(the $Y$ for an $n$-year deferred whole life annuity)

$=$ (the $Y$ for a whole life annuity)

$-$ (the $Y$ for an $n$-year temporary life annuity)

and that taking expectations would yield (5.3.17) again.

One way to calculate the variance of $Y$ for the deferred annuity is the following:

$$\text{Var}[Y] = \int_n^\infty v^{2n} \; \bar{a}_{\overline{t-n}|}^2 \; _tp_x \; \mu_{x+t} \; dt - \left( _{n|}\bar{a}_x \right)^2$$

$$= v^{2n} \; _np_x \int_0^\infty \bar{a}_{\overline{s}|}^2 \; _sp_{x+n} \; \mu_{x+n+s} \; ds - \left( _{n|}\bar{a}_x \right)^2,$$

by Theorem 3.1,

$$= v^{2n} \; _np_x \int_0^\infty 2 \, \bar{a}_{\overline{s}|} \, v^s \; _sp_{x+n} \; ds - \left( _{n|}\bar{a}_x \right)^2$$

$$= \frac{2}{\delta} v^{2n} \; _np_x \int_0^\infty (v^s - v^{2s}) \; _sp_{x+n} \; ds - \left( _{n|}\bar{a}_x \right)^2$$

$$= \frac{2}{\delta} v^{2n} \; _np_x \left[ \bar{a}_{x+n} - {}^2\bar{a}_{x+n} \right] - \left( _{n|}\bar{a}_x \right)^2. \tag{5.3.20}$$

For an alternative development of this formula, see Exercise 5.40.

The actuarial present value of a deferred temporary life annuity of 1 per annum payable continuously while $(x)$ survives between ages $x + m$ and $x + m + n$ is denoted by $_{m|n}\bar{a}_x$. Then

$$_{m|n}\bar{a}_x = \int_m^{m+n} v^t \; _tp_x \; dt \tag{5.3.21}$$

$$= \bar{a}_{x:\overline{m+n}|} - \bar{a}_{x:\overline{m}|} \tag{5.3.22}$$

$$= \frac{\bar{A}_{x:\overline{m}|} - \bar{A}_{x:\overline{m+n}|}}{\delta} \tag{5.3.23}$$

$$= \; _mE_x \; \bar{a}_{x+m:\overline{n}|}. \tag{5.3.24}$$

# Chapter 5
## LIFE ANNUITIES

Analogous to the function

$$\bar{s}_{\overline{n}|} = \int_0^n (1 + i)^{n-t} \, dt$$

in the theory of interest, we have here

$$\bar{s}_{x:\overline{n}|} = \frac{1}{{}_nE_x} \bar{a}_{x:\overline{n}|} = \int_0^n \frac{{}_tE_x}{{}_nE_x} \, dt = \int_0^n \frac{1}{{}_{n-t}E_{x+t}} \, dt, \qquad (5.3.25)$$

representing the actuarial accumulated value at the end of the term of an $n$-year temporary life annuity of 1 per year payable continuously while $(x)$ survives. Such accumulated value is available at age $x + n$ only if $(x)$ survives.

As a final comment on continuous life annuities, we obtain an expression for $d\bar{a}_x/dx$ by differentiating the integral in formula (5.3.2B), thus

$$\frac{d\bar{a}_x}{dx} = \int_0^\infty v^t \left( \frac{\partial}{\partial x} \, {}_tp_x \right) dt = \int_0^\infty v^t \, {}_tp_x (\mu_x - \mu_{x+t}) \, dt$$

$$= \mu_x \bar{a}_x - \bar{A}_x$$

$$= \mu_x \bar{a}_x - (1 - \delta \bar{a}_x),$$

thus

$$\frac{d\bar{a}_x}{dx} = (\mu_x + \delta) \bar{a}_x - 1. \qquad (5.3.26)$$

The interpretation of (5.3.26) is that the actuarial present value changes at a rate that is a combination of the rate of interest income $\delta \bar{a}_x$, the rate of survivorship benefit $\mu_x \bar{a}_x$ and the rate of payment outgo.

**Example 5.6:** Obtain formulas for

a. $\dfrac{\partial}{\partial x} \, \bar{a}_{x:\overline{n}|}$  b. $\dfrac{\partial}{\partial n} \, {}_{n|}\bar{a}_x.$

**Solution:**
a. Proceeding as in the development of (5.3.26), we obtain

$$\frac{\partial}{\partial x} \bar{a}_{x:\overline{n}|} = \mu_x \bar{a}_{x:\overline{n}|} - \bar{A}^1_{x:\overline{n}|}$$

$$= \mu_x \bar{a}_{x:\overline{n}|} - (1 - \delta \bar{a}_{x:\overline{n}|} - {}_nE_x)$$

$$= (\mu_x + \delta) \bar{a}_{x:\overline{n}|} - (1 - {}_nE_x).$$

b. $\dfrac{\partial}{\partial n} \, {}_{n|}\bar{a}_x = \dfrac{\partial}{\partial n} \displaystyle\int_n^\infty v^t \, {}_tp_x \, dt = -v^n \, {}_np_x$ ▼

Table 5.1 summarizes concepts for continuous life annuities.

**Table 5.1
Summary of
Continuous
Life Annuities
(Annuity of 1 per
annum payable
continuously)**

| Annuity Name | Present Value Random Variable $Y$ | Actuarial Present Value $E[Y]$ equal to |
|---|---|---|
| Whole Life Annuity | $\bar{a}_{\overline{T}}\quad T \geq 0$ | $\bar{a}_x = \int_0^\infty v^t\ {}_tp_x\,dt$ |
| $n$-year Temporary Life Annuity | $\begin{cases}\bar{a}_{\overline{T}} & 0 \leq T < n \\ \bar{a}_{\overline{n}} & T \geq n\end{cases}$ | $\bar{a}_{x:\overline{n}} = \int_0^n v^t\ {}_tp_x\,dt$ |
| $n$-year Deferred Whole Life Annuity | $\begin{cases}0 & 0 \leq T < n \\ \bar{a}_{\overline{T}} - \bar{a}_{\overline{n}} & T \geq n\end{cases}$ | ${}_{n|}\bar{a}_x = \int_n^\infty v^t\ {}_tp_x\,dt$ |
| $m$-year Deferred, $n$-year Temporary Life Annuity | $\begin{cases}0 & 0 \leq T < m \\ \bar{a}_{\overline{T}} - \bar{a}_{\overline{m}} & m \leq T < m+n \\ \bar{a}_{\overline{m+n}} - \bar{a}_{\overline{m}} & T \geq m+n\end{cases}$ | ${}_{m|n}\bar{a}_x = \int_m^{m+n} v^t\ {}_tp_x\,dt$ |

Additional relations are
- $1 = \delta\bar{a}_x + \bar{A}_x$
- $1 = \delta\bar{a}_{x:\overline{n}} + \bar{A}_{x:\overline{n}}$
- ${}_{n|}\bar{a}_x = \bar{a}_x - \bar{a}_{x:\overline{n}}$
- $\bar{s}_{x:\overline{n}} = \dfrac{\bar{a}_{x:\overline{n}}}{{}_nE_x} = \int_0^n (1+i)^{n-t}\dfrac{l_{x+t}}{l_{x+n}}\,dt.$

## 5.4 Discrete Life Annuities

The theory of discrete life annuities is analogous, step-by-step, to the theory of continuous life annuities, with integrals replaced by sums, integrands by summands, and differentials by differences. For continuous annuities there was no distinction between payments at the beginnings of payment intervals or at the ends, that is, between annuities-due and annuities-immediate. For discrete annuities the distinction is meaningful, and we will start with annuities-due as they have the more prominent role in actuarial applications. For example, most individual life insurances are purchased by an annuity-due of periodic premiums.

Let us consider $\ddot{a}_x$, the actuarial present value of a whole life annuity-due of 1 payable at the beginning of each year while $(x)$ survives. Since the actuarial present value of the payment due at time $k$ is

$$_kE_x = v^k\ {}_kp_x,$$

we have by the current payment technique

$$\ddot{a}_x = \sum_{k=0}^\infty v^k\ {}_kp_x. \tag{5.4.1}$$

In terms of the survivorship function, $l_x$, formula (5.4.1) is

$$\ddot{a}_x = \frac{1}{l_x}\sum_{k=0}^\infty v^k\ l_{x+k}. \tag{5.4.2}$$

# Chapter 5

## LIFE ANNUITIES

Thus, by the survivorship group interpretation of the life table, $\ddot{a}_x$ is the amount that each of $l_x$ lives at age $x$ should contribute to a fund in order that the fund, with interest, could pay out 1 to each of the $l_{x+k}$ survivors at age $x + k$; $k = 0, 1, 2, \ldots$.

To use the aggregate payment technique, we consider the present-value random variable $Y = \ddot{a}_{\overline{K+1}|}$ of the annuity payments, where the random variable $K$ is the curtate-future-lifetime of $(x)$. Then

$$\ddot{a}_x = E[Y] = E[\ddot{a}_{\overline{K+1}|}]$$

$$= \sum_{k=0}^{\infty} \ddot{a}_{\overline{k+1}|} \, _{k|}q_x, \tag{5.4.3}$$

since $\Pr[K = k] = \,_{k|}q_x$. By Theorem 3.2, and use of the relation

$$\Delta \ddot{a}_{\overline{k+1}|} = v^{k+1},$$

(5.4.3) converts to

$$\ddot{a}_x = 1 + \sum_{k=0}^{\infty} v^{k+1} \, _{k+1}p_x,$$

which is equivalent to (5.4.1).

From (5.4.3) we obtain in succession

$$\ddot{a}_x = E\left[\frac{1 - v^{K+1}}{d}\right]$$

$$= \frac{1}{d}[1 - A_x], \tag{5.4.4}$$

and

$$\ddot{a}_x = \ddot{a}_{\overline{\infty}|} - \ddot{a}_{\overline{\infty}|} A_x, \tag{5.4.5}$$

$$1 = d\,\ddot{a}_x + A_x. \tag{5.4.6}$$

These should be compared with their continuous counterparts (5.3.6), (5.3.7) and (5.3.4). Formula (5.4.6) indicates that a unit invested now will produce interest-in-advance of $d$ per year while $(x)$ survives plus the repayment of the unit at the end of the year of death of $(x)$.

The variance formula is

$$\text{Var}[\ddot{a}_{\overline{K+1}|}] = \text{Var}\left[\frac{1 - v^{K+1}}{d}\right] = \frac{1}{d^2}\text{Var}[v^{K+1}]$$

$$= \frac{1}{d^2}[{}^2A_x - A_x^2]. \tag{5.4.7}$$

[See (5.3.8).]

The actuarial present value of an $n$-year temporary life annuity of 1 payable at the beginning of each year while $(x)$ survives is denoted by $\ddot{a}_{x:\overline{n}|}$. The current payment technique yields the formula

$$\ddot{a}_{x:\overline{n}|} = \sum_{k=0}^{n-1} {}_kE_x = \sum_{k=0}^{n-1} v^k \, {}_kp_x. \tag{5.4.8}$$

For the aggregate payment approach, we define

$$Y = \begin{cases} \ddot{a}_{\overline{K+1}|} & 0 \le K < n \\ \ddot{a}_{\overline{n}|} & K \ge n \end{cases} \tag{5.4.9}$$

and set

$$\ddot{a}_{x:\overline{n}|} = E[Y].$$

But since $Y = (1 - Z)/d$ where

$$Z = \begin{cases} v^{K+1} & 0 \le K < n \\ v^n & K \ge n \end{cases}$$

is the present-value random variable for a unit of endowment insurance, payable at the end of the year of death, or at maturity, we have

$$\ddot{a}_{x:\overline{n}|} = \frac{1}{d}(1 - E[Z]) = \frac{1}{d}(1 - A_{x:\overline{n}|}). \tag{5.4.10}$$

[See (5.3.13).]

Rearrangement of (5.4.10) yields

$$1 = d\,\ddot{a}_{x:\overline{n}|} + A_{x:\overline{n}|} \tag{5.4.11}$$

[see (5.3.11)].

To calculate the variance, one can use

$$\mathrm{Var}\,[Y] = \frac{1}{d^2}\mathrm{Var}\,[Z] = \frac{1}{d^2}[{}^2A_{x:\overline{n}|} - A_{x:\overline{n}|}^2] \tag{5.4.12}$$

[see Table 4.2, footnote (1)].

The actuarial present value of a deferred life anuity of 1 payable at the beginning of each year while $(x)$ survives from age $x + n$ onward is denoted by ${}_{n|}\ddot{a}_x$. Here

$$_{n|}\ddot{a}_x = \sum_{k=n}^{\infty} v^k \, {}_kp_x \tag{5.4.13}$$

$$= \ddot{a}_x - \ddot{a}_{x:\overline{n}|} \tag{5.4.14}$$

$$= \frac{A_{x:\overline{n}|} - A_x}{d} \tag{5.4.15}$$

$$= {}_nE_x \, \ddot{a}_{x+n} \tag{5.4.16}$$

[see (5.3.16)–(5.3.19)].

The actuarial accumulated value at the end of the term of an $n$-year temporary life annuity-due of 1 per annum, payable while $(x)$ survives, is denoted by $\ddot{s}_{x:\overline{n}|}$. Formulas for this function are

$$\ddot{s}_{x:\overline{n}|} = \frac{1}{{}_nE_x}\ddot{a}_{x:\overline{n}|} \tag{5.4.17}$$

$$= \sum_{k=0}^{n-1} \frac{{}_kE_x}{{}_nE_x}$$

$$= \sum_{k=0}^{n-1} \frac{1}{{}_{n-k}E_{x+k}}, \tag{5.4.18}$$

which are analogous to formulas for $\ddot{s}_{\overline{n}|}$ in the theory of interest.

For annuities-immediate, with payments at the ends of the payment periods, the notations $\ddot{a}$ and $\ddot{s}$ are replaced by $a$ and $s$. Thus $a_x$ denotes the actuarial present value of an annuity of 1 at the end of each year while $(x)$ survives. Formulas for $a_x$ can be obtained by methods similar to those already used for annuities-due, or one can use relations between the values of the two types of annuities. Since the life annuity-immediate differs from the life annuity-due by only the initial payment,

$$a_x = \ddot{a}_x - 1 \tag{5.4.19}$$

$$= \sum_{k=1}^{\infty} v^k \, {}_kp_x. \tag{5.4.20}$$

Alternatively,

$$a_x = \mathrm{E}[a_{\overline{K}|}] \tag{5.4.21}$$

$$= \sum_{k=1}^{\infty} a_{\overline{K}|} \, {}_{k|}q_x.$$

From formula (5.4.21), it follows that

$$a_x = \mathrm{E}\left[\frac{1 - v^K}{i}\right]$$

$$= \mathrm{E}\left[\frac{1 - (1+i)v^{K+1}}{i}\right]$$

$$= \frac{1}{i}[1 - (1+i)A_x],$$

which can be rewritten either as

$$a_x = a_{\overline{\infty}|} - \ddot{a}_{\overline{\infty}|}A_x, \tag{5.4.22}$$

or as

$$1 = i\,a_x + (1+i)A_x. \tag{5.4.23}$$

Formula (5.4.23) has significance for estate tax statutes. For each unit of an estate, define $i\,a_x$ as the **life estate** and $(1+i)A_x = 1 - i\,a_x$ as the **remainder**.

The actuarial present value of an $n$-year temporary annuity of 1 at the end of each year for $n$ years while $(x)$ survives is denoted by $a_{x:\overline{n}|}$, and can be expressed as

$$a_{x:\overline{n}|} = \sum_{k=1}^{n} v^k \, _k p_x , \qquad (5.4.24)$$

or as

$$a_{x:\overline{n}|} = \ddot{a}_{x:\overline{n}|} - 1 + {}_n E_x . \qquad (5.4.25)$$

In the latter formula, ${}_n E_x$ is the actuarial present value of the payment due at the end of $n$ years under the annuity-immediate but not under the annuity-due. The formula can be rearranged as

$$\ddot{a}_{x:\overline{n}|} = 1 + a_{x:\overline{n-1}|} . \qquad (5.4.26)$$

For a deferred annuity of 1 payable at the end of each year while $(x)$ survives after age $x + n$, we denote the actuarial present value by ${}_{n|}a_x$ and have the formulas

$$_{n|}a_x = \sum_{k=n+1}^{\infty} v^k \, _k p_x \qquad (5.4.27)$$

$$= a_x - a_{x:\overline{n}|} \qquad (5.4.28)$$

$$= {}_n E_x \, a_{x+n} . \qquad (5.4.29)$$

This section will conclude with formulas relating $\ddot{a}$, $a$ and $A$ functions. We have

$$A_x = \mathrm{E}[v^{K+1}]$$

$$= \mathrm{E}[a_{\overline{K+1}|} - a_{\overline{K}|}]$$

$$= \mathrm{E}[v\,\ddot{a}_{\overline{K+1}|} - a_{\overline{K}|}]$$

$$= v\,\ddot{a}_x - a_x . \qquad (5.4.30)$$

To interpret (5.4.30), we note that payments of $v$ at the beginning of each year while $(x)$ survives, provided by $v\,\ddot{a}_x$, will be offset by the equivalent payments of 1 at the end of each year, provided by $a_x$, except in the year of death. Thus the right-hand side of (5.4.30) is equivalent to 1 at the end of the year of death of $(x)$, that is, to $A_x$.

For an $n$-year term insurance, the corresponding relation is

$$A^1_{x:\overline{n}|} = v\,\ddot{a}_{x:\overline{n}|} - a_{x:\overline{n}|} . \qquad (5.4.31)$$

Also, for an $n$-year endowment insurance

$$A_{x:\overline{n}|} = A^1_{x:\overline{n}|} + {}_n E_x .$$

Substitution from (5.4.31) and use of the relation

$$a_{x:\overline{n}|} = a_{x:\overline{n-1}|} + {}_n E_x$$

lead to

$$A_{x:\overline{n}|} = v\,\ddot{a}_{x:\overline{n}|} - a_{x:\overline{n-1}|}. \tag{5.4.32}$$

Table 5.2 summarizes concepts for discrete life annuities.

**Table 5.2**
**Summary of Discrete Life Annuities [Annuity of 1 per annum payable at the beginning of each year (annuity-due) or at the end of each year (annuity-immediate)]**

| Annuity Name | Present Value Random Variable $Y$ | Actuarial Present Value $E[Y]$ equal to |
|---|---|---|
| Whole Life Annuity | | |
| —due | $\ddot{a}_{\overline{K+1}|}$ $\quad K \geq 0$ | $\ddot{a}_x = \sum\limits_{k=0}^{\infty} v^k\,{}_k p_x$ |
| —immediate | $a_{\overline{K}|}$ $\quad K \geq 0$ | $a_x = \sum\limits_{k=1}^{\infty} v^k\,{}_k p_x$ |
| $n$-year Temporary Life Annuity | | |
| —due | $\ddot{a}_{\overline{K+1}|}$ $\quad 0 \leq K < n$ $\ddot{a}_{\overline{n}|}$ $\quad K \geq n$ | $\ddot{a}_{x:\overline{n}|} = \sum\limits_{k=0}^{n-1} v^k\,{}_k p_x$ |
| —immediate | $a_{\overline{K}|}$ $\quad 0 \leq K < n$ $a_{\overline{n}|}$ $\quad K \geq n$ | $a_{x:\overline{n}|} = \sum\limits_{k=1}^{n} v^k\,{}_k p_x$ |
| $n$-year Deferred Whole Life Annuity | | |
| —due | $0$ $\quad 0 \leq K < n$ $\ddot{a}_{\overline{K+1}|} - \ddot{a}_{\overline{n}|}$ $\quad K \geq n$ | ${}_{n|}\ddot{a}_x = \sum\limits_{k=n}^{\infty} v^k\,{}_k p_x$ |
| —immediate | $0$ $\quad 0 \leq K < n$ $a_{\overline{K}|} - a_{\overline{n}|}$ $\quad K \geq n$ | ${}_{n|}a_x = \sum\limits_{k=n+1}^{\infty} v^k\,{}_k p_x$ |

Additional relations are
- $1 = d\,\ddot{a}_x + A_x$
- $A_x = v\,\ddot{a}_x - a_x$
- $1 = d\,\ddot{a}_{x:\overline{n}|} + A_{x:\overline{n}|}$
- $\ddot{a}_{x:\overline{n}|} = 1 + a_{x:\overline{n-1}|}$
- $A^1_{x:\overline{n}|} = v\,\ddot{a}_{x:\overline{n}|} - a_{x:\overline{n}|}$

- $A_{x:\overline{n}|} = v\,\ddot{a}_{x:\overline{n}|} - a_{x:\overline{n-1}|}$
- ${}_{n|}\ddot{a}_x = \ddot{a}_x - \ddot{a}_{x:\overline{n}|}$
- $\ddot{s}_{x:\overline{n}|} = \dfrac{\ddot{a}_{x:\overline{n}|}}{{}_n E_x}$

$$= \sum\limits_{k=0}^{n-1} (1+i)^{n-k} \frac{l_{x+k}}{l_{x+n}}.$$

## 5.5 Life Annuities with *m*thly Payments

In practice, life annuities are often payable on a monthly, quarterly or semiannual basis. Analogous to annuity-certain notation, the actuarial present value of a life annuity of 1 per year, payable in installments of $1/m$ at the beginning of each $m$th of a year while $(x)$ survives, is denoted by $\ddot{a}_x^{(m)}$. By the current payment technique,

$$\ddot{a}_x^{(m)} = \frac{1}{m} \sum_{h=0}^{\infty} v^{h/m} \,_{h/m}p_x. \tag{5.5.1}$$

We could proceed from (5.5.1), but it is more convenient to utilize the relations

$$1 = d\,\ddot{a}_x + A_x = d^{(m)}\ddot{a}_x^{(m)} + A_x^{(m)}. \tag{5.5.2}$$

These follow from the fact that an investment of 1 will produce interest-in-advance at the beginning of each interest period and repayment of the unit at the end of the interest period in which death occurs. (For further justification of the relations (5.5.2), see (5.4.4), (5.4.6) and Exercise 5.14.)

From the two right members of (5.5.2), we obtain

$$\ddot{a}_x^{(m)} = \frac{d}{d^{(m)}} \ddot{a}_x - \frac{1}{d^{(m)}} [A_x^{(m)} - A_x]$$

$$= \ddot{a}_{\overline{1}|}^{(m)} \ddot{a}_x - \ddot{a}_{\overline{\infty}|}^{(m)} [A_x^{(m)} - A_x]. \tag{5.5.3}$$

This can be interpreted as follows: The $m$thly payment life annuity is equivalent to a series of one-year annuities-certain in each year that $(x)$ begins, with cancellation in the year of death of installments payable beyond the $m$th (month, quarter, half-year) of death. The cancellation is accomplished by an $m$thly payment perpetuity beginning at the end of the $m$th of death less a similar perpetuity beginning at the end of the year of death.

Alternatively, we might from (5.5.2) write

$$\ddot{a}_x^{(m)} = \frac{1 - A_x^{(m)}}{d^{(m)}} = \ddot{a}_{\overline{\infty}|}^{(m)} - \ddot{a}_{\overline{\infty}|}^{(m)} A_x^{(m)}, \tag{5.5.4}$$

which is left to the reader to interpret.

Now let us assume a uniform distribution of deaths in each year of age and recall that under this assumption

$$A_x^{(m)} = \frac{i}{i^{(m)}} A_x = s_{\overline{1}|}^{(m)} A_x$$

(see Exercise 4.15). Then (5.5.3) becomes

$$\ddot{a}_x^{(m)} = \ddot{a}_{\overline{1}|}^{(m)} \ddot{a}_x - \frac{s_{\overline{1}|}^{(m)} - 1}{d^{(m)}} A_x, \tag{5.5.5}$$

which exhibits the cancellation term for the year of death in terms of the standard function $A_x$.

By substituting $1 - d\,\ddot{a}_x$ for $A_x$ in (5.5.5) and noting that $d^{(m)} \ddot{a}_{\overline{1}|}^{(m)} = d$, we obtain a formula involving only annuity functions, namely,

$$\ddot{a}_x^{(m)} = \frac{1 - s_{\overline{1}|}^{(m)}(1 - d\,\ddot{a}_x)}{d^{(m)}}$$

$$= s_{\overline{1}|}^{(m)}\,\ddot{a}_{\overline{1}|}^{(m)}\,\ddot{a}_x - \frac{s_{\overline{1}|}^{(m)} - 1}{d^{(m)}}. \tag{5.5.6}$$

Formula (5.5.6) is not readily interpretable but has the advantage that it expresses $\ddot{a}_x^{(m)}$ in terms of annuity functions only. Also it is more comparable with the traditional approximation for $\ddot{a}_x^{(m)}$. The traditional approximation for $\ddot{a}_x^{(m)}$ can be obtained by applying Wool-house's summation formula to the right-hand side of (5.5.1) to obtain

$$\ddot{a}_x^{(m)} \cong \ddot{a}_x - \frac{m-1}{2m} - \frac{m^2-1}{12m^2}(\mu_x + \delta). \tag{5.5.7}$$

In practice, this is usually curtailed to

$$\ddot{a}_x^{(m)} \cong \ddot{a}_x - \frac{m-1}{2m}, \tag{5.5.8}$$

which also follows from assuming that the commutation function

$$D_{x+h/m} = v^{x+h/m}\,l_{x+h/m}$$

is a linear function,

$$D_x - \frac{h}{m}[D_x - D_{x+1}],$$

in each year of age (see Exercise 5.15). It should be noted that linearity of $D_{x+h/m}$ in each year of age is not the same as linearity of $l_{x+h/m}$ in each year of age, which is the case under the uniform distribution of deaths assumption. Consistent use of the assumption of a uniform distribution of deaths in each year of age assures that relations such as

$$1 = d^{(m)}\,\ddot{a}_x^{(m)} + A_x^{(m)}$$

are satisfied exactly. It also has been observed that formulas derived from (5.5.8) can, for high rates of interest and low rates of mortality, produce distorted annuity values such as $\ddot{a}_{x:\overline{1}|}^{(12)} > \ddot{a}_{\overline{1}|}^{(12)}$. For these reasons, (5.5.5) and the equivalent (5.5.6) are presented as replacements for the traditional approximation (5.5.8).

It is convenient for writing purposes to express (5.5.6) in the form

$$\ddot{a}_x^{(m)} = \alpha(m)\,\ddot{a}_x - \beta(m) \tag{5.5.9}$$

where

$$\alpha(m) = s_{\overline{1}|}^{(m)}\,\ddot{a}_{\overline{1}|}^{(m)} = \frac{i\,d}{i^{(m)}\,d^{(m)}}, \tag{5.5.10}$$

and

$$\beta(m) = \frac{s_{\overline{1}|}^{(m)} - 1}{d^{(m)}} = \frac{i - i^{(m)}}{i^{(m)} d^{(m)}}. \tag{5.5.11}$$

We note that $\alpha(m)$ and $\beta(m)$ depend only on $m$ and the rate of interest, and are independent of the year of age. Further, for $m = 1$, (5.5.9) is an identity where $\alpha(1) = 1$ and $\beta(1) = 0$. Also, $\beta(m)$ is the coefficient of the cancellation term in (5.5.5); that is, (5.5.5) can be written as

$$\ddot{a}_x^{(m)} = \ddot{a}_{\overline{1}|}^{(m)} \ddot{a}_x - \beta(m) A_x. \tag{5.5.12}$$

For series expansions of $\alpha(m)$ and $\beta(m)$, see Exercise 5.44.

**Example 5.7:** On the basis of the Illustrative Life Table, with interest at the effective annual rate of 6%, calculate the actuarial present value of a whole life annuity-due of 1000 per month for a retiree aged 65.

**Solution:**
Here

$$\alpha(12) = s_{\overline{1}|}^{(12)} \ddot{a}_{\overline{1}|}^{(12)} = (1.02721070)(0.97378368) = 1.0002810$$

$$\beta(12) = \frac{s_{\overline{1}|}^{(12)} - 1}{d^{(12)}} = 0.46811951$$

$$\frac{11}{24} = 0.45833333.$$

Observe that $\alpha(12) \cong 1$, and $\beta(12)$ is fairly close to the 11/24 that appears in the traditional approximation.

By the Illustrative Life Table, as defined by (3.7.1), with interest at 6%,

$$\ddot{a}_{65} = 9.89693$$

$$A_{65} = 1 - d\,\ddot{a}_{65} = 0.4397965$$

$$1000\,\mu_{65} = 0.7 + 0.05\,(10^{0.04})^{65} = 20.605359.$$

Then, $12{,}000\,\ddot{a}_{65}^{(12)}$ can be calculated as follows:

By (5.5.12),  $12{,}000\,[\ddot{a}_{\overline{1}|}^{(12)}\,\ddot{a}_{65} - \beta(12)\,A_{65}]$

$$= 12{,}000\,[(0.97378368)\,(9.89693)$$

$$- (0.46811951)\,(0.4397965)] = 113{,}179.$$

By (5.5.9),  $12{,}000\,[\alpha(12)\,\ddot{a}_{65} - \beta(12)]$

$$= 12{,}000\,[(1.0002810)\,(9.89693) - 0.46811951]$$

$$= 113{,}179.$$

By (5.5.8),  $12{,}000\,\left[\ddot{a}_{65} - \frac{11}{24}\right] = 113{,}263.$

By (5.5.7),      $12{,}000 \left[ \ddot{a}_{65} - \dfrac{11}{24} - \dfrac{143}{1728} (\mu_{65} + \delta) \right] = 113{,}185.$

Formulas (5.5.12) and (5.5.9) are algebraically equivalent and therefore should produce the same value. Formula (5.5.8) is an abbreviated version of (5.5.7) and the relatively small disparity in results is clear. There is no reason to expect that the formulas based on a uniform distribution of deaths, (5.5.12) and (5.5.9), would produce identical results to those based on Woolhouse's formula, (5.5.8) and (5.5.7). However, the example illustrates that, usually, the differences are relatively small.  ▼

Now that formulas have been established for $m$thly payment whole life annuities, it is easy to develop formulas for temporary and for deferred annuities. Thus from (5.5.12), we have

$$\ddot{a}^{(m)}_{x:\overline{n}|} = \ddot{a}^{(m)}_x - {}_nE_x\, \ddot{a}^{(m)}_{x+n}$$

$$= \ddot{a}^{(m)}_{\overline{1}|}\, \ddot{a}_x - \beta(m)\, A_x - {}_nE_x [\ddot{a}^{(m)}_{\overline{1}|}\, \ddot{a}_{x+n} - \beta(m)\, A_{x+n}]$$

$$= \ddot{a}^{(m)}_{\overline{1}|}\, \ddot{a}_{x:\overline{n}|} - \beta(m)\, A^1_{x:\overline{n}|}. \qquad (5.5.13)$$

Similarly,

$$_{n|}\ddot{a}^{(m)}_x = \ddot{a}^{(m)}_{\overline{1}|}\, {}_{n|}\ddot{a}_x - \beta(m)\, {}_{n|}A_x, \qquad (5.5.14)$$

and from (5.5.9)

$$\ddot{a}^{(m)}_{x:\overline{n}|} = \alpha(m)\, \ddot{a}_{x:\overline{n}|} - \beta(m)\, [1 - {}_nE_x] \qquad (5.5.15)$$

$$_{n|}\ddot{a}^{(m)}_x = \alpha(m)\, {}_{n|}\ddot{a}_x - \beta(m)\, {}_nE_x. \qquad (5.5.16)$$

The values of life annuities-immediate with $m$thly payments can be obtained by adjusting the values of the corresponding life annuities-due, for instance,

$$a^{(m)}_x = \ddot{a}^{(m)}_x - \frac{1}{m}$$

$$a^{(m)}_{x:\overline{n}|} = \ddot{a}^{(m)}_{x:\overline{n}|} - \frac{1}{m}(1 - {}_nE_x).$$

Alternatively, one may develop formulas for $m$thly payment annuities-immediate in terms of functions for annual payment annuities-immediate, by means of relations such as

$$1 = i\, a_x + (1 + i)\, A_x = i^{(m)}\, a^{(m)}_x + \left( 1 + \frac{i^{(m)}}{m} \right) A^{(m)}_x \qquad (5.5.17)$$

[analogous to relations (5.5.2)]. The meaning here is that an investment of 1 will produce interest at the end of each interest period plus the repayment of the unit together with interest then due at the end of the interest period in which death occurs. This will be explored

## 5.6 Commutation Function Formulas for Annuities with Level Payments

further in Exercises 5.17–5.20. Traditional formulas are presented in Exercise 5.21.

The function $D_x = v^x l_x$ was introduced in Chapter 4 for the valuation of insurances. We shall now reexamine its role in the valuation of payments contingent on survival. In (4.6.2), $A_{x:\overline{n}|}^{\,1} = {}_nE_x$ was expressed as $D_{x+n}/D_x$. Hence, (5.2.3) can be written as

$$\frac{1}{{}_nE_x} = \frac{v^x l_x}{v^{x+n} l_{x+n}} = \frac{D_x}{D_{x+n}}. \qquad (5.6.1)$$

More generally, the actuarial value at age $x$ of a payment $b$ at age $y$ is

$$\frac{b D_y}{D_x}. \qquad (5.6.2)$$

The reader should verify this formula for the case $x < y$ where it represents an actuarial present value, and for the case $x > y$ where it represents an actuarial accumulated value.

We now consider a life annuity for $(x)$ with payments as indicated on the line diagram, Figure 5.1.

**Figure 5.1
Line Diagram for a
Level Payment
Annuity**

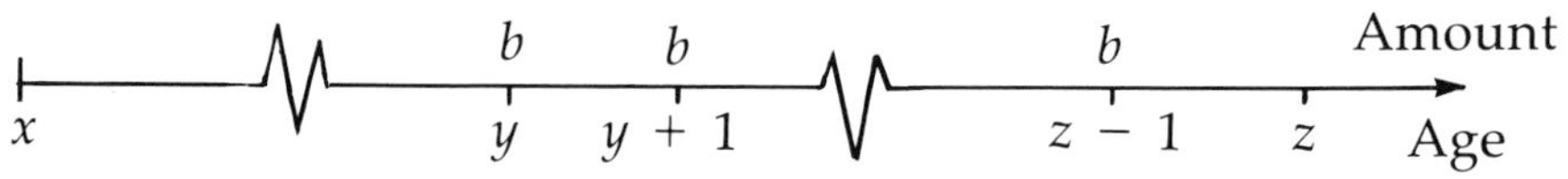

By (5.6.2), the actuarial value at age $x$ of the life annuity payments at ages $y, y+1, \ldots, z-1$ is

$$\frac{b}{D_x} \sum_{u=y}^{z-1} D_u.$$

Now, on introducing the function $N_x = \sum_{u=x}^{\infty} D_u$, we find the value of the annuity expressed as

$$\frac{b}{D_x}(N_y - N_z). \qquad (5.6.3)$$

Here $x$ is the age at which the actuarial value is to be calculated, $y$ is the age at which the first annual payment, $b$, is made, and $z$ is the age as of 1 year after the last annual payment, $b$. We note that $x$ could have any relation to $y$ and $z$; that is, $x$ could be less than, equal to or greater than either $y$ or $z$.

The usefulness of commutation functions is almost completely restricted to applications where a constant rate of interest and a specified life table are assumed. Where more general assumptions are made, more basic functions may be required. Where constant rates are assumed, such basic functions may still be preferred. However, if tables for the functions $D_x$ and $N_x$ are available, one has a very flexible and ready means for calculating life annuity values by utilizing formulas such as (5.6.3). Instead of rewriting formulas in terms of $D_x$ and $N_x$ for the various forms of life annuities, we shall simply note that the general formulas (5.6.2) and (5.6.3) are sufficient for most purposes where commutation functions are used for valuing annual payment life annuities.

For valuing $m$thly payment life annuities, we observe that (5.5.1) can be written as

$$\ddot{a}_x^{(m)} = \frac{1}{m D_x} \sum_{h=0}^{\infty} D_{x+h/m},$$ (5.6.4)

which suggests the introduction of a function

$$N_x^{(m)} = \frac{1}{m} \sum_{h=0}^{\infty} D_{x+h/m}.$$ (5.6.5)

Then

$$\ddot{a}_x^{(m)} = \frac{N_x^{(m)}}{D_x}.$$

If we now assume a uniform distribution of deaths in each year of age, we have

$$\ddot{a}_x^{(m)} = \alpha(m)\,\ddot{a}_x - \beta(m)$$

$$= \frac{\alpha(m)\,N_x - \beta(m)\,D_x}{D_x},$$

and on comparing the two formulas for $\ddot{a}_x^{(m)}$ obtain a formula for $N_x^{(m)}$, namely,

$$N_x^{(m)} = \alpha(m)\,N_x - \beta(m)\,D_x.$$ (5.6.6)

On the basis of (5.5.8), the approximation

$$N_x^{(m)} \cong N_x - \frac{m-1}{2m}D_x$$ (5.6.7)

is also used in practice. However, (5.6.6) consistently follows the assumption of a uniform distribution of deaths in each year of age.

With the function $N_x^{(m)}$ available, a general valuation formula for annuities with level $m$thly payments, in analogy to (5.6.3), is

$$\frac{b}{D_x}(N_y^{(m)} - N_z^{(m)})$$ (5.6.8)

where $b$ is the level annual income and $b/m$ is the $m$thly payment.

# LIFE ANNUITIES

**Example 5.8:** Express, in terms of commutation functions, the actuarial present value for (25) of a deferred life annuity of 1000 per month, first payment at age 65.

**Solution:**
The annual income is 12,000, and the required value is

$$\frac{12,000\, N_{65}^{(12)}}{D_{25}}$$

where $N_{65}^{(12)} = \alpha(12)\, N_{65} - \beta(12)\, D_{65}$. ▼

**Example 5.9:** Express, in terms of commutation functions, the actuarial accumulated value at age 65 of monthly payments of 100 at the beginning of each month during survival of (25) from age 25 to age 65.

**Solution:**
Application of (5.6.8) here yields

$$\frac{1200}{D_{65}}[N_{25}^{(12)} - N_{65}^{(12)}].$$ ▼

Returning now to (5.6.4) and letting $m \to \infty$, we obtain

$$\bar{a}_x = \frac{1}{D_x}\int_0^\infty D_{x+t}\,dt,$$ (5.6.9)

which suggests the definition

$$\bar{N}_x = \int_0^\infty D_{x+t}\,dt = \int_x^\infty D_y\,dy.$$ (5.6.10)

Further, under an assumption of a uniform distribution of deaths in each year of age, we have, as for (5.6.6),

$$\bar{N}_x = \alpha(\infty)\, N_x - \beta(\infty)\, D_x$$

where, from (5.5.10) and (5.5.11),

$$\alpha(\infty) = \bar{s}_{\overline{1}|}\bar{a}_{\overline{1}|} = \frac{id}{\delta^2}$$ (5.6.11)

$$\beta(\infty) = \frac{i - \delta}{\delta^2}.$$ (5.6.12)

For series expansions of $\alpha(\infty)$, $\beta(\infty)$, see Exercise 5.44.

The formula,

$$\bar{N}_x \cong N_x - \frac{1}{2}D_x,$$ (5.6.13)

is used in practice, and can be obtained by applying the trapezoidal rule to evaluate the integral in (5.6.9), or by letting $m \to \infty$ in (5.6.7).

# LIFE ANNUITIES

With these new functions, a general formula for valuing level income continuous life annuities is

$$\frac{b}{D_x}(\bar{N}_y - \bar{N}_z). \tag{5.6.14}$$

## 5.7
## Varying Annuities

Here we consider the problem of valuing annuities for which the annual income, payable in $m$thly installments, changes yearly. Let us assume that the sequence of annual incomes is $b_x, b_{x+1}, \ldots, b_y, \ldots, b_{x+n-1}$ and that payments are made at the beginnings of the $m$thly intervals ceasing at age $x + n$. The actuarial present value at age $y$ of the payments to be made during the year of age $(y, y + 1)$ is $b_y \ddot{a}_{y:\overline{1}|}^{(m)}$, and the actuarial present value, $(apv)_x$, at age $x$, of the whole annuity can be expressed as

$$(apv)_x = \sum_{y=x}^{x+n-1} b_y \ddot{a}_{y:\overline{1}|}^{(m)} {}_{y-x}E_x. \tag{5.7.1}$$

If a uniform distribution of deaths in each year of age is assumed, we have from (5.5.15)

$$(apv)_x = \sum_{y=x}^{x+n-1} b_y [\alpha(m) - \beta(m)(1 - {}_1E_y)] {}_{y-x}E_x. \tag{5.7.2}$$

If one prefers to work with commutation functions, one can rewrite (5.7.2) in the form

$$(apv)_x = \frac{1}{D_x} \sum_{y=x}^{x+n-1} b_y [\alpha(m) D_y - \beta(m)(D_y - D_{y+1})]. \tag{5.7.3}$$

If we define

$$D_y^{(m)} = N_y^{(m)} - N_{y+1}^{(m)},$$

we see from (5.6.6) that

$$D_y^{(m)} = \alpha(m) D_y - \beta(m)(D_y - D_{y+1}). \tag{5.7.4}$$

Hence, (5.7.3) becomes

$$(apv)_x = \frac{1}{D_x} \sum_{y=x}^{x+n-1} b_y D_y^{(m)}. \tag{5.7.5}$$

Parallel formulas for varying life annuities-immediate will be outlined. The formula corresponding to (5.7.1) is

$$(apv)_x = \sum_{y=x}^{x+n-1} b_y a_{y:\overline{1}|}^{(m)} {}_{y-x}E_x. \tag{5.7.6}$$

On the assumption of a uniform distribution of deaths in each year of age,

$$a_{y:\overline{1}|}^{(m)} = \ddot{a}_{y:\overline{1}|}^{(m)} - \frac{1}{m}(1 - {}_1E_y) = \alpha(m) - \left[\beta(m) + \frac{1}{m}\right][1 - {}_1E_y].$$

Corresponding to (5.7.3), there is now

$$(apv)_x = \frac{1}{D_x} \sum_{y=x}^{x+n-1} b_y \left\{ \alpha(m) D_y - \left[ \beta(m) + \frac{1}{m} \right] [D_y - D_{y+1}] \right\}, \quad (5.7.7)$$

which suggests the definition

$$\tilde{D}_y^{(m)} = \alpha(m) D_y - \left[ \beta(m) + \frac{1}{m} \right] [D_y - D_{y+1}]. \quad (5.7.8)$$

Then (5.7.7) becomes

$$(apv)_x = \frac{1}{D_x} \sum_{y=x}^{x+n-1} b_y \tilde{D}_y^{(m)}. \quad (5.7.9)$$

For applications, see Exercise 5.24.

When the annual incomes are level, that is, $b_y = b$ (a constant), (5.7.5) simplifies to $(b/D_x)[N_x^{(m)} - N_{x+n}^{(m)}]$. In other special cases, where the annual incomes $b_y$ are linear in $y$, it may be useful to introduce a commutation function $S_y^{(m)}$ where

$$N_y^{(m)} = S_y^{(m)} - S_{y+1}^{(m)},$$

or

$$S_x^{(m)} = \sum_{y=x}^{\infty} N_y^{(m)}. \quad (5.7.10)$$

Formulas for these special cases will not be elaborated, but some will be explored in Exercises 5.25–5.27.

**Example 5.10:**

On the basis of the Illustrative Life Table, with interest at the effective annual rate of 6%, calculate
a. $N_{70}^{(12)}$ and $S_{70}^{(12)}$
b. the actuarial present value of an annuity to (70) with monthly payments of 100 in the first year, 110 in the second year, and so on, the monthly income increasing by 10 in each successive year.

**Solution:**
a. By (5.6.6),

$$N_{70}^{(12)} = \alpha(12) N_{70} - \beta(12) D_{70}$$

$$= (1.0002810)(9597.05) - (0.46811951)(1119.94)$$

$$= 9075.48.$$

Similarly,

$$S_{70}^{(12)} = \alpha(12) S_{70} - \beta(12) N_{70}$$

$$= 62,643.28.$$

# LIFE ANNUITIES

b. The actuarial present value can be written as

$$\frac{12\,[90\,N_{70}^{(12)} + 10\,S_{70}^{(12)}]}{D_{70}} = 15{,}464.$$

▼

**5.8
Recursion
Equations**

Let us again consider a varying $m$thly payment life annuity-due with annual incomes $b_x$, $b_{x+1}$, ..., $b_{x+n-1}$. Let $(apv)_y$ denote the actuarial present value at age $y$ of the annuity payments from age $y$ to age $x + n$; then, as can be seen from (5.7.1),

$$(apv)_y = b_y\,\ddot{a}_{y:\overline{1}|}^{(m)} + {}_1E_y\,(apv)_{y+1} \tag{5.8.1}$$

is a recursion equation for the successive calculation of the values of $(apv)_y$, $y = x + n - 1, x + n - 2, ..., x$, with starting value $(apv)_{x+n} = 0$. Such a recursive calculation, yielding all values of $(apv)_y$, $y = x, x + 1, ..., x + n - 1$, may be preferred to the calculation of the single value $(apv)_x$ by formulas such as (5.7.1) or (5.7.5). However, the latter formulas may be useful for checking error accumulation in the recursive calculation.

As an example, if one wants a table of values of $\ddot{a}_x^{(m)}$ for $x = c, c + 1, ..., \omega - 1$, one can proceed by the recursion equation

$$\ddot{a}_y^{(m)} = \ddot{a}_{y:\overline{1}|}^{(m)} + {}_1E_y\,\ddot{a}_{y+1}^{(m)}. \tag{5.8.2}$$

Under the assumption of a uniform distribution of deaths in each year of age,

$$\ddot{a}_{y:\overline{1}|}^{(m)} = \ddot{a}_{\overline{1}|}^{(m)} - \beta(m)\,v\,q_y$$

[see (5.5.13)]. Then

$$\ddot{a}_y^{(m)} = \ddot{a}_{\overline{1}|}^{(m)} - \beta(m)\,v\,q_y + v\,p_y\,\ddot{a}_{y+1}^{(m)} \tag{5.8.3}$$

provides a recursive means of calculating, from an initial starting value of $\ddot{a}_\omega^{(m)} = 0$, the successive values $\ddot{a}_y^{(m)}$, $y = \omega - 1, \omega - 2, ..., c + 1, c$. For $m = 1$, the formulas simplify to

$$\ddot{a}_\omega = 0$$

$$\ddot{a}_y = 1 + v\,p_y\,\ddot{a}_{y+1}, \tag{5.8.4}$$

which can be readily interpreted.

**Example 5.11:**

Show that (5.8.3) can be rearranged to

$$\ddot{a}_y^{(m)}\,(1 + i) - \ddot{s}_{\overline{1}|}^{(m)} + q_y\,[\beta(m) + \ddot{a}_{y+1}^{(m)}] = \ddot{a}_{y+1}^{(m)}. \tag{5.8.5}$$

Give a verbal interpretation of this formula.

**Solution:**
Multiply (5.8.3) by $(1 + i)$, substitute $1 - q_y$ for $p_y$, then transpose terms to obtain (5.8.5).

If the traditional approximation,

$$\ddot{a}_y^{(m)} \cong \ddot{a}_y - \frac{m-1}{2m},$$

is used, the formula comparable to (5.8.5) is

$$\ddot{a}_y^{(m)}(1+i) - \left(1 + \frac{m+1}{2m}i\right) + q_y\left(\frac{m-1}{2m} + \ddot{a}_{y+1}^{(m)}\right) \cong \ddot{a}_{y+1}^{(m)}. \quad (5.8.6)$$

Formula (5.8.6) is used in gain and loss analysis of pension systems. Formula (5.8.5) indicates that

(the actuarial present value, $\ddot{a}_y^{(m)}$, accumulated under interest for a year)

$-$ (the accumulated value of the $m$thly installments for the year)

$+$ (the values of the $m$thly installments of the current and future years expected to be canceled by death in the current year)

$=$ (the actuarial present value for the annuity from age $y + 1$).

Formula (5.8.6) has a similar interpretation under the assumption

$$D_{x+t} = (1-t)D_x + tD_{x+1} \quad 0 \le t \le 1,$$

while (5.8.5) is based on the uniform distribution of deaths. ▼

## 5.9 Complete Annuities- Immediate and Apportionable Annuities-Due

In the case of continuous annuities, the income is payable continuously up to the moment of death, and there is no final adjustment payment. With discrete annuities, particularly those with annual payments, a question may arise about having a pro rata adjustment taking account of the date of death. For instance, if a life annuity-immediate provides annual payments of 5000, and the annuitant dies 1 month before the due date of the next payment, there may be a final fractional payment for the 11 months that the annuitant has survived since the last payment. As another example, if a life insurance contract is being purchased by annual premiums of 1000 payable on the anniversaries of the issue date, and if the insured dies 1 month after an anniversary date, there may be a refund of premium for the 11 months the insured did not complete in the policy year.

We denote by $\mathring{a}_x^{(m)}$ the actuarial present value of a complete life annuity of 1 per year payable in installments of $1/m$ at the end of each $m$th of a year while $(x)$ survives, plus an adjustment payment to take account of the period between the date of the last $m$thly payment and the date of death. To complete the definition of the annuity we need to decide on the adjustment payment. Since a payment of $1/m$ at the end of an $m$th of a year is equivalent to continous payments at the rate

## LIFE ANNUITIES

$$\frac{1}{m} \frac{1}{\bar{s}_{\overline{1/m}|}}$$

per annum during the $m$th, we shall choose

$$\frac{1}{m} \frac{\bar{s}_{\overline{t}|}}{\bar{s}_{\overline{1/m}|}} \qquad (5.9.1)$$

to be the adjustment payment if death occurs at time $t$ in the $m$th of death, $0 < t < 1/m$. With this definition of the adjustment payment, the complete life annuity-immediate is exactly equivalent to a continuous life annuity with payments at the per annum rate of

$$\frac{1}{m} \frac{1}{\bar{s}_{\overline{1/m}|}} = \frac{1}{m} \frac{\delta}{(1 + i)^{1/m} - 1} = \frac{\delta}{i^{(m)}}. \qquad (5.9.2)$$

This can be seen by noting that, in any $m$th of a year through which $(x)$ survives, the continuous life annuity provides payments of value

$$\frac{1}{m \, \bar{s}_{\overline{1/m}|}} \bar{s}_{\overline{1/m}|} = \frac{1}{m}$$

at the end of the $m$th. And, in the $m$th of death, the continuous life annuity provides payments equivalent to

$$\frac{1}{m \, \bar{s}_{\overline{1/m}|}} \bar{s}_{\overline{t}|}$$

at time of death, as does the complete annuity. Hence, we now have

$$\mathring{a}_x^{(m)} = \frac{\delta}{i^{(m)}} \bar{a}_x, \qquad (5.9.3)$$

which is analogous to the relation

$$a_{\overline{n}|}^{(m)} = \frac{\delta}{i^{(m)}} \bar{a}_{\overline{n}|}$$

in compound interest theory.

In practice, the adjustment payment may be taken as $t$, approximating (5.9.1). However, a simpler theory results if interest is taken into account and the adjustment is as in (5.9.1). For example, we note that in this latter case

$$1 - i^{(m)} \mathring{a}_x^{(m)} = 1 - \delta \bar{a}_x = \bar{A}_x,$$
$$1 = i^{(m)} \mathring{a}_x^{(m)} + \bar{A}_x. \qquad (5.9.4)$$

The interpretation of (5.9.4) is that 1 invested during the lifetime of $(x)$ will produce interest of $i^{(m)}/m$ at the end of each $m$th of a year while $(x)$ survives, plus an adjustment of

$$i^{(m)} \frac{\bar{s}_{\bar{t}|}}{m\,\bar{s}_{\overline{1/m}|}} = \delta\bar{s}_{\bar{t}|} = (1+i)^t - 1$$

for interest in the $m$th of death, plus the repayment of 1 at death. (For further insight into the adjustment payment under $\mathring{a}_x^{(m)}$, see Exercise 5.31 for the case $m = 1$.)

Let us now look at the parallel theory for annuities-due. We denote by $\ddot{a}_x^{\{m\}}$ the actuarial present value of an apportionable life annuity of 1 per year payable in installments of $1/m$ at the beginning of each $m$th of a year while $(x)$ survives, with a refund at death to the payer to take account of the period between the date of death and the date of the next $m$thly payment. Since a payment of $1/m$ at the beginning of an $m$th of a year is equivalent to continuous payments at the rate

$$\frac{1}{m} \frac{1}{\bar{a}_{\overline{1/m}|}}$$

per annum during the $m$th, we choose

$$\frac{1}{m} \frac{\bar{a}_{\overline{1/m-t}|}}{\bar{a}_{\overline{1/m}|}} \tag{5.9.5}$$

to be the refund payment if death occurs at time $t$ in the $m$th of death, $0 < t < 1/m$. Expression (5.9.5) represents the equitable refund at the time of death of the unearned portion of the payment of $1/m$ at the beginning of the $m$th of death. With this definition of the refund payment, the apportionable life annuity-due is exactly equivalent to a continuous life annuity with payments at the per annum rate of

$$\frac{1}{m} \frac{1}{\bar{a}_{\overline{1/m}|}} = \frac{1}{m} \frac{\delta}{1 - v^{1/m}} = \frac{\delta}{d^{(m)}}. \tag{5.9.6}$$

That is,

$$\ddot{a}_x^{\{m\}} = \frac{\delta}{d^{(m)}} \bar{a}_x \tag{5.9.7}$$

and

$$1 - d^{(m)} \ddot{a}_x^{\{m\}} = 1 - \delta\bar{a}_x = \bar{A}_x,$$

or

$$1 = d^{(m)} \ddot{a}_x^{\{m\}} + \bar{A}_x, \tag{5.9.8}$$

which is left to the reader to interpret.

**Example 5.12:**

Establish the formulas:

a. $\mathring{a}_{x:\overline{n}|}^{(m)} = \dfrac{\delta}{i^{(m)}} \bar{a}_{x:\overline{n}|}$ 　　 b. $\ddot{a}_{x:\overline{n}|}^{\{m\}} = \dfrac{\delta}{d^{(m)}} \bar{a}_{x:\overline{n}|}$

c. $\ddot{a}_{x:\overline{n}|}^{\{m\}} = (1+i)^{1/m} \mathring{a}_{x:\overline{n}|}^{(m)}$.

**Solution:**

a. $\mathring{a}_{x:\overline{n}|}^{(m)} = \mathring{a}_x^{(m)} - {}_nE_x \, \mathring{a}_{x+n}^{(m)} = \dfrac{\delta}{i^{(m)}}[\bar{a}_x - {}_nE_x \, \bar{a}_{x+n}] = \dfrac{\delta}{i^{(m)}}\bar{a}_{x:\overline{n}|}$

b. $\ddot{a}_{x:\overline{n}|}^{\{m\}} = \ddot{a}_x^{\{m\}} - {}_nE_x \, \ddot{a}_{x+n}^{\{m\}} = \dfrac{\delta}{d^{(m)}}[\bar{a}_x - {}_nE_x \, \bar{a}_{x+n}] = \dfrac{\delta}{d^{(m)}}\bar{a}_{x:\overline{n}|}$

c. $\ddot{a}_{x:\overline{n}|}^{\{m\}} = \dfrac{\delta}{d^{(m)}}\bar{a}_{x:\overline{n}|} = \dfrac{\delta}{v^{1/m}\,i^{(m)}}\bar{a}_{x:\overline{n}|} = (1+i)^{1/m}\,\mathring{a}_{x:\overline{n}|}^{(m)}$

The interpretation of (c) is that both $\ddot{a}_{x:\overline{n}|}^{\{m\}}$ and $\mathring{a}_{x:\overline{n}|}^{(m)}$ provide an $m$thly payment income of 1 per year, adjusted up to the date of death. However, $\ddot{a}_{x:\overline{n}|}^{\{m\}}$ pays installments at the beginning of the $m$thly intervals and $\mathring{a}_{x:\overline{n}|}^{(m)}$ at the ends. It is an interesting, but not obvious, exercise to see how, in the $m$th of death, the payments under $\ddot{a}_{x:\overline{n}|}^{\{m\}}$ (consisting of $1/m$ at the beginning of the $m$th less the refund at death) are worth $(1+i)^{1/m}$ times the adjustment payment provided by $\mathring{a}_{x:\overline{n}|}^{(m)}$. ▼

From (5.9.3), (3.5.2), and the fact that $\lim_{\delta \to 0} (\delta/i) = 1$, we observe that for $\delta = 0$

$$\mathring{a}_x = \bar{a}_x = \mathring{e}_x = \bar{a}_{\overline{\mathring{e}_x}|}.$$

In this special case,

(the actuarial present value of a life annuity at age $x$)

$= $ (the present value of an annuity-certain for a term equal to the expectation of life at age $x$).

It is a popular misconception that this equality also holds when $\delta > 0$, but the following example shows that it does not.

**Example 5.13:**  For $\delta > 0$, show that

a. $\bar{a}_x < \bar{a}_{\overline{\mathring{e}_x}|}$  b. $a_x < a_{\overline{e_x}|}$,  $x < \omega - 1$.

**Solution:**

a. Here it is convenient to use Jensen's inequality exhibited in Figure 1.2. We replace the random variable $X$ by the future-lifetime variable $T$, and $u(X)$ by $\bar{a}_{\overline{T}|}$, and note that

$$\frac{d^2}{dt^2}\bar{a}_{\overline{t}|} = -\delta e^{-\delta t} < 0$$

for $\delta > 0$. Then from (5.3.1), (1.3.2) and (3.5.1), we have

$$\bar{a}_x = \mathrm{E}[\bar{a}_{\overline{T}|}] < \bar{a}_{\overline{\mathrm{E}[T]}|} = \bar{a}_{\overline{\mathring{e}_x}|},$$

which shows the inequality.

b. The analogous argument for the discrete annuity begins with the curtate-future-lifetime variable $K$ and the function $a_{\overline{K}|}$, $K = 0,1,2,\dots$ . The proof of Jensen's inequality does not depend on the type of probability distribution (continuous, discrete, or mixed), but it does assume that the function $u(x)$ is differentiable with $u''(x) < 0$. In our example, we are dealing with the function $a_{\overline{t}|} = (1 - e^{-\delta t})/i$, which is differentiable to any order and has

$$\frac{d^2}{dt^2} a_{\overline{t}|} = -\frac{\delta^2}{i} v^t < 0 \qquad \delta > 0.$$

Then, by Jensen's inequality,

$$a_x = \mathrm{E}[a_{\overline{K}|}] \le a_{\overline{\mathrm{E}[K]|}} = a_{\overline{e_x}|}.$$

The inequality is strict except when $K$ is constant. For instance, when $x = \omega - 1$, $K$ is 0 and the equality holds. For $x < \omega - 1$ and $\delta > 0$, we have $a_x < a_{\overline{e_x}|}$. ▼

The relation of $\bar{a}_x$ to $\bar{a}_{\overline{\hat{e}_x}|}$ is further explored in Exercise 5.45.

**5.10
Notes and
References**

Some references for Woolhouse's summation formula are Kellison (1975) or Jordan (1967). Examples of the distortion of annuity values based on the traditional approximation are given in the January and April, 1977, issues of *The Actuary*. Taylor (1952) presented new formulas analogous to (5.5.3). Various inquiries into the probability distribution of annuity costs have been made by Boermeester (1956), Fretwell and Hickman (1964) and Bowers (1967). Mereu (1962) has given a means of calculating annuity values directly from Makeham constants. Complete and apportionable annuities are involved, explicitly or implicitly, in the papers by Rasor and Greville (1952), Lauer (1967) and Scher (1974), and in the discussions thereof.

**Exercises**

*Section 5.2*

5.1. Calculate the actuarial present value of 1000 due at the end of 20 years if a life aged 50 survives. Use the Illustrative Life Table with interest at the effective annual rate of 6%.

5.2. What is the future value of 1000 accumulated from age 50 to age 70 with interest at the effective annual rate of 6% and with survivorship given by the Illustrative Life Table?

5.3. Prove and interpret the relation

$$_nE_x + {_nE_x}[(1 + i)^n - 1] + {_nE_x}(1 + i)^n \frac{l_x - l_{x+n}}{l_{x+n}} = 1.$$

*Section 5.3*

5.4. Using the assumption of a uniform distribution of deaths in each year of age and the Illustrative Life Table with interest at the effective annual rate of 6%, calculate
   a. $\bar{a}_{20}, \bar{a}_{50}, \bar{a}_{80}$
   b. $\mathrm{Var}\,[\bar{a}_{\overline{T}|}]$ for $x = 20, 50, 80$.
   [Hint: Use (5.3.6) and (4.4.2).]

# Chapter 5
## LIFE ANNUITIES

5.5. Using the values obtained in Exercise 5.4, calculate the standard deviation and the coefficient of variation, $\sigma/\mu$, of the following present-value random variables.
   a. Individual annuities issued at ages 20, 50, 80 with life incomes of 1000 per year payable continuously.
   b. A group of 100 annuities, each issued at age 50, with life income of 1000 per year payable continuously.

5.6. Show that $\text{Var}[\bar{a}_{\overline{T}|}]$ can be expressed as

$$\frac{2}{\delta}[\bar{a}_x - {}^2\bar{a}_x] - \bar{a}_x^2$$

where ${}^2\bar{a}_x$ is based on the force of interest $2\delta$.

5.7. Calculate $\text{Cov}[\delta\bar{a}_{\overline{T}|}, v^T]$.

5.8. If a deterministic (rate function) approach is adopted, (5.3.26) could be taken as the starting point for the development of a theory of continuous life annuities. For this, one would begin with

$$\frac{d\bar{a}_y}{dy} = (\mu_y + \delta)\,\bar{a}_y - 1 \qquad x \le y < \omega$$

$$\bar{a}_y = 0 \qquad \omega \le y.$$

   a. Use the integrating factor $\exp[-\int_0^y (\mu_z + \delta)\,dz]$ to solve the differential equation to obtain (5.3.1).
   b. Use the integrating factor $e^{-\delta y}$ to obtain the curious equation

$$\bar{a}_x = \bar{a}_{\overline{\omega-x}|} - \int_x^\omega e^{-\delta(y-x)}\,\bar{a}_y\,\mu_y\,dy,$$

   and give a verbal interpretation of it.

*Section 5.4*

5.9. Define ${}_{m|n}\ddot{a}_x$ and write formulas for it that are analogous to (5.3.21)–(5.3.24) for ${}_{m|n}\bar{a}_x$.

5.10. Show that

$$\text{Var}[a_{\overline{K}|}] = \text{Var}[\ddot{a}_{\overline{K+1}|}] = \frac{1}{d^2}\,\text{Var}[v^{K+1}].$$

5.11. Prove and interpret the given relations.
   a. $a_{x:\overline{n}|} = {}_1E_x\,\ddot{a}_{x+1:\overline{n}|}$

   b. ${}_{n|}a_x = \dfrac{A_{x:\overline{n}|} - A_x}{d} - {}_nE_x$

5.12. Prove (5.4.32) algebraically starting from (5.4.11).

5.13. Is

$$1 = i\,a_{x:\overline{n}|} + (1 + i)\,A_{x:\overline{n}|}$$

a correct formula? If not, correct it.

*Section 5.5*

5.14. Consider

$$\ddot{a}_x^{(m)} = E[\ddot{a}_{\overline{K+J_m}}^{(m)}]$$

where $K$ is the curtate-future-lifetime of $(x)$ and

$$J_m = \frac{j+1}{m}$$

when

$$\frac{j}{m} < S \le \frac{j+1}{m} \quad j = 0,1,\ldots,m-1$$

where $S$ is as in (3.6.1). Using Exercise 4.15, show that
a. $1 = d^{(m)}\ddot{a}_x^{(m)} + A_x^{(m)}$
b. $J_m = [mS+1]/m$, except when $S = (j+1)/m$.
The brackets indicate the greatest integer function. [Note that $\Pr(S = (j+1)/m) = 0$.]

5.15. Making the assumption that

$$D_{y+h/m} = D_y - \frac{h}{m}(D_y - D_{y+1}) \quad h = 0,1,\ldots,m-1,$$

in each year of age, verify that

$$\ddot{a}_x^{(m)} = \ddot{a}_x - \frac{m-1}{2m}.$$

5.16. Write the traditional formulas corresponding to (5.5.15) and (5.5.16) and verify them by use of (5.5.8).

5.17. Show that the annuity-immediate analogue for (5.5.3) is

$$a_x^{(m)} = s_{\overline{1}|}^{(m)} a_x + \frac{1}{i^{(m)}}\left[(1+i)A_x - \left(1+\frac{i^{(m)}}{m}\right)A_x^{(m)}\right],$$

and that under the assumption of a uniform distribution of deaths in each year of age, this becomes

$$a_x^{(m)} = s_{\overline{1}|}^{(m)} a_x + (1+i)\frac{1-\ddot{a}_{\overline{1}|}^{(m)}}{i^{(m)}}A_x.$$

5.18. Show that the annuity-immediate analogues for formulas (5.5.4) are

$$a_x^{(m)} = \frac{1 - [1+i^{(m)}/m]A_x^{(m)}}{i^{(m)}} = a_{\overline{\infty}|}^{(m)} - \ddot{a}_{\overline{\infty}|}^{(m)} A_x^{(m)}$$

and that under the assumption of a uniform distribution of deaths in each year of age these become

$$a_x^{(m)} = \alpha(m)a_x + \gamma(m)$$

where $\gamma(m) = (1-\ddot{a}_{\overline{1}|}^{(m)})/i^{(m)}$.

# LIFE ANNUITIES

5.19. Since, under the assumption of a uniform distribution of deaths in each year of age,

$$\ddot{a}_x^{(m)} = \alpha(m)\,\ddot{a}_x - \beta(m)$$

$$a_x^{(m)} = \alpha(m)\,a_x + \gamma(m),$$

and since

$$\ddot{a}_x^{(m)} - a_x^{(m)} = \frac{1}{m}$$

$$\ddot{a}_x - a_x = 1,$$

it follows that

$$\gamma(m) = \alpha(m) - \beta(m) - \frac{1}{m}.$$

Verify this relation by substituting for $\alpha(m)$, $\beta(m)$.

5.20. a. Using (5.5.1) as starting point, verify that

$$\lim_{m\to\infty} \ddot{a}_x^{(m)} = \bar{a}_x.$$

b. Use (5.5.8) and the result in (a) to show

$$\bar{a}_x \cong a_x + \frac{1}{2}.$$

c. Start with (5.3.2B) to show that the trapezoidal rule for approximate integration yields the result in (b).

5.21. Using the traditional approximation given in (5.5.8), establish the following:

a. $a_x^{(m)} \cong a_x + \dfrac{m-1}{2m}$

b. $a_{x:\overline{n}|}^{(m)} \cong a_{x:\overline{n}|} + \dfrac{m-1}{2m}(1 - {}_nE_x)$

c. ${}_{n|}a_x^{(m)} \cong {}_{n|}a_x + \dfrac{m-1}{2m}\,{}_nE_x.$

5.22. a. Develop a formula for $\ddot{s}_{25:\overline{40}|}^{(m)}$ in terms of $\ddot{s}_{25:\overline{40}|}$.

b. On the basis of the Illustrative Life Table with interest at the effective annual rate of 6%, calculate the values of

(i) $\ddot{a}_{25:\overline{40}|}^{(12)}$      (ii) $\ddot{s}_{25:\overline{40}|}^{(12)}.$

*Section 5.6*

5.23. Give formulas, in terms of commutation functions, for

a. $\ddot{a}_x$              b. $a_x$           c. $\ddot{a}_{x:\overline{n}|}$

d. $a_{x:\overline{n}|}$          e. ${}_{n|}\ddot{a}_x$          f. ${}_{n|}a_x$

g. $\ddot{a}_{x:\overline{n}|}^{(m)}$         h. ${}_{n|}\ddot{a}_x^{(m)}.$

5.24. For evaluating life annuities-immediate with annual income $b$, one can use the special commutation function

$$\tilde{N}_x^{(m)} = \alpha(m)\, N_{x+1} + \gamma(m)\, D_x = \alpha(m)\, N_x - \left[\beta(m) + \frac{1}{m}\right] D_x$$

and the general formula

$$\frac{b}{D_x}[\tilde{N}_y^{(m)} - \tilde{N}_z^{(m)}].$$

Write formulas in terms of $\tilde{N}_x^{(12)}$ for

a. $a_{60}^{(12)}$　　　　　　b. $a_{40:\overline{25|}}^{(12)}$　　　　　　c. $_{30|}a_{40}^{(12)}$.

*Section 5.7*

5.25. The actuarial present value of a standard increasing temporary life annuity in respect to $(x)$ with
   * yearly income of 1 in the first year, 2 in the second year, and so on, ending with $n$ in the $n$th year,
   * payments made $m$thly on a due basis,
   is denoted by $(I\ddot{a})_{x:\overline{n|}}^{(m)}$. Show that $(I\ddot{a})_{x:\overline{n|}}^{(m)}$ can be expressed in the following ways.

a. $\displaystyle\sum_{k=0}^{n-1} {}_{k|}\ddot{a}_{x:\overline{n-k|}}^{(m)}$

b. $\displaystyle\frac{1}{D_x}\sum_{k=0}^{n-1} (k+1)\, D_{x+k}^{(m)}$

c. $\displaystyle\frac{1}{D_x}\sum_{k=0}^{n-1} [N_{x+k}^{(m)} - N_{x+n}^{(m)}]$

d. $\displaystyle\frac{1}{D_x}[S_x^{(m)} - S_{x+n}^{(m)} - n\, N_{x+n}^{(m)}]$

5.26. The actuarial present value of a decreasing temporary life annuity in respect to $(x)$ with
   * yearly income of $n$ in the first year, $n-1$ in the second year, and so on, ending with 1 in the $n$th year,
   * payments made $m$thly on a due basis,
   is denoted by $(D\ddot{a})_{x:\overline{n|}}^{(m)}$. Show that $(D\ddot{a})_{x:\overline{n|}}^{(m)}$ can be expressed in the following ways.

a. $\displaystyle\sum_{k=1}^{n} \ddot{a}_{x:\overline{k|}}^{(m)}$

b. $\displaystyle\frac{1}{D_x}\sum_{k=0}^{n-1} (n-k)\, D_{x+k}^{(m)}$

c. $\displaystyle\frac{1}{D_x}\sum_{k=1}^{n} [N_x^{(m)} - N_{x+k}^{(m)}]$

d. $\displaystyle\frac{1}{D_x}[n\, N_x^{(m)} - (S_{x+1}^{(m)} - S_{x+n+1}^{(m)})]$

# Chapter 5
## LIFE ANNUITIES

5.27. If, in Exercise 5.25, the yearly income does not cease at age $x + n$ but continues at the level $n$ while $(x)$ survives thereafter, the actuarial present value is denoted by $(I_{\overline{n}|}\ddot{a})_x^{(m)}$. Show that for $(I_{\overline{n}|}\ddot{a})_x^{(m)}$ the following expressions hold.

a. $\displaystyle\sum_{k=0}^{n-1} {}_{k|}\ddot{a}_x^{(m)}$

b. $\dfrac{1}{D_x}\left[\displaystyle\sum_{k=0}^{n-1} (k+1)\,D_{x+k}^{(m)} + n\,N_{x+n}^{(m)}\right]$

c. $\dfrac{1}{D_x}\displaystyle\sum_{k=0}^{n-1} N_{x+k}^{(m)}$

d. $\dfrac{1}{D_x}[S_x^{(m)} - S_{x+n}^{(m)}]$

5.28. Verify the formula

$$\delta\,(\bar{I}\bar{a})_{\overline{T}|} + T\,v^T = \bar{a}_{\overline{T}|}$$

where $T$ represents the future lifetime of $(x)$. Use it to prove that

$$\delta\,(\bar{I}\bar{a})_x + (\bar{I}\bar{A})_x = \bar{a}_x$$

where $(\bar{I}\bar{a})_x$ is the actuarial present value of a life annuity to $(x)$ under which payments are being made continuously at the rate of $t$ per annum at time $t$.

*Section 5.8*

5.29. a. Show that, when $m = 1$, formula (5.8.6) becomes

$$\ddot{a}_y\,(1+i) - (1+i) + q_y\,\ddot{a}_{y+1} = \ddot{a}_{y+1}.$$

b. Express the formula in part (a) in terms of annuity-immediate values to obtain the following.
 (i) $a_y\,(1+i) + q_y\,(1+a_{y+1}) = 1 + a_{y+1}$
 (ii) $1 = i\,a_y + q_y\,(1 + a_{y+1}) + a_y - a_{y+1}$
 Give verbal interpretations of each.

5.30. Show that, for given $n$ and $x$, the following recursions hold for $h = 0,1,\ldots,n-1$.
 a. $(D\ddot{a})_{x+h:\overline{n-h}|}^{(12)} = (n-h)\,\ddot{a}_{x+h:\overline{1}|}^{(12)} + {}_1E_{x+h}\,(D\ddot{a})_{x+h+1:\overline{n-h-1}|}^{(12)}$
 b. $(apv)_{x+h} = (h+1)\,\ddot{a}_{x+h:\overline{1}|}^{(12)} + {}_1E_{x+h}\,(apv)_{x+h+1}$
 where $(apv)_{x+h} = h\,\ddot{a}_{x+h:\overline{n-h}|}^{(12)} + (I\ddot{a})_{x+h:\overline{n-h}|}^{(12)}$.

*Section 5.9*

5.31. a. Show that, for the aggregate payment technique in evaluating $\overset{\circ}{a}_x$, the present-value random variable is

$$a_{\overline{K}|} + \frac{v^T\,\bar{s}_{\overline{T-K}|}}{\bar{s}_{\overline{1}|}} = a_{\overline{K}|} + v^T\,\frac{\delta}{i}\,\bar{s}_{\overline{T-K}|}$$

# LIFE ANNUITIES

where $K$, $T$ are the curtate- and complete-future-lifetimes of $(x)$, respectively, and that this reduces to

$$\frac{1 - v^T}{i} = a_{\overline{T}|}.$$

b. Hence, show

$$\mathring{a}_x = \mathrm{E}\left[\frac{1 - v^T}{i}\right] = \frac{\delta}{i}\bar{a}_x,$$

and obtain a formula for

$$\mathrm{Var}\left[\frac{1 - v^T}{i}\right].$$

5.32. a. Show that for $\ddot{a}_x^{\{1\}}$ the present-value random variable is

$$\ddot{a}_{\overline{K+1}|} - v^T \frac{\delta}{d}\bar{a}_{\overline{K+1-T}|}$$

and that this reduces to

$$\frac{1 - v^T}{d} = \ddot{a}_{\overline{T}|}.$$

b. Hence, show that

$$\ddot{a}_x^{\{1\}} = \frac{\delta}{d}\bar{a}_x.$$

*Miscellaneous*

5.33. For $0 \le t \le 1$ and the assumption of a uniform distribution of deaths in each year of age, show that

a. $\ddot{a}_{x+t} = \dfrac{(1 + it)\,\ddot{a}_x - t\,(1 + i)}{1 - t\,q_x}$

b. $_{t|}\ddot{a}_x = v^t\left[(1 + it)\,\ddot{a}_x - t\,(1 + i)\right]$

c. $_{1-t|}\ddot{a}_{x+t} = \dfrac{(1 + i)^t}{1 - t\,q_x}(\ddot{a}_x - 1)$

d. $A_{x+t} = \dfrac{1 + it}{1 - t\,q_x}A_x - \dfrac{t\,q_x}{1 - t\,q_x}.$

5.34. Obtain formulas for the evaluation of a life annuity-due to $(x)$ with an initial payment of 1 and with annual payments increasing thereafter by
a. 3% of the initial annual payment
b. 3% of the previous year's annual payment.

5.35. Express $(\bar{D}\bar{a})_{x:\overline{n}|}$ as an integral and prove the equation

$$\frac{\partial}{\partial n}(\bar{D}\bar{a})_{x:\overline{n}|} = \bar{a}_{x:\overline{n}|}.$$

# Chapter 5
## LIFE ANNUITIES

5.36. Give an expression for the actuarial accumulated value at age 70 of an annuity with the following monthly payments:
- 100 at the end of each month from age 30 to 40,
- 200 at the end of each month from age 40 to 50,
- 500 at the end of each month from age 50 to 60,
- 1000 at the end of each month from age 60 to 70.

5.37. Derive a simplified expression of the net single premium for a 25-year term insurance payable immediately on the death of (35), under which the death benefit in case of death at age $35 + t$ is $\bar{s}_{\overline{t}|}$, $0 \le t \le 25$. Interpret your result.

5.38. Derive a simplified expression of the net single premium for an $n$-year term insurance payable at the end of the year of death of $(x)$, under which the death benefit in case of death in year $k + 1$ is $\ddot{s}_{\overline{k+1}|}$, $0 \le k < n$. Interpret your result.

5.39. Obtain a simplified expression for
$$(I\ddot{a})^{(12)}_{x:\overline{25}|} - (Ia)^{(12)}_{x:\overline{25}|}.$$

5.40. Consider an $n$-year deferred continuous life annuity of 1 per year as an insurance with probability of claim, $_np_x$, and random amount of claim, $v^n \bar{a}_{\overline{T}|}$. Here $T$ has p.d.f. $_tp_{x+n}\,\mu_{x+n+t}$. Apply (2.2.13) to show that the variance of the insurance equals
$$v^{2n}\,_np_x\,(1 - _np_x)\,\bar{a}^2_{x+n} + v^{2n}\,_np_x\,\frac{^2\bar{A}_{x+n} - \bar{A}^2_{x+n}}{\delta^2},$$
and verify that this reduces to (5.3.20).

5.41. Write the discrete analogue of the variance formula in Exercise 5.40.

5.42. Let $I_k$ be the indicator random variable with $\Pr(I_k = 1) = _kp_x$, $\Pr(I_k = 0) = _kq_x$. Show the following:
a. The actuarial present value of a life annuity to $(x)$, with annual payment $b_k$ on survival to age $x + k$, $k = 0,1,2,\ldots$ can be written as
$$\mathrm{E}\left[\sum_{k=0}^{\infty} v^k b_k I_k\right].$$

b. $\mathrm{E}[I_j I_k] = _kp_x \quad j \le k$
$\mathrm{Cov}[I_j, I_k] = _kp_x\,_jq_x \quad j \le k.$

c. $\mathrm{Var}\left[\sum_{k=0}^{\infty} v^k b_k I_k\right]$
$$= \sum_{k=0}^{\infty} v^{2k} b_k^2\,_kp_x\,_kq_x + 2\sum_{k=0}^{\infty}\sum_{j<k} v^{j+k}\,b_j\,b_k\,_kp_x\,_jq_x.$$

5.43. If a left superscript 2 indicates that interest is at force $2\,\delta$, show that
a. $^2A_x = 1 - (2d - d^2)\,^2\ddot{a}_x$
b. $\mathrm{Var}[v^{K+1}] = 2d\,(\ddot{a}_x - {}^2\ddot{a}_x) - d^2\,(\ddot{a}_x^2 - {}^2\ddot{a}_x)$

c. $\text{Var}\,[\ddot{a}_{\overline{K+1}|}] = \dfrac{2}{d}(\ddot{a}_x - {}^2\ddot{a}_x) - (\ddot{a}_x^2 - {}^2\ddot{a}_x).$

5.44. a. Expand, in terms of powers of $\delta$, the annuity coefficients $\alpha(m)$ and $\beta(m)$.

b. What do the expansions in (a) become for $m = \infty$?

5.45. If $g(x)$ is a nonnegative function and $X$ is a random variable with p.d.f. $f(x)$, justify the inequality

$$E[g(X)] = \int_{-\infty}^{\infty} g(x)\,f(x)\,dx \geq k\,\Pr\,[g(X) \geq k] \qquad k > 0,$$

and use it to show that

$$\bar{a}_x \geq \bar{a}_{\overline{\mathring{e}_x}|}\,\Pr\,(\bar{a}_{\overline{T}|} \geq \bar{a}_{\overline{\mathring{e}_x}|}) = \bar{a}_{\overline{\mathring{e}_x}|}\,\Pr\,(T \geq \mathring{e}_x).$$

5.46. A unit is to be used to purchase a combination benefit consisting of a life income of $I$ per year payable continuously while $(x)$ survives and an insurance of $J$ payable immediately on the death of $(x)$. Write the present-value random variable for this combination, and give its mean and variance.

5.47. Using the assumption of a uniform distribution of deaths in each year of age and the Illustrative Life Table with interest at the effective annual rate of 6%, calculate

a. $\ddot{a}_{40}^{(12)}$          b. $\ddot{a}_{40:\overline{30}|}^{(12)}$          c. ${}_{30|}\ddot{a}_{40}^{(12)}.$

5.48. Show that, if $q_x < \left(\dfrac{i^{(2)}}{2}\right)^2$, the traditional approximation

$$\ddot{a}_{x:\overline{n}|}^{(m)} = \ddot{a}_{x:\overline{n}|} - \dfrac{m-1}{2m}(1 - {}_nE_x)$$

in the special case with $n = 1$, $m = 2$ leads to

$$\ddot{a}_{x:\overline{1}|}^{(2)} > \ddot{a}_{\overline{1}|}^{(2)}.$$

5.49. If $A''_{x:\overline{m}|}$ and $\ddot{a}''_{x:\overline{m}|}$ are actuarial present values calculated using
• an interest rate of $i$ for the first $n$ years, $n < m$, and
• an interest rate $i'$ for the remaining $m - n$ years,
show algebraically and interpret

a. $A''_{x:\overline{m}|} = 1 - d\,\ddot{a}_{x:\overline{n}|} - v^n\,{}_np_x\,d'\,\ddot{a}'_{x+n:\overline{m-n}|}$

b. $A''_{x:\overline{m}|} = 1 - d'\,\ddot{a}''_{x:\overline{m}|} + (d' - d)\,\ddot{a}_{x:\overline{n}|}.$

5.50. Show that

$$\dfrac{d\ddot{a}_x}{di} = -v\,(Ia)_x$$

where

$$(Ia)_x = \sum_{t=1}^{\infty} t\,v^t\,{}_tp_x,$$

and interpret the relation.

5.51. If, in Example 5.10, the annuity payments level off after
   a. 10 increases,
   b. 20 increases,
   find the actuarial present value of the annuity.

5.52. Show that a constant increase in the force of mortality has the same effect on $\ddot{a}_x$ as a constant increase in the force of interest, but that this is not the case for $\ddot{a}_x^{(m)}$ evaluated by $\alpha(m)\ddot{a}_x - \beta(m)$.

5.53. Show that
   a. $\alpha(m) - \beta(m)\,d = \ddot{a}_{\overline{1}|}^{(m)}$
   b. the recursion formula (5.8.3) can be rewritten as
   $$\ddot{a}_y^{(m)} = \alpha(m) - \beta(m)\,(1 - v\,p_y) + v\,p_y\,\ddot{a}_{y+1}^{(m)}.$$

5.54. Consider the following portfolio of annuities-due currently being paid from the assets of a pension fund.

| Age | Number of Annuitants |
|-----|----------------------|
| 65  | 30                   |
| 75  | 20                   |
| 85  | 10                   |

Each annuity has an annual payment of 1 as long as the annuitant survives. Assume an earned interest rate of 6% and a mortality as given in the Illustrative Life Table. For the present value of these obligations of the pension fund, calculate
   a. the expectation
   b. the variance
   c. the 95th percentile of the distribution.
For parts (b) and (c), assume the lives are mutually independent.

# Chapter 6
## NET PREMIUMS

**6**

## 6.1
## Introduction

In Chapters 4 and 5 we discussed the actuarial present values of the payments of various life insurances and annuities. These ideas will be combined in this chapter, for in practice an individual life insurance is usually purchased by a life annuity of gross premiums. Gross premiums provide for the benefits of the life insurance, the expenses of initiating and maintaining the insurance, and margins for profit and for offsetting possible unfavorable experience. This chapter covers net annual premiums that provide for only the benefit payments. Such net annual premiums will form a life annuity beginning when the insurance is issued.

In Chapter 1 we discussed the idea that determination of the insurance premium requires the adoption of a premium principle. Example 6.1 illustrates the application of two premium principles. One of these will determine the premium to cover only the expected present value of the insurance benefits.

**Example 6.1:**

An insurer is planning to issue a policy to a life aged 0 whose curtate-future-lifetime, $K$, is governed by the p.f.

$$_{k|}q_0 = \frac{1}{4} \quad k = 0, 1, 2, 3.$$

The policy will pay 1 unit at the end of the year of death in exchange for the payment of a premium $P$ at the beginning of each year, provided the life survives. Find the annual premium, $P$, as determined by

a. Principle I: $P$ shall be such that the expectation of the present value, at policy issue, of the financial loss is 0.

b. Principle II: $P$ shall be the least amount such that the probability of a positive financial loss is at most 1/4.

For both parts assume the insurer will use an annual effective rate of $i = 0.06$.

**Solution:**
For $K = k$ and an arbitrary premium, $P$, the present value of the financial loss at policy issue is $v^{k+1} - P\ddot{a}_{\overline{k+1}|}$.

a. According to Principle I, $P$ should be chosen such that

$$\sum_{k=0}^{3} (v^{k+1} - P\ddot{a}_{\overline{k+1}|}) \Pr(K = k) = 0, \tag{6.1.1}$$

which gives $P = 0.3667$.

b. Since $v^j - P\ddot{a}_{\overline{j}|}$ decreases as $j$ increases, the requirement of Principle II will hold if $P$ is such that $v^2 - P\ddot{a}_{\overline{2}|} = 0$. Then the financial loss is positive for only $K = 0$. Thus, for this principle, $P = 0.4580$.

These results are summarized below.

| Outcome $k$ | Probability $_{k\|}q_0$ | Present Value of Financial Loss | | |
|---|---|---|---|---|
| | | General Formula | Premium by Principle | |
| | | | I | II |
| 0 | 1/4 | $v - P\ddot{a}_{\overline{1}\|}$ | 0.5767 | 0.4854 |
| 1 | 1/4 | $v^2 - P\ddot{a}_{\overline{2}\|}$ | 0.1774 | 0.0000 |
| 2 | 1/4 | $v^3 - P\ddot{a}_{\overline{3}\|}$ | -0.1993 | -0.4580 |
| 3 | 1/4 | $v^4 - P\ddot{a}_{\overline{4}\|}$ | -0.5547 | -0.8900 |
| | | The premium is | 0.3667 | 0.4580 |

▼

From now on, Principle I will be followed for the determination of premiums. To formalize its concepts, we define the insurer's loss, $L$, as the random variable of the present value of benefits to be paid by the insurer less the random variable of the present value of the annuity of premiums to be paid by the insured. Principle I is called the *equivalence principle* and has the requirement that

$$E[L] = 0. \qquad (6.1.2)$$

We will speak of net premiums as those satisfying (6.1.2). These net premiums will be such that

E[present value of benefits − present value of net premiums] = 0,

which is equivalent to

E[present value of benefits] = E[present value of net premiums].

In other words, the net premiums are chosen so that the actuarial present value of the benefits equals the actuarial present value of the net premiums. The methods developed in Chapters 4 and 5 for calculating these actuarial present values can be used to reduce this equality to a form that can be solved for the premiums. For instance, when the benefits and premiums are constant, as in Example 6.1, equation (6.1.1) can be rewritten as $A_0 = P\ddot{a}_0$, and $\ddot{a}_0$ can be calculated as

$$\sum_{k=0}^{3} v^k \,_k p_0.$$

When the equivalence principle is used to determine the single premium to be collected at policy issue for a life insurance or a life annuity, the premium is equal to the actuarial present value of the payments and is called the net single premium.

## 6.2 Fully Continuous Premiums

The basic concepts involved in the determination of net annual premiums using the equivalence principle will be illustrated first for the case of the fully continuous net level annual premium for a unit whole life insurance payable immediately on the death of $(x)$. For any continuously paid premium, $\bar{P}$, consider

$$l(t) = v^t - \bar{P}\bar{a}_{\overline{t}|}, \tag{6.2.1}$$

the present value of the loss to the insurer if death occurs at time $t$.

We note that $l(t)$ is a decreasing function of $t$ with $l(0) = 1$ and $l(t)$ approaching $-\bar{P}/\delta$ as $t \to \infty$. If $t_0$ is the time when $l(t_0) = 0$, death before $t_0$ results in a loss while death after $t_0$ produces a negative loss, that is, a gain.

We now consider the loss random variable,

$$L = l(T) = v^T - \bar{P}\bar{a}_{\overline{T}|}, \tag{6.2.2}$$

corresponding to the loss function $l(t)$. If the insurer determines his premium by the equivalence principle, the premium is denoted by $\bar{P}(\bar{A}_x)$ and is such that

$$E[L] = 0. \tag{6.2.3}$$

It follows from (4.2.6) and (5.3.2) that

$$\bar{A}_x - \bar{P}(\bar{A}_x)\bar{a}_x = 0,$$

or

$$\bar{P}(\bar{A}_x) = \frac{\bar{A}_x}{\bar{a}_x}. \tag{6.2.4}$$

The variance of $L$ can be used as a measure of the variability of losses on an individual whole life insurance due to the random nature of time-until-death. Since $E[L] = 0$,

$$\text{Var}[L] = E[L^2]. \tag{6.2.5}$$

For the loss in (6.2.2), we have

$$\begin{aligned}
\text{Var}[v^T - \bar{P}\bar{a}_{\overline{T}|}] &= \text{Var}\left[v^T - \frac{\bar{P}(1 - v^T)}{\delta}\right] \\
&= \text{Var}\left[v^T\left(1 + \frac{\bar{P}}{\delta}\right) - \frac{\bar{P}}{\delta}\right] \\
&= \text{Var}\left[v^T\left(1 + \frac{\bar{P}}{\delta}\right)\right] \tag{6.2.6} \\
&= \text{Var}[v^T]\left(1 + \frac{\bar{P}}{\delta}\right)^2 \\
&= (^2\bar{A}_x - \bar{A}_x^2)\left(1 + \frac{\bar{P}}{\delta}\right)^2.
\end{aligned}$$

For the premium determined by the equivalence principle, we can use (6.2.4) and (5.3.4), $\delta\bar{a}_x + \bar{A}_x = 1$, to rewrite (6.2.6) as

$$\text{Var}[L] = \frac{^2\bar{A}_x - \bar{A}_x^2}{(\delta\bar{a}_x)^2}. \tag{6.2.7}$$

**Example 6.2:**

Under the assumptions stated in Example 5.5, calculate $\bar{P}(\bar{A}_x)$ and $\text{Var}[L]$.

**Solution:**

Example 5.5 involves a constant force of mortality, $\mu = 0.04$, and a constant force of interest, $\delta = 0.06$. These assumptions yield $\bar{a}_x = 10$, $\bar{A}_x = 0.4$, and $^2\bar{A}_x = 0.25$. Using (6.2.4), we obtain

$$\bar{P}(\bar{A}_x) = \frac{\bar{A}_x}{\bar{a}_x} = 0.04,$$

and from (6.2.7)

$$\text{Var}[L] = \frac{0.25 - 0.16}{(0.6)^2} = 0.25. \qquad \blacktriangledown$$

By reference to (6.2.6) we can see that the numerator of this last expression can be interpreted as the variance of the loss, $v^T - \bar{A}_x$, associated with a single premium whole life insurance. This latter variance is 0.09, and hence the standard deviation of the loss associated with this annual premium insurance is $\sqrt{0.25/0.09} = 5/3$ times the standard deviation of the loss in the single premium case. Additional uncertainty about the present value of the net premium income increased the variability of losses due to the random nature of time-until-death.

In Example 6.2, $\bar{P}(\bar{A}_x) = 0.04$, the constant force of mortality. We can confirm this as a general result by using parts of Examples 4.2 and 5.5. Under the constant force of mortality assumption,

$$\bar{A}_x = \frac{\mu}{\mu + \delta}$$

and

$$\bar{a}_x = \frac{1}{\mu + \delta},$$

thus

$$\bar{P}(\bar{A}_x) = \frac{\mu(\mu + \delta)^{-1}}{(\mu + \delta)^{-1}} = \mu,$$

which does not depend on the force of interest or the age at issue.

Using the equivalence principle, as in (6.1.2), we can determine formulas for net annual premiums of a variety of fully continuous life insurances. Our general loss is

$$b_T v_T - \bar{P}Y = Z - \bar{P}Y \qquad (6.2.8)$$

where

- $b_t$ and $v_t$ are, respectively, the benefit amount and discount factor defined in connection with (4.2.1),

# Chapter 6
## NET PREMIUMS

- $\bar{P}$ is a general symbol for a fully continuous net annual premium,
- $Y$ is a continuous annuity random variable as defined, for example, in (5.3.12), and
- $Z$ is defined by (4.2.2).

Application of the equivalence principle yields

$$E[b_T v_T - \bar{P} Y] = 0$$

or

$$\bar{P} = \frac{E[b_T v_T]}{E[Y]}.$$

These ideas are used to display annual premium formulas in Table 6.1.

It is of interest to note how the pattern follows for an $n$-year deferred whole life annuity of 1 per year payable continuously. In this case $b_T v_T = 0$, $T \leq n$ and $b_T v_T = \bar{a}_{\overline{T-n}|} v^n$, $T > n$. Then,

$$E[b_T v_T] = {}_n p_x \, E[\bar{a}_{\overline{T-n}|} v^n | T > n]$$

$$= v^n \, {}_n p_x \, \bar{a}_{x+n} = A_{x:\overline{n}|}^{\ 1} \, \bar{a}_{x+n}.$$

**Table 6.1**
**Fully Continuous Net Annual Premiums**

| Plan | Loss Components $b_T v_T$ | $\bar{P} Y$ where $Y$ is | Premium Formula $\bar{P} = \dfrac{E[b_T v_T]}{E[Y]}$ |
|---|---|---|---|
| Whole Life Insurance | $1 v^T$ | $\bar{a}_{\overline{T}|}$ | $\bar{P}(\bar{A}_x) = \dfrac{\bar{A}_x}{\bar{a}_x}$ |
| $n$-Year Term Insurance | $1 v^T$ <br> $0$ | $\bar{a}_{\overline{T}|}, \ T \leq n$ <br> $\bar{a}_{\overline{n}|}, \ T > n$ | $\bar{P}(\bar{A}_{x:\overline{n}|}^{\ 1}) = \dfrac{\bar{A}_{x:\overline{n}|}^{\ 1}}{\bar{a}_{x:\overline{n}|}}$ |
| $n$-Year Endowment Insurance | $1 v^T$ <br> $1 v^n$ | $\bar{a}_{\overline{T}|}, \ T \leq n$ <br> $\bar{a}_{\overline{n}|}, \ T > n$ | $\bar{P}(\bar{A}_{x:\overline{n}|}) = \dfrac{\bar{A}_{x:\overline{n}|}}{\bar{a}_{x:\overline{n}|}}$ |
| $h$-Payment* Whole Life Insurance | $1 v^T$ <br> $1 v^T$ | $\bar{a}_{\overline{T}|}, \ T \leq h$ <br> $\bar{a}_{\overline{h}|}, \ T > h$ | ${}_h\bar{P}(\bar{A}_x) = \dfrac{\bar{A}_x}{\bar{a}_{x:\overline{h}|}}$ |
| $h$-Payment,* $n$-Year Endowment Insurance | $1 v^T$ <br> $1 v^T$ <br> $1 v^n$ | $\bar{a}_{\overline{T}|}, \ T \leq h$ <br> $\bar{a}_{\overline{h}|}, \ h < T \leq n$ <br> $\bar{a}_{\overline{n}|}, \ T > n$ | ${}_h\bar{P}(\bar{A}_{x:\overline{n}|}) = \dfrac{\bar{A}_{x:\overline{n}|}}{\bar{a}_{x:\overline{h}|}}$ |
| $n$-Year Pure Endowment | $0$ <br> $1 v^n$ | $\bar{a}_{\overline{T}|}, \ T \leq n$ <br> $\bar{a}_{\overline{n}|}, \ T > n$ | $\bar{P}(A_{x:\overline{n}|}^{\ \ 1}) = \dfrac{A_{x:\overline{n}|}^{\ \ 1}}{\bar{a}_{x:\overline{n}|}}$ |
| $n$-Year Deferred Whole Life Annuity | $0$ <br> $\bar{a}_{\overline{T-n}|} v^n$ | $\bar{a}_{\overline{T}|}, \ T \leq n$ <br> $\bar{a}_{\overline{n}|}, \ T > n$ | $\bar{P}({}_n|\bar{a}_x) = \dfrac{A_{x:\overline{n}|}^{\ 1} \, \bar{a}_{x+n}}{\bar{a}_{x:\overline{n}|}}$ |

*The insurances described in the fourth and fifth rows provide for a premium paying period that is shorter than the period over which death benefits are paid.

In practice, however, deferred life annuities usually provide some type of death benefit during the deferment period. One contract of this type is examined later in Example 6.12.

**Example 6.3:** Express the variance of the loss, $L$, associated with an $n$-year endowment insurance, in terms of net single premiums, (see the third row of Table 6.1).

**Solution:**
Using the notation of (4.2.8), we have

$$\text{Var}[L] = \text{Var}\left[Z_3\left(1 + \frac{\bar{P}(\bar{A}_{x:\overline{n}|})}{\delta}\right) - \frac{\bar{P}(\bar{A}_{x:\overline{n}|})}{\delta}\right].$$

We now use (4.2.10) to obtain

$$\text{Var}[L] = \left[1 + \frac{\bar{P}(\bar{A}_{x:\overline{n}|})}{\delta}\right]^2 [^2\bar{A}_{x:\overline{n}|} - \bar{A}_{x:\overline{n}|}^2].$$

Formula (5.3.11) can be rewritten as

$$(\delta\,\bar{a}_{x:\overline{n}|})^{-1} = 1 + \frac{\bar{P}(\bar{A}_{x:\overline{n}|})}{\delta},$$

which implies that

$$\text{Var}[L] = \frac{^2\bar{A}_{x:\overline{n}|} - \bar{A}_{x:\overline{n}|}^2}{(\delta\,\bar{a}_{x:\overline{n}|})^2}.\qquad\blacktriangledown$$

The two identities, (5.3.4) and (5.3.11), can be used to derive relationships among continuous net premiums. For example, starting with (5.3.4)

$$\delta\,\bar{a}_x + \bar{A}_x = 1$$

$$\delta + \bar{P}(\bar{A}_x) = \frac{1}{\bar{a}_x}$$

$$\bar{P}(\bar{A}_x) = \frac{1}{\bar{a}_x} - \delta \qquad (6.2.9)$$

$$= \frac{1 - \delta\,\bar{a}_x}{\bar{a}_x}$$

$$= \frac{\delta\,\bar{A}_x}{1 - \bar{A}_x}.$$

Starting with (5.3.11) we obtain

$$\delta \bar{a}_{x:\overline{n}|} + \bar{A}_{x:\overline{n}|} = 1$$

$$\delta + \bar{P}(\bar{A}_{x:\overline{n}|}) = \frac{1}{\bar{a}_{x:\overline{n}|}}$$

$$\bar{P}(\bar{A}_{x:\overline{n}|}) = \frac{1}{\bar{a}_{x:\overline{n}|}} - \delta \qquad (6.2.10)$$

$$= \frac{1 - \delta \bar{a}_{x:\overline{n}|}}{\bar{a}_{x:\overline{n}|}}$$

$$= \frac{\delta \bar{A}_{x:\overline{n}|}}{1 - \bar{A}_{x:\overline{n}|}}.$$

Verbal interpretations of the discrete analogues of (6.2.9) and (6.2.10) are given in Example 6.7.

## 6.3
## Fully Discrete
## Premiums

In Section 6.2 we discussed the theory of fully continuous net annual premiums. In this section we shall consider annual premium insurances like the one that appeared in Example 6.1. That is, the sum insured is payable at the end of the policy year in which death occurs and the first premium is payable when the insurance is issued. Subsequent premiums are payable on anniversaries of the policy issue date while the insured survives during the contractual premium payment period. The set of annual premiums form a life annuity-due. This model does not conform to practice but is of historic importance in the development of actuarial theory.

Under these circumstances, the net level annual premium for a unit whole life insurance is denoted by $P_x$, where the absence of $(\bar{A}_x)$ means that the insurance is payable at the end of the policy year of death. The loss for this insurance is

$$L = v^{K+1} - P_x \ddot{a}_{\overline{K+1}|} \qquad K = 0, 1, 2, \ldots. \qquad (6.3.1)$$

The equivalence principle requires that $E[L] = 0$, or

$$E[v^{K+1}] - P_x\, E[\ddot{a}_{\overline{K+1}|}] = 0,$$

which yields

$$P_x = \frac{A_x}{\ddot{a}_x}. \qquad (6.3.2)$$

This is the discrete analogue of (6.2.4).

Using (5.4.6) in place of (5.3.4), in steps parallel to those taken in obtaining formula (6.2.6), we obtain

$$\mathrm{Var}\,[L] = \frac{{}^{2}A_x - A_x^2}{(d\,\ddot{a}_x)^2}. \qquad (6.3.3)$$

**Example 6.4:**

If

$$_{k|}q_x = c\,(0.96)^{k+1} \qquad k = 0, 1, 2, \ldots$$

where $c = 0.04/0.96$ and $i = 0.06$, calculate $P_x$ and $\text{Var}[L]$.

**Solution:**
First we exhibit the components of (6.3.2),

$$A_x = c \sum_{k=0}^{\infty} (1.06)^{-k-1} (0.96)^{k+1} = 0.40$$

$$\ddot{a}_x = \frac{1 - A_x}{d} = 10.60.$$

Then using (6.3.2) we obtain

$$P_x = \frac{A_x}{\ddot{a}_x} = 0.0377.$$

For $\text{Var}[L]$, we calculate

$$^2A_x = c \sum_{k=0}^{\infty} [(1.06)^2]^{-k-1} (0.96)^{k+1} = 0.2445.$$

Therefore,

$$\text{Var}[L] = \frac{0.2445 - 0.1600}{[(0.06)(10.60)/(1.06)]^2} \qquad = \frac{{}^2A_x - A_x^2}{(d\,\ddot{a}_x)^2}$$

$$= 0.2347. \qquad \blacktriangledown$$

There is a connection between Examples 6.2 and 6.4. Since

$$_{k|}q_x = \int_k^{k+1} {}_t p_x\, \mu_{x+t}\, dt \qquad k = 0, 1, 2, \ldots, \tag{6.3.4}$$

for the situation described in Example 6.4, we have

$$\frac{0.04}{0.96}(0.96)^{k+1} = \int_k^{k+1} {}_t p_x\, \mu_{x+t}\, dt.$$

If the force of mortality is a constant, $\mu$, it follows that

$$\frac{0.04}{0.96}(0.96)^{k+1} = e^{-(k+1)\mu}(e^{\mu} - 1),$$

and then $e^{-\mu} = 0.96$ and $\mu = 0.0408$. The geometric distribution, with p.f.

$$_{k|}q_x = \frac{0.04}{0.96}(0.96)^{k+1},$$

is a discrete version of the exponential distribution with $\mu = 0.0408$. Formula (6.3.4) provides the bridge between the discrete and contin-

## NET PREMIUMS

uous versions. The fully continuous net annual premium corresponding to $P_x = 0.0377$ in Example 6.4 would be $\bar{P}(\bar{A}_x) = \mu = 0.0408$.

Continuing to use the equivalence principle, we can determine formulas for net annual premiums for a variety of fully discrete life insurances. Our general loss will be

$$b_{K+1}v_{K+1} - PY$$

where

- $b_{k+1}$ and $v_{k+1}$ are, respectively, the benefit and discount functions defined in (4.3.1),
- $P$ is a general symbol for an annual premium paid at the beginning of each policy year during the premium paying period while the insured survives, and
- $Y$ is a discrete annuity random variable as defined, for example, in (5.4.9).

Application of the equivalence principle yields

$$E[b_{K+1}v_{K+1} - PY] = 0,$$

or

$$P = \frac{E[b_{K+1}v_{K+1}]}{E[Y]}.$$

These ideas are used in Table 6.2 to display premium formulas for fully discrete insurances.

**Example 6.5:**  Express the variance of the loss, $L$, associated with an $n$-year endowment insurance, in terms of net single premiums (see the third row of Table 6.2).

**Solution:**
We start with the notation of Table 6.2. Let

$$Z = \begin{cases} v^{K+1} & K = 0,1,\ldots,n-1 \\ v^n & K = n,n+1,\ldots. \end{cases}$$

Then we can write, by reference to the third row of Table 6.2,

$$L = Z - P_{x:\overline{n}|}\frac{1-Z}{d},$$

hence we have

$$\text{Var}[L] = \text{Var}\left[Z\left(1 + \frac{P_{x:\overline{n}|}}{d}\right) - \frac{P_{x:\overline{n}|}}{d}\right].$$

We can use Theorem 4.1 to find $\text{Var}[Z]$, as indicated in Table 4.2, then obtain

$$\text{Var}[L] = \left(1 + \frac{P_{x:\overline{n}|}}{d}\right)^2 ({}^2A_{x:\overline{n}|} - A^2_{x:\overline{n}|}).$$

# NET PREMIUMS

**Table 6.2
Fully Discrete Net
Annual Premiums**

| Plan | $b_{K+1}v_{K+1}$ | $PY$ where $Y$ is | $P = \dfrac{E[b_{K+1}v_{K+1}]}{E[Y]}$ |
|---|---|---|---|
| | **Loss Components** | | **Premium Formula** |
| Whole Life Insurance | $1\,v^{K+1}$ | $\ddot{a}_{\overline{K+1}\rceil},\ K=0,1,2,\ldots$ | $P_x = \dfrac{A_x}{\ddot{a}_x}$ |
| $n$-Year Term Insurance | $1\,v^{K+1}$ <br> $0$ | $\ddot{a}_{\overline{K+1}\rceil},\ K=0,1,\ldots,n-1$ <br> $\ddot{a}_{\overline{n}\rceil},\ K=n,\,n+1,\ldots$ | $P^1_{x:\overline{n}\rceil} = \dfrac{A^1_{x:\overline{n}\rceil}}{\ddot{a}_{x:\overline{n}\rceil}}$ |
| $n$-Year Endowment Insurance | $1\,v^{K+1}$ <br> $1\,v^n$ | $\ddot{a}_{\overline{K+1}\rceil},\ K=0,1,\ldots,n-1$ <br> $\ddot{a}_{\overline{n}\rceil},\ K=n,n+1,\ldots$ | $P_{x:\overline{n}\rceil} = \dfrac{A_{x:\overline{n}\rceil}}{\ddot{a}_{x:\overline{n}\rceil}}$ |
| $h$-Payment Whole Life Insurance | $1\,v^{K+1}$ <br> $1\,v^{K+1}$ | $\ddot{a}_{\overline{K+1}\rceil},\ K=0,1,\ldots,h-1$ <br> $\ddot{a}_{\overline{h}\rceil},\ K=h,h+1,\ldots$ | $_hP_x = \dfrac{A_x}{\ddot{a}_{x:\overline{h}\rceil}}$ |
| $h$-Payment, $n$-Year Endowment Insurance | $1\,v^{K+1}$ <br> $1\,v^{K+1}$ <br> $1\,v^n$ | $\ddot{a}_{\overline{K+1}\rceil},\ K=0,1,\ldots,h-1$ <br> $\ddot{a}_{\overline{h}\rceil},\ K=h,\ldots,n-1$ <br> $\ddot{a}_{\overline{h}\rceil},\ K=n,n+1,\ldots$ | $_hP_{x:\overline{n}\rceil} = \dfrac{A_{x:\overline{n}\rceil}}{\ddot{a}_{x:\overline{h}\rceil}}$ |
| $n$-Year Pure Endowment | $0$ <br> $1\,v^n$ | $\ddot{a}_{\overline{K+1}\rceil},\ K=0,1,\ldots,n-1$ <br> $\ddot{a}_{\overline{n}\rceil},\ K=n,n+1,\ldots$ | $P^{\ 1}_{x:\overline{n}\rceil} = \dfrac{A^{\ 1}_{x:\overline{n}\rceil}}{\ddot{a}_{x:\overline{n}\rceil}}$ |
| $n$-Year Deferred Whole Life Annuity | $0$ <br> $\ddot{a}_{\overline{K+1-n}\rceil}\,v^n$ | $\ddot{a}_{\overline{K+1}\rceil},\ K=0,1,\ldots,n-1$ <br> $\ddot{a}_{\overline{n}\rceil},\ K=n,n+1,\ldots$ | $P(_{n|}\ddot{a}_x) = \dfrac{A^{\ 1}_{x:\overline{n}\rceil}\,\ddot{a}_{x+n}}{\ddot{a}_{x:\overline{n}\rceil}}$ |

Formula (5.4.11) and the entry from the third row of Table 6.2, can be combined as follows:

$$d\,\ddot{a}_{x:\overline{n}\rceil} + A_{x:\overline{n}\rceil} = 1$$

$$1 + \frac{P_{x:\overline{n}\rceil}}{d} = \frac{1}{d\,\ddot{a}_{x:\overline{n}\rceil}}.$$

Therefore, the variance we seek is

$$\frac{^2A_{x:\overline{n}\rceil} - A^2_{x:\overline{n}\rceil}}{(d\,\ddot{a}_{x:\overline{n}\rceil})^2}. \tag{6.3.5}$$

▼

**Example 6.6:**

Consider a 10,000 fully discrete whole life insurance. Let $\pi$ denote an annual premium for this policy and $L(\pi)$ denote the loss-at-issue random variable for one such policy on the basis of the Illustrative Life Table, 6% interest and issue age 35.

a. Determine the premium, $\pi_a$, such that the distribution of $L(\pi_a)$ has mean 0. Calculate the variance of $L(\pi_a)$.

b. Approximate the lowest premium, $\pi_b$, such that the probability is less than 0.5 that the loss $L(\pi_b)$ is positive. Find the variance of $L(\pi_b)$.

# Chapter 6
## NET PREMIUMS

c. Determine the premium, $\pi_c$, such that the probability of a positive total loss on 100 such independent policies is 0.05 by the normal approximation.

**Solution:**
a. By the equivalence principle, (6.1.2),

$$\pi_a = 10,000\, P_{35} = 10,000\frac{A_{35}}{\ddot{a}_{35}}$$

$$= \frac{1287.194}{15.39262}$$

$$= 83.62.$$

From (6.3.3)

$$\text{Var}\,[L(\pi_a)] = (10,000)^2\,\frac{{}^{2}A_{35} - A_{35}^{2}}{(d\,\ddot{a}_{35})^2}$$

$$= 10^8\,\frac{0.0348843 - (0.1287194)^2}{[(0.06/1.06)\,(15.39262)]^2}$$

$$= \frac{1,831,562}{0.7591295}$$

$$= 2,412,713.$$

b. We want $\pi_b$ such that

$$\Pr\,[L(\pi_b) > 0] < 0.5,$$

or in terms of curtate-future-lifetime, $K$,

$$\Pr\,(10,000\,v^{K+1} - \pi_b\,\ddot{a}_{\overline{K+1}|} > 0) < 0.5.$$

From the Illustrative Life Table, $_{42}p_{35} = 0.5125101$ and $_{43}p_{35} = 0.4808964$. Therefore, if $\pi_b$ is chosen so that

$$10,000\,v^{43} - \pi_b\,\ddot{a}_{\overline{43}|} = 0,$$

then $\Pr\,[L(\pi_b) > 0)] = \Pr\,(K < 42) < 0.5$. Thus,

$$\pi_b = \frac{10,000}{\ddot{s}_{\overline{43}|}} = 50.31.$$

Using the fully discrete analogue of (6.2.6) we can write

$$\text{Var}\,[L(\pi_b)] = (10,000)^2\,({}^{2}A_{35} - A_{35}^{2})\left[1 + \frac{\pi_b}{10,000}\frac{1}{d}\right]^2$$

$$= (1,831,562)\,(1.18567)$$

$$= 2,171,630.$$

c. With a premium $\pi_c$, the loss on one policy is

$$L(\pi_c) = 10{,}000\,v^{K+1} - \pi_c\ddot{a}_{\overline{K+1|}} = \left(10{,}000 + \frac{\pi_c}{d}\right)v^{K+1} - \frac{\pi_c}{d};$$

its expectation and variance are as follows:

$$E[L(\pi_c)] = \left(10{,}000 + \frac{\pi_c}{d}\right)A_{35} - \frac{\pi_c}{d}$$

$$= (0.1287194)\left(10{,}000 + \frac{\pi_c}{d}\right) - \frac{\pi_c}{d}$$

and

$$\text{Var}\,[L(\pi_c)] = \left(10{,}000 + \frac{\pi_c}{d}\right)^2 (^2A_{35} - A_{35}^2)$$

$$= \left(10{,}000 + \frac{\pi_c}{d}\right)^2 (0.01831562).$$

For each of 100 such policies we have the loss $L_i(\pi_c) = L(\pi_c)$, $i = 1$, 2, ..., 100 and

$$S = \sum_{i=1}^{100} L_i(\pi_c)$$

for the total loss on the portfolio. Then

$$E[S] = 100\,E[L(\pi_c)],$$

and, using the assumption of independent policies,

$$\text{Var}\,[S] = 100\,\text{Var}\,[L(\pi_c)].$$

To determine $\pi_c$ so that $\Pr\,(S > 0) = 0.05$ by the normal approximation, we want

$$\frac{0 - E[S]}{\sqrt{\text{Var}\,[S]}} = 1.645$$

$$10\left(\frac{-E[L(\pi_c)]}{\sqrt{\text{Var}\,[L(\pi_c)]}}\right) = 1.645$$

$$10\left[\frac{-A_{35}\left(10{,}000 + \dfrac{\pi_c}{d}\right) + \dfrac{\pi_c}{d}}{\left(10{,}000 + \dfrac{\pi_c}{d}\right)\sqrt{^2A_{35} - A_{35}^2}}\right] = 1.645.$$

Thus

$$= \frac{b_t \, d}{\sqrt{\# \, policy}} \left( \qquad \qquad \right)$$

$$\pi_c = 10,000 \, d \left[ \frac{(0.1645) \sqrt{{}^2A_{35} - A_{35}^2} + A_{35}}{1 - \left( A_{35} + 0.1645 \sqrt{{}^2A_{35} - A_{35}^2} \right)} \right]$$

$$= 100.66.$$

The two identities, (5.4.6) and (5.4.11), can be used to derive relationships among discrete premiums. For example, starting with (5.4.6), we have for whole life insurances

$$d \, \ddot{a}_x + A_x = 1$$

$$d + P_x = \frac{1}{\ddot{a}_x}$$

$$P_x = \frac{1}{\ddot{a}_x} - d \qquad \qquad (6.3.6)$$

$$= \frac{1 - d \, \ddot{a}_x}{\ddot{a}_x}$$

$$= \frac{d \, A_x}{1 - A_x}.$$

Starting with (5.4.11) we obtain a similar chain of equalities for $n$-year discrete endowment insurances:

$$d \, \ddot{a}_{x:\overline{n}|} + A_{x:\overline{n}|} = 1$$

$$d + P_{x:\overline{n}|} = \frac{1}{\ddot{a}_{x:\overline{n}|}}$$

$$P_{x:\overline{n}|} = \frac{1}{\ddot{a}_{x:\overline{n}|}} - d \qquad \qquad (6.3.7)$$

$$= \frac{1 - d \, \ddot{a}_{x:\overline{n}|}}{\ddot{a}_{x:\overline{n}|}}$$

$$= \frac{d \, A_{x:\overline{n}|}}{1 - A_{x:\overline{n}|}}.$$

**Example 6.7:** Give verbal interpretations of the following equations from the (6.3.6) set:

$$\frac{1}{\ddot{a}_x} = P_x + d \qquad \qquad (6.3.8)$$

and

$$P_x = \frac{d \, A_x}{1 - A_x}. \qquad \qquad (6.3.9)$$

**Solution:**

We shall use the word equivalent to mean equal in terms of actuarial present value. For (6.3.8), first note that a unit now is equivalent to a life annuity of $\ddot{a}_x^{-1}$ payable at the beginning of each year while $(x)$ survives. A unit now is also equivalent to interest-in-advance of $d$ at the beginning of each year while $(x)$ survives with the repayment of the unit at the end of the year of $(x)$'s death. The repayment of the unit at the end of the year of death is, in turn, equivalent to a life annuity-due of $P_x$ while $(x)$ survives. Therefore, the unit now is equivalent to $P_x + d$ at the beginning of each year during the lifetime of $(x)$. Then $\ddot{a}_x^{-1} = P_x + d$, for each side of the equality, represents the annual payment of a life annuity produced by a unit available now.

For (6.3.9), we consider an insured $(x)$ who borrows the net single premium $A_x$ for the purchase of a single premium unit whole life insurance. The insured agrees to pay interest-in-advance in the amount of $dA_x$ on the loan at the beginning of each year during survival and to repay the $A_x$ from the unit death benefit at the end of the year of death. In essence, the insured is paying a net annual premium of $dA_x$ for an insurance of amount $1 - A_x$. Then for a full unit of insurance, the net annual premium must be $dA_x/(1 - A_x)$. ▼

Similar interpetations exist for corresponding relationships involving endowment insurances as given in the second and fifth equalities in the (6.3.7) set. There is analogy between (6.3.8), the corresponding formula involving endowment insurances,

$$\ddot{a}_{x:\overline{n}|}^{-1} = P_{x:\overline{n}|} + d,$$

and the interest only formula,

$$\ddot{a}_{\overline{n}|}^{-1} = \ddot{s}_{\overline{n}|}^{-1} + d.$$

**Example 6.8:**

Prove and interpret the formula

$$P_{x:\overline{n}|} = {}_nP_x + P_{x:\overline{n}|}^{\;1}(1 - A_{x+n}). \qquad (6.3.10)$$

**Solution:**

The proof is completed using entries from Table 6.2:

$$P_{x:\overline{n}|}\, \ddot{a}_{x:\overline{n}|} = A_{x:\overline{n}|} = A_{x:\overline{n}|}^{1} + A_{x:\overline{n}|}^{\;\;1}$$

$$_nP_x\, \ddot{a}_{x:\overline{n}|} = A_x = A_{x:\overline{n}|}^{1} + A_{x:\overline{n}|}^{\;\;1}\, A_{x+n}.$$

By subtraction,

$$(P_{x:\overline{n}|} - {}_nP_x)\, \ddot{a}_{x:\overline{n}|} = A_{x:\overline{n}|}^{\;\;1}(1 - A_{x+n}),$$

from which (6.3.10) follows.

The interpretation is that both $P_{x:\overline{n}|}$ and $_nP_x$ are payable during the survival of $(x)$ to a maximum of $n$ years. During these years, both insurances provide a death benefit of 1 payable at the end of the year of the death of $(x)$. If $(x)$ survives the $n$ years, $P_{x:\overline{n}|}$ provides a maturity benefit of 1, while $_nP_x$ provides whole life insurance without further premiums, that is, an insurance with an actuarial present value of $A_{x+n}$. Hence, the difference $P_{x:\overline{n}|} - {_nP_x}$ is the level annual premium for a pure endowment of $1 - A_{x+n}$. ▼

In practice, life insurances are payable soon after death rather than at the end of the policy year of death, so there is a need for annual payment, semicontinuous net premiums. Such premiums, following the same order used in Tables 6.1 and 6.2, will be denoted by $P(\bar{A}_x)$, $P(\bar{A}^1_{x:\overline{n}|})$, $P(\bar{A}_{x:\overline{n}|})$, $_hP(\bar{A}_x)$, and $_hP(\bar{A}_{x:\overline{n}|})$. There is no need for a semicontinuous annual premium $n$-year pure endowment since no death benefit is involved. The equivalence principle can be applied to produce formulas like those in Table 6.2, but with the general symbol $A$ replaced by $\bar{A}$. For example,

$$P(\bar{A}_x) = \frac{\bar{A}_x}{\ddot{a}_x}. \qquad (6.3.11)$$

We observe that the notation for this premium is not $\bar{P}_x$, the annual premium payable continuously for a unit whole life insurance benefit payable at the end of the year of death and equal to $A_x/\bar{a}_x$. If a uniform distribution of deaths is assumed over each year of age, we can use the notions of Section 4.4 to write

$$P(\bar{A}_x) = \frac{i}{\delta}\frac{A_x}{\ddot{a}_x} = \frac{i}{\delta}P_x$$

$$P(\bar{A}^1_{x:\overline{n}|}) = \frac{i}{\delta}P^1_{x:\overline{n}|} \qquad (6.3.12)$$

and

$$P(\bar{A}_{x:\overline{n}|}) = \frac{i}{\delta}P^1_{x:\overline{n}|} + P_{x:\frac{1}{n}|}.$$

## 6.4 True mthly Payment Premiums

If premiums are payable $m$ times a policy year, rather than annually, with no adjustment in the death benefit, the resulting premiums are called *true fractional premiums*. Thus $P^{(m)}_x$ denotes the *true net level annual premium,* payable in $m$thly installments, for a unit whole life insurance payable at the end of the year of death. The symbol $P^{(m)}(\bar{A}_x)$ would have the same interpretation except that the insurance is payable at the moment of death. Typically, $m$ is 2, 4 or 12.

The development in this section will stress the payment of insurance benefits at the end of the policy year of death. Table 6.3 specifies the symbols and formulas for true fractional premiums for common life insurances. The premium formulas can be obtained by applying the equivalence principle.

In some applications it is useful to write the $m$thly payment premium as a multiple of the annual premium. This will be illustrated for

**Table 6.3**
**True Fractional**
**Premiums\***

| | Payment of Proceeds | |
|---|---|---|
| **Plan** | **At end of policy year** | **At moment of death** |
| Whole Life Insurance | $P_x^{(m)} = \dfrac{A_x}{\ddot{a}_x^{(m)}}$ | $P^{(m)}(\bar{A}_x) = \dfrac{\bar{A}_x}{\ddot{a}_x^{(m)}}$ |
| $n$-Year Term Insurance | $P^1{}_{x:\overline{n}|}^{(m)} = \dfrac{A^1_{x:\overline{n}|}}{\ddot{a}_{x:\overline{n}|}^{(m)}}$ | $P^{(m)}(\bar{A}^1_{x:\overline{n}|}) = \dfrac{\bar{A}^1_{x:\overline{n}|}}{\ddot{a}_{x:\overline{n}|}^{(m)}}$ |
| $n$-Year Endowment Insurance | $P_{x:\overline{n}|}^{(m)} = \dfrac{A_{x:\overline{n}|}}{\ddot{a}_{x:\overline{n}|}^{(m)}}$ | $P^{(m)}(\bar{A}_{x:\overline{n}|}) = \dfrac{\bar{A}_{x:\overline{n}|}}{\ddot{a}_{x:\overline{n}|}^{(m)}}$ |
| $h$-Payment Years, Whole Life Insurance | $_hP_x^{(m)} = \dfrac{A_x}{\ddot{a}_{x:\overline{h}|}^{(m)}}$ | $_hP^{(m)}(\bar{A}_x) = \dfrac{\bar{A}_x}{\ddot{a}_{x:\overline{h}|}^{(m)}}$ |
| $h$-Payment Years, $n$-Year Endowment Insurance | $_hP_{x:\overline{n}|}^{(m)} = \dfrac{A_{x:\overline{n}|}}{\ddot{a}_{x:\overline{h}|}^{(m)}}$ | $_hP^{(m)}(\bar{A}_{x:\overline{n}|}) = \dfrac{\bar{A}_{x:\overline{n}|}}{\ddot{a}_{x:\overline{h}|}^{(m)}}$ |

\*The actual amount of each fractional premium, payable $m$ times each policy year, during the premium paying period and the survival of $(x)$, is $P^{(m)}/m$. Note that here $h$ refers to the number of payment years, not to the number of payments.

$_hP_{x:\overline{n}|}^{(m)}$, the premium for a rather general insurance. The resulting formula can be modified to produce premium formulas for other common insurances. From the last row of Table 6.3 we have

$$_hP_{x:\overline{n}|}^{(m)} = \frac{A_{x:\overline{n}|}}{\ddot{a}_{x:\overline{h}|}^{(m)}}. \qquad (6.4.1)$$

Since

$$A_{x:\overline{n}|} = {_hP_{x:\overline{n}|}}\,\ddot{a}_{x:\overline{h}|},$$

(6.4.1) can be rearranged as

$$_hP_{x:\overline{n}|}^{(m)} = \frac{_hP_{x:\overline{n}|}\,\ddot{a}_{x:\overline{h}|}}{\ddot{a}_{x:\overline{h}|}^{(m)}}. \qquad (6.4.2)$$

Formula (6.4.2) will be used in the next chapter. It expresses the $m$thly payment premium as equal to the corresponding annual payment premium times a ratio of annuity values. This ratio can be arranged in various ways, each corresponding to a different formula used to express the relationship between $\ddot{a}_{x:\overline{h}|}^{(m)}$ and $\ddot{a}_{x:\overline{h}|}$ (see Exercise 6.11).

**Example 6.9:**

a. Calculate the net level annual premium payable in semiannual installments for a 10,000, 20-year endowment insurance with proceeds paid at the end of the policy year of death (discrete) issued to (50), on the basis of the Illustrative Life Table with interest at the effective annual rate of 6%.

b. Determine the corresponding premium with proceeds paid at the moment of death (semicontinuous).

# Chapter 6
## NET PREMIUMS

For both parts, assume a uniform distribution of deaths in each year of age.

**Solution:**

a. We require $10{,}000\,P^{(2)}_{50:\overline{20}|}$. As preliminary steps we calculate

$$d = 0.056603774,$$

$$i^{(2)} = 0.059126028,$$

$$d^{(2)} = 0.057428275,$$

$$\ddot{a}^{(2)}_{\overline{1}|} = 0.98564294,$$

$$s^{(2)}_{\overline{1}|} = 1.01478151,$$

$$\alpha(2) = s^{(2)}_{\overline{1}|}\ddot{a}^{(2)}_{\overline{1}|} = 1.0002122,$$

$$\beta(2) = \frac{s^{(2)}_{\overline{1}|} - 1}{d^{(2)}} = 0.25739081,$$

and the following premiums:

$$\ddot{a}_{50:\overline{20}|} = 11.291832,$$

$$A^{1}_{50:\overline{20}|} = 0.13036536,$$

$$P^{1}_{50:\overline{20}|} = 0.01154510,$$

$$_{20}E_{50} = 0.23047353,$$

$$A_{50:\overline{20}|} = 0.36083889,$$

$$P_{50:\overline{20}|} = 0.03195574.$$

Then, under the assumption of a uniform distribution of deaths for each year of age, the required premium can be calculated by use of (6.4.1), with $x = 50$, $n = 20$, $h = 20$ and $m = 2$. For this purpose, we calculate

$$\ddot{a}^{(2)}_{50:\overline{20}|} = \alpha(2)\,\ddot{a}_{50:\overline{20}|} - \beta(2)\,(1 - {}_{20}E_{50}) = 11.096159,$$

and then

$$10{,}000\,P^{(2)}_{50:\overline{20}|} = 325.19.$$

b. The corresponding semicontinuous premium can be obtained by multiplying the values in (a) by the ratio

$$\frac{P(\bar{A}_{50:\overline{20}|})}{P_{50:\overline{20}|}} = \frac{\bar{A}_{50:\overline{20}|}}{A_{50:\overline{20}|}}.$$

Under the uniform distribution of deaths assumption this ratio is

$$\frac{(i/\delta)\,P^{1}_{50:\overline{20}|} + P_{50:\overline{20}|}^{\ \ 1}}{P_{50:\overline{20}|}}, \tag{6.4.3}$$

and the result is

$$10{,}000\, P^{(2)}(\bar{A}_{50:\overline{20}|}) = 328.68. \qquad \blacktriangledown$$

## 6.5 Apportionable Premiums

A second type of fractional premium is the *apportionable premium.* Here, at death, a refund is made of a portion of the premium related to the length of time between the time of death and the time of the next scheduled premium payment. In practice this may be on a pro rata basis without interest. In this section we will consider interest, and will view the sequence of $m$thly premiums as an apportionable life annuity-due in the sense of Section 5.9. The symbols used to denote these net level apportionable annual premiums payable $m$thly will be like the symbols for true fractional premiums on the semicontinuous basis. They differ in that the superscript $m$ will be enclosed in braces rather than parentheses, e.g., $P^{\{m\}}(\bar{A}_x)$. In view of the premium refund feature, it is natural to assume that the death benefit is payable at the moment of death.

Again we shall use an $h$-payment years, $n$-year endowment insurance to illustrate the development of formulas for apportionable premiums paid $m$thly. The equivalence principle leads to the formulas

$$_hP^{\{m\}}(\bar{A}_{x:\overline{n}|})\, \ddot{a}^{\{m\}}_{x:\overline{h}|} = \bar{A}_{x:\overline{n}|}$$

and

$$_hP^{\{m\}}(\bar{A}_{x:\overline{n}|}) = \frac{\bar{A}_{x:\overline{n}|}}{\ddot{a}^{\{m\}}_{x:\overline{h}|}}. \qquad (6.5.1)$$

Utilizing part (b) of Example 5.12, we obtain

$$_hP^{\{m\}}(\bar{A}_{x:\overline{n}|}) = \frac{\bar{A}_{x:\overline{n}|}}{(\delta/d^{(m)})\,\bar{a}_{x:\overline{h}|}} = \frac{d^{(m)}}{\delta}\, _h\bar{P}(\bar{A}_{x:\overline{n}|}). \qquad (6.5.2)$$

This implies that the $m$thly installment is

$$\frac{1}{m}\, _hP^{\{m\}}(\bar{A}_{x:\overline{n}|}) = \, _h\bar{P}(\bar{A}_{x:\overline{n}|})\frac{1-v^{1/m}}{\delta} = \, _h\bar{P}(\bar{A}_{x:\overline{n}|})\,\bar{a}_{\overline{1/m}|}, \qquad (6.5.3)$$

and in particular, for $m = 1$,

$$_hP^{\{1\}}(\bar{A}_{x:\overline{n}|}) = \, _h\bar{P}(\bar{A}_{x:\overline{n}|})\,\bar{a}_{\overline{1}|}. \qquad (6.5.4)$$

Formulas (6.5.3) and (6.5.4) demonstrate that these apportionable premiums are equivalent to fully continuous premiums, discounted for interest to the start of each payment period. Similar formulas exist for other types of insurance. For example, by letting $h$ and $n \to \infty$, (6.5.4) becomes

$$P^{\{1\}}(\bar{A}_x) = \bar{P}(\bar{A}_x)\,\bar{a}_{\overline{1}|}. \qquad (6.5.5)$$

The apportionable net premium $P^{\{1\}}(\bar{A}_x)$ and the semicontinuous net premium $P(\bar{A}_x)$ are both payable annually at the beginning of each year while $(x)$ survives. Each insurance provides a unit at the death of $(x)$. The two insurances differ only in respect to the refund provided by $P^{\{1\}}(\bar{A}_x)$. Thus, the difference

$$P^{\{1\}}(\bar{A}_x) - P(\bar{A}_x) \tag{6.5.6}$$

is a net level annual premium paid at the beginning of each year for the refund-of-premium feature. We shall verify this assertion about the expression in (6.5.6) in the following analysis.

From Exercise 5.32, we note that the random variable for the present value of the refund-of-premium feature is

$$\frac{P^{\{1\}}(\bar{A}_x)\, v^T\, \bar{a}_{\overline{K+1-T}|}}{\bar{a}_{\overline{1}|}}$$

where $K$ and $T$ are defined as in Chapter 3. By the equivalence principle, the net single premium for this feature is

$$\bar{A}_x^{PR} = P^{\{1\}}(\bar{A}_x)\, \mathrm{E}\!\left[ v^T \frac{\bar{a}_{\overline{K+1-T}|}}{\bar{a}_{\overline{1}|}} \right].$$

Using (6.5.5) we obtain

$$\bar{A}_x^{PR} = \bar{P}(\bar{A}_x)\, \mathrm{E}\!\left[ \frac{v^T - v^{K+1}}{\delta} \right]$$

$$= \bar{P}(\bar{A}_x)\left( \frac{\bar{A}_x - A_x}{\delta} \right). \tag{6.5.7}$$

The net level annual premium is then

$$P(\bar{A}_x^{PR}) = \frac{\bar{P}(\bar{A}_x)(\bar{A}_x - A_x)}{\delta\, \ddot{a}_x}. \tag{6.5.8}$$

Formula (6.5.7) has the following interpretation: The actuarial present value of the refund feature is the difference between the value of a continuous perpetuity of $\bar{P}(\bar{A}_x)$ per year beginning at the death of $(x)$, and the value of a continuous perpetuity of $\bar{P}(\bar{A}_x)$ payable from the end of the year of death of $(x)$.

We return now to (6.5.6) where, by (6.5.5), we have

$$P^{\{1\}}(\bar{A}_x) - P(\bar{A}_x) = \bar{P}(\bar{A}_x)\frac{d}{\delta} - \frac{\bar{A}_x}{\ddot{a}_x}$$

$$= \bar{P}(\bar{A}_x)\left( \frac{d}{\delta} - \frac{\bar{a}_x}{\ddot{a}_x} \right)$$

$$= \bar{P}(\bar{A}_x)\frac{d\,\ddot{a}_x - \delta\,\bar{a}_x}{\delta\,\ddot{a}_x} \tag{6.5.9}$$

$$= \bar{P}(\bar{A}_x)\frac{\bar{A}_x - A_x}{\delta\,\ddot{a}_x}$$

$$= P(\bar{A}_x^{PR}),$$

as we obtained in (6.5.8). This confirms our assertion about (6.5.6).

This analysis can be extended to $m$thly payment premiums and to other life insurance in addition to whole life. In general,

$$P^{\{m\}}(\bar{A}) - P^{(m)}(\bar{A})$$

is an $m$thly payment premium for the refund feature.

**Example 6.10:**

If the policy of Example 6.9(b) is to have apportionable premiums, what increase occurs in the net annual premium?

**Solution:**

The apportionable annual premium per unit of insurance is given by (6.5.2),

$$P^{\{2\}}(\bar{A}_{50:\overline{20}|}) = \bar{P}(\bar{A}_{50:\overline{20}|}) \frac{d^{(2)}}{\delta} = \frac{\bar{A}_{50:\overline{20}|}}{\bar{a}_{50:\overline{20}|}} \frac{d^{(2)}}{\delta}.$$

Under the assumption of a uniform distribution of deaths in each age interval, this becomes

$$= \frac{(i/\delta)\, A^1_{50:\overline{20}|} + A_{50:\overline{20}|}^{\phantom{1}1}}{\alpha(\infty)\,\ddot{a}_{50:\overline{20}|} - \beta(\infty)\,(1 - {}_{20}E_{50})} \frac{d^{(2)}}{\delta}$$

$$= \frac{(i/\delta)\, P^1_{50:\overline{20}|} + P_{50:\overline{20}|}^{\phantom{1}1}}{\alpha(\infty) - \beta(\infty)\,(P^1_{50:\overline{20}|} + d)} \frac{d^{(2)}}{\delta}.$$

Here $\alpha(\infty) = \bar{s}_{\overline{1}|}\,\bar{a}_{\overline{1}|} = i\,d/\delta^2 = 1.00028$, $\beta(\infty) = (\bar{s}_{\overline{1}|} - 1)/\delta = 0.50985$. Using other values available in Example 6.9 we find

$$10{,}000\, P^{\{2\}}(\bar{A}_{50:\overline{20}|}) = 329.69.$$

Then the increase in annual premium is

$$10{,}000\,[P^{\{2\}}(\bar{A}_{50:\overline{20}|}) - P^{(2)}(\bar{A}_{50:\overline{20}|})] = 1.01,$$

which is the net annual premium payable semiannually for the refund feature. ▼

**6.6
Commutation
Functions**

We have seen that net annual premiums can be expressed in terms of life insurance net single premiums and actuarial present values of annuities. In Chapters 4 and 5 formulas for these premiums and annuities were given in terms of commutation functions. We can now write the net annual premiums in terms of commutation functions. The fully continuous net annual premium for an $h$-payment years, $n$-year endowment insurance for $(x)$ is expressed as

$$_h\bar{P}(\bar{A}_{x:\overline{n}|}) = \frac{\bar{M}_x - \bar{M}_{x+n} + D_{x+n}}{\bar{N}_x - \bar{N}_{x+h}}. \tag{6.6.1}$$

Special cases of (6.6.1) include, for $n = \omega - x$,

$$_h\bar{P}(\bar{A}_x) = \frac{\bar{M}_x}{\bar{N}_x - \bar{N}_{x+h}} \tag{6.6.2}$$

# Chapter 6

## NET PREMIUMS

and, for $h = n = \omega - x$,

$$\bar{P}(\bar{A}_x) = \frac{\bar{M}_x}{\bar{N}_x}.$$ (6.6.3)

For term insurance, we have formulas such as

$$\bar{P}(\bar{A}^1_{x:\overline{n|}}) = \frac{\bar{M}_x - \bar{M}_{x+n}}{\bar{N}_x - \bar{N}_{x+n}}$$ (6.6.4)

and

$$_h\bar{P}(D\bar{A})^1_{x:\overline{n|}} = \frac{n\,\bar{M}_x - \bar{R}_{x+1} + \bar{R}_{x+n+1}}{\bar{N}_x - \bar{N}_{x+h}}.$$ (6.6.5)

For annual payment life insurances with the death benefit payable at the end of the year of death, formulas corresponding to (6.6.1), (6.6.2) and (6.6.4) are

$$_hP_{x:\overline{n|}} = \frac{M_x - M_{x+n} + D_{x+n}}{N_x - N_{x+h}}$$ (6.6.6)

$$_hP_x = \frac{M_x}{N_x - N_{x+h}}$$ (6.6.7)

$$P^1_{x:\overline{n|}} = \frac{M_x - M_{x+n}}{N_x - N_{x+n}}.$$ (6.6.8)

For true $m$thly payment premiums on insurances payable at the end of the year of death, we have formulas such as

$$_hP^{(m)}_{x:\overline{n|}} = \frac{M_x - M_{x+n} + D_{x+n}}{N^{(m)}_x - N^{(m)}_{x+h}}$$ (6.6.9)

[see (5.6.6) and (5.6.7)].

Formulas for apportionable $m$thly premiums can be written as discounted fully continuous premiums as shown in (6.5.3) and (6.5.4).

**Example 6.11:** Express, in terms of commutation functions, the initial net annual premium for a unit of whole life insurance for $(x)$ if after 5 years the net annual premium is double that payable during the first 5 years. A fully discrete model is used.

**Solution:**
Let $P$ be the initial net annual premium. The equation of value, derived from the equivalence principle, used to determine $P$ is

$$P\,(N_x - N_{x+5}) + 2\,P\,N_{x+5} = M_x.$$

Thus

$$P = \frac{M_x}{N_x + N_{x+5}}.$$

▼

## 6.7
## Accumulation
## Type Benefits

The analysis in this section will be in terms of annual premiums for insurances payable at the end of the year of death. An analogous development is possible for fully continuous premiums and, with some adjustment, for semicontinuous premiums. We first seek the net single premium for an $n$-year term insurance on $(x)$ for which the sum insured, in case death occurs in year $k + 1$, is $\ddot{s}_{\overline{k+1}|j}$. The present-value random variable of this benefit, at policy issue, is

$$W = \begin{cases} v^{K+1}\ddot{s}_{\overline{K+1}|j} = \dfrac{1}{d_{(j)}}[v^{K+1}(1+j)^{K+1} - v^{K+1}] & 0 \le K < n \\ \\ 0 & K \ge n \end{cases}$$

where the insurer's present values are computed at interest rate $i$ and $d_{(j)}$ is the discount rate equivalent to interest rate $j$. By the equivalence principle, the net single premium is

$$E[W] = \frac{A'^{1}_{x:\overline{n}|} - A^{1}_{x:\overline{n}|}}{d_{(j)}} \tag{6.7.1}$$

where $A'^{1}_{x:\overline{n}|}$ is calculated at the rate of interest $i' = (i - j)/(1 + j)$.

If $i = j$, then $i' = 0$ and the net single premium is

$$\frac{{}_{n}q_x - A^{1}_{x:\overline{n}|}}{d} = \frac{1 - {}_{n}p_x - A_{x:\overline{n}|} + v^n\,{}_{n}p_x}{d}$$

$$= \ddot{a}_{x:\overline{n}|} - {}_{n}p_x\,\ddot{a}_{\overline{n}|}$$

$$= \ddot{a}_{x:\overline{n}|} - {}_{n}E_x\,\ddot{s}_{\overline{n}|}. \tag{6.7.2}$$

Formula (6.7.2) indicates that, when $j = i$, this special term insurance is equivalent to an $n$-year life annuity-due except for the event that $(x)$ survives the $n$ years. Then the term insurance would provide a benefit of 0 while the life annuity payments, given survival for $n$ years, would have value $\ddot{s}_{\overline{n}|}$ at time $n$.

Now let us consider the situation where $(x)$ has the choice of purchasing an $n$-year unit endowment insurance with an annual premium of $P_{x:\overline{n}|}$ or of establishing a savings fund with deposits of $1/\ddot{s}_{\overline{n}|}$ at the beginning of each of $n$ years and purchasing a special decreasing term insurance. The special insurance will provide, in the event of death in year $k + 1$, the difference,

$$1 - \frac{\ddot{s}_{\overline{k+1}|}}{\ddot{s}_{\overline{n}|}} \qquad k = 0, 1, 2, \ldots, n - 1,$$

between the unit benefit under the endowment insurance and the accumulation in the savings fund. We suppose further that the same interest rate $i$ is applicable in valuing all these transactions. The same benefits are provided by the endowment insurance and by the combination of the special term insurance and the savings fund. Therefore one would anticipate that

# Chapter 6

## NET PREMIUMS

(the net annual premium $P_{x:\overline{n}|}$ for the endowment insurance)

= (the net annual premium for the special term insurance)

+ (the annual savings fund deposit $1/\ddot{s}_{\overline{n}|}$).

To verify this conjecture, we consider the present-value random variable for the special decreasing term insurance,

$$\tilde{W} = \begin{cases} v^{K+1}\left(1 - \dfrac{\ddot{s}_{\overline{K+1}|}}{\ddot{s}_{\overline{n}|}}\right) = v^{K+1} - \dfrac{\ddot{a}_{\overline{K+1}|}}{\ddot{s}_{\overline{n}|}} & 0 \le K < n \\ 0 & K \ge n. \end{cases} \tag{6.7.3}$$

By an application of the equivalence principle the net single premium, denoted by $\tilde{A}^1_{x:\overline{n}|}$, is given by

$$\tilde{A}^1_{x:\overline{n}|} = E[\tilde{W}]$$

$$= A^1_{x:\overline{n}|} - \dfrac{\ddot{a}_{x:\overline{n}|} - {}_n p_x\, \ddot{a}_{\overline{n}|}}{\ddot{s}_{\overline{n}|}}$$

$$= A^1_{x:\overline{n}|} - \dfrac{\ddot{a}_{x:\overline{n}|} - {}_n E_x\, \ddot{s}_{\overline{n}|}}{\ddot{s}_{\overline{n}|}}$$

[see (6.7.2)].

The net annual premium for the special term insurance is therefore

$$\tilde{P}^1_{x:\overline{n}|} = \dfrac{\tilde{A}^1_{x:\overline{n}|}}{\ddot{a}_{x:\overline{n}|}} = P^1_{x:\overline{n}|} - \dfrac{1}{\ddot{s}_{\overline{n}|}} + P_{x:\overline{n}|}^{\phantom{1}1}$$

$$= P_{x:\overline{n}|} - \dfrac{1}{\ddot{s}_{\overline{n}|}}.$$

Then

$$P_{x:\overline{n}|} = \tilde{P}^1_{x:\overline{n}|} + \dfrac{1}{\ddot{s}_{\overline{n}|}}. \tag{6.7.4}$$

We have already seen that

$$P_{x:\overline{n}|} = P^1_{x:\overline{n}|} + P_{x:\overline{n}|}^{\phantom{1}1},$$

and now (6.7.4) provides an alternative decomposition of $P_{x:\overline{n}|}$. The components are the annual premium for the special term insurance and the annual savings fund deposits, $1/\ddot{s}_{\overline{n}|}$, which will accumulate to 1 at the end of $n$ years.

**Example 6.12:** Derive formulas for the net annual premium for a 5000, 20-year term insurance on $(x)$ providing, in case of death within the 20 years, the return of the net annual premiums paid

a. without interest

b. accumulated at the interest rate used in the determination of premiums.

In each case, the return of premiums is in addition to the 5000 sum insured and benefit payments are made at the end of the year of death.

**Solution:**

a. Let $\pi_a$ be the net premium. Then

$$\pi_a \ddot{a}_{x:\overline{20|}} = 5000\, A^1_{x:\overline{20|}} + \pi_a\, (IA)^1_{x:\overline{20|}}$$

and

$$\pi_a = 5000\, \frac{A^1_{x:\overline{20|}}}{\ddot{a}_{x:\overline{20|}} - (IA)^1_{x:\overline{20|}}}.$$

b. Let $\pi_b$ be the net premium. We use (6.7.2) to obtain

$$\pi_b \ddot{a}_{x:\overline{20|}} = 5000\, A^1_{x:\overline{20|}} + \pi_b\, [\ddot{a}_{x:\overline{20|}} - {}_{20}E_x\, \ddot{s}_{\overline{20|}}]$$

$$\pi_b\, {}_{20}E_x\, \ddot{s}_{\overline{20|}} = 5000\, A^1_{x:\overline{20|}}$$

$$\pi_b = 5000\, \frac{A^1_{x:\overline{20|}}}{{}_{20}E_x\, \ddot{s}_{\overline{20|}}}$$

$$= 5000\, \frac{A^1_{x:\overline{20|}}}{{}_{20}p_x\, \ddot{a}_{\overline{20|}}}.$$

In practice, gross annual premiums would be refunded, and the formulas would take this into account. ▼

**Example 6.13:** A deferred annuity issued to $(x)$ for an annual income of 1 commencing at age $x + n$ is to be paid for by net annual premiums during the deferral period. The benefit for death during the premium paying period is the return of net annual premiums accumulated with interest at the rate used for the premium. Assuming the death benefit is paid at the end of the year of death, determine the net annual premium.

**Solution:**
Equating the actuarial present value of the net annual premiums, $\pi$, to the actuarial present value of the benefits, we have

$$\pi \ddot{a}_{x:\overline{n|}} = {}_nE_x\, \ddot{a}_{x+n} + \pi\, (\ddot{a}_{x:\overline{n|}} - {}_nE_x\, \ddot{s}_{\overline{n|}})$$

where the second term on the right-hand side comes from (6.7.2). Solving for $\pi$ yields

$$\pi = \frac{\ddot{a}_{x+n}}{\ddot{s}_{\overline{n|}}}.$$
▼

**6.8
Notes and
References**

Lukacs (1945) provides a survey of the development of the equivalence principle. Premiums derived by an application of the equivalence principle are often called actuarial premiums in the literature of the economics of uncertainty. Fractional premiums of various types are important in practice. Scher (1974) has discussed developments

Chapter 6

# NET PREMIUMS

in this area, namely, the relations among fully continuous, apportionable and semicontinuous premiums. The decomposition of an endowment insurance premium appeared in a paper by Linton (1919).

**Exercises**

*Section 6.1*

6.1. Calculate the expectation and the variance of the present value of the financial loss for the insurance in Example 6.1, when the premium is determined by Principle I.

*Section 6.2*

6.2. If the force of mortality strictly increases with age, show that $\bar{P}(\bar{A}_x) > \mu_x$. [Hint: Show that $\bar{P}(\bar{A}_x)$ is a weighted average of $\mu_{x+t}$, $t > 0$.]

6.3. Following Example 6.2, derive a general expression for

$$\frac{{}^2\bar{A}_x - \bar{A}_x^2}{(\delta \bar{a}_x)^2}$$

where $\mu_{x+t} = \mu$ and $\delta$ is the force of interest for $t > 0$.

6.4. If $\delta = 0$, show that

$$\bar{P}(\bar{A}_x) = \frac{1}{\overset{\circ}{e}_x}.$$

6.5. Prove that the variance of the loss associated with a net single premium whole life insurance is less than the variance of the loss associated with an annual premium whole life insurance. Assume immediate payment of claims on death and continuous payment of net annual premiums.

6.6. Show that

$$\left(1 + \frac{d\bar{a}_x}{dx}\right)\bar{P}(\bar{A}_x) - \frac{d\bar{A}_x}{dx} = \mu_x.$$

*Section 6.3*

6.7. On the basis of the Illustrative Life Table and an interest rate of 6%, calculate values for the annual premiums in the following table. Note any patterns of inequalities that appear in the matrix of results.

| Fully Continuous | Semicontinuous | Fully Discrete |
|---|---|---|
| $\bar{P}(\bar{A}_{35:\overline{10}})$ | $P(\bar{A}_{35:\overline{10}})$ | $P_{35:\overline{10}}$ |
| $\bar{P}(\bar{A}_{35:\overline{30}})$ | $P(\bar{A}_{35:\overline{30}})$ | $P_{35:\overline{30}}$ |
| $\bar{P}(\bar{A}_{35:\overline{60}})$ | $P(\bar{A}_{35:\overline{60}})$ | $P_{35:\overline{60}}$ |
| $\bar{P}(\bar{A}_{35})$ | $P(\bar{A}_{35})$ | $P_{35}$ |
| $\bar{P}(\bar{A}^1_{35:\overline{30}})$ | $P(\bar{A}^1_{35:\overline{30}})$ | $P^1_{35:\overline{30}}$ |
| $\bar{P}(\bar{A}^1_{35:\overline{10}})$ | $P(\bar{A}^1_{35:\overline{10}})$ | $P^1_{35:\overline{10}}$ |

6.8. Show that

$$_{20}P^1_{x:\overline{30}} - P^1_{x:\overline{20}} = {}_{20}P\left({}_{20|10}A_x\right).$$

6.9. Generalize Example 6.4 where
$$_{k|}q_x = (1 - r)\, r^k \qquad k = 0, 1, 2, \ldots.$$
That is, derive expressions in terms of $r$ and $i$ for $A_x$, $\ddot{a}_x$, $P_x$ and $(^2A_x - A_x^2)/(d\,\ddot{a}_x)^2$.

*Section 6.4*

6.10. Using the information given in Example 6.9, calculate the value $P^{(2)}_{50}$.

6.11. Using various formulas for $\ddot{a}^{(m)}_{x:\overline{n}|}$, show that the ratio

$$\frac{\ddot{a}_{x:\overline{h}|}}{\ddot{a}^{(m)}_{x:\overline{h}|}}$$

in (6.4.2) can be expressed as the reciprocal of

a. $\ddot{a}^{(m)}_{\overline{1}|} - \beta(m)\, P^1_{x:\overline{h}|}$

b. $\alpha(m) - \beta(m)\, (P^1_{x:\overline{h}|} + d)$

c. $1 - \dfrac{m-1}{2m}\, (P^1_{x:\overline{h}|} + d)$.

6.12. Refer to Example 6.9(b) and directly calculate

$$P^{(2)}(\bar{A}_{50:\overline{20}|}) = \frac{\bar{A}_{50:\overline{20}|}}{\ddot{a}^{(2)}_{50:\overline{20}|}}$$

using the Illustrative Life Table for the net single endowment premium in the numerator and for the life annuity value in the denominator.

6.13. If

$$\frac{P^{1\ (12)}_{x:\overline{20}|}}{P^1_{x:\overline{20}|}} = 1.032$$

and $P_{x:\overline{20}|} = 0.040$, what is the value of $P^{(12)}_{x:\overline{20}|}$?

*Section 6.5*

6.14. Arrange in order of magnitude. Indicate your reasoning.
$$P^{(2)}(\bar{A}_{40:\overline{25}|}),\ \bar{P}(\bar{A}_{40:\overline{25}|}),\ P^{\{4\}}(\bar{A}_{40:\overline{25}|}),\ P(\bar{A}_{40:\overline{25}|}),\ \dot{P}^{\{12\}}(\bar{A}_{40:\overline{25}|})$$

6.15. Given that

$$\frac{d}{d^{(12)}} = \frac{99}{100},$$

evaluate

$$\frac{P^{\{12\}}(\bar{A}_x)}{P^{\{1\}}(\bar{A}_x)}.$$

6.16. If $\bar{P}(\bar{A}_x) = 0.03$, and if interest is at the effective annual rate of 5%, calculate the semiannual net premium for a 50,000 whole life insurance on $(x)$ where premiums are apportionable.

6.17. Show that

$$P^{\{m\}}(\bar{A}_{x:\overline{n}|}) - P^{(m)}(\bar{A}_{x:\overline{n}|}) = \bar{P}(\bar{A}_{x:\overline{n}|})\left[\frac{\bar{A}_{x:\overline{n}|} - A^{(m)}_{x:\overline{n}|}}{\delta\ddot{a}^{(m)}_{x:\overline{n}|}}\right].$$

*Section 6.6*

6.18. Give formulas, in terms of commutation functions, for

   a. $_{20}P^{(12)}(\bar{A}_{x:\overline{30}|})$   b. $_{20}\bar{P}(\bar{A}_{x:\overline{30}|})$

   c. $_{20}P^{\{4\}}(\bar{A}_{x:\overline{30}|})$   d. $_{20}P(_{40|}\ddot{a}_{25})$.

6.19. Using appropriate commutation functions, write an equation in the form of (6.6.1) for the net annual apportionable premium, payable annually for 20 years, on a decreasing term insurance for a life aged 30. The sum insured is initially 200,000, decreasing by 5000 at the end of each year until age 70 when the insurance terminates.

*Section 6.7*

6.20. Express

$$1 - \frac{\ddot{s}_{\overline{20}|}}{\ddot{s}_{45:\overline{20}|}}$$

as an annual premium. Interpret your result.

6.21. On the basis of the Illustrative Life Table and an interest rate of 6%, calculate the components of the two decompositions

   a. $1000\,P_{50:\overline{20}|} = 1000\,(P^1_{50:\overline{20}|} + P_{50:\overline{20}|}^{\phantom{1}})$

   b. $1000\,P_{50:\overline{20}|} = 1000\left(\bar{P}^1_{50:\overline{20}|} + \dfrac{1}{\ddot{s}_{\overline{20}|}}\right).$

6.22. Consider the continuous random variable analogue of (6.7.3),

$$\tilde{W} = \begin{cases} v^T\left(1 - \dfrac{\bar{s}_{\overline{T}|}}{\bar{s}_{\overline{n}|}}\right) & 0 \le T < n \\ 0 & T \ge n. \end{cases}$$

The loss,

$$L = \tilde{W} - \tilde{\bar{A}}^1_{x:\overline{n}|},$$

can be used with the equivalence principle to determine $\tilde{\bar{A}}^1_{x:\overline{n}|}$, the net single premium for this special policy. Show that

   a. $\tilde{\bar{A}}^1_{x:\overline{n}|} = \bar{A}^1_{x:\overline{n}|} - \dfrac{\bar{a}_{x:\overline{n}|} - {}_np_x\,\bar{a}_{\overline{n}|}}{\bar{s}_{\overline{n}|}}$

   b. $\mathrm{E}[\tilde{W}^2] = \dfrac{(1+i)^{2n}\,{}^2\bar{A}^1_{x:\overline{n}|} - 2(1+i)^n\,\bar{A}^1_{x:\overline{n}|} + (1 - {}_np_x)}{[(1+i)^n - 1]^2}.$

*Miscellaneous*

6.23. Express

$$A_{40} P_{40:\overline{25}|} + (1 - A_{40}) P_{40}$$

as a net annual premium. Interpret your result.

6.24. a. Show that

$$\frac{1}{\ddot{a}_{65:\overline{10}|}} - \frac{1}{\ddot{s}_{65:\overline{10}|}} = P^1_{65:\overline{10}|} + d.$$

b. What is the corresponding formula for

$$\frac{1}{\ddot{a}^{(12)}_{65:\overline{10}|}} - \frac{1}{\ddot{s}^{(12)}_{65:\overline{10}|}}?$$

c. Show that the amount of annual income provided by a single net premium of 100,000 where
   - the income is payable at the beginning of each month while (65) survives during the next 10 years, and
   - the single premium is returned at the end of 10 years if (65) reaches age 75,
   
   is given by

$$100,000 \left( \frac{1}{\ddot{a}^{(12)}_{65:\overline{10}|}} - \frac{1}{\ddot{s}^{(12)}_{65:\overline{10}|}} \right) = 100,000\,(\beta)$$

   where $(\beta)$ denotes the answer to part (b) of this exercise.

d. In terms of commutation functions, show that the annual income of part (c) can be expressed as

$$100,000 \frac{D_{65} - D_{75}}{N^{(12)}_{65} - N^{(12)}_{75}}.$$

6.25. An insurance issued to (35) with level premiums to age 65 provides
   - 100,000 in case the insured survives to age 65, and
   - the return of the gross annual premiums with interest at the valuation rate to the end of the year of death if the insured dies before age 65.
   
   If the gross annual premium $G$ is $1.1\,\pi$ where $\pi$ is the net annual premium, write an expression for $\pi$.

6.26. If $_{15}P_{45} = 0.038$, $P_{45:\overline{15}|} = 0.056$ and $A_{60} = 0.625$, calculate $P^1_{45:\overline{15}|}$.

6.27. A 20-payment life policy is designed to return, in the event of death, 10,000 plus all gross premiums without interest. The return-of-premium feature applies during both the premium paying period and after. Premiums are annual and death claims are paid at the end of the year of death. Calculate, in terms of commutation functions, for a policy issued to $(x)$, the gross annual premium if it is to be 110% of the net premium plus 25.

6.28. Calculate, in terms of commutation functions, the initial net annual premium for a whole life insurance issued to (25), subject to the following provisions:
  • The face amount is to be 1 for the first 10 years and 2 thereafter.
  • Each premium during the first 10 years is 1/2 of each premium payable thereafter.
  • Premiums are payable annually to age 65.
  • Claims are paid at the end of the year of death.

6.29. Rewrite, in terms of commutation functions, the premiums in Table 6.3 with proceeds payable at moment of death.

6.30. Let $L_1$ be the insurer's loss on a unit of whole life insurance, issued to $(x)$ on a fully continuous net premium basis. Let $L_2$ be the loss to $(x)$ on a continuous life annuity purchased for a net single premium of 1. Show that $L_1 \equiv L_2$, and give a verbal explanation.

6.31. An ordinary life contract for a unit amount on a fully discrete basis is issued to a person aged $x$ with an annual premium of 0.048. Assume $d = 0.06$, $A_x = 0.4$ and $^2A_x = 0.2$. Let $L$ be the insurer's loss function at issue of this policy.
  a. Calculate $E[L]$.
  b. Calculate $\text{Var}[L]$.
  c. Now consider a portfolio of 100 policies of this type with face amounts given below.

| Face amount | Number of policies |
|-------------|--------------------|
| 1 | 80 |
| 4 | 20 |

Assume the losses are independent and use a normal approximation to calculate the probability that the present value of gains for the portfolio will exceed 20.

# Chapter 7
## NET PREMIUM RESERVES

**7.1 Introduction**

In Chapter 6 we introduced the equivalence principle. As used in our discussions there, an equivalence relation is established on the date a long-term contract is entered into by two parties who agree to exchange sets of payments. For example, under an amortized loan, a borrower may pay a series of equal monthly payments equivalent to the single payment by a lender at the date of the loan. An insured may pay a series of net premiums to an insurer equivalent, at the date of policy issue, to the sum insured upon the death of the insured, or on survival of the insured to the maturity date. An individual may purchase a deferred life annuity by means of level premiums payable to an annuity organization equivalent, at the date of contract agreement, to monthly payments by the annuity organization to the individual when that person survives beyond a specified age. Equivalence in the loan example is in terms of present value while in the insurance and annuity examples it is an equivalence between two actuarial present values.

After a period of time, however, there will no longer be an equivalence between the future financial obligations of the two parties. A borrower may have payments remaining to be made while the lender has already performed his responsibilities. In other settings both parties may still have obligations. The insured may still be required to pay further net premiums while the insurer has the duty to pay the face amount on maturity or the death of the insured. In our deferred annuity example above, the individual may have completed his payments while the annuity organization still has monthly remunerations to make.

In this chapter we will apply the equivalence principle to payments in time periods beyond the date of initiation. For this, a balancing item will be required, and this item will be a liability for one of the parties and an asset for the other. In the loan case, the balancing item is the outstanding principal, an asset for the lender and a liability for the borrower. In the other two cases, the balancing item will be called the ***net premium reserve.*** This is a liability that should be recognized in any financial statement of an insurer or annuity organization as the case may be. It is also an asset for the insured or individual purchasing the annuity.

A number of sections here will parallel sections of Chapter 6 on net premiums. Also, we will assume that the mortality and interest rates adopted at policy issue for the determination of net premiums will continue to be appropriate and will be used for the determination of premium reserves.

**Example 7.1:**

Assume that an insured is still alive 1 year after entering into the insurance agreement of Example 6.1. Evaluate the present values of future financial obligations at that time. Use the annual premium, 0.3667, determined in Example 6.1.

**Solution:**

The p.f. for $K$, the curtate-future-lifetime, was given as equal to $1/4$ for $k = 0,1,2,3$. The conditional p.f. for $K$, given that $K \geq 1$, is

$$\Pr[K = k | K \geq 1] = \frac{\Pr(K = k)}{\Pr(K \geq 1)} = \frac{1/4}{3/4} = \frac{1}{3} \qquad k = 1,2,3.$$

The required present values are indicated below.

| | | Present Value (1 year after policy issue, $i = 0.06$) of Future Obligations of | | |
|---|---|---|---|---|
| Outcome $k$ | Conditional Probability | Insurer | Insured | Insurer's Prospective Loss |
| 1 | 1/3 | $v = 0.9434$ | $P = 0.3667$ | 0.5767 |
| 2 | 1/3 | $v^2 = 0.8900$ | $P\ddot{a}_{\overline{2}|} = 0.7126$ | 0.1774 |
| 3 | 1/3 | $v^3 = 0.8396$ | $P\ddot{a}_{\overline{3}|} = 1.0390$ | $-0.1994$ |

The actuarial present value of the insurer's obligations is

$$\frac{1}{3}(0.9434 + 0.8900 + 0.8396) = 0.8910.$$

Similarly, the actuarial present value of the insured's obligations is 0.7061. The balancing item,

$$0.8910 - 0.7061 = 0.1849,$$

is the net premium reserve 1 year after policy issue (time 1), immediately before the second premium is paid.

Alternatively, we can examine the expected value of the prospective loss. For each value of $K$, the prospective loss is the difference between the present values of the obligations of the insurer and the insured. The expected value of the prospective loss is

$$\frac{1}{3}(0.5767 + 0.1774 - 0.1994) = 0.1849. \qquad \blacktriangledown$$

## 7.2 Fully Continuous Net Premium Reserves

We now develop the reserve ideas related to the net premiums discussed in Section 6.2.

Let us consider reserves for a unit whole life insurance issued to $(x)$ on a fully continuous basis with an annual premium of $\bar{P}(\bar{A}_x)$. The corresponding reserve for an insured surviving at the end of $t$ years is denoted by $_t\bar{V}(\bar{A}_x)$. To determine $_t\bar{V}(\bar{A}_x)$ under the equivalence principle, we introduce the random variable $U$, the time-until-death of $(x + t)$, with p.d.f. given by

$$_u p_{x+t} \; \mu_{x+t+u} \qquad u \geq 0.$$

We then define the ***prospective loss*** at time $t$ as

$$_tL = v^U - \bar{P}(\bar{A}_x)\,\bar{a}_{\overline{U}|}. \tag{7.2.1}$$

The net premium reserve is defined as the expectation of the prospective loss. Thus we have

$$_t\bar{V}(\bar{A}_x) = \mathrm{E}[v^U] - \bar{P}(\bar{A}_x)\,\mathrm{E}[\bar{a}_{\overline{U}|}]$$

$$= \bar{A}_{x+t} - \bar{P}(\bar{A}_x)\,\bar{a}_{x+t}. \tag{7.2.2}$$

This formula states that

$$\begin{aligned}
&\text{(the reserve)}\\[4pt]
=\ &\text{(the actuarial present value for the}\\
&\quad\text{whole life insurance from age } x + t)\\[4pt]
-\ &\text{(the actuarial present value of future}\\
&\quad\text{net premiums payable at an annual rate of } \bar{P}(\bar{A}_x)).
\end{aligned}$$

The formulations of $\bar{P}(\bar{A}_x)$ and $_t\bar{V}(\bar{A}_x)$ are related. When $t = 0$, formula (7.2.2) yields $_0V(A_x) = 0$. This is a consequence of applying the equivalence principle at the time net premiums are determined. Note that the distribution of $U$ is the conditional distribution of $T - t$, given that $T > t$. That is, the d.f. of $U$ is

$$1 - \frac{_{t+u}p_x}{_tp_x} = {_uq_{x+t}},$$

and its p.d.f. is

$$\frac{_{t+u}p_x\,\mu_{x+t+u}}{_tp_x} = {_up_{x+t}}\,\mu_{x+t+u}.$$

By steps analogous to those used to obtain (6.2.6), we determine

$$_tL = v^U\left[1 + \frac{\bar{P}(\bar{A}_x)}{\delta}\right] - \frac{\bar{P}(\bar{A}_x)}{\delta}, \tag{7.2.3}$$

thus

$$\mathrm{Var}[_tL] = \left[1 + \frac{\bar{P}(\bar{A}_x)}{\delta}\right]^2 \mathrm{Var}[v^U]$$

$$= \left[1 + \frac{\bar{P}(\bar{A}_x)}{\delta}\right]^2 ({}^2\bar{A}_{x+t} - \bar{A}_{x+t}^2). \tag{7.2.4}$$

Note the relation to (6.2.6).

**Example 7.2:**  Follow up Example 6.2 by calculating $_t\bar{V}(\bar{A}_x)$ and $\mathrm{Var}[_tL]$.

**Solution:**
Since $\bar{A}_x$, $\bar{a}_x$ and $\bar{P}(\bar{A}_x)$ are independent of age $x$, (7.2.2) becomes

$$_t\bar{V}(\bar{A}_x) = \bar{A}_x - \bar{P}(\bar{A}_x)\,\bar{a}_x = 0 \quad t \geq 0.$$

In this case, future premiums are always equivalent to future benefits and no reserve is needed to balance.

Also, in this case, (7.2.4) reduces to

$$\text{Var}\left[{}_tL\right] = \left[1 + \frac{\bar{P}(\bar{A}_x)}{\delta}\right]^2 ({}^2\bar{A}_x - \bar{A}_x^2) = \text{Var}\left[L\right] = 0.25,$$

as in Example 6.2. Here the variance depends on neither the age $x$ nor the duration $t$.  ▼

**Example 7.3:**

If mortality follows the de Moivre law with $l_x = 100 - x$ and the interest rate is 6%, calculate

a. $\bar{P}(\bar{A}_{35})$

b. ${}_t\bar{V}(\bar{A}_{35})$ and $\text{Var}\left[{}_tL\right]$ for $t = 0,10,20,\ldots,60$.

**Solution:**
a. From $l_x = 100 - x$, we obtain ${}_tp_{35} = 1 - t/65$ and ${}_tp_{35}\,\mu_{35+t} = 1/65$ for $0 \le t < 65$. It follows that

$$\bar{A}_{35} = \int_0^{65} v^t \frac{1}{65} dt = \frac{\bar{a}_{\overline{65}|}}{65} = 0.258047$$

and

$$\bar{a}_{35} = \frac{1 - \bar{A}_{35}}{\log 1.06} = 12.7333.$$

Then

$$\bar{P}(\bar{A}_{35}) = \frac{0.258047}{12.7333} = 0.020266.$$

b. At age $35 + t$, we have $\bar{A}_{35+t} = \bar{a}_{\overline{65-t}|}/(65 - t)$ and

$${}_t\bar{V}(\bar{A}_{35}) = \bar{A}_{35+t} - 0.020266\frac{1 - \bar{A}_{35+t}}{\log 1.06}.$$

Further,

$${}^2\bar{A}_{35+t} = \int_0^{65-t} v^{2u} \frac{1}{65-t} du = \frac{{}^2\bar{a}_{\overline{65-t}|}}{65-t}$$

and, from (7.2.4),

$$\text{Var}\left[{}_tL\right] = \left(1 + \frac{0.020266}{\log 1.06}\right)^2 ({}^2\bar{A}_{35+t} - \bar{A}_{35+t}^2).$$

Applying these formulas, we obtain the following results.

| $t$ | $_t\bar{V}(\bar{A}_{35})$ | $\mathrm{Var}[_tL]$ |
|---|---|---|
| 0 | 0.0000 | 0.1187 |
| 10 | 0.0557 | 0.1201 |
| 20 | 0.1289 | 0.1174 |
| 30 | 0.2271 | 0.1073 |
| 40 | 0.3619 | 0.0861 |
| 50 | 0.5508 | 0.0508 |
| 60 | 0.8214 | 0.0097 |

▼

By analogy to level benefit and net premiums, we can define the prospective loss for a general, fully continuous insurance as

$$_tL = b_{t+u}\, v^u - \int_0^u \pi_{t+s}\, v^s\, ds$$

where $b_{t+u}$ is the benefit amount payable if death occurs at time $t + U$ and $\pi_{t+s}$ is the annual rate of payment at time $t + s$ of the fully continuous net premium. The net premium reserve for this general case, denoted by $_t\bar{V}$, is then

$$_t\bar{V} = \mathrm{E}[_tL] = \int_0^\infty \left( b_{t+u}\, v^u - \int_0^u \pi_{t+s}\, v^s\, ds \right) {_up_{x+t}}\, \mu_{x+t+u}\, du$$

$$= \int_0^\infty b_{t+u}\, v^u\, {_up_{x+t}}\, \mu_{x+t+u}\, du - \int_0^\infty \pi_{t+s}\, v^s\, {_sp_{x+t}}\, ds \quad (7.2.6)$$

where the second integral in (7.2.6) is obtained by applying Theorem 3.1 or, alternatively, by reversing the order of integration. In other words, $_t\bar{V}$ can be expressed as the actuarial present value of future benefits less the actuarial present value of future net premiums.

Corresponding to Table 6.1, we present Table 7.1 for reserves. We have not tabulated details of the prospective loss, $_tL$, nor are explicit formulas for $\mathrm{Var}[_tL]$, corresponding to the several reserves, displayed.

## 7.3 Other Formulas for Fully Continuous Reserves

So far we have developed only one method to write formulas for fully continuous reserves, namely, the **prospective method** stating that the reserve is the difference between the actuarial present values of future benefits and future net premiums. From the prospective method, we can easily develop three other general formulas for policies with level premium rates. We illustrate these for the case of $n$-year endowment insurances.

The **premium-difference formula** for $_t\bar{V}(\bar{A}_{x:\overline{n}|})$ is obtained by factoring $\bar{a}_{x+t:\overline{n-t}|}$ out of the Table 7.1 formula for $_t\bar{V}(\bar{A}_{x:\overline{n}|})$:

$$_t\bar{V}(\bar{A}_{x:\overline{n}|}) = \left[ \frac{\bar{A}_{x+t:\overline{n-t}|}}{\bar{a}_{x+t:\overline{n-t}|}} - \bar{P}(\bar{A}_{x:\overline{n}|}) \right] \bar{a}_{x+t:\overline{n-t}|} \quad (7.3.1)$$

$$= [\bar{P}(\bar{A}_{x+t:\overline{n-t}|}) - \bar{P}(\bar{A}_{x:\overline{n}|})] \bar{a}_{x+t:\overline{n-t}|}.$$

# NET PREMIUM RESERVES

**Table 7.1**
**Fully Continuous Net**
**Premium Reserves**
**Age-at-Issue $x$;**
**Duration $t$;**
**Unit Amount**

| Plan | Reserve Notation | Prospective Formula | |
|---|---|---|---|
| Whole Life Insurance | $_t\bar{V}(\bar{A}_x)$ | $\bar{A}_{x+t} - \bar{P}(\bar{A}_x)\,\bar{a}_{x+t}$ | |
| $n$-Year Term Insurance | $_t\bar{V}(\bar{A}^1_{x:\overline{n}})$ | $\bar{A}^1_{x+t:\overline{n-t}} - \bar{P}(\bar{A}^1_{x:\overline{n}})\,\bar{a}_{x+t:\overline{n-t}}$ <br> $0$ | $t < n$ <br> $t = n$ |
| $n$-Year Endowment Insurance | $_t\bar{V}(\bar{A}_{x:\overline{n}})$ | $\bar{A}_{x+t:\overline{n-t}} - \bar{P}(\bar{A}_{x:\overline{n}})\,\bar{a}_{x+t:\overline{n-t}}$ <br> $1$ | $t < n$ <br> $t = n$ |
| $h$-Payment Years Whole Life Insurance | $_t^h\bar{V}(\bar{A}_x)$ | $\bar{A}_{x+t} - {_h}\bar{P}(\bar{A}_x)\,\bar{a}_{x+t:\overline{h-t}}$ <br> $\bar{A}_{x+t}$ | $t < h$ <br> $t \geq h$ |
| $h$-Payment Years $n$-Year Endowment Insurance | $_t^h\bar{V}(\bar{A}_{x:\overline{n}})$ | $\bar{A}_{x+t:\overline{n-t}} - {_h}\bar{P}(\bar{A}_{x:\overline{n}})\,\bar{a}_{x+t:\overline{h-t}}$ <br> $\bar{A}_{x+t:\overline{n-t}}$ <br> $1$ | $t < h$ <br> $h \leq t < n$ <br> $t = n$ |
| $n$-Year Pure Endowment | $_t\bar{V}(A_{x:\overline{n}}^{\ 1})$ | $A_{x+t:\overline{n-t}}^{\ 1} - \bar{P}(A_{x:\overline{n}}^{\ 1})\,\bar{a}_{x+t:\overline{n-t}}$ <br> $1$ | $t < n$ <br> $t = n$ |
| $n$-Year Deferred Annuity | $_t\bar{V}(_{n|}\bar{a}_x)$ | $A_{x+t:\overline{n-t}}^{\ 1}\,\bar{a}_{x+n} - \bar{P}(_{n|}\bar{a}_x)\,\bar{a}_{x+t:\overline{n-t}}$ <br> $\bar{a}_{x+t}$ | $t < n$ <br> $t \geq n$ |

This exhibits the reserve as the actuarial present value of a premium difference payable over the remaining premium-payment term. The premium difference is obtained by subtracting the original net annual premium from the similar premium on an insurance issued at the attained age $x + t$ for the remaining benefits.

A second formula is obtained by factoring the actuarial present value of future benefits out of the prospective formula. Thus, for $_t\bar{V}(\bar{A}_{x:\overline{n}})$ we have

$$
_t\bar{V}(\bar{A}_{x:\overline{n}}) = \left[ 1 - \bar{P}(\bar{A}_{x:\overline{n}}) \frac{\bar{a}_{x+t:\overline{n-t}}}{\bar{A}_{x+t:\overline{n-t}}} \right] \bar{A}_{x+t:\overline{n-t}}
$$

$$
= \left[ 1 - \frac{\bar{P}(\bar{A}_{x:\overline{n}})}{\bar{P}(\bar{A}_{x+t:\overline{n-t}})} \right] \bar{A}_{x+t:\overline{n-t}}.
$$

(7.3.2)

This exhibits the reserve as the actuarial present value of a portion of the remaining future benefits, that portion which is not funded by the net premiums still to be collected. Note that $\bar{P}(\bar{A}_{x+t:\overline{n-t}})$ is the net premium required if the future benefits were to be funded from the future net premiums, but $\bar{P}(\bar{A}_{x:\overline{n}})$ is the net premium actually payable. Thus, $\bar{P}(\bar{A}_{x:\overline{n}})/\bar{P}(\bar{A}_{x+t:\overline{n-t}})$ is the portion of future benefits funded by future premiums. This is called a ***paid-up insurance formula***, named from the paid-up insurance nonforfeiture benefit to be discussed in Chapter 15. Formulas analogous to (7.3.1) and (7.3.2) exist for a wide variety of insurance reserves.

A third expression is the *retrospective formula.* We develop this from a more general relationship. We have, from Exercise 4.12 and from (5.3.22), (5.3.24), for $t < n - s$,

$$\bar{A}_{x+s:\overline{n-s}|} = \bar{A}^{\;1}_{x+s:\bar{t}|} + {}_tE_{x+s}\,\bar{A}_{x+s+t:\overline{n-s-t}|},$$

$$\bar{a}_{x+s:\overline{n-s}|} = \bar{a}_{x+s:\bar{t}|} + {}_tE_{x+s}\,\bar{a}_{x+s+t:\overline{n-s-t}|}.$$

Substituting these expressions into the prospective formula for ${}_s\bar{V}(\bar{A}_{x:\overline{m}|})$ we obtain

$${}_s\bar{V}(\bar{A}_{x:\overline{m}|}) = \bar{A}^{\;1}_{x+s:\bar{t}|} - \bar{P}(\bar{A}_{x:\overline{m}|})\,\bar{a}_{x+s:\bar{t}|}$$

$$+ {}_tE_{x+s}\,[\bar{A}_{x+s+t:\overline{n-s-t}|} - \bar{P}(\bar{A}_{x:\overline{m}|})\,\bar{a}_{x+s+t:\overline{n-s-t}|}] \quad (7.3.3)$$

$$= \bar{A}^{\;1}_{x+s:\bar{t}|} + {}_tE_{x+s}\;{}_{s+t}\bar{V}(\bar{A}_{x:\overline{m}|}) - \bar{P}(\bar{A}_{x:\overline{m}|})\,\bar{a}_{x+s:\bar{t}|}.$$

Thus the reserves at the beginning and end of an interval are connected by the following argument:

(the reserve at the beginning)

$=$ (the actuarial present value of benefits payable during the interval)

$+$ (the actuarial present value of a pure endowment for the amount of reserve at the end of the interval)

$-$ (the actuarial present value of net premiums payable during the interval).

The rearranged symbolic form,

$${}_s\bar{V}(\bar{A}_{x:\overline{m}|}) + \bar{P}(\bar{A}_{x:\overline{m}|})\,\bar{a}_{x+s:\bar{t}|} = \bar{A}^{\;1}_{x+s:\bar{t}|} + {}_tE_{x+s}\;{}_{s+t}\bar{V}(\bar{A}_{x:\overline{m}|}), \quad (7.3.4)$$

shows that the actuarial present values of the insurer's resources and requirements are equal.

The retrospective formula is obtained from (7.3.4) by setting $s = 0$, noting that ${}_0\bar{V}(\bar{A}_{x:\overline{m}|}) = 0$ by the equivalence principle, and solving for ${}_t\bar{V}(\bar{A}_{x:\overline{m}|})$. Thus,

$${}_t\bar{V}(\bar{A}_{x:\overline{m}|}) = \frac{1}{{}_tE_x}\,[\bar{P}(\bar{A}_{x:\overline{m}|})\,\bar{a}_{x:\bar{t}|} - \bar{A}^{\;1}_{x:\bar{t}|}].$$

Further, $\bar{s}_{x:\bar{t}|} = \bar{a}_{x:\bar{t}|}/{}_tE_x$ so that the formula reduces to

$${}_t\bar{V}(\bar{A}_{x:\overline{m}|}) = \bar{P}(\bar{A}_{x:\overline{m}|})\,\bar{s}_{x:\bar{t}|} - {}_t\bar{k}_x. \quad (7.3.5)$$

Here

$${}_t\bar{k}_x = \frac{\bar{A}^{\;1}_{x:\bar{t}|}}{{}_tE_x} \quad (7.3.6)$$

is called the ***accumulated cost of insurance.*** One notes that

$$_t\bar{k}_x = \int_0^t \frac{v^s \, _sp_x \, \mu_{x+s}}{v^t \, _tp_x} \, ds$$

$$= \frac{\int_0^t (1 + i)^{t-s} \, l_{x+s} \, \mu_{x+s} \, ds}{l_{x+t}}.$$

(7.3.7)

This can be interpreted as the assessment against each of the $l_{x+t}$ survivors to provide for the accumulated value of the death claims in the survivorship group between ages $x$ and $x + t$. Thus, the reserve can be viewed as the difference between the net premiums, accumulated with interest and shared among only the survivors at age $x + t$, and the accumulated cost of insurance.

The question may arise as to whether a prospective or a retrospective formula should be used for numerical calculations. Two guidelines are the following:

- The prospective formula is more convenient for durations beyond the premium-paying period. In such cases, the reserve simplifies to the actuarial present value, at the attained age, of future benefits. For example, for $t \geq h$, $_t^h\bar{V}(\bar{A}_x) = \bar{A}_{x+t}$.
- The retrospective formula is more convenient in a deferred period during which no benefits have been provided. The reserve in this case simplifies to the actuarial accumulated value of past net premiums. For example, for $t < n$, $_t\bar{V}(_{n|}\ddot{a}_x^{(12)}) = \bar{P}(_{n|}\ddot{a}_x^{(12)}) \, \bar{s}_{x:\bar{t}|}$.

We conclude this section with some special formulas for whole life insurance reserves. Analogous formulas hold for $n$-year endowment insurance reserves, but do not hold for insurance reserves in general. The first of these follows from formula (6.2.9), $\bar{P}(\bar{A}_x) = (1/\bar{a}_x) - \delta$. Thus,

$$_t\bar{V}(\bar{A}_x) = 1 - \delta\bar{a}_{x+t} - \left(\frac{1}{\bar{a}_x} - \delta\right)\bar{a}_{x+t}$$

$$= 1 - \frac{\bar{a}_{x+t}}{\bar{a}_x}.$$

(7.3.8)

Further, using (7.3.1) gives

$$_t\bar{V}(\bar{A}_x) = [\bar{P}(\bar{A}_{x+t}) - \bar{P}(\bar{A}_x)]\bar{a}_{x+t}$$

$$= \frac{\bar{P}(\bar{A}_{x+t}) - \bar{P}(\bar{A}_x)}{\bar{P}(\bar{A}_{x+t}) + \delta}.$$

(7.3.9)

Finally, we can rewrite (7.3.8) using $\bar{A}_{x+t} = 1 - \delta\bar{a}_{x+t}$ to obtain

$$_t\bar{V}(\bar{A}_x) = 1 - \frac{1 - \bar{A}_{x+t}}{1 - \bar{A}_x} = \frac{\bar{A}_{x+t} - \bar{A}_x}{1 - \bar{A}_x}.$$

(7.3.10)

# NET PREMIUM RESERVES

## 7.4 Fully Discrete Net Premium Reserves

The reserves discussed here are related to the net annual premiums discussed in Section 6.3, that is, for the case of annual premium payment and payment of the benefit at the end of the year of death. Let us consider a unit whole life insurance with net premium $P_x$. For this case, the reserve at the end of $k$ years is denoted by $_kV_x$. Following the development in Sections 6.3 and 7.2, we define the random variable $J$ as the curtate-future-lifetime of $(x+k)$ with p.f. $_jp_{x+k}\,q_{x+k+j}$, $j = 0,1,2,\ldots$. The prospective loss is then defined as

$$_kL = v^{J+1} - P_x\,\ddot{a}_{\overline{J+1}|},\tag{7.4.1}$$

and the definition that $_kV_x = E[_kL]$ produces

$$_kV_x = A_{x+k} - P_x\,\ddot{a}_{x+k}.\tag{7.4.2}$$

This prospective formula for $_kV_x$ is the actuarial present value of the whole life insurance from age $x+k$ less the actuarial present value of future net premiums $P_x$. Comparing this with the development in Section 7.2, we observe that $J = K - k$ with p.f.

$$_jp_{x+k}\,q_{x+k+j} = \frac{_{k+j}p_x\,q_{x+k+j}}{_kp_x}.$$

Here we are dealing with probabilities conditional on $(x)$ surviving to age $x+k$.

Analogous to (7.2.4), we have

$$\begin{aligned}
\text{Var}\,[_kL] &= \text{Var}\left[v^{J+1}\left(1 + \frac{P_x}{d}\right)\right] \\
&= \left[1 + \frac{P_x}{d}\right]^2 \text{Var}\,[v^{J+1}].
\end{aligned}\tag{7.4.3}$$

**Example 7.4:**

Follow up Example 6.4 by calculating $_kV_x$ and $\text{Var}\,[_kL]$.

> **Solution:**
> Here $A_x$, $\ddot{a}_x$ and $P_x$ are independent of age $x$ so that $A_{x+k} = A_x$ and
>
> $$_kV_x = A_x - P_x\,\ddot{a}_x = 0 \quad k = 0,1,2,\ldots.$$
>
> Also from (7.4.3), $\text{Var}\,[_kL] = \text{Var}\,[L] = 0.2347.$ ▼

We now consider a more general fully discrete insurance on $(x)$ under which
- the death benefit is payable at the end of the policy year of death;
- premiums are payable annually, at the beginning of the policy year;
- the death benefit in the $j$th policy year is $b_j$, $j = 1,2,\ldots$;
- the premium payment in the $j$th policy year is $\pi_{j-1}$, for $j = 1,2,\ldots$.

The prospective loss, from the end of policy year $k$, is now

$$_kL = b_{k+J+1}v^{J+1} - \sum_{h=0}^{J} \pi_{k+h}v^h.\tag{7.4.4}$$

# NET PREMIUM RESERVES

The net premium reserve, denoted by $_kV$, is defined as

$$_kV = \mathrm{E}[_kL] = \sum_{j=0}^{\infty} \left[ b_{k+j+1}\, v^{j+1} - \sum_{h=0}^{j} \pi_{k+h}\, v^h \right] {_jp_{x+k}}\, q_{x+k+j}$$

$$= \sum_{j=0}^{\infty} b_{k+j+1}\, v^{j+1}\, {_jp_{x+k}}\, q_{x+k+j} - \sum_{h=0}^{\infty} \pi_{k+h}\, v^h\, {_hp_{x+k}} \qquad (7.4.5)$$

where the second sum in (7.4.5) is obtained by applying Theorem 3.2 or by reversing the order of summation. Thus, as for other reserves, $_kV$ is the actuarial present value of future benefits less the actuarial present value of future net premiums.

The reserve formulas tabulated in Table 7.2 correspond to the net premiums in Table 6.2 and are analogous to the reserves in Table 7.1.

**Table 7.2**
**Fully Discrete Net Premium Reserves**
**Age-at-Issue $x$;**
**Duration $k$;**
**Unit Amount**

| Plan | Reserve Notation | Prospective Formula | |
|---|---|---|---|
| Whole Life Insurance | $_kV_x$ | $A_{x+k} - P_x\, \ddot{a}_{x+k}$ | |
| $n$-Year Term Insurance | $_kV^1_{x:\overline{n}|}$ | $A^1_{x+k:\overline{n-k}|} - P^1_{x:\overline{n}|}\, \ddot{a}_{x+k:\overline{n-k}|}$ <br> $0$ | $k < n$ <br> $k = n$ |
| $n$-Year Endowment Insurance | $_kV_{x:\overline{n}|}$ | $A_{x+k:\overline{n-k}|} - P_{x:\overline{n}|}\, \ddot{a}_{x+k:\overline{n-k}|}$ <br> $1$ | $k < n$ <br> $k = n$ |
| $h$-Payment Years Whole Life Insurance | $^h_kV_x$ | $A_{x+k} - {_hP_x}\, \ddot{a}_{x+k:\overline{h-k}|}$ <br> $A_{x+k}$ | $k < h$ <br> $k \geq h$ |
| $h$-Payment Years, $n$-Year Endowment Insurance | $^h_kV_{x:\overline{n}|}$ | $A_{x+k:\overline{n-k}|} - {_hP_{x:\overline{n}|}}\, \ddot{a}_{x+k:\overline{h-k}|}$ <br> $A_{x+k:\overline{n-k}|}$ <br> $1$ | $k < h$ <br> $h \leq k < n$ <br> $k = n$ |
| $n$-Year Pure Endowment | $_kV^{\;1}_{x:\overline{n}|}$ | $A^{\;1}_{x+k:\overline{n-k}|} - P^{\;1}_{x:\overline{n}|}\, \ddot{a}_{x+k:\overline{n-k}|}$ <br> $1$ | $k < n$ <br> $k = n$ |
| $n$-Year Deferred Annuity | $_kV({_n|\ddot{a}_x})$ | $A^{\;1}_{x+k:\overline{n-k}|}\, \ddot{a}_{x+n} - P({_n|\ddot{a}_x})\, \ddot{a}_{x+k:\overline{n-k}|}$ <br> $\ddot{a}_{x+k}$ | $k < n$ <br> $k \geq n$ |

**Example 7.5:** Determine $\mathrm{Var}\,[_kL]$ for an $n$-year endowment insurance.

**Solution:**

$$_kL = v^{J+1}\left[ 1 + \frac{P_{x:\overline{n}|}}{d} \right] - \frac{P_{x:\overline{n}|}}{d} \qquad J < n - k$$

$$= v^{n-k}\left[ 1 + \frac{P_{x:\overline{n}|}}{d} \right] - \frac{P_{x:\overline{n}|}}{d} \qquad J \geq n - k$$

# NET PREMIUM RESERVES

$J$ has p.f. $_j p_{x+k} \, q_{x+k+j}$, $j = 0,1,\dots$. From this we get

$$\text{Var}\,[_kL] = \left[1 + \frac{P_{x:\overline{n}|}}{d}\right]^2 [^2A_{x+k:\overline{n-k}|} - A^2_{x+k:\overline{n-k}|}].$$   ▼

In cases other than whole life or endowment insurances with premiums payable throughout the insurance term, the expressions of the variance of loss contain many terms. In such cases, the results of Section 7.10 may facilitate calculations.

Formulas similar to those of Section 7.3 can be developed for fully discrete net premium reserves. We shall illustrate these by writing the formulas for $_kV_{x:\overline{n}|}$ with a minimum of discussion. Verbal interpretations and algebraic manipulations closely parallel those for fully continuous net premium reserves.

The premium difference formula is

$$_kV_{x:\overline{n}|} = (P_{x+k:\overline{n-k}|} - P_{x:\overline{n}|})\ddot{a}_{x+k:\overline{n-k}|}. \tag{7.4.6}$$

The paid-up insurance formula is

$$_kV_{x:\overline{n}|} = \left[1 - \frac{P_{x:\overline{n}|}}{P_{x+k:\overline{n-k}|}}\right] A_{x+k:\overline{n-k}|}. \tag{7.4.7}$$

For the retrospective formula, we first establish a result analogous to (7.3.3), namely, for $h < n - j$,

$$_jV_{x:\overline{n}|} = A^{\,1}_{x+j:\overline{h}|} - P_{x:\overline{n}|}\,\ddot{a}_{x+j:\overline{h}|} + {}_hE_{x+j}\,_{j+h}V_{x:\overline{n}|}. \tag{7.4.8}$$

Then, if $j = 0$, we have, since $_0V_{x:\overline{n}|} = 0$,

$$_hV_{x:\overline{n}|} = \frac{1}{_hE_x}[P_{x:\overline{n}|}\,\ddot{a}_{x:\overline{h}|} - A^{\,1}_{x:\overline{h}|}]$$

$$= P_{x:\overline{n}|}\,\ddot{s}_{x:\overline{h}|} - _hk_x. \tag{7.4.9}$$

Here the accumulated cost of insurance is $_hk_x = A^{\,1}_{x:\overline{h}|}/_hE_x$, and a survivorship group interpretation is possible.

An interesting observation follows from the retrospective formula for the reserve. Let us consider two different policies issued to $(x)$, each for a unit of insurance during the first $h$ years. Here, $h$ is less than or equal to the shorter of the two premium-payment periods. The retrospective formulas for the reserves are

$$_hV_1 = P_1\,\ddot{s}_{x:\overline{h}|} - _hk_x$$

and

$$_hV_2 = P_2\,\ddot{s}_{x:\overline{h}|} - _hk_x.$$

It follows that

$$_hV_1 - _hV_2 = (P_1 - P_2)\ddot{s}_{x:\overline{h}|}, \tag{7.4.10}$$

which shows that the difference in the two reserves equals the actuarial accumulated value of the difference $P_1 - P_2$ in the net premiums. Since

$$\frac{1}{\ddot{s}_{x:\overline{h}|}} = \frac{{}_hE_x}{\ddot{a}_{x:\overline{h}|}} = P_{x:\overline{h}|}^{\phantom{x:}1},$$

formula (7.4.10) can be rearranged as

$$P_1 - P_2 = P_{x:\overline{h}|}^{\phantom{x:}1}({}_hV_1 - {}_hV_2). \tag{7.4.11}$$

Now, the difference in the net premiums is expressed as the net premium for an $h$-year pure endowment of the difference in the reserves at the end of $h$ years. Formula (6.3.10) is a special case of (7.4.11) with ${}_nV_{x:\overline{n}|} = 1$ and ${}_n^hV_x = A_{x+n}$. Another illustration is

$$P_x = P_{x:\overline{n}|}^1 + P_{x:\overline{n}|}^{\phantom{x:}1}{}_nV_x \tag{7.4.12}$$

since ${}_nV_{x:\overline{n}|}^1 = 0$.

As in the fully continuous case, there are special formulas for whole life and endowment insurance reserves in the fully discrete case. Parallel to (7.3.8)–(7.3.10), we have by use of the relations $A_y = 1 - d\ddot{a}_y$ and $1/\ddot{a}_y = P_y + d$

$$_kV_x = 1 - d\ddot{a}_{x+k} - \left(\frac{1}{\ddot{a}_x} - d\right)\ddot{a}_{x+k}$$

$$= 1 - \frac{\ddot{a}_{x+k}}{\ddot{a}_x}, \tag{7.4.13}$$

$$_kV_x = 1 - \frac{1 - A_{x+k}}{1 - A_x} = \frac{A_{x+k} - A_x}{1 - A_x} \tag{7.4.14}$$

and

$$_kV_x = 1 - \frac{P_x + d}{P_{x+k} + d} = \frac{P_{x+k} - P_x}{P_{x+k} + d}.^* \tag{7.4.15}$$

**Example 7.6:**   Assume that a 5-year term life insurance of 1000 is issued on a fully discrete basis to each member of a group of $l_{50}$ persons at age 50. Trace the cash flow expected for this group on the basis of the Illustrative Life Table with interest at 6%, and, as a by-product, obtain the net premium reserves.

   **Solution:**
   We first calculate the net annual premium, $\pi = 1000\,P_{50:\overline{5}|}^1 = 6.55692$. Then the expected accumulation of funds for the group through

---

*Similar special formulas also hold for $n$-year endowment insurance reserves, but not for insurance reserves in general.

# NET PREMIUM RESERVES

the collection of premiums, the crediting of interest and the payment of claims is as stated in the following.

| (1) Year $h$ | (2) Expected Premiums at Beginning of Year $l_{50+h-1}\,\pi$ | (3) Expected Fund at Beginning of Year $(2)_h + (6)_{h-1}$ | (4) Expected Interest $(0.06)(3)_h$ | (5) Expected Death Claims $1000\,d_{50+h-1}$ | (6) Expected Fund at End of Year $(3)_h + (4)_h - (5)_h$ | (7) Expected Number of Survivors at End of Year $l_{50+h}$ | (8) $1000\,_hV^1_{50:\overline{5}|}$ $(6)_h \div (7)_h$ |
|---|---|---|---|---|---|---|---|
| 1 | 586 903 | 586 903 | 35 214 | 529 884 | 92 233 | 88 979.11 | 1.04 |
| 2 | 583 429 | 675 662 | 40 540 | 571 432 | 144 770 | 88 407.68 | 1.64 |
| 3 | 579 682 | 724 452 | 43 467 | 616 416 | 151 503 | 87 791.26 | 1.73 |
| 4 | 575 640 | 727 143 | 43 629 | 665 065 | 105 707 | 87 126.20 | 1.21 |
| 5 | 571 280 | 676 987 | 40 619 | 717 606 | 0 | 86 408.60 | 0.00 |

▼

**Example 7.7:** Assume that a 5-year endowment insurance of 1000 is issued on a fully discrete basis to each member of a group of $l_{50}$ persons at age 50. Trace the cash flow expected for this group on the basis of the Illustrative Life Table with interest at 6%, and as a by-product, obtain the net premium reserves.

**Solution:**
Here the net annual premium is $\pi = 1000\,P_{50:\overline{5}|} = 170.083$. The expected cash flow is displayed in the following table.

| (1) Year $h$ | (2) Expected Premiums at Beginning of Year $l_{50+h-1}\,\pi$ | (3) Expected Fund at Beginning of Year $(2)_h + (6)_{h-1}$ | (4) Expected Interest $(0.06)(3)_h$ | (5) Expected Death Claims $1000\,d_{50+h-1}$ | (6) Expected Fund at End of Year $(3)_h + (4)_h - (5)_h$ | (7) Expected Number of Survivors at End of Year $l_{50+h}$ | (8) $1000\,_hV_{50:\overline{5}|}$ $(6)_h \div (7)_h$ |
|---|---|---|---|---|---|---|---|
| 1 | 15 223 954 | 15 223 954 | 913 437 | 529 884 | 15 607 507 | 88 979.11 | 175.41 |
| 2 | 15 133 829 | 30 741 336 | 1 844 480 | 571 432 | 32 014 384 | 88 407.68 | 362.12 |
| 3 | 15 036 638 | 47 051 022 | 2 823 061 | 616 416 | 49 257 667 | 87 791.26 | 561.08 |
| 4 | 14 931 796 | 64 189 463 | 3 851 368 | 665 065 | 67 375 766 | 87 126.20 | 773.31 |
| 5 | 14 818 680 | 82 194 446 | 4 931 667 | 717 606 | 86 408 507 | 86 408.60 | 1 000.00 |

▼

Figures 7.1 and 7.2 display the expected premiums and expected death claims for the preceding two examples. In Example 7.6, expected premiums exceed expected death claims for 2 years, but thereafter are less than claims. The excess premiums accumulate a fund in the early years to be drawn on in the later years when claims are higher. At the end of 5 years, the fund is expected to be exhausted.

For the 5-year endowment case of Example 7.7, the picture is much different. As shown in Figure 7.2, the expected premiums remain far in excess of expected death claims throughout. The expected fund at the end of 5 years is sufficient to provide 1000 in maturity payments to each of the expected survivors.

**Figure 7.1
Expected Premiums
and Expected Death
Claims for
Example 7.6**

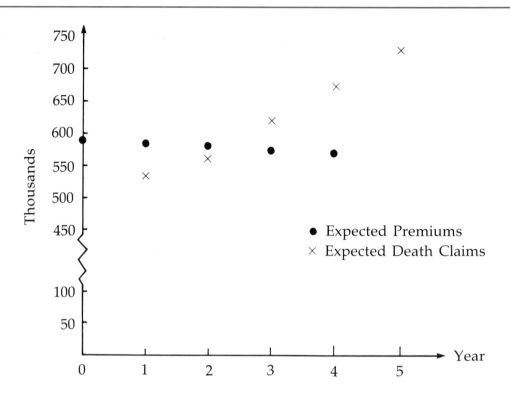

**Figure 7.2
Expected Premiums
and Expected Death
Claims for
Example 7.7**

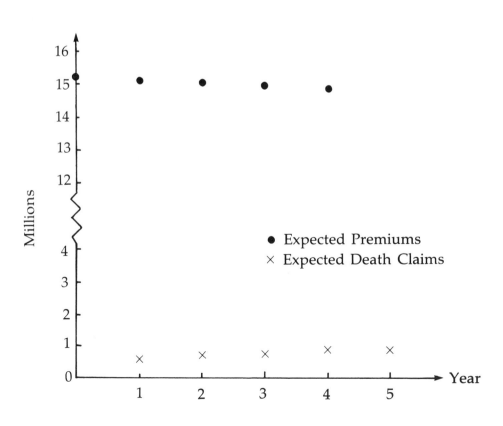

The 5-year term policy exemplifies a low premium, low accumulation life insurance, while the 5-year endowment exemplifies a high premium, high accumulation form. Most life insurances would fall between these two extremes.

## 7.5 Reserves on a Semicontinuous Basis

It was noted at the end of Section 6.3 that, in practice, there is a need for semicontinuous net annual premiums $P(\bar{A}_x)$, $P(\bar{A}^1_{x:\overline{n}|})$, $P(\bar{A}_{x:\overline{n}|})$, $_hP(\bar{A}_x)$ and $_hP(\bar{A}_{x:\overline{n}|})$ to take account of immediate payment of death claims. In such cases, the reserve formulas in Table 7.2 need to be revised by replacement of $A$ by $\bar{A}$ and of $P$ by $P(\bar{A})$. Thus, for example, for an $h$-payment years, $n$-year endowment insurance

$$_k^hV(\bar{A}_{x:\overline{n}|}) = \begin{cases} \bar{A}_{x+k:\overline{n-k}|} - {}_hP(\bar{A}_{x:\overline{n}|})\,\ddot{a}_{x+k:\overline{h-k}|} & k < h \\ \bar{A}_{x+k:\overline{n-k}|} & h \le k < n. \end{cases} \tag{7.5.1}$$

If a uniform distribution of deaths over each year of age is assumed, we have, from (4.4.2) and (6.3.12),

$$_k^hV(\bar{A}_{x:\overline{n}|}) = \frac{i}{\delta}\,_k^hV^1_{x:\overline{n}|} + {}_k^hV\,{}_{x:\overline{n}|}^{\ 1}. \tag{7.5.2}$$

Under this circumstance reserves on a semicontinuous basis are easily calculated from the corresponding fully discrete reserves.

## 7.6 Reserves Based on True *m*thly Premiums

In this section we examine the reserve formulas corresponding to the formulas for true $m$thly premiums discussed in Section 6.4. By the prospective method, one can write a direct formula for $_k^hV^{(m)}_{x:\overline{n}|}$, namely,

$$_k^hV^{(m)}_{x:\overline{n}|} = A_{x+k:\overline{n-k}|} - {}_hP^{(m)}_{x:\overline{n}|}\,\ddot{a}^{(m)}_{x+k:\overline{h-k}|} \qquad k < h. \tag{7.6.1}$$

This can be evaluated after obtaining $_hP^{(m)}_{x:\overline{n}|}$ by means of (6.4.1) or (6.4.2), and $\ddot{a}^{(m)}_{x+k:\overline{h-k}|}$ by means of (5.5.13) or (5.5.15).

We now consider the difference between $_k^hV^{(m)}_{x:\overline{n}|}$ and $_k^hV_{x:\overline{n}|}$ in the general case of a limited payment endowment insurance. We have, for $k < h$,

$$\begin{aligned} _k^hV^{(m)}_{x:\overline{n}|} - {}_k^hV_{x:\overline{n}|} &= {}_hP_{x:\overline{n}|}\,\ddot{a}_{x+k:\overline{h-k}|} - {}_hP^{(m)}_{x:\overline{n}|}\,\ddot{a}^{(m)}_{x+k:\overline{h-k}|} \\ &= {}_hP^{(m)}_{x:\overline{n}|}\,\frac{\ddot{a}^{(m)}_{x:\overline{h}|}}{\ddot{a}_{x:\overline{h}|}}\,\ddot{a}_{x+k:\overline{h-k}|} - {}_hP^{(m)}_{x:\overline{n}|}\,\ddot{a}^{(m)}_{x+k:\overline{h-k}|}. \end{aligned} \tag{7.6.2}$$

Under the assumption of a uniform distribution of deaths in each year of age, (7.6.2) becomes

$$_k^hV^{(m)}_{x:\overline{n}|} - {}_k^hV_{x:\overline{n}|} = {}_hP^{(m)}_{x:\overline{n}|}\left\{ \frac{\ddot{a}^{(m)}_{\overline{1}|}\,\ddot{a}_{x:\overline{h}|} - \beta(m)\,A^1_{x:\overline{h}|}}{\ddot{a}_{x:\overline{h}|}}\,\ddot{a}_{x+k:\overline{h-k}|} \right.$$
$$\left. - [\ddot{a}^{(m)}_{\overline{1}|}\,\ddot{a}_{x+k:\overline{h-k}|} - \beta(m)\,A^{\ 1}_{x+k:\overline{h-k}|}] \right\}.$$

The terms involving $\ddot{a}_{\overline{1}|}^{(m)}$ cancel to yield

$$_k^hV_{x:\overline{n}|}^{(m)} - {}_k^hV_{x:\overline{n}|} = \beta(m)\, {}_hP_{x:\overline{n}|}^{(m)}\, [A_{x+k:\overline{h-k}|}^{\,1} - P_{x:\overline{h}|}^1\, \ddot{a}_{x+k:\overline{h-k}|}]$$

$$= \beta(m)\, {}_hP_{x:\overline{n}|}^{(m)}\, {}_kV_{x:\overline{h}|}^1. \qquad (7.6.3)$$

Thus,

(the reserve for an insurance with true $m$thly premiums)

= (the corresponding fully discrete reserve)

(a fully discrete reserve for term insurance over
+ the premium paying period for a fraction, $\beta(m)$, of the
true $m$thly premium for the plan of insurance).

A similar result holds for reserves on a semicontinuous basis with true $m$thly premiums under the assumption of uniform distribution of deaths in each year of age. By the prospective method, we have for $k < h$,

$$_k^hV^{(m)}(\bar{A}_{x:\overline{n}|}) = \bar{A}_{x+k:\overline{n-k}|} - {}_hP^{(m)}(\bar{A}_{x:\overline{n}|})\, \ddot{a}_{x+k:\overline{h-k}|}^{(m)}. \qquad (7.6.4)$$

By steps analogous to those connecting (7.6.1) and (7.6.3), we obtain

$$_k^hV^{(m)}(\bar{A}_{x:\overline{n}|}) = {}_k^hV(\bar{A}_{x:\overline{n}|}) + \beta(m)\, {}_hP^{(m)}(\bar{A}_{x:\overline{n}|})\, {}_kV_{x:\overline{h}|}^1. \qquad (7.6.5)$$

Further, by letting $m \to \infty$ above, we obtain for a fully continuous basis

$$_k^h\bar{V}(\bar{A}_{x:\overline{n}|}) = {}_k^hV(\bar{A}_{x:\overline{n}|}) + \beta(\infty)\, {}_h\bar{P}(\bar{A}_{x:\overline{n}|})\, {}_kV_{x:\overline{h}|}^1. \qquad (7.6.6)$$

Note again that the term reserve is on a fully discrete basis.

**Example 7.8:**

For the 20-year endowment insurance of Example 6.9 with true semi-annual premiums, calculate

a. the reserve at the end of 10 years on a fully discrete basis

b. the corresponding reserve on a semicontinuous basis.

Also verify (7.6.5) in relation to the reserve in part (b).

**Solution:**

a. In addition to the values calculated in Example 6.9, we require

$$A_{60:\overline{10}|}^1 = 0.13678852$$

$$A_{60:\overline{10}|} = 0.58798425$$

$$\ddot{a}_{60:\overline{10}|} = 7.2789425$$

$$_{10}V_{50:\overline{20}|}^1 = A_{60:\overline{10}|}^1 - P_{50:\overline{20}|}^1\, \ddot{a}_{60:\overline{10}|} = 0.052752$$

$$_{10}V_{50:\overline{20}|} = A_{60:\overline{10}|} - P_{50:\overline{20}|}\, \ddot{a}_{60:\overline{10}|} = 0.355380.$$

Then, under the assumption of a uniform distribution of deaths in each year of age, we have

$$\ddot{a}_{60:\overline{10}|}^{(2)} = \alpha(2)\, \ddot{a}_{60:\overline{10}|} - \beta(2)\, (1 - {}_{10}E_{60}) = 7.1392299.$$

The reserve, $_{10}V^{(2)}_{50:\overline{20}|}$, can be calculated using either

$$(7.6.1): \quad A_{60:\overline{10}|} - P^{(2)}_{50:\overline{20}|} \ddot{a}^{(2)}_{60:\overline{10}|} = 0.355822$$

or

$$(7.6.3): \quad _{10}V_{50:\overline{20}|} + \beta(2)\, P^{(2)}_{50:\overline{20}|}\, _{10}V^1_{50:\overline{20}|} = 0.355822.$$

b. We need additional calculated values,

$$\frac{i}{\delta} A^1_{50:\overline{20}|} = 0.13423835 \qquad P^{(2)}(\bar{A}_{50:\overline{20}|}) = \frac{\bar{A}_{50:\overline{20}|}}{\ddot{a}^{(2)}_{50:\overline{20}|}} = 0.03286830$$

$$\frac{i}{\delta} A^1_{60:\overline{10}|} = 0.14085233 \qquad\qquad \bar{A}_{50:\overline{20}|} = 0.36471188$$

$$P(\bar{A}_{50:\overline{20}|}) = \frac{\bar{A}_{50:\overline{20}|}}{\ddot{a}_{50:\overline{20}|}} = 0.03229873 \qquad \bar{A}_{60:\overline{10}|} = 0.59204806$$

$$_{10}V(\bar{A}_{50:\overline{20}|}) = \bar{A}_{60:\overline{10}|} - P(\bar{A}_{50:\overline{20}|})\, \ddot{a}_{60:\overline{10}|} = 0.3569475$$

$$_{10}V^{(2)}(\bar{A}_{50:\overline{20}|}) = \bar{A}_{60:\overline{10}|} - P^{(2)}(\bar{A}_{50:\overline{20}|})\, \ddot{a}^{(2)}_{60:\overline{10}|} = 0.3573937$$

$$\beta(2)\, P^{(2)}(\bar{A}_{50:\overline{20}|})\, _{10}V^1_{50:\overline{20}|} = 0.000446.$$

This last value is the difference between the two directly above it, as stated in (7.6.5). ▼

## 7.7 Reserves on an Apportionable or Discounted Continuous Basis

In Section 6.5 we discussed apportionable, or discounted continuous, premiums and now consider the corresponding reserves. For integer $k$, we have by the prospective method

$$_{k}^{h}V^{\{m\}}(\bar{A}_{x:\overline{n}|}) = \bar{A}_{x+k:\overline{n-k}|} - _{h}P^{\{m\}}(\bar{A}_{x:\overline{n}|})\, \ddot{a}^{\{m\}}_{x+k:\overline{h-k}|} \qquad k < h. \qquad (7.7.1)$$

But by (6.5.2),

$$_{h}P^{\{m\}}(\bar{A}_{x:\overline{n}|}) = \frac{d^{(m)}}{\delta}\, _{h}\bar{P}(\bar{A}_{x:\overline{n}|}),$$

and by (5.9.7),

$$\ddot{a}^{\{m\}}_{x+k:\overline{h-k}|} = \frac{\delta}{d^{(m)}}\, \bar{a}_{x+k:\overline{h-k}|}.$$

Substitution into (7.7.1) yields

$$_{k}^{h}V^{\{m\}}(\bar{A}_{x:\overline{n}|}) = \bar{A}_{x+k:\overline{n-k}|} - _{h}\bar{P}(\bar{A}_{x:\overline{n}|})\, \bar{a}_{x+k:\overline{h-k}|} = _{k}^{h}\bar{V}(\bar{A}_{x:\overline{n}|}). \qquad (7.7.2)$$

This means that fully continuous reserves can be used for all apportionable cases, independent of the premium-paying mode.

In Section 6.5, it was noted that the apportionable premium could be decomposed as

$$P^{\{1\}}(\bar{A}_x) = P(\bar{A}_x) + P(\bar{A}^{PR}_x) \qquad (7.7.3)$$

where the superscript $PR$ is used to denote an insurance for the premium refund feature. One would expect a similar decomposition to hold for the reserves. To verify this, one can use the prospective method and (6.5.7) to write

$$_kV(\bar{A}_x^{PR}) = \bar{P}(\bar{A}_x)\frac{\bar{A}_{x+k} - A_{x+k}}{\delta} - P(\bar{A}_x^{PR})\ddot{a}_{x+k}$$

$$= \bar{P}(\bar{A}_x)\frac{d\ddot{a}_{x+k} - \delta\bar{a}_{x+k}}{\delta} - [P^{\{1\}}(\bar{A}_x) - P(\bar{A}_x)]\ddot{a}_{x+k}.$$

Since

$$\frac{d}{\delta}\bar{P}(\bar{A}_x) = P^{\{1\}}(\bar{A}_x),$$

the expression can be reduced to

$$_kV(\bar{A}_x^{PR}) = -\bar{P}(\bar{A}_x)\bar{a}_{x+k} + P(\bar{A}_x)\ddot{a}_{x+k}$$

$$= \bar{A}_{x+k} - \bar{P}(\bar{A}_x)\bar{a}_{x+k} - [\bar{A}_{x+k} - P(\bar{A}_x)\ddot{a}_{x+k}]$$

$$= _k\bar{V}(\bar{A}_x) - _kV(\bar{A}_x)$$

$$= _kV^{\{1\}}(\bar{A}_x) - _kV(\bar{A}_x).$$

Thus we have

$$_kV^{\{1\}}(\bar{A}_x) = _kV(\bar{A}_x) + _kV(\bar{A}_x^{PR}). \qquad (7.7.4)$$

## 7.8 Recursive Formulas for Fully Discrete Reserves

In Section 7.4 we considered a general insurance for $(x)$ providing a death benefit of $b_{j+1}$ at the end of policy year $j + 1$, purchased by net annual premiums, $\pi_j$, $j = 0,1,\ldots$, with $\pi_j$ payable at the beginning of policy year $j + 1$. The reserve $_{h-1}V$ at the end of the policy year $h - 1$ is given by (7.4.5),

$$_{h-1}V = \sum_{j=0}^{\infty} b_{h+j}v^{j+1}\,_jp_{x+h-1}\,q_{x+h-1+j} - \sum_{j=0}^{\infty} \pi_{h+j-1}\,v^j\,_jp_{x+h-1}. \qquad (7.8.1)$$

We can split off the first terms in the summations to obtain

$$_{h-1}V = b_h v\, q_{x+h-1} - \pi_{h-1} + v\, p_{x+h-1}\left\{\sum_{j=1}^{\infty} b_{h+j}\,v^j\,_{j-1}p_{x+h}\,q_{x+h+j-1}\right.$$

$$\left. - \sum_{j=1}^{\infty} \pi_{h+j-1}\,v^{j-1}\,_{j-1}p_{x+h}\right\}.$$

The expression in the braces is equal to $_hV$, hence

$$_{h-1}V = b_h v\, q_{x+h-1} - \pi_{h-1} + v\, p_{x+h-1}\,_hV,$$

or

$$_{h-1}V + \pi_{h-1} = b_h v\, q_{x+h-1} + _hV\, v\, p_{x+h-1}. \qquad (7.8.2)$$

In words, the resources required at the beginning of policy year $h$ equal the actuarial present value of year-end requirements.

# NET PREMIUM RESERVES

Formula (7.8.2) can be rearranged to separate the premium $\pi_{h-1}$ into components for policy year $h$, namely,

$$\pi_{h-1} = b_h \, v \, q_{x+h-1} + ({}_hV \, v \, p_{x+h-1} - {}_{h-1}V). \tag{7.8.3}$$

The first component on the right-hand side of (7.8.3) is the 1-year term insurance net premium for the sum insured $b_h$. The second component, ${}_hV \, v \, p_{x+h-1} - {}_{h-1}V$, represents the amount which, if added to ${}_{h-1}V$ at the beginning of the year, would accumulate under interest and survivorship to ${}_hV$ at the end of the year.

For the purpose of subsequent comparison with formulas for a fully continuous insurance, we multiply both sides of (7.8.3) by $1 + i$ and rearrange the formula to

$$\pi_{h-1} + ({}_{h-1}V + \pi_{h-1})i + {}_hV q_{x+h-1} = b_h \, q_{x+h-1} + \Delta({}_{h-1}V). \tag{7.8.4}$$

To indicate that ${}_{h-1}V$ and ${}_hV$ are year-end reserves, they are referred to as the **terminal reserves** for policy years $h-1$ and $h$. The sum ${}_{h-1}V + \pi_{h-1}$ is called the **initial reserve** for policy year $h$. The left-hand side of (7.8.4) indicates resources for policy year $h$, namely, the premium, interest for the year on the initial reserve and the expected release by death of terminal reserve. The right-hand side consists of the expected payment of the death benefit at the end of the year and the increment ${}_hV - {}_{h-1}V$ in the reserve.

A different analysis results if one considers that the reserve ${}_hV$ is to be available to offset the death benefit $b_h$, and that only the **net amount at risk,** $b_h - {}_hV$, needs to be covered by 1-year term insurance. For this analysis we have, on substituting $1 - q_{x+h-1}$ for $p_{x+h-1}$ in (7.8.2) and multiplying through by $1 + i$,

$$_hV = ({}_{h-1}V + \pi_{h-1})(1 + i) - (b_h - {}_hV)q_{x+h-1}. \tag{7.8.5}$$

Corresponding to (7.8.3), we now have

$$\pi_{h-1} = (b_h - {}_hV) \, v \, q_{x+h-1} + v \, {}_hV - {}_{h-1}V. \tag{7.8.6}$$

The first component on the right-hand side is the 1-year term insurance net premium for the net amount of risk. The second component, $v \, {}_hV - {}_{h-1}V$, is the amount which, if added to ${}_{h-1}V$ at the beginning of the year, would accumulate under interest only to ${}_hV$ at the end of the year. Here, ${}_hV$ is used, in case of death, to offset the death benefit. Consequently, the reserve accumulates as a savings fund. This is shown again by the formula corresponding to (7.8.4), namely,

$$\pi_{h-1} + ({}_{h-1}V + \pi_{h-1}) \, i = (b_h - {}_hV) \, q_{x+h-1} + \Delta({}_{h-1}V), \tag{7.8.7}$$

which is left for the reader to interpret.

The first analysis, (7.8.3), does not use the reserve to offset the death benefit and, consequently, the reserve accumulates under interest and survivorship. Both components of the right-hand side of (7.8.3) involve mortality risk, while in (7.8.6) only the first component does. We shall see in Section 7.10 that (7.8.6) is related to a flexible means for calculating variance of loss.

**Example 7.9:**

A deferred annuity issued to $(x)$ for an annual income of 1 commencing at age $x + n$ is to be paid for by net annual premiums during the deferral period. The benefit for death prior to age $x + n$ is the net premium reserve. Assuming the death benefit is paid at the end of the year of death, determine the net annual premium and the net premium reserve at the end of year $k$ for $k \leq n$.

**Solution:**
From (7.8.6) and the fact that $b_h = {}_hV$ for $h = 1, 2, \ldots, n$,

$$\pi = v\,{}_hV - {}_{h-1}V.$$

On multiplication by $v^{h-1}$, we have

$$\pi v^{h-1} = v^h\,{}_hV - v^{h-1}\,{}_{h-1}V = \Delta(v^{h-1}\,{}_{h-1}V). \qquad (7.8.8)$$

Summing over $h = 1, 2, \ldots, n$, we obtain

$$v^n\,{}_nV - v^0\,{}_0V = \pi \sum_{h=1}^{n} v^{h-1} = \pi \ddot{a}_{\overline{n}|}$$

and, since ${}_0V = 0$ while ${}_nV = \ddot{a}_{x+n}$, it follows that

$$\pi = \frac{v^n\,\ddot{a}_{x+n}}{\ddot{a}_{\overline{n}|}} = \frac{\ddot{a}_{x+n}}{\ddot{s}_{\overline{n}|}}.$$

Thus, this annuity is identical to that described in Example 6.13. The reserve at the end of $k$ years can be found by summing (7.8.8) over $h = 1, 2, \ldots, k$ to give

$$v^k\,{}_kV = \pi \ddot{a}_{\overline{k}|}$$

from which

$${}_kV = \pi \ddot{s}_{\overline{k}|}. \qquad \blacktriangledown$$

**Example 7.10:**

An insurance on $(x)$ provides, in case of death within $n$ years, a payment of 1 plus the net premium reserve at the end of the year of death. Obtain formulas for the net level annual premium and the net premium reserve at the end of $k$ years, given that the maturity value is 1.

**Solution:**
In this case $b_h = 1 + {}_hV$, and the net amount at risk has constant value 1. Denoting the net level annual premium by $\pi$ and using (7.8.6), we have

$$v\,{}_hV - {}_{h-1}V = \pi - v\,q_{x+h-1}.$$

On multiplication by $v^{h-1}$, this becomes

$$\Delta(v^{h-1}\,{}_{h-1}V) = \pi v^{h-1} - v^h q_{x+h-1}. \qquad (7.8.9)$$

Summing this over $h = 1, 2, \ldots, n$, we obtain

$$v^n\,{}_nV = \pi\,\ddot{a}_{\overline{n}|} - \sum_{h=1}^{n} v^h q_{x+h-1}$$

# NET PREMIUM RESERVES

so that, with $_nV = 1$,

$$\pi = \frac{v^n + \sum_{h=1}^{n} v^h\, q_{x+h-1}}{\ddot{a}_{\overline{n}|}}.$$

By summing (7.8.9) over $h = 1,2,\ldots,k$, and solving for $_kV$, we find

$$_kV = \pi\, \ddot{s}_{\overline{k}|} - \sum_{h=1}^{k} (1 + i)^{k-h}\, q_{x+h-1}. \qquad \blacktriangledown$$

## 7.9
## Reserves at Fractional Durations

We again consider a general insurance on $(x)$ for a death benefit of $b_{j+1}$ at the end of policy year $j + 1$, purchased by net annual premiums of $\pi_j$, $j = 0,1,\ldots$, with $\pi_j$ payable at the beginning of policy year $j + 1$. The reserve at duration $k + s$ where $k$ is an integer, and $0 < s < 1$, is given prospectively by

$$_{k+s}V = b_{k+1}\, v^{1-s}\, {}_{1-s}q_{x+k+s} + {}_{k+1}V\, v^{1-s}\, {}_{1-s}p_{x+k+s}. \qquad (7.9.1)$$

Under the assumption of a uniform distribution of deaths in each year of age

$$_sp_{x+k}\, {}_{1-s}q_{x+k+s} = {}_{s|1-s}q_{x+k} = (1 - s)\, q_{x+k},$$

thus

$$_{1-s}q_{x+k+s} = \frac{(1 - s)\, q_{x+k}}{1 - s\, q_{x+k}} \qquad (7.9.2)$$

$$_{1-s}p_{x+k+s} = \frac{p_{x+k}}{1 - s\, q_{x+k}}. \qquad (7.9.3)$$

Then (7.9.1) can be rewritten as

$$_{k+s}V = \frac{v^{1-s}}{1 - s\, q_{x+k}} [b_{k+1}(1 - s)\, q_{x+k} + {}_{k+1}V\, p_{x+k}].$$

However, (7.8.2) shows us that

$$b_{k+1}\, q_{x+k} = (_kV + \pi_k)(1 + i) - {}_{k+1}V\, p_{x+k},$$

so we can express the reserve as

$$_{k+s}V = \frac{v^{1-s}}{1 - s\, q_{x+k}} [(1 - s)(_kV + \pi_k)(1 + i) + s\, {}_{k+1}V\, p_{x+k}]. \qquad (7.9.4)$$

A simple approximation to this formula is widely used in practice. One way to obtain it from (7.9.4) is to assume that $i$ and $q_{x+k}$ are small so that $1 + i$, $p_{x+k}$, $v^{1-s}$ and $1 - s\, q_{x+k}$ can each be approximated by 1. The result is

$$_{k+s}V \cong (1 - s)(_kV + \pi_k) + s\, {}_{k+1}V. \qquad (7.9.5)$$

This expression is a linear interpolation between the initial reserve $_kV + \pi_k$ and the terminal reserve $_{k+1}V$. Another way of viewing this approximation is as the sum of the interpolated terminal reserve,

$$(1 - s)\,_kV + s\,_{k+1}V,$$

and the ***unearned net premium***, $(1 - s)\,\pi_k$. In general,

> (the unearned net premium at any time during the year)

> = (the net premium for that year)

> $\times$ (the difference between the time through which the premium has been paid and the current time).

Thus, on an annual premium basis, the premium has been paid to the end of the year so that at time $s$, the unearned net premium is $(1 - s)\,\pi_k$. This notion of an unearned net premium will be used in discussing reserve approximations when premiums are collected more frequently than on an annual basis.

We consider only one such case, that of true semiannual premiums with claims paid at the end of the policy year of death. For $0 < s \leq 1/2$, we have (with $\pi_k^{(2)}$ denoting the annual premium)

$$_{k+s}V^{(2)} = b_{k+1}\,v^{1-s}\,_{1-s}q_{x+k+s}$$

$$+ \,_{k+1}V^{(2)}\,v^{1-s}\,_{1-s}p_{x+k+s} - \frac{\pi_k^{(2)}}{2}\,v^{1/2-s}\,_{1/2-s}p_{x+k+s}. \qquad (7.9.6)$$

It can be shown (see Exercise 7.44) that under the assumption of a uniform distribution of deaths in each year of age, (7.9.6) becomes

$$_{k+s}V^{(2)} = \frac{v^{1-s}}{1 - s\,q_{x+k}}\left\{(1 - s)\,_kV^{(2)}\,(1 + i) + s\,_{k+1}V^{(2)}\,p_{x+k}\right.$$

$$\left. + \frac{\pi_k^{(2)}}{2}[(1 + i)(1 - s) - s(1 + i)^{1/2}\,_{1/2}p_{x+k}]\right\}, \qquad (7.9.7)$$

and this can be approximated as

$$_{k+s}V^{(2)} \cong (1 - s)\,_kV^{(2)} + s\,_{k+1}V^{(2)} + \left(\frac{1}{2} - s\right)\pi_k^{(2)}. \qquad (7.9.8)$$

Here, in addition to the interpolated terminal reserve, there is an unearned net premium equal to a fraction of the annual premium rate, the fraction being the difference between the time through which the premiums are paid (in this case $1/2$) and the current time $s$.

For $1/2 < s < 1$, the reserve expression is of the same form as (7.9.1) and by steps similar to those leading to (7.9.4) can be expressed as

$$_{k+s}V^{(2)} = \frac{v^{1-s}}{1 - s\,q_{x+k}}\left\{(1 - s)\,_kV^{(2)}\,(1 + i) + s\,_{k+1}V^{(2)}\,p_{x+k}\right.$$

$$\left. + (1 - s)(1 + i)^{1/2}\frac{\pi_k^{(2)}}{2}[(1 + i)^{1/2} + \,_{1/2}p_{x+k}]\right\};$$

# NET PREMIUM RESERVES

it can be approximated as

$$_{k+s}V^{(2)} \cong (1-s) \, _kV^{(2)} + s \, _{k+1}V^{(2)} + (1-s) \, \pi_k^{(2)}. \qquad (7.9.9)$$

This again is the interpolated terminal reserve plus the unearned net premium as of time $s$.

**7.10
Allocation of the
Loss to the
Policy Years**

We have seen in (7.8.6) that for each policy year the net annual premium for a life insurance can be split into a 1-year term insurance net premium to cover the net amount at risk and a deposit into a savings fund for the accumulation of the reserve. There is no mortality risk in regard to the savings fund. Hence, we might anticipate that variances associated with the given insurance can be expressed in terms of the variances in regard to the 1-year term insurances. This is the case. A by-product is a flexible means of calculating variances associated with the given insurance.

For the general fully discrete insurance introduced in Section 7.4, the loss $L = {_0}L$ is, by (7.4.4),

$$L = b_{K+1} v^{K+1} - \sum_{h=0}^{K} \pi_h \, v^h \qquad (7.10.1)$$

where $K$ is the curtate-future-lifetime of $(x)$. In this expression, $L$ is the present value, at policy issue, of the financial result of this insurance when death occurs in policy year $K+1$. We now seek to allocate a part of this result to each of the first $K+1$ years. The basis of this allocation is the second analysis in Section 7.8 where the reserve is considered as a savings fund and the mortality risk in a given year is in regard to a 1-year term insurance for the net amount at risk. For this purpose, we introduce a loss, valued at time $h$ and depending implicitly on $K$, to be allocated to policy year $h+1$, namely,

$$\Lambda_h = \begin{cases} 0 & K \leq h-1 \\ v\,b_{h+1} - ({_h}V + \pi_h) & K = h \\ v\,_{h+1}V - ({_h}V + \pi_h) & K \geq h+1 \end{cases} \qquad (7.10.2)$$

for $h = 0,1,2,\ldots$. Note that the first case relates to the policyholder dying before year $h+1$, the second case to death in year $h+1$, and the third case to survival to the end of year $h+1$.

From (7.8.2), with $h$ replaced by $h+1$, we can reformulate $\Lambda_h$ as

$$\Lambda_h = \begin{cases} 0 & K \leq h-1 \\ \dfrac{(b_{h+1} - {_{h+1}}V)\,v\,p_{x+h}}{= (b_{h+1} - {_{h+1}}V)\,v - (b_{h+1} - {_{h+1}}V)\,v\,q_{x+h}} & K = h \\ \dfrac{- (b_{h+1} - {_{h+1}}V)\,v\,q_{x+h}}{= 0 - (b_{h+1} - {_{h+1}}V)\,v\,q_{x+h}} & K \geq h+1. \end{cases} \qquad (7.10.3)$$

Since $(b_{h+1} - {_{h+1}}V)\,v\,q_{x+h}$ is the premium for a 1-year term insurance for the net amount at risk in year $h+1$, we see that the nonzero values of $\Lambda_h$ express the loss associated with that 1-year term

# NET PREMIUM RESERVES

insurance, namely, the present value at time $h$ of benefits under the term insurance less the net single premium.

Consequently, from (7.10.3),

$$\text{E}[\Lambda_h] = v\,(b_{h+1} - {}_{h+1}V)\,[p_{x+h}\,{}_hp_x\,q_{x+h} + (-1)\,q_{x+h}\,{}_hp_x\,p_{x+h}] = 0. \quad (7.10.4)$$

Then

$$\text{Var}\,[\Lambda_h] = \text{E}[\Lambda_h^2] = v^2\,(b_{h+1} - {}_{h+1}V)^2\,[p_{x+h}^2\,{}_hp_x\,q_{x+h}$$
$$+ (-1)^2\,q_{x+h}^2\,{}_hp_x\,p_{x+h}]$$
$$= v^2\,(b_{h+1} - {}_{h+1}V)^2\,{}_hp_x\,p_{x+h}\,q_{x+h}. \quad (7.10.5)$$

It follows by general reasoning that the total loss can be obtained by summing up the present value of the losses allocated to the individual policy years,

$$L = \sum_{h=0}^{\infty} v^h\,\Lambda_h. \quad (7.10.6)$$

For illustrative purposes, we present an algebraic derivation of (7.10.6) by noting that

$$\sum_{h=0}^{\infty} v^h\,\Lambda_h = \sum_{h=0}^{K-1} v^h\,\Lambda_h + v^K\,\Lambda_K + \sum_{h=K+1}^{\infty} v^h\,\Lambda_h.$$

In the first sum $K \geq h+1$, and in the second sum $K \leq h-1$, so by (7.10.2) we have

$$\sum_{h=0}^{\infty} v^h\,\Lambda_h = \sum_{h=0}^{K-1} (v^{h+1}\,{}_{h+1}V - v^h\,{}_hV - v^h\,\pi_h)$$

$$+ v^{K+1}\,b_{K+1} - v^K\,{}_KV - v^K\,\pi_K + 0.$$

All terms involving $v^j\,{}_jV$, $j = 1,2,\ldots$, cancel, and ${}_0V = 0$, so that the expression reduces to

$$\sum_{h=0}^{\infty} v^h\,\Lambda_h = v^{K+1}\,b_{K+1} - \sum_{h=0}^{K} v^h\,\pi_h = L.$$

With the summation starting at $h = k$, this argument can be used to show that

$$\sum_{h=k}^{\infty} v^h\,\Lambda_h = v^k\,{}_kL - v^k\,{}_kV \qquad k = 0,1,2,\ldots.$$

Solving for ${}_kL$ we obtain

$${}_kL = \sum_{h=0}^{\infty} v^h\,\Lambda_{k+h} + {}_kV \qquad k = 0,1,2,\ldots. \quad (7.10.7)$$

# NET PREMIUM RESERVES

Using these expressions at $k$ and $k + j$, we have

$$_kL = \sum_{h=0}^{j-1} v^h \, \Lambda_{k+h} + v^j \, _{k+j}L$$

$$+ (_kV - v^j \, _{k+j}V) \qquad k = 0,1,\ldots, j = 0,1,\ldots. \qquad (7.10.8)$$

From (7.10.4) and (7.10.6), we confirm that $E[L] = 0$. The following result, due to Hattendorf, provides a means for calculating the variance of $L$. Its real significance is that the variance of $L$ can be allocated to the individual policy years.

**Theorem 7.1:**

a. $\text{Cov}[\Lambda_h, \Lambda_j] = 0 \qquad h \neq j$

b. $\text{Var}[L] = \sum_{h=0}^{\infty} v^{2h} \, \text{Var}[\Lambda_h]$

**Proof:**
From (7.10.4), $E[\Lambda_h] = 0$. Therefore, $\text{Cov}[\Lambda_h, \Lambda_j] = E[\Lambda_h \Lambda_j]$. We seek to show that this latter expectation is 0. Without loss of generality, we can assume $j < h$. Then, whenever $\Lambda_h \neq 0$, we know that $K \geq h \geq j + 1$, and it follows that $\Lambda_j$ has the constant value $v \, _{j+1}V - (_jV + \pi_j)$. Hence

$$E[\Lambda_h \Lambda_j] = [v \, _{j+1}V - (_jV + \pi_j)] \, E[\Lambda_h].$$

But, by (7.10.4), the right-hand side vanishes.

From (7.10.6) and part (a), it follows that, with all covariances equal to 0, the variance of the sum, $L$, is the sum of the variances of $v^h \Lambda_h$, $h = 0,1,\ldots$, which yields part (b). ∎

The $\Lambda_h$, $h = 0,1,\ldots$, are dependent but uncorrelated random variables; that permits the variance of $L$ to be allocated to the individual policy years.

Theorem 7.1 also allows us to calculate the variance of $_kL$, $k = 1,2,\ldots$ [see (7.4.4)]. For this purpose, we consider an insurance with issue age $x + k$, initial premium $\pi_0' = {}_kV + \pi_k$, subsequent premiums $\pi_h' = \pi_{k+h}$, benefits $b_h' = b_{k+h}$, reserves $_hV' = {}_{k+h}V$, for $h = 1,2,\ldots$, and loss variables $L'$ and $\Lambda_h'$ for $h = 0,1,2,\ldots$. Then, by (7.4.4)

$$_kL = b_{k+J+1} \, v^{J+1} - \sum_{h=0}^{J} \pi_{k+h} \, v^h$$

$$= b_{J+1}' \, v^{J+1} - \sum_{h=0}^{J} \pi_h' \, v^h + {}_kV = L' + {}_kV.$$

Since $_kL$ and $L'$ differ by a constant $_kV$,

$$\text{Var}[_kL] = \text{Var}[L'] = \sum_{h=0}^{\infty} v^{2h} \, \text{Var}[\Lambda_h'],$$

# NET PREMIUM RESERVES

and from (7.10.5),

$$= \sum_{h=0}^{\infty} v^{2h} \, v^2 \, (b'_{h+1} - \,_{h+1}V')^2 \,\,_h p_{x+k} \, p_{x+k+h} \, q_{x+k+h}$$

$$= \sum_{h=0}^{\infty} v^{2h} \,\,_h p_{x+k} \, [v^2 \, (b_{k+h+1} - \,_{k+h+1}V)^2 \, p_{x+k+h} \, q_{x+k+h}]. \quad (7.10.9)$$

Formula (7.10.9) makes sense because the Hattendorf theorem uses the concept of the reserve as a savings fund and relates the variances of loss for the given insurance to the variances of losses in regard to future yearly term insurances for the net amounts at risk, these latter variances being exemplified for year $k + h + 1$ by the expression in square brackets.

A relationship between $\text{Var}\,[_k L]$ and $\text{Var}\,[_{k+j} L]$, $j = 0,1,\ldots$, can be established by first writing (7.10.9) as

$$\text{Var}\,[_k L] = \sum_{h=0}^{j-1} v^{2h} \,\,_h p_{x+k} \, [v^2 \, (b_{k+h+1} - \,_{k+h+1}V)^2 \, p_{x+k+h} \, q_{x+k+h}]$$

$$+ \sum_{h=j}^{\infty} v^{2h} \,\,_h p_{x+k} \, [v^2 \, (b_{k+h+1} - \,_{k+h+1}V)^2 \, p_{x+k+h} \, q_{x+k+h}].$$

Now in the second summation replace the summation variable, $h$, by $l + j$, which transforms it to

$$v^{2j} \,\,_j p_{x+k} \sum_{l=0}^{\infty} v^{2l} \,\,_l p_{x+k+j} \, [v^2 \, (b_{k+j+l+1} - \,_{k+j+l+1}V)^2 \, p_{x+k+j+l} \, q_{x+k+j+l}].$$

Comparing this to (7.10.9) shows that this summation is $\text{Var}\,[_{k+j} L]$ so we have

$$\text{Var}\,[_k L] = \sum_{h=0}^{j-1} v^{2h} \,\,_h p_{x+k} \, [v^2 \, (b_{k+h+1} - \,_{k+h+1}V)^2 \, p_{x+k+h} \, q_{x+k+h}]$$

$$+ v^{2j} \,\,_j p_{x+k} \, \text{Var}\,[_{k+j} L]. \quad (7.10.10)$$

Just as the expression for $\text{Var}\,[L]$ in Theorem 7.1 was derived from $L = \sum_{h=0}^{\infty} v^h \, \Lambda_h$, the expressions (7.10.9) and (7.10.10) for $\text{Var}\,[_k L]$ can also be derived directly by using (7.10.7) and (7.10.8).

The following two examples illustrate the application of the Hattendorf theorem, Theorem 7.1.

**Example 7.11:**

Consider an insured from Example 7.6 who has survived to the end of the second policy year. In respect to this insured, evaluate

a. $\text{Var}\,[_2 L]$, directly
b. $\text{Var}\,[_2 L]$, by means of the Hattendorf theorem
c. $\text{Var}\,[_3 L]$
d. $\text{Var}\,[_4 L]$.

# NET PREMIUM RESERVES

**Solution:**

a. For the direct calculation, we need a table of values for $_2L$.

| Outcome $j$ | $_2L = \begin{cases} 1000\,v^{j+1} - 6.55692\,\ddot{a}_{\overline{j+1}}, j = 0,1,2 \\ 0 - 6.55692\,\ddot{a}_{\overline{3}}, j = 3,4,\ldots \end{cases}$ | Conditional Probability of Outcome $_jp_{52}\,q_{52+j} = d_{52+j}/l_{52}$, $j = 0,1,2$ $_3p_{52} = l_{55}/l_{52}$, $j = 3,4,\ldots$ |
|---|---|---|
| 0 | 936.84 | 0.0069724 |
| 1 | 877.25 | 0.0075227 |
| 2 | 821.04 | 0.0081170 |
| $\geq 3$ | $-18.58$ | 0.9773879 |

Then $E[_2L] = 1.64$, in agreement with the value shown in Example 7.6, and

$$\text{Var}\,[_2L] = E[_2L^2] - (E[_2L])^2$$

$$= 17{,}717.82 - (1.64)^2$$

$$= 17{,}715.1.$$

b. To apply the Hattendorf theorem, we can use the reserves from Example 7.6 to calculate the variances of the losses associated with the 1-year term insurances.

| $h$ | $q_{52+h}$ | $v^2(1000 - 1000\,_{2+h+1}V^1_{\overline{50:5}})^2\,p_{52+h}\,q_{52+h}$ |
|---|---|---|
| 0 | 0.0069724 | 6 140.842 |
| 1 | 0.0075755 | 6 674.910 |
| 2 | 0.0082364 | 7 269.991 |

Then by (7.10.9),

$$\text{Var}\,[_2L] = 6140.842 + (1.06)^{-2}(6674.910)\,p_{52}$$

$$+ (1.06)^{-4}(7269.991)\,_2p_{52} = 17{,}715.1,$$

which agrees with the value found by the direct calculation in part (a).

Note that in the direct method it was necessary to consider the gain in the event of survival to age 55; but for the Hattendorf theorem, we need to consider only the losses associated with the 1-year term insurances for the net amounts at risk in the remaining policy years. Thereafter, the net amount at risk is 0 and the corresponding terms in (7.10.9) vanish.

Also note that the standard deviation, $\sqrt{17{,}751.1} = 133.1$, for a single policy is over 80 times the reserve, $E[_2L] = 1.64$.

Similarly, we use (7.10.9) to calculate

c. $\text{Var}[_3L] = 6674.910 + (1.06)^{-2}(7269.991)\,p_{53} = 13096.2$

d. $\text{Var}[_4L] = 7269.991$, or after rounding, 7270.0.                  ▼

**Example 7.12:**

Consider a portfolio of 1500 policies of the type described in Example 7.6 and discussed in Example 7.11. Assume all policies have annual premiums due immediately. Further, assume 750 policies are at duration 2, 500 are at duration 3 and 250 are at duration 4, and that the policies in each group are evenly divided between those with 1000 face amount and those with 3000 face amount.

a. Calculate the aggregate reserve.
b. Calculate the variance of the prospective losses over the remaining periods of coverage of the policies, assuming such losses are independent. Also, calculate the amount which, on the basis of the normal distribution, will give the insurer a probability of 0.95 of meeting the future obligations to this block of business.
c. Calculate the variance of the losses associated with the 1-year term insurances for the net amounts at risk under the policies and the amount of supplement to the aggregate reserve which, on the basis of the normal distribution, will give the insurer a probability of 0.95 of meeting the obligations to this block of business for the 1-year period.
d. Redo (b) and (c) with each set of policies increased 100-fold in number.

**Solution:**
a. Let $Z$ be the sum of the prospective losses on the 1500 policies. Using the results of Example 7.6, we have for the aggregate reserve

$$E[Z] = [375\,(1) + 375\,(3)]\,(1.64) + [250\,(1) + 250\,(3)]\,(1.73)$$
$$+ [125\,(1) + 125\,(3)]\,(1.21)$$
$$= 4795.$$

b. From Example 7.11, we have

$$\text{Var}[Z] = [375\,(1) + 375\,(9)]\,(17{,}715.1)$$
$$+ [250\,(1) + 250\,(9)]\,(13{,}096.2)$$
$$+ [125\,(1) + 125\,(9)]\,(7270.0)$$
$$= (1.0825962)\,10^8$$

and $\sigma_Z = 10{,}404.8$.

Then if

$$0.05 = \Pr[Z > c] = \Pr\left[\frac{Z - 4795.0}{10{,}404.8} > \frac{c - 4795.0}{10{,}404.8}\right],$$

the normal distribution implies

$$\frac{c - 4795.0}{10{,}404.8} = 1.645,$$

# Chapter 7
## NET PREMIUM RESERVES

or

$$c = 21{,}911,$$

which is 4.6 times the aggregate reserve, $E[Z]$.

c. Here we take account of only the next year's risk. For each policy, we consider a variable equal to the loss associated with a 1-year term insurance for the net amount at risk. Let $Z_1$ be the sum of these loss variables. The expected loss for each of the 1-year term insurances is 0, hence $E[Z_1] = 0$.

From the table in part (b) of Example 7.11, we can obtain the variances of the losses in regard to the 1-year term insurances, and hence

$$\text{Var}[Z_1] = [375\,(1) + 375\,(9)]\,(6140.8) + [250\,(1) + 250\,(9)]\,(6674.9)$$
$$+ [125\,(1) + 125\,(9)]\,(7270.0)$$
$$= (4.880275)\,10^7$$

and

$$\sigma_{Z_1} = 6985.9.$$

If $c_1$ is the required supplement to the aggregate reserve, then

$$0.05 = \text{Pr}\,(Z_1 > c_1) = \text{Pr}\left[\frac{Z_1 - 0}{6985.9} > \frac{c_1 - 0}{6985.9}\right],$$

and we determine

$$c_1 = (1.645)\,(6985.9) = 11{,}492,$$

which is 2.4 times the aggregate reserve, 4795.

d. In this case, $E[Z] = 479{,}500$ and $\text{Var}[Z] = (1.0825962)\,10^{10}$. The amount $c$ required to provide a probability of 0.95 that all future obligations will be met is

$$479{,}500 + 1.645\,\sqrt{1.0825962}\,10^5 = 650{,}659,$$

which is 1.36 times the aggregate reserve, $E[Z]$.

Also, $\text{Var}[Z_1]$ is now $(4.880275)\,10^9$. The amount $c_1$ of supplement to the aggregate reserve required to give a 0.95 probability that the insurer can meet policy obligations for the next year is $1.645\,\sqrt{4.880275}\,10^{4.5} = 114{,}918$, or 24% of the aggregate reserve. ▼

## 7.11 Differential Equations for Fully Continuous Reserves

The results here parallel those in Section 7.8 for the fully discrete case and will be developed more briefly. The general insurance for $(x)$ is now on a fully continuous basis with amount insured $b_t$ payable if death occurs at time $t$, and with annual rate of premium payment $\pi_t$ at time $t$, $t \geq 0$. This last specification implies that premiums of $\pi_t\,dt$ are payable in the time interval $(t, t + dt)$. The reserve $_t\bar{V}$ at time $t$ is given by the formula

$$_t\bar{V} = \int_0^\infty b_{t+s}\, v^s\, {}_sp_{x+t}\, \mu_{x+t+s}\, ds - \int_0^\infty \pi_{t+s}\, v^s\, {}_sp_{x+t}\, ds. \qquad (7.11.1)$$

To simplify calculation, we set $u = t + s$ and combine the two integrals, thus

$$_t\bar{V} = \int_t^\infty (b_u\, \mu_{x+u} - \pi_u)\, e^{\delta(t-u)}\, {}_{u-t}p_{x+t}\, du. \qquad (7.11.2)$$

Since

$$\frac{d}{dt}\, {}_{u-t}p_{x+t} = \frac{d}{dt} \exp\left[-\int_{x+t}^{x+u} \mu_y\, dy\right] = \mu_{x+t}\, {}_{u-t}p_{x+t},$$

the derivative of $_t\bar{V}$ is a combination of three terms,

$$\frac{d\,_t\bar{V}}{dt} = -(b_t\, \mu_{x+t} - \pi_t) + \delta I + \mu_{x+t}I$$

where $I$ denotes the integral in (7.11.2). But $I = {}_t\bar{V}$, and hence

$$\frac{d\,_t\bar{V}}{dt} = \pi_t + (\delta + \mu_{x+t})\,_t\bar{V} - b_t\, \mu_{x+t}. \qquad (7.11.3)$$

Here the rate of change of the reserve is made up of three components: the premium rate, the rate of increase of the reserve under interest and survivorship and the rate of benefit outgo, $b_t\, \mu_{x+t}$. A formula corresponding to (7.8.4) is

$$\pi_t + {}_t\bar{V}\, \delta + {}_t\bar{V}\, \mu_{x+t} = b_t\, \mu_{x+t} + \frac{d\,_t\bar{V}}{dt}. \qquad (7.11.4)$$

This balances income rates with the rate of benefit outgo and the rate of increase in the reserve.

If the reserve is treated as a savings fund, available to offset the death benefit, we have

$$\pi_t + {}_t\bar{V}\, \delta = (b_t - {}_t\bar{V})\, \mu_{x+t} + \frac{d\,_t\bar{V}}{dt}. \qquad (7.11.5)$$

Here the income rates are in respect to premiums and to interest on the reserve, and these balance with the benefit outgo rate $(b_t - {}_t\bar{V})\, \mu_{x+t}$, based on the net amount at risk and the rate of increase in the reserve.

## 7.12 Reserve Formulas in Terms of Commutation Functions

In previous sections, we have expressed prospective formulas for the reserve in terms of the actuarial present values of future benefits and future net premiums. Retrospective formulas have been derived in terms of the actuarial accumulated value of past premiums and the accumulated cost of past benefits. In Chapters 4 and 5, expressions in terms of commutation functions were given for these insurance and annuity values. Consequently, it is easy to write reserve formulas in terms of commutation functions, especially if, for simplicity,

# NET PREMIUM RESERVES

the premium is indicated by the appropriate symbol rather than by its expression in commutation functions. This is done in Table 7.3 for reserves on a semicontinuous basis. Analogous formulas can be written for the fully continuous and the various discrete bases.

**Table 7.3**
**Semicontinuous Net Premium Reserves; Age at Issue $x$; Duration $k$; Unit Amount**

| Plan | Reserve Notation | Numerator (Denominator is always $D_{x+k}$) | |
|---|---|---|---|
| | | Prospective Formula | Retrospective Formula |
| Whole Life Insurance | $_kV(\bar{A}_x)$ | $\bar{M}_{x+k} - P(\bar{A}_x) N_{x+k}$ | $P(\bar{A}_x)(N_x - N_{x+k}) - (\bar{M}_x - \bar{M}_{x+k})$ |
| $n$-Year Term Insurance | $_kV(\bar{A}^1_{x:\overline{n}\rceil})$ | $\bar{M}_{x+k} - \bar{M}_{x+n} - P(\bar{A}^1_{x:\overline{n}\rceil})(N_{x+k} - N_{x+n})$ | $P(\bar{A}^1_{x:\overline{n}\rceil})(N_x - N_{x+k}) - (\bar{M}_x - \bar{M}_{x+k})$ |
| $n$-Year Endowment Insurance | $_kV(\bar{A}_{x:\overline{n}\rceil})$ | $\bar{M}_{x+k} - \bar{M}_{x+n} + D_{x+n} - P(\bar{A}_{x:\overline{n}\rceil})(N_{x+k} - N_{x+n})$ | $P(\bar{A}_{x:\overline{n}\rceil})(N_x - N_{x+k}) - (\bar{M}_x - \bar{M}_{x+k})$ |
| $h$-Payment Years, Whole Life Insurance | $^h_kV(\bar{A}_x)$ | $\bar{M}_{x+k} - {}_hP(\bar{A}_x)(N_{x+k} - N_{x+h}), \quad k < h$ <br> $\bar{M}_{x+k} \qquad\qquad\qquad\qquad k \geq h$ | ${}_hP(\bar{A}_x)(N_x - N_{x+k}) - (\bar{M}_x - \bar{M}_{x+k})$ <br> $k < h$ <br> (use prospective formula for $k \geq h$) |
| $h$-Payment Years, $n$-Year Endowment Insurance | $^h_kV(\bar{A}_{x:\overline{n}\rceil})$ | $\bar{M}_{x+k} - \bar{M}_{x+n} + D_{x+n}$ <br> $\quad - {}_hP(\bar{A}_{x:\overline{n}\rceil})(N_{x+k} - N_{x+h}) \quad k < h$ <br> $\bar{M}_{x+k} - \bar{M}_{x+n} + D_{x+n} \qquad h \leq k < n$ | ${}_hP(\bar{A}_{x:\overline{n}\rceil})(N_x - N_{x+k}) - (\bar{M}_x - \bar{M}_{x+k})$ <br> $k < h$ <br> (use prospective formula for $h \leq k < n$) |
| $n$-Year Pure Endowment | $_kV^{\;\;1}_{x:\overline{n}\rceil}$ | $D_{x+n} - P^{\;\;1}_{x:\overline{n}\rceil}(N_{x+k} - N_{x+n})$ | $P^{\;\;1}_{x:\overline{n}\rceil}(N_x - N_{x+k})$ |

**Example 7.13:**

a. A decreasing term insurance is issued to (45) for which the benefit payable immediately on death is 100,000 in the first year, thereafter decreasing by 5000 per year until expiring at the end of 20 years. On the basis of the Illustrative Life Table with interest of 6%, calculate the net level annual premium payable for 20 years, and the net premium reserve at the end of the first, second and third years.

b. Redo as part (a) with premiums payable for 15 years.

**Solution:**
a. The net level premium is given by

$$\frac{100{,}000\,\bar{M}_{45} - 5000\,(\bar{R}_{46} - \bar{R}_{66})}{N_{45} - N_{65}} = 5000\,\frac{i}{\delta}\frac{20\,M_{45} - (R_{46} - R_{66})}{N_{45} - N_{65}}$$

$$= 391.577.$$

By means of the Fackler reserve accumulation formula (see Exercise 7.19), the reserve at the end of the first year is

$$391.577\,\frac{D_{45}}{D_{46}} - 100{,}000\,\frac{i}{\delta}\frac{C_{45}}{D_{46}} = 3.551;$$

at the end of the second year it is

$$(3.551 + 391.577)\frac{D_{46}}{D_{47}} - 95,000\frac{i}{\delta}\frac{C_{46}}{D_{47}} = -3.199;$$

and at the end of the third year it is

$$(-3.199 + 391.577)\frac{D_{47}}{D_{48}} - 90,000\frac{i}{\delta}\frac{C_{47}}{D_{48}} = -20.473.$$

The reserves thereafter remain nonpositive until the end of the insurance term.

b.  The net premium is now

$$5000\frac{i}{\delta}\frac{20\,M_{45} - (R_{46} - R_{66})}{N_{45} - N_{60}} = 455.221$$

and the reserves computed as in part (a) are now 71.281, 136.664 and 196.255 at the ends of the first, second and third years respectively. The reserves now remain nonnegative throughout the term of the policy.                                              ▼

Negative net premium reserves occur when the actuarial present value of future benefits is less than that of future net premiums. Such a situation could induce the insured to terminate the insurance and leave the insurer bearing the deficit. As we have seen in Example 7.13, negative net premium reserves may occur for a decreasing term insurance with premium payable for the whole term. By shortening the premium term, the reserves can be increased to nonnegative levels. If one considers the matter retrospectively, one sees that negative reserves occur when the actuarial accumulated value of past premiums is less than the accumulated cost of past benefits. Shortening of the premium-payment term, thereby raising the net premiums, can keep the accumulated premiums ahead of the accumulated cost of benefits.

**7.13
Notes and
References**

The concept of loss and the equivalence principle used in Chapter 6 to define net premiums has been followed up in this chapter by the concept of prospective loss and the definition of reserve as the expectation of prospective loss. Consequently, the theory and formulas in the earlier sections of this chapter are closely related to patterns established for premiums in the corresponding sections of Chapter 6. A variety of formulas for reserves, in particular, the retrospective formula involving the concept of accumulated cost of past benefits, ramify the theory. So do the relations developed for reserves based on true fractional premiums and on apportionable premiums, a reference for the latter being the paper by Scher (1974). Recursive formulas for fully discrete reserves and differential equations for fully continuous reserves provide basic insights into long-term insurance and annuity processes. In particular, one of these recursive formulas is applied to develop Hattendorf's theorem (1868) [for references, see

# NET PREMIUM RESERVES

Steffensen (1929), Hickman (1964), Gerber (1976)]. This formula allocates the variance of the loss to the separate policy years. Another application is to the formulation of interim reserves at fractional durations, which was discussed for the fully discrete case.

**Exercises**

*Section 7.2*

7.1. For an $n$-year unit endowment insurance issued on a fully continuous basis to $(x)$, define $_tL$, the prospective loss after duration $t$. Confirm that

$$\text{Var}[_tL] = \frac{^2\bar{A}_{x+t:\overline{n-t}|} - \bar{A}^2_{x+t:\overline{n-t}|}}{(\delta\bar{a}_{x:\overline{m}|})^2}.$$

7.2. The prospective loss, after duration $t$, for a single premium continuous temporary life annuity of 1 per annum issued to $(x)$ is given by

$$_tL = \begin{cases} \bar{a}_{\overline{U}|} & 0 \le U < n - t \\ \bar{a}_{\overline{n-t}|} & U \ge n - t. \end{cases}$$

Calculate $E[_tL]$ and $\text{Var}[_tL]$.

7.3. Write prospective formulas for
   a. $_{10}^{20}\bar{V}(\bar{A}_{35:\overline{30}|})$
   b. the reserve at the end of 5 years for a unit 10-year term insurance issued to $(45)$ on a single premium basis.

*Section 7.3*

7.4. Write four formulas for $_{10}^{20}\bar{V}(\bar{A}_{40})$.

7.5. Write seven formulas for $_{10}\bar{V}(\bar{A}_{40:\overline{20}|})$.

7.6. Give the retrospective formula for $_{20}^{30}\bar{V}(_{30|}\bar{a}_{35})$.

7.7. Show that for $0 < t \le m$,
   a. $\bar{P}(\bar{A}_{x:\overline{m+n}|}) = \bar{P}(\bar{A}^1_{x:\overline{m}|}) + \bar{P}_{x:\overline{m}|}^{\;1}\;_m\bar{V}(\bar{A}_{x:\overline{m+n}|})$
   b. $_t\bar{V}(\bar{A}_{x:\overline{m+n}|}) = {}_t\bar{V}(\bar{A}^1_{x:\overline{m}|}) + {}_t\bar{V}_{x:\overline{m}|}^{\;1}\;_m\bar{V}(\bar{A}_{x:\overline{m+n}|})$
   and give verbal interpretations.

7.8. State what formula in Section 7.3 the following equation is related to, and give a verbal interpretation.
$$_{10}^{20}\bar{V}(\bar{A}_{30}) = \bar{A}^1_{40:\overline{5}|} + {}_5E_{40}\;_{15}^{20}\bar{V}(\bar{A}_{30}) - {}_{20}\bar{P}(\bar{A}_{30})\,\bar{a}_{40:\overline{5}|}$$

*Section 7.4*

7.9. Write four formulas for $_{10}^{20}V_{40}$.

7.10. Write seven formulas for $_{10}V_{40:\overline{20}|}$.

7.11. Show that, for $0 < k \le m$,
$$_kV_{x:\overline{m+n}|} = {}_kV^1_{x:\overline{m}|} + {}_kV_{x:\overline{m}|}^{\;1}\;_mV_{x:\overline{m+n}|}.$$

7.12. If $k < n/2$, $_kV_{x:\overline{n}|} = 1/6$ and $\ddot{a}_{x:\overline{n}|} + \ddot{a}_{x+2k:\overline{n-2k}|} = 2\ddot{a}_{x+k:\overline{n-k}|}$, calculate $_kV_{x+k:\overline{n-k}|}$.

*Section 7.5*

7.13. On the basis of the Illustrative Life Table and interest of 6%, calculate values for the reserves in the following table. (See Exercise 6.7.)

| Fully Continuous | Semicontinuous | Fully Discrete |
|---|---|---|
| $_{10}\bar{V}(\bar{A}_{35:\overline{30}\vert})$ | $_{10}V(\bar{A}_{35:\overline{30}\vert})$ | $_{10}V_{35:\overline{30}\vert}$ |
| $_{10}\bar{V}(\bar{A}_{35})$ | $_{10}V(\bar{A}_{35})$ | $_{10}V_{35}$ |
| $_{10}\bar{V}(\bar{A}^1_{35:\overline{30}\vert})$ | $_{10}V(\bar{A}^1_{35:\overline{30}\vert})$ | $_{10}V^1_{35:\overline{30}\vert}$ |

7.14. Under the assumption of a uniform distribution of deaths in each year of age, which of the following are correct?

a. $_{k}V(\bar{A}_{x:\overline{n}\vert}) = \dfrac{i}{\delta}\,_{k}V_{x:\overline{n}\vert}$

b. $_{k}V(\bar{A}_{x}) = \dfrac{i}{\delta}\,_{k}V_{x}$

c. $_{k}V(\bar{A}^1_{x:\overline{n}\vert}) = \dfrac{i}{\delta}\,_{k}V^1_{x:\overline{n}\vert}.$

*Section 7.6*

7.15. Show that, under the assumption of a uniform distribution of deaths in each year of age,

$$\frac{_5V^{(4)}_{30:\overline{20}\vert} - \,_5V_{30:\overline{20}\vert}}{^{20}_5V^{(4)}_{30} - \,^{20}_5V_{30}} = \frac{A_{30:\overline{20}\vert}}{A_{30}}.$$

(The assumption is sufficient but not necessary.)

7.16. Which of the following are correct formulas for $_{15}V^{(m)}_{40}$?

 a. $[P^{(m)}_{55} - P^{(m)}_{40}]\ddot{a}^{(m)}_{55}$   c. $P^{(m)}_{40}\,\ddot{s}^{(m)}_{40:\overline{15}\vert} - \,_{15}k_{40}$

 b. $\left[1 - \dfrac{P^{(m)}_{40}}{P^{(m)}_{55}}\right]A_{55}$   d. $1 - \dfrac{\ddot{a}^{(m)}_{55}}{\ddot{a}^{(m)}_{40}}.$

*Section 7.7*

7.17. Which of the following are correct formulas for $_{15}V^{\{4\}}(\bar{A}_{40})$?

 a. $_{15}\bar{V}(\bar{A}_{40})$   b. $[P^{\{4\}}(\bar{A}_{55}) - P^{\{4\}}(\bar{A}_{40})]\ddot{a}^{\{4\}}_{55}$

 c. $[\bar{P}(\bar{A}_{55}) - \bar{P}(\bar{A}_{40})]\bar{a}_{55}$   d. $\left[1 - \dfrac{\bar{P}(\bar{A}_{40})}{\bar{P}(\bar{A}_{55})}\right]\bar{A}_{55}$

 e. $1 - \dfrac{\bar{a}_{55}}{\bar{a}_{40}}$   f. $\bar{P}(\bar{A}_{40})\,\bar{s}_{40:\overline{15}\vert} - \,_{15}\bar{k}_{40}.$

7.18. Show that

a. $P^{\{m\}}(\bar{A}_{x:\overline{n}|}) = {}_nP^{\{m\}}(\bar{A}_x) + (1 - \bar{A}_{x+n})P^{\{m\}}{}_{x:\overline{n}|}^{1}$

b. ${}_kV^{\{m\}}(\bar{A}_{x:\overline{n}|}) = {}_k^nV^{\{m\}}(\bar{A}_x) + (1 - \bar{A}_{x+n}) {}_kV^{\{m\}}{}_{x:\overline{n}|}^{1}$.

Give verbal interpretations.

*Section 7.8*

7.19. Show that (7.8.2), with $h$ replaced by $h + 1$, can be rearranged as

$$_{h+1}V = ({}_hV + \pi_h)\frac{1 + i}{p_{x+h}} - b_{h+1}\frac{q_{x+h}}{p_{x+h}}.$$

Give a verbal interpretation. (This is called the *Fackler reserve* accumulation formula, after the American actuary, David Parks Fackler.)

7.20. For a whole life insurance of 1 issued to $(x)$, prove that

a. $_kV_x = \displaystyle\sum_{h=0}^{k-1} \frac{P_x - vq_{x+h}}{{}_{k-h}E_{x+h}}$

b. $_kV_x = \displaystyle\sum_{h=0}^{k-1} [P_x - vq_{x+h}(1 - {}_{h+1}V_x)](1 + i)^{k-h}$.

Give verbal interpretations of the formulas.

7.21. If $b_{h+1} = {}_{h+1}V$, $_0V = 0$ and $\pi_h = \pi$, $h = 0,1,\ldots,k-1$, prove that $_kV = \pi\ddot{s}_{\overline{k}|}$. [Hint: Use (7.8.6).]

7.22. Show that if $\pi$ is the net level annual premium for an $n$-year term insurance with $b_h = \ddot{a}_{\overline{n-h}|}$, $h = 1,2,\ldots,n$, $_0V = {}_nV = 0$, then

a. $\pi = \dfrac{\ddot{a}_{\overline{n}|} - \ddot{a}_{x:\overline{n}|}}{\ddot{a}_{x:\overline{n}|}}$

b. $_kV = \ddot{a}_{\overline{n-k}|} - \ddot{a}_{x+k:\overline{n-k}|} - \pi\ddot{a}_{x+k:\overline{n-k}|}$.

[Hint: This can be shown directly, or by use of (7.8.3).]

*Section 7.9*

7.23. Starting with (7.9.1), establish the equation

$$_sp_{x+k \ k+s}V + v^{1-s} {}_sq_{x+k}b_{k+1} = (1 + i)^s ({}_kV + \pi_k) \qquad 0 < s < 1.$$

Explain the result by general reasoning.

7.24. Interpret the formulas,

a. $_{k+(h/m)+r}V^{(m)} \cong \left(1 - \dfrac{h}{m} - r\right)_kV^{(m)}$

$$+ \left(\dfrac{h}{m} + r\right)_{k+1}V^{(m)} + \left(\dfrac{1}{m} - r\right)P^{(m)}$$

b. $_{k+(h/m)+r}V^{\{m\}} \cong \left(1 - \dfrac{h}{m} - r\right)\,_{k}V^{\{m\}}$

$$+ \left(\dfrac{h}{m} + r\right)\,_{k+1}V^{\{m\}} + \left(\dfrac{1}{m} - r\right)P^{\{m\}}$$

where $0 < r < 1/m$.

7.25. For each of the following reserves, develop formulas similar to one or more of (7.9.5), (7.9.8) and (7.9.9).

a. $_{20^{1/2}}V(\bar{A}_{x:\overline{40}|})$      b. $_{20^{1/2}}\bar{V}(\bar{A}_{x:\overline{40}|})$

c. $_{20^{1/2}}V^{(2)}(\bar{A}_{x:\overline{40}|})$      d. $_{20^{2/3}}V^{(2)}(\bar{A}_{x:\overline{40}|})$

e. $_{20^{1/2}}V^{\{2\}}(\bar{A}_{x:\overline{40}|})$      f. $_{20^{2/3}}V^{\{2\}}(\bar{A}_{x:\overline{40}|})$

7.26. On the basis of the Illustrative Life Table and interest of 6%, approximate

$$_{10^{1/6}}V^{\{4\}}(\bar{A}_{25}).$$

7.27. Show that (7.9.4) can be written as

$$_{k+s}V = \dfrac{1-s}{1 - s\,q_{x+k}}\,(_{k}V + \pi_{k})\,(1+i)^{s} + \left(1 - \dfrac{1-s}{1 - s\,q_{x+k}}\right)_{k+1}V\,v^{1-s}.$$

*Section 7.10*

7.28. For a fully discrete whole life insurance of amount 1 issued to $(x)$ with premiums payable for life, show that

a. $\text{Var}\,[L] = \displaystyle\sum_{h=0}^{\infty} \left(\dfrac{\ddot{a}_{x+h+1}}{\ddot{a}_{x}}\right)^{2} v^{2(h+1)}\,{}_{h}p_{x}\,p_{x+h}\,q_{x+h}$

b. $\text{Var}\,[_{k}L] = \displaystyle\sum_{h=0}^{\infty} \left(\dfrac{\ddot{a}_{x+k+h+1}}{\ddot{a}_{x}}\right)^{2} v^{2(h+1)}\,{}_{h}p_{x+k}\,p_{x+k+h}\,q_{x+k+h}.$

7.29. For a life annuity-due of 1 per annum payable while $(x)$ survives, consider the whole life loss

$$L = \ddot{a}_{\overline{K+1}|} - \ddot{a}_{x} \qquad K = 0,1,2,\ldots$$

and the loss $\Lambda_{h}$, valued at time $h$, that is allocated to annuity year $h$, namely,

$$\Lambda_{h} = \begin{cases} 0 & K \leq h - 1 \\ -(\ddot{a}_{x+h} - 1) = -v\,p_{x+h}\,\ddot{a}_{x+h+1} & K = h \\ v\,\ddot{a}_{x+h+1} - (\ddot{a}_{x+h} - 1) = v\,q_{x+h}\,\ddot{a}_{x+h+1} & K \geq h + 1. \end{cases}$$

a. Interpret the formulas for $\Lambda_{h}$.

b. Show that

(i) $L = \displaystyle\sum_{h=0}^{\infty} v^{h}\,\Lambda_{h}$

(ii) $E[\Lambda_{h}] = 0$

(iii) $\text{Var}\,[\Lambda_{h}] = v^{2}\,(\ddot{a}_{x+h+1})^{2}\,{}_{h}p_{x}\,p_{x+h}\,q_{x+h}.$

7.30.  a. For the insurance of Example 7.10, establish that

$$\text{Var}\,[L] = \sum_{h=0}^{n-1} v^{2(h+1)} \,_h p_x \, p_{x+h} \, q_{x+h}.$$

   b. If $\delta = 0.05$, $n = 20$ and $\mu_{x+t} = 0.01$, $t \geq 0$, calculate $\text{Var}\,[L]$ for the insurance in (a).

7.31.  A 20-payment life policy with unit face amount was issued on a fully discrete basis to a person aged 25. On the basis of the Illustrative Life Table and interest of 6%, calculate

   a. $_{20}P_{25}$        b. $_{19}^{20}V_{25}$        c. $_{20}^{20}V_{25}$
   d. $\text{Var}\,[_{20}L]$        e. $\text{Var}\,[_{18}L]$, using Theorem 7.1.

*Section 7.11*

7.32.  Interpret the differential equations:

   a. $\dfrac{d}{dt}\,_t\bar{V} = \pi_t + (\delta + \mu_{x+t})\,_t\bar{V} - b_t\,\mu_{x+t}$

   b. $\dfrac{d}{dt}\,_t\bar{V} = \pi_t + \delta\,_t\bar{V} - (b_t - \,_t\bar{V})\,\mu_{x+t}.$

7.33.  If $b_t = \,_t\bar{V}$, $_0\bar{V} = 0$, and $\pi_t = \pi$, $t \geq 0$, show that $_t\bar{V} = \pi\,\bar{s}_{\overline{t}|}.$

7.34.  Evaluate $\dfrac{d}{dt}\{[1 - \,_t\bar{V}(\bar{A}_x)]\,_t p_x\}.$

*Section 7.12*

7.35.  A decreasing term insurance to age 65 with immediate payment of death claims is issued to (30) with the following benefits.

| For death between ages: | 30–50 | 50–55 | 55–60 | 60–65 |
|---|---|---|---|---|
| Benefit: | 100,000 | 90,000 | 80,000 | 60,000 |

Write formulas, in terms of commutation functions, for
   a. the net annual apportionable premium, payable semiannually
   b. The reserve at the end of 30 years, if net premiums are as in part (a).

7.36.  A single premium insurance contract issued to (35) provides 100,000 in case the insured survives to age 65, and returns (at the end of the year of death) the net single premium without interest if the insured dies before age 65. If the net single premium is denoted by $S$, write expressions, in terms of commutation functions, for
   a. $S$
   b. the prospective formula for the reserve at the end of $k$ years
   c. the retrospective formula for the reserve at the end of $k$ years.

7.37. In terms of $P = {}_{20}P^{(12)}(\bar{A}_{30:\overline{35}|})$ and commutation functions, write prospective and retrospective formulas for the following:

a. ${}_{10}^{20}V^{(12)}(\bar{A}_{30:\overline{35}|})$

b. ${}_{25}^{20}V^{(12)}(\bar{A}_{30:\overline{35}|})$.

*Miscellaneous*

7.38. Calculate the value of $P^1_{x:\overline{n}|}$ if ${}_nV_x = 0.080$, $P_x = 0.024$ and $P_{x:\overline{n}|}^{\phantom{x}1} = 0.2$.

7.39. If ${}_{10}V_{35} = 0.150$ and ${}_{20}V_{35} = 0.354$, calculate ${}_{10}V_{45}$.

7.40. A whole life insurance issued to (25) pays a unit benefit at the end of the year of death. Premiums are payable annually to age 65. The net premium for the first 10 years is $P_{25}$ followed by an increased level annual premium for the next 30 years. Express the following in commutation functions:
a. The net annual premium payable at ages 35 through 64.
b. The tenth-year terminal reserve.
c. The amount, $B$, under the following option: At the end of ten years the policyholder may continue with the net premium $P_{25}$ until age 65 in return for reducing the death benefit to $B$ for death after age 35.
d. The twentieth-year terminal reserve, if the option in (c) is selected.

7.41. Use (7.11.3) to write expressions for

a. $\dfrac{d}{dt}({}_tp_x \; {}_tV)$      b. $\dfrac{d}{dt}(v^t \; {}_tV)$      c. $\dfrac{d}{dt}(v^t \; {}_tp_x \; {}_tV)$

and interpret the results.

7.42. Show that the formula equivalent to (7.9.1) under the Balducci assumption for mortality within the year of age is

$$_{k+s}V = v^{1-s}[(1-s)({}_kV + \pi_k)(1+i) + s \; {}_{k+1}V].$$

7.43. Assuming $\delta = 0.05$, $q_x = 0.05$ and a uniform distribution of deaths in the year of age, calculate

a. $(\bar{I}\bar{A})^1_{x:\overline{1}|}$      b. $_{1/2}V(\bar{I}\bar{A})^1_{x:\overline{1}|}$.

7.44.*Using the assumption of a uniform distribution of deaths in the year of age, and the following reserve growth equation in case of true semiannual premiums,

$$\left[ {}_kV^{(2)} + \frac{\pi^{(2)}_k}{2} \right](1+i) + \frac{\pi^{(2)}_k}{2} \; {}_{1/2}p_{x+k} \, (1+i)^{1/2} = p_{x+k \; k+1}V^{(2)} + q_{x+k} \, b_{k+1},$$

obtain (7.9.7) from (7.9.6).

# Chapter 7

## NET PREMIUM RESERVES

7.45.\*Prove that

$$\int_0^\infty (v^t - \bar{P}(\bar{A}_x)\,\bar{a}_{\bar{t}|})^2 \;_t p_x\,\mu_{x+t}\,dt = \int_0^\infty [1 - \;_t\bar{V}(\bar{A}_x)]^2\,v^{2t}\;_t p_x\,\mu_{x+t}\,dt$$

and interpret the result.

7.46.\*If

$$_{k,m}L = \begin{cases} b_{k+J+1}\,v^{J+1} - \;_kV - \displaystyle\sum_{h=0}^{J} \pi_{k+h}\,v^h & 0 \leq J \leq m-1 \\[2em] _{k+m}V\,v^m - \;_kV - \displaystyle\sum_{h=0}^{m-1} \pi_{k+h}\,v^h & J \geq m, \end{cases}$$

and, for $h = 0,1,\ldots,m-1$,

$$\Lambda_{k+h} = \begin{cases} 0 & J \leq h-1 \\ v\,b_{k+h+1} - (_{k+h}V + \pi_{k+h}) & J = h \\ v\;_{k+h+1}V - (_{k+h}V + \pi_{k+h}) & J \geq h+1, \end{cases}$$

show that

a. $_{k,m}L = \displaystyle\sum_{h=0}^{m-1} v^h\,\Lambda_{k+h}$

b. $\mathrm{Var}\,[_{k,m}L] = \displaystyle\sum_{h=0}^{m-1} v^{2h}\,\mathrm{Var}\,[\Lambda_{k+h}]$.

7.47. Repeat Example 7.11 in terms of an insured from Example 7.7 who has survived to the end of the second policy year.

7.48. Repeat Example 7.12 in terms of a portfolio of 1500 policies of the type described in Example 7.7 and discussed in Exercise 7.47.

7.49. In Exercise 7.48 there is no uncertainty about the amount or time of payment for the insureds who have survived to the end of the fourth policy year. Redo Exercise 7.48 for just those insureds at durations 2 and 3.

7.50. What changes should be made in line five of Table 7.3 if the insurance is
a. on a fully continuous basis
b. on a fully discrete basis.

7.51. Write a formula, in terms of premium and terminal reserve symbols, for the net premium reserve at the middle of the eleventh policy year for a 10,000 ordinary life insurance with apportionable net premiums payable annually issued to (30).

7.52. A 3-year endowment policy for a face amount of 3 has the death benefit payable at the end of the year of death and a net premium, determined by the equivalence principle, of 0.94

payable annually. Using an interest rate of 20%, the following reserves are generated:

| End of Year | Reserve |
|---|---|
| 1 | 0.66 |
| 2 | 1.56 |
| 3 | 3.00 |

Calculate

a. $q_x$          b. $q_{x+1}$

c. the variance of the loss at policy issue, $_0L$

d. the variance of the loss at the end of the first year, $_1L$.

# Chapter 8
## MULTIPLE LIFE FUNCTIONS

## 8.1
## Introduction

In Chapters 3 through 7 we developed a theory for the analysis of financial benefits contingent on the time of death of a single life. We can extend this theory to benefits involving several lives. An application of this extension commonly found in pension plans is the joint-and-survivor annuity option. A participant may elect to change his benefit from a specific amount payable as long as he is alive to a lesser amount payable while either the participant or his beneficiary is alive.

The applications of multiple life actuarial calculations are common. In estate and gift taxation, for example, the investment income from a trust can be paid to a group of heirs as long as at least one of the group survives. Upon the last death, the principal from the trust is to be donated to a university. The amount of the charitable deduction allowed for inheritance tax purposes will be determined by an actuarial calculation. There are family policies in which benefits differ due to the order of the deaths of the insured and the spouse, and there are insurance policies issued on a joint-life basis providing cash for estate planning.

In this chapter we will restrict our discussion to situations involving two lives. We will not discuss annual premiums, reserves or the problem of selection inherent in two-life combinations. These topics will be discussed in Chapter 17 of this work. Here we will concentrate on the basic benefits and apply the concepts and techniques developed in Chapters 3 through 5.

A useful abstraction in the theory of life contingencies, particularly as it is applied to several lives, is that of *status* for which there are definitions of survival and failure. A single life aged $x$ defines a status that survives while $(x)$ lives. Thus, the random variable $T(x)$, used in Chapter 3 to denote the future lifetime of $(x)$, can be interpreted as the period of survival of the status and also as the time-until-failure of the status. A term certain, $\overline{n}|$, defines a status surviving for exactly $n$ years and then failing. More complex statuses can be defined in terms of several lives in various ways. Survival can mean that all members survive or, alternatively, that at least one member survives. Still more complicated statuses can be in regard to two men and two women with the status considered to survive only as long as at least one man and at least one woman survive.

After a status and its survival have been defined, we can apply the definition to develop models for annuities and insurances. An annuity is payable as long as the status survives, while an insurance is payable upon the failure of the status. Insurances also can be restricted so they are payable only if the individuals die in a specific order.

## 8.2
## The Joint-Life Status

A status that exists as long as all members survive and fails upon the first death is known as a *joint-life status.* It is denoted by $(x_1 x_2 \cdots x_m)$ where $x_i$ represents the age of member $i$ of the group and $m$ represents the number of members. Notation introduced in Chapters 3, 4 and 5 will be used here with the subscript listing several ages rather

# MULTIPLE LIFE FUNCTIONS

than a single age. For example, $A_{xy}$ and $_tp_{xy}$ will have the same meaning for the joint-life status $(xy)$ as $A_x$ and $_tp_x$ have for the single life $(x)$.

We now consider the distribution of the random variable $T$, the time-until-failure of a status. For the joint-life status, $T = \min[T(x_1), T(x_2),\ldots,T(x_m)]$ where $T(x_i)$ is the time of death of individual $i$. For the future lifetime of a status, the concepts and relationships established in Sections 3.2.2 through 3.5 (excluding the life table example in Section 3.3.2) apply to the distribution of $T$. These concepts will be used here without new proofs.

In applications, a mortality law or life table is not directly specified for the future lifetime of the joint-life status. When we want to express probabilities of survival or failure of the joint-life status we will do so in terms of the probabilities for the individual lives in the group. Realistically, the individuals covered by a joint-life insurance or annuity contract have some association, implying that the time-until-death random variables are not independent. However, the dependence of these time-until-death random variables is very difficult to quantify, and no effort to do so will be made. Consequently, whenever we express life table functions for the joint-life status in terms of those for the individual lives, we will be using an assumption of independence.

We begin by defining the distribution function of $T$ for $t > 0$ and restrict our attention to the two-life case with $x_1 = x$ and $x_2 = y$, so that $T = T(xy)$, thus,

$$\begin{aligned} F_T(t) &= \Pr(T \le t) \\ &= \Pr[\min[T(x), T(y)] \le t] \\ &= 1 - \Pr[T(x) > t \quad \text{and} \quad T(y) > t]. \end{aligned}$$
(8.2.1)

Then, by independence,

$$\begin{aligned} F_T(t) &= 1 - \Pr[T(x) > t]\, \Pr[T(y) > t] \\ &= 1 - {}_tp_x\,{}_tp_y. \end{aligned}$$
(8.2.2)

Thus, independence implies that the probability of the joint-life status $(xy)$ surviving to time $t$, $_tp_{xy}$, is

$$_tp_{xy} = {}_tp_x\,{}_tp_y.$$
(8.2.3)

The p.d.f. for $T$ is obtained by differentiating $F_T(t)$ with respect to $t$ and, for independent future lifetimes, is

$$\begin{aligned} f_T(t) &= \frac{d}{dt}(1 - {}_tp_x\,{}_tp_y) \\ &= -{}_tp_x\,(-{}_tp_y\,\mu_{y+t}) - {}_tp_y\,(-{}_tp_x\,\mu_{x+t}) \\ &= {}_tp_x\,{}_tp_y\,(\mu_{x+t} + \mu_{y+t}). \end{aligned}$$
(8.2.4)

The distribution of $T = T(xy)$ can also be specified by the forces of mortality of the associated lives. To do so, we first consider a notation for the force of failure of the status at time $t$. A common notation for this force is $\mu_{x+t:y+t}$ (in analogy with $\mu_{x+t}$) but, in preparation for discussing more general statuses, we shall use the notation $\mu_{xy}(t)$. By analogy with the first formula of (3.2.12) with $f(x)$ and $F(x)$ replaced by $f_{T(xy)}(t)$ and $F_{T(xy)}(t)$, we have

$$\mu_{xy}(t) = \frac{f_{T(xy)}(t)}{1 - F_{T(xy)}(t)}. \tag{8.2.5}$$

For independent $T(x)$, $T(y)$, we then have, from (8.2.2) and (8.2.4),

$$\mu_{xy}(t) = \mu_{x+t} + \mu_{y+t}. \tag{8.2.6}$$

In words, the force of failure for the joint-life status is the sum of the forces of mortality for the individuals if their future lifetimes are independent. As in Chapter 3 with the single life case, we can characterize the distribution of $T(xy)$ by the p.d.f., the d.f. or the force of mortality.

The probability that the joint-life status fails during the time $k$ to $k + 1$ is determined using the distribution function by

$$\begin{aligned} \Pr(k < T \le k + 1) &= \Pr(T \le k + 1) - \Pr(T \le k) \\ &= {}_k p_{xy} - {}_{k+1} p_{xy} \\ &= {}_k p_{xy}\, q_{x+k:y+k}. \end{aligned} \tag{8.2.7}$$

Note that the probability of the joint-life status $(x + k:y + k)$ failing within the next year can be written in terms of the probabilities of independent failure of the individual lives as follows:

$$\begin{aligned} q_{x+k:y+k} &= 1 - p_{x+k:y+k} \\ &= 1 - p_{x+k}\, p_{y+k} \\ &= 1 - (1 - q_{x+k})(1 - q_{y+k}) \\ &= q_{x+k} + q_{y+k} - q_{x+k}\, q_{y+k}. \end{aligned} \tag{8.2.8}$$

From the discussion of curtate-future-lifetime of $(x)$ in Section 3.2.3, we see that (8.2.7) also provides the p.f. of the random variable $K$, the number of years completed prior to failure of the status, that is, for $k = 0,1,2,\ldots,$

$$\begin{aligned} \Pr(K = k) &= \Pr(k \le T < k + 1) \\ &= \Pr(k < T \le k + 1) \\ &= {}_k p_{xy}\, q_{x+k:y+k} \\ &= {}_{k|}q_{xy}. \end{aligned} \tag{8.2.9}$$

## 8.3
## The Last-Survivor
## Status

In addition to benefits defined in terms of the time of the first death, there are those defined in terms of the time of the last death. In this section we will examine situations in which the random variable is the time of the last death.

A status that exists as long as at least one member is alive and fails upon the last death is called a *last-survivor status.* It is denoted by $(\overline{x_1 x_2 \cdots x_m})$ where $x_i$ represents the age of member $i$ and $m$ represents the number of members.

We consider the distribution of the random variable $T$, the time-until-failure of the status. In the last-survivor status, $T = \max [T(x_1), T(x_2), \ldots, T(x_m)]$ where $T(x_i)$ is the time-until-death of individual $i$. As in the development of the joint-life status, when we want to express functions and characteristics of $T$'s distribution in terms of those of the individual lives, we assume $T(x_1)$, $T(x_2)$, ..., $T(x_m)$ are mutually independent. For two lives, we have

$$F_T(t) = \Pr(T \le t)$$

$$= \Pr[\max[T(x), T(y)] \le t] \qquad (8.3.1)$$

$$= \Pr[T(x) \le t \quad \text{and} \quad T(y) \le t].$$

Then, by independence,

$$F_T(t) = \Pr[T(x) \le t] \Pr[T(y) \le t]$$

$$= (1 - {}_tp_x)(1 - {}_tp_y) \qquad (8.3.2)$$

$$= 1 - {}_tp_x - {}_tp_y + {}_tp_x \, {}_tp_y.$$

Thus,

$$_t p_{\overline{xy}} = {}_tp_x + {}_tp_y - {}_tp_x \, {}_tp_y. \qquad (8.3.3)$$

(See Exercise 8.39 for a direct derivation.)

We can differentiate (8.3.2) with respect to $t$ to express the p.d.f. of $T = T(\overline{xy})$ in terms of life functions for the individual lives under the independence assumption:

$$f_T(t) = \frac{d}{dt}[(1 - {}_tp_x)(1 - {}_tp_y)]$$

$$= (1 - {}_tp_x) \, {}_tp_y \, \mu_{y+t} + (1 - {}_tp_y) \, {}_tp_x \, \mu_{x+t} \qquad (8.3.4A)$$

$$= {}_tp_x \, \mu_{x+t} + {}_tp_y \, \mu_{y+t} - {}_tp_x \, {}_tp_y \, (\mu_{x+t} + \mu_{y+t}). \qquad (8.3.4B)$$

A more general relationship exists among $T(xy)$, $T(\overline{xy})$, $T(x)$ and $T(y)$. Even if $T(x)$ and $T(y)$ are not independent, $T(\overline{xy})$ equals either $T(x)$ or $T(y)$ and $T(xy)$ equals the other for every outcome, so we have the following equations:

$$T(xy) + T(\overline{xy}) = T(x) + T(y) \qquad (8.3.5A)$$

$$F_{T(xy)}(t) + F_{T(\overline{xy})}(t) = F_{T(x)}(t) + F_{T(y)}(t) \qquad (8.3.5B)$$

$$f_{T(xy)}(t) + f_{T(\overline{xy})}(t) = f_{T(x)}(t) + f_{T(y)}(t). \qquad (8.3.5C)$$

From (8.3.5B) it follows that

$$_tp_{\overline{xy}} = {}_tp_x + {}_tp_y - {}_tp_{xy} \tag{8.3.5D}$$

and from (8.3.5C) and (8.2.5A) that

$$f_{T(\overline{xy})}(t) = {}_tp_x\,\mu_{x+t} + {}_tp_y\,\mu_{y+t} - {}_tp_{xy}\,\mu_{xy}(t). \tag{8.3.5E}$$

We note that (8.3.4B) and (8.3.5E) differ only in the third term. Equation (8.3.5E) can be written as (8.3.4B) if $T(x)$ and $T(y)$ are independent.

By analogy with the first formula of (3.2.13), with $f(x)$ and $F(x)$ replaced by $f_{T(\overline{xy})}(t)$ and $F_{T(\overline{xy})}(t)$, we have

$$\mu_{\overline{xy}}(t) = \frac{f_{T(\overline{xy})}(t)}{1 - F_{T(\overline{xy})}(t)}.$$

It follows from (8.3.5D) and (8.3.5E) that

$$\mu_{\overline{xy}}(t) = \frac{{}_tp_x\,\mu_{x+t} + {}_tp_y\,\mu_{y+t} - {}_tp_{xy}\,\mu_{xy}(t)}{{}_tp_x + {}_tp_y - {}_tp_{xy}}. \tag{8.3.6}$$

The p.f. of the random variable $K$, the number of years completed prior to failure of the status, or for the last-survivor status, the number of years completed prior to the last death, can now be determined by matching the elements of the pair $[K(xy), K(\overline{xy})]$ with those of the pair $[K(x), K(y)]$. For $k = 0,1,2,\ldots$ we have

$$\Pr[K(\overline{xy}) = k] + \Pr[K(xy) = k] = \Pr[K(x) = k] + \Pr[K(y) = k],$$

thus

$$\Pr[K(\overline{xy}) = k] = {}_kp_x\,q_{x+k} + {}_kp_y\,q_{y+k} - {}_kp_{xy}\,q_{x+k:y+k}. \tag{8.3.7}$$

For independent lives, (8.2.3) and (8.2.7) allow us to write (8.3.7) as

$$\Pr[K(\overline{xy}) = k] = {}_kp_x\,q_{x+k} + {}_kp_y\,q_{y+k}$$
$$- {}_kp_x\,{}_kp_y\,(q_{x+k} + q_{y+k} - q_{x+k}\,q_{y+k}) \tag{8.3.8}$$
$$= (1 - {}_kp_y)\,{}_kp_x\,q_{x+k} + (1 - {}_kp_x)\,{}_kp_y\,q_{y+k}$$
$$+ {}_kp_x\,{}_kp_y\,q_{x+k}\,q_{y+k}.$$

The first two terms are the probability that only the second death occurs between times $k$ and $k+1$. The third term is the probability that both deaths occur during that year. This expression for $\Pr[K(\overline{xy}) = k]$ is analogous to (8.3.4A) for the p.d.f. of $T(\overline{xy})$ where, since the probability that two deaths occur in the same instant is 0, there are only two terms.

## 8.4 Probabilities and Expectations

In Sections 2 and 3 we expressed the p.d.f.'s and the d.f.'s of the future lifetimes of the joint-life status and the last-survivor status in terms of functions for the independent single lives. In this section we will use these expressions to solve probability problems and to obtain expectations, variances and the covariance of the joint- and last-survivor future lifetimes.

**Example 8.1:**

Assuming the future lifetimes of (80) and (85) are independent, obtain an expression for the probability that their

a. first death occurs after 5 and before 10 years from now

b. last death occurs after 5 and before 10 years from now.

**Solution:**

a. With $T = T(80:85)$ we obtain

$$\Pr(5 < T \le 10) = \Pr(T > 5) - \Pr(T > 10)$$

$$= {}_5p_{80:85} - {}_{10}p_{80:85}$$

$$= {}_5p_{80}\,{}_5p_{85} - {}_{10}p_{80}\,{}_{10}p_{85}.$$

Note that the independence assumption is used only in the last step.

b. With $T = T(\overline{80:85})$ we use (8.3.5D) to obtain

$$\Pr(5 < T \le 10) = \Pr(T > 5) - \Pr(T > 10)$$

$$= {}_5p_{\overline{80:85}} - {}_{10}p_{\overline{80:85}}$$

$$= {}_5p_{80} - {}_{10}p_{80} + {}_5p_{85} - {}_{10}p_{85} - ({}_5p_{80:85} - {}_{10}p_{80:85}).$$

Using the independence assumption, we can substitute ${}_5p_{80}\,{}_5p_{85}$ for ${}_5p_{80:85}$ and ${}_{10}p_{80}\,{}_{10}p_{85}$ for ${}_{10}p_{80:85}$. ▼

The results of Section 3.5 concerning expected values of the distribution of $T$, the time-until-the death of $(x)$, are also valid if $T = T(u)$ is the time-until-failure of a general status $(u)$.

For example, from (3.5.2) we have that $\overset{\circ}{e}_u = E[T(u)]$, which for a general status $(u)$ can be obtained from the formula

$$\overset{\circ}{e}_u = \int_0^\infty {}_tp_u\,dt. \tag{8.4.1}$$

If $(u)$ is the joint-life status $(xy)$, then

$$\overset{\circ}{e}_{xy} = \int_0^\infty {}_tp_{xy}\,dt, \tag{8.4.2}$$

and for the last-survivor status $(\overline{xy})$ we have

$$\overset{\circ}{e}_{\overline{xy}} = \int_0^\infty {}_tp_{\overline{xy}}\,dt. \tag{8.4.3}$$

Upon substituting (8.3.5D) into this last result, we see that

$$\overset{\circ}{e}_{\overline{xy}} = \overset{\circ}{e}_x + \overset{\circ}{e}_y - \overset{\circ}{e}_{xy}. \tag{8.4.4}$$

From (3.5.5), the expected value of $K = K(u)$ is

$$e_u = \sum_{k=1}^\infty {}_kp_u$$

# Chapter 8

## MULTIPLE LIFE FUNCTIONS

for a general status, $(u)$. Special cases include

$$e_{xy} = \sum_{k=1}^{\infty} {}_k p_{xy}$$

and

$$e_{\overline{xy}} = \sum_{k=1}^{\infty} {}_k p_{\overline{xy}}.$$

It follows from these special cases and (8.3.5D) that

$$e_{\overline{xy}} = e_x + e_y - e_{xy}.$$

The variance formulas derived in Section 3.5 can be used to calculate the variance of the future lifetime, or curtate-future-lifetime, of any status, $(u)$. Thus,

$$\mathrm{Var}\,[T(xy)] = 2 \int_0^{\infty} t \; {}_t p_{xy} \, dt - (\mathring{e}_{xy})^2$$

and

$$\mathrm{Var}\,[T(\overline{xy})] = 2 \int_0^{\infty} t \; {}_t p_{\overline{xy}} \, dt - (\mathring{e}_{\overline{xy}})^2.$$

To express the covariance of $T(xy)$ and $T(\overline{xy})$ in terms of life table functions for the individual lives, we start with

$$\mathrm{Cov}\,[T(xy), T(\overline{xy})] = \mathrm{E}[T(xy)\,T(\overline{xy})] - \mathrm{E}[T(xy)]\,\mathrm{E}[T(\overline{xy})].$$

On the same basis as for (8.3.5A)

$$T(xy)\,T(\overline{xy}) = T(x)\,T(y),$$

thus

$$\mathrm{E}[T(xy)\,T(\overline{xy})] = \mathrm{E}[T(x)\,T(y)].$$

If $T(x)$ and $T(y)$ are independent, then

$$\mathrm{E}[T(x)\,T(y)] = \mathrm{E}[T(x)]\,\mathrm{E}[T(y)].$$

Thus

$$\mathrm{Cov}\,[T(xy), T(\overline{xy})] = \mathring{e}_x \mathring{e}_y - \mathring{e}_{xy} \mathring{e}_{\overline{xy}}. \tag{8.4.5}$$

Substituting (8.4.4) into (8.4.5) and rearranging terms, we have

$$\mathrm{Cov}\,[T(xy), T(\overline{xy})] = (\mathring{e}_x - \mathring{e}_{xy})(\mathring{e}_y - \mathring{e}_{xy}). \tag{8.4.6}$$

Since both factors of (8.4.6) must be nonnegative, we can see that $T(xy)$ and $T(\overline{xy})$ are positively correlated except in trivial cases where $\mathring{e}_x$ or $\mathring{e}_y$ equals $\mathring{e}_{xy}$.

## 8.5
## Insurance and
## Annuity Benefits

Insurances and annuities, previously discussed for an individual life, can be defined for the general status, $(u)$. With the single-life status, $(x)$, replaced by the general status, $(u)$, the models and formulas of Chapters 4 and 5 are applicable here. Expressions for the actuarial present values and variances, in terms of the distribution of the future lifetime of $(u)$, are immediately available. The relationships of Section 8.3 can then be used to put these expressions in terms of functions for the individual lives of the general status.

For an insurance of unit amount payable at the end of the year in which the general status fails, the model and formulas of Section 4.3 apply. Thus if $K$ denotes the curtate-future-lifetime of $(u)$, then the

- time of payment is $K + 1$,
- present value at issue of the payment is $Z = v^{K+1}$,
- net single premium, $A_u$, is $E[Z] = \sum_{k=0}^{\infty} v^{k+1} \Pr(K = k)$,   (8.5.1)
- $\text{Var}[Z] = {}^2A_u - (A_u)^2$.   (8.5.2)

As an illustration, consider a unit sum insured payable at the end of the year in which the last survivor of $(x)$ and $(y)$ dies. From (8.3.7) and (8.5.1) we have

$$A_{\overline{xy}} = \sum_{k=0}^{\infty} v^{k+1} \left( {}_kp_x\, q_{x+k} + {}_kp_y\, q_{y+k} - {}_kp_{xy}\, q_{x+k:y+k} \right),$$

which can be used at forces of interest $\delta$ and $2\delta$ to obtain the variance by (8.5.2).

The numerous formulas for discrete annuities in Section 5.4 are valid when the annuity payments are contingent on the survival of a general status. For example, if we replace $x$ with $u$ to emphasize that $K$ is the curtate-future-lifetime of the general status, $(u)$, we can restate the following formulas for an $n$-year temporary life annuity in regard to $(u)$:

$$Y = \begin{cases} \ddot{a}_{\overline{K+1|}} & 0 \le K < n \\ \ddot{a}_{\overline{n|}} & K \ge n \end{cases} \qquad (5.4.9)\,\text{restated}$$

$$\ddot{a}_{u:\overline{n|}} = E[Y] = \sum_{k=0}^{n-1} \ddot{a}_{\overline{k+1|}}\; {}_{k|}q_u + \ddot{a}_{\overline{n|}}\; {}_np_u$$

$$\ddot{a}_{u:\overline{n|}} = \sum_{k=0}^{n-1} {}_kE_u = \sum_{k=0}^{n-1} v^k\; {}_kp_u \qquad (5.4.8)\,\text{restated}$$

$$\ddot{a}_{u:\overline{n|}} = \frac{1}{d}(1 - A_{u:\overline{n|}}) \qquad (5.4.10)\,\text{restated}$$

$$\text{Var}[Y] = \frac{1}{d^2}[{}^2A_{u:\overline{n|}} - (A_{u:\overline{n|}})^2]. \qquad (5.4.12)\,\text{restated}$$

As an illustration, consider an annuity of 1, payable at the beginning of each year to which both $(x)$ and $(y)$ survive during the next $n$

# MULTIPLE LIFE FUNCTIONS

years. This is an annuity to the joint-life status $(xy)$. By substituting $_tp_{xy}$, or $_tp_x\,_tp_y$ if the lifetimes are independent, for $_tp_u$ in the above formulas, one can obtain the actuarial present value of the annuity. For the variance in (5.4.12), one can use

$$A_{xy:\overline{n|}} = 1 - d\,\ddot{a}_{xy:\overline{n|}}$$

and

$$^2A_{xy:\overline{n|}} = 1 - (2d - d^2)\,^2\ddot{a}_{xy:\overline{n|}}$$

or can calculate the net single premiums directly.

We can establish relations among the models for annuities and insurances on the last-survivor status and the joint-life status. Similar to the argument used for (8.3.5A), we have that, for each outcome, $K(\overline{xy})$ equals either $K(x)$ or $K(y)$ and $K(xy)$ equals the other. Therefore,

$$v^{K(\overline{xy})+1} + v^{K(xy)+1} = v^{K(x)+1} + v^{K(y)+1} \tag{8.5.3}$$

$$\ddot{a}_{\overline{K(\overline{xy})+1|}} + \ddot{a}_{\overline{K(xy)+1|}} = \ddot{a}_{\overline{K(x)+1|}} + \ddot{a}_{\overline{K(y)+1|}} \tag{8.5.4}$$

$$v^{K(xy)+1}\,v^{K(\overline{xy})+1} = v^{K(x)+1}\,v^{K(y)+1}. \tag{8.5.5}$$

By taking the expectations of both sides of (8.5.3) and (8.5.4), we have

$$A_{\overline{xy}} + A_{xy} = A_x + A_y$$

and

$$\ddot{a}_{\overline{xy}} + \ddot{a}_{xy} = \ddot{a}_x + \ddot{a}_y.$$

These formulas allow us to express the actuarial present values of last-survivor annuities and insurances in terms of those for the individual lives and the joint-life status.

We now consider continuous insurances and annuities. If $T$, the future-lifetime random variable in Sections 4.2 and 5.3, is reinterpreted as $T(u)$, the time-until-failure of the general status, $(u)$, the formulas of those sections for present values, actuarial present values and variances hold for insurances and annuities in respect to the status $(u)$.

For an insurance paying a unit amount at the moment of failure of $(u)$, the present value at policy issue, the net single premium and the variance are given by

$$Z = v^T$$

$$\bar{A}_u = \int_0^\infty v^t\,_tp_u\,\mu_{u+t}\,dt \qquad (4.2.6)\text{ restated}$$

$$\text{Var}[Z] = {}^2\bar{A}_u - \bar{A}_u^2.$$

As an illustration, the restated (4.2.6) for the last survivor of $(x)$ and $(y)$ would be

# MULTIPLE LIFE FUNCTIONS

$$\bar{A}_{\overline{xy}} = \int_0^\infty v^t \, {}_t p_{\overline{xy}} \, \mu_{\overline{xy}}(t) \, dt.$$

By (8.3.6) this is

$$\bar{A}_{\overline{xy}} = \int_0^\infty v^t \, [{}_t p_x \, \mu_{x+t} + {}_t p_y \, \mu_{y+t} - {}_t p_{xy} \, \mu_{xy}(t)] \, dt.$$

For an annuity payable continuously at the rate of 1 per annum until $T$, the time-of-failure of $(u)$, we have

$$Y = \bar{a}_{\overline{T}|}$$

$$\bar{a}_u = \int_0^\infty \bar{a}_{\overline{T}|} \, {}_t p_u \, \mu_{u+t} \, dt \qquad \text{(5.3.2A) restated}$$

$$= \int_0^\infty v^t \, {}_t p_u \, dt \qquad \text{(5.3.2B) restated}$$

$$\text{Var}[Y] = \frac{{}^2\bar{A}_u - \bar{A}_u^2}{\delta^2}. \qquad \text{(5.3.8) restated}$$

The interest identity,

$$\delta \bar{a}_{\overline{T}|} + v^T = 1, \qquad \text{(5.3.9) restated}$$

is also available for $T = T(u)$ and provides the connection between the models for insurances and annuities.

As an application, consider an annuity payable continuously at the rate of 1 per year as long as at least one of $(x)$ or $(y)$ survives. This is an annuity in respect to $(\overline{xy})$, so we have from the above formulas with $T = T(\overline{xy})$

$$Y = \bar{a}_{\overline{T}|}$$

$$\bar{a}_{\overline{xy}} = \int_0^\infty \bar{a}_{\overline{T}|} \, [{}_t p_x \, \mu_{x+t} + {}_t p_y \, \mu_{y+t} - {}_t p_{xy} \, \mu_{xy}(t)] \, dt$$

$$= \int_0^\infty v^t \, {}_t p_{\overline{xy}} \, dt$$

$$\text{Var}[Y] = \frac{{}^2\bar{A}_{\overline{xy}} - \bar{A}_{\overline{xy}}^2}{\delta^2}.$$

Formulas (8.5.3)–(8.5.5) hold with the curtate-future-lifetime, $K$, replaced by the future lifetime, $T$, thus,

$$v^{T(\overline{xy})} + v^{T(xy)} = v^{T(x)} + v^{T(y)} \qquad (8.5.6)$$

$$\bar{a}_{\overline{T(\overline{xy})}|} + \bar{a}_{\overline{T(xy)}|} = \bar{a}_{\overline{T(x)}|} + \bar{a}_{\overline{T(y)}|} \qquad (8.5.7)$$

$$v^{T(\overline{xy})} \, v^{T(xy)} = v^{T(x)} \, v^{T(y)}.$$

# MULTIPLE LIFE FUNCTIONS

These identities can be used to obtain the relations among the net single premiums, actuarial present values, variances and covariances of insurances and annuities for the various statuses. For example, taking the expectations of both sides of (8.5.6) and (8.5.7), we obtain

$$\bar{A}_{\overline{xy}} + \bar{A}_{xy} = \bar{A}_x + \bar{A}_y \qquad (8.5.8)$$

$$\bar{a}_{\overline{xy}} + \bar{a}_{xy} = \bar{a}_x + \bar{a}_y. \qquad (8.5.9)$$

In the same way that $\text{Cov}\,[T(\overline{xy}), T(xy)]$ was expressed in terms of the expected future lifetimes for independent $T(x)$ and $T(y)$, we can show that

$$\text{Cov}\,[v^{T(\overline{xy})}, v^{T(xy)}] = (\bar{A}_x - \bar{A}_{xy})(\bar{A}_y - \bar{A}_{xy}) \qquad (8.5.10)$$

holds for independent lifetimes. Both factors of (8.5.10) are nonpositive, so this covariance is nonnegative. It will be 0 only in the trivial case where $\bar{A}_x$ or $\bar{A}_y$ equals $\bar{A}_{xy}$.

**Example 8.2:**

Calculate the net single premium for an $n$-year term insurance paying a death benefit of 1 at the moment of the last death of $(x)$ and $(y)$ if this death occurs before time $n$. If at least one individual survives to time $n$, no payment is made.

**Solution:**
By restating (4.2.3), and using (8.3.6), we have

$$\bar{A}^1_{\overline{xy}:\overline{n}|} = \int_0^n v^t \,_t p_{\overline{xy}} \, \mu_{\overline{xy}}(t) \, dt$$

$$= \int_0^n v^t \,[_t p_x \, \mu_{x+t} + \,_t p_y \, \mu_{y+t} - \,_t p_{xy} \, \mu_{xy}(t)] \, dt$$

$$= \bar{A}^1_{x:\overline{n}|} + \bar{A}^1_{y:\overline{n}|} - \bar{A}^1_{\overline{xy}:\overline{n}|}$$

The symbol $\bar{A}^1_{\overline{xy}:\overline{n}|}$ represents the net single premium for an $n$-year term insurance payable at the failure of the joint-life status. ▼

**Example 8.3:**

An annuity is payable at the rate of
- 1 per year while both $(x)$ and $(y)$ are alive,
- 2/3 per year while one of $(x)$ or $(y)$ is alive and the other is dead.

Assuming that $T(x)$ and $T(y)$ are independent, derive expressions for

      a. the annuity's present-value random variable
      b. the annuity's actuarial present value
      c. the variance of the random variable in (a).

**Solution:**
a. The annuity is a combination of one that is payable at the rate of 2/3 per year while at least one of $(x)$ and $(y)$ is alive [until time $T(\overline{xy})$] and one that is payable at the rate of 1/3 per year while both individuals are alive [until time $T(xy)$]. The present value of the payments is

# MULTIPLE LIFE FUNCTIONS

$$Z = \frac{2}{3}\bar{a}_{\overline{T(\overline{xy})}|} + \frac{1}{3}\bar{a}_{\overline{T(xy)}|}.$$

b. The actuarial present value is

$$E[Z] = \frac{2}{3}\bar{a}_{\overline{xy}} + \frac{1}{3}\bar{a}_{xy}.$$

Using (8.5.9) to substitute for $\bar{a}_{\overline{xy}}$, we have

$$E[Z] = \frac{2}{3}\bar{a}_x + \frac{2}{3}\bar{a}_y - \frac{1}{3}\bar{a}_{xy}.$$

Alternatively, from (5.3.2B) restated, we have

$$E[Z] = \frac{2}{3}\int_0^\infty v^t \, _tp_{\overline{xy}} \, dt + \frac{1}{3}\int_0^\infty v^t \, _tp_{xy} \, dt.$$

Then, by considering the three mutually exclusive cases as to which of the lives are surviving when $(\overline{xy})$ is surviving at time $t$, and assuming $T(x)$ and $T(y)$ are independent, we can write

$$_tp_{\overline{xy}} = \, _tp_{xy} + \, _tp_x \, (1 - \, _tp_y) + \, _tp_y \, (1 - \, _tp_x).$$

Substitution of this expression into the first integral gives

$$E[Z] = \int_0^\infty v^t \, _tp_{xy} \, dt + \frac{2}{3}\int_0^\infty v^t \, _tp_x \, (1 - \, _tp_y) \, dt$$

$$+ \frac{2}{3}\int_0^\infty v^t \, _tp_y \, (1 - \, _tp_x) \, dt.$$

This expression for $E[Z]$ can be directly obtained by considering the three cases. The first term is the present value of the payments at the rate of 1 per year while both $(x)$ and $(y)$ survive. The second term is the present value of the payments at the rate of 2/3 per year at those times $t$ when $(x)$ is alive [with probability $_tp_x$] and $(y)$ is dead [with probability $(1 - \, _tp_y)$]. The third term has a similar interpretation.

c. $Var[Z] = Var\left[\dfrac{2}{3}\bar{a}_{\overline{T(\overline{xy})}|} + \dfrac{1}{3}\bar{a}_{\overline{T(xy)}|}\right]$

$$= \frac{4}{9}Var[\bar{a}_{\overline{T(\overline{xy})}|}] + \frac{1}{9}Var[\bar{a}_{\overline{T(xy)}|}] + \frac{4}{9}Cov[\bar{a}_{\overline{T(\overline{xy})}|}, \bar{a}_{\overline{T(xy)}|}]$$

But, by (8.5.10),

$$Cov[\bar{a}_{\overline{T(\overline{xy})}|}, \bar{a}_{\overline{T(xy)}|}] = \frac{Cov[v^{T(\overline{xy})}, v^{T(xy)}]}{\delta^2}$$

$$= \frac{(\bar{A}_x - \bar{A}_{xy})(\bar{A}_y - \bar{A}_{xy})}{\delta^2}.$$

# MULTIPLE LIFE FUNCTIONS

Hence

$$\text{Var}[Z] = \frac{(4/9)\,(^2\bar{A}_{\overline{xy}} - \bar{A}_{\overline{xy}}^2) + (1/9)\,(^2\bar{A}_{xy} - \bar{A}_{xy}^2) + (4/9)\,(\bar{A}_x - \bar{A}_{xy})(\bar{A}_y - \bar{A}_{xy})}{\delta^2}. \quad \blacktriangledown$$

**Example 8.4:**         Calculate the actuarial present value of an annuity payable continuously at the rate of

1. 1 per year with certainty until time $n$,
2. 1 per year after time $n$ if both $(x)$ and $(y)$ are alive,
3. 3/4 per year after time $n$ if $(x)$ is alive and $(y)$ is dead, and
4. 1/2 per year after time $n$ if $(y)$ is alive and $(x)$ is dead.

**Solution:**
In this example, the present-value random variable is awkward. But, if only the actuarial present value is desired, it can be easily obtained by use of the current payment technique. Thereby, we obtain an expression for the expectation of $Y$, the present value of the annuity payments, in each case covered by the annuity.

Case 1: $$\int_0^n v^t\, dt = \bar{a}_{\overline{n}|}$$

Case 2: $$\int_n^\infty v^t\, {}_t p_{xy}\, dt = \int_0^\infty v^t\, {}_t p_{xy}\, dt - \int_0^n v^t\, {}_t p_{xy}\, dt$$

$$= \bar{a}_{xy} - \bar{a}_{xy:\overline{n}|}$$

Case 3: $$\frac{3}{4} \int_n^\infty v^t\, {}_t p_x\, (1 - {}_t p_y)\, dt$$

$$= \frac{3}{4}(\bar{a}_x - \bar{a}_{x:\overline{n}|}) - \frac{3}{4}(\bar{a}_{xy} - \bar{a}_{xy:\overline{n}|})$$

Case 4: $$\frac{1}{2} \int_n^\infty v^t\, (1 - {}_t p_x)\, {}_t p_y\, dt$$

$$= \frac{1}{2}(\bar{a}_y - \bar{a}_{y:\overline{n}|}) - \frac{1}{2}(\bar{a}_{xy} - \bar{a}_{xy:\overline{n}|})$$

Adding, we obtain the required actuarial present value,

$$\bar{a}_{\overline{n}|} + \frac{3}{4}\bar{a}_x + \frac{1}{2}\bar{a}_y - \frac{1}{4}\bar{a}_{xy} - \frac{3}{4}\bar{a}_{x:\overline{n}|} - \frac{1}{2}\bar{a}_{y:\overline{n}|} + \frac{1}{4}\bar{a}_{xy:\overline{n}|}. \quad \blacktriangledown$$

In this section we have examined a variety of benefits involving integral expressions. In the next two sections we will study several assumptions about the p.d.f. of $T$ that will simplify the evaluation of integrals involving multiple lives.

## 8.6 Evaluation-Special Mortality Laws

Here we examine the assumption that mortality follows Makeham's law, or its important special case, Gompertz's law, and the implications for the computations of net single premiums and actuarial present values in respect to multiple life statuses.

We begin with the assumption that mortality for each life follows Gompertz's law, $\mu_x = Bc^x$. We seek to substitute a single-life status $(w)$ for the joint-life status $(xy)$, and consider

$$\mu_{xy}(s) = \mu_{w+s} \qquad s \geq 0. \tag{8.6.1}$$

That is,

$$Bc^{x+s} + Bc^{y+s} = Bc^{w+s},$$

or

$$c^x + c^y = c^w, \tag{8.6.2}$$

which defines the desired $w$. It follows that for $t > 0$,

$$
\begin{aligned}
{}_tp_w &= \exp\left(-\int_0^t \mu_{w+s}\, ds\right) \\
&= \exp\left(-\int_0^t \mu_{xy}(s)\, ds\right) \tag{8.6.3} \\
&= {}_tp_{xy}.
\end{aligned}
$$

Thus for $w$ defined in (8.6.2), all probabilities, expected values and variances for the joint-life status $(xy)$ equal those for the single life $(w)$. For tabled values, the need for a two-dimensional array has been replaced by the need for a one-dimensional array, but typically $w$ will be nonintegral and therefore the determination of its values will require interpolation in the single array.

The assumption that mortality for each life follows Makeham's law (see Table 3.6) makes the procedure more complex. The force of mortality for the joint-life status is

$$\mu_{xy}(s) = \mu_{x+s} + \mu_{y+s} = 2A + Bc^s(c^x + c^y). \tag{8.6.4}$$

We cannot substitute a single life for the two lives because of the $2A$. Instead, we replace $(xy)$ with another joint-life status $(ww)$. Then

$$\mu_{ww}(s) = 2\mu_{w+s} = 2(A + Bc^s c^w), \tag{8.6.5}$$

and we choose $w$ such that

$$2c^w = c^x + c^y. \tag{8.6.6}$$

Unlike the Gompertz case where the one-dimensional array is based on functions from a single life table, this one-dimensional array is

# Chapter 8
## MULTIPLE LIFE FUNCTIONS

based on functions for a joint-life status $(ww)$ involving equal-aged lives.

**Example 8.5:**

Use (3.7.1) and the $\ddot{a}_{xx}$ values based on the Illustrative Life Table with interest at 6% to calculate the value of $\ddot{a}_{60:70}$. Compare your result with the values of $\ddot{a}_{60:70}$ in the table of $\ddot{a}_{x:x+10}$.

**Solution:**
From $c = 10^{0.04}$ and $c^{60} + c^{70} = 2c^w$, we obtain $w = 66.11276$. Then $\ddot{a}_{60:70} = 0.88724\,\ddot{a}_{66:66} + 0.11276\,\ddot{a}_{67:67} = 7.55637$. The value by the $\ddot{a}_{x:x+10}$ table is 7.55633. ▼

## 8.7 Evaluation- Uniform Distribution of Deaths

We now consider the assumption of a uniform distribution of deaths in each year of age for each individual in the joint-life status. With this additional assumption, we can evaluate net single premiums of insurance benefits payable at the moment of death and the actuarial present value of annuities payable more frequently than once a year.

We recall from Table 3.5 that, under the assumption of a uniform distribution of deaths for each year of age, $_tp_x = 1 - tq_x$ and

$$_tp_x\,\mu_{x+t} = \frac{d}{dt}(1 - {_tp_x}) = q_x. \tag{8.7.1}$$

When we apply this assumption to a joint-life status $(xy)$, with independent $T(x)$ and $T(y)$, we obtain, for $0 \le t \le 1$,

$$
\begin{aligned}
_tp_{xy}\,\mu_{xy}(t) &= {_tp_x}\,{_tp_y}\,(\mu_{x+t} + \mu_{y+t}) \\
&= {_tp_y}\,({_tp_x}\,\mu_{x+t}) + {_tp_x}\,({_tp_y}\,\mu_{y+t}) \\
&= (1 - tq_y)\,q_x + (1 - tq_x)\,q_y \tag{8.7.2} \\
&= q_x + q_y - q_x q_y + (1 - 2t)\,q_x q_y \\
&= q_{xy} + (1 - 2t)\,q_x q_y.
\end{aligned}
$$

On the basis of (4.4.1), the net single premium for an insurance benefit in regard to a general status, $(u)$, can be written as

$$\bar{A}_u = \sum_{k=0}^{\infty} v^{k+1}\,{_kp_u}\int_0^1 (1 + i)^{1-s}\,\frac{_{k+s}p_u}{_kp_u}\,\mu_u(k + s)\,ds.$$

Using (8.7.2), we can rewrite this for the joint-life status, $(xy)$, as

$$
\begin{aligned}
\bar{A}_{xy} &= \sum_{k=0}^{\infty} v^{k+1}\,{_kp_{xy}}\left[ q_{x+k:y+k}\int_0^1 (1 + i)^{1-s}\,ds \right. \\
&\qquad \left. + q_{x+k}\,q_{y+k}\int_0^1 (1 + i)^{1-s}\,(1 - 2s)\,ds \right] \\
&= \frac{i}{\delta}A_{xy} + \frac{i}{\delta}\left(1 - \frac{2}{\delta} + \frac{2}{i}\right)\sum_{k=0}^{\infty} v^{k+1}\,{_kp_{xy}}\,q_{x+k}\,q_{y+k}. \tag{8.7.3}
\end{aligned}
$$

# MULTIPLE LIFE FUNCTIONS

To interpret the right-hand side of (8.7.3), we see from (4.4.2) that the first term is equal to $\bar{A}_{xy}$ if $T(xy)$, the time-until-failure of $(xy)$, is uniformly distributed in each year of future lifetime. Such is not the case for $T(xy) = [\min(T(x), T(y))]$ when $T(x)$ and $T(y)$ are distributed independently and uniformly over such years. Under this latter assumption, the conditional distribution of $T(xy)$, given that $T(x)$ and $T(y)$ are in different yearly intervals, is also uniform over each year of future lifetime. However, given that $T(x)$ and $T(y)$ are within the same interval, the distribution of their minimum will be shifted toward the beginning of the interval (see Exercise 8.27). A consequence of this shift is to require the second term in (8.7.3) to cover the additional expected costs of the earlier claims in those years. The second term, which is the product of an interest term that is close to $i/6$ (see Exercise 8.28) and a net single premium for an insurance payable if both individuals die in the same future year, is very small. We usually approximate $\bar{A}_{xy}$ by ignoring the small correction term, thereby simplifying (8.7.3) to

$$\bar{A}_{xy} \cong \frac{i}{\delta} A_{xy}, \tag{8.7.4}$$

which is exact, as noted previously, if $T(xy)$ is uniformly distributed in each year of future lifetime.

To evaluate $\bar{a}_{xy}$, we have from (5.3.6), with status $(x)$ replaced by $(xy)$,

$$\bar{a}_{xy} = \frac{1}{\delta}(1 - \bar{A}_{xy}),$$

and, on substitution from (8.7.3), obtain

$$\bar{a}_{xy} = \frac{1}{\delta}\left\{1 - \frac{i}{\delta}\left[A_{xy} + \left(1 - \frac{2}{\delta} + \frac{2}{i}\right)\sum_{k=0}^{\infty} v^{k+1}\,_kp_{xy}\,q_{x+k}\,q_{y+k}\right]\right\}.$$

Now, on the basis of (5.4.6) for the status $(xy)$, we substitute $1 - d\ddot{a}_{xy}$ for $A_{xy}$ and use (5.6.11), (5.6.12) to write

$$\bar{a}_{xy} = \alpha(\infty)\ddot{a}_{xy} - \beta(\infty) - \frac{i}{\delta^2}\left(1 - \frac{2}{\delta} + \frac{2}{i}\right)\sum_{k=0}^{\infty} v^{k+1}\,_kp_{xy}\,q_{x+k}\,q_{y+k}. \tag{8.7.5}$$

Formula (8.7.5) follows from the assumption that $T(x)$ and $T(y)$ are distributed independently and uniformly over future years. If we assume that $T(xy)$ itself is uniformly distributed over each future year, then from the continuous case, $m = \infty$, of (5.5.9), we would have immediately

$$\bar{a}_{xy} = \alpha(\infty)\ddot{a}_{xy} - \beta(\infty). \tag{8.7.6}$$

Formula (8.7.6) differs from (8.7.5) by a small amount, which approximates the product of $i/(6\delta)$ and the net single premium for an insurance payable if both individuals die in the same future year.

To use the same approach to evaluate the actuarial present value of an annuity-due payable $m$thly, we need an expression for $A_{xy}^{(m)}$ under

# MULTIPLE LIFE FUNCTIONS

the assumption of a uniform distribution of deaths for each of the individuals in each year of age. In analogy to the continuous case, we start with

$$A_{xy}^{(m)} = \sum_{k=0}^{\infty} v^k \, {}_kp_{xy} \sum_{j=1}^{m} v^{j/m} \left( {}_{(j-1)/m}p_{x+k:y+k} - {}_{j/m}p_{x+k:y+k} \right). \quad (8.7.7)$$

In Exercise 8.29 this expression, under the assumption that $T(x)$ and $T(y)$ are independently and uniformly distributed over each year of age, is reduced to

$$A_{xy}^{(m)} = \frac{i}{i^{(m)}} A_{xy} + \frac{i}{i^{(m)}} \left( 1 + \frac{1}{m} - \frac{2}{d^{(m)}} + \frac{2}{i} \right) \sum_{k=0}^{\infty} v^{k+1} \, {}_kp_{xy} \, q_{x+k} \, q_{y+k}. \quad (8.7.8)$$

As $m \to \infty$, the expressions in (8.7.8) approach their counterparts in (8.7.3). To interpret the right-hand side of (8.7.8), we see by analogy to (8.7.4) that the first term is the usual approximation for $A_{xy}^{(m)}$ and is exact if $T(xy)$ is uniformly distributed in each year. Then

$$\frac{i}{i^{(m)}} \left( 1 + \frac{1}{m} - \frac{2}{d^{(m)}} + \frac{2}{i} \right) \cong \frac{m^2 - 1}{6 m^2} \, i,$$

which is less than $i/6$.

By substituting (8.7.8) into (5.5.2) restated for $(xy)$, and replacing $A_{xy}$ by $1 - d\ddot{a}_{xy}$, we obtain the formula for $\ddot{a}_{xy}^{(m)}$ that is analogous to (8.7.5). If the second term of (8.7.8) is ignored, the formula for $\ddot{a}_{xy}^{(m)}$ reduces to

$$\ddot{a}_{xy}^{(m)} = \alpha(m) \ddot{a}_{xy} - \beta(m). \quad (8.7.9)$$

Again by (5.5.9), this is exact under the assumption that the distribution of $T(xy)$ is uniform over each year of future lifetime.

## 8.8 Simple Contingent Functions

In this section we study insurances that, in addition to being dependent on the time of failure of the status, are contingent on the order of the deaths of the individuals in the group.

We begin with an evaluation of the probability that $(x)$ dies before $(y)$ and before $n$ years from now. This probability is denoted by ${}_nq_{xy}^1$, where the 1 over the $x$ indicates the probability is for an event in which $(x)$ dies before $(y)$, and the $n$ indicates that the event occurs within $n$ years. Then ${}_nq_{xy}^1$ is equal to the double integral of the joint p.d.f. of $T(x)$ and $T(y)$ over the set of outcomes such that $T(x) \le T(y)$ and $T(x) \le n$. Under the assumption that $T(x)$ and $T(y)$ are independent, the integrand is the product of the single life p.d.f.'s and we have

$$_nq_{xy}^1 = \int_0^n \int_t^{\infty} {}_sp_y \, \mu_{y+s} \, {}_tp_x \, \mu_{x+t} \, ds \, dt. \quad (8.8.1)$$

Moving ${}_tp_x \, \mu_{x+t}$ outside the inner integral we see that the inner integral is ${}_tp_y$, thus (8.8.1) can be written

$$_n q_{xy}^1 = \int_0^n {}_t p_{xy}\, \mu_{x+t}\, dt.  \qquad (8.8.2)$$

An interpretation of this expression involves three elements. First, because $t$ is the time of death of $(x)$, the probability ${}_t p_{xy}$ indicates that both $(x)$ and $(y)$ survive to time $t$. Second, $\mu_{x+t}\, dt$ is the probability that $(x)$, now aged $x + t$, will die in the interval $dt$, and finally the probabilities are summed for all times $t$ between 0 and $n$.

We can also evaluate the probability that $(y)$ dies after $(x)$ and before $n$ years from now. This probability is denoted by $_n q_{xy}^2$, the 2 above the $y$ indicating that $(y)$ dies second, the $n$ requiring that this occurs within $n$ years. To evaluate $_n q_{xy}^2$, we integrate the joint p.d.f. of $T(x)$ and $T(y)$ over the event $[0 \le T(x) \le T(y) \le n]$ using $T(y)$ as the variable for the outside integral,

$$_n q_{xy}^2 = \int_0^n \int_0^t {}_s p_x\, \mu_{x+s}\, {}_t p_y\, \mu_{y+t}\, ds\, dt$$

$$= \int_0^n (1 - {}_t p_x)\, {}_t p_y\, \mu_{y+t}\, dt  \qquad (8.8.3)$$

$$= {}_n q_y - {}_n q_{xy}^1.$$

In the second expression the integrand is the product

$$\Pr\left[(x)\text{ predeceases }(y)\,\middle|\,(y)\text{ dies at }t\right]\Pr\left[(y)\text{ dies at }t\right].$$

Similar integrals can be written for net single premiums for contingent insurances.

We can also use $T(x)$ as the variable for the outside integral. This gives

$$_n q_{xy}^2 = \int_0^n \int_s^n {}_s p_x\, \mu_{x+s}\, {}_t p_y\, \mu_{y+t}\, dt\, ds$$

$$= \int_0^n ({}_s p_y - {}_n p_y)\, {}_s p_x\, \mu_{x+s}\, ds  \qquad (8.8.4)$$

$$= {}_n q_{xy}^1 - {}_n p_y\, {}_n q_x.$$

The second expression is interpreted as $(x)$ dies at time $s$ with $0 < s < n$, and $(y)$ survives to time $s$ but not to time $n$. Moreover, we now have that

$$_n q_{xy}^1 = {}_n q_{xy}^2 + {}_n p_y\, {}_n q_x.$$

This implies

$$_n q_{xy}^1 \ge {}_n q_{xy}^2.$$

Similar integrals can be written for net single premiums on

# Chapter 8
# MULTIPLE LIFE FUNCTIONS

contingent insurances, but the analogue of the double integral in (8.8.4) does not simplify to the same extent. The following examples illustrate net single premiums for contingent insurances.

**Example 8.6:** Derive the net single premium for an insurance of 1 payable at the time of the death of $(x)$ provided that $(y)$ is still alive.

**Solution:**
The net single premium, denoted by $\bar{A}^1_{xy}$, is $E[Z]$ where

$$Z = \begin{cases} v^{T(x)} & T(x) \le T(y) \\ 0 & T(x) > T(y). \end{cases}$$

Since $Z$ is a function of $T(x)$ and $T(y)$, we can write an integral for the expectation of $Z$ by using the joint distribution of $T(x)$ and $T(y)$,

$$\bar{A}^1_{xy} = \int_0^\infty \int_t^\infty v^t \, {}_sp_y \, \mu_{y+s} \, {}_tp_x \, \mu_{x+t} \, ds \, dt$$

$$= \int_0^\infty v^t \, {}_tp_{xy} \, \mu_{x+t} \, dt.$$

The final expression can be interpreted as follows: If $(x)$ dies at any future time $t$ and $(y)$ is still surviving, then a payment of 1 with present value $v^t$ is made. ▼

**Example 8.7:** Derive the net single premium for an insurance of 1 payable at the moment of the death of $(y)$ if predeceased by $(x)$.

**Solution:**
The net single premium, denoted by $\bar{A}^2_{xy}$, is $E[Z]$ where

$$Z = \begin{cases} v^{T(y)} & T(x) \le T(y) \\ 0 & T(x) > T(y). \end{cases}$$

Again, $Z$ is a function of $T(x)$ and $T(y)$ so we can use their joint p.d.f. to obtain $E[Z]$,

$$\bar{A}^2_{xy} = \int_0^\infty \int_0^t v^t \, {}_sp_x \, \mu_{x+s} \, {}_tp_y \, \mu_{y+t} \, ds \, dt$$

$$= \int_0^\infty v^t \, (1 - {}_tp_x) \, {}_tp_y \, \mu_{y+t} \, dt$$

$$= \bar{A}_y - \bar{A}^1_{xy}.$$

We note here that we can express the net single premium for a simple contingent insurance, payable on a death other than the first death, in terms of net single premiums for insurances payable on the first death. This is the initial step in the numerical evaluation of simple contingent insurances.

Another expression can be obtained by reversing the order of integration in the double integral, that is, proceed as in (8.8.4). We have

$$\bar{A}_{xy}^{2} = \int_{0}^{\infty} \int_{s}^{\infty} v^{t} \, _{t}p_{y} \, \mu_{y+t} \, _{s}p_{x} \, \mu_{x+s} \, dt \, ds.$$

We now replace $t$ with $r+s$ in the inner integral, rewrite the expression and evaluate it.

$$\bar{A}_{xy}^{2} = \int_{0}^{\infty} \int_{0}^{\infty} v^{r+s} \, _{r+s}p_{y} \, \mu_{y+r+s} \, _{s}p_{x} \, \mu_{x+s} \, dr \, ds$$

$$= \int_{0}^{\infty} v^{s} \, _{s}p_{y} \, _{s}p_{x} \, \mu_{x+s} \left( \int_{0}^{\infty} v^{r} \, _{r}p_{y+s} \, \mu_{y+s+r} \, dr \right) ds$$

$$= \int_{0}^{\infty} v^{s} \, \bar{A}_{y+s} \, _{s}p_{y} \, _{s}p_{x} \, \mu_{x+s} \, ds.$$

This last integral is an application of the general result given in (2.2.10), $E[W] = E[E[W|V]]$. Here $V = T(x)$, $W = Z$ and we see that the conditional expectation of $Z$, given $T(x) = s$, is the net single premium, $v^{s} \, _{s}p_{y} \, \bar{A}_{y+s}$, for a pure endowment for an amount $\bar{A}_{y+s}$ sufficient to fund a unit insurance on $(y + s)$. ▼

In this section we have discussed only contingent insurances. Contingent annuities, called ***reversionary annuities,*** will be covered in Chapter 17. These commence payment upon the failure of a given status if a second status exists, and continue payment until failure of the second status. (See Examples 8.3 and 8.4 for preliminary illustrations.)

## 8.9 Evaluation-Simple Contingent Functions

We now turn to the evaluation of simple contingent probabilities and net single premiums, noting the effects of assuming Gompertz's law, Makeham's law and a uniform distribution of deaths.

**Example 8.8:**

Assuming Gompertz's law for the forces of mortality, calculate

a. the net single premium for an $n$-year term contingent insurance paying a unit amount at the moment of death of $(x)$ only if $(x)$ dies before $(y)$

b. the probability that $(x)$ dies within $n$ years and predeceases $(y)$.

**Solution:**

a. $\bar{A}_{xy:\overline{n}|}^{1} = \int_{0}^{n} v^{t} \, _{t}p_{xy} \, \mu_{x+t} \, dt$

# MULTIPLE LIFE FUNCTIONS

Under Gompertz's law,

$$\bar{A}^1_{xy:\overline{n}|} = \int_0^n v^t \, {}_tp_{xy} \, B c^x \, c^t \, dt$$

$$= \frac{c^x}{c^x + c^y} \int_0^n v^t \, {}_tp_{xy} \, B (c^x + c^y) c^t \, dt \qquad (8.9.1)$$

$$= \frac{c^x}{c^x + c^y} \int_0^n v^t \, {}_tp_{xy} \, \mu_{x+t:y+t} \, dt$$

$$= \frac{c^x}{c^x + c^y} \, \bar{A}^1_{\overline{xy}:\overline{n}|}.$$

Furthermore, if (8.6.2) holds, then

$$\bar{A}^1_{\overline{xy}:\overline{n}|} = \bar{A}^1_{w:\overline{n}|},$$

and

$$\bar{A}^1_{xy:\overline{n}|} = \frac{c^x}{c^w} \, \bar{A}^1_{w:\overline{n}|}. \qquad (8.9.2)$$

b. Referring to (8.8.2) we see that ${}_nq^1_{xy}$ is $\bar{A}^1_{xy:\overline{n}|}$ with $v = 1$. Thus, it follows from (8.9.2) that, under Gompertz's law,

$$_nq^1_{xy} = \frac{c^x}{c^w} \, {}_nq_w \qquad (8.9.3)$$

where $c^w = c^x + c^y$. ▼

**Example 8.9:** Assuming Makeham's law for the forces of mortality, repeat Example 8.8.

**Solution:**

a. $\bar{A}^1_{xy:\overline{n}|} = \int_0^n v^t \, {}_tp_{xy} \, (A + B c^x c^t) \, dt$

$$= A \int_0^n v^t \, {}_tp_{xy} \, dt + \frac{c^x}{c^x + c^y} \int_0^n v^t \, {}_tp_{xy} \, B (c^x + c^y) c^t \, dt$$

$$= A \left(1 - \frac{2c^x}{c^x + c^y}\right) \int_0^n v^t \, {}_tp_{xy} \, dt$$

$$+ \frac{c^x}{c^x + c^y} \int_0^n v^t \, {}_tp_{xy} \, [2A + B(c^x + c^y)c^t] \, dt$$

$$= A \left(1 - \frac{2c^x}{c^x + c^y}\right) \bar{a}_{xy:\overline{n}|} + \frac{c^x}{c^x + c^y} \, \bar{A}^1_{\overline{xy}:\overline{n}|}$$

# MULTIPLE LIFE FUNCTIONS

Then by using (8.6.6) we obtain

$$\bar{A}^1_{xy:\overline{n}|} = A\left(1 - \frac{c^x}{c^w}\right) \bar{a}_{ww:\overline{n}|} + \frac{c^x}{2\,c^w}\,\bar{A}^1_{\overline{ww}:\overline{n}|}. \tag{8.9.4}$$

b. Again we set $v = 1$ in the result of part (a) to have

$$_nq^1_{xy} = A\left(1 - \frac{c^x}{c^w}\right) \mathring{e}_{ww:\overline{n}|} + \frac{c^x}{2\,c^w}\,_nq_{ww}. \tag{8.9.5}$$

▼

The net single premium for a contingent insurance paying at the end of the year of death is

$$A^1_{xy} = \sum_{k=0}^{\infty} v^{k+1}\,_kp_{xy}\, q^1_{\overline{x+k}:y+k}. \tag{8.9.6}$$

Under the assumption of a uniform distribution of deaths for each individual, we have

$$q^1_{\overline{x+k}:y+k} = \int_0^1 {}_sp_{x+k:y+k}\, \mu_{x+k+s}\, ds$$

$$= \int_0^1 q_{x+k}(1 - s\,q_{y+k})\, ds \tag{8.9.7}$$

$$= q_{x+k}\left(1 - \frac{1}{2}q_{y+k}\right).$$

We can now rewrite ${}_sp_{x+k:y+k}\, \mu_{x+k+s}$ in terms of $q^1_{\overline{x+k}:y+k}$,

$${}_sp_{x+k:y+k}\, \mu_{x+k+s} = q_{x+k}(1 - s\,q_{y+k})$$

$$= q_{x+k}\left(1 - \frac{1}{2}q_{y+k}\right) + \left(\frac{1}{2} - s\right)q_{x+k}q_{y+k} \tag{8.9.8}$$

$$= q^1_{\overline{x+k}:y+k} + \left(\frac{1}{2} - s\right)q_{x+k}q_{y+k}.$$

For the immediate payment of claims, the net single premium is

$$\bar{A}^1_{xy} = \sum_{k=0}^{\infty} v^k\,_kp_{xy} \int_0^1 v^s\,{}_sp_{x+k:y+k}\, \mu_{x+k+s}\, ds$$

$$= \sum_{k=0}^{\infty} v^{k+1}\,_kp_{xy}\left[q^1_{\overline{x+k}:y+k}\int_0^1 (1+i)^{1-s}\, ds\right.$$

$$\left. + q_{x+k}\,q_{y+k}\int_0^1 (1+i)^{1-s}\left(\frac{1}{2} - s\right) ds\right] \tag{8.9.9}$$

$$= \frac{i}{\delta}A^1_{xy} + \frac{1}{2}\frac{i}{\delta}\left(1 - \frac{2}{\delta} + \frac{2}{i}\right)\sum_{k=0}^{\infty} v^{k+1}\,_kp_{xy}\, q_{x+k}\, q_{y+k}.$$

# Chapter 8
## MULTIPLE LIFE FUNCTIONS

The second term in (8.9.9) is very small relative to the total premium. It is 1/2 of the second term in (8.7.3).

## 8.10
## Notes and References

The concept of the future-lifetime random variable, developed for a single life in previous chapters, has been extended to a general status, particular cases of which are statuses defined by several lives. Probability distributions, actuarial present values, net single premiums, variances and covariances based on these new random variables were obtained for statuses defined by two lives by adaptation of the single life theory. These concepts will be developed for more than two lives in Chapter 17.

Discussions of the ideas of this chapter without the use of random variables can be found in Chapters 9–13 of Jordan (1967) and Chapters 7–8 of Neill (1977). A general analysis of laws of mortality, which simplify the formulas for actuarial functions based on more than one life, is given by Greville (1956).

## Exercises

Unless otherwise indicated, all lives in question are subject to the same table of mortality rates and their times-until-death are independent random variables.

*Section 8.2*

8.1. In terms of the single life probabilities $_np_x$ and $_np_y$, express
   a. the probability that $(xy)$ will survive $n$ years
   b. the probability that exactly one of the lives $(x)$ and $(y)$ will survive $n$ years
   c. the probability that at least one of the lives $(x)$ and $(y)$ will survive $n$ years
   d. the probability that $(xy)$ will fail within $n$ years
   e. the probability that at least one of the lives will die within $n$ years
   f. the probability that both lives will die within $n$ years.

8.2. Show that the probability that $(x)$ survives $n$ years and $(y)$ survives $n - 1$ years may be expressed either as

$$\frac{_np_{x:y-1}}{p_{y-1}}$$

or as

$$p_x \,_{n-1}p_{x+1:y}.$$

8.3. Evaluate

$$\int_0^n {}_tp_{xx}\,\mu_{xx}(t)\,dt.$$

*Section 8.3*

8.4. Show

$$_tp_{\overline{xy}} = {}_tp_{xy} + {}_tp_x\,(1 - {}_tp_y) + {}_tp_y\,(1 - {}_tp_x)$$

algebraically and by general reasoning.

8.5. Find the probability that at least one of two lives $(x)$ and $(y)$ will die in the year $(n+1)$. Is this the same as $_{n|}q_{\overline{xy}}$? Explain.

*Section 8.4*

8.6. Given that $_{25}p_{25:50} = 0.2$ and $_{15}p_{25} = 0.9$, calculate the probability that a person aged 40 will survive to age 75.

8.7. If $\mu_x = 1/(100-x)$ for $0 \le x < 100$, calculate
   a. $_{10}p_{40:50}$      e. $\mathrm{Var}[T(40:50)]$
   b. $_{10}p_{\overline{40:50}}$      f. $\mathrm{Var}[T(\overline{40:50})]$
   c. $\mathring{e}_{40:50}$      g. $\mathrm{Cov}[T(40:50),\ T(\overline{40:50})]$
   d. $\mathring{e}_{\overline{40:50}}$      h. the correlation between $T(40:50)$ and $T(\overline{40:50})$.

8.8. Evaluate $\dfrac{d\mathring{e}_{xx}}{dx}$.

8.9. Show that the probability of two lives (30) and (40) dying in the same year can be expressed as

$$1 + e_{30:40} - p_{30}(1 + e_{31:40}) - p_{40}(1 + e_{30:41}) + p_{30:40}(1 + e_{31:41}).$$

8.10. Show that the probability of two lives (30) and (40) dying at the same age last birthday can be expressed as

$$_{10}p_{30}(1 + e_{40:40}) - 2\ _{11}p_{30}(1 + e_{40:41}) + p_{40}\ _{11}p_{30}(1 + e_{41:41}).$$

8.11. Assume that the forces of mortality that apply to individuals I and II are

$$\mu_x^{\mathrm{I}} = \log\frac{10}{9},\ \text{for all } x$$

and

$$\mu_x^{\mathrm{II}} = (10 - x)^{-1},\ \text{for } 0 \le x < 10.$$

Evaluate the probability that, if both individuals are of exact age 1, the first death will occur between exact ages 3 and 5.

*Section 8.5*

8.12. Show that

$$a_{\overline{xy}:\overline{n}|} = a_{\overline{n}|} + {}_{n|}a_{xy}.$$

Describe the underlying benefit.

8.13. For a net single premium denoted by $\bar{A}_{x:\overline{n}|}$, describe the benefit. Show that

$$\bar{A}_{x:\overline{n}|} = \bar{A}_x - \bar{A}_{x:\overline{n}|} + v^n.$$

8.14. For independent lifetimes $T(x)$ and $T(y)$, show that

$$\mathrm{Cov}[v^{T(\overline{xy})},\ v^{T(xy)}] = (\bar{A}_x - \bar{A}_{xy})(\bar{A}_y - \bar{A}_{xy}).$$

8.15. Express, in terms of single- and joint-life annuity values, the actuarial present value of an annuity payable continuously at a rate of 1 per year while at least one of (25) and (30) survives and is below age 50.

8.16. Express, in terms of single- and joint-life annuity values, the actuarial present value of a deferred annuity of 1 payable at the end of any year as long as either (25) or (30) is living after age 50.

8.17. Calculate the actuarial present value of an $n$-year temporary annuity-due, payable in respect to $(\overline{xy})$, providing annual payments of 1 while both lives survive, reducing to $1/2$ on the death of $(x)$ and to $1/3$ on the death of $(y)$.

8.18. An annuity-immediate of 1 is payable to $(x)$ as long as he lives jointly with $(y)$ and for $n$ years after the death of $(y)$, except that in no event will payments be made after $m$ years from the present time, $m > n$. Show that the actuarial present value is

$$a_{x:\overline{n}|} + {}_nE_x\, a_{x+n:y:\overline{m-n}|}.$$

8.19. Obtain an expression for the actuarial present value of a continuous annuity of 1 per annum payable while at least one of two lives (40) and (55) is living and is over age 60, but not if (40) is alive and under age 55.

8.20. A qualified joint-and-survivor annuity to $(x)$ and $(y)$ is payable at an initial rate per year while $(x)$ lives, and, if $(y)$ survives $(x)$, is continued at the fraction $p, 1/2 \leq p \leq 1$, of the initial rate per year during the lifetime of $(y)$ following the death of $(x)$.
   a. Express the actuarial present value of such an annuity-due with an initial rate of 1 per year, payable in $m$thly installments, in terms of the actuarial present values of single-life and joint-life annuities.
   b. A qualified joint-and-survivor annuity to $(x)$ and $(y)$ and a life annuity to $(x)$ are said to be actuarially equivalent on the basis of stated assumptions if they have equal actuarial present values on such basis. Derive an expression for the ratio of the initial payment of the qualified joint-and-survivor annuity to the payment rate of the actuarially equivalent life annuity.

*Section 8.6*

8.21. When, under Makeham's Law, the status $(xy)$ is replaced by the status $(ww)$, show that

$$w - y = \frac{\log(c^{\Delta} + 1) - \log 2}{\log c}$$

where $\Delta = x - y \geq 0$. (This indicates that $w$ can be obtained from the younger age $y$ by adding an amount that is a function of $\Delta = x - y$. Such a property is referred to as a *law of uniform seniority*.)

8.22. On the basis of the Illustrative Life Table with interest of 6%, calculate $\ddot{a}_{50:60:\overline{10}|}$. In your solution, use
   a. values interpolated in the $\ddot{a}_{xx}$ table
   b. values from the $\ddot{a}_{x:x+10}$ table.

8.23. Given a mortality table that follows Makeham's law and ages $x$ and $y$ for which $(ww)$ is the equivalent equal-age status, show that
   a. $_tp_w$ is the geometric mean of $_tp_x$ and $_tp_y$
   b. $_tp_x + {_tp_y} > 2\,_tp_w$ for $x \neq y$
   c. $a_{\overline{xy}} > a_{\overline{ww}}$ for $x \neq y$.

8.24. Given a mortality table that follows Makeham's law, show that $\bar{a}_{xy}$ is equal to the actuarial present value of an annuity with a single life $(w)$ where $c^w = c^x + c^y$ and force of interest $\delta' = \delta + A$. Further, show that

$$\bar{A}_{xy} = \bar{A}'_w + A\,\bar{a}'_w$$

where the primed functions are evaluated at force of interest $\delta'$.

8.25. Consider two mortality tables, one for males, $M$, and one for females, $F$, with

$$\mu^M_z = 3a + \frac{3bz}{2} \quad \text{and} \quad \mu^F_z = a + bz.$$

We wish to use a table of actuarial present values for two lives, one male and one female, each of age $w$, to evaluate the actuarial present value of a joint-life annuity for a male aged $x$ and a female aged $y$. Express $w$ in terms of $x$ and $y$.

*Section 8.7*

8.26. Find $\overset{\circ}{e}_{xy}$ if $q_x = q_y = 1$ and the deaths are uniformly distributed over the year of age for each of $(x)$ and $(y)$.

8.27. Let $T(x)$ and $T(y)$ be independent and uniformly distributed in the next year of age. Given that both $(x)$ and $(y)$ die within the next year, demonstrate that the time-of-failure of $(xy)$ is not uniformly distributed over the year. [Hint: Show that $\Pr\left[T(xy) \leq t \mid \{(T(x) \leq 1) \cap (T(y) \leq 1)\}\right] = 2t - t^2$.]

8.28. Show

$$\frac{1}{\delta} = \frac{1}{i\left[1 - (i/2 - i^2/3 + i^3/4 - i^4/5 + \cdots)\right]}$$

$$= \frac{1}{i}\left(1 + \frac{i}{2} - \frac{i^2}{12} + \frac{i^3}{24} - \frac{19\,i^4}{720} + \cdots\right).$$

Hence, show

$$\frac{i}{\delta}\left(1 - \frac{2}{\delta} + \frac{2}{i}\right) \cong \frac{i}{6} - \frac{i^3}{360} + \cdots.$$

8.29. Show that if deaths are uniformly distributed over each year of age, then

# Chapter 8
## MULTIPLE LIFE FUNCTIONS

$$_{(j-1)/m}p_{xy} - {}_{j/m}p_{xy} = \frac{1}{m}q_{xy} + \frac{m+1-2j}{m^2}q_x q_y$$

for any $x$ and $y$ and $j = 1,2,3,\ldots,m$. Hence, verify expression (8.7.8).

*Section 8.8*

8.30. Show by general reasoning that

$$_nq^1_{xy} = {}_nq^2_{xy} + {}_nq_x \, {}_np_y.$$

When $n \to \infty$, what does the equation become?

8.31. Show that the net single premium for an insurance of 1 payable at the end of the year of death of $(x)$, provided that $(y)$ survives to the time of payment, can be expressed as $v p_y \ddot{a}_{x:y+1} - a_{xy}$.

8.32. Show that $A^1_{xy} - A^2_{xy} = A_{xy} - A_y$.

8.33. Express, in terms of net single premiums for single life and first death contingent insurances, the net single premium for an insurance of 1 payable at the moment of death of (50), provided that (20), at that time, has died or attained age 40.

8.34. Express, in terms of net single premiums for pure endowment and first death contingent insurances, the net single premium for an insurance of 1 payable at the time of the death of $(x)$ after $(y)$, providing $(y)$ died during the $n$ years preceding the death of $(x)$.

8.35. If $\mu_x = 1/(100 - x)$ for $0 \le x < 100$, calculate $_{25}q^2_{25:50}$.

*Section 8.9*

8.36. In a mortality table known to follow Makeham's law, you are given that $A = 0.003$ and $c^{10} = 3$.
   a. If $\mathring{e}_{40:50} = 17$, calculate $_\infty q^1_{40:50}$.
   b. Express $\bar{A}^1_{40:50}$ in terms of $\bar{A}_{40:50}$ and $\bar{a}_{40:50}$.

8.37. Given that mortality follows Gompertz's law with $\mu_x = 10^{-4} \, 2^{x/8}$ for $x > 35$ and that by (8.9.2)

$$\bar{A}^1_{40:48:\overline{10|}} = f\bar{A}^1_{w:\overline{10|}},$$

calculate $f$ and $w$.

*Miscellaneous*

8.38. The status $(\overline{n|})$ is one that exists for exactly $n$ years. It has been used in conjunction with life statuses, for example, in $\bar{A}_{x:\overline{n|}}$, $\bar{A}^1_{x:\overline{n|}}$, $\bar{A}_{x:\overline{n|}}^{\phantom{1}1}$, $\ddot{a}_{x:\overline{n|}}$, $A_{xy:\overline{n|}}$. Simplify and interpret the following:
   a. $\bar{a}_{x:\overline{n|}}$
   b. $\bar{A}^2_{x:\overline{n|}}$.

8.39. Use the probability rule $\Pr(A \cup B) = \Pr(A) + \Pr(B) - \Pr(A \cap B)$ to obtain (8.3.5D).

8.40. Evaluate $\dfrac{\partial}{\partial x}\mathring{e}_{xy}$.

# Chapter 9
## MULTIPLE DECREMENT MODELS

## 9.1
## Introduction

In Chapter 8 we extended the theory of Chapters 3 through 7 from an individual life to multiple lives, subject to a single contingency of death. We now return to the case of a single life, but here subject to multiple contingencies. As an application of this extension, we observe that the number of workers for an employer will be reduced when an employee withdraws, becomes disabled, dies or retires. In manpower planning, it might be necessary to estimate only the numbers of those presently at work who will remain active to various years into the future. For this task, the model for survivorship developed in Chapter 3 would be adequate, with time-until-termination of employment rather than time-until-death as the interpretation of the basic random variable. However, actuaries require models for employee benefit plans in which the benefits paid on termination of employment may depend on the cause of termination. For example, the benefits on retirement will often differ from those payable on death or disability. Therefore, survivorship models for employee benefit systems will include random variables for both time-of-termination and cause of termination. Also, the benefit structure often depends on earnings, which is another and different kind of uncertainty that will be discussed in Chapter 10.

As another application, most individual life insurances provide payment of a nonforfeiture benefit if premiums stop before the end of the specified premium payment term. A comprehensive model for such insurances will incorporate both time-until-termination and cause of termination as random variables.

Disability income insurance provides periodic payments to insureds who satisfy the definition of disability contained in the policy. In some cases, the amount of the periodic payments may depend on whether the disability was caused by illness or accident. A person may cease to be an active insured by dying, withdrawing, becoming disabled or reaching the end of the coverage period. A complete model for disability insurance will incorporate a random variable for time-until-termination, when the insured ceases to be a member of the active insureds, as well as a random variable for the cause of termination.

In public health planning, there is interest in the analysis of mortality and survivorship in terms of cause of death. Public health goals may be set by a study of joint distribution of time-until-death and cause of death. Priorities in cardiovascular and cancer research were established by this type of analysis.

The main purpose of this chapter is to build a theory for studying the distribution of two random variables in regard to a single life: time-until-termination from a given status and cause of the termination. The resulting model is used in each of the applications described in this section. Within actuarial science, the termination from a given status is called *decrement* and the subject of this chapter is called *multiple decrement theory*. Within biostatistics it is referred to as the *theory of competing risks*.

**9.2
Two Random
Variables**

It is also possible to develop multiple decrement theory in terms of deterministic rates and rate functions. There will be some recapitulation of the theory from this point of view in Section 9.4.

Chapter 3 was devoted in part to methods for specifying and using the distribution of the continuous random variable $T(x)$, the time-until-death of $(x)$. The same methods can be used to study time-until-termination from a status, such as employment with a particular employer, with only minor changes in vocabulary. In fact, we shall use the same notation $T(x)$, or more briefly $T$, to denote the time random variable in this new setting.

In this section, we shall expand the basic model by introducing a second random variable, cause of decrement, to be denoted by $J(x) = J$. We shall assume that $J$ is a discrete random variable.

The applications in Section 9.1 provide examples of these random variables. For employee benefit plan applications, the random variable $J$ could be assigned the values 1, 2, 3 or 4 depending on whether termination is due to withdrawal, disability, death or retirement respectively. In the life insurance application, $J$ could be assigned the values 1 or 2, depending on whether the insured dies or chooses to terminate payment of premiums. For the disability insurance application, $J$ could be assigned the values 1, 2, 3 or 4 depending on whether the insured dies, withdraws, becomes disabled or reaches the end of the coverage period. Finally, in the public health application, there are many possibilities for causes of decrement. For example, in a given study, $J$ could be assigned the values 1, 2, 3 or 4 depending on whether death was caused by cardiovascular disease, cancer, accident or all other causes.

Now our purpose is to describe the joint distribution of $T$ and $J$ and the related marginal and conditional distributions. We shall denote the joint p.d.f. of $T$ and $J$ by $f(t,j)$, the marginal p.f. of $J$ by $h(j)$, and the marginal p.d.f. of $T$ by $g(t)$. Figure 9.1 illustrates these distributions. They may seem strange at first because $J$ is a discrete random variable and $T$ is continuous.

The joint p.d.f. of $T$ and $J$, $f(t,j)$, can be pictured as falling on $m$ parallel sheets, as illustrated in Figure 9.1 for 3 causes of decrement ($m = 3$). There is a separate sheet for each of the $m$ causes of decrement recognized in the model. In Figure 9.1 the following relations hold:

$$\sum_{j=1}^{3} h(j) = 1$$

and

$$\int_{0}^{\infty} g(t)\, dt = 1.$$

The p.d.f. $f(t,j)$ can be used in the usual ways to calculate the

Chapter 9
## MULTIPLE DECREMENT MODELS

**Figure 9.1**
**Graph of $f(t,j)$**

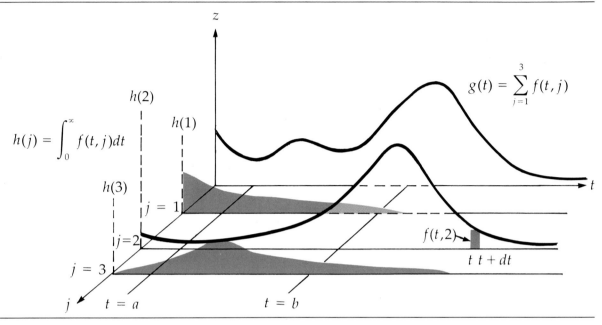

probabilities of events defined by $T$ and $J$. For example,

$$f(t,j)\,dt = \Pr[t < T \le t + dt, J = j]. \tag{9.2.1}$$

$$\Pr(a < T \le b) = \sum_{j=1}^{m} \int_{a}^{b} f(t,j)\,dt,$$

and

$$\Pr(0 < T \le t, J = j) = \int_{0}^{t} f(s,j)\,ds. \tag{9.2.2}$$

The probability of decrement before time $t$ due to cause $j$ given in (9.2.2) has the special symbol

$$_tq_x^{(j)} = \int_{0}^{t} f(s,j)\,ds \qquad t \ge 0, j = 1,2,\ldots,m, \tag{9.2.3}$$

which is illustrative of the use of the superscript to denote the cause of decrement in multiple decrement theory.

By the definition of the marginal distribution for $J$, appearing as $h(j)$ in the $(j,z)$ plane of Figure 9.1, we have

$$h(j) = \int_{0}^{\infty} f(s,j)\,ds = {}_\infty q_x^{(j)} \qquad j = 1,2,\ldots,m. \tag{9.2.4}$$

This is new and without a counterpart in Chapter 3, unlike the marginal p.d.f. for $T$, $g(t)$, in the $(t,z)$ plane of Figure 9.1. For $g(t)$, and the d.f., $G(t)$, we have for $t \geq 0$

$$g(t) = \sum_{j=1}^{m} f(t,j)$$

and                                                                 (9.2.5)

$$G(t) = \int_0^t g(s)\,ds.$$

The notations introduced in Chapter 3 can be extended to accommodate the random variable $T$. Using the superscript $(\tau)$ to indicate that a function refers to all causes, or total force, of decrement, we obtain

$$_tq_x^{(\tau)} = \Pr(T \leq t) = G(t) = \int_0^t g(s)\,ds, \qquad (9.2.6)$$

$$_tp_x^{(\tau)} = \Pr(T > t) = 1 - {}_tq_x^{(\tau)}, \qquad (9.2.7)$$

and

$$\mu_{x+t}^{(\tau)} = \frac{g(t)}{1 - G(t)} = \frac{1}{{}_tp_x^{(\tau)}}\frac{d}{dt}\,{}_tq_x^{(\tau)}$$

$$= -\frac{1}{{}_tp_x^{(\tau)}}\frac{d}{dt}\,{}_tp_x^{(\tau)} \qquad (9.2.8)$$

$$= -\frac{d}{dt}\log {}_tp_x^{(\tau)}.$$

Mathematically, these functions for the random variable $T$ of this chapter are identical to those for the $T$ of Chapter 3; the difference is in their interpretation in the applications.

As with the applications in previous chapters, the statement in (9.2.1) can be analyzed by conditioning on survival in the given status to time $t$. In this way, we have

$$f(t,j)\,dt = \Pr[T > t]\,\Pr[\{(t < T \leq t + dt) \cap (J = j)\}|T > t]. \quad (9.2.9)$$

By analogy with (3.2.12) this suggests the definition of the force of decrement due to cause $j$ as

$$\mu_{x+t}^{(j)} = \frac{f(t,j)}{1 - G(t)} = \frac{f(t,j)}{{}_tp_x^{(\tau)}}. \qquad (9.2.10)$$

The force of decrement at age $x + t$ due to cause $j$ has a conditional probability interpretation. It is the value of the joint conditional p.d.f. of $T$ and $J$ at $x + t$, given survival to $x + t$. Then (9.2.9) can be rewritten as

$$f(t,j)\,dt = {}_tp_x^{(\tau)}\,\mu_{x+t}^{(j)}\,dt \qquad j = 1,2,\ldots,m,\ t \geq 0. \quad (9.2.9)\text{ restated}$$

# Chapter 9
## MULTIPLE DECREMENT MODELS

In words,

(the joint probability of decrement between $t$ and $t + dt$ due to cause $j$)

$=$ (the probability, $_tp_x^{(\tau)}$, that $(x)$ remains in the given status until time $t$)

$\times$ (the conditional probability, $\mu_{x+t}^{(j)}\, dt$, that decrement occurs between $t$ and $t + dt$ due to cause $j$, given that decrement has not occurred before time $t$).

It follows, from differentiation of (9.2.3) and use of (9.2.10), that

$$\mu_{x+t}^{(j)} = \frac{1}{_tp_x^{(\tau)}} \frac{d}{dt}\, {}_tq_x^{(j)}. \tag{9.2.11}$$

Now, from (9.2.6), (9.2.5) and (9.2.3)

$$_tq_x^{(\tau)} = \int_0^t g(s)\, ds = \int_0^t \sum_{j=1}^m f(s,j)\, ds$$

$$= \sum_{j=1}^m \int_0^t f(s,j)\, ds = \sum_{j=1}^m {}_tq_x^{(j)}. \tag{9.2.12}$$

That the first and last members of (9.2.12) are equal is immediately interpretable. Combining (9.2.8), (9.2.12) and (9.2.11), we have

$$\mu_{x+t}^{(\tau)} = \sum_{j=1}^m \mu_{x+t}^{(j)}, \tag{9.2.13}$$

that is, the total force of decrement is the sum of the forces of decrement due to the $m$ causes.

We can summarize the definitions here by expressing the joint p.d.f., marginals and conditionals in actuarial notation and repeating the defining equation number:

$$f(t,j) = {}_tp_x^{(\tau)}\, \mu_{x+t}^{(j)} \qquad \text{(9.2.10) restated}$$

$$h(j) = {}_\infty q_x^{(j)} \qquad \text{(9.2.4) restated}$$

$$g(t) = {}_tp_x^{(\tau)}\, \mu_{x+t}^{(\tau)}. \qquad \text{(9.2.8) restated}$$

The conditional p.f. of $J$, given decrement at time $t$, is

$$h(j|T = t) = \frac{f(t,j)}{g(t)} = \frac{_tp_x^{(\tau)}\, \mu_{x+t}^{(j)}}{_tp_x^{(\tau)}\, \mu_{x+t}^{(\tau)}}$$

$$= \frac{\mu_{x+t}^{(j)}}{\mu_{x+t}^{(\tau)}}. \tag{9.2.14}$$

Finally, we note that the probability in (9.2.3) can be rewritten as

$$_tq_x^{(j)} = \int_0^t {}_sp_x^{(\tau)}\,\mu_{x+s}^{(j)}\,ds. \qquad (9.2.3)\,\text{restated}$$

**Example 9.1:**    Consider a multiple decrement model with 2 causes of decrement, the forces of decrement given by

$$\mu_{x+t}^{(1)} = \frac{t}{100} \qquad t \geq 0$$

$$\mu_{x+t}^{(2)} = \frac{1}{100} \qquad t \geq 0.$$

For this model, calculate the p.f. (or p.d.f.) for the joint, marginal and conditional distributions.

**Solution:**

Since

$$\mu_{x+s}^{(\tau)} = \mu_{x+s}^{(1)} + \mu_{x+s}^{(2)} = \frac{s+1}{100},$$

the survival probability $_tp_x^{(\tau)}$ is

$$_tp_x^{(\tau)} = \exp\left[-\int_0^t [(s+1)/100]\,ds\right]$$

$$= \exp[-(t^2 + 2t)/200] \qquad t \geq 0,$$

and the joint p.d.f. of $T$ and $J$ is

$$f(t,j) = \begin{cases} \dfrac{t}{100}\,\exp[-(t^2+2t)/200] & t \geq 0, j = 1 \\[2ex] \dfrac{1}{100}\,\exp[-(t^2+2t)/200] & t \geq 0, j = 2. \end{cases}$$

The marginal p.d.f. of $T$ is

$$g(t) = \sum_{j=1}^{2} f(t,j) = \frac{t+1}{100}\,\exp[-(t^2+2t)/200] \qquad t \geq 0$$

and the marginal p.f. of $J$ is

$$h(j) = \begin{cases} \displaystyle\int_0^\infty f(t,1)\,dt & j = 1 \\[3ex] \displaystyle\int_0^\infty f(t,2)\,dt & j = 2. \end{cases}$$

It is somewhat easier to evaluate $h(2)$. In the following

development, $\Phi(x)$ is the d.f. for the standard normal distribution $N(0,1)$. By completing the square we have

$$h(2) = \frac{1}{100} e^{0.005} \int_0^\infty \exp\left[-(t+1)^2/200\right] dt$$

$$= \frac{1}{100} e^{0.005} \sqrt{2\pi}\, 10 \int_0^\infty \frac{1}{\sqrt{2\pi}\, 10} \exp\left[-(t+1)^2/200\right] dt.$$

We now make the change of variable $z = (t+1)/10$ and obtain

$$h(2) = \frac{1}{10} e^{0.005} \sqrt{2\pi} \int_{0.1}^\infty \frac{1}{\sqrt{2\pi}} \exp\left(-z^2/2\right) dz$$

$$= \frac{1}{10} e^{0.005} \sqrt{2\pi}\, [1 - \Phi(0.1)]$$

$$= 0.1159.$$

Therefore $h(1) = 0.8841$. Finally the conditional p.f. of $J$, given decrement at $t$, is derived from (9.2.14) as

$$h(1|t) = \frac{t}{t+1}$$

and

$$h(2|t) = \frac{1}{t+1}. \qquad \blacktriangledown$$

**Example 9.2:**

For the joint distribution of $T$ and $J$ specified in Example 9.1, calculate $E[T]$ and $E[T|J = 2]$.

**Solution:**
Using the marginal p.d.f. $g(t)$, we have

$$E[T] = \int_0^\infty t \left\{ \frac{t+1}{100} \exp\left[-(t^2 + 2t)/200\right] \right\} dt.$$

Integration by parts, as in Theorem 3.1, yields

$$E[T] = -t \exp\left[-(t^2 + 2t)/200\right]\Big|_0^\infty$$

$$+ \int_0^\infty \exp\left[-(t^2 + 2t)/200\right] dt$$

$$= 0 + 100\, h(2),$$

hence

$$E[T] = 11.59.$$

# MULTIPLE DECREMENT MODELS

Using the conditional p.d.f. $f(t,2)/h(2)$, we have

$$E[T|J = 2] = \int_0^\infty t\{100^{-1}\exp[-(t^2 - 2t)/200]\}(0.1159)^{-1}\,dt.$$

This integral may be evaluated as follows:

$$E[T|J = 2] = E[(T + 1) - 1|J = 2]$$

$$= (0.1159)^{-1}\int_0^\infty \frac{t + 1}{100}\exp[-(t^2 + 2t)/200]\,dt - 1$$

$$= -(0.1159)^{-1}\exp[-(t^2 + 2t)/200]\big|_0^\infty - 1$$

$$= 7.63.$$

The point of Examples 9.1 and 9.2 is that once the joint distribution of $T$ and $J$ is specified, marginal and conditional distributions can be derived and the moments of these distributions determined. ▼

In some instances, a particular application may require a modification of the above model. A continuous distribution for time-until-termination, $T$, is inadequate in applications where there is a time at which there is a positive probability of decrement.

One example of this is a pension plan with a mandatory retirement age, an age at which all remaining active employees must retire. A second example is term life insurance in which there is typically no benefit paid on withdrawal. Thus, after a premium is paid, none of the remaining insureds will withdraw until the next premium due date. Here we shall not attempt to extend the notation to cover such situations. However, in Section 9.7 we shall describe extended models for each of these examples.

The random variable $K$, the curtate-future-years before decrement of $(x)$ is defined, as in Chapter 3, to be the greatest integer less than $T$. The joint p.f. of $K$ and $J$ is given by

$$\Pr[K = k, J = j] = \Pr[k < T \le k + 1, J = j]$$

$$= \int_k^{k+1} {}_tp_x^{(\tau)}\,\mu_{x+t}^{(j)}\,dt$$

$$= {}_kp_x^{(\tau)}\int_0^1 {}_sp_{x+k}^{(\tau)}\,\mu_{x+k+s}^{(j)}\,ds$$

$$= {}_kp_x^{(\tau)}\,q_{x+k}^{(j)} \qquad\qquad (9.2.15)$$

where

$$q_{x+k}^{(j)} = \int_0^1 {}_sp_{x+k}^{(\tau)}\,\mu_{x+k+s}^{(j)}\,ds \qquad\qquad (9.2.16)$$

(compare with (9.2.3) restated). The probability of decrement from all causes between ages $x + k$ and $x + k + 1$, given survival to age $x + k$,

# MULTIPLE DECREMENT MODELS

is denoted by $q_{x+k}^{(\tau)}$, and it follows that

$$
\begin{aligned}
q_{x+k}^{(\tau)} &= \int_0^1 {}_sp_{x+k}^{(\tau)}\, \mu_{x+k+s}^{(\tau)}\, ds \\
&= \int_0^1 {}_sp_{x+k}^{(\tau)} \sum_{j=1}^m \mu_{x+k+s}^{(j)}\, ds \\
&= \sum_{j=1}^m q_{x+k}^{(j)}.
\end{aligned}
\tag{9.2.17}
$$

An examination of (9.2.16) and (9.2.17) discloses why multiple decrement theory is also called the theory of competing risks. The probability of decrement between ages $x+k$ and $x+k+1$ due to cause $j$ depends on ${}_sp_{x+k}^{(\tau)}$, $0 \le s \le 1$, and thus on all the component forces. When the forces for other decrements are increased, ${}_sp_{x+k}^{(\tau)}$ is reduced, and then $q_{x+k}^{(j)}$ is also decreased.

## 9.3 Random Survivorship Group

Let us consider a group of $l_a^{(\tau)}$ lives aged $a$ years. Each life is assumed to have a distribution of time-until-decrement and cause of decrement specified by the p.d.f.

$$
f(t,j) = {}_tp_a^{(\tau)}\, \mu_{a+t}^{(j)} \qquad t \ge 0,\ j = 1, 2, \ldots, m.
$$

We shall denote by ${}_n\mathcal{D}_x^{(j)}$ the random variable equal to the number of lives who will leave the group between ages $x$ and $x+n$, $x \ge a$, from cause $j$. We denote $E[{}_n\mathcal{D}_x^{(j)}]$ by ${}_nd_x^{(j)}$ and obtain

$$
\begin{aligned}
{}_nd_x^{(j)} &= E[{}_n\mathcal{D}_x^{(j)}] \tag{9.3.1A} \\
&= l_a^{(\tau)} \int_{x-a}^{x+n-a} {}_tp_a^{(\tau)}\, \mu_{a+t}^{(j)}\, dt.
\end{aligned}
$$

As usual, if $n = 1$, we delete the prefixes on ${}_n\mathcal{D}_x^{(j)}$ and ${}_nd_x^{(j)}$. We note that

$$
{}_n\mathcal{D}_x^{(\tau)} = \sum_{j=1}^m {}_n\mathcal{D}_x^{(j)}
$$

and define

$$
{}_nd_x^{(\tau)} = E[{}_n\mathcal{D}_x^{(\tau)}] = \sum_{j=1}^m {}_nd_x^{(j)}.
\tag{9.3.1B}
$$

Then, using (9.3.1A), we have

$$
\begin{aligned}
{}_nd_x^{(\tau)} &= l_a^{(\tau)} \sum_{j=1}^m \int_{x-a}^{x+n-a} {}_tp_a^{(\tau)}\, \mu_{a+t}^{(j)}\, dt \\
&= l_a^{(\tau)} \int_{x-a}^{x+n-a} {}_tp_a^{(\tau)}\, \mu_{a+t}^{(\tau)}\, dt.
\end{aligned}
\tag{9.3.2}
$$

If $\mathcal{L}^{(\tau)}(x)$ is defined as the random variable equal to the number of survivors at age $x$ out of the $l_a^{(\tau)}$ lives in the original group at age $a$,

# MULTIPLE DECREMENT MODELS

then by analogy with (3.3.1) we can write

$$l_x^{(\tau)} = E[\mathcal{L}^{(\tau)}(x)]$$

$$= l_a^{(\tau)} \,_{x-a}p_a^{(\tau)}. \tag{9.3.3}$$

We can rewrite (9.3.1) for the case $n = 1$ and with $s = t - (x - a)$ as

$$d_x^{(j)} = l_a^{(\tau)} \int_0^1 \,_{s+x-a}p_a^{(\tau)} \, \mu_{x+s}^{(j)} \, ds.$$

Then, by use of (9.3.3) and (9.2.16),

$$d_x^{(j)} = l_a^{(\tau)} \,_{x-a}p_a^{(\tau)} \int_0^1 \,_s p_x^{(\tau)} \, \mu_{x+s}^{(j)} \, ds$$

$$= l_x^{(\tau)} \, q_x^{(j)}. \tag{9.3.4}$$

This result enables us to display a table of $p_x^{(\tau)}$ and $q_x^{(j)}$ values in a corresponding table of $l_x^{(\tau)}$ and $d_x^{(j)}$ values. Either table is called a **multiple decrement table**.

**Example 9.3:**  Construct a table of $l_x^{(\tau)}$ and $d_x^{(j)}$ values corresponding to the probabilities of decrement given below.

| $x$ | $q_x^{(1)}$ | $q_x^{(2)}$ |
|---|---|---|
| 65 | 0.02 | 0.05 |
| 66 | 0.03 | 0.06 |
| 67 | 0.04 | 0.07 |
| 68 | 0.05 | 0.08 |
| 69 | 0.06 | 0.09 |
| 70 | 0.00 | 1.00 |

Although this display is designed for computational ease, it may be roughly suggestive of a double decrement situation with cause 1 related to death and cause 2 to retirement. It appears that, in this case, 70 is the mandatory retirement age.

**Solution:**
We assume the arbitrary value of $l_{65}^{(\tau)} = 1000$ and use (9.3.4) as indicated below.

| $x$ | $q_x^{(1)}$ | $q_x^{(2)}$ | $q_x^{(\tau)}$ | $p_x^{(\tau)}$ | $l_x^{(\tau)} = l_{x-1}^{(\tau)} p_{x-1}^{(\tau)}$ | $d_x^{(1)} = l_x^{(\tau)} q_x^{(1)}$ | $d_x^{(2)} = l_x^{(\tau)} q_x^{(2)}$ |
|---|---|---|---|---|---|---|---|
| 65 | 0.02 | 0.05 | 0.07 | 0.93 | 1 000.00 | 20.00 | 50.00 |
| 66 | 0.03 | 0.06 | 0.09 | 0.91 | 930.00 | 27.90 | 55.80 |
| 67 | 0.04 | 0.07 | 0.11 | 0.89 | 846.30 | 33.85 | 59.24 |
| 68 | 0.05 | 0.08 | 0.13 | 0.87 | 753.21 | 37.66 | 60.26 |
| 69 | 0.06 | 0.09 | 0.15 | 0.85 | 655.29 | 39.32 | 58.98 |
| 70 | 0.00 | 1.00 | 1.00 | 0.00 | 557.00 | 0.00 | 557.00 |

Note, as a check on the calculations, that $l_{x+1}^{(\tau)} = l_x^{(\tau)} - d_x^{(1)} - d_x^{(2)}$, except for rounding error.

# Chapter 9
## MULTIPLE DECREMENT MODELS

We continue this example with the evaluation, from first principles, of several probabilities:

$$_2p_{65}^{(\tau)} = p_{65}^{(\tau)} p_{66}^{(\tau)} = (0.93)(0.91) = 0.8463$$

$$_{2|}q_{66}^{(1)} = p_{66}^{(\tau)} p_{67}^{(\tau)} q_{68}^{(1)} = (0.91)(0.89)(0.05) = 0.0405$$

$$_2q_{67}^{(2)} = q_{67}^{(2)} + p_{67}^{(\tau)} q_{68}^{(2)} = 0.07 + (0.89)(0.08) = 0.1412.$$

The last three columns of the above table may be used to obtain the same probabilities. The answers agree to four decimal places:

$$_2p_{65}^{(\tau)} = \frac{l_{67}^{(\tau)}}{l_{65}^{(\tau)}} = \frac{846.30}{1000.00} = 0.8463$$

$$_{2|}q_{66}^{(1)} = \frac{d_{68}^{(1)}}{l_{66}^{(\tau)}} = \frac{37.66}{930.00} = 0.0405$$

$$_2q_{67}^{(2)} = \frac{d_{67}^{(2)} + d_{68}^{(2)}}{l_{67}^{(\tau)}} = \frac{59.24 + 60.26}{846.30} = 0.1412. \qquad \blacktriangledown$$

## 9.4 Deterministic Survivorship Group

The total force of decrement can also be viewed as a total (nominal annual) rate of decrement rather than as a conditional probability density. In this view, where we assume a continuous model, a group of $l_a^{(\tau)}$ lives advance through age subject to deterministic forces of decrement $\mu_y^{(\tau)}$, $y \geq a$. The number of survivors to age $x$ from the original group of $l_a^{(\tau)}$ lives at age $a$ is given by

$$l_x^{(\tau)} = l_a^{(\tau)} \exp\left[-\int_a^x \mu_y^{(\tau)} dy\right], \qquad (9.4.1)$$

and the total decrement between ages $x$ and $x+1$ is

$$
\begin{aligned}
d_x^{(\tau)} &= l_x^{(\tau)} - l_{x+1}^{(\tau)} \\
&= l_x^{(\tau)}\left[1 - \frac{l_{x+1}^{(\tau)}}{l_x^{(\tau)}}\right] \\
&= l_x^{(\tau)}\left\{1 - \exp\left[-\int_x^{x+1} \mu_y^{(\tau)} dy\right]\right\} \qquad (9.4.2) \\
&= l_x^{(\tau)}[1 - p_x^{(\tau)}] \\
&= l_x^{(\tau)} q_x^{(\tau)}.
\end{aligned}
$$

Further, by definition or from differentiating (9.4.1), we have

$$\mu_x^{(\tau)} = -\frac{1}{l_x^{(\tau)}} \frac{dl_x^{(\tau)}}{dx}. \qquad (9.4.3)$$

These formulas are analogous to those for life tables in Section 3.4. Here $q_x^{(\tau)}$ is the effective annual total rate of decrement for the year of age $x$ to $x+1$ equivalent to the forces $\mu_y^{(\tau)}$, $x \leq y \leq x+1$.

Let us now consider $m$ causes of decrement and assume that the $l_x^{(\tau)}$ survivors to age $x$ will, at future ages, be fully depleted by these $m$ forms of decrement. Then the $l_x^{(\tau)}$ survivors can be visualized as falling into distinct subgroups $l_x^{(j)}$, $j = 1, 2, \ldots, m$, where $l_x^{(j)}$ denotes the number from the $l_x^{(\tau)}$ survivors who will terminate at future ages due to cause $j$, so that

$$l_x^{(\tau)} = \sum_{j=1}^{m} l_x^{(j)}. \tag{9.4.4}$$

We can now define the force of decrement at age $x$ due to cause $j$ by

$$\mu_x^{(j)} = \lim_{h \to 0} \frac{l_x^{(j)} - l_{x+h}^{(j)}}{h \, l_x^{(\tau)}}$$

where $l_x^{(\tau)}$, not $l_x^{(j)}$, appears in the denominator. This yields

$$\mu_x^{(j)} = -\frac{1}{l_x^{(\tau)}} \frac{dl_x^{(j)}}{dx}. \tag{9.4.5}$$

From (9.4.3)–(9.4.5) it follows that

$$\mu_x^{(\tau)} = -\frac{1}{l_x^{(\tau)}} \frac{d}{dx} \sum_{j=1}^{m} l_x^{(j)} = \sum_{j=1}^{m} \mu_x^{(j)}. \tag{9.4.6}$$

Formula (9.4.5), with a change of variable, can be written as

$$-dl_y^{(j)} = l_y^{(\tau)} \, \mu_y^{(j)} \, dy$$

and integration from $y = x$ to $y = x + 1$ gives

$$l_x^{(j)} - l_{x+1}^{(j)} = d_x^{(j)} = \int_x^{x+1} l_y^{(\tau)} \, \mu_y^{(j)} \, dy. \tag{9.4.7}$$

Summation over $j = 1, 2, \ldots, m$ yields

$$l_x^{(\tau)} - l_{x+1}^{(\tau)} = d_x^{(\tau)} = \int_x^{x+1} l_y^{(\tau)} \, \mu_y^{(\tau)} \, dy. \tag{9.4.8}$$

Further, from division of formula (9.4.7) by $l_x^{(\tau)}$, one has

$$\frac{d_x^{(j)}}{l_x^{(\tau)}} = \int_x^{x+1} {}_{y-x}p_x^{(\tau)} \, \mu_y^{(j)} \, dy = q_x^{(j)} \tag{9.4.9}$$

where $q_x^{(j)}$ is the proportion of the $l_x^{(\tau)}$ survivors to age $x$ who terminate due to cause $j$ before age $x + 1$ when all $m$ causes of decrement are operating.

As was the case for life tables, the deterministic model provides an alternative language and conceptual framework for multiple decrement theory.

## 9.5
## Associated Single Decrement Tables

For each of the causes of decrement recognized in a multiple decrement model, it is possible to define a single decrement model that depends only on the particular cause of decrement. We define the associated single decrement model functions as follows:

$$_tp_x'^{(j)} = \exp\left[-\int_0^t \mu_{x+s}^{(j)}\,ds\right],$$

$$_tq_x'^{(j)} = 1 - {_tp_x'^{(j)}}. \qquad (9.5.1)$$

Quantities such as $_tq_x'^{(j)}$ are called **net probabilities of decrement** in biostatistics as they are net of other causes of decrement. However, many other names have been given to the same quantity. One is **independent rate of decrement,** chosen because cause $j$ does not compete with other causes in determining $_tq_x'^{(j)}$. The term we shall use for $_tq_x'^{(j)}$ is **absolute rate of decrement.** The use of the word rate in describing $_tq_x'^{(j)}$ stems from a desire to avoid the word probability. The symbol $_tq_x^{(j)}$ denotes a probability of decrement for cause $j$ between ages $x$ and $x+t$ and we shall show that it differs from $_tq_x'^{(j)}$. In addition, $_tp_x'^{(j)}$, unlike $_tp_x^{(\tau)}$, is not necessarily a survival function for it is not required that $\lim_{t\to\infty} {_tp_x'^{(j)}} = 0$.

While

$$\int_0^\infty \mu_{x+t}^{(\tau)}\,dt = \infty,$$

we can conclude from (9.2.13) only that

$$\int_0^\infty \mu_{x+t}^{(j)}\,dt = \infty$$

for at least one $j$. There may be causes of decrement for which this integral is finite.

One seldom has an opportunity to observe the operation of a random survival system in which a single cause of decrement operates. In an employee benefit plan, retirement, disabilities and voluntary terminations make it impossible to directly observe the operation of a single decrement model for mortality during active service. In biostatistical applications random withdrawals from observation and arbitrary ending of the period of study may prevent the observation of mortality alone operating on a group of lives.

As we shall see in Section 9.6, a usual first step in constructing a multiple decrement model is to select absolute rates of decrement and to make assumptions concerning the incidence of the decrements within any single year of age in order to obtain probabilities $q_x^{(j)}$. The converse problem of obtaining absolute rates from the probabilities is a difficult one. It involves assumptions about incidence of the decrements. These assumptions are implicit in the statistical problem of estimating absolute rates.

In the following four subsections we shall examine a number of relationships between a multiple decrement table and its associated single decrement tables. We shall then look at a number of special assumptions about incidence of decrement over the year of age and note some implied relationships.

## 9.5.1 Basic Relationships

First, we note that since

$$_tp_x^{(\tau)} = \exp\left\{-\int_0^t [\mu_{x+s}^{(1)} + \mu_{x+s}^{(2)} + \ldots + \mu_{x+s}^{(m)}] ds\right\},$$

we have

$$_tp_x^{(\tau)} = \prod_{i=1}^m {}_tp_x'^{(i)}. \tag{9.5.2}$$

This result does not involve any approximation and we shall require that it hold for any method used to construct a multiple decrement table from a set of absolute rates of decrement.

Now let us compare the size of the absolute rates and the probabilities. From (9.5.2) we see, if some cause other than $j$ is operating, that

$$_tp_x'^{(j)} \geq {}_tp_x^{(\tau)}.$$

This implies

$$_tp_x'^{(j)} \mu_{x+t}^{(j)} \geq {}_tp_x^{(\tau)} \mu_{x+t}^{(j)},$$

and if these functions are integrated with respect to $t$ over the interval $(0,1)$, we obtain

$$q_x'^{(j)} = \int_0^1 {}_tp_x'^{(j)} \mu_{x+t}^{(j)} dt \geq \int_0^1 {}_tp_x^{(\tau)} \mu_{x+t}^{(j)} dt = q_x^{(j)}. \tag{9.5.3}$$

The magnitude of other forces of decrement can cause $_tp_x'^{(j)}$ to be considerably greater than $_tp_x^{(\tau)}$ and thus there can be corresponding differences between the absolute rates and the probabilities.

## 9.5.2 Central Rates of Multiple Decrement

There is a function of the multiple decrement model that is quite close to the corresponding function for an associated single decrement model. To introduce this function, we return to a mortality table and recall the central rate of mortality, or central-death-rate at age $x$, denoted by $m_x$ and defined in formula (3.5.9) by

$$m_x = \frac{\displaystyle\int_0^1 {}_tp_x\, \mu_{x+t}\, dt}{\displaystyle\int_0^1 {}_tp_x\, dt} = \frac{\displaystyle\int_0^1 l_{x+t}\, \mu_{x+t}\, dt}{\displaystyle\int_0^1 l_{x+t}\, dt} = \frac{d_x}{L_x}. \tag{9.5.4}$$

Thus, $m_x$ is a weighted average of the force of mortality between ages $x$ and $x+1$ and this justifies the terminology central rate.

# MULTIPLE DECREMENT MODELS

Such central rates can be defined in a multiple decrement context. The *central rate of decrement from all causes* is defined by

$$m_x^{(\tau)} = \frac{\int_0^1 {}_t p_x^{(\tau)} \, \mu_{x+t}^{(\tau)} \, dt}{\int_0^1 {}_t p_x^{(\tau)} \, dt} \tag{9.5.5}$$

and is a weighted average of $\mu_{x+t}^{(\tau)}$, $0 \le t < 1$. Similarly, the *central rate of decrement from cause j* is

$$m_x^{(j)} = \frac{\int_0^1 {}_t p_x^{(\tau)} \, \mu_{x+t}^{(j)} \, dt}{\int_0^1 {}_t p_x^{(\tau)} \, dt} \tag{9.5.6}$$

and is a weighted average of $\mu_{x+t}^{(j)}$, $0 \le t < 1$. Clearly

$$m_x^{(\tau)} = \sum_{j=1}^{m} m_x^{(j)}.$$

The corresponding central rate for the associated single decrement table is given by

$$m_x^{\prime(j)} = \frac{\int_0^1 {}_t p_x^{\prime(j)} \, \mu_{x+t}^{(j)} \, dt}{\int_0^1 {}_t p_x^{\prime(j)} \, dt}. \tag{9.5.7}$$

This is again a weighted average of $\mu_{x+t}^{(j)}$ over the same age range, the weights now being ${}_t p_x^{\prime(j)}$ rather than ${}_t p_x^{(\tau)}$. If the force $\mu_{x+t}^{(j)}$ is constant for $0 \le t < 1$, we have $m_x^{(j)} = m_x^{\prime(j)} = \mu_x^{(j)}$. If $\mu_{x+t}^{(j)}$ is an increasing function of $t$, then ${}_t p_x^{\prime(j)}$ gives more weight to higher values than does ${}_t p_x^{(\tau)}$, and $m_x^{\prime(j)} > m_x^{(j)}$. If $\mu_{x+t}^{(j)}$ is a decreasing function of $t$, then $m_x^{\prime(j)} < m_x^{(j)}$. See Exercise 9.31 for a more formal treatment of these statements.

Central rates provide a convenient but approximate means of proceeding from the $q_x^{\prime(j)}$ to the $q_x^{(j)}$, $j = 1, 2, \ldots, m$, and vice versa. This is illustrated in Exercise 9.17.

## 9.5.3
## Constant Force
## Assumption

Let us examine specific assumptions concerning the incidence of decrements. First, let us use an assumption of a constant force for each decrement over each year of age. This implies

$$\mu_{x+t}^{(j)} = \mu_x^{(j)}$$

and

$$\mu_{x+t}^{(\tau)} = \mu_x^{(\tau)} \qquad 0 \le t < 1.$$

Then we have

$$q_x^{(j)} = \int_0^1 {}_tp_x^{(\tau)}\, \mu_x^{(j)}\, dt$$

$$= \frac{\mu_x^{(j)}}{\mu_x^{(\tau)}} \int_0^1 {}_tp_x^{(\tau)}\, \mu_x^{(\tau)}\, dt = \frac{\mu_x^{(j)}}{\mu_x^{(\tau)}}\, q_x^{(\tau)}. \tag{9.5.8}$$

But also, under the constant force assumption,

$$\mu_x^{(\tau)} = -\log p_x^{(\tau)}$$

and

$$\mu_x^{(j)} = -\log p_x'^{(j)},$$

so that from (9.5.8)

$$q_x^{(j)} = \frac{\log p_x'^{(j)}}{\log p_x^{(\tau)}}\, q_x^{(\tau)}. \tag{9.5.9}$$

This formula, together with (9.5.2), can be used for calculating $q_x^{(j)}$ from given values of $q_x'^{(j)}$, $j = 1, 2, \ldots, m$.

Equation (9.5.9) can be solved for $q_x'^{(j)}$ to give

$$q_x'^{(j)} = 1 - \left[1 - q_x^{(\tau)}\right]^{(q_x^{(j)}/q_x^{(\tau)})}. \tag{9.5.10}$$

This result is useful for obtaining absolute rates from a given set of probabilities of decrement. Note that for (9.5.9) and (9.5.10) special treatment is required if $p_x'^{(j)}$ or $p_x^{(\tau)}$ equals 0.

**9.5.4
Uniform
Distribution
Assumption
for Multiple
Decrements**

Formula (9.5.10) holds under an alternative assumption, namely, that each of the decrements in a multiple decrement context has a uniform distribution in each year of age. Thus we assume that

$$_tq_x^{(j)} = t\, q_x^{(j)} \quad j = 1, 2, \ldots, m, \; 0 \le t \le 1$$

and by summation that

$$_tq_x^{(\tau)} = 1 - {}_tp_x^{(\tau)} = t\, q_x^{(\tau)}.$$

Also, under the given assumption, we see from (9.2.11)

$$_tp_x^{(\tau)}\, \mu_{x+t}^{(j)} = q_x^{(j)} \tag{9.5.11}$$

and

$$\mu_{x+t}^{(j)} = \frac{q_x^{(j)}}{{}_tp_x^{(\tau)}} = \frac{q_x^{(j)}}{1 - t\, q_x^{(\tau)}}.$$

Then

$$q_x'^{(j)} = 1 - \exp\left[-\int_0^1 \mu_{x+t}^{(j)}\, dt\right]$$

$$= 1 - \exp\left[-\int_0^1 \frac{q_x^{(j)}}{1 - t\,q_x^{(\tau)}}\, dt\right]$$

$$= 1 - \exp\left[\frac{q_x^{(j)}}{q_x^{(\tau)}} \log\left(1 - q_x^{(\tau)}\right)\right],$$

which is formula (9.5.10) again. Formula (9.5.9) now follows by solving for $q_x^{(j)}$. Exercise 9.21 provides additional insights into the connection between the developments in Sections 9.5.3 and 9.5.4.

**Example 9.4:**

Continue Example 9.3 by evaluating $q_x'^{(1)}$ and $q_x'^{(2)}$ by (9.5.10).

**Solution:**
By (9.5.10), the following results are obtained.

| $x$ | $q_x^{(1)}$ | $q_x^{(2)}$ | $q_x'^{(1)}$ | $q_x'^{(2)}$ |
|---|---|---|---|---|
| 65 | 0.02 | 0.05 | 0.02052 | 0.05052 |
| 66 | 0.03 | 0.06 | 0.03095 | 0.06094 |
| 67 | 0.04 | 0.07 | 0.04149 | 0.07147 |
| 68 | 0.05 | 0.08 | 0.05215 | 0.08213 |
| 69 | 0.06 | 0.09 | 0.06294 | 0.09291 |
| 70 | 0.00 | 1.00 | — | — |

At age 70, the rates depend on mandatory retirement and there is no particular need for $q_{70}'^{(1)}$, $q_{70}'^{(2)}$ although they could be identified, respectively, using $q_{70}^{(1)}$ and $q_{70}^{(2)}$. ▼

## 9.6 Construction of a Multiple Decrement Table

In building a multiple decrement model it is best if data, including that on age and cause of decrement for the population under study, can be used to directly estimate the probabilities $q_x^{(j)}$. Large, well established employee benefit plans may have such data. For other plans, such data are frequently not available. An alternative is to construct the model from associated single decrement rates assumed appropriate for the population under study. The adequacy of the model should then be tested by reviewing data as they become available.

Once satisfactory associated single decrement tables are selected, the results of Section 9.5 can be used to complete the construction of the multiple decrement table. The availability of a set of $p_x'^{(j)}$, for $j = 1, 2, \ldots, m$ and all values of $x$, will permit the computation of $p_x^{(\tau)}$ by (9.5.2) and of $q_x^{(\tau)}$ by $q_x^{(\tau)} = 1 - p_x^{(\tau)}$.

The remaining step is to break $q_x^{(\tau)}$ into its components $q_x^{(j)}$ for $j = 1, 2, \ldots, m$. If either the constant force or the uniform distribution of decrement assumption is adopted in the model, (9.5.9) can be used for the calculation of the $q_x^{(j)}$.

**Example 9.5:**

Use (9.5.2) and (9.5.9) to obtain the multiple decrement table corresponding to absolute rates of decrement given below. Presumably, the actuary has examined the characteristics of the participant group and has decided that associated single decrement tables yielding these rates are appropriate for the group under study. It is also assumed

# MULTIPLE DECREMENT MODELS

that cause 3 is retirement that can occur between ages 65 and 70 and is mandatory at 70.

| $x$ | $q_x'^{(1)}$ | $q_x'^{(2)}$ | $q_x'^{(3)}$ |
|---|---|---|---|
| 65 | 0.020 | 0.02 | 0.04 |
| 66 | 0.025 | 0.02 | 0.06 |
| 67 | 0.030 | 0.02 | 0.08 |
| 68 | 0.035 | 0.02 | 0.10 |
| 69 | 0.040 | 0.02 | 0.12 |

**Solution:**
The following table contains the results of the calculation of the probabilities of decrement. Formula (9.5.2) can be rewritten as

$$q_x^{(\tau)} = 1 - \prod_{j=1}^{3} (1 - q_x'^{(j)}),$$

while (9.5.9), and the mandatory retirement condition, give the probabilities. The multiple decrement table is constructed as in Example 9.3.

| $x$ | $q_x^{(\tau)}$ | $q_x^{(1)}$ | $q_x^{(2)}$ | $q_x^{(3)}$ | $l_x^{(\tau)}$ | $d_x^{(1)}$ | $d_x^{(2)}$ | $d_x^{(3)}$ |
|---|---|---|---|---|---|---|---|---|
| 65 | 0.07802 | 0.01940 | 0.01940 | 0.03921 | 1 000.00 | 19.40 | 19.40 | 39.21 |
| 66 | 0.10183 | 0.02401 | 0.01916 | 0.05867 | 921.99 | 22.14 | 17.67 | 54.09 |
| 67 | 0.12545 | 0.02851 | 0.01891 | 0.07803 | 828.09 | 23.61 | 15.66 | 64.62 |
| 68 | 0.14887 | 0.03290 | 0.01866 | 0.09731 | 724.20 | 23.83 | 13.51 | 70.47 |
| 69 | 0.17210 | 0.03720 | 0.01841 | 0.11649 | 616.39 | 22.93 | 11.35 | 71.80 |
| 70 | 1.00000 | 0.00000 | 0.00000 | 1.00000 | 510.31 | 0.00 | 0.00 | 510.31 |

▼

It has been noted that (9.5.9) and (9.5.10) will not be used if $p_x'^{(j)}$ or $p_x^{(\tau)} = 0$. Some alternative device will be necessary. One such method, which handles this indeterminacy and lends itself to special adjustments, is based on assumed distributions of decrement in the associated single decrement tables rather than on assumptions about multiple decrement probabilities as in Section 9.5.4. We shall first examine an assumption of uniform distribution of decrement (in each year of age) in each of these tables. We shall restrict our attention to situations with 3 decrements, but the method and formulas easily extend for $m > 3$. Under the stated assumption,

$$_t p_x'^{(j)} = 1 - t q_x'^{(j)} \qquad j = 1,2,3; 0 \le t \le 1 \qquad (9.6.1)$$

and

$$_t p_x'^{(j)} \ \mu_{x+t}^{(j)} = \frac{d}{dt}(- \ _t p_x'^{(j)}) = q_x'^{(j)}. \qquad (9.6.2)$$

# Chapter 9
## MULTIPLE DECREMENT MODELS

It follows that

$$
\begin{aligned}
q_x^{(1)} &= \int_0^1 {}_t p_x^{(\tau)} \, \mu_{x+t}^{(1)} \, dt \\
&= \int_0^1 {}_t p_x'^{(1)} \, \mu_{x+t}^{(1)} \, {}_t p_x'^{(2)} \, {}_t p_x'^{(3)} \, dt \\
&= q_x'^{(1)} \int_0^1 (1 - t\,q_x'^{(2)}) \, (1 - t\,q_x'^{(3)}) \, dt \\
&= q_x'^{(1)} \left[ 1 - \frac{1}{2}[q_x'^{(2)} + q_x'^{(3)}] + \frac{1}{3} q_x'^{(2)} q_x'^{(3)} \right].
\end{aligned}
\tag{9.6.3}
$$

Similar formulas hold for $q_x^{(2)}$, $q_x^{(3)}$ and it can be verified that

$$
\begin{aligned}
q_x^{(1)} + q_x^{(2)} + q_x^{(3)} &= q_x'^{(1)} + q_x'^{(2)} + q_x'^{(3)} \\
&\quad - [q_x'^{(1)} q_x'^{(2)} + q_x'^{(1)} q_x'^{(3)} + q_x'^{(2)} q_x'^{(3)}] \\
&\quad + q_x'^{(1)} q_x'^{(2)} q_x'^{(3)} \\
&= 1 - [1 - q_x'^{(1)}][1 - q_x'^{(2)}][1 - q_x'^{(3)}] = q_x^{(\tau)}.
\end{aligned}
\tag{9.6.4}
$$

**Example 9.6:**  Obtain the probabilities of decrement for ages 65–69 from the data in Example 9.5, under the assumption of a uniform distribution of decrement in each year of age in each of the associated single decrement tables.

**Solution:**
This is an application of (9.6.3).

| $x$ | $q_x'^{(1)}$ | $q_x'^{(2)}$ | $q_x'^{(3)}$ | $q_x^{(1)}$ | $q_x^{(2)}$ | $q_x^{(3)}$ |
|-----|------|------|------|---------|---------|---------|
| 65 | 0.020 | 0.02 | 0.04 | 0.01941 | 0.01941 | 0.03921 |
| 66 | 0.025 | 0.02 | 0.06 | 0.02401 | 0.01916 | 0.05866 |
| 67 | 0.030 | 0.02 | 0.08 | 0.02852 | 0.01892 | 0.07802 |
| 68 | 0.035 | 0.02 | 0.10 | 0.03292 | 0.01867 | 0.09727 |
| 69 | 0.040 | 0.02 | 0.12 | 0.03723 | 0.01843 | 0.11643 |

These probabilities are close to those obtained by (9.5.9), displayed in Example 9.5.  ▼

We conclude this section with another example illustrating the use of a special distribution for one of the decrements. Special distributions are sometimes required by the facts of the situation being modeled.

**Example 9.7:**  Consider a situation with 3 causes of decrement: mortality, disability and withdrawal. Assume mortality and disability are uniformly distributed in each year of age in the associated single decrement tables with absolute rates of $q_x'^{(1)}$, $q_x'^{(2)}$ respectively. Further, assume that withdrawals occur only at the end of the year with an absolute rate of $q_x^{\prime\,(3)}$.

a. Give formulas for the probabilities of decrement in the year of age $x$ to $x+1$ for the 3 causes.

b. Reformulate the probabilities under the assumptions that
   - in the associated single decrement model, withdrawals occur only at the age's midyear or year end,
   - equal proportions, namely $(1/2)q_x^{\prime\,(3)}$, of those beginning the year withdraw at the midyear and at the year end.

**Remark:**

Up to now our multiple decrement models have been fully continuous, except possibly to recognize a mandatory retirement age. Moreover, our theory began with a multiple decrement model and, after defining the forces $\mu_{x+t}^{(j)}$, $j = 1,2,\ldots,m$, proceeded to the associated single decrement tables. In this example we are starting with the single decrement tables, and in one of these tables the decrement takes place discretely at the ends of stated intervals. We shall not attempt to define a force of decrement for this discrete case, but will proceed by direct methods to build, from the single decrement tables, a multiple decrement model possessing the relationships (9.2.17) and (9.5.2) established in our prior theory.

**Solution:**

a. Figure 9.2A displays survival factors for the given single decrement tables and for a multiple decrement table where

$$_tp_x^{(\tau)} = {_tp_x'^{(1)}}\,{_tp_x'^{(2)}}\,{_tp_x'^{(3)}}$$

for nonintegral $t \geq 0$. At $t = 1$, $_tp_x'^{(3)}$ and $_tp_x^{(\tau)}$ are discontinuous, so we consider

$$\lim_{t\to1-} {_tp_x^{(\tau)}} = p_x'^{(1)}\,p_x'^{(2)}\,1$$

and

$$p_x^{(\tau)} = p_x'^{(1)}\,p_x'^{(2)}(1 - q_x'^{(3)}).$$

We shall also require that, for our multiple decrement table,

$$q_x^{(\tau)} = q_x^{(1)} + q_x^{(2)} + q_x^{(3)} = 1 - p_x^{(\tau)} = 1 - p_x'^{(1)}p_x'^{(2)}[1 - q_x'^{(3)}].$$

We set

$$q_x^{(1)} = \int_0^1 {_tp_x^{(\tau)}}\,\mu_{x+t}^{(1)}\,dt$$

$$= \int_0^1 {_tp_x'^{(1)}}\,{_tp_x'^{(2)}}\,(1)\,\mu_{x+t}^{(1)}\,dt$$

# MULTIPLE DECREMENT MODELS

$$= q_x'^{(1)} \int_0^1 [1 - t\, q_x'^{(2)}]\, dt$$

$$= q_x'^{(1)} \left[ 1 - \frac{1}{2} q_x'^{(2)} \right].$$

Similarly, we set

$$q_x^{(2)} = q_x'^{(2)} \left[ 1 - \frac{1}{2} q_x'^{(1)} \right].$$

Then

$$q_x^{(3)} = q_x^{(\tau)} - [q_x^{(1)} + q_x^{(2)}]$$

$$= 1 - p_x'^{(1)} p_x'^{(2)} [1 - q_x'^{(3)}] - q_x'^{(1)} - q_x'^{(2)} + q_x'^{(1)} q_x'^{(2)},$$

**Figure 9.2A**
**Survival Factors,**
$_t p_x'^{(j)}$, $j = 1, 2, 3$ **and**
$_t p_x^{(\tau)}$

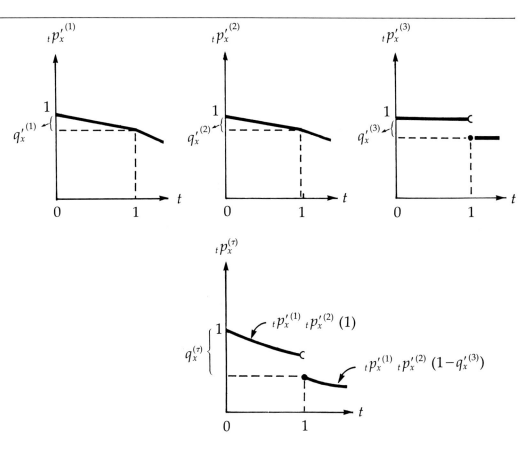

and, since

$$1 - q_x'^{(1)} - q_x'^{(2)} + q_x'^{(1)} q_x'^{(2)} = p_x'^{(1)} p_x'^{(2)},$$

$$q_x^{(3)} = p_x'^{(1)} p_x'^{(2)} q_x'^{(3)}.$$

Note that

$$\lim_{t \to 1-} {}_t p_x^{(\tau)} - \lim_{t \to 1+} {}_t p_x^{(\tau)} = p_x'^{(1)} p_x'^{(2)} q_x'^{(3)} = q_x^{(3)};$$

that is, the discontinuity at $t = 1$ equals $q_x^{(3)}$.

b. Here ${}_t p_x'^{(1)}$ and ${}_t p_x'^{(2)}$ are as in Figure 9.2A, but ${}_t p_x'^{(3)}$ and ${}_t p_x^{(\tau)}$ now have discontinuities at $t = 1/2$ and $t = 1$, as shown in Figure 9.2B.

**Figure 9.2B Survival Factors, ${}_t p_x'^{(3)}$ and ${}_t p_x^{(\tau)}$**

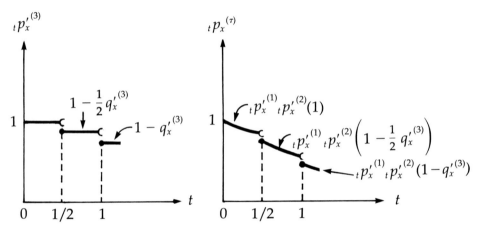

Proceeding as in (a), but taking account of the intervals $[0, 1/2)$ and $[1/2, 1)$, we set

$$q_x^{(1)} = q_x'^{(1)} \int_0^{1/2} [1 - t \, q_x'^{(2)}] \, dt + q_x'^{(1)} \left[ 1 - \frac{1}{2} q_x'^{(3)} \right] \int_{1/2}^1 [1 - t \, q_x'^{(2)}] \, dt$$

$$= q_x'^{(1)} \left[ 1 - \frac{1}{2} q_x'^{(2)} - \frac{1}{4} q_x'^{(3)} + \frac{3}{16} q_x'^{(2)} q_x'^{(3)} \right].$$

Similarly, we set

$$q_x^{(2)} = q_x'^{(2)} \left( 1 - \frac{1}{2} q_x'^{(1)} - \frac{1}{4} q_x'^{(3)} + \frac{3}{16} q_x'^{(1)} q_x'^{(3)} \right).$$

Then

$$q_x^{(3)} = 1 - p_x^{(\tau)} - q_x^{(1)} - q_x^{(2)}$$

$$= 1 - p_x'^{(1)} p_x'^{(2)} [1 - q_x'^{(3)}] - q_x^{(1)} - q_x^{(2)},$$

which reduces to

$$q_x^{(3)} = q_x'^{(3)} \left[ 1 - \frac{3}{4} q_x'^{(1)} - \frac{3}{4} q_x'^{(2)} + \frac{5}{8} q_x'^{(1)} q_x'^{(2)} \right].$$

▼

## 9.7
## Net Single Premiums and their Numerical Evaluation

Examples 9.5–9.7 illustrate how the actuary can custom build a multiple decrement model from associated single decrement tables to fit the purpose on hand.

Actuarial applications of multiple decrement models arise when the amount of benefit payment depends on the mode of exit from the group of active insureds. We let $B_{x+t}^{(j)}$ denote the value of a benefit at age $x + t$ for a decrement at that age by cause $j$. Then a net single premium, denoted in general by $\bar{A}$, will be defined by

$$\bar{A} = \sum_{j=1}^{m} \int_0^\infty B_{x+t}^{(j)} \, v^t \, {}_t p_x^{(\tau)} \, \mu_{x+t}^{(j)} \, dt. \qquad (9.7.1)$$

If $m = 1$ and $B_{x+t}^{(j)} = 1$, $\bar{A}$ reduces to $\bar{A}_x$, the net single premium for whole life insurance with immediate payment of claims. More appropriate for this chapter is the example of a **double indemnity provision** providing for the death benefit to be doubled when death is caused by accidental means. Let $J = 1$ for death by accidental means and $J = 2$ for death by other means, and take $B_{x+t}^{(1)} = 2$, $B_{x+t}^{(2)} = 1$. The net single premium for an $n$-year insurance is given by

$$\bar{A} = 2 \int_0^n v^t \, {}_t p_x^{(\tau)} \, \mu_{x+t}^{(1)} \, dt + \int_0^n v^t \, {}_t p_x^{(\tau)} \, \mu_{x+t}^{(2)} \, dt. \qquad (9.7.2)$$

Writing the net single premium in integral form does not complete the task of numerical evaluation. The first step is to break the expression into separate integrals for each of the years involved. Restricting ourselves to the first integral, we get

$$\int_0^n v^t \, {}_t p_x^{(\tau)} \, \mu_{x+t}^{(1)} \, dt = \sum_{k=0}^{n-1} v^k \, {}_k p_x^{(\tau)} \int_0^1 v^s \, {}_s p_{x+k}^{(\tau)} \, \mu_{x+k+s}^{(1)} \, ds.$$

If now we assume, as for (9.5.11), that each decrement in the multiple decrement context has a uniform distribution in each year of age, we have

$$\int_0^n v^t \, {}_t p_x^{(\tau)} \, \mu_{x+t}^{(1)} \, dt = \sum_{k=0}^{n-1} v^{k+1} \, {}_k p_x^{(\tau)} \, q_{x+k}^{(1)} \int_0^1 (1 + i)^{1-s} \, ds$$

$$= \frac{i}{\delta} \sum_{k=0}^{n-1} v^{k+1} \, {}_k p_x^{(\tau)} \, q_{x+k}^{(1)}.$$

Applying a similar argument for the second integral and combining, we get

$$\bar{A} = \frac{i}{\delta} \left[ \sum_{k=0}^{n-1} v^{k+1} \, {}_k p_x^{(\tau)} \left( 2 q_{x+k}^{(1)} + q_{x+k}^{(2)} \right) \right]$$

$$= \frac{i}{\delta} \sum_{k=0}^{n-1} v^{k+1} \, {}_k p_x^{(\tau)} \, q_{x+k}^{(1)} + \frac{i}{\delta} \sum_{k=0}^{n-1} v^{k+1} \, {}_k p_x^{(\tau)} \, q_{x+k}^{(\tau)} \qquad (9.7.3)$$

$$= \bar{A}_{x:\overline{n}|}^{1(1)} + \bar{A}_{x:\overline{n}|}^{1}$$

where $\bar{A}^{1(1)}_{x:\overline{n}|}$ is the net single premium for a term insurance of 1 covering death from accidental means and $\bar{A}^{1}_{x:\overline{n}|}$ is the net single premium for a term insurance of 1 covering death from all causes. Here $_{k}p^{(\tau)}_{x}$ could be taken as the survivorship function from a mortality table, and if values of $q^{(1)}_{x+k}$ are available, it would be unnecessary to develop the full double decrement table in order to calculate (9.7.3).

This example is particularly simple because the benefit amount does not change as a function of age at decrement and, in particular, it does not change within a year of age. To study this more complex situation, we examine a multiple decrement model with 2 decrements. For simplicity, we take $B^{(1)}_{x+t} = t$ and $B^{(2)}_{x+t} = 0$ for $t > 0$. In this case,

$$\bar{A} = \int_0^\infty t\, v^t\, {}_{t}p^{(\tau)}_{x}\, \mu^{(1)}_{x+t}\, dt$$

$$= \sum_{k=0}^\infty v^k\, {}_{k}p^{(\tau)}_{x} \int_0^1 (k+s)\, v^s\, {}_{s}p^{(\tau)}_{x+k}\, \mu^{(1)}_{x+k+s}\, ds.$$

We again make the assumption that each decrement in the multiple decrement context has a uniform distribution in each year of age, and obtain

$$\bar{A} = \sum_{k=0}^\infty v^{k+1}\, {}_{k}p^{(\tau)}_{x}\, q^{(1)}_{x+k} \int_0^1 (k+s)\,(1+i)^{1-s}ds$$

$$= \sum_{k=0}^\infty v^{k+1}\, {}_{k}p^{(\tau)}_{x}\, q^{(1)}_{x+k}\, \frac{i}{\delta}\left(k + \frac{1}{\delta} - \frac{1}{i}\right). \tag{9.7.4}$$

The quantity

$$k + \frac{1}{\delta} - \frac{1}{i} \cong k + \frac{1}{2}$$

can be viewed as an effective mean benefit amount for the year $k+1$, while the familiar $i/\delta$ term can be viewed as the correction needed to provide immediate payment of claims. The value by (9.7.4) is closely approximated by

$$\sum_{k=0}^\infty v^{k+1/2}\, {}_{k}p^{(\tau)}_{x}\, q^{(1)}_{x+k}\left(k + \frac{1}{2}\right), \tag{9.7.5}$$

which can be obtained by using the midpoint rule for evaluating

$$\int_0^1 (k+s)\,(1+i)^{1-s}ds.$$

In practice, formulas such as (9.7.5) are widely used in cases where $B^{(j)}_{x+t}$ is a complicated function, possibly requiring some degree of approximation. For example, if we apply the uniform distribution assumption to the $j$th integral in (9.7.1), we obtain

Chapter 9

# MULTIPLE DECREMENT MODELS

$$\sum_{k=0}^{\infty} v^{k+1} \,_{k}p_x^{(\tau)} \, q_{x+k}^{(j)} \int_0^1 B_{x+k+s}^{(j)} \, (1+i)^{1-s} \, ds.$$

Then, use of the midpoint rule yields

$$\sum_{k=0}^{\infty} v^{k+1/2} \,_{k}p_x^{(\tau)} \, q_{x+k}^{(j)} \, B_{x+k+1/2}^{(j)} \qquad (9.7.6)$$

as a practical formula for the evaluation of the integral.

In Section 9.6 we discussed situations where a uniform distribution of decrement assumption was not appropriate. For such situations, special adjustments to the net single premiums should be made. We reexamine Example 9.7 where, in the associated single decrement model for withdrawals, equal proportions, namely $(1/2)q_x'^{(3)}$, of those beginning the year withdraw at midyear and at year end. The net single premium for a withdrawal benefit with amount $B_{x+t}^{(3)}$ payable for withdrawal at age $x+t$, $t > 0$, is given by

$$\bar{A} = \sum_{k=0}^{\infty} v^k \,_{k}p_x^{(\tau)} \left\{ \frac{1}{2} q_{x+k}'^{(3)} v^{1/2} B_{x+k+1/2}^{(3)} \left[ 1 - \frac{1}{2}q_{x+k}'^{(1)} \right] \left[ 1 - \frac{1}{2}q_{x+k}'^{(2)} \right] \right.$$

$$\left. + \frac{1}{2} q_{x+k}'^{(3)} v \, B_{x+k+1}^{(3)} [1 - q_{x+k}'^{(1)(1)}] [1 - q_{x+k}'^{(2)}] \right\}.$$

Here we are dealing with the distribution of decrement in the context of the associated single decrement tables, rather than in the multiple decrement context. A possible approximation here would be to take an average value of the interest factor, such as $v^{3/4}$, and an average value of the withdrawal benefit, such as

$$\hat{B}_{x+k} = \frac{1}{2}[B_{x+k+1/2}^{(3)} + B_{x+k+1}^{(3)}].$$

If the interest and benefit amount terms are replaced by their geometric and arithmetic averages respectively, and then factored out, the expression for $q_{x+k}^{(3)}$ obtained in Example 9.7 remains inside the braces. Thus,

$$\bar{A} \cong \sum_{k=0}^{\infty} v^{k+3/4} \,_{k}p_x^{(\tau)} \, q_{x+k}^{(3)} \, \hat{B}_{x+k}$$

$$= (1+i)^{1/4} \sum_{k=0}^{\infty} v^{k+1} \,_{k}p_x^{(\tau)} \, q_{x+k}^{(3)} \, \hat{B}_{x+k}.$$

The last expression can be interpreted as providing a withdrawal benefit of $\hat{B}_{x+k}$ at the end of the year and then adjusting by $(1+i)^{1/4}$ to recognize that, on the average, withdrawal benefits are paid $1/4$ year earlier.

We have only scratched the surface of actuarial applications of multiple decrement models. Further examples, which are more detailed and practical, are the subject of the next chapter.

**Remark:**

In this chapter we have not used the format employed in Chapter 6 to state premium determination problems. This was done to achieve brevity. The premium problems of this section could have been approached by formulating a loss function and invoking the equivalence principle.

For example, suppose that the net single premium $\bar{A}$ is required for an insurance to $(x)$ paying $2B$ upon death due to an accident and $B$ upon death due to all other causes, if death occurs before age $r$. If death, from any cause, occurs after age $r$, the amount $B$ is paid. Two causes of decrement are recognized, $j = 1$, the accidental cause, and $j = 2$, the nonaccident cause. The loss function is

$$L = \begin{cases} \begin{rcases} 2B v^T - \bar{A} & J = 1 \\ B v^T - \bar{A} & J = 2 \end{rcases} & 0 < T \leq r - x \\ B v^T - \bar{A} & J = 1,2 \quad T > r - x. \end{cases}$$

The equivalence principle yields $E[L] = 0$, or

$$\bar{A} = B \int_0^{r-x} v^t \, _t p_x^{(\tau)} \, \mu_{x+t}^{(1)} \, dt + B \int_0^\infty v^t \, _t p_x^{(\tau)} \, \mu_{x+t}^{(\tau)} \, dt.$$

A measure of the dispersion due to the random natures of time and cause of death is provided by $\mathrm{Var}[L] = E[L^2]$. One can verify that, for this case,

$$\mathrm{Var}[L] = B^2 \left[ 3 \int_0^{r-x} v^{2t} \, _t p_x^{(\tau)} \, \mu_{x+t}^{(1)} \, dt + \int_0^\infty v^{2t} \, _t p_x^{(\tau)} \, \mu_{x+t}^{(\tau)} \, dt \right] - \bar{A}^2.$$

In the general case, with net single premium given by (9.7.1), we have

$$\mathrm{Var}[L] = E[L^2] = \sum_{j=1}^m \int_0^\infty [B_{x+t}^{(j)} v^t - \bar{A}]^2 \, _t p_x^{(\tau)} \, \mu_{x+t}^{(j)} \, dt,$$

which can be reduced to

$$\mathrm{Var}[L] = \sum_{j=1}^m \int_0^\infty [B_{x+t}^{(j)} v^t]^2 \, _t p_x^{(\tau)} \, \mu_{x+t}^{(j)} \, dt - \bar{A}^2. \tag{9.7.7}$$

**9.8
Notes and
References**

The history of multiple decrement theory was reviewed by Seal (1977). Chiang (1968) developed the theory using the language of competing risks. The foundation for the actuarial theory of multiple decrement models was built by Makeham (1874). Menge (1932) and Nesbitt and Van Eenam (1948) provided insight into the deterministic interpretation of forces of decrement and of increment. Bicknell and Nesbitt (1956) developed a very general theory for individual insurances using a deterministic multiple decrement model. Hickman (1964) redeveloped this theory using the language of the stochastic model, and this redevelopment is the basis for much of the current chapter. The analysis of life tables by cause of death is the subject of papers by Greville (1948) and Preston, Keyfitz and Schoen (1973).

# Chapter 9
## MULTIPLE DECREMENT MODELS

**Exercises**

*Section 9.2*

9.1. Let $\mu_{x+t}^{(j)} = \mu_x^{(j)}$, $j = 1, 2, \ldots, m$, $t \geq 0$. Obtain expressions for
a. $f(t,j)$      b. $h(j)$      c. $g(t)$.
The functions called for in (a) and (c) are p.d.f.'s and the function in (b) is a p.f. Show that $T$ and $J$ are independent random variables here.

9.2. A multiple decrement model with 2 causes of decrement has forces of decrement given by

$$\mu_{x+t}^{(1)} = \frac{1}{100 - (x + t)}$$

and

$$\mu_{x+t}^{(2)} = \frac{2}{100 - (x + t)} \qquad t < 100 - x.$$

If $x = 50$, obtain expressions for
a. $f(t, j)$      b. $g(t)$      c. $h(j)$      d. $h(j|t)$.

*Section 9.3*

9.3. Using the multiple decrement probabilities given in Example 9.3, evaluate the following:
a. $_3p_{65}^{(\tau)}$      b. $_{3|}q_{65}^{(1)}$      c. $_3q_{65}^{(2)}$.

9.4. The following multiple decrement probabilities apply to students entering a four-year college.

| Curtate duration, at beginning of academic year | Probability of | | |
|---|---|---|---|
| | Academic failure, $j = 1$ | Withdrawal for all other reasons, $j = 2$ | Survival through the academic year |
| 0 | 0.15 | 0.25 | 0.60 |
| 1 | 0.10 | 0.20 | 0.70 |
| 2 | 0.05 | 0.15 | 0.80 |
| 3 | 0.00 | 0.10 | 0.90 |

An entering class has 1000 members.
a. What is the expectation of the number of graduates? What is the variance?
b. What is the expected number of those who will fail sometime during the four-year program? What is the variance of the number of students who will fail?

9.5. Construct a multiple decrement table on the basis of the data in Exercise 9.4 and use it to exhibit
a. the marginal distribution of the random variable $J$ (mode of exit), which takes on values for academic failure, withdrawal and graduation
b. the conditional distribution of the mode of termination, given that a student has terminated in the third year.

*Section 9.4*

9.6. Given that $\mu_x^{(1)} = 1/(a-x)$, $0 \le x < a$, and $\mu_x^{(2)} = 1$, derive expressions for

   a. $l_x^{(\tau)}$       b. $d_x^{(1)}$       c. $d_x^{(2)}$.

   Assume $l_0^{(\tau)} = a$.

9.7. Given $\mu_x^{(1)} = 2x/(a-x^2)$, $0 \le x < \sqrt{a}$, and $\mu_x^{(2)} = c$, $c > 0$, and $l_0^{(\tau)} = 1000$, derive an expression for $l_x^{(\tau)}$.

9.8. Derive expressions for the following derivatives:

   a. $\dfrac{d}{dx} \, _tq_x^{(\tau)}$       b. $\dfrac{d}{dx} \, _tq_x^{(j)}$       c. $\dfrac{d}{dt} \, _tq_x^{(j)}$.

*Section 9.5*

9.9. Using the data in Exercise 9.4, and assuming a uniform distribution of decrements in the multiple decrement model, calculate a table of $q_k'^{(j)}$, $j = 1,2$, $k = 0,1,2,3$ (where $k$ is the curtate duration).

9.10. If $\mu_{x+t}^{(1)}$ is a constant $c$ for $0 \le t \le 1$, derive expressions in terms of $c$ and $_tp_x^{(\tau)}$ for

   a. $q_x'^{(1)}$       b. $m_x^{(1)}$       c. $q_x^{(1)}$.

9.11. Show that under appropriate assumptions of a uniform distribution of decrements

   a. $m_x^{(\tau)} = \dfrac{q_x^{(\tau)}}{1 - (1/2)q_x^{(\tau)}}$       b. $m_x^{(j)} = \dfrac{q_x^{(j)}}{1 - (1/2)q_x^{(\tau)}}$

   c. $m_x'^{(j)} = \dfrac{q_x'^{(j)}}{1 - (1/2)q_x'^{(j)}}$

   and, conversely,

   d. $q_x^{(\tau)} = \dfrac{m_x^{(\tau)}}{1 + (1/2)m_x^{(\tau)}}$       e. $q_x^{(j)} = \dfrac{m_x^{(j)}}{1 + (1/2)m_x^{(\tau)}}$

   f. $q_x'^{(j)} = \dfrac{m_x'^{(j)}}{1 + (1/2)m_x'^{(j)}}$.

9.12. Order in terms of magnitude. State your reasons.

$$q_x'^{(j)}, \quad q_x^{(j)}, \quad m_x'^{(j)}$$

9.13. Given, for a double decrement table, that $q_{40}'^{(1)} = 0.02$ and $q_{40}'^{(2)} = 0.04$, calculate $q_{40}^{(\tau)}$ to four decimal places.

9.14. For a double decrement table you are given that $m_{40}^{(\tau)} = 0.2$ and $q_{40}'^{(1)} = 0.1$. Calculate $q_{40}'^{(2)}$ to four decimal places assuming a

   a. uniform distribution of decrements in the multiple decrement model

   b. uniform distribution of decrements in the associated single decrement tables.

9.15. Using the data in Exercise 9.4 and assuming a uniform distribution of decrements in the multiple decrement model, construct a table of $m_k^{(j)}$, $j = 1,2$, $k = 0,1,2,3$ (where $k$ is the curtate duration). Calculate each result to five decimal places.

9.16. Given that decrement may be due to death, 1, disability, 2, or retirement, 3, use (9.5.9) to construct a multiple decrement table based on the following absolute rates:

| Age $x$ | $q_x'^{(1)}$ | $q_x'^{(2)}$ | $q_x'^{(3)}$ |
|---|---|---|---|
| 62 | 0.020 | 0.030 | 0.200 |
| 63 | 0.022 | 0.034 | 0.100 |
| 64 | 0.028 | 0.040 | 0.120 |

9.17. Recalculate the multiple decrement table from the absolute rates of decrement in Exercise 9.16 by means of the **central rate bridge.** [Hint: To use the central rate bridge, first calculate $m_x'^{(j)}$ by the formula

$$m_x'^{(j)} \cong \frac{q_x'^{(j)}}{1 - (1/2)q_x'^{(j)}} \quad j = 1,2,3,$$

which holds if there is a uniform distribution of decrement in the associated single decrement tables. Next, assume $m_x^{(j)} \cong m_x'^{(j)}$, $j = 1,2,3$, and proceed to $q_x^{(j)}$ by

$$q_x^{(j)} = \frac{d_x^{(j)}}{l_x^{(\tau)}} = \frac{d_x^{(j)}}{l_x^{(\tau)} - (1/2)d_x^{(\tau)} + (1/2)d_x^{(\tau)}} = \frac{m_x^{(j)}}{1 + (1/2)m_x^{(\tau)}}.$$

This second relation holds if there is a uniform distribution of total decrement in the multiple decrement table. But then

$$_tp_x^{(\tau)} = 1 - tq_x^{(\tau)} \neq {}_tp_x'^{(1)} {}_tp_x'^{(2)} {}_tp_x'^{(3)}$$
$$= [1 - tq_x'^{(1)}][1 - tq_x'^{(2)}][1 - tq_x'^{(3)}]$$

under the condition of a uniform distribution in the associated single decrement tables. Thus there is an inconsistence in the stated conditions, but the calculations may be accurate enough for the purpose on hand.]

9.18. Indicate arguments for the following relations:
a. $m_x'^{(j)} \cong m_x^{(j)}$

b. $\dfrac{q_x'^{(j)}}{1 - (1/2)q_x'^{(j)}} \cong \dfrac{q_x^{(j)}}{1 - (1/2)q_x^{(\tau)}}.$

Show that these lead to

c. $q_x^{(j)} \cong \dfrac{q_x'^{(j)}[1 - (1/2)q_x^{(\tau)}]}{1 - (1/2)q_x'^{(j)}}$

d. $q_x'^{(j)} \cong \dfrac{q_x^{(j)}}{1 - (1/2)(q_x^{(\tau)} - q_x^{(j)})}.$

Compare (c) and (d) to (9.5.9) and (9.5.10).

9.19. Use the values of $q_x^{(j)}$, $q_x'^{(j)}$ from Example 9.4 to calculate values of $m_x^{(j)}$, $m_x'^{(j)}$, $j = 1,2$, $x = 65,\ldots,69$, under appropriate assumptions of uniform distribution of decrements (see Exercise 9.11).

9.20. Which of the following statements would you accept? Revise where necessary.

a. $q_x^{(j)} \cong \dfrac{m_x^{(j)}}{1 + (1/2)\,m_x^{(j)}}$

b. $\displaystyle\int_0^1 l_{x+t}^{(\tau)}\, dt \cong \dfrac{l_x^{(\tau)}}{1 + (1/2)\,m_x^{(\tau)}}$

c. $q_x^{(1)} = q_x'^{(1)}(1 - (1/2)\,q_x'^{(2)})$ in a double decrement table where there is a uniform distribution of decrement for the year of age $x$ to $x+1$ in each of the associated single decrement tables.

9.21. a. For a certain age $x$, particular cause of decrement $j$ and constant $K_j$, show that the following conditions are equivalent.
   (i) $_tq_x^{(j)} = K_j \,{}_tq_x^{(\tau)}$    $0 \le t \le 1$
   (ii) $\mu_{x+t}^{(j)} = K_j \,\mu_{x+t}^{(\tau)}$    $0 \le t \le 1$
   (iii) $1 - {}_tq_x'^{(j)} = [1 - {}_tq_x^{(\tau)}]^{K_j}$    $0 \le t \le 1$
   [Hint: Show (i) $\Rightarrow$ (ii) $\Rightarrow$ (iii) $\Rightarrow$ (ii) $\Rightarrow$ (i).]

   b. Verify that, in a multiple decrement table, where either

   • $\mu_{x+t}^{(j)} = \mu_x^{(j)}$    $0 \le t \le 1, j = 1,2,\ldots,m$

   (the constant force assumption for each cause of decrement) or

   • $_tq_x^{(j)} = t\,q_x^{(j)}$    $0 \le t \le 1, j = 1,2,\ldots,m$

   (the uniform distribution for each cause of decrement), then

   $_tq_x^{(j)} = K_j \,{}_tq_x^{(\tau)}$    $0 \le t \le 1, j = 1,2,\ldots,m$.

*Section 9.6*

9.22. Redo Exercise 9.9 by use of the formula for $q_x'^{(j)}$ in Exercise 9.18.

9.23. Show that $\mu_{x+1/2}^{(j)} = m_x^{(j)}$, under the assumption of a uniform distribution of each decrement in each year of age in a multiple decrement context.

9.24. How would you proceed to construct the multiple decrement table if the given rates were
a. $q_x'^{(1)}, q_x'^{(2)}, q_x^{(3)}$
b. $q_x'^{(1)}, q_x^{(2)}, q_x^{(3)}$?

9.25. In Example 9.6 suppose that decrement 3 at age 69 is not uniformly distributed but follows the pattern

$$_tp_{69}'^{(3)} = \begin{cases} 1 - 0.12t & 0 < t < 1 \\ 0 & t = 1. \end{cases}$$

In words, the cause 3 absolute rate is 0.12 during the year. Then, just before age 70, all remaining survivors terminated due to cause 3. This is consistent with an assumption that $q_{69}^{\prime(3)} = 1$. What then is the value of $q_{69}^{(3)}$?

9.26. In a double decrement table where cause 1 is death and cause 2 is withdrawal, it is assumed that
 • deaths in the year from age $h$ to age $h+1$ are uniformly distributed,
 • withdrawals in the year from age $h$ to age $h+1$ occur immediately after the attainment of age $h$.
 From this table, it is noted that, at age 50, $l_{50}^{(\tau)} = 1000$, $q_{50}^{(2)} = 0.2$ and $d_{50}^{(1)} = 0.06\, d_{50}^{(2)}$. Determine $q_{50}^{\prime(1)}$.

*Section 9.7*

9.27. Employees enter a benefit plan at age 30. If an employee remains in service until mandatory retirement at age 70, the member receives an annual pension of 300 times years of service. If the employee dies in service before mandatory retirement, the beneficiary is paid 20,000 immediately. If the employee withdraws before mandatory retirement for any reason except death, the member receives a deferred life annuity, starting at age 70, with annual income of 300 times years of service. Give an expression, in terms of integrals and continuous annuities, for the actuarial present value of these benefits for an employee at age 30.

*Miscellaneous*

9.28. On the basis of a triple decrement table, what is the probability that (20) will not terminate before age 65 for cause 2?

9.29. a. You are given $q_x^{\prime(1)}$, $q_x^{\prime(2)}$, $m_x^{(3)}$, $m_x^{(4)}$. How would you proceed to construct a multiple decrement table where active service of an employee group is subject to decrement from death, 1, withdrawal, 2, disability, 3, and retirement, 4?
 b. On the basis of the table in (a), give an expression for the probability that, in the future, an active member aged $y$ will not retire but will terminate from service for some other cause.

9.30. Prove and interpret the relation

$$q_x^{(j)} = q_x^{\prime(j)} - \sum_{k \neq j} \int_0^1 {}_t p_x^{(\tau)}\, \mu_{x+t}^{(k)}\, {}_{1-t}q_{x+t}^{\prime(j)}\, dt.$$

9.31. Let

$$w^{(\tau)}(t) = \frac{{}_t p_x^{(\tau)}}{\displaystyle\int_0^1 {}_t p_x^{(\tau)}\, dt}$$

and

# MULTIPLE DECREMENT MODELS

$$w^{(j)}(t) = \frac{{}_tp_x'^{(j)}}{\displaystyle\int_0^1 {}_tp_x'^{(j)}\,dt} \qquad 0 \le t \le 1.$$

Assume that $j$ and at least one other cause have positive forces of decrement on the interval $0 \le t \le 1$.

a. Show that
   (i) $w^{(\tau)}(0) > w^{(j)}(0)$
   (ii) $w^{(\tau)}(1) < w^{(j)}(1)$
   (iii) there exists a unique number $r$, $0 < r < 1$, such that $w^{(\tau)}(r) = w^{(j)}(r)$.

b. Let

$$-I = \int_0^r [w^{(j)}(t) - w^{(\tau)}(t)]\,dt.$$

Show that

$$I = \int_r^1 [w^{(j)}(t) - w^{(\tau)}(t)]\,dt.$$

c. Assume that $\mu_{x+t}^{(j)}$ is an increasing function on the interval $0 \le t \le 1$. Use the mean value theorem for integrals to establish the following inequalities:

$$m_x'^{(j)} - m_x^{(j)} = \int_0^1 [w^{(j)}(t) - w^{(\tau)}(t)]\,\mu_{x+t}^{(j)}\,dt$$

$$= \int_0^r [w^{(j)}(t) - w^{(\tau)}(t)]\,\mu_{x+t}^{(j)}\,dt$$

$$+ \int_r^1 [w^{(j)}(t) - w^{(\tau)}(t)]\,\mu_{x+t}^{(j)}\,dt$$

$$= -\mu_{x+t_0}^{(j)}\,I + \mu_{x+t_1}^{(j)}\,I \qquad 0 < t_0 < r < t_1 < 1$$

$$= I\,(\mu_{x+t_1}^{(j)} - \mu_{x+t_0}^{(j)}) > 0.$$

9.32. The joint distribution of $T$ and $J$ is specified by

$$
\left.
\begin{aligned}
\mu_{x+t}^{(1)} &= \frac{\theta\,t^{\alpha-1}e^{-\beta t}}{\displaystyle\int_t^\infty s^{\alpha-1}e^{-\beta s}\,ds} \\[2em]
\mu_{x+t}^{(2)} &= \frac{(1-\theta)\,t^{\alpha-1}e^{-\beta t}}{\displaystyle\int_t^\infty s^{\alpha-1}e^{-\beta s}\,ds}
\end{aligned}
\right\}
\quad
\begin{aligned}
&0 < \theta < 1 \\
&\alpha > 0 \\
&\beta > 0 \\
&t \ge 0.
\end{aligned}
$$

# MULTIPLE DECREMENT MODELS

a. Obtain expressions for $f(t, j)$, $h(j)$ and $g(t)$, the joint p.d.f. of $T$ and $J$, the p.f. of $J$ and the p.d.f. of $T$.
b. Express $E[T]$ and $\text{Var}[T]$ in terms of $\alpha$ and $\beta$.
c. An insurance to $(x)$ provides a benefit of 1 if decrement is by cause 1 and a benefit of 0 if the decrement is by cause 2. The force of interest is $\delta$.
   (i) Exhibit the loss function associated with this insurance if it is to be funded by a single premium denoted by $\bar{A}$.
   (ii) Use the equivalence principle and obtain an expression for $\bar{A}$.
   (iii) Obtain a formula for the variance of the loss function in (i).

## Chapter 10
## VALUATION THEORY FOR PENSION PLANS

### 10.1
### Introduction

A major application of multiple decrement models in actuarial work is in pension plans. In this chapter we shall consider basic methods used in calculating the actuarial present values of benefits and contributions for a participant in a pension plan. The participants of a plan may be the employees of a single employer, or they may be the employees of a group of employers engaged in similar activities. A plan, upon retirement, typically provides pensions for age and service or for disability. In case of withdrawal from employment, there may be a return of accumulated employee contributions or a deferred pension. For death occurring before the other contingencies, there may be a lump sum or income payable to a beneficiary. Payments to meet the costs of the benefits are referred to as contributions, not premiums as for insurance, and are payable in various proportions by the participants and the plan sponsor.

A pension plan can be regarded as a system for purchasing deferred life annuities (payable during retirement) and certain ancillary benefits by some form of temporary annuity of contributions during active service. The balancing of the actuarial present values of benefits and contributions may be on an individual basis, but more often is on some aggregate basis for the whole group of participants. Methods to accomplish this balance are the content of the theory of pension funding. Here we shall be concerned with only the separate *valuation* of the pension plan's actuarial present values of benefits and contributions with respect to a typical participant. Aggregate values can then be obtained by summation over all participants. The basic tools for valuing the benefits of, and the contributions to, a pension plan will be presented here, but their application to the possible funding methods for a plan will be deferred to Chapter 19.

### 10.2
### Basic Functions

A starting point is a multiple decrement (service) table constructed to represent a survivorship group of participants subject, in the various years of active service, to given probabilities of
- withdrawal from service,
- death in service,
- retirement for disability,
- retirement for age-service.

The notations for these probabilities for the year of age $x$ to $x + 1$ are $q_x^{(w)}$, $q_x^{(d)}$, $q_x^{(i)}$ and $q_x^{(r)}$ respectively. These are consistent with the notations developed in Chapter 9. Also, we shall use the survivorship function $l_x^{(\tau)}$ from Chapter 9. If $a$ is the initial age and $l_a^{(\tau)}$ is assigned an arbitrary value, we have

$$l_{x+1}^{(\tau)} = l_x^{(\tau)}[1 - (q_x^{(w)} + q_x^{(d)} + q_x^{(i)} + q_x^{(r)})] = l_x^{(\tau)} p_x^{(\tau)}.$$

This function can be used to evaluate such expressions as $_k p_x^{(\tau)}$, thus

$$_k p_x^{(\tau)} = \frac{l_{x+k}^{(\tau)}}{l_x^{(\tau)}}.$$

One can also proceed by direct recursion, namely,

$$_k p_x^{(\tau)} = {}_{k-1}p_x^{(\tau)} \; p_{x+k-1}^{(\tau)}.$$

The forces of decrement related to a service table will be continuous at most ages. They will be denoted by $\mu_x^{(w)}$, $\mu_x^{(d)}$, $\mu_x^{(i)}$ and $\mu_x^{(r)}$. At some ages, discontinuities may occur, primarily at age $\alpha$, the first eligible age for retirement, or at the limiting age $\omega$ beyond which there are no further active members. We shall usually assume that $l_\omega^{(\tau)} = 0$, but where $\omega$ represents a mandatory retirement age, it may be appropriate to assume that $l_\omega^{(\tau)} \neq 0$ and that all retirements for members attaining age $\omega$ occur at that age. Otherwise, we shall generally assume that decrements are spread across each year of age.

In the early years of service, withdrawal rates tend to be high, and the benefit for withdrawal may be only the participant's contributions, if any, accumulated with interest. After a period of time, for example, 5 years, withdrawal rates will be somewhat lower and the withdrawing participant may be eligible for a deferred pension. If these conditions hold, it may be necessary to use select rates of withdrawal for an appropriate number of years. Conditions for disability retirement may also indicate a need for a select basis. The mathematical modifications to a select basis are relatively easy to make, and the theory is more adaptable if select functions are used. In this chapter we shall denote the age at entry by $x$, but shall not otherwise indicate whether an aggregate table, a select table, or a select-and-ultimate table is intended.

The Illustrative Service Table in Appendix 2B illustrates a service table for entry age 30, earliest age for retirement $\alpha = 60$, and limiting age for active service $\omega = 71$. Here $l_{71}^{(\tau)} = 0$.

As noted earlier, the principal benefits under a pension plan are annuities to eligible beneficiaries. For the valuation of such annuity benefits, it is necessary to adopt appropriate mortality tables that will differ if retirement is for disability or for age-service. The corresponding annuity values will be indicated by post-fixed superscripts, $\bar{a}_{x+t}^i$ if retirement is for disability and $\bar{a}_{x+t}^r$ if retirement is for age-service. The continuous annuity value is used as a convenient means of approximating the actual form of pension payment that will normally be monthly, but may have particular conditions as to initial and final payments.

Some pension plans, particularly those for hourly paid workers, define benefits as flat amounts of income per year of service. Other plans define benefits as percentages of final average salary. Such formulas are often used for plans involving salaried employees. In these cases, it is necessary to project future salaries in order to evaluate benefits. Sponsor contributions are often expressed as a percentage of salary, so here also a projection of future salaries is important. For such a projection, we define the following salary functions:

$(AS)_{x+h}$ is the actual annual salary rate at age $x + h$, for a participant who entered at age $x$ and is now at attained age $x + h$;

Chapter 10

# VALUATION THEORY FOR PENSION PLANS

$(ES)_{x+h+t}$ is the projected annual salary rate at age $x + h + t$.

Further, we shall assume that we have a salary scale function $S_y$, to use for these projections, such that

$$(ES)_{x+h+t} = (AS)_{x+h} \frac{S_{x+h+t}}{S_{x+h}}. \qquad (10.2.1)$$

Here the salary function $S_y$ reflects not only merit and seniority increases in salary, but also those increases caused by inflation. For example, in the Illustrative Service Table, $S_y = s_y(1.06)^{y-30}$ where the $s_y$ factor represents the progression of salary due to individual merit and experience increases, and the 6% accumulation factor is to allow for long-term effects of inflation and of increases in productivity of all members of the plan. As was the case for the $l_x^{(\tau)}$ function, one of the values of $S_y$ can be chosen arbitrarily, for instance, in the Illustrative Service Table, $S_{30}$ is taken as unity. The $S_y$ function is usually assumed to be a step function, with constant level throughout any given year of age.

A multiple decrement model, a salary scale, an assumption concerning investment return, and appropriate annuity values for disability and age-service retirements are the essential factors needed to determine the actuarial present values of pension plan benefits and of contributions to support these benefits. In the following sections, we shall discuss the basic formulas for the valuation of pension plan contributions and various types of benefits. This will be followed by a reformulation in terms of pension commutation functions.

## 10.3 Contributions

There are two simple patterns of contributions: a flat rate per participant and a flat percentage of salary per participant. For each of these patterns we shall evaluate the actuarial present value of future contributions with respect to a participant who has attained age $x + h$.

The actuarial present value of future contributions paid continuously at a rate of $c$ per year can be written as

$$c \int_0^{\omega-x-h} v^t \, {}_tp_{x+h}^{(\tau)} \, dt = c \sum_{k=0}^{\omega-x-h-1} v^k \, {}_kp_{x+h}^{(\tau)} \int_0^1 v^s \, {}_sp_{x+h+k}^{(\tau)} \, ds. \qquad (10.3.1)$$

The right member of (10.3.1) results from replacing $t$ by $k + s$ where $k$ is an integer and $0 \le s \le 1$. If we approximate each integral of the right-hand side by a midpoint formula, we obtain the approximate value

$$c \sum_{k=0}^{\omega-x-h-1} v^k \, {}_kp_{x+h}^{(\tau)} \, v^{1/2} \, {}_{1/2}p_{x+h+k}^{(\tau)} = c \sum_{k=0}^{\omega-x-h-1} v^{k+1/2} \, {}_{k+1/2}p_{x+h}^{(\tau)}. \qquad (10.3.2)$$

Note that (10.3.2) can be obtained directly by assuming that payments take place at the middle of age years.

If contributions are expressed as a fraction $c$ of the salary, then the actuarial present value of future contributions in respect to a

# VALUATION THEORY FOR PENSION PLANS

participant currently being paid at an annual rate of $(AS)_{x+h}$ is expressible as

$$c(AS)_{x+h} \int_0^{\omega-x-h} v^t {}_t p_{x+h}^{(\tau)} \frac{S_{x+h+t}}{S_{x+h}} dt$$

$$= \frac{c(AS)_{x+h}}{S_{x+h}} \sum_{k=0}^{\omega-x-h-1} v^k {}_k p_{x+h}^{(\tau)} \int_0^1 v^s {}_s p_{x+h+k}^{(\tau)} S_{x+h+k+s} \, ds. \qquad (10.3.3)$$

If the $S_y$ function is assumed to be constant within any year of age, then it can also be removed from the integrals. Further, if we approximate each of the integrals by a midpoint formula, we obtain as the actuarial present value

$$\frac{c(AS)_{x+h}}{S_{x+h}} \sum_{k=0}^{\omega-x-h-1} v^{k+1/2} {}_{k+1/2} p_{x+h}^{(\tau)} S_{x+h+k}. \qquad (10.3.4)$$

Formulas (10.3.3) and (10.3.4) for the actuarial present value of contributions can be adapted to variations of these simple patterns as illustrated in the following examples.

**Example 10.1:**

On the basis of the Illustrative Service Table and interest at the effective annual rate of 6%, give formulas for the actuarial present value of future contributions to a pension plan in respect to a participant now aged 50 if the contribution rate is
a. level at 1200 per year
b. assumed to increase by 100 per year from an initial level of 1200
c. assumed to increase yearly at a compound rate of 4% from an initial level of 1200.

**Solution:**
In the Illustrative Service Table $\omega = 71$, which determines the range in the following summations.

a. $1200 \sum_{k=0}^{20} v^{k+1/2} {}_{k+1/2} p_{50}^{(\tau)}$

b. $100 \sum_{k=0}^{20} (12 + k) \, v^{k+1/2} {}_{k+1/2} p_{50}^{(\tau)}$

c. $1200 \sum_{k=0}^{20} (1.04)^k \, v^{k+1/2} {}_{k+1/2} p_{50}^{(\tau)}$

The last expression can be rearranged as

$$1200 \, (1.04)^{-1/2} \sum_{k=0}^{20} (v')^{k+1/2} {}_{k+1/2} p_{50}^{(\tau)}$$

where $v' = 1.04/1.06$ is based on the rate of interest

$$i' = \frac{1.06}{1.04} - 1 = \frac{0.02}{1.04} = 0.019.$$

▼

**Example 10.2:**

In an *excess-type plan,* benefits and contributions are to be payable in respect to salaries in excess of a sequence of earnings levels, namely, $H_0, H_1, \ldots, H_k, \ldots$ where $H_k$ applies in future year $k+1$. On the basis of the Illustrative Service Table, give a formula for the actuarial present value of contributions of 5% of the future excess salaries in respect to an employee now aged 50 with a salary of 30,000. Assume $30,000 > H_0$ and that future salaries will remain above the earnings level $H_k$, $k = 1,2,\ldots$.

**Solution:**
The required actuarial present value is

$$0.05 \sum_{k=0}^{20} \left[ 30{,}000 \frac{S_{50+k}}{S_{50}} - H_k \right] v^{k+1/2} {}_{k+1/2}p_{50}^{(\tau)}. \qquad \blacktriangledown$$

## 10.4 Age-Service Retirement Benefits

The principal benefit under a pension plan is normally the deferred annuity for age-service retirement. In *defined contribution plans,* the actuarial present value is simply the accumulation under interest of contributions made for the participant, and the benefit is an annuity that can be purchased by such accumulation. In such plans, the determination of the actuarial present value is accomplished by an accumulation process. In other plans, the retirement income is defined by formula, and it is for such *defined benefit plans* that we seek to express actuarial present values. We shall do so first for a general case and shall then specialize to some of the more useful patterns for defined benefits.

For this purpose, we introduce the function $R(x,h,t)$ to denote the (annual) income benefit rate for an employee aged $x+h$ who entered at age $x$ and who $t$ years from now at age $x+h+t$ qualifies for immediate or deferred income benefits. We assume that the income remains level, and in case of retirement, for example, we express its actuarial present value at time of retirement by $R(x,h,t)\,\ddot{a}^r_{x+h+t}$. It should be noted that in Section 9.7, benefits were lump sums, $B_{x+h+t}$, and the corresponding quantity here is the annuity value, $R(x,h,t)\,\ddot{a}^r_{x+h+t}$, the calculation of which is a preliminary step in the valuation process. We can then write an integral expression for the actuarial present value of the age-service retirement benefit for an active employee now at status $x+h < \alpha$,

$$APV = \int_{\alpha-x-h}^{\omega-x-h} v^t\, {}_tp_{x+h}^{(\tau)}\, \mu_{x+h+t}^{(r)}\, R(x,h,t)\, \ddot{a}^r_{x+h+t}\, dt. \qquad (10.4.1)$$

As in Section 9.7, we approximate the integral for practical calculation of the actuarial present value. To do so, we write

$$APV = \sum_{k=\alpha-x-h}^{\omega-x-h-1} v^k\, {}_kp_{x+h}^{(\tau)} \int_0^1 v^s\, {}_sp_{x+h+k}^{(\tau)}\, \mu_{x+h+k+s}^{(r)}\, R(x,h,k+s)\, \ddot{a}^r_{x+h+k+s}\, ds.$$

By assuming a uniform distribution of retirements in each year of age, we can rewrite this as

$$APV = \sum_{k=\alpha-x-h}^{\omega-x-h-1} v^k \, {}_kp_{x+h}^{(\tau)} \, q_{x+h+k}^{(r)} \int_0^1 v^s \, R(x,h,k+s) \, \bar{a}_{x+h+k+s}^r \, ds.$$

Using the midpoint approximation for the remaining integrals gives

$$APV \cong \sum_{k=\alpha-x-h}^{\omega-x-h-1} v^{k+1/2} \, {}_kp_{x+h}^{(\tau)} \, q_{x+h+k}^{(r)} \, R(x,h,k+1/2) \, \bar{a}_{x+h+k+1/2}^r. \quad (10.4.2)$$

Formula (10.4.2) is the general means by which we will calculate the actuarial present values of age-service retirement benefits.

We proceed to consider several common types of income benefit rate functions $R(x,h,t)$. These fall into three groups. First, there are functions that do not depend on salary levels. Second, there are those that depend on either the final salary rate or on an average salary rate over the last several years prior to retirement. Finally, there are functions that depend on the average salary over the career with the plan sponsor.

**10.4.1**
**$R(x,h,t)$**
**Independent**
**of Salary**

Let us consider an income benefit of $b$ times the total number of years of service, including any final fraction. In this case $R(x,h,t) = b(h+t)$. If only whole years of service are to be counted, then $R(x,h,t) = b(h+k)$ where $k$ is the greatest integer in $t$. Another variation would be to apply a lower rate for service in excess of a number of years, for example, 30 years. In this case, the income benefit rate would be

$$R(x,h,t) = \begin{cases} b_1(h+t) & h+t \le 30 \\ 30\,b_1 + b_2(h+t-30) & h+t > 30. \end{cases}$$

**Example 10.3:**

A pension plan provides a basic benefit of 15 per month for each year of service plus a supplementary benefit, payable to age 65, of 10 per month for each year of service. Give a formula for the actuarial present value of these benefits for a participant aged 40 who entered service at age 30, assuming the Illustrative Service Table is to be applied.

**Solution:**
From (10.4.2), the actuarial present value of the basic benefit is

$$180 \sum_{k=20}^{30} v^{k+1/2} \, {}_kp_{40}^{(\tau)} \, q_{40+k}^{(r)} \left( 10 + k + \frac{1}{2} \right) \bar{a}_{40+k+1/2}^r$$

and of the supplementary benefit is

$$120 \sum_{k=20}^{24} v^{k+1/2} \, {}_kp_{40}^{(\tau)} \, q_{40+k}^{(r)} \left( 10 + k + \frac{1}{2} \right) \bar{a}_{40+k+1/2:\overline{25-k-1/2}|}^r. \qquad \blacktriangledown$$

**Example 10.4:**

If in Example 10.3, no more than 35 years of service are to count for the benefit, how would the formulas be modified?

# VALUATION THEORY FOR PENSION PLANS

**Solution:**
For the basic benefit, the income benefit rate would be

$$R\left(30,10,k + \frac{1}{2}\right) = \begin{cases} 180 \left(10 + k + \frac{1}{2}\right) & k < 25 \\ 6300 & 25 \leq k \leq 30. \end{cases}$$

The formula for the supplementary benefit would be unchanged. ▼

## 10.4.2
## $R(x,h,t)$
## Dependent on
## Final Salary

We first consider the case where the income benefit rate is a fixed fraction $g$ of the final salary rate, thus

$$R(x,h,t) = g\,(ES)_{x+h+t}$$

$$= g\,(AS)_{x+h}\frac{S_{x+h+t}}{S_{x+h}}.$$

More often, the income benefit rate is based on the average salary rate over the last $m$ years, for example, over the last 5 years. In this case, if $t > m$,

$$R(x,h,t) = g\frac{1}{m}\int_{t-m}^{t} (ES)_{x+h+s}\,ds$$

$$= g\frac{(AS)_{x+h}}{m}\int_{t-m}^{t} \frac{S_{x+h+s}}{S_{x+h}}\,ds. \tag{10.4.3}$$

If $t < m$, the exact expression for $R(x,h,t)$ involves some known salaries and is given by

$$g\frac{1}{m}\left[\int_{t-m}^{0} (AS)_{x+h+s}\,ds + \int_{0}^{t} (AS)_{x+h}\frac{S_{x+h+s}}{S_{x+h}}\,ds\right].$$

This second formulation requires special handling.

For numerical evaluation of (10.4.3), we utilize yearly intervals for $t$; for $k \leq t < k + 1$, we use the midyear value. Thus

$$R\left(x,h,k + \frac{1}{2}\right) = g\frac{(AS)_{x+h}}{S_{x+h}}\frac{1}{m}\int_{k+1/2-m}^{k+1/2} S_{x+h+s}\,ds.$$

Under the usual assumption that $S_y$ is a step function, constant over each year of age, we have

$$R\left(x,h,k + \frac{1}{2}\right) = g\frac{(AS)_{x+h}}{S_{x+h}}\frac{1}{m}\left(\frac{1}{2}S_{x+h+k-m} + S_{x+h+k-m+1}\right.$$

$$\left. + \cdots + S_{x+h+k-1} + \frac{1}{2}S_{x+h+k}\right).$$

## VALUATION THEORY FOR PENSION PLANS

By introducing the notation

$$_mZ_y = \frac{1}{m}\left(\frac{1}{2}S_{y-m} + S_{y-m+1} + \cdots + S_{y-1} + \frac{1}{2}S_y\right), \qquad (10.4.4)$$

we can rewrite the formula as

$$R\left(x,h,k+\frac{1}{2}\right) = g\,(AS)_{x+h}\,\frac{_mZ_{x+h+k}}{S_{x+h}}. \qquad (10.4.5)$$

A more common form of the final salary benefit is to base the income benefit rate on the product of the final average salary and the number of years of service at retirement. A typical formula would be

$$R(x,h,t) = f\,(h+t)\,(AS)_{x+h}\left[\frac{1}{m}\int_{t-m}^{t}\frac{S_{x+h+s}}{S_{x+h}}\,ds\right]$$

where $f$ is a designated fraction such as 0.02. For numerical approximation, one might proceed as in (10.4.5) to write

$$R\left(x,h,k+\frac{1}{2}\right) = f\left(h+k+\frac{1}{2}\right)(AS)_{x+h}\,\frac{_mZ_{x+h+k}}{S_{x+h}}. \qquad (10.4.6)$$

In some cases, only completed years of service are counted, and in that case

$$R\left(x,h,k+\frac{1}{2}\right) = f\,(h+k)\,(AS)_{x+h}\,\frac{_mZ_{x+h+k}}{S_{x+h}}. \qquad (10.4.7)$$

Some variations are indicated in the following examples.

**Example 10.5:**

In a *step-rate plan,*

    (the income benefit rate for retirement in year $k+1$)

  = (the number of years of service)

      $\times$ [($1\frac{1}{4}\%$ of the first $H_k$ of the 3-year final average salary)

        + ($1\frac{3}{4}\%$ of the 3-year final average salary in excess of $H_k$)].

For a participant who is entering now at age 30 with salary of 20,000, give a formula for the midyear income benefit rate in case of retirement between ages 63 and 64. Assume that the 3-year final average salary will be in excess of $H_{33}$.

**Solution:**

$$R(30,0,33\tfrac{1}{2}) = 33.5\left[0.0125\,H_{33} + 0.0175\left(20,000\,\frac{_3Z_{63}}{S_{30}} - H_{33}\right)\right]$$

$$= 33.5\left[350\,\frac{_3Z_{63}}{S_{30}} - 0.005\,H_{33}\right]$$

▼

# VALUATION THEORY FOR PENSION PLANS

**Example 10.6:**

In an *offset plan,* the income benefit rate is first calculated as 2% of the 3-year final average salary times the number of years of service, and then an offset based on the participant's social insurance benefit is subtracted. The offset is equal to 50% of the participant's initial retirement income from social insurance. For a participant aged 40, who entered service at age 30 and now has salary of 30,000, the estimated income benefit rate from social insurance for retirement at age 65 is $P$. Give a formula for the income benefit rate from the offset plan if retirement occurs at exact age 65.

**Solution:**

$$R(30,10,25) = 35 \left[ 0.02\,(30,000) \frac{3\tilde{Z}_{65}}{S_{40}} \right] - 0.5\,P$$

$$= 21,000 \frac{3\tilde{Z}_{65}}{S_{40}} - 0.5\,P$$

where

$$3\tilde{Z}_{65} = \frac{S_{62} + S_{63} + S_{64}}{3}.$$

▼

**Example 10.7:**

An *add-on plan* provides a basic income benefit rate of $1\frac{1}{2}$% of 5-year final average compensation for each year of service plus a supplement payable to age 65 of 1/2% of 5-year final average compensation for each year of service in case a participant retires before age 65. For a participant aged 40, who entered service at age 30 and has a salary of 30,000, give a formula for the actuarial present value of the participant's benefit if the earliest retirement age is 60, retirement is mandatory at age 70, and some participants remain in service until attainment of age 70.

**Solution:**
Here $q_{40+k}^{(r)} = 0$, $k = 0,1,2,\ldots,19$ and $_{30}p_{40}^{(\tau)} \neq 0$. The actuarial present value is

$$\sum_{k=20}^{29} v^{k+1/2}\,_{k}p_{40}^{(\tau)}\, q_{40+k}^{(r)} \left(10 + k + \frac{1}{2}\right) \frac{5\tilde{Z}_{40+k}}{S_{40}}\, 450\, \ddot{a}_{40+k+1/2}^{r}$$

$$+ v^{30}\,_{30}p_{40}^{(\tau)} \frac{5\tilde{Z}_{70}}{S_{40}}\, 18,000\, \ddot{a}_{70}^{r}$$

$$+ \sum_{k=20}^{24} v^{k+1/2}\,_{k}p_{40}^{(\tau)}\, q_{40+k}^{(r)} \left(10 + k + \frac{1}{2}\right) \frac{5\tilde{Z}_{40+k}}{S_{40}}\, 150\, \ddot{a}_{40+k+1/2:\overline{25-k-1/2|}}^{r}$$

where

$$5\tilde{Z}_{70} = \frac{S_{65} + S_{66} + S_{67} + S_{68} + S_{69}}{5}.$$

▼

**Example 10.8:**

How does the formula for the actuarial present value of the benefit for the participant in Example 10.7 change if the service to be credited in the income benefit rate is limited to 30 years?

**Solution:**
For this particular participant, who by age 60 will have completed 30 years of service, the formula for the actuarial present value simplifies to

$$13,500 \left\{ \sum_{k=20}^{29} v^{k+1/2} \; {}_k p_{40}^{(\tau)} \; q_{40+k}^{(r)} \; \frac{{}_5 Z_{40+k}}{S_{40}} \; \bar{a}_{40+k+1/2}^r + v^{30} \; {}_{30} p_{40}^{(\tau)} \; \frac{{}_5 \tilde{Z}_{70}}{S_{40}} \; \bar{a}_{70}^r \right.$$

$$\left. + \frac{1}{3} \sum_{k=20}^{24} v^{k+1/2} \; {}_k p_{40}^{(\tau)} \; q_{40+k}^{(r)} \; \frac{{}_5 Z_{40+k}}{S_{40}} \; \bar{a}_{40+k+1/2:\overline{25-k-1/2|}}^r \right\}.$$                ▼

**Example 10.9:**

Give a formula for the actuarial present value of the retirement benefit associated with service between ages 30 and 40 by the participant in Example 10.7.

**Solution:**
The participant has 10 years of service between ages 30 and 40 and the actuarial present value of the associated benefit is 1/3 of the actuarial present value of Example 10.8, which was based on 30 years of service credit. The only change required is to replace 13,500 by 4500.                ▼

## 10.4.3
## $R(x,h,t)$
## Determined
## by Career
## Average Salary

Another type of income benefit rate is a fraction $f$ of the entire career earnings of the retiree. This income benefit rate can be viewed as $f$ times the product of the number of years of service and the average salary over the entire career. For this reason, such benefits are called *career average benefits.*

The calculation of actuarial present values of career average retirement benefits breaks naturally into two parts, one for past service for which the salary information is known and one for future service where salaries must be estimated. Here, past salaries enter into the valuation of benefits for all participants and not just for participants who are near retirement. Thus, unlike the situation mentioned in connection with (10.4.3), it is usual here to use actual past salaries. If the total of past salaries for a participant at status $x+h$ is denoted by $(TPS)_{x+h}$, the benefit rate for past service is $f\,(TPS)_{x+h}$ and the actuarial present value of the past service benefit is

$$f\,(TPS)_{x+h} \sum_{k=\alpha-x-h}^{\omega-x-h-1} v^{k+1/2} \; {}_k p_{x+h}^{(\tau)} \; q_{x+h+k}^{(r)} \; \bar{a}_{x+h+k+1/2}^r .$$      (10.4.8)

The income benefit rate based on future service is given by

$$f \int_0^t (ES)_{x+h+s} \, ds = f \frac{(AS)_{x+h}}{S_{x+h}} \int_0^t S_{x+h+s} \, ds.$$

For numerical evaluation, if $S_{x+h+s}$ is a step function with yearly steps, we have

# VALUATION THEORY FOR PENSION PLANS

$$f \frac{(AS)_{x+h}}{S_{x+h}} \left( \sum_{j=0}^{k-1} S_{x+h+j} + \frac{1}{2} S_{x+h+k} \right) \qquad (10.4.9)$$

where $k$ is the greatest integer in $t$. The actuarial present value of the future service benefit is thus

$$f \frac{(AS)_{x+h}}{S_{x+h}} \left[ \sum_{k=\alpha-x-h}^{\omega-x-h-1} v^{k+1/2} \; {}_k p_{x+h}^{(\tau)} \; q_{x+h+k}^{(r)} \; \bar{a}_{x+h+k+1/2}^r \left( \sum_{j=0}^{k-1} S_{x+h+j} + \frac{1}{2} S_{x+h+k} \right) \right].$$
$$(10.4.10)$$

Since $q_{x+h+k}^{(r)} = 0$ for $k < \alpha - x - h$, (10.4.10) can be rewritten as

$$f \frac{(AS)_{x+h}}{S_{x+h}} \left[ \sum_{k=0}^{\omega-x-h-1} v^{k+1/2} \; {}_k p_{x+h}^{(\tau)} \; q_{x+h+k}^{(r)} \; \bar{a}_{x+h+k+1/2}^r \left( \sum_{j=0}^{k-1} S_{x+h+j} + \frac{1}{2} S_{x+h+k} \right) \right].$$
$$(10.4.11)$$

Figure 10.1 shows those combinations of $j$ and $k$ values over which the summation is made. Lattice points where the term has a multiplicative coefficient of $1/2$ are marked $\circ$.

By changing the order of summation, (10.4.11) becomes

$$f \frac{(AS)_{x+h}}{S_{x+h}} \left[ \sum_{j=0}^{\omega-x-h-1} S_{x+h+j} \left( \frac{1}{2} v^{j+1/2} \; {}_j p_{x+h}^{(\tau)} \; q_{x+h+j}^{(r)} \; \bar{a}_{x+h+j+1/2}^r \right. \right.$$

$$\left. \left. + \sum_{k=j+1}^{\omega-x-h-1} v^{k+1/2} \; {}_k p_{x+h}^{(\tau)} \; q_{x+h+k}^{(r)} \; \bar{a}_{x+h+k+1/2}^r \right) \right]. \qquad (10.4.12)$$

Note that the inner sum is 0 when $j = \omega - x - h - 1$.

**Figure 10.1
Points in the
Summations for
Formulas (10.4.11)
and (10.4.12)**

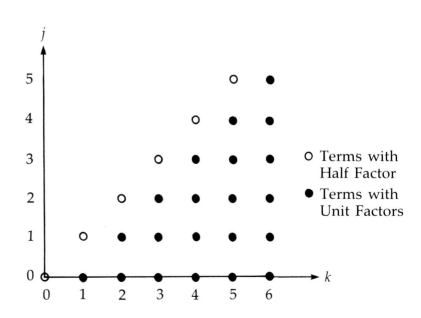

Expression (10.4.12) can be interpreted by considering that service in year $j+1$ provides a full unit of benefit,

$$f \frac{(AS)_{x+h}}{S_{x+h}} S_{x+h+j},$$

if retirement occurs after year $j+1$ and an average of 1/2 unit of benefit if retirement occurs in year $j+1$ itself.

Instead of valuing the total benefit for future service, one may be interested in determining the actuarial present value of the benefit credited for service in the year from age $x+h$ to $x+h+1$. This is simply the first summand in (10.4.12), which, after cancellation of $S_{x+h}$, is

$$f (AS)_{x+h} \left[ \frac{1}{2} v^{1/2} q^{(r)}_{x+h} \bar{a}^r_{x+h+1/2} + \sum_{k=1}^{\omega-x-h-1} v^{k+1/2} \; _kp^{(\tau)}_{x+h} \, q^{(r)}_{x+h+k} \, \bar{a}^r_{x+h+k+1/2} \right].$$

(10.4.13)

This actuarial present value can be interpreted as the cost allocated to current service under the career average plan for the participant aged $x+h$.

**Example 10.10:**

a. A career average plan provides a retirement income of 2% of aggregate salary during a participant's years of service. For a participant aged 40 who entered at age 30, has 200,000 of total past salaries, and has a current salary of 25,000, write an expression for the participant's total income benefit rate in case of retirement between ages 67 and 68.

b. Give alternative formulas for the actuarial present value of this participant's future service benefit, assuming the Illustrative Service Table is to be used.

c. Express the actuarial present value of the benefit credited for this participant's service from age 40 to 41, again assuming the Illustrative Service Table.

**Solution:**
a. The total midyear income benefit rate is

$$R(30,10,27^1/_2) = 0.02 \left[ 200,000 + 25,000 \frac{\sum_{j=0}^{26} S_{40+j} + (1/2) S_{67}}{S_{40}} \right]$$

$$= 4000 + 500 \frac{\sum_{j=0}^{26} S_{40+j} + (1/2) S_{67}}{S_{40}}.$$

b. By (10.4.10), the actuarial present value is

$$\frac{500}{S_{40}} \sum_{k=20}^{30} v^{k+1/2} \; _kp^{(\tau)}_{40} \, q^{(r)}_{40+k} \left( \sum_{j=0}^{k-1} S_{40+j} + \frac{1}{2} S_{40+k} \right) \bar{a}^r_{40+k+1/2}.$$

Alternatively, the expression by (10.4.12) is

$$\frac{500}{S_{40}} \left[ \sum_{j=0}^{30} S_{40+j} \left( \frac{1}{2} v^{j+1/2} \, _{j}p_{40}^{(\tau)} \, q_{40+j}^{(r)} \, \bar{a}_{40+j+1/2}^{r} \right. \right.$$

$$\left. \left. + \sum_{k=j+1}^{30} v^{k+1/2} \, _{k}p_{40}^{(\tau)} \, q_{40+k}^{(r)} \, \bar{a}_{40+k+1/2}^{r} \right) \right].$$

Since $q_{40+k}^{(r)} = 0$ for $k < 20$, a number of summands will be 0.

c. After the 0-valued terms are dropped, the required result from (10.4.13) is

$$500 \sum_{k=20}^{30} v^{k+1/2} \, _{k}p_{40}^{(\tau)} \, q_{40+k}^{(r)} \, \bar{a}_{40+k+1/2}^{r}. \qquad \blacktriangledown$$

## 10.5 Disability Benefits

A process similar to that used in the previous section can be used in the valuation of disability pensions. Such pensions are usually based on salary at date of disability, might involve a minimum benefit, and might be payable only to some age such as 65 at which time the pension is changed to an age-service retirement pension. We shall illustrate the process by a disability pension payable at a rate of $f$ times the salary in the year of disability retirement times the number of years credited service including any fractional credit. It is assumed that the participant must have served at least 5 years and be below age 65 to be eligible for disability retirement, but if disability retirement occurs during this period, the benefit will be at least $10f$ times the annual salary on the date of disability. The income benefit rate function for a new entrant aged $x$ is given by

$$R(x,0,t) = \begin{cases} 0 & 0 \le t < 5 \text{ or } t \ge 65 - x \\ 10f(ES)_{x+t} = 10f(AS)_x \dfrac{S_{x+t}}{S_x} & 5 \le t < 10 \\ tf(ES)_{x+t} = tf(AS)_x \dfrac{S_{x+t}}{S_x} & 10 \le t < 65 - x. \end{cases}$$

(10.5.1)

The actuarial present value for these disability benefits (here assumed payable for life) is given by

$$\int_{5}^{65-x} v^t \, _tp_x^{(\tau)} \, \mu_{x+t}^{(i)} \, R(x,0,t) \, \bar{a}_{x+t}^i \, dt, \qquad (10.5.2)$$

and is approximated by

$$\sum_{k=5}^{64-x} v^{k+1/2} \, _kp_x^{(\tau)} \, q_{x+k}^{(i)} \, R\left(x,0,k+\frac{1}{2}\right) \bar{a}_{x+k+1/2}^i. \qquad (10.5.3)$$

The differences between these expressions and (10.4.1) and (10.4.2) are the use of the force of disability decrement and the probability of disability retirement, the integration and summation limits, and the use of disability annuity values.

**Example 10.11:**

A pension plan provides a disability income benefit of 50% of final salary, but not more than 70% of final salary less the initial amount of disability income payable under a social insurance system. To qualify for the benefit, a participant must have served at least 3 years and have retired for disability before age 65. For a participant entering at age 30 with a salary of 15,000, and with estimated initial social insurance disability income of $I_y$ for disability retirement in the year of age $y$ to $y + 1$, $30 \le y < 65$, express the disability income benefit rate payable through the pension plan.

**Solution:**

If $k = 0,1,2$, $R(30,0,k + 1/2) = 0$. If $3 \le k \le 34$,

$$R\left(30,0,k + \frac{1}{2}\right) = \text{the lesser of} \begin{cases} 7500\dfrac{S_{30+k}}{S_{30}} \\[2ex] 10{,}500\dfrac{S_{30+k}}{S_{30}} - I_{30+k} \end{cases}$$

provided this quantity is positive, otherwise $R(30,0,k + 1/2) = 0$. ▼

## 10.6 Withdrawal Benefits

There are, in general, two types of withdrawal benefits. After a number of years, for example, 10 years, the withdrawing participant may be eligible for a deferred annuity. As an example, we consider a withdrawal benefit of a deferred annuity starting at age 60. The income rate is $f$ times the number of years of service at withdrawal times the salary rate payable in the year of withdrawal. In this case we have

$$R(x,h,t) = \begin{cases} 0 & h + t < 10 \\ f(h + t)(ES)_{x+h+t} & 10 \le h + t < 60 - x. \end{cases}$$

The actuarial present value of this benefit is approximated by

$$\sum_{k=l}^{59-x-h} v^{k+1/2} \, {}_kp^{(\tau)}_{x+h} \, q^{(w)}_{x+h+k} \, R\left(x,h,k + \frac{1}{2}\right) {}_{60-x-h-k-1/2|}\bar{a}^r_{x+h+k+1/2} \quad (10.6.1)$$

where $l$ is the greater of $10 - h$ or 0. The use of $\bar{a}^r$ in (10.6.1) is on the assumption that the retired life mortality table is suitable for deferred retirement calculations.

The other type of withdrawal benefit applies to plans that include participant contributions. These plans, which often involve public employees, usually provide for the return of participant contributions, accumulated with interest, as a lump sum if the participant withdraws before becoming eligible for a pension benefit. A similar benefit is often paid on the death of the participant while in active

# Chapter 10
## VALUATION THEORY FOR PENSION PLANS

service, but in this case there may also be provision for an income benefit to a survivor. Here we shall confine ourselves to consideration of refund benefits payable on withdrawal. We shall also consider only refunds in regard to past contributions and to the current year's contribution, both of which are based on known salaries. We could go on to career average formulas for the valuation of refunds of future contributions, but such formulas are complex and may be avoided in practice.

To value the refund benefit of past contributions, we let $(ATPC)_{x+h}$ denote the past contributions, accumulated with interest to date, with respect to a participant currently aged $x + h$. On the assumption that participant contributions will accumulate at the effective annual rate $j$ in the future, the size of the lump-sum benefit payable for withdrawal at age $x + h + t$ is given by

$$B(x,h,t) = (ATPC)_{x+h} (1 + j)^t.$$

The approximating sum for the actuarial present value of the refund benefit in respect to past contributions is then

$$(ATPC)_{x+h} \sum_{k=0}^{\beta-x-h-1} v^{k+1/2} \, {}_kp_{x+h}^{(\tau)} \, q_{x+h+k}^{(w)} (1 + j)^{k+1/2} \qquad (10.6.2)$$

where $\beta$ is the age at which eligibility for pension (deferred or immediate) is established and $x + h < \beta$. It is assumed here that no refunds are made after age $\beta$ is obtained.

The refund in regard to a participant's current contribution of $c\%$ of salary will be approximated by $(1/2)(0.01c)(AS)_{x+h}$ for withdrawal in the current year, and by $(0.01c)(AS)_{x+h}(1 + j)^k$ for withdrawal in year $k + 1$. Then the actuarial present value of the refund benefit with respect to the participant's current contribution is

$$0.01 \, c \, (AS)_{x+h} \left\{ \frac{1}{2} v^{1/2} q_{x+h}^{(w)} + \sum_{k=1}^{\beta-x-h-1} v^{k+1/2} \, {}_kp_{x+h}^{(\tau)} \, q_{x+h+k}^{(w)} (1 + j)^k \right\} \qquad (10.6.3)$$

where $x + h < \beta$.

**Example 10.12:**

For $j = i$, simplify (10.6.2) and (10.6.3).

**Solution:**
When $j = i$, (10.6.2) becomes

$$(ATPC)_{x+h} \sum_{k=0}^{\beta-x-h-1} {}_kp_{x+h}^{(\tau)} \, q_{x+h+k}^{(w)}$$

$$= (ATPC)_{x+h} \Pr\left[(x + h) \text{ will withdraw before pension eligibility}\right]$$

$$= (ATPC)_{x+h} \frac{l_{x+h}^{(w)} - l_{\beta}^{(w)}}{l_{x+h}^{(\tau)}}$$

where $l_y^{(w)}$ is the number from $l_y^{(\tau)}$ actives at age $y$ who are expected to withdraw in the future.

Formula (10.6.3) is now

$$(0.01\,c)\,(AS)_{x+h}\,v^{1/2}\left[\frac{1}{2}q^{(w)}_{x+h} + \sum_{k=1}^{\beta-x-h-1} {}_{k}p^{(\tau)}_{x+h}\,q^{(w)}_{x+h+k}\right]$$

$$= (0.01\,c)\,(AS)_{x+h}\,v^{1/2}\frac{(1/2)\,(l^{(w)}_{x+h} - l^{(w)}_{x+h+1}) + l^{(w)}_{x+h+1} - l^{(w)}_{\beta}}{l^{(\tau)}_{x+h}}$$

$$= (0.01\,c)\,(AS)_{x+h}\,v^{1/2}\frac{(1/2)\,(l^{(w)}_{x+h} + l^{(w)}_{x+h+1}) - l^{(w)}_{\beta}}{l^{(\tau)}_{x+h}}. \qquad \blacktriangledown$$

## 10.7 Commutation Functions

Special commutation functions provide a traditional notation and storage method for the numerical evaluation of actuarial present values for pension plans. These functions may be useful if a large number of valuations are to be made using the same set of actuarial assumptions. Commutation functions for pension calculations are not included in the International Actuarial Notation, but several forms have been widely used in practice. In this section we shall define and indicate the application of a number of such functions.

We start with the definition

$$D^{(\tau)}_{x} = v^{x}l^{(\tau)}_{x}. \qquad (10.7.1)$$

This is analogous to the $D_x$ function used in Chapters 4 and 5. The superscript $(\tau)$ indicates that it is constructed using the $l^{(\tau)}_{x}$ function from a multiple decrement table. Our formulas for numerical evaluation frequently involve factors such as $v^{k+1/2}{}_{k+1/2}p^{(\tau)}_{x}$, and we write

$$v^{k+1/2}{}_{k+1/2}p^{(\tau)}_{x} = \frac{\bar{D}^{(\tau)}_{x+k}}{D^{(\tau)}_{x}}$$

where

$$\bar{D}^{(\tau)}_{y} = D^{(\tau)}_{y+1/2}. \qquad (10.7.2)$$

Additional functions for the valuation of contributions are

$$^{S}\bar{D}^{(\tau)}_{y} = S_{y}\bar{D}^{(\tau)}_{y} \qquad (10.7.3)$$

and

$$\bar{N}^{(\tau)}_{x} = \sum_{y=x}^{\omega-1}\bar{D}^{(\tau)}_{y}$$

$$^{S}\bar{N}^{(\tau)}_{x} = \sum_{y=x}^{w-1}{}^{S}\bar{D}^{(\tau)}_{y}. \qquad (10.7.4)$$

For the valuation of benefits, the basic function is

$$\bar{C}^{h}_{y} = D^{(\tau)}_{y}v^{1/2}q^{(h)}_{y}, \qquad (10.7.5)$$

which, as in Chapter 4, includes a $D$ function and the probability of a decrement, $q^{(h)}_{y}$. The decrement involved, $h$, is indicated by a post-fixed superscript. The bar over the $C$ indicates that payments are made at the moment of decrement and, consistent with our approximations, requires the factor $v^{1/2}$. Additional functions for the valuation of benefits are

$$^{a}\bar{C}_{y}^{h} = \bar{C}_{y}^{h}\,\bar{a}_{y+1/2}^{h} \tag{10.7.6}$$

$$^{Sa}\bar{C}_{y}^{h} = S_{y}\,{}^{a}\bar{C}_{y}^{h} \tag{10.7.7}$$

$$^{Za}\bar{C}_{y}^{h} = {}_{m}Z_{y}\,{}^{a}\bar{C}_{y}^{h}. \tag{10.7.8}$$

Corresponding $\bar{M}$ and $\bar{R}$ functions may be used, for example

$$^{Za}\bar{M}_{x}^{h} = \sum_{y=x}^{\omega-1} {}^{Za}\bar{C}_{y}^{h} \tag{10.7.9}$$

$$^{Za}\bar{R}_{x}^{h} = \sum_{y=x}^{\omega-1} {}^{Za}\bar{M}_{y}^{h}. \tag{10.7.10}$$

If, in these functions, the annuity value is for other than a whole life annuity, we will indicate this variation by a prime on the $a$ superscript. Note also that $^{Za}\bar{C}_{y}^{r} = 0$ and $^{Za}\bar{M}_{y}^{r} = {}^{Za}\bar{M}_{\alpha}^{r}$ for $y < \alpha$, where $\alpha$ is the first age for retirement.

We shall now develop formulas in terms of pension commutation functions for actuarial present values corresponding to various formulas in previous sections. For the actuarial present value of future contributions paid continuously at a rate of $c$ per year, we start with (10.3.2) rearranged to

$$c \sum_{k=0}^{\omega-x-h-1} \frac{v^{x+h+k+1/2}\,l_{x+h+k+1/2}^{(\tau)}}{v^{x+h}\,l_{x+h}^{(\tau)}}$$

to obtain

$$c\,\frac{\bar{N}_{x+h}^{(\tau)}}{D_{x+h}^{(\tau)}}. \tag{10.7.11}$$

If contributions are expressed as a fraction of salary, we start from (10.3.4) rearranged to

$$c\,(AS)_{x+h} \sum_{k=0}^{\omega-x-h-1} \frac{v^{x+h+k+1/2}\,l_{x+h+k+1/2}^{(\tau)}\,S_{x+h+k}}{v^{x+h}\,l_{x+h}^{(\tau)}\,S_{x+h}} = c\,(AS)_{x+h} \sum_{k=0}^{\omega-x-h-1} \frac{{}^{S}\bar{D}_{x+h+k}^{(\tau)}}{{}^{S}D_{x+h}^{(\tau)}}$$

and end with

$$c\,\frac{(AS)_{x+h}\,{}^{S}\bar{N}_{x+h}^{(\tau)}}{{}^{S}D_{x+h}^{(\tau)}}. \tag{10.7.12}$$

By (10.7.5) and (10.7.6), the expression $v^{k+1/2}\,{}_{k}p_{x+h}^{(\tau)}\,q_{x+h+k}^{(r)}\,\bar{a}_{x+h+k+1/2}^{r}$ can be rewritten as $^{a}\bar{C}_{x+h+k}^{r}/D_{x+h}^{(\tau)}$. Then the general formula (10.4.2) for the actuarial present value of the age-service retirement benefit, in terms

# VALUATION THEORY FOR PENSION PLANS

of commutation functions, is, for $x + h \leq \alpha$,

$$\sum_{k=\alpha-x-h}^{\omega-x-h-1} \frac{R(x,h,k + 1/2)\ {}^{a}\bar{C}^{r}_{x+h+k}}{D^{(\tau)}_{x+h}}. \tag{10.7.13}$$

In particular, when $R(x,h,k + 1/2)$ is given by (10.4.5), we obtain

$$g\,(AS)_{x+h} \sum_{k=\alpha-x-h}^{\omega-x-h-1} \frac{{}_{m}Z_{x+h+k}}{S_{x+h}} \frac{{}^{a}\bar{C}^{r}_{x+h+k}}{D^{(\tau)}_{x+h}}$$

$$= g\,(AS)_{x+h} \sum_{k=\alpha-x-h}^{\omega-x-h-1} \frac{{}^{Z\,a}\bar{C}^{r}_{x+h+k}}{{}^{S}D^{(\tau)}_{x+h}}$$

$$= g\,(AS)_{x+h} \frac{{}^{Z\,a}\bar{M}^{r}_{\alpha}}{{}^{S}D^{(\tau)}_{x+h}}. \tag{10.7.14}$$

Since $0 = q^{(r)}_{y} = \bar{C}^{r}_{y} = {}^{Z\,a}\bar{C}^{r}_{y}$, for $y < \alpha$, we can express the actuarial present value as

$$g\,(AS)_{x+h} \sum_{k=0}^{\omega-x-h-1} \frac{{}^{Z\,a}\bar{C}^{r}_{x+h+k}}{{}^{S}D^{(\tau)}_{x+h}} = g\,(AS)_{x+h} \frac{{}^{Z\,a}\bar{M}^{r}_{x+h}}{{}^{S}D^{(\tau)}_{x+h}}. \tag{10.7.15}$$

This alternative formula is valid whether $x + h \leq \alpha$ or $x + h > \alpha$. This advantage of the reformulation of the sum will be seen again when $R(x,h,k + 1/2)$ depends on years of service.

An example of this is given by (10.4.6) where

$$R\left(x,h,k + \frac{1}{2}\right) = f\left(h + k + \frac{1}{2}\right)(AS)_{x+h} \frac{{}_{m}Z_{x+h+k}}{S_{x+h}}.$$

Then the actuarial present value of the retirement benefit can be expressed by a summation, starting at $k = 0$, as

$$f(AS)_{x+h} \sum_{k=0}^{\omega-x-h-1} \frac{(h + k + 1/2)\,{}^{Z\,a}\bar{C}^{r}_{x+h+k}}{{}^{S}D^{(\tau)}_{x+h}}$$

$$= f(AS)_{x+h} \frac{(h + 1/2)\,{}^{Z\,a}\bar{M}^{r}_{x+h} + {}^{Z\,a}\bar{R}^{r}_{x+h+1}}{{}^{S}D^{(\tau)}_{x+h}}. \tag{10.7.16}$$

This holds for any $x + h$, while a summation starting with $k = \alpha - x - h$ would produce the formula

$$f(AS)_{x+h} \frac{(\alpha - x + 1/2)\,{}^{Z\,a}\bar{M}^{r}_{\alpha} + {}^{Z\,a}\bar{R}^{r}_{\alpha+1}}{{}^{S}D^{(\tau)}_{x+h}},$$

which would have to be supplemented by (10.7.16) for $x + h > \alpha$.

If only full years of service are counted, as in (10.4.7), the actuarial present value is

$$f(AS)_{x+h} \frac{h\,{}^{Z\,a}\bar{M}^{r}_{x+h} + {}^{Z\,a}\bar{R}^{r}_{x+h+1}}{{}^{S}D^{(\tau)}_{x+h}}, \tag{10.7.17}$$

## VALUATION THEORY FOR PENSION PLANS

which follows from (10.7.16) by dropping the average fraction 1/2 for any incomplete year of service.

The actuarial present value (10.4.8) for the past service benefit in the career average salary case is expressible as

$$f(TPS)_{x+h}\left(\frac{{}^a\bar{M}^r_{x+h}}{D^{(\tau)}_{x+h}}\right). \tag{10.7.18}$$

A formula corresponding directly to (10.4.10) for the future service benefit is

$$f(AS)_{x+h}\sum_{k=\alpha-x-h}^{\omega-x-h-1}\frac{\left(\sum_{j=0}^{k-1}S_{x+h+j}+(1/2)\,S_{x+h+k}\right){}^a\bar{C}^r_{x+h+k}}{{}^SD^{(\tau)}_{x+h}}. \tag{10.7.19}$$

To obtain an expression, in pension commutation functions, corresponding to the alternative formula (10.4.12), we write it as

$$f(AS)_{x+h}\frac{(1/2)\displaystyle\sum_{j=0}^{\omega-x-h-1}{}^{Sa}\bar{C}^r_{x+h+j}+\sum_{j=0}^{\omega-x-h-1}S_{x+h+j}\sum_{k=j+1}^{\omega-x-h-1}{}^a\bar{C}^r_{x+h+k}}{{}^SD^{(\tau)}_{x+h}}$$

$$=f(AS)_{x+h}\frac{(1/2)\,{}^{Sa}\bar{M}^r_{x+h}+\displaystyle\sum_{j=0}^{\omega-x-h-1}S_{x+h+j}\,{}^a\bar{M}^r_{x+h+j+1}}{{}^SD^{(\tau)}_{x+h}}.$$

We now define

$$^{S'a}\bar{M}^r_y = S_{y-1}\,{}^a\bar{M}^r_y. \tag{10.7.20}$$

This enables us to express the actuarial present value as

$$f(AS)_{x+h}\frac{(1/2)\,{}^{Sa}\bar{M}^r_{x+h}+{}^{S'a}\bar{R}^r_{x+h+1}}{{}^SD^{(\tau)}_{x+h}}. \tag{10.7.21}$$

Steps similar to those indicated for retirement benefits apply for annuity benefits available upon disability or withdrawal. Thus (10.5.3), for the actuarial present value of a disability benefit, can be written in terms of commutation functions as

$$\sum_{k=5}^{64-x}\frac{R(x,0,k+1/2)\,{}^a\bar{C}^i_{x+k}}{D^{(\tau)}_x} \tag{10.7.22}$$

where ${}^a\bar{C}^i_y = v^{1/2}D^{(\tau)}_y\,q^{(i)}_y\,\bar{a}^i_{y+1/2}$. Similarly, (10.6.1) can be written in terms of commutation functions as

$$f(AS)_{x+h}\sum_{k=l}^{59-x-h}\frac{(h+k+1/2)\,{}^{Sa'}\bar{C}^w_{x+h+k}}{{}^SD^{(\tau)}_{x+h}} \tag{10.7.23}$$

where ${}^{Sa'}\bar{C}^w_y = S_y\,\bar{C}^w_y\,{}_{60-y-1/2|}\bar{a}^r_{y+1/2}$. If desired, one could also express this actuarial present value in terms of ${}^{Sa'}\bar{M}^w_y$ and ${}^{Sa'}\bar{R}^w_y$.

By introducing the notation ${}^{j}\bar{C}_{y}^{w} = (1+j)^{y}\,\bar{C}_{y}^{w}$, we can rewrite (10.6.3) as

$$0.01\,c\,(AS)_{x+h}\frac{(1/2)\,{}^{j}\bar{C}_{x+h}^{w} + \sum_{k=1}^{\beta-x-h-1} {}^{j}\bar{C}_{x+h+k}^{w}}{(1+j)^{x+h}\,D_{x+h}^{(\tau)}}$$

$$= 0.01\,c\,(AS)_{x+h}\frac{(1/2)\,{}^{j}\bar{C}_{x+h}^{w} + {}^{j}M_{x+h+1}^{w} - {}^{j}\bar{M}_{\beta}^{w}}{(1+j)^{x+h}\,D_{x+h}^{(\tau)}}. \qquad (10.7.24)$$

Further illustrations of the commutation function method are in Exercises 10.12–10.18.

**10.8
Notes and
References**

While there are many papers and a number of texts dealing with pension fund mathematics, it seems useful for the purposes of this introductory treatment to refer only to other actuarial texts with similar chapters. Three such references are Hooker and Longley-Cook (1957), Jordan (1967) and Neill (1977). These texts stress the formulation of actuarial present values in terms of pension commutation functions, and the use of tables of such functions to carry out the computations.

In contrast, a major portion of our presentation has been in terms of integrals and approximating sums, with the integrands or summands expressed in terms of basic functions. These approximating sums can be computed by various processes that may or may not make use of commutation functions. For pension benefits determined by complex eligibility or income conditions, it may be more flexible and efficient to calculate by processes not requiring extensive formulation by commutation functions. An opposite view, indicating the power of commutation functions for expressing actuarial present values and controlling their computation, is given by Chamberlin (1982).

We have not defined insurer's losses and studied their variances in this chapter. Formula (9.7.7) gives a means of doing so if one considers the total benefits for all causes of decrement. If one considers only a single benefit, such as the retirement benefit, there is more than one way of defining losses. The usual concept is that premiums and reserves, for a benefit in regard to a particular cause of decrement, apply only to that decrement. Thus, if decrement due to a second cause occurs, then, with respect to the first cause, there is 0 benefit and a gain emerges. An insurer's loss based on this concept would lead to (10.4.2). However, losses defined in this way may have nonzero covariances, so that the loss variance for all benefits is not the sum of the loss variances for the individual benefits.

Alternatively, one may consider that when a particular cause of decrement occurs, the reserves accumulated for the benefits in regard to all the other causes are released to offset the benefit outgo for the given cause. In this case, the losses defined for the benefits for each cause of decrement have 0-valued covariances, and the loss variance for all benefits is the sum of the loss variances for the individual benefits. However, the premiums and reserves for the individual benefits are more difficult to compute on this second basis, and individually differ significantly from those on the usual basis. For insight into these matters, see Hickman (1964).

## Exercises

*Sections 10.2 and 10.3*

10.1. It is assumed that, for a new participant entering at age 30, there will be annual increases in salary at the rate of 5% per year to take account of the effects of inflation and increases in productivity. In addition, it is assumed that promotion raises of 10% of existing salary will occur at ages 40, 50 and 60.
   a. Construct a salary scale function, $S_{30+k}$, to express these assumptions.
   b. Write an expression for the actuarial present value of contributions of 10% of future salary for a new entrant at age 30 with initial salary of 12,000, and with increases in salary according to the scale constructed in part (a).

10.2. Every year, a plan sponsor contributes 10% of that portion of each participant's salary that is in excess of a certain amount. That amount is 10,000 this year and will increase by 5% annually. Express the actuarial present value of the sponsor's contribution for a participant entering now at age 35 with a salary of 25,000.

*Section 10.4*

10.3. In Example 10.3, assume that all retirements take place at exact age 63 (instead of following the Illustrative Service Table). To what do the actuarial present values simplify?

10.4. A new participant aged 25 has a current salary of 12,000. For this participant, express the income benefit rate function for a step-rate plan providing, in case of retirement in year $k+1$,

   (an income)

   = (the number of completed years of service)

   $\times$ [(0.01 of the 3-year final average salary up to $15{,}000\,(1.04)^k$)

   + (0.015 of the excess, if any, of the 3-year final average salary over $15{,}000\,(1.04)^k$)].

10.5. For an offset plan, the offset is determined as the number of years of service times 2% of social insurance income, but in no case more than 50% of the social insurance income. The plan income benefit rate, before the offset is applied, equals the number of years of service times 2% of the 3-year final average salary. For a new entrant at age 40 with a salary of 30,000, give formulas for the income benefit rate after the offset is applied if retirement is
   a. at exact age 65 with estimated social insurance income of $I_{65}$

b. between ages 68 and 69 with estimated social insurance income of $I_{68^{1/2}}$.

10.6. A plan provides for an income benefit rate of 2% of the 3-year final average salary for each year of service, payable to age 65. Thereafter the income benefit rate is $1^{1/3}$% of the 3-year final average salary for each year of service. For a participant aged 50, who entered service at age 30 and has a salary of 36,000, express the actuarial present value of the participant's benefit if the earliest retirement age is 55 and all retirements are completed by age 68.

10.7. In Exercise 10.6, assume the maximum years to be credited is 35. What does the formula for the actuarial present value of the benefit become?

10.8. Write a formula for the actuarial present value of the income benefit associated with the service between ages 30 and 50 of the participant in Exercise 10.6.

10.9. A career average plan provides a retirement income of 2% of aggregate salary during a participant's years of service. The earliest age for retirement is 58 and all retirements are completed by age 68. For a participant aged 50, who entered service at age 30, and has a 400,000 total of past salaries with a current salary of 36,000, write expressions for
   a. the participant's total income benefit rate in case of retirement at exact age 65
   b. the participant's midyear total income benefit rate in case of retirement between ages 65 and 66
   c. the actuarial present value of this participant's retirement benefit for past service
   d. the actuarial present value of this participant's retirement benefit for future service.

*Section 10.5*

10.10. For the disability benefit of Example 10.11, in respect to a participant now aged 50 with 20 years of service and a salary of 25,000, what would be the actuarial present value incurred at time of disability for the benefit if the participant becomes disabled at the middle of the current year and $I_{50} = 8000$?

*Section 10.6*

10.11. A participant aged 35 has accumulated a total of 5000 from his past contributions. This participant will be entitled to full vesting of his deferred annuity upon reaching age 40. Write an expression for the actuarial present value of the refund of the accumulated total of this participant's past contributions in case of withdrawal before age 40, assuming that contributions accumulate at an effective rate of 6% per year.

Chapter 10

# VALUATION THEORY FOR PENSION PLANS

---

10.12  a. In the development of (10.6.3), rewrite the term for withdrawal in the current year,

$$0.01\ c\ (AS)_{x+h}\ \frac{1}{2}\ v^{1/2}\ q^{(w)}_{x+h},$$

as a double integral with one variable for the time of earning a salary increment and the other as time of withdrawal. Credit interest at rate $j$ from the time of earning the salary increment to the time of withdrawal.
  b. Under the assumption of a uniform distribution of withdrawal in the multiple decrement context, evaluate the integral of part (a).
  c. Using $i = 0.06$ and $j = 0.04$, evaluate the term as given in (10.6.3) and in the integral in part (b). Compare the results.

*Section 10.7*

10.13. Express, in terms of commutation functions, the actuarial present value formulas in the following Exercises:
  a. 10.1(b)       b. 10.2       c. 10.3
  d. 10.7          e. 10.9(c)    f. 10.9(d).

10.14. For a participant with a salary of 12,000, who enters a pension plan at age $x < \alpha$, express, in terms of pension commutation functions, the actuarial present value of
  a. a retirement annuity of 1% of the 3-year final average salary for each completed year of service
  b. a retirement annuity of 1% of the 3-year final average salary for each year of service including any fraction.

10.15. If, in Exercise 10.14(b), there is an additional condition that, in order to qualify for retirement, the participant must have served at least 10 years, what does the formula become?

10.16. If contributions of a level percent $c$ of future salaries are to be equivalent to the retirement benefit in Exercise 10.14(b), obtain a formula for $c$ in terms of pension commutation functions.

10.17. Express the formulas given in Example 10.1 in terms of pension commutation functions.

10.18. Express the formula given in Example 10.2 in terms of pension commutation functions.

10.19. Rewrite the formulas given in
  a. Example 10.7
  b. Example 10.9
  in terms of pension commutation functions.

*Miscellaneous*

10.20. Express the actuarial present value of the benefit credited in the year from age 62 to 63 for a participant aged 62 who is covered by the plan of Example 10.10 and has a salary of 30,000.

# VALUATION THEORY FOR PENSION PLANS

10.21. Assuming an increasing salary scale, which of the following two actuarial present values, in respect to a new participant at age 25 with salary of 20,000, is the larger?

A. $400 \dfrac{(1/2)\, ^{Z\,a}\bar{M}^r_{25} + \, ^{Z\,a}\bar{R}^r_{26}}{^SD^{(\tau)}_{25}}$

where $m = 5$ for $_mZ_y$.

B. $400 \dfrac{(1/2)\, ^{S\,a}\bar{M}^r_{25} + \, ^{S'a}\bar{R}^r_{26}}{^SD^{(\tau)}_{25}}$.

# Chapter 11
## COLLECTIVE RISK MODELS FOR A SINGLE PERIOD

## 11.1
## Introduction

In Chapters 3 through 10 we considered models for long-term insurances. The inclusion of interest in these models was essential. In this chapter we return to a topic introduced in Chapter 2, namely, short-term insurance policies. Consequently interest will be ignored. The purpose of this chapter is to present an alternative to the individual policy model discussed in Chapter 2.

The individual risk model developed in Chapter 2 is built by considering individual policies and the claims produced by each policy. Then aggregate claims are obtained by summing over all the policies in the portfolio.

In the *collective risk model* the basic concept is that of a random process that generates claims for a portfolio of policies. This process is characterized in terms of the portfolio as a whole rather than in terms of the individual policies comprising the portfolio. The mathematical formulation is as follows: Let $N$ denote the number of claims produced by a portfolio of policies in a given time period. Let $X_1$ denote the amount of the first claim, $X_2$ the amount of the second claim and so on. Then

$$S = X_1 + X_2 + \cdots + X_N \qquad (11.1.1)$$

represents the aggregate claims generated by the portfolio for the period under study. The number of claims, $N$, is a random variable and is associated with the frequency of claim. In addition, the individual claim amounts $X_1$, $X_2$, ... are also random variables and are said to measure the severity of claims.

In order to make the model tractable, we make two fundamental assumptions:

1. $X_1$, $X_2$, ... are identically distributed random variables.

2. The random variables $N$, $X_1$, $X_2$, ... are mutually independent.

The expression (11.1.1) will be called a random sum, and assumptions (1) and (2) will always be made concerning its components.

A first step in exploring this alternative model will be the study of the distribution of $S$ in terms of the distribution of $N$ and of the common distribution of the $X_i$'s. The expected value, variance and m.g.f. for $S$ will be expressed in terms of the corresponding items for the basic distributions. Also, a formula will be given expressing the d.f. of $S$ by means of the distribution of $N$ and of convolutions of the claim amount distribution.

A second step, pursued in Section 11.3, is the discussion of choices for the distribution of $N$ and the common distribution of the $X_i$'s. For $N$, a Poisson or a negative binomial distribution is often selected. For the claim amount distribution, a normal, gamma or other, perhaps empirical, distribution may be used. When a Poisson distribution is chosen for $N$, the distribution of $S$ is called a *compound Poisson distribution;* when a negative binomial distribution is selected for $N$, the distribution of $S$ is called a ***compound negative binomial distribution.*** These two classes of distributions provide a considerable choice for modeling the distribution of the aggregate claims $S$.

Compound Poisson distributions have a number of useful properties presented in two theorems in Section 11.4. The first theorem shows that the combination of a number of portfolios, each of which has a compound Poisson distribution of aggregate claims, also has a compound Poisson distribution of aggregate claims. The second theorem lays the groundwork for simplified calculations of compound Poisson distributions.

In the final section it is noted that if $S$ has a compound Poisson or compound negative binomial distribution, then the standardized variable

$$\frac{S - E[S]}{\sqrt{\text{Var}[S]}}$$

has approximately a standard normal distribution when the expected number of claims is large. This can be interpreted as a version of the central limit theorem. Thus the normal distribution provides an approximation for the distribution of $S$ itself when the expected number of claims is large. A second way of approximating the distribution of $S$ is by means of a translated gamma distribution. This has the advantage of recognizing skewness in the distribution of $S$ and, in fact, fitting would be accomplished by equating the first three moments.

A principal tool for developing the theory of this chapter is the moment generating function. These functions provide a simple but powerful means for the reader to gain a working knowledge of the collective theory of risk. For a reader who has not worked with them recently, it would be well to review the m.g.f.'s, means and variances of the widely used probability distributions summarized in Appendix 5.

**11.2
The Distribution
of Aggregate
Claims**

In this section we shall see how the distribution of aggregate claims in a fixed time period can be obtained from the distribution of the number of claims and the distribution of individual claim amounts.

Let $P(x)$ denote the common d.f. of the independent and identically distributed $X_i$'s. Let $X$ be a random variable with this d.f.; let

$$p_k = E[X^k] \tag{11.2.1}$$

denote the $k$th moment about the origin and

$$M_X(t) = E[e^{tX}] \tag{11.2.2}$$

the m.g.f. of $X$. In addition, let

$$M_N(t) = E[e^{tN}] \tag{11.2.3}$$

denote the m.g.f. of the distribution of number of claims, and let

$$M_S(t) = E[e^{tS}] \tag{11.2.4}$$

denote the m.g.f. of aggregate claims. The d.f. of aggregate claims will be denoted by $F(x)$.

## Chapter 11

## COLLECTIVE RISK MODELS FOR A SINGLE PERIOD

Using (2.2.10) and (2.2.11), in conjunction with assumptions (1) and (2) of Section 11.1, we obtain

$$E[S] = E[E[S|N]] = E[p_1 N] = p_1 E[N] \qquad (11.2.5)$$

and

$$\begin{aligned} Var[S] &= E[Var[S|N]] + Var[E[S|N]] \\ &= E[N\,Var[X]] + Var[p_1 N] \\ &= E[N]\,Var[X] + p_1^2\,Var[N] \qquad (11.2.6) \end{aligned}$$

where $Var[X] = p_2 - p_1^2$.

The result stated in (11.2.5), that the expected value of aggregate claims is the product of the expected individual claim amount and the expected number of claims, is not surprising. Expression (11.2.6) for the variance of aggregate claims also has a natural interpretation. The variance of aggregate claims is the sum of two components where the first is attributed to the variability of individual claim amounts and the second to the variability of the number of claims.

In a similar fashion we derive an expression for the m.g.f. of $S$:

$$\begin{aligned} M_S(t) &= E[e^{tS}] = E[E[e^{tS}|N]] \\ &= E[M_X(t)^N] = E[e^{N\log M_X(t)}] \\ &= M_N(\log M_X(t)). \qquad (11.2.7) \end{aligned}$$

**Example 11.1:**

Assume that $N$ has a geometric distribution, that is, the p.f. of $N$ is given by

$$Pr(N = n) = pq^n \qquad n = 0,1,2,\ldots \qquad (11.2.8)$$

where $0 < q < 1$ and $p = 1 - q$. Determine $M_S(t)$ in terms of $M_X(t)$.

**Solution:**
Since

$$M_N(t) = E[e^{tN}] = \sum_{n=0}^{\infty} p(qe^t)^n = \frac{p}{1 - qe^t},$$

formula (11.2.7) tells us

$$M_S(t) = \frac{p}{1 - qM_X(t)}. \qquad (11.2.9)$$

▼

To derive the d.f. of $S$ we distinguish according to how many claims occur and use the law of total probability,

$$\begin{aligned} F(x) = Pr(S \le x) &= \sum_{n=0}^{\infty} Pr(S \le x|N = n)\,Pr(N = n) \\ &= \sum_{n=0}^{\infty} Pr(X_1 + X_2 + \cdots + X_n \le x)\,Pr(N = n). \qquad (11.2.10) \end{aligned}$$

But, in terms of the convolution operation defined in Section 2.3, we can write

$$\Pr(X_1 + X_2 + \cdots + X_n \leq x) = P * P * P * \cdots * P(x)$$

$$= P^{*n}(x), \qquad (11.2.11)$$

called the $n$th convolution of $P$. Thus (11.2.10) becomes

$$F(x) = \sum_{n=0}^{\infty} P^{*n}(x) \Pr(N = n). \qquad (11.2.12)$$

If the individual claim amount distribution is discrete with a p.f. $p(x) = \Pr(X = x)$, the distribution of aggregate claims is also discrete. By analogy with the above derivation, the p.f. of $S$ can be obtained directly as

$$f(x) = \sum_{n=0}^{\infty} p^{*n}(x) \Pr(N = n) \qquad (11.2.13)$$

where

$$p^{*n}(x) = p * p * \cdots * p(x) = \Pr(X_1 + X_2 + \cdots + X_n = x). \qquad (11.2.11A)$$

Here the inequality sign in the probability symbol in (11.2.11) has been replaced by the equality sign.

**Example 11.2:**

Consider an insurance portfolio that will produce 0,1,2 or 3 claims in a fixed time period with probabilities 0.1, 0.3, 0.4 and 0.2 respectively. An individual claim will be of amount 1, 2 or 3 with probabilities 0.5, 0.4 and 0.1 respectively. Calculate the p.f. and d.f. of the aggregate claims.

**Solution:**
The calculations are summarized below. Only nonzero entries are exhibited.

| (1) $x$ | (2) $p^{*0}(x)$ | (3) $p^{*1}(x) = p(x)$ | (4) $p^{*2}(x)$ | (5) $p^{*3}(x)$ | (6) $f(x)$ | (7) $F(x)$ |
|---|---|---|---|---|---|---|
| 0 | 1.0 | — | — | — | 0.1000 | 0.1000 |
| 1 | — | 0.5 | — | — | 0.1500 | 0.2500 |
| 2 | — | 0.4 | 0.25 | — | 0.2200 | 0.4700 |
| 3 | — | 0.1 | 0.40 | 0.125 | 0.2150 | 0.6850 |
| 4 | — | — | 0.26 | 0.300 | 0.1640 | 0.8490 |
| 5 | — | — | 0.08 | 0.315 | 0.0950 | 0.9440 |
| 6 | — | — | 0.01 | 0.184 | 0.0408 | 0.9848 |
| 7 | — | — | — | 0.063 | 0.0126 | 0.9974 |
| 8 | — | — | — | 0.012 | 0.0024 | 0.9998 |
| 9 | — | — | — | 0.001 | 0.0002 | 1.0000 |
| $n$ | 0 | 1 | 2 | 3 | — | — |
| $\Pr(N = n)$ | 0.1 | 0.3 | 0.4 | 0.2 | — | — |

Since there are at most 3 claims and each produces a claim amount of at most 3, we can limit the calculations to $x = 0,1,2,\ldots,9$.

# COLLECTIVE RISK MODELS FOR A SINGLE PERIOD

Column (2) lists the p.f. of a degenerate distribution with all the probability mass at 0. Column (3) lists the p.f. of the individual claim amount random variable. Columns (4) and (5) are obtained recursively by applying

$$p^{*(n+1)}(x) = \Pr(X_1 + X_2 + \cdots + X_{n+1} = x)$$

$$= \sum_y \Pr(X_{n+1} = y)\Pr(X_1 + X_2 + \cdots + X_n = x - y)$$

$$= \sum_y p(y)\, p^{*n}(x - y). \tag{11.2.14}$$

Since only 3 different claim amounts are possible, the evaluation of (11.2.14) will involve a sum of 3 or fewer terms. Next, (11.2.13) is used to compute the p.f. displayed in Column (6). For this step, it is convenient to record the p.f. of $N$ in the last row of the results. Finally, the elements of Column (7) are obtained as partial sums of Column (6). An alternative approach, not illustrated here, would have been to perform the convolutions in terms of the d.f.'s, obtain $F(x)$ from (11.2.12), and finally calculate $f(x) = F(x) - F(x-1)$. ▼

If the claim amount distribution is continuous, it cannot be concluded that the distribution of $S$ is continuous. If $\Pr(N = 0) > 0$, the distribution of $S$ will be of the mixed type, that is, it will have a mass of probability at 0 and be continuous elsewhere. This idea is illustrated in the following.

**Example 11.3:**

In Example 11.1, add the assumption that

$$P(x) = 1 - e^{-x} \qquad x > 0;$$

that is, the individual claim amount distribution is exponential with mean 1. Then show that

$$M_S(t) = p + q\frac{p}{p - t} \tag{11.2.15}$$

and interpret the formula.

**Solution:**
First we rewrite (11.2.9) as follows:

$$M_S(t) = p + q\frac{p\,M_X(t)}{1 - q\,M_X(t)}.$$

Then we substitute

$$M_X(t) = \int_0^\infty e^{tx}e^{-x}dx = (1 - t)^{-1}$$

to obtain (11.2.15).

Since 1 is the m.g.f. of the constant 0 and $p/(p-t)$ is the m.g.f. of the exponential distribution with d.f. $1 - e^{-px}$, $x > 0$, formula (11.2.15) can be interpreted as a weighted average (with weights $p$ and $q$ respectively). It follows that the d.f. of $S$ is the corresponding weighted average of distributions. Thus, for $x > 0$

$$F(x) = p(1) + q(1 - e^{-px}) = 1 - qe^{-px}. \qquad (11.2.16)$$

This distribution is of the mixed type. Its d.f. is pictured in Figure 11.1.

**Figure 11.1**
**Graph of $F(x)$**

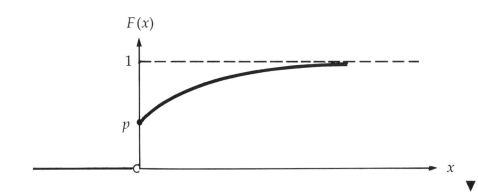

**11.3**
**Selection of Basic Distributions**

In this section we discuss the process of selecting the distribution of the number of claims $N$ and the common distribution of the $X_i$'s. As different considerations apply to these two selections, a separate subsection will be devoted to each.

**11.3.1**
**The Distribution of $N$**

One choice for the distribution of $N$ is the Poisson with p.f. given by

$$\Pr(N = n) = \frac{\lambda^n e^{-\lambda}}{n!} \qquad n = 0,1,2,\dots \qquad (11.3.1)$$

where $\lambda > 0$. For the Poisson distribution $E[N] = \text{Var}[N] = \lambda$. With this choice for the distribution of $N$, the distribution of $S$ is a compound Poisson distribution. Using (11.2.5) and (11.2.6), we have that

$$E[S] = \lambda \, p_1 \qquad (11.3.2)$$

and

$$\text{Var}[S] = \lambda \, p_2. \qquad (11.3.3)$$

Substituting the m.g.f. of the Poisson distribution

$$M_N(t) = e^{\lambda(e^t - 1)} \qquad (11.3.4)$$

into (11.2.7), we obtain the m.g.f. of the compound Poisson distribution,

$$M_S(t) = e^{\lambda[M_X(t) - 1]}. \qquad (11.3.5)$$

# COLLECTIVE RISK MODELS FOR A SINGLE PERIOD

The compound Poisson distribution has many attractive features, some of which will be discussed in Section 11.4.

When the variance of the number of claims exceeds its mean, the Poisson distribution is not appropriate. In this situation, the use of the negative binomial distribution has been suggested. The negative binomial distribution has a p.f. given by

$$\Pr(N = n) = \binom{r+n-1}{n} p^r q^n \qquad n = 0,1,2,\ldots. \qquad (11.3.6)$$

This distribution has two parameters: $r > 0$; $0 < p < 1$, $q = 1 - p$. For this distribution, we have

$$M_N(t) = \left(\frac{p}{1 - q\,e^t}\right)^r \qquad (11.3.7)$$

$$E[N] = \frac{rq}{p} \qquad (11.3.8)$$

and

$$\mathrm{Var}\,[N] = \frac{rq}{p^2}. \qquad (11.3.9)$$

When a negative binomial distribution is chosen for $N$, the distribution of $S$ is a compound negative binomial distribution. Substituting from (11.3.8) and (11.3.9) into (11.2.5) and (11.2.6), we have

$$E[S] = \frac{rq}{p}\, p_1 \qquad (11.3.10)$$

and

$$\mathrm{Var}\,[S] = \frac{rq}{p}\, p_2 + \frac{rq^2}{p^2}\, p_1^2. \qquad (11.3.11)$$

Substituting from (11.3.7) into (11.2.7), we obtain

$$M_S(t) = \left[\frac{p}{1 - q\,M_X(t)}\right]^r. \qquad (11.3.12)$$

We observe that the family of geometric distributions used in Examples 11.1 and 11.3 is contained as a special case ($r = 1$) of the two parameter family of negative binomial distributions.

A family of distributions for the number of claims can be generated by assuming that the Poisson parameter $\Lambda$ is a random variable with p.d.f. $u(\lambda)$, $\lambda > 0$, and that the conditional distribution of $N$, given $\Lambda = \lambda$, is Poisson with parameter $\lambda$. There are several situations in which this might be a useful way to consider the distribution of $N$. For example, consider a population of insureds where various classes of insureds within the population generate numbers of claims according to Poisson distributions, but the Poisson parameters may be different for the various classes. If the relative frequency of the values of $\lambda$ is given by $u(\lambda)$, we may adopt this idea. Using the law of total probability, we have

$$\Pr(N = n) = \int_0^\infty \Pr(N = n | \Lambda = \lambda) u(\lambda) \, d\lambda$$

$$= \int_0^\infty \frac{e^{-\lambda} \lambda^n}{n!} u(\lambda) \, d\lambda. \tag{11.3.13}$$

Furthermore, using (2.2.10) and (2.2.11), we have

$$E[N] = E[E[N|\Lambda]] = E[\Lambda] \tag{11.3.14}$$

$$\mathrm{Var}[N] = E[\mathrm{Var}[N|\Lambda]] + \mathrm{Var}[E[N|\Lambda]]$$

$$= E[\Lambda] + \mathrm{Var}[\Lambda] \tag{11.3.15}$$

and

$$M_N(t) = E[e^{tN}] = E[E[e^{tN}|\Lambda]] = E[e^{\Lambda(e^t - 1)}] = M_\Lambda(e^t - 1). \tag{11.3.16}$$

The equality,

$$E[e^{tN}|\Lambda] = e^{\Lambda(e^t - 1)},$$

follows from the hypothesis that the conditional distribution of $N$, given $\Lambda$, is Poisson with parameter $\Lambda$.

Thus, as in the case of the negative binomial distribution, $E[N] < \mathrm{Var}[N]$. In fact, the negative binomial distribution can be derived in this fashion, which will be shown in the following example.

**Example 11.4:**

Assume that $u(\lambda)$ is the gamma p.d.f. with parameters $\alpha$ and $\beta$,

$$u(\lambda) = \frac{\beta^\alpha}{\Gamma(\alpha)} \lambda^{\alpha - 1} e^{-\beta\lambda} \qquad \lambda > 0 \tag{11.3.17}$$

where

$$\Gamma(\alpha) = \int_0^\infty y^{\alpha - 1} e^{-y} \, dy.$$

Show that

a. the marginal distribution of $N$ is negative binomial with parameters

$$r = \alpha, \qquad p = \frac{\beta}{1 + \beta} \tag{11.3.18}$$

b. $E[\Lambda] = \alpha/\beta$ and $\mathrm{Var}(\Lambda) = \alpha/\beta^2$, and by substitution in (11.3.14) and (11.3.15), verify (11.3.8) and (11.3.9).

**Solution:**
Recall that the m.g.f. for the random variable $\Lambda$ with gamma p.d.f. as in (11.3.17) is

# Chapter 11
## COLLECTIVE RISK MODELS FOR A SINGLE PERIOD

$$M_\Lambda(t) = \left(\frac{\beta}{\beta - t}\right)^\alpha. \tag{11.3.19}$$

a.  Using this form in (11.3.16) we have

$$M_N(t) = M_\Lambda(e^t - 1) = \left[\frac{\beta}{\beta - (e^t - 1)}\right]^\alpha = \left[\frac{\beta/(\beta + 1)}{1 - [1 - \beta/(\beta + 1)]\, e^t}\right]^\alpha.$$

Comparison of this final expression with (11.3.7) confirms that the distribution of $N$ is negative binomial with parameters $r = \alpha$,

$$p = \frac{\beta}{1 + \beta} \tag{11.3.20}$$

$$q = 1 - p = \frac{1}{1 + \beta}.$$

b.  Again using (11.3.19),

$$E[\Lambda] = \frac{d}{dt} M_\Lambda(t)\bigg|_{t=0} = \frac{\alpha}{\beta} \tag{11.3.21}$$

$$\mathrm{Var}\,[\Lambda] = \frac{d^2}{dt^2} M_\Lambda(t)\bigg|_{t=0} - \left(\frac{\alpha}{\beta}\right)^2 = \frac{\alpha}{\beta^2}. \tag{11.3.22}$$

Substitution of these into (11.3.14) and (11.3.15) yields

$$E[N] = \frac{\alpha}{\beta} = \frac{rq}{p}$$

as in (11.3.8) and

$$\mathrm{Var}\,[N] = \frac{\alpha}{\beta} + \frac{\alpha}{\beta^2} = \frac{rq}{p}\left[1 + \frac{q}{p}\right] = \frac{rq}{p^2}$$

as in (11.3.9).  ▼

Table 11.1 summarizes pertinent information on the compound distributions resulting from the selections for $N$ discussed here.

## 11.3.2 The Individual Claim Amount Distribution

On the basis of (11.2.12) we see that convolutions of the individual claim amount distribution may be required. Thus, when possible, it is convenient to select that distribution from a family of distributions for which convolutions may be calculated easily either by formula or numerically. For example, if the claim amount has the normal distribution with mean $\mu$ and variance $\sigma^2$, then its $n$th convolution is the normal distribution with mean $n\mu$ and variance $n\sigma^2$. For many types of insurance, the claim amount random variable is only positive and its distribution is skewed to the right. For these insurances we might choose a gamma distribution that also has these properties. The $n$th convolution of a gamma distribution with parameters $\alpha$ and $\beta$ is also a gamma distribution but with parameters $n\alpha$ and $\beta$. This fact can be confirmed by noting from (11.3.19) that $M_X(t) = [\beta/(\beta - t)]^\alpha$

**Table 11.1**
**Compound Distributions of $S$**

$$S = \sum_{j=1}^{N} X_j$$

$N, X_1, X_2, \ldots$ are
independent random variables.
Each $X_j$ has d.f. $P(x)$,
m.g.f. $M_X(t)$ and
$p_k = E[X^k] \quad k = 1,2,\ldots$

$$P^{*0}(x) = \begin{bmatrix} 1 & x \geq 0 \\ 0 & \text{elsewhere.} \end{bmatrix}$$

$$P^{*n}(x) = \begin{cases} \displaystyle\sum_{j=0}^{x} p(x-j)\,P^{*(n-1)}(j), \text{ or} \\ \displaystyle\int_0^x p(x-y)\,P^{*(n-1)}(y)\,dy \end{cases}$$

| Definitions | Distribution Function, $F_S(x)$ | Restrictions on Parameters | Moment Generating Function, $M(t)$ | Mean | Variance |
|---|---|---|---|---|---|
| General | $\displaystyle\sum_{n=0}^{\infty} \Pr(N=n)\,P^{*n}(x)$ | — | $M_N(\log M_X(t))$ | $p_1\,E[N]$ | $E[N](p_2 - p_1^2) + p_1^2\,\text{Var}[N]$ |
| Compound Poisson | $\displaystyle\sum_{n=0}^{\infty} \frac{e^{-\lambda}\lambda^n}{n!}P^{*n}(x)$ | $\lambda > 0$ | $e^{\lambda[M_X(t)-1]}$ | $\lambda\,p_1$ | $\lambda\,p_2$ |
| Compound Negative Binomial | $\displaystyle\sum_{n=0}^{\infty}\binom{r+n-1}{n}p^r q^n P^{*n}(x)$ | $0<p<1$ $q=1-p$ $r>0$ | $\left[\dfrac{p}{1-q\,M_X(t)}\right]^r,$ $q\,M_X(t)<1$ | $\dfrac{rq\,p_1}{p}$ | $\dfrac{rq\,p_2}{p}+\dfrac{rq^2 p_1^2}{p^2}$ |

and hence the m.g.f. associated with $P^{*n}(x)$ is

$$M_X(t)^n = \left(\frac{\beta}{\beta - t}\right)^{n\alpha} \quad t < \beta. \tag{11.3.23}$$

If the claim amounts have an exponential distribution with parameter 1, the p.d.f. is given by

$$p(x) = e^{-x} \quad x > 0.$$

This can be considered a gamma distribution with $\alpha = \beta = 1$. Then by using (11.3.19), we may conclude that the $n$th convolution is a gamma distribution with parameters $\alpha = n$, $\beta = 1$; that is,

$$p^{*n}(x) = \frac{x^{n-1}e^{-x}}{(n-1)!} \quad x > 0. \tag{11.3.24}$$

To obtain an expression for $P^{*n}(x)$, we perform integration by parts $n$ times as follows:

$$1 - P^{*n}(x) = \int_x^{\infty} \frac{y^{n-1}e^{-y}}{(n-1)!}dy$$

$$= -\frac{y^{n-1}}{(n-1)!}e^{-y}\Big|_x^{\infty} + \int_x^{\infty}\frac{y^{n-2}e^{-y}}{(n-2)!}dy$$

## COLLECTIVE RISK MODELS FOR A SINGLE PERIOD

$$= \frac{x^{n-1}}{(n-1)!} e^{-x} + [1 - P^{*(n-1)}(x)]$$

$$= e^{-x} \sum_{i=0}^{n-1} \frac{x^i}{i!}. \tag{11.3.25}$$

Then, using formula (11.2.12), we have

$$1 - F(x) = \sum_{n=1}^{\infty} \Pr(N = n) \, e^{-x} \sum_{i=0}^{n-1} \frac{x^i}{i!} \quad x > 0. \tag{11.3.26}$$

This exponential distribution case shows that even with simple assumed distributions, the distribution of aggregate claims may not have a simple form. Therefore, it may be more practical to select a discrete claim amount distribution and calculate the required convolutions numerically. For compound Poisson distributions it has been established that the convolution method can be shortened or, alternatively, it can be bypassed by use of a recursive formula for directly calculating the distribution function of $S$. These computational shortcuts are discussed in the following section.

## 11.4
## Properties of the Compound Poisson Distribution

In this section we shall discuss some mathematical properties of the compound Poisson distribution. Two theorems will be presented. The first concerns the sum of independent random variables, each having a compound Poisson distribution. The theorem shows that the sum also has a compound Poisson distribution, and this has some immediate practical consequences. The second theorem will lead to a method of evaluating the compound Poisson distribution that is an alternative to the basic method illustrated in Example 11.2.

Furthermore, we shall see that there is an alternative way to define the compound Poisson distribution when the claim amount distribution is discrete. Instead of specifying the parameter $\lambda$ and the d.f. $P(x)$, we may define the distribution in terms of the discrete values taken by individual claim amounts and the parameters of independent Poisson random variables associated with each possible claim amount.

**Theorem 11.1:**

If $S_1, S_2, \ldots, S_m$ are mutually independent random variables such that $S_i$ has a compound Poisson distribution with parameter $\lambda_i$ and d.f. of claim amount $P_i(x)$, $i = 1, 2, \ldots, m$, then $S = S_1 + S_2 + \cdots + S_m$ has a compound Poisson distribution with

$$\lambda = \sum_{i=1}^{m} \lambda_i \tag{11.4.1}$$

and

$$P(x) = \sum_{i=1}^{m} \frac{\lambda_i}{\lambda} P_i(x). \tag{11.4.2}$$

**Proof:**
We let $M_i(t)$ denote the m.g.f. of $P_i(x)$. According to (11.3.5), the m.g.f. of $S_i$ is

$$M_{S_i}(t) = \exp\{\lambda_i [M_i(t) - 1]\}.$$

Because of the assumed independence of $S_1, \ldots, S_m$, the m.g.f. of their sum is

$$M_S(t) = \prod_{i=1}^{m} M_{S_i}(t) = \exp\left\{ \sum_{i=1}^{m} \lambda_i [M_i(t) - 1] \right\}.$$

Finally, we rewrite the exponent to obtain

$$M_S(t) = \exp\left\{ \lambda \left[ \sum_{i=1}^{m} \frac{\lambda_i}{\lambda} M_i(t) - 1 \right] \right\} \qquad (11.4.3)$$

where

$$\lambda = \sum_{i=1}^{m} \lambda_i.$$

Since this is the m.g.f. of the compound Poisson distribution, specified by (11.4.1) and (11.4.2), the theorem follows. ∎

This result has two important consequences for building insurance models. First, if we combine $m$ insurance portfolios, where the aggregate claims of the respective portfolios have compound Poisson distributions and are mutually independent, then the aggregate claims for the combined portfolio will again have a compound Poisson distribution. Second, we can consider a single insurance portfolio for a period of $m$ years. Here we shall assume independence among the $m$ annual aggregate claims and that the aggregate claims for each year has a compound Poisson distribution. It is not necessary that the annual aggregate claims distributions be identical. Then it follows from Theorem 11.1 that the total claims for the $n$-year period will have a compound Poisson distribution.

**Example 11.5:**

Let $x_1, x_2, \ldots, x_m$ be $m$ different numbers and suppose that $N_1, N_2, \ldots, N_m$ are mutually independent random variables. Further, suppose that $N_i$ ($i = 1, 2, \ldots, m$) has a Poisson distribution with parameter $\lambda_i$. What is the distribution of

$$x_1 N_1 + x_2 N_2 + \cdots + x_m N_m? \qquad (11.4.4)$$

**Solution:**
By interpreting $x_i N_i$ to have a compound Poisson distribution with Poisson parameter $\lambda_i$ and a degenerate claim amount distribution at $x_i$, we can apply Theorem 11.1 to establish that the sum in (11.4.4) has a compound Poisson distribution with

$$\lambda = \sum_{i=1}^{m} \lambda_i$$

# COLLECTIVE RISK MODELS FOR A SINGLE PERIOD

and p.f. of claim amount $p(x)$ where

$$p(x) = \begin{cases} \dfrac{\lambda_i}{\lambda} & x = x_i,\ i = 1,2,\ldots,m \\[2mm] 0 & \text{elsewhere.} \end{cases} \tag{11.4.5}$$

▼

We shall now verify that every compound Poisson distribution with a discrete claim amount distribution can be represented as a sum of the form (11.4.4). We let $x_1,x_2,\ldots,x_m$ denote the discrete values for individual claim amounts and let

$$\pi_i = p(x_i) \qquad i = 1,2,\ldots,m \tag{11.4.6}$$

denote their respective probabilities. Let $N_i$ be the number of terms in (11.1.1) that are equal to $x_i$. Then by collecting terms we see that

$$S = x_1 N_1 + x_2 N_2 + \cdots + x_m N_m. \tag{11.4.7}$$

In general, the $N_i$'s of (11.4.7) are dependent random variables. However, in the special case of a compound Poisson distribution for $S$, they are independent, as will be shown in Theorem 11.2.

Before stating Theorem 11.2, we will cite some properties of the **multinomial distribution** that will be used in the proof. For the multinomial, each of $n$ independent trials will result in one of $m$ different outcomes. The probability that a trial ends in outcome $i$ is denoted by $\pi_i$. We shall denote the random variable that counts the number of outcomes $i$ in $n$ trials by $N_i$. Then

$$1 = \sum_{i=1}^{m} \pi_i, \qquad n = \sum_{i=1}^{m} N_i,$$

and the joint p.f. of $N_1,N_2,\ldots,N_m$ is given by

$$\Pr[N_1 = n_1,\ N_2 = n_2,\ \ldots,\ N_m = n_m]$$

$$= \frac{n!}{n_1!\,n_2!\cdots n_m!}\,\pi_1^{n_1}\,\pi_2^{n_2}\cdots\pi_m^{n_m}; \tag{11.4.8}$$

by using (11.4.8) we obtain

$$E\left[\exp\left(\sum_{i=1}^{m} t_i N_i\right)\right] = [\pi_1 e^{t_1} + \pi_2 e^{t_2} + \cdots + \pi_m e^{t_m}]^n. \tag{11.4.9}$$

The multivariate discrete distribution with p.f. given by (11.4.8) and m.g.f. given by (11.4.9) is called a multinomial distribution with parameters $n,\pi_1,\ldots,\pi_m$.

# COLLECTIVE RISK MODELS FOR A SINGLE PERIOD

**Theorem 11.2:**   If $S$, as given in (11.4.7), has a compound Poisson distribution with parameter $\lambda$ and p.f. of claim amounts given by the discrete p.f. exhibited in (11.4.6), then

a. $N_1, N_2, \ldots, N_m$ are mutually independent.

b. $N_i$ has a Poisson distribution with parameter $\lambda_i = \lambda \pi_i$, $i = 1, 2, \ldots, m$.

**Proof:**
We start by defining the m.g.f. of the joint distribution of $N_1, N_2, \ldots, N_m$ by use of (2.2.10) for conditional expectations. Note that for a fixed number of independent claims (trials) where each claim results in 1 of $m$ claim amounts, the numbers of claims of each amount have a multinomial distribution with parameters $n, \pi_1, \pi_2, \ldots, \pi_m$. Hence, given

$$N = \sum_{i=1}^{m} N_i = n,$$

the conditional distribution of $N_1, N_2, \ldots, N_m$ is this multinomial distribution. For this case, we use (11.4.9) to obtain

$$E\left[\exp\left(\sum_{i=1}^{m} t_i N_i\right)\right]$$

$$= \sum_{n=0}^{\infty} E\left[\exp\left(\sum_{i=1}^{m} t_i N_i\right) \middle| N = n\right] \Pr(N = n)$$

$$= \sum_{n=0}^{\infty} (\pi_1 e^{t_1} + \cdots + \pi_m e^{t_m})^n \frac{e^{-\lambda} \lambda^n}{n!}. \qquad (11.4.10)$$

We now perform the required summation by recognizing (11.4.10) as a Taylor series expansion of an exponential function. We obtain

$$E\left[\exp\left(\sum_{i=1}^{m} t_i N_i\right)\right] = \exp(-\lambda) \exp\left(\lambda \sum_{i=1}^{m} \pi_i e^{t_i}\right)$$

$$= \prod_{i=1}^{m} \exp[\lambda \pi_i (e^{t_i} - 1)]. \qquad (11.4.11)$$

Since this is the product of $m$ functions each of a single variable $t_i$, formula (11.4.11) shows the mutual independence of the $N_i$'s. Furthermore, if we set $t_i = t$, and $t_j = 0$ for $j \neq i$ in (11.4.11), we obtain

$$E[\exp(t N_i)] = \exp[\lambda \pi_i (e^t - 1)], \qquad (11.4.12)$$

which is the m.g.f. of the Poisson distribution with parameter $\lambda \pi_i$. This proves statement (b).  ∎

Formula (11.4.7) and Theorem 11.2 provide an alternative method for tabulating a compound Poisson distribution with a discrete claim amount distribution. First, we compute the p.f.'s of $x_1 N_1, x_2 N_2, \ldots, x_m N_m$. Since the nonzero entries for the p.f. of $x_i N_i$ are at multiples

# Chapter 11
## COLLECTIVE RISK MODELS FOR A SINGLE PERIOD

of $x_i$, and are Poisson probabilities, this is an easy task. Then the convolution of these $m$ distributions is calculated to obtain the p.f. of $S$. This method is particularly convenient if $m$, the number of different claim amounts, is small. Even if a continuous distribution has been selected for the individual claim amounts, a discrete approximation can sometimes be used with the alternative method to produce a satisfactory approximation to the distribution of $S$. The basic and the alternative methods for tabulating the distribution of $S$ are compared in the following example.

**Example 11.6:**

Suppose that $S$ has a compound Poisson distribution with $\lambda = 0.8$ and individual claim amounts that are 1, 2 or 3 with probabilities 0.25, 0.375 and 0.375 respectively. Compute $f(x) = \Pr[S = x]$ for $x = 0, 1, \ldots, 6$.

**Solution:**

For the basic method the calculations parallel those in Example 11.2 and are summarized below.

### Basic Method Calculations

| (1) $x$ | (2) $p^{*0}(x)$ | (3) $p(x)$ | (4) $p^{*2}(x)$ | (5) $p^{*3}(x)$ | (6) $p^{*4}(x)$ | (7) $p^{*5}(x)$ | (8) $p^{*6}(x)$ | (9) $f(x)$ |
|---|---|---|---|---|---|---|---|---|
| 0 | 1 | — | — | — | — | — | — | 0.449329 |
| 1 | — | 0.25 | — | — | — | — | — | 0.089866 |
| 2 | — | 0.375 | 0.0625 | — | — | — | — | 0.143785 |
| 3 | — | 0.375 | 0.1875 | 0.015625 | — | — | — | 0.162357 |
| 4 | — | — | 0.328125 | 0.070313 | 0.003906 | — | — | 0.049905 |
| 5 | — | — | 0.281250 | 0.175781 | 0.023438 | 0.000977 | — | 0.047360 |
| 6 | — | — | 0.140625 | 0.263672 | 0.076172 | 0.007324 | 0.000244 | 0.030923 |

| $n$ | 0 | 1 | 2 | 3 | 4 | 5 | 6 |
|---|---|---|---|---|---|---|---|
| $e^{-0.8}\dfrac{(0.8)^n}{n!}$ | 0.449329 | 0.359463 | 0.143785 | 0.038343 | 0.007669 | 0.001227 | 0.000164 |

For the alternative method outlined in this section, the calculations are displayed below.

### Alternative Method Calculations

| (1) $x$ | (2) $\Pr[N_1 = x]$ | (3) $\Pr[2N_2 = x]$ | (4) $\Pr[3N_3 = x]$ | (5) $\Pr[N_1 + 2N_2 = x]$ = (2)*(3) | (6) $\Pr[N_1 + 2N_2 + 3N_3 = x]$ = (4)*(5) = $f(x)$ |
|---|---|---|---|---|---|
| 0 | 0.818731 | 0.740818 | 0.740818 | 0.606531 | 0.449329 |
| 1 | 0.163746 | — | — | 0.121306 | 0.089866 |
| 2 | 0.016375 | 0.222245 | — | 0.194090 | 0.143785 |
| 3 | 0.001092 | — | 0.222245 | 0.037201 | 0.162358 |
| 4 | 0.000055 | 0.033337 | — | 0.030974 | 0.049906 |
| 5 | 0.000002 | — | — | 0.005703 | 0.047360 |
| 6 | 0.000000 | 0.003334 | 0.033337 | 0.003288 | 0.030923 |

| $i$ | 1 | 2 | 3 |
|---|---|---|---|
| $\lambda_i$ | 0.2 | 0.3 | 0.3 |
| | $\dfrac{e^{-0.2}(0.2)^x}{x!}$ | $\dfrac{e^{-0.3}(0.3)^{x/2}}{(x/2)!}$ | $\dfrac{e^{-0.3}(0.3)^{x/3}}{(x/3)!}$ |

For the application of the formulas of this section, we note that $m = 3$, $x_1 = 1$, $x_2 = 2$, $x_3 = 3$, $\lambda_1 = \lambda\, p(1) = 0.2$, $\lambda_2 = \lambda\, p(2) = 0.3$ and $\lambda_3 = \lambda\, p(3) = 0.3$. First, we compute Columns (2), (3) and (4). The nonzero entries are Poisson probabilities. Then we obtain the convolution of the p.f.'s in Columns (2) and (3) and record the result in Column (5). Finally, we convolute the p.f.'s displayed in Columns (4) and (5) and record the result in Column (6).

Remember that the complete p.f. is not displayed in either set of calculations. The example required probabilities for only $x = 0, 1, \ldots, 6$. However, $\Pr[S \le 6] = f(0) + f(1) + \cdots + f(6) = 0.97325$. ▼

Formula (11.4.7) and Theorem 11.2 have another implication. Instead of defining a compound Poisson distribution of $S$ by specifying the parameter $\lambda$ and the d.f. $P(x)$ of the discrete individual claim amounts, we can define the distribution in terms of the possible individual claim amounts $x_1, x_2, \ldots, x_m$ and the parameters $\lambda_1, \lambda_2, \ldots, \lambda_m$ of the associated Poisson distributions described in part (b) of Theorem 11.2. Thus for $x_i$ there is an associated Poisson distribution of $N_i$ with parameter $\lambda_i$. In terms of this new definition of the distribution of $S$, we have from $E[N_i] = \mathrm{Var}[N_i] = \lambda_i$ and the independence of the $N_i$'s that

$$E[S] = E\left[\sum_{i=1}^{m} x_i N_i\right] = \sum_{i=1}^{m} x_i \lambda_i \qquad (11.4.13)$$

and

$$\mathrm{Var}[S] = \mathrm{Var}\left[\sum_{i=1}^{m} x_i N_i\right] = \sum_{i=1}^{m} x_i^2 \lambda_i. \qquad (11.4.14)$$

Formula (11.4.13) could be obtained by starting from (11.3.2) and noting that

$$\lambda\, p_1 = \lambda \sum_{i=1}^{m} x_i \pi_i = \sum_{i=1}^{m} x_i \lambda_i.$$

Similarly we can obtain (11.4.14) from (11.3.3).

In some cases it is useful, as in Example 11.5, to regard $S$ as a sum of mutually independent random variables $x_i N_i$, $i = 1, 2, \ldots, m$, where $x_i N_i$ has a compound Poisson distribution with parameter $\lambda_i$ and degenerate claim amount distribution at $x_i$. This interpretation follows from Theorem 11.2 and underlies the alternative method illustrated in Example 11.6.

There is a third way, the *recursive method,* for evaluating a compound Poisson distribution. For this method, it is assumed that the possible claim amounts are positive integers, and we set $\lambda_i = \lambda\, p(i)$, $i = 1, 2, \ldots$. The recursive method is based on the recursive formula

$$f(x) = \sum_{i=1}^{\infty} \frac{i}{x} \lambda_i f(x - i) \qquad x = 1, 2, \ldots. \qquad (11.4.15)$$

# COLLECTIVE RISK MODELS FOR A SINGLE PERIOD

Then, starting with $f(0) = \Pr(N = 0) = e^{-\lambda}$, $f(1)$, $f(2)$, ... are calculated in succession.

Note that the sum in (11.4.15) has only a finite number of nonzero terms, since $f(x - i) = 0$ for $i > x$. Also, if there is a largest possible claim amount, say $m$, the factor $\lambda_i$ vanishes for $i > m$. Thus the upper summation limit will be the minimum of $x$ and $m$.

To establish (11.4.15), we first consider the conditional expectations $E[X_k | X_1 + X_2 + \cdots + X_{n+1} = x]$ for $k = 1, 2, \ldots, n+1$. For reasons of symmetry, these quantities are the same for all these $k$. Furthermore, their sum is $x$. Hence, each is $x/(n+1)$. Thus, for example, $E[X_1 | X_1 + X_2 + \cdots + X_{n+1} = x] = x/(n+1)$. Expressing this conditional expectation in terms of the common p.f. of the $X_k$'s, we obtain the formula

$$\frac{\sum_{i=1}^{\infty} i\, p(i)\, p^{*n}(x - i)}{p^{*(n+1)}(x)} = \frac{x}{n+1}. \qquad (11.4.16)$$

Now we start with the right-hand side of (11.4.15) and proceed as follows:

$$\sum_{i=1}^{\infty} \frac{i}{x} \lambda_i f(x - i)$$

$$= \sum_{i=1}^{\infty} \frac{i}{x} \lambda_i \sum_{n=0}^{\infty} e^{-\lambda} \frac{\lambda^n}{n!} p^{*n}(x - i).$$

By changing the order of summation, we obtain

$$\sum_{n=0}^{\infty} e^{-\lambda} \frac{\lambda^{n+1}}{n!} \sum_{i=1}^{\infty} \frac{i}{x} p(i)\, p^{*n}(x - i),$$

which, by use of (11.4.16) rearranged for the second sum, becomes

$$\sum_{n=0}^{\infty} e^{-\lambda} \frac{\lambda^{n+1}}{(n+1)!} p^{*(n+1)}(x) = f(x).$$

**Example 11.6 (recomputed):**

For the compound Poisson distribution of this example, compute $f(x) = \Pr(S = x)$ by the recursive method.

**Solution:**
Substituting the values of $\lambda_i$, $i = 1, 2, 3$, used for the alternative method of calculation into (11.4.15) yields

$$f(x) = \frac{1}{x}[0.2\, f(x - 1) + 0.6\, f(x - 2) + 0.9\, f(x - 3)] \qquad x = 1, 2, \ldots.$$

Recalling that $f(x) = 0$, $x < 0$, and $f(0) = e^{-\lambda} = 0.449329$, we readily reproduce the values of $f(x)$ given in the basic method calculations. ▼

# COLLECTIVE RISK MODELS FOR A SINGLE PERIOD

**11.5
Approximations
to the
Distribution of
Aggregate Claims**

In Section 2.4 the normal distribution was employed as an approximation to the distribution of aggregate claims in the individual model. The normal approximation will be the first developed for use with the collective model.

For the compound Poisson distribution, the two parameters of the normal approximation are given by (11.3.2) and (11.3.3). For the compound negative binomial distribution the parameters are given by (11.3.10) and (11.3.11). In each of the two cases the approximation is better when the expected number of claims is large, or, in other words, when $\lambda$ is large for the compound Poisson case and when $r$ is large for the negative binomial. These two results are contained in Theorem 11.3, which may be interpreted as a version of the central limit theorem.

**Theorem 11.3:**

a. If $S$ has a compound Poisson distribution, specified by $\lambda$ and $P(x)$, then the distribution of

$$Z = \frac{S - \lambda p_1}{\sqrt{\lambda p_2}} \qquad (11.5.1)$$

converges to the standard normal distribution as $\lambda \to \infty$.

b. If $S$ has a compound negative binomial distribution, specified by $r$, $p$ and $P(x)$, then the distribution of

$$Z = \frac{S - r(q/p)\, p_1}{\sqrt{r(q/p)\, p_2 + r(q^2/p^2)\, p_1^2}} \qquad (11.5.2)$$

converges to the standard normal distribution as $r \to \infty$.

**Proof:**
We shall prove statement (a) by showing that

$$\lim_{\lambda \to \infty} M_Z(t) = e^{t^2/2}.$$

Statement (b) can be proved using a similar strategy, but the proof involves additional steps.

From (11.5.1), it follows that

$$M_Z(t) = M_S\left(\frac{t}{\sqrt{\lambda p_2}}\right) \exp\left\{-\frac{\lambda p_1 t}{\sqrt{\lambda p_2}}\right\}.$$

Now, we use (11.3.5) to obtain

$$M_Z(t) = \exp\left\{\lambda\left[M_X\left(\frac{t}{\sqrt{\lambda p_2}}\right) - 1\right] - \frac{\lambda p_1 t}{\sqrt{\lambda p_2}}\right\}, \qquad (11.5.3)$$

and substitute the expansion

$$M_X(t) = 1 + \frac{p_1 t}{1!} + \frac{p_2 t^2}{2!} + \cdots, \qquad (11.5.4)$$

# COLLECTIVE RISK MODELS FOR A SINGLE PERIOD

with $t/\sqrt{\lambda\, p_2}$ in place of $t$, into (11.5.3) to obtain

$$M_Z(t) = \exp\left\{\frac{1}{2}t^2 + \frac{1}{6}\frac{1}{\sqrt{\lambda}}\frac{p_3}{p_2^{3/2}}t^3 + \cdots\right\}. \qquad (11.5.5)$$

Then as $\lambda \to \infty$, $M_Z(t)$ approaches $e^{t^2/2}$, the m.g.f. of the standard normal distribution. ∎

The normal distribution is symmetric and consequently its third central moment is 0, however, the distribution of aggregate claims is often skewed. Table 11.2 shows that the third central moment of $S$ under each of the compound Poisson and compound negative binomial distributions is not 0. For positive claim amount distributions, $P(0) = 0$, and the third central moment of $S$ is positive in each case.

In completing Table 11.2 we have used properties of the logarithm of a m.g.f., for example,

$$\left.\frac{d}{dt}\log M_X(t)\right|_{t=0} = \frac{M_X'(0)}{M_X(0)} = \mu$$

and

$$\left.\frac{d^2}{dt^2}\log M_X(t)\right|_{t=0} = \frac{M_X''(0)\,M_X(0) - M_X'(0)^2}{M_X(0)^2} = \sigma^2.$$

In Exercise 11.19(a), the student is asked to confirm the relation used in the last row of Table 11.2.

**Table 11.2**
**Calculation of Third Central Moment of $S$**

| Step | Distribution of S — Compound Poisson | Compound Negative Binomial |
|---|---|---|
| $M_S(t)$ | $\exp\{\lambda[M_X(t) - 1]\}$ | $\left[\dfrac{p}{1 - q\,M_X(t)}\right]^r$ |
| $\log M_S(t)$ | $\lambda[M_X(t) - 1]$ | $r\log p - r\log[1 - q\,M_X(t)]$ |
| $\dfrac{d^3}{dt^3}\log M_S(t)$ | $\lambda\,M_X'''(t)$ | $\dfrac{rq\,M_X'''(t)}{1 - q\,M_X(t)} + \dfrac{3\,rq^2\,M_X'(t)\,M_X''(t)}{[1 - q\,M_X(t)]^2} + \dfrac{2\,rq^3\,M_X'(t)^3}{[1 - q\,M_X(t)]^3}$ |
| $E[(S - E[S])^3]$ | | |
| $= \left.\dfrac{d^3}{dt^3}\log M_S(t)\right|_{t=0}$ * | $\lambda\,p_3$ | $\dfrac{rq\,p_3}{p} + \dfrac{3\,rq^2\,p_1\,p_2}{p^2} + \dfrac{2\,rq^3\,p_1^3}{p^3}$ |

*For $k \geq 4$, $\left.\dfrac{d^k}{dt^k}\log M(t)\right|_{t=0}$ is not the $k$th central moment.

# COLLECTIVE RISK MODELS FOR A SINGLE PERIOD

Thus we require a more general approximation to the distribution of aggregate claims, one that accommodates skewness. For this second approximation, we begin with a gamma distribution. This choice is motivated by the fact that the gamma distribution has a positive third central moment as do the compound Poisson and compound negative binomial distributions with positive claim amounts. We let $G(x:\alpha,\beta)$ denote the d.f. of the gamma distribution with parameters $\alpha$ and $\beta$; that is,

$$G(x:\alpha,\beta) = \int_0^x \frac{\beta^\alpha}{\Gamma(\alpha)} t^{\alpha-1} e^{-\beta t} dt. \qquad (11.5.6)$$

Then for any $x_0$ we define a new d.f., denoted by $H(x:\alpha,\beta,x_0)$, as

$$H(x:\alpha,\beta,x_0) = G(x - x_0:\alpha,\beta). \qquad (11.5.7)$$

This amounts to a translation of the distribution $G(x:\alpha,\beta)$ by $x_0$. Figure 11.2 illustrates this for the case $x_0 > 0$ where $g(x)$, $x \geq 0$, and $h(x)$, $x \geq x_0$, denote, respectively, the p.d.f.'s associated with $G(x:\alpha,\beta)$ and $H(x:\alpha,\beta,x_0)$.

The second approximation consists of approximating the distribution of aggregate claims $S$ by a translated gamma distribution where the parameters $\alpha$, $\beta$ and $x_0$ are selected by equating the first moment and second and third central moments of $S$ with the corresponding items for the translated gamma distribution. Since central moments of the translated gamma are the same as for the basic gamma distribution, this procedure imposes the requirements

$$E[S] = x_0 + \frac{\alpha}{\beta} \qquad (11.5.8)$$

$$Var[S] = \frac{\alpha}{\beta^2} \qquad (11.5.9)$$

**Figure 11.2
Translated Gamma
Distribution**

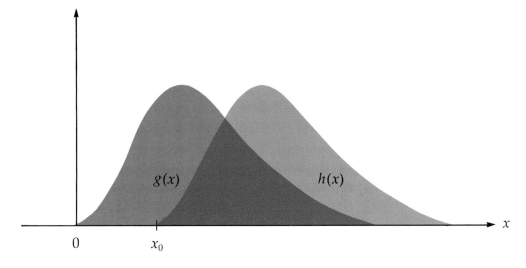

# COLLECTIVE RISK MODELS FOR
# A SINGLE PERIOD

$$E[(S - E[S])^3] = \frac{2\alpha}{\beta^3}. \qquad (11.5.10)$$

From these we obtain

$$\beta = 2\frac{\text{Var}[S]}{E[(S - E[S])^3]} \qquad (11.5.11)$$

$$\alpha = 4\frac{(\text{Var}[S])^3}{E[(S - E[S])^3]^2} \qquad (11.5.12)$$

$$x_0 = E[S] - 2\frac{(\text{Var}[S])^2}{E[(S - E[S])^3]}. \qquad (11.5.13)$$

For a compound Poisson distribution this procedure leads to

$$\alpha = 4\lambda\frac{p_2^3}{p_3^2} \qquad (11.5.14)$$

$$\beta = 2\frac{p_2}{p_3} \qquad (11.5.15)$$

$$x_0 = \lambda p_1 - 2\lambda\frac{p_2^2}{p_3}. \qquad (11.5.16)$$

**Remark:**

We can show that if $\alpha \to \infty$, $\beta \to \infty$ and $x_0 \to -\infty$ such that

$$x_0 + \frac{\alpha}{\beta} = \mu \text{ (constant)} \qquad (11.5.17)$$

$$\frac{\alpha}{\beta^2} = \sigma^2 \text{ (constant)},$$

the distribution $H(x:\alpha,\beta,x_0)$ converges to the $N(\mu,\sigma^2)$ distribution. Therefore, the family of normal distributions is contained, as limiting distributions, within this family of three parameter gamma distributions. In this sense, this approximation is a generalization of the normal approximation.

**Example 11.7:** Consider the Poisson distribution with parameter $\lambda = 16$. This is the same as the compound Poisson distribution with $\lambda = 16$ and a degenerate claim amount distribution at 1. Compare this distribution with approximations by

a. a translated gamma distribution

b. a normal distribution.

**Solution:**
a. Here $p_k = 1$, $k = 1,2,3$, and from (11.5.14)–(11.5.16), we have $\alpha = 64$, $\beta = 2$, $x_0 = -16$. Note that, unlike the case in Figure 11.2, $x_0$ is negative.

b. For the normal approximation, we use $\mu = 16$ and $\sigma = 4$.

The results given below compare the three distributions. In the approximations, the half-integer discontinuity correction was used to approximate $F(x)$ for $x = 5, 10, \dots, 40$.

| | Exact | Approximations | |
|---|---|---|---|
| $x$ | $\sum\limits_{y=0}^{x} \dfrac{e^{-16}(16)^y}{y!}$ | $G(x + 16.5 : 64, 2)$ | $\Phi\left(\dfrac{x + 0.5 - 16}{4}\right)$ |
| 5  | 0.001384 | 0.001636 | 0.004332 |
| 10 | 0.077396 | 0.077739 | 0.084566 |
| 15 | 0.466745 | 0.466560 | 0.450262 |
| 20 | 0.868168 | 0.868093 | 0.869705 |
| 25 | 0.986881 | 0.986604 | 0.991226 |
| 30 | 0.999433 | 0.999378 | 0.999856 |
| 35 | 0.999988 | 0.999985 | 0.999999 |
| 40 | 1.000000 | 1.000000 | 1.000000 |

▼

In the case of the compound negative binomial distribution there is an additional argument that supports the use of a gamma approximation. The argument is outlined in the Appendix to this chapter.

**11.6
Notes and
References**

Chapter 2 of Seal (1969) contains an extensive survey of the literature on collective risk models, including the pioneering work of Lundberg on the compound Poisson distribution. Several authors, for example, Dropkin (1959) and Simon (1960), have used the negative binomial distribution to model the number of automobile accidents by a collection of policyholders in a fixed period.

In Example 11.4 we derived the negative binomial distribution by assuming that the unknown Poisson parameter has a gamma distribution. This idea goes back at least as far as Greenwood and Yule's work on accident proneness (1920). An alternative derivation in terms of a contagion model is due to Polya and Eggenberger and may be found in Chapter 2 of Bühlmann (1970). In the special case where $r$ is an integer, the negative binomial can be obtained as the distribution of the number of Bernoulli trials that end in failure prior to the $r$th success. This development may be found in most probability texts, but has little relevance to the subject of this chapter.

Theorem 11.2 has been known for some time and can be studied in Section 2, Chapter 2 of Feller (1968). The alternative method for computing probabilities for a compound Poisson distribution, which is based on Theorem 11.2, was suggested by Pesonen (1967) and implemented by Halmstad (1976) in the calculation of stop-loss premiums. Theorem 11.2 has a converse, which was not stated in Section 11.4. Renyi (1962) shows that the mutual independence of $N_1, N_2, \dots, N_m$ implies that $N$ has a Poisson distribution. Hence the alternative method of computing will work only for the compound Poisson distribution.

# COLLECTIVE RISK MODELS FOR A SINGLE PERIOD

The alternative method of computation may also be adopted to build a simulation model for aggregate claims. Instead of determining the individual claim amounts, one simulates $N_1, N_2, \ldots, N_m$ and obtains a realization of $S$ directly from formula (11.4.7). For one determination of $S$, the expected number of random numbers required is $1 + \lambda$ under the basic method. If the alternative method is used, exactly $m$ random numbers are required for each determination of a value of $S$.

There are several more elaborate methods of approximating the distribution of aggregate claims. The normal power and Esscher approximations are described in Beard, Pesonen and Pentikäinen (1977). Several of the approximation methods have been compared by Bohman and Esscher (1963, 1964). Seal (1978) presents the case for the translated gamma approximation and illustrates its excellent performance. Bowers (1966) approximated the distribution of aggregate claims by a sum of orthogonal functions, the first term of which is the gamma distribution. The result, stated in the Appendix to this chapter, that the gamma distribution can be obtained as a limit from the compound negative binomial is due to Lundberg (1940).

Sometimes the distribution of aggregate claims can be obtained from a numerical inversion of its m.g.f., this is developed in Chapter 3 of Seal (1978).

## Appendix

**Theorem 11.4:**

If the random variables $S_k$, $k = 0,1,2,\ldots$, have compound negative binomial distributions with parameters $r$ and $p(k)$ and claim amount d.f. $P(x)$, and if the parameters of the negative binomial distributions are such that

$$\frac{q(k)}{p(k)} = k\frac{q}{p}$$

for $k = 1,2,3,\ldots$, where $q = 1 - p$ is a constant, then the distribution of

$$\frac{S_k}{E[S_k]}$$

approaches $G(x:r,r)$ as $k \to \infty$.

**Proof:**
Using (11.2.9), we find the m.g.f. of $S_k/E[S_k]$ to be

$$\left[\frac{p(k)}{1 - q(k)\,M_X(t/E[S_k])}\right]^r. \tag{11.A.1}$$

We also have

$$M_X(t/E[S_k]) = 1 + \frac{p_1}{E[S_k]}t + \frac{p_2}{2\,E[S_k]^2}t^2 + \cdots. \tag{11.A.2}$$

If (11.A.2) is substituted into (11.A.1), we obtain

$$\left[\frac{p(k)}{1 - q(k) - (q(k)\, p_1/\mathrm{E}[S_k])\, t - (q(k)\, p_2/2\,\mathrm{E}[S_k]^2)\, t^2 - \cdots}\right]^r. \quad (11.A.3)$$

Now, since

$$\mathrm{E}[S_k] = r\frac{q(k)\, p_1}{p(k)} = r\frac{kq\, p_1}{p},$$

we see that the m.g.f. of $S_k/\mathrm{E}[S_k]$ is

$$\left[1 - \frac{1}{r}t - \frac{p_2}{2\,r^2\, p_1^2(q/p)\, k}\, t^2 - \cdots\right]^{-r}$$

$$= \left[1 - \frac{1}{r}t - R(k)\right]^{-r}$$

where the remainder term $R(k)$ is such that $\lim_{k\to\infty} R(k) = 0$. There-

fore,

$$\lim_{k\to\infty} \mathrm{E}\left[\exp\left(t\frac{S_k}{\mathrm{E}[S_k]}\right)\right] = \left(\frac{r}{r - t}\right)^r, \quad (11.A.4)$$

which is the m.g.f. of a $G(x{:}r,r)$ distribution.   ∎

It follows from (11.A.4) that the m.g.f. of $S_k$ itself is approximately

$$\left(\frac{r}{r - \mathrm{E}[S_k]t}\right)^r = \left(\frac{r}{r - (r\,q(k)/p(k))\, p_1 t}\right)^r = \left(\frac{p(k)/[q(k)p_1]}{(p(k)/[q(k)\, p_1]) - t}\right)^r,$$

which is the m.g.f. of $G(x{:}r,(p(k)/q(k)\, p_1))$. Thus, when $k$ is large, which under the hypothesis of Theorem 11.4 implies that the expected number of claims, $r\,q(k)/p(k) = rk(q/p)$, is large, the distribution of aggregate claims is approximately a gamma distribution.

Theorem 11.4 is presented to provide an argument supporting the use of gamma distributions to approximate the distribution of aggregate claims. Comparison of the main ideas in Theorem 11.3(b) and Theorem 11.4 leads to insights. Theorem 11.3(b) follows closely the pattern of the central limit theorem. If in (11.5.2) one writes

$$Z = \frac{S/r - (q/p)\, p_1}{\sqrt{(q/p)\, p_2 + (q^2/p^2)\, p_1^2}/\sqrt{r}},$$

the correspondence is clear, with the parameter $r$ playing the role of $n$ in the central limit theorem.

In Theorem 11.4 the parameter $r$ of the negative binomial distribution remains fixed. The expected number of claims changes in proportion to a size parameter $k$, by compensating changes in $q(k)$ and $p(k) = 1 - q(k)$. Under the hypothesis of Theorem 11.4

# Chapter 11

## COLLECTIVE RISK MODELS FOR A SINGLE PERIOD

---

$$\text{Var}[S_k] = \frac{rkq}{p}p_2 + r\frac{k^2q^2}{p^2}p_1^2$$

and

$$\text{Var}\left[\frac{S_k}{E[S_k]}\right] = \frac{p}{rkqp_1^2}p_2 + \frac{1}{r}.$$

As the size parameter $k \to \infty$,

$$\text{Var}\left[\frac{S_k}{E[S_k]}\right] \to \frac{1}{r},$$

as indicated by Theorem 11.4. Thus the gamma approximation may be considered in the negative binomial case when the expected number of claims is large and the claim amount distribution has relatively small dispersion.

**Exercises**

*Section 11.1*

11.1. Let $S$ denote the number of people crossing a certain intersection by car in a given hour. How would you model $S$ as a random sum?

11.2. Let $S$ denote the total amount of rain that falls at a weather station in a given month. How would you model $S$ as a random sum?

*Section 11.2*

11.3. Suppose $N$ has a binomial distribution with parameters $n$ and $p$. Express each of the following in terms of $n$, $p$, $p_1$, $p_2$ and $M_X(t)$.
   a. $E[S]$          b. $\text{Var}[S]$          c. $M_S(t)$

11.4. For the distribution specified in Example 11.2, calculate
   a. $E[N]$          b. $\text{Var}[N]$          c. $E[X]$
   d. $\text{Var}[X]$          e. $E[S]$          f. $\text{Var}[S]$.

*Section 11.3*

11.5. Suppose that the claim amount distribution is the same as in Example 11.2, but that $N$ has a Poisson distribution with $E[N] = 1.7$. Calculate
   a. $E[S]$          b. $\text{Var}[S]$.

11.6. Suppose that $S$ has a compound Poisson distribution with $\lambda = 2$ and $p(x) = 0.1x$, $x = 1,2,3,4$. Calculate probabilities that aggregate claims equal 0,1,2,3 and 4.

11.7. Consider the family of negative binomial distributions with parameters $r$ and $p$. Let $r \to \infty$ and $p \to 1$ such that $r(1-p) = \lambda$ remains constant. Show that the limit obtained is the Poisson distribution with parameter $\lambda$. [Hint: Note that $p^r = [1-(\lambda/r)]^r \to e^{-\lambda}$ as $r \to \infty$, and consider the convergence of the m.g.f.].

# COLLECTIVE RISK MODELS FOR A SINGLE PERIOD

11.8. Suppose that $S$ has a compound Poisson distribution with Poisson parameter $\lambda$ and claim amount p.f.

$$p(x) = [-\log(1-c)]^{-1}\frac{c^x}{x} \quad x = 1,2,3,\ldots, 0 < c < 1.$$

Consider the m.g.f. of $S$ and show that $S$ has a negative binomial distribution with parameters $p$ and $r$. Express $p$ and $r$ in terms of $c$ and $\lambda$.

11.9. Let

$$g(x) = 3^{18} x^{17}\frac{e^{-3x}}{17!}$$

and

$$h(x) = 3^6 x^5\frac{e^{-3x}}{5!} \quad x > 0$$

be two p.d.f.'s. Write the convolution of these two distributions, that is, exhibit $g*h(x)$. [Hint: Proceed directly from the definition of convolution in Section 2.3, or make use of (11.3.19)].

11.10. Suppose that the number of accidents incurred by an insured driver in a single year has a Poisson distribution with parameter $\lambda$. If an accident happens, the probability is $p$ that the damage amount will exceed a deductible amount. On the assumption that the number of accidents is independent of the severity of the accidents, derive the distribution of the number of accidents that result in a claim payment.

*Section 11.4*

11.11. Suppose that $S_1$ has a compound Poisson distribution with Poisson parameter $\lambda = 2$ and claim amounts that are 1, 2 or 3 with probabilities 0.2, 0.6 and 0.2 respectively. In addition, $S_2$ has a compound Poisson distribution with Poisson parameter $\lambda = 6$ and claim amounts that are either 3 or 4 with probability 0.5 for each. If $S_1$ and $S_2$ are independent, what is the distribution of $S_1 + S_2$?

11.12. Suppose that $N_1$, $N_2$, $N_3$ are mutually independent and that $N_i$ has a Poisson distribution with $E[N_i] = i^2$, $i = 1,2,3$. What is the distribution of $S = -2N_1 + N_2 + 3N_3$?

11.13. If $N$ has a Poisson distribution with parameter $\lambda$, express $\Pr(N = n + 1)$ in terms of $\Pr(N = n)$.

Note that this recursive formula may be useful in calculations such as those for successive entries in Columns (2), (3) and (4) of the alternate method calculations of Example 11.6.

11.14. Suppose that $S$ has a compound Poisson distribution with parameter $\lambda$ and discrete p.f. $p(x)$, $x > 0$. Let $0 < \alpha < 1$.

Consider $\tilde{S}$ with a distribution that is compound Poisson with
Poisson parameter $\tilde{\lambda} = \lambda/\alpha$ and claim amount p.f. $\tilde{p}(x)$ where

$$\tilde{p}(x) = \begin{cases} \alpha p(x) & x > 0 \\ 1 - \alpha & x = 0. \end{cases}$$

This means we are allowing for claim amounts of 0 (as could
happen if there is a deductible) and are modifying the distributions accordingly. Show that $S$ and $\tilde{S}$ have the same distribution by
a. comparing the m.g.f.'s of $S$ and $\tilde{S}$
b. comparing the definition of the distribution of $S$ and $\tilde{S}$ in
terms of possible claim amounts and the Poisson param-
eters of the distributions of their frequencies.

11.15. In Example 11.2, let $N_1$ be the random number of claims of
amount 1 and $N_2$ the random number of claims of amount 2.
Compute
a. $\Pr(N_1 = 1)$     b. $\Pr(N_2 = 1)$     c. $\Pr(N_1 = 1, N_2 = 1)$.
Are $N_1$ and $N_2$ independent?

*Section 11.5*

11.16. Show that, if $N$ has a Poisson distribution with parameter $\lambda$,
the distribution of

$$Z = \frac{N - \lambda}{\sqrt{\lambda}}$$

approaches a $N(0,1)$ distribution as $\lambda \to \infty$.

11.17. Use $\log M_S(t)$ as given in Table 11.2 to verify (11.3.3) and
(11.3.11).

11.18. Suppose that the d.f. of $S$ is $G(x:\alpha,\beta)$. Use the m.g.f. [see
(11.3.19)] to show that

$$E[S^h] = \frac{\alpha(\alpha + 1)(\alpha + 2) \cdots (\alpha + h - 1)}{\beta^h} \quad h = 1,2,3, \ldots.$$

11.19. a. Verify that

$$\left. \frac{d^3}{dt^3} \log M_X(t) \right|_{t=0} = E[(X - E[X])^3].$$

b. Use (a) to show that if $S$ has a $G(x:\alpha,\beta)$ distribution, then

$$E[(S - E[S])^3] = \frac{2\alpha}{\beta^3}.$$

11.20. a. For a given $\alpha$, determine $\beta$ and $x_0$ so that $H(x:\alpha,\beta,x_0)$ has
mean 0 and variance 1.
b. What is the limit of $H(x:\alpha, \sqrt{\alpha}, -\sqrt{\alpha})$ as $\alpha \to \infty$?

11.21. Suppose that $S$ has a compound Poisson distribution with $\lambda = 12$ and claim amounts that are uniformly distributed between 0 and 1. Approximate $\Pr(S < 10)$ using
a. the normal approximation
b. the translated gamma approximation.

*Miscellaneous*

11.22. The loss ratio for a collection of insurance policies over a single premium period is defined as $R = S/G$ where $S$ is aggregate claims and $G$ is aggregate premiums. Assume that $G = p_1 E[N] (1 + \theta)$, $\theta > 0$.
a. Show that

$$E[R] = (1 + \theta)^{-1}$$

and that

$$\text{Var}[R] = \frac{E[N]\,\text{Var}[X] + p_1^2\,\text{Var}[N]}{[p_1 E[N](1 + \theta)]^2}.$$

b. Develop an expression for $\text{Var}[R]$ if
   (i) $N$ has a Poisson distribution
   (ii) $N$ has a negative binomial distribution.

11.23. Suppose that the distribution of $S_1$ is compound Poisson, given by $\lambda$ and $P_1(x)$, and that the distribution of $S_2$ is compound negative binomial, given by $r$, $p$ with $q = 1 - p$, and $P_2(x)$. Show that $S_1$ and $S_2$ have the same distribution provided that $\lambda = -r \log p$ and

$$P_1(x) = \frac{\displaystyle\sum_{k=1}^{\infty} \frac{q^k}{k} P_2^{*k}(x)}{-\log p}.$$

[Hint: Show equality of the m.g.f.'s.]
Note that, in the sense of this exercise, every compound negative binomial distribution can be considered as compound Poisson.

Chapter 12

## COLLECTIVE RISK MODELS OVER AN EXTENDED PERIOD

**12**

**12.1
Introduction**

The purpose of this chapter is to present a mathematical model for the variations in the amount of an insurer's *surplus* over an extended period of time. By surplus we will mean the excess of some initial fund plus premiums collected over claims paid. As should be noted, this is a convenient mathematical, but not accounting, definition of surplus.

For $t \geq 0$, let $U(t)$ denote the surplus of the insurer at time $t$. We assume premiums are received continuously at a constant rate, $c > 0$, and let $S(t)$ denote the aggregate claims up to time $t$. If $U(0) = u$ is the surplus on hand at time 0, perhaps as a result of past operations, then

$$U(t) = u + ct - S(t) \quad t \geq 0. \tag{12.1.1}$$

Note that in this model we ignore interest and factors other than premiums and claims that could affect surplus. For example, we are ignoring expenses and dividends to policyholders or stockholders. A typical outcome of this *surplus process* $\{U(t), t \geq 0\}$ is shown in Figure 12.1. The word *process* indicates that we are interested in a family of random variables, one for each value of $t$, $t \geq 0$, and in the interconnections between their distributions. This is in contrast to Chapter 11 where we considered the distribution of one random variable for a single time period.

Note that the surplus increases linearly (with slope $c$) except at those times when a claim occurs. Then the surplus drops by the amount of the claim. If the initial surplus $u$ was increased or decreased by an amount $h$, the graph of $U(t)$ would be raised or lowered $h$ units of height but would be unchanged otherwise. As illustrated in Figure 12.1, the surplus might become negative at certain times. When this first happens, we speak of *ruin* having occurred. This technical term is not equivalent to *insolvency.* In a real-life situation, the event of ruin may not be as hopeless as the name suggests since, when all factors are considered, the insurer's funds may be positive, or it may be possible to restore surplus to a positive position. However, a useful measure of the financial risk in an insurance organization is obtained by calculating the probability of ruin as a consequence of the variation in the amount of surplus.

**Figure 12.1
A Typical Outcome
of the Surplus
Process**

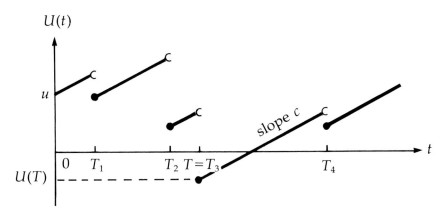

# COLLECTIVE RISK MODELS OVER AN EXTENDED PERIOD

Let us define

$$T = \min\{t : t \geq 0 \text{ and } U(t) < 0\} \qquad (12.1.2)$$

as the time when ruin occurs (with the understanding that $T = \infty$ is symbolic for $U(t) \geq 0$ for all $t \geq 0$; that is, ruin does not occur). Further, we denote by

$$\psi(u) = \Pr(T < \infty) \qquad (12.1.3)$$

the probability of ruin considered as a function of the initial surplus $u$. We shall also be interested in $U(T)$, the negative surplus at the time ruin occurs.

In practice, most insurers are interested in ruin only over a long—but finite—period like 20 years and are not really concerned about an infinite horizon. More precisely, consideration would be limited to

$$\psi(u,t) = \Pr(T < t), \qquad (12.1.4)$$

the probability of ruin before time $t$. We shall discuss, however, only the probability of ruin over an infinite horizon, $\psi(u)$, which is more tractable mathematically. Of course, $\psi(u)$ is an upper bound for $\psi(u,t)$.

The ideas in this chapter can be used to provide an early warning system for the guidance of an insurance organization. Necessarily, a model must be selected to represent the risk process of such an organization. The probability of ruin, on the basis of that model, warns management of the insurance organization regarding some of the risks involved. Again, the particular models developed in this chapter make simplifying assumptions to keep the mathematics tractable. The effects of dividends, interest and experience rating are ignored. Nevertheless, these models provide an initial means of analyzing the risk process of an insurance organization. In practice, they would be supplemented by additional analyses.

## 12.2 Claims Processes

In this section we shall formulate the ruin model using two random processes, the claim number process and the aggregate claims process. We shall model the first with a Poisson process and the second by a compound Poisson process.

For a certain portfolio of insurance policies, let $N(t)$ denote the number of claims and $S(t)$ the aggregate claims up to time $t$. We start the count at time 0; that is, $N(0) = 0$. Furthermore, $S(t) = 0$ as long as $N(t) = 0$. As in Chapter 11, we let $X_i$ denote the amount of the $i$th claim. Then

$$S(t) = X_1 + X_2 + \cdots + X_{N(t)}. \qquad (12.2.1)$$

The process $\{N(t), t \geq 0\}$ is called the **claim number process,** while $\{S(t), t \geq 0\}$ is called the **aggregate claim process.** As mentioned previously, the collection of random variables is called a process since we are interested in the distributions at all times $t \geq 0$. This is in contrast to Chapter 11 where we were interested in the number of claims and aggregate claims for a single period.

# COLLECTIVE RISK MODELS OVER AN EXTENDED PERIOD

Let $t \geq 0$ and $h > 0$. From the definitions it follows that $N(t+h) - N(t)$ is the number of claims and $S(t+h) - S(t)$ is the aggregate of claims that occur in the time interval between $t$ and $t+h$. Let $T_i$ denote the time when the $i$th claim occurs. Thus $T_1, T_2, \ldots$ are random variables with $T_1 < T_2 < T_3 < \cdots$. These inequalities are strict, thus excluding the possibility that two or more claims occur at the same time. Then the waiting time (or time elapsed) between successive claims is denoted by $W_1 = T_1$ and

$$W_i = T_i - T_{i-1} \qquad i > 1. \qquad (12.2.2)$$

Typical outcomes of the claim number process and the aggregate claim process are depicted in Figures 12.2 and 12.3. Note that $N(t)$ and $S(t)$ are step functions. The discontinuities are at the times $T_i$ when the claims occur, and the size of the steps at these times is 1 for $N(t)$ and is the corresponding claim amount $X_i$ for $S(t)$.

**Figure 12.2**
**A Typical Outcome of the Claim Number Process**

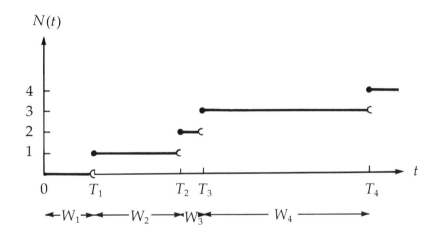

**Figure 12.3**
**A Typical Outcome of the Aggregate Claim Process**

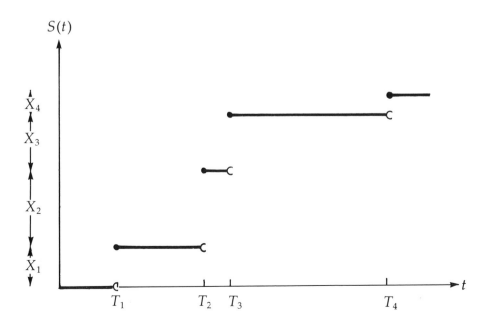

There are three methods to define a claim number process:

a. The **global method:** For $t \geq 0$ and $h > 0$ we specify the distribution of $N(t + h) - N(t)$. This distribution may depend on the values of $N(s)$ for $s \leq t$.

b. The **infinitesimal method:** We specify the probability that $N(t + dt) = N(t) + 1$, that is, the probability for a claim occurrence in the infinitesimal interval between $t$ and $t + dt$. This probability is proportional to $dt$ and may depend on the observations up to time $t$, that is, on $N(s)$ for $s \leq t$. The method is restricted to processes where

$$\lim_{\Delta t \to 0} \frac{\Pr[N(t + \Delta t) > N(t) + 1]}{\Delta t} = 0$$

and thus may be less general than the other two methods.

c. The **discrete** (or **waiting time**) **method:** We specify the joint distribution of $W_1, W_2, W_3, \ldots$ or, equivalently, that of $T_1, T_2, T_3, \ldots$.

**Example 12.1:**   Consider $n$ people aged $x$ at time 0. Let $N(t)$ denote the number of deaths that have occurred by time $t$ and $T_i$ denote the time when the $i$th death occurs ($i = 1, 2, \ldots, n$). As in Chapter 8, we assume independence of the times-until-death. Specify the process $\{N(t), t \geq 0\}$ by each of the three methods above.

**Solution:**

a. The conditional distribution of $N(t + h) - N(t)$, given $N(t) = i$, is binomial with parameters $n - i$ and $_hq_{x+t}$, $i = 0, 1, \ldots, n - 1$. Thus

$$\Pr[N(t + h) - N(t) = k \mid N(t) = i]$$
$$= \binom{n-i}{k} (_hq_{x+t})^k (1 - _hq_{x+t})^{n-i-k} \qquad k = 0, 1, \ldots, n - i.$$

If $N(t) = n$, then $N(t + h) = n$.

b. $\Pr[N(t + dt) - N(t) = 1 \mid N(t) = i] = (n - i)\,\mu_{x+t}dt$, $i = 0, 1, \ldots, n$. This follows from method (a) by replacing $_hq_{x+t}$ with $\mu_{x+t}dt$ and setting $k = 1$. Alternatively, the force operating on the joint-life status of the remaining $n - i$ lives, all aged $x + t$, is $(n - i)\,\mu_{x+t}$ for the interval $dt$.

c. For $i = 1, 2, \ldots, n$

$$\Pr(W_{i+1} > t \mid T_i = s) = (_tp_{x+s})^{n-i}$$

and $W_{n+1} = \infty$. Formally, this can be obtained from method (a) by

$$\Pr(T_{i+1} > s + t \mid T_i = s) = \Pr[N(s + t) - N(s) = 0 \mid N(s) = i]$$
$$= (1 - _tq_{x+s})^{n-i}. \qquad \blacktriangledown$$

The definition of a **Poisson process** by method (a) is as follows: The number of claims that occur in any interval of length $h$ has a Poisson distribution with parameter $\lambda h$, regardless of the location of the in-

# Chapter 12

## COLLECTIVE RISK MODELS OVER AN EXTENDED PERIOD

terval and the observed history. Thus, the conditional probability that $N(t + h) - N(t) = k$, given the observed history up to time $t$, that is, given $N(s)$ for all $s \le t$, is

$$\Pr[N(t + h) - N(t) = k \,|\, N(s) \text{ for all } s \le t]$$

$$= \frac{e^{-\lambda h}(\lambda h)^k}{k!} \quad k = 0, 1, 2, \ldots \quad (12.2.3)$$

for all $t \ge 0$ and $h > 0$. From this property it follows that the Poisson process has **independent increments**; that is, if $(t_1, t_1 + h_1)$, $(t_2, t_2 + h_2)$, ..., $(t_n, t_n + h_n)$ are disjoint time intervals, the random variables $N(t_1 + h_1) - N(t_1)$, $N(t_2 + h_2) - N(t_2)$, ..., $N(t_n + h_n) - N(t_n)$ are mutually independent. Furthermore, these increments are **stationary**; that is, the distribution of $N(t_i + h_i) - N(t_i)$, which is Poisson with parameter $\lambda h_i$, does not depend on $t_i$.

For $k = 1$, and any $t \ge 0$ and $h > 0$, we have from (12.2.3)

$$\Pr[N(t + h) - N(t) = 1 \,|\, N(s) \text{ for all } s \le t] = e^{-\lambda h} \lambda h.$$

Now we replace $h$ by the infinitesimal $dt$ to see that

$$\Pr[N(t + dt) - N(t) = 1 \,|\, N(s) \text{ for all } s \le t] = \lambda \, dt, \quad (12.2.4)$$

which is the definition of the Poisson process under method (b). It states that the probability of the occurrence of a claim in an infinitesimal interval of length $dt$ is $\lambda \, dt$ and is independent of the location of the interval and the observed history of the process.

Under method (c) we need to obtain the distribution of the waiting times between successive claims. We have

$$\Pr[W_{i+1} > h \,|\, T_i = t, N(s) \text{ for } s \le t]$$

$$= \Pr[N(t + h) - N(t) = 0 \,|\, T_i = t, N(s) \text{ for } s \le t]$$

$$= e^{-\lambda h} \quad (12.2.5)$$

by (12.2.3). Thus $W_{i+1}$ has an exponential distribution with parameter $\lambda$ and is independent of $N(s)$ for $s \le T_i$. In other words, $W_{i+1}$ is independent of $W_1, W_2, \ldots, W_i$. Then the definition of a Poisson process under method (c) is as follows: If $W_1, W_2, \ldots$ are mutually independent random variables with a common exponential distribution (parameter $\lambda > 0$), the process $\{N(t), t \ge 0\}$ is said to be a Poisson process with parameter $\lambda$.

We now define a compound Poisson process in this context. If for $S(t)$, defined in (12.2.1), the $X_1, X_2, X_3, \ldots$ are independent, identically distributed random variables with common d.f. $P(x)$, and if they are also independent of the process $\{N(t), t \ge 0\}$, assumed to be a Poisson process, the process $\{S(t), t \ge 0\}$ is said to be a **compound Poisson process**. If the aggregate claims process is a compound Poisson process given by $\lambda$ and $P(x)$, the following properties correspond to the properties of the underlying claim number process.

a. If $t \geq 0$ and $h > 0$, the distribution of $S(t + h) - S(t)$ is compound Poisson with specifications $\lambda h$ and $P(x)$, that is,

$$\Pr[S(t + h) - S(t) \leq x] = \sum_{k=0}^{\infty} \frac{e^{-\lambda h}(\lambda h)^k}{k!} P^{*k}(x)$$

where $P^{*k}(x)$ is the $k$-fold convolution of the d.f. $P(x)$.

b. In an infinitesimal time interval of length $dt$, there is either 1 claim with probability $\lambda \, dt$ and with $P(x)$ as the d.f. of its amount, or there is no claim.

c. At any time $h$, the probability that the next claim occurs between $h + t$ and $h + t + dt$ and that the claim amount is less than or equal to $x$ is $e^{-\lambda t}(\lambda \, dt) P(x)$.

Furthermore, the process $\{S(t), t \geq 0\}$ has independent and stationary increments. The aggregate claims of disjoint time intervals are independent random variables, and the distribution of each of these depends only on the length of the corresponding time interval and not on its location.

If $S(t)$ denotes a compound Poisson process and the value of $t$ is fixed, $S(t)$ will have a compound Poisson distribution. This distribution was studied in Chapter 11; formulas (11.3.2) and (11.3.3) give the mean and variance. Applying these formulas with $\lambda$ replaced by $\lambda t$, we obtain

$$E[S(t)] = \lambda t p_1 \qquad\qquad (12.2.6)$$

$$\mathrm{Var}[S(t)] = \lambda t p_2. \qquad\qquad (12.2.7)$$

## 12.3
## The Adjustment
## Coefficient

The surplus process $\{U(t), t \geq 0\}$ can be studied by its relation, given in (12.1.1), to the claim process $S(t)$. Now that we have a complete model of the surplus process, we will develop a special concept. This tool can be used to find upper and lower bounds on $\psi(u)$ in general and in explicit form in the particular case of an exponential distribution of individual claims.

First, we will assume that the rate of premium collection $c$ exceeds the expected claim payments per unit time, which is $\lambda p_1$. Further, we define a relative security loading $\theta$ by the equation $c = (1 + \theta) \lambda p_1$ where $\theta$ is positive. When we come to Theorem 12.1 in the next section, we shall see that $\theta \to 0$ or $\theta < 0$ implies $\psi(u) = 1$, that is, certainty of ruin.

Next, let $(-\infty, \gamma)$ denote the largest open interval for which the m.g.f. of $P(x)$ exists. It is assumed that $\gamma$ is positive. In the case of the exponential distribution with parameter $\beta$, $\gamma$ is equal to $\beta$, while for any bounded claim amount distribution $\gamma$ is $+\infty$.

Furthermore, we shall assume that $M_X(r)$ tends to $\infty$ as $r \to \gamma$. (This assumption does not always hold for finite $\gamma$; for an example, consider the distribution that is concentrated on the interval $x > 1$ where its p.d.f. is proportional to $x^{-2}e^{-x}$.)

## Chapter 12
# COLLECTIVE RISK MODELS OVER AN EXTENDED PERIOD

**Figure 12.4
Definition of the
Adjustment
Coefficient**

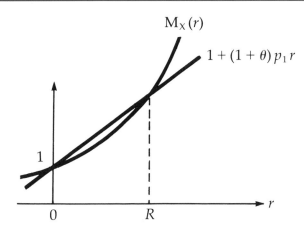

For notational convenience, we shall also assume that $P(x)$ is continuous and has a p.d.f. $p(x)$; if $P(x)$ is discrete and has a p.f. $p(x)$, integrals will be replaced by sums in the following.

For a compound Poisson process, we consider the equation

$$\lambda + cr = \lambda \int_0^\infty e^{rx} p(x)\, dx = \lambda M_X(r) \qquad r < \gamma \qquad (12.3.1)$$

or the equivalent expression, using $c = (1 + \theta)\lambda p_1$,

$$1 + (1 + \theta) p_1 r = M_X(r) \qquad r < \gamma. \qquad (12.3.2)$$

Here, the left-hand side is a linear function of $r$, while the right-hand side is a positive increasing function that tends to $\infty$ as $r \to \gamma$. Furthermore, the second derivative of the right-hand side is positive so that its graph is concave upward. The assumption that $c > \lambda p_1$ (equivalent to $\theta > 0$) means that the slope, $(1 + \theta)p_1$, of the left-hand side of (12.3.2) exceeds the slope, $M_X'(0) = p_1$, of the right-hand side at $r = 0$. From Figure 12.4, we see that equation (12.3.2) has two solutions. Aside from the trivial solution $r = 0$, there is a positive solution $r = R$, which is called the **adjustment coefficient.** The motivation for considering (12.3.1) and its solution $R$ will become clear from Theorem 12.1 and its proof in the Appendix to this chapter.

**Example 12.2:**

Determine the adjustment coefficient if the claim amount distribution is exponential with parameter $\beta$.

**Solution:**
The adjustment coefficient is obtained from (12.3.2) and here becomes

$$1 + \frac{(1 + \theta) r}{\beta} = \frac{\beta}{\beta - r}$$

or, as a quadratic equation in $r$,

$$(1 + \theta) r^2 - \theta \beta r = 0.$$

# COLLECTIVE RISK MODELS OVER AN EXTENDED PERIOD

As expected, $r = 0$ is a solution while the adjustment coefficient solution is

$$R = \frac{\theta \beta}{1 + \theta}.$$

In most cases, equation (12.3.2) cannot be solved explicitly. In these cases, it must be solved by an appropriate method of numerical analysis. From Figure 12.4 we see that if

$$M_X(r) - 1 - (1 + \theta)p_1 r \qquad (12.3.3)$$

is positive for some value of $r > 0$, it follows that $R < r$. Similarly, if (12.3.3) is negative for some value of $r$, $R > r$. We can use this information to determine $R$ by either trial and error or successive interval bisection. In Exercise 12.4 it is shown that $R < 2\theta p_1/p_2$, so that $r = 0$ and $r = 2\theta p_1/p_2$ can be used as starting values for the successive interval bisection method.

**Example 12.3:**

Calculate the adjustment coefficient if all claims are of size 1.

**Solution:**
Formula (12.3.2) gives the adjustment coefficient as the positive root of

$$1 + (1 + \theta)r = e^r.$$

The results of numerical evaluation of the above equation for several values of $\theta$ are displayed below.

| $\theta$ | $R$ |
|------|-------|
| 0.2 | 0.354 |
| 0.4 | 0.639 |
| 0.6 | 0.876 |
| 0.8 | 1.079 |
| 1.0 | 1.256 |
| 1.2 | 1.413 |

In general, the adjustment coefficient is an increasing function of the relative security loading, $\theta$. This can be seen from Figure 12.4. As $\theta$ is increased, the slope of the straight line through the point $(0,1)$ is increased so that the point of intersection of the line and the curve moves to the right and upward.

There is an intrinsic connection between the adjustment coefficient and the probability of ruin given in the following theorem, proved in the Appendix to this chapter.

**Theorem 12.1:**

For $u \geq 0$,

$$\psi(u) = \frac{e^{-Ru}}{\mathrm{E}[e^{-RU(T)}|T < \infty]}. \qquad (12.3.4)$$

In words, the denominator is calculated with respect to the condi-

# COLLECTIVE RISK MODELS OVER AN EXTENDED PERIOD

tional distribution of the negative surplus, $U(T)$, given that ruin occurs; that is, $T < \infty$.

From Figure 12.4, we see that if $\theta \to 0$, the secant approaches the tangent to $M_X(r)$ at $r = 0$, which implies $R \to 0$. But then, from (12.3.4), $\psi(u) = 1$, or ruin is certain. Further, $U(t)$, $t > 0$, for the case where $\theta < 0$, will always be less than the corresponding $U(t)$ for $\theta \to 0$, and hence, since ruin is certain for $\theta \to 0$, ruin is also certain for $\theta < 0$. For these reasons, we shall remain with the assumption that $\theta > 0$.

In general, an explicit evaluation of the denominator of (12.3.4) is not possible. Exceptions are the case $u = 0$ (see Exercise 12.10) and the case where the claim amount distribution is exponential (see Example 12.4). However, the theorem can be used to derive inequalities. Since $U(T)$, given $T < \infty$, is necessarily negative, the denominator in (12.3.4) exceeds 1. It follows that

$$\psi(u) < e^{-Ru}. \tag{12.3.5}$$

If the claim amount distribution is bounded so that $P(m) = 1$ for some finite $m$, it follows, given $T < \infty$, that $U(T) > -m$ since the surplus just before the claim must have been positive. Therefore, $e^{-RU(T)} < e^{Rm}$, so

$$E[e^{-RU(T)} \mid T < \infty] < e^{Rm}.$$

Thus

$$\psi(u) > e^{-Ru}e^{-Rm} = e^{-R(u+m)}. \tag{12.3.6}$$

Some authors suggest the use of the approximation

$$\psi(u) \cong e^{-Ru}, \tag{12.3.7}$$

which, in view of (12.3.5), overstates the probability of ruin.

We now examine a special case where Theorem 12.1 can be applied to obtain an explicit expression for the ruin probability $\psi(u)$.

**Example 12.4:** Calculate the probability of ruin in the case that the claim amount distribution is exponential with parameter $\beta > 0$.

**Solution:**
Ruin, if it occurs, is assumed to take place at time $T$. Let $\hat{u}$ be the amount of surplus just prior to $T$. The event that $-U(T) > y$ can be restated as the event that $X$, the size of the claim causing ruin, exceeds $\hat{u} + y$, given that it exceeds $\hat{u}$. The conditional probability of this event is given by

$$\frac{\beta \int_{\hat{u}+y}^{\infty} e^{-\beta x}\, dx}{\beta \int_{\hat{u}}^{\infty} e^{-\beta x}\, dx} = e^{-\beta y},$$

so that the p.d.f. of $-U(T)$, given $T < \infty$, is

$$\frac{d}{dy}(1 - e^{-\beta y}) = \beta e^{-\beta y}.$$

Therefore

$$E[e^{-RU(T)} | T < \infty] = \beta \int_0^\infty e^{Ry} e^{-\beta y} \, dy$$

$$= \frac{\beta}{\beta - R}.$$

From Example 12.2, we know that the adjustment coefficient in this case is $R = \theta \beta / (1 + \theta)$. Combining this with (12.3.4) gives us

$$\psi(u) = \frac{\beta - R}{\beta} e^{-Ru}$$

$$= \frac{1}{1 + \theta} \exp \left\{ \frac{-\theta \beta}{1 + \theta} u \right\}$$

$$= \frac{1}{1 + \theta} \exp \left\{ -\frac{\theta}{1 + \theta} \frac{u}{p_1} \right\}. \qquad (12.3.8)$$

▼

## 12.4 Discrete Time Model

In this section we examine a model that can be considered to be the discrete time analogue of the model developed in the preceding sections.

Let $U_n$ denote the insurer's surplus at time $n$, $n = 0,1,2,\dots$. We assume that

$$U_n = u + nc - S_n \qquad (12.4.1)$$

where $u = U_0$ is the initial surplus, $c$ is the amount of premiums received each period and $S_n$ is the sum of all the claims in the first $n$ periods. We also assume that

$$S_n = W_1 + W_2 + \cdots + W_n \qquad (12.4.2)$$

where $W_i$ is the sum of the claims in period $i$ and $W_1, W_2, \dots, W_n$ are independent, identically distributed random variables. Furthermore, $\mu = E[W] < c$ where $W$ is a random variable distributed as the $W_i$. Let

$$\tilde{T} = \min \{n : U_n < 0\} \qquad (12.4.3)$$

denote the time of ruin (again with the understanding that $\tilde{T} = \infty$ if $U_n \geq 0$ for all $n$), and let

$$\tilde{\psi}(u) = \Pr(\tilde{T} < \infty) \qquad (12.4.4)$$

denote the probability of ruin in this context.

## Chapter 12

# COLLECTIVE RISK MODELS OVER AN EXTENDED PERIOD

This model generates a result analogous to Theorem 12.1. To formulate it, we must first define the adjustment coefficient $\tilde{R}$ for the new model. We define $\tilde{R}$ as the positive solution of the equation

$$e^{-cr} M_W(r) = 1 \qquad (12.4.5)$$

(see Figure 12.5). The graph of $e^{-cr} M_W(r)$ can be traced by observing that

$$\frac{d}{dr}[e^{-cr} M_W(r)] = \frac{d}{dr} E[e^{(W-c)r}] = E[(W-c) e^{(W-c)r}]$$

and

$$\frac{d^2}{dr^2}[e^{-cr} M_W(r)] = E[(W-c)^2 e^{(W-c)r}].$$

The first of these observations shows that the slope at $r = 0$ is $\mu - c$, a negative quantity, and the second shows that the graph is concave upward. Further, provided $W$ has positive probability over values in excess of $c$, the first derivative will, for some large enough $r$, become positive and remain so. Thus, $e^{-cr} M_W(r)$ will have a minimum as indicated in Figure 12.5 and $\tilde{R}$ is positive as shown.

**Figure 12.5**
**The Definition of $\tilde{R}$**

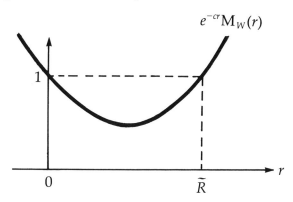

We note that (12.4.5) can be rewritten as

$$\log M_W(r) - cr = 0. \qquad (12.4.6)$$

If we look at the special case where the $W_i$'s common distribution is compound Poisson, then $\log M_W(r) = \lambda(M_X(r) - 1)$ and (12.4.6) is the same as (12.3.1), the definition of $R$ for the continuous time model. Hence, when the claims process is compound Poisson, $\tilde{R} = R$ so that $\tilde{R}$ can be considered to be a generalization of $R$.

**Example 12.5:**

Derive an expression for $\tilde{R}$ in the special case where the $W_i$'s common distribution is $N(\mu, \sigma^2)$.

**Solution:**
Here

$$\log M_W(r) = \mu r + \frac{1}{2}\sigma^2 r^2.$$

Hence, the positive solution of (12.4.6) is

$$\tilde{R} = \frac{2(c - \mu)}{\sigma^2}$$

where, as assumed above, $\mu < c$.                                    ▼

The analogue to Theorem 12.1 is the following result.

**Theorem 12.2:**

For $u > 0$

$$\tilde{\psi}(u) = \frac{\exp(-\tilde{R}\,u)}{\mathrm{E}[\exp(-\tilde{R}\,U_{\tilde{T}})\,|\,\tilde{T} < \infty]}. \tag{12.4.7}$$

Since $U_{\tilde{T}} < 0$ by definition, it follows that

$$\tilde{\psi}(u) < \exp(-\tilde{R}\,u). \tag{12.4.8}$$

The proof of Theorem 12.2 is similar to that of Theorem 12.3, presented in the Appendix to this chapter.

We shall now derive an approximation for $\tilde{R}$. In the presentation of Table 11.2 we have seen that for a random variable $X$

$$\frac{d}{dt} \log \mathrm{M}_X(t)\big|_{t=0} = \mathrm{E}[X]$$

and

$$\frac{d^2}{dt^2} \log \mathrm{M}_X(t)\big|_{t=0} = \mathrm{Var}[X].$$

Hence, using the Maclaurin series expansion, we have

$$\log \mathrm{M}_W(r) = \mu r + \frac{1}{2}\sigma^2 r^2 + \cdots$$

where $\sigma^2 = \mathrm{Var}[W]$. If we use only the first two terms of this expansion in (12.4.6), we obtain the approximation

$$\tilde{R} \cong \frac{2(c - \mu)}{\sigma^2}. \tag{12.4.9}$$

Comparing this with Example 12.5, we observe that (12.4.9) is exact in the case where the $W_i$'s common distribution is normal. Furthermore, if $W$ has a compound distribution and the relative security loading $\theta$ is given by $c = (1 + \theta)\mu$, then (11.2.5) and (11.2.6) yield

$$\tilde{R} \cong \frac{2\theta p_1 \mathrm{E}[N]}{(p_2 - p_1^2)\,\mathrm{E}[N] + p_1^2\,\mathrm{Var}[N]} \tag{12.4.10}$$

where $N$ is a random variable distributed as the number of claims in a period.

Chapter 12

# COLLECTIVE RISK MODELS OVER AN EXTENDED PERIOD

**Example 12.6:**

Approximate $\tilde{R}$ if

a. $N$ has a Poisson distribution with parameter $\lambda$

b. $N$ has a negative binomial distribution with parameters $r$ and $p$.

**Solution:**
a. Here $E[N] = \text{Var}[N] = \lambda$, and (12.4.10) reduces to

$$\tilde{R} \cong \frac{2\,\theta p_1}{p_2}. \tag{12.4.11}$$

We have already noted that, in this case, $\tilde{R} = R$, and it will follow from Exercise 12.4 that the right-hand side of (12.4.11) is actually an upper bound.

b. In this case,

$$E[N] = \frac{rq}{p}$$

$$\text{Var}[N] = \frac{rq}{p^2},$$

so it follows from (12.4.10) that

$$\tilde{R} \cong \frac{2\,\theta p_1}{p_2 + p_1^2[(1/p) - 1]}. \tag{12.4.12}$$

Note that for $p \to 1$, the result in (a) is obtained. ▼

Up to now it has been assumed that the total amounts of claims in different periods are independent random variables. In many cases, this assumption may be unrealistic. To investigate a situation of this type, we now consider an autoregressive model for the insurer's claim costs which generalizes the model previously considered and allows for correlation between the claims of successive periods.

We assume that $W_i$, the sum of claims in period $i$, is of the form

$$W_i = Y_i + a\,W_{i-1} \qquad i = 1,2,\ldots. \tag{12.4.13}$$

Here $-1 < a < 1$, and $Y_1, Y_2, \ldots$ are independent and identically distributed random variables with $E[Y_i] < (1-a)c$. The initial value $W_0 = w$ completes the description of this first order autoregressive model for the $W_i$'s.

The insurer's surplus $U_n$ at time $n$ is defined as in (12.4.1) and $\tilde{T}$, the time of ruin, as in (12.4.3). Note that the probability of ruin,

$$\tilde{\psi}(u,w) = \Pr(\tilde{T} < \infty), \tag{12.4.14}$$

is now a function of two variables. This generalizes the model considered previously, which corresponds to the special case $a = 0$.

# COLLECTIVE RISK MODELS OVER AN EXTENDED PERIOD

Now we use the iterative rule in (12.4.13) to obtain

$$W_i = Y_i + a Y_{i-1} + \cdots + a^{i-1} Y_1 + a^i w. \qquad (12.4.15)$$

Thus the total of the claims in the first $n$ periods is

$$
\begin{aligned}
S_n &= Y_n + (1 + a) Y_{n-1} + \cdots + (1 + a + \cdots + a^{n-1}) Y_1 \\
&\quad + (a + a^2 + \cdots + a^n) w \\
&= Y_n + \frac{1 - a^2}{1 - a} Y_{n-1} + \cdots + \frac{1 - a^n}{1 - a} Y_1 + a \frac{1 - a^n}{1 - a} w. \qquad (12.4.16)
\end{aligned}
$$

This shows that $Y_1$ will ultimately contribute $Y_1/(1 - a)$ to the total claims. Hence we assume that $c > E(Y_1)/(1 - a)$, and in analogy to (12.4.5) we define the adjustment coefficient as the positive solution of the equation

$$e^{-cr} M_{Y/(1-a)}(r) = 1. \qquad (12.4.17)$$

Thus $\tilde{R}$ is a positive number with the property that

$$\log E\left[ \exp\left( \frac{\tilde{R} Y}{1 - a} \right) \right] - c\tilde{R} = 0. \qquad (12.4.18)$$

Note that $\tilde{R}$ depends on the common distribution of the $Y_i$'s and on the values of $a$ and $c$.

In the Appendix to this chapter, the following result will be derived.

**Theorem 12.3:**

$$\tilde{\psi}(u, w) = \frac{\exp(-\tilde{R} \hat{u})}{E[\exp(-\tilde{R} \hat{U}_{\tilde{T}}) \mid \tilde{T} < \infty]} \qquad (12.4.19)$$

Here we have used the notation

$$\hat{U}_n = U_n - \frac{a}{1 - a} W_n \qquad \hat{u} = \hat{U}_0. \qquad (12.4.20)$$

In a sense, $\hat{U}_n$ is a modified surplus. It is the actual surplus $U_n$ adjusted by all future claims that are related to $W_n$. This interpretation of $\hat{U}_n$ is developed in Exercise 12.9.

If $a \geq 0$, it follows that $\hat{U}_{\tilde{T}} \leq U_{\tilde{T}} < 0$. Thus, in this case, the denominator of (12.4.19) is greater than 1 and we get a simplified upper bound for the probability of ruin.

**Corollary to Theorem 12.3:**

If $0 \leq a < 1$, then

$$\tilde{\psi}(u, w) \leq \exp(-\tilde{R} \hat{u}). \qquad (12.4.21)$$

Note that this generalizes (12.4.8).

# COLLECTIVE RISK MODELS OVER AN EXTENDED PERIOD

**12.5
The First Surplus
Below the Initial
Level**

We now return to the continuous time model developed in Sections 12.1–12.3 for which additional results are available.

Specifically, we will consider the amount of the surplus at the time it first falls below the initial level (this may, of course, never happen). As an application, we find a simple expression for $\psi(0)$, the probability of ruin if the initial surplus is 0.

The main theorem of this section, proved in the Appendix to this chapter, is the following.

**Theorem 12.4:**

For a compound Poisson process, the probability that the surplus will ever fall below its initial level $u$, and will be between $u - y$ and $u - y - dy$ when it happens for the first time, is

$$\frac{\lambda}{c}[1 - P(y)]\,dy = \frac{1 - P(y)}{(1 + \theta)\,p_1}\,dy \quad y > 0.$$

As an application of Theorem 12.4, we note that the probability that the surplus will ever fall below its original level is

$$\frac{1}{(1 + \theta)\,p_1} \int_0^\infty [1 - P(y)]\,dy = \frac{1}{1 + \theta} \qquad (12.5.1)$$

since

$$\int_0^\infty [1 - P(y)]\,dy = p_1.$$

Thus, if $u = 0$, $1/(1 + \theta)$ is the probability that the surplus will ever drop below 0, that is, ruin occurs. Hence

$$\psi(0) = \frac{1}{1 + \theta}. \qquad (12.5.2)$$

It is remarkable that $\psi(0)$ depends on the relative security loading $\theta$ and not on the specific form of the claim amount distribution.

We note that

$$\frac{\lambda}{c}[1 - P(y)] = \frac{1 - P(y)}{(1 + \theta)\,p_1} \quad y > 0$$

is not a p.d.f. since it does not integrate to 1. However, there is a related p.d.f. in the proper sense. Let $L_1$ be a random variable denoting the amount by which the surplus falls below the initial level for the first time, given that this ever happens. The p.d.f. for $L_1$ is obtained by dividing

$$\frac{1 - P(y)}{(1 + \theta)\,p_1}$$

by

$$\psi(0) = \frac{1}{1 + \theta}$$

and is

$$f_{L_1}(y) = \frac{1}{p_1}[1 - P(y)] \quad y > 0. \tag{12.5.3}$$

The relationship between the m.g.f. of $L_1$ and that of the distribution of claim size $X$ can be obtained by integration by parts:

$$M_{L_1}(r) = \frac{1}{p_1}\int_0^\infty e^{ry}[1 - P(y)]\, dy$$

$$= \frac{1}{p_1}\left\{\frac{e^{ry}}{r}[1 - P(y)]\Big|_0^\infty + \frac{1}{r}\int_0^\infty e^{ry}p(y)\, dy\right\}$$

$$= \frac{1}{p_1 r}[M_X(r) - 1]. \tag{12.5.4}$$

We will illustrate further applications of Theorem 12.4 by means of the following examples.

**Example 12.7:**

Write an expression for the distribution of the surplus level at the first time surplus falls below the initial level $u$, given that it does fall below $u$, if all claims are of size 2.

**Solution:**
We have

$$1 - P(y) = \begin{cases} 1 & 0 \le y < 2 \\ 0 & y \ge 2 \end{cases}.$$

Thus the p.d.f. for $L_1$ is

$$\frac{1}{p_1}[1 - P(y)] = \begin{cases} \dfrac{1}{2} & 0 \le y < 2 \\ 0 & \text{elsewhere.} \end{cases}$$

Therefore, $L_1$ is uniformly distributed between 0 and 2 so the surplus level after the first such drop is uniformly distributed between $u - 2$ and $u$.  ▼

**Example 12.8:**

Write an expression for the distribution of $L_1$ if the size of the individual claims has an exponential distribution with parameter $\beta$.

**Solution:**
Since $1 - P(y) = e^{-\beta y}$ for $y > 0$, the p.d.f. of $L_1$ is

$$\frac{1}{p_1}[1 - P(y)] = \beta e^{-\beta y} \quad y > 0.$$

# COLLECTIVE RISK MODELS OVER AN EXTENDED PERIOD

Hence, the distribution of $L_1$ is also exponential with parameter $\beta$. ▼

## 12.6 The Maximal Aggregate Loss

A new random variable, the *maximal aggregate loss*, is defined as

$$L = \max_{t \geq 0} \{S(t) - ct\}, \tag{12.6.1}$$

that is, as the maximal excess of aggregate claims over premiums received. Since $S(t) - ct = 0$ for $t = 0$, it follows that $L \geq 0$.

Theorem 12.2 will be used in the proof of another theorem that gives an explicit formula for the m.g.f. of $L$. This can be used to provide information about $\psi(u)$. As an application, $\psi(u)$ is expressed for the case where the individual claim amount distribution is a weighted sum of exponential distributions.

To obtain the d.f. of the random variable $L$ we consider, for $u \geq 0$, that

$$1 - \psi(u) = \Pr[U(t) \geq 0 \text{ for all } t]$$

$$= \Pr[u + ct - S(t) \geq 0 \text{ for all } t]$$

$$= \Pr[S(t) - ct \leq u \text{ for all } t].$$

But the right-hand side is equivalent to $\Pr(L \leq u)$, so we have

$$1 - \psi(u) = \Pr(L \leq u) \quad u \geq 0. \tag{12.6.2}$$

It follows that $1 - \psi(u)$, the complement of the probability of ruin, can be interpreted as the d.f. of $L$. In particular, we have

$$1 - \psi(0) = \Pr(L \leq 0) = \Pr(L = 0) \tag{12.6.3}$$

since $L \geq 0$. In this case, the maximum loss is attained at time $t = 0$. Also, the distribution of $L$ is of mixed type. There is a point mass of $1 - \psi(0)$ at the origin with the remaining probability distributed continuously over positive values of $L$.

The main result of this section is the following explicit formula for the m.g.f. of $L$, which, in view of (12.6.2), can be used to obtain information about $\psi(u)$.

**Theorem 12.5:**

$$\mathrm{M}_L(r) = \frac{\theta p_1 r}{1 + (1 + \theta) p_1 r - \mathrm{M}_X(r)} \tag{12.6.4}$$

An equivalent formula is

$$\mathrm{M}_L(r) = \frac{\theta}{1 + \theta} + \frac{1}{1 + \theta} \frac{\theta[\mathrm{M}_X(r) - 1]}{1 + (1 + \theta) p_1 r - \mathrm{M}_X(r)}, \tag{12.6.4A}$$

which reflects the point mass at the origin more directly, since the contribution to the m.g.f. of the probability at $L = 0$ is

$$1 - \psi(0) = \frac{\theta}{1 + \theta}$$

# COLLECTIVE RISK MODELS OVER
# AN EXTENDED PERIOD

**Figure 12.6
A Typical
Outcome of
the Aggregate
Loss Process**

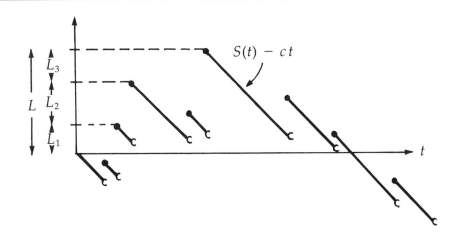

by (12.5.2). Notice that the equation used to define the adjustment coefficient is obtained by equating the denominator of (12.6.4) to 0.

**Proof:**

The proof of the theorem involves the consideration of the times when the aggregate loss process assumes new record highs. An outcome of the aggregate loss process is shown in Figure 12.6. In this outcome a new record high is established three times. After each record high there is a probability of $1 - \psi(0)$ that this record will not be broken and a probability of $\psi(0)$ that it will be broken. In making this statement we are relying on the fact that a compound Poisson process has stationary and independent increments.

If it is broken, the p.d.f. of the increase is that of $L_1$, which is given in (12.5.3). The figure illustrates that we can represent $L$ as a sum of a random number of random variables, a random sum, thus

$$L = L_1 + L_2 + \cdots + L_N. \tag{12.6.5}$$

Here $N$ is the number of new record highs and has a geometric distribution with

$$\Pr(N = n) = [1 - \psi(0)] \, [\psi(0)]^n$$

$$= \theta \left( \frac{1}{1 + \theta} \right)^{n+1} \qquad n = 0,1,2,\ldots, \tag{12.6.6}$$

and m.g.f. given by

$$M_N(r) = \frac{\theta}{1 + \theta - e^r}. \tag{12.6.7}$$

The random variables $L_1, L_2, \ldots$ are mutually independent and independent of $N$. Their common p.d.f. is given by (12.5.3). According to (11.2.7), the m.g.f. of $L$ is

$$M_L(r) = M_N\left(\log M_{L_1}(r)\right)$$

$$= \frac{\theta}{1 + \theta - M_{L_1}(r)}. \tag{12.6.8}$$

# COLLECTIVE RISK MODELS OVER AN EXTENDED PERIOD

Formula (12.5.4) gives $M_{L_1}(r)$ in terms of $M_X(r)$ and thus

$$M_L(r) = \frac{\theta}{1 + \theta - \{1/(p_1 r)\}[M_X(r) - 1]}$$

$$= \frac{\theta p_1 r}{1 + (1 + \theta)p_1 r - M_X(r)},$$

which was to be shown. The alternative formula (12.6.4A) can be verified by collecting terms over a common denominator. ∎

Observe that since $1 - \psi(u)$ is the d.f. of the random variable $L$ [see (12.6.2) above] where $L$ has a point mass at the origin and a continuous density for positive values of $u$, we have

$$M_L(r) = 1 - \psi(0) + \int_0^\infty e^{ur}[-\psi'(u)]\, du$$

$$= \frac{\theta}{1 + \theta} + \int_0^\infty e^{ur}[-\psi'(u)]\, du.$$

Hence (12.6.4A) states that

$$\int_0^\infty e^{ur}[-\psi'(u)]\, du = \frac{1}{1 + \theta}\frac{\theta[M_X(r) - 1]}{1 + (1 + \theta)p_1 r - M_X(r)}. \quad (12.6.9)$$

This formula can be used to find explicit expressions for $\psi(u)$ for certain families of claim amount distributions. One such family consists of mixtures of exponential distributions of the form

$$p(x) = \sum_{i=1}^n A_i \beta_i e^{-\beta_i x} \quad x > 0, \quad (12.6.10)$$

$$\beta_i > 0,\ A_i > 0,\ A_1 + A_2 + \cdots + A_n = 1.$$

Then

$$M_X(r) = \sum_{i=1}^n A_i \frac{\beta_i}{\beta_i - r}. \quad (12.6.11)$$

Originally, $M_X(r)$ is defined as an expectation and exists only for $r < \gamma = \min\{\beta_1, \ldots, \beta_n\}$. However, this function can be extended in a natural way to all $r \neq \beta_i$. For simplicity, we use the same symbol, $M_X(r)$, for these functions.

We substitute (12.6.11) into (12.6.9) and recognize that the right-hand side of the result is a rational function of $r$, which, by applying the method of partial fractions, we can write in the following form

$$\int_0^\infty e^{ur}[-\psi'(u)]\, du = \sum_{i=1}^n \frac{C_i r_i}{r_i - r}. \quad (12.6.12)$$

The only function that satisfies this and $\psi(\infty) = 0$ is

$$\psi(u) = \sum_{i=1}^n C_i e^{-r_i u}. \quad (12.6.13)$$

# COLLECTIVE RISK MODELS OVER AN EXTENDED PERIOD

It follows that the probability of ruin is given by this expression. We illustrate this procedure with two examples.

**Example 12.9:**

Derive an expression for $\psi(u)$ if the $X_i$'s have an exponential claim amount distribution; that is, $n = 1$ in (12.6.10).

**Solution:**
Since

$$M_X(r) = \frac{\beta}{\beta - r} = \frac{1}{1 - p_1 r},$$

the right-hand side of (12.6.9) is

$$\left(\frac{1}{1 + \theta}\right)\left(\frac{\theta(1/(1 - p_1 r) - 1)}{1 + (1 + \theta)p_1 r - 1/(1 - p_1 r)}\right) = \left(\frac{1}{1 + \theta}\right)\left(\frac{\theta}{\theta - (1 + \theta)p_1 r}\right)$$

$$= C_1 \frac{r_1}{r_1 - r}$$

where $C_1 = 1/(1 + \theta)$ and $r_1 = \theta/[(1 + \theta)p_1]$. Then

$$\psi(u) = C_1 e^{-r_1 u}.$$

This formula was established previously in Example 12.4, formula (12.3.8).  ▼

**Example 12.10:**

Given that $\theta = 2/5$ and $p(x)$ is given by

$$p(x) = \frac{3}{2}e^{-3x} + \frac{7}{2}e^{-7x} \quad x > 0,$$

calculate $\psi(u)$.

**Solution:**
From $p(x)$ we have

$$M_X(r) = \frac{3/2}{3 - r} + \frac{7/2}{7 - r}$$

and

$$p_1 = \left(\frac{1}{2}\right)\left(\frac{1}{3}\right) + \left(\frac{1}{2}\right)\left(\frac{1}{7}\right) = \frac{5}{21}.$$

We substitute these expressions into the right-hand side of (12.6.9), which, after some simplification, becomes

$$\left(\frac{6}{7}\right)\left(\frac{5 - r}{6 - 7r + r^2}\right).$$

The roots of the denominator are $r_1 = 1$ and $r_2 = 6$. Hence this expression, rewritten in the form of (12.6.12), is

$$\frac{C_1}{1 - r} + \frac{6C_2}{6 - r}.$$

## COLLECTIVE RISK MODELS OVER AN EXTENDED PERIOD

The coefficients are determined to be

$$C_1 = \frac{24}{35}$$

$$C_2 = \frac{1}{35}.$$

Thus

$$\psi(u) = \frac{24}{35}e^{-u} + \frac{1}{35}e^{-6u} \quad u \geq 0.$$ ▼

In Figure 12.7 a graph illustrates the points $r_i$ satisfying the equation

$$1 + (1 + \theta)p_1 r = M_X(r) \tag{12.6.14}$$

where the distribution of $X$ is a mixture of exponentials. The function $M_X(r)$ is given in (12.6.11) with $n = 3$.

The right-hand side of (12.6.11) has discontinuities at $\beta_1$, $\beta_2$, ..., and at each of these arguments the value of the function shifts from $+\infty$ to $-\infty$. The figure illustrates that, in general, the $r_i$'s will satisfy a condition of the form

$$r_1 = R < \beta_1 < r_2 < \beta_2 < \ldots < r_n < \beta_n. \tag{12.6.15}$$

Figure 12.4 illustrates that part of Figure 12.7 to the left of $\beta_1 = \gamma$. Practical problems will necessitate consideration of claim distributions that are not mixtures of exponential distributions. For some distributions it may even be difficult to calculate the adjustment coefficient so as to be able to approximate ruin probabilities. A method based on the first two moments of the claim amount distribution is easy to apply and seems to give satisfactory results for moderate values of $u$.

**Figure 12.7
The Solution of
Equation (12.6.14)
for $n = 3$**

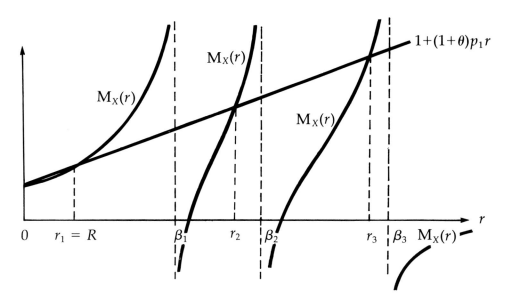

# COLLECTIVE RISK MODELS OVER AN EXTENDED PERIOD

The first moment for the distribution of $L$ is obtained in Exercise 12.13(b). The result is

$$E[L] = \frac{p_2}{2\,\theta\,p_1}. \qquad (12.6.16)$$

Further we know from (12.5.2) that $\psi(0) = 1/(1 + \theta)$ and from (12.3.5) that $\psi(u) < e^{-Ru}$. The approximation proposed here is that

$$1 - F_L(u) = \psi(u) \cong \frac{1}{1+\theta} e^{-Ku} \qquad u > 0$$

where $K$ is chosen so that the approximated value of $E[L]$ is equal to that given in (12.6.16). But

$$E[L] = \int_0^\infty [1 - F_L(u)]\, du \cong \frac{1}{1+\theta}\frac{1}{K},$$

so that

$$K = \frac{2\,\theta\,p_1}{(1+\theta)\,p_2}$$

will give us the required equality. Thus our approximation is

$$\psi(u) \cong \frac{1}{1+\theta} \exp\left\{ -\frac{2\,\theta\,p_1\,u}{(1+\theta)\,p_2} \right\} \qquad u > 0.$$

It is to be noted that if the claim distribution is exponential with mean $p_1$, so that $p_2 = 2p_1^2$, the result is exact [see (12.3.8)]. This method is extended in Exercise 12.19 to give an improved approximation.

## 12.7 Notes and References

General references are the texts by
• Beard, Pentikäinen and Pesonen (1977),
• Beekman (1974),
• Bühlmann (1970),
• Gerber (1979), and
• Seal (1969).

Ruin theory has been developed by the Scandinavian school (F. Lundberg, Cramér) and by the Italian school (DeFinetti); this development is accurately described in the text by Dubourdieu (1952).

We did not discuss the famous asymptotic formula for the probability of ruin,

$$\psi(u) \cong C e^{-Ru} \qquad u \to \infty \qquad (12.7.1)$$

where $C$ is some constant. In view of Theorem 12.1, this formula is quite plausible; it means that the denominator in formula (12.3.4) has a limit as $u \to \infty$ with the $C$ in formula (12.7.1) as the reciprocal of this limit. In the case where the claim amount distribution is a mixture of exponential distributions, this asymptotic form is illustrated by formula (12.6.13).

# Chapter 12
# COLLECTIVE RISK MODELS OVER AN EXTENDED PERIOD

The equation in Exercise 12.11 is called a defective renewal equation. Feller (1966) discussed the solutions of equations of this type; in particular, he proves (12.7.1). By the same technique, Gerber (1974) finds the limit of the conditional distribution of $-U(T)$, given $T < \infty$, for $u \to \infty$.

If we modify the model by assuming that the surplus earns interest at a constant force $\delta > 0$, we have to replace $c$ by $c + \delta u$ in the integro-differential equation (12.A.7) in the Appendix to this chapter. In the case of exponential claim amounts, the resulting equation has an explicit solution in terms of the gamma function.

If the roles of premiums and claims are interchanged, with premiums representing payments by the insurer and claims representing payments to the insurer, so that

$$U(t) = u - ct + S(t)$$

where it is now assumed that $c < \lambda p_1$, there is an explicit formula,

$$\psi(u) = e^{-Ru}.$$

To prove this, one establishes a result like Theorem 12.1 and observes that the surplus at the time of ruin is necessarily 0. It has been suggested that this model could be used for a portfolio of annuities where a death frees the reserve of the policyholder and leads to a negative claim.

Seal (1978) discusses numerical methods for evaluating the probability of ruin in a finite time interval. Beekman and Bowers (1972) approximate $\psi(u,t)$ by matching moments. Gerber (1974) and DeVylder (1978) give upper bounds for $\psi(u,t)$ by martingale arguments.

## Appendix

**Proof of Theorem 12.1:**
For $t > 0$ and $r > 0$, we consider

$$E[e^{-rU(t)}] = E[e^{-rU(t)}|T \le t] \Pr(T \le t)$$
$$+ E[e^{-rU(t)}|T > t] \Pr(T > t). \quad (12.A.1)$$

Since $U(t) = u + ct - S(t)$, the term on the left-hand side is

$$\exp\{-ru - rct + \lambda t[M_X(r) - 1]\}. \quad (12.A.2)$$

In the first term on the right-hand side, we write

$$U(t) = U(T) + [U(t) - U(T)]$$
$$= U(T) + c(t - T) - [S(t) - S(T)].$$

For a given $T$, the term in brackets is independent of $U(T)$ and has a compound Poisson distribution with Poisson parameter $\lambda(t - T)$. Hence the first term on the right-hand side of (12.A.1) can be written as

$$E[\exp(-rU(T))\exp\{-rc(t - T) + \lambda(t - T)[M_X(r) - 1]\}|T \le t]\Pr(T \le t). \quad (12.A.3)$$

# COLLECTIVE RISK MODELS OVER AN EXTENDED PERIOD

Expressions (12.A.2) and (12.A.3) can be greatly simplified if we choose $r$ such that

$$-rc + \lambda [M_X(r) - 1] = 0.$$

Two solutions exist (see Figure 12.4). The solution $r = 0$ gives a trivial identity when substituted into (12.A.1), but the other solution, $r = R$, will serve our purpose. If, with $r = R$, we substitute the simplified expressions into (12.A.1), we obtain

$$e^{-Ru} = E[e^{-RU(T)}|T \leq t] \Pr(T \leq t)$$
$$+ E[e^{-RU(t)}|T > t] \Pr(T > t). \tag{12.A.4}$$

Now we let $t \to \infty$. The first term on the right-hand side converges to

$$E[e^{-RU(T)}|T < \infty] \psi(u).$$

Hence Theorem 12.1 follows if we can show that the second term on the right-hand side vanishes for $t \to \infty$. We shall show this as follows:

Let $\alpha = c - \lambda p_1$, $\beta^2 = \lambda p_2$. Thus, from (12.2.6) and (12.2.7)

$$E[U(t)] = E[u + ct - S(t)] = u + \alpha t$$
$$\text{Var}[U(t)] = \text{Var}[S(t)] = \beta^2 t.$$

We consider $u + \alpha t - \beta t^{2/3}$, which is positive for $t$ sufficiently large. Now we split the second term on the right-hand side of (12.A.4) by distinguishing whether $U(t)$ is less than or greater than $u + \alpha t - \beta t^{2/3}$. With this splitting, we have

$$E[e^{-RU(t)}|T > t, 0 \leq U(t) \leq u + \alpha t - \beta t^{2/3}] \Pr[T > t, 0 \leq U(t) \leq u + \alpha t - \beta t^{2/3}]$$
$$+ E[e^{-RU(t)}|T > t, U(t) > u + \alpha t - \beta t^{2/3}] \Pr[T > t, U(t) > u + \alpha t - \beta t^{2/3}]$$
$$\leq \Pr[U(t) \leq u + \alpha t - \beta t^{2/3}] + \exp[-R(u + \alpha t - \beta t^{2/3})]$$
$$\leq t^{-1/3} + \exp[-R(u + \alpha t - \beta t^{2/3})]$$

by Chebychev's inequality. But with this upper bound, the second term on the right-hand side of (12.A.4) vanishes for $t \to \infty$. $\blacksquare$

**Proof of Theorem 12.3:**
The following calculation yields a simple recursion formula for the modified surplus:

$$\hat{U}_i = U_i - \frac{a}{1-a} W_i$$

$$= U_{i-1} + c - W_i - \frac{a}{1-a} W_i$$

$$= U_{i-1} + c - \frac{1}{1-a} W_i$$

## COLLECTIVE RISK MODELS OVER AN EXTENDED PERIOD

$$= U_{i-1} + c - \frac{1}{1-a}(Y_i + a W_{i-1})$$

$$= \hat{U}_{i-1} + c - \frac{Y_i}{1-a} \qquad i = 1,2,\ldots . \qquad (12.A.5)$$

From (12.A.5), (12.4.17) and the independence of the $Y_i's$ it follows that for any $n$

$$E[\exp\{-R(\hat{U}_n - \hat{U}_i)\}] = 1 \qquad i = 0,1,\ldots,n. \qquad (12.A.6)$$

Now consider the identity

$$E[\exp(-R\hat{U}_n)] = \sum_{i=1}^{n} E[\exp(-R\hat{U}_n)|\tilde{T} = i]\,\Pr(\tilde{T} = i)$$

$$+ E[\exp(-R\hat{U}_n)|\tilde{T} > n]\,\Pr(\tilde{T} > n). \qquad (12.A.7)$$

From (12.A.6) for $i = 0$, it follows that the expression on the left-hand side of (12.A.7) is $\exp(-\tilde{R}\hat{u})$. In the summation on the right-hand side we replace $\hat{U}_n$ by $\hat{U}_i + (\hat{U}_n - \hat{U}_i)$. The difference, $\hat{U}_n - \hat{U}_i$, is independent of $\hat{U}_1, \hat{U}_2, \ldots \hat{U}_i$. This can be confirmed by using (12.A.5) and the independence of the $Y's$. In particular $(\hat{U}_n - \hat{U}_i)$ is independent of the event $\tilde{T} = i$. It follows from (12.A.6) that

$$E[\exp(-R\hat{U}_n)|\tilde{T} = i] = E[\exp(-R\hat{U}_i)|\tilde{T} = i].$$

Thus (12.A.7) can be written as

$$\exp(-R\hat{u}) = \sum_{i=1}^{n} E[\exp(-R\hat{U}_i)|\tilde{T} = i]\,\Pr(\tilde{T} = i)$$

$$+ E[\exp(-R\hat{U}_n)|\tilde{T} > n]\,\Pr(\tilde{T} > n), \qquad (12.A.8)$$

which is similar to (12.A.4). Now we let $n \to \infty$. Then the first term on the right-hand side of (12.A.8) converges to

$$\sum_{i=1}^{\infty} E[\exp(-R\hat{U}_i)|\tilde{T} = i]\,\Pr(\tilde{T} = i) = E[\exp(-R\hat{U}_T)|\tilde{T} < \infty]\,\Pr(\tilde{T} < \infty).$$

Thus to complete the proof of Theorem 12.3 we have to show that the second term on the right-hand side of (12.A.8) vanishes for $n \to \infty$. We do this as follows.

From (12.4.16) it follows that

$$E[S_n] = n\frac{E[Y]}{1-a} - a\frac{1-a^n}{1-a}\left\{\frac{E[Y]}{1-a} - w\right\}.$$

Since $c > E[Y]/(1-a)$, there is a positive number $\alpha$ such that $E[U_n] > u + \alpha n$ if $n$ is sufficiently large. Furthermore, it follows from (12.4.16) that there is a number $\beta^2$ such that $\text{Var}[U_n] < \beta^2 n$. Now we can use the same reasoning we used at the end of the proof of Theorem 12.1 to show that the second term on the right-hand side of (12.A.8) converges to 0 for $n \to \infty$. ∎

**Proof of Theorem 12.4:**

For this proof we introduce a new concept that is of interest in itself. Let $w(x)$, $x < 0$, be a function with $w(x) \geq 0$. We define

$$\psi(u;w) = E[w(U(T))|T < \infty]\,\psi(u), \qquad (12.A.9)$$

considered as a function of the initial surplus, $u$. We may interpret $w(x)$ as a **penalty** if the surplus at the time of ruin is $x$. In this case $\psi(u;w)$ is the expected value of the penalty. Examples are

a. if $w(x) = e^{-Rx}$, then (12.3.4) shows that $\psi(u;w) = e^{-Ru}$

b. if $w(x) = 1$, then (12.A.9) shows that $\psi(u;w) = \psi(u)$

c. if

$$w_h(x) = \begin{cases} 1 & x < -h \\ 0 & -h \leq x \leq 0, \end{cases}$$

then

$$\psi(0;w_h) = \Pr[U(T) < -h|T < \infty]\,\psi(0).$$

We start the proof by showing that, for every bounded function $w(x)$, we have

$$\psi(0;w) = \frac{\lambda}{c} \int_0^\infty w(-y)\,[1 - P(y)]\,dy. \qquad (12.A.10)$$

From property (b) in the definition of the compound Poisson process in Section 12.2 and the law of total probability, we see that for $u \geq 0$

$$\psi(u;w) = (1 - \lambda\,dt)\,\psi(u + c\,dt;w) \qquad (12.A.11)$$

$$+ \lambda\,dt\left\{\int_0^u \psi(u - x;w)\,p(x)\,dx + \int_u^\infty w(u - x)\,p(x)\,dx\right\}.$$

We substitute $\psi(u + c\,dt;w) = \psi(u;w) + c\,dt\,\psi'(u;w)$, subtract $\psi(u;w)$ from both sides, and divide by $c\,dt$ to obtain

$$\psi'(u;w) = \frac{\lambda}{c}\psi(u;w) - \frac{\lambda}{c}\int_0^u \psi(u - x;w)\,p(x)\,dx$$

$$-\frac{\lambda}{c}\int_u^\infty w(u - x)\,p(x)\,dx. \qquad (12.A.12)$$

We shall now integrate this equation over $u$ from 0 to $z$. The resulting double integrals can be reduced to single integrals by a change in variables. For the first integral we replace $x$ and $u$ by $x$ and $y = u - x$. Then

$$\int_0^z \int_0^u \psi(u - x;w)\,p(x)\,dx\,du = \int_0^z \int_0^{z-y} \psi(y;w)\,p(x)\,dx\,dy$$

$$= \int_0^z \psi(y;w)\,P(z - y)\,dy.$$

# COLLECTIVE RISK MODELS OVER AN EXTENDED PERIOD

In the second integral we replace $x$ and $u$ by $x$ and $y = x - u$. Then

$$\int_0^z \int_u^\infty w(u - x)\, p(x)\, dx\, du = \int_0^\infty \int_y^{y+z} w(-y)\, p(x)\, dx\, dy$$

$$= \int_0^\infty w(-y)\, [P(y + z) - P(y)]\, dy.$$

Thus (12.A.12), integrated from 0 to $z$, gives

$$\psi(z;w) - \psi(0;w) = \frac{\lambda}{c} \int_0^z \psi(y;w)\, [1 - P(z - y)]\, dy$$

$$- \frac{\lambda}{c} \int_0^\infty w(-y)\, [P(y + z) - P(y)]\, dy. \quad (12.A.13)$$

For $z \to \infty$, the first terms on both sides vanish leaving

$$-\psi(0;w) = -\frac{\lambda}{c} \int_0^\infty w(-y)\, [1 - P(y)]\, dy.$$

Now let $w_h(x)$ be defined as in Example (c), that is,

$$w_h(x) = \begin{cases} 1 & x < -h \\ 0 & -h \le x \le 0, \end{cases}$$

then

$$\Pr[U(T) < -h|T < \infty]\, \psi(0) = \psi(0;w_h) = \frac{\lambda}{c} \int_h^\infty [1 - P(y)]\, dy.$$

Hence, when $u = 0$, the probability that the surplus ever falls below 0, and will be between $-h$ and $-h - dh$ when it happens, is

$$\frac{\lambda}{c} [1 - P(h)]\, dh.$$

If $u > 0$, an event with equal probability is that the surplus will ever fall below $u$, and will be between $u - h$ and $u - h - dh$ when it happens. This proves Theorem 12.4. ∎

## Exercises

*Section 12.2*

12.1. Suppose that $W_1, W_2, \ldots$ are independent, identically distributed random variables with common d.f. $F(x)$ and p.d.f. $f(x)$, $x \ge 0$. Given $N(t) = i$ and $T_i = s$ ($s < t$), what is the probability of the occurrence of a claim between times $t$ and $t + dt$? (This generalization of the Poisson process is called a *renewal process*.)

12.2. Let $\{N(t), t \ge 0\}$ be a Poisson process with parameter $\lambda$ and $p_n(t) = \Pr[N(t) = n]$.

a. Show that

$$p_0'(t) = -\lambda p_0(t)$$

$$p_n'(t) = -\lambda p_n(t) + \lambda p_{n-1}(t) \qquad n \geq 1.$$

b. Interpret these formulas.

*Section 12.3*

12.3. Calculate $\lim_{c \to \lambda p_1} R$ and $\lim_{c \to \infty} R$.

12.4. Use

$$e^{rx} > 1 + rx + \frac{1}{2}(rx)^2 \qquad r > 0, x > 0$$

to show that

$$R < \frac{2\theta p_1}{p_2}.$$

12.5. Suppose that $\theta = 2/5$ and

$$p(x) = \frac{3}{2}e^{-3x} + \frac{7}{2}e^{-7x} \qquad x > 0,$$

calculate

a. $\gamma$                          b. $R$.

12.6. Suppose that the claim amount distribution is discrete with $p(1) = 1/4$ and $p(2) = 3/4$. If $R = \log 2$, calculate $\theta$.

12.7. Show that the adjustment coefficient can also be obtained as the unique solution of the equation

$$\int_0^\infty e^{rx}[1 - P(x)]\,dx = \frac{c}{\lambda} \qquad r < \gamma.$$

*Section 12.4*

12.8. Suppose that $W_i$ assumes only the values $0$ and $+2$ and that $\Pr(W = 0) = p$, $\Pr(W = 2) = q$ where $p + q = 1$. Assume that $c = 1$, $p > 1/2$ and that $u$ is an integer. For this case, determine
a. $U(\tilde{T})$                          b. $\tilde{\psi}(u)$ in terms of $\tilde{R}$
c. $\tilde{R}$ in terms of $p, q$          d. $\tilde{\psi}(u)$ in terms of $p, q$.

12.9. Consider the claims in periods $n + 1$, $n + 2$, ..., $n + m$ and denote their total by $S_{n,m}$; that is,

$$S_{n,m} = W_{n+1} + W_{n+2} + \cdots + W_{n+m}.$$

The claim amount for each period is generated by the stochastic process described in (12.4.13). Verify the following:

a. $\displaystyle S_{n,m} = \sum_{i=1}^{m} Y_{n+i} \sum_{j=0}^{m-i} a^j + W_n \sum_{j=1}^{m} a^j$

$\displaystyle = \sum_{i=1}^{m} \left( \frac{1 - a^{(m-i+1)}}{1 - a} \right) Y_{n+i} + \left( \frac{a - a^{m+1}}{1 - a} \right) W_n$

# Chapter 12

## COLLECTIVE RISK MODELS OVER AN EXTENDED PERIOD

b. As $m \to \infty$ the final term on the right-hand side of the expression in (a) converges to

$$\frac{a W_n}{1 - a}.$$

c. $E[S_{n,m} | W_1 = w_1, W_2 = w_2, \ldots, W_n = w_n]$

$$= \left[ \frac{m(1 - a) - a + a^{m+1}}{(1 - a)^2} \right] \mu + \left( \frac{a - a^{m+1}}{1 - a} \right) w_n$$

where $E(Y_{n+i}) = \mu$.

*Section 12.5*

12.10. Use Theorem 12.4 to evaluate the denominator in (12.3.4) in the case $u = 0$. Is your result consistent with (12.5.2)?

12.11. Show by interpretation that $\psi(u)$, $u \geq 0$, satisfies

$$\psi(u) = \frac{\lambda}{c} \int_0^u [1 - P(y)] \psi(u - y) \, dy + \frac{\lambda}{c} \int_u^\infty [1 - P(y)] \, dy.$$

[Hint: Use Theorem 12.4.]

12.12. Substitute

$$M_X(r) = 1 + p_1 r + p_2 \frac{r^2}{2} + p_3 \frac{r^3}{6} + \cdots$$

into (12.5.4) to derive expressions for
a. $E[L_1]$      b. $E[L_1^2]$      c. $\text{Var}[L_1]$.

*Section 12.6*

12.13. a. For $N$ as in (12.6.5), show that $E[N] = 1/\theta$ and $\text{Var}[N] = (1 + \theta)/\theta^2$.
b. Use the result of Exercise 12.12 to derive expressions for $E[L]$ and $\text{Var}[L]$. [Hint: Formulas (12.6.5), (11.2.5) and (11.2.6), with $p_1 = E[L_1]$, $\text{Var}[X] = \text{Var}[L_1]$, are helpful. For an alternative derivation, expand $M_L(r)$ in (12.6.4) in powers of $r$.]

12.14. Define the m.g.f. of $L$ if all claims are of size 2.

12.15. Under certain assumptions, the probability of ruin is
$$\psi(u) = (0.3) e^{-2u} + (0.2) e^{-4u} + (0.1) e^{-7u} \qquad u \geq 0.$$
Calculate
a. $\theta$      b. $R$.

12.16. What is the expected claim size for a distribution of the form (12.6.10)?

12.17. Suppose that $\lambda = 3$, $c = 1$ and
$$p(x) = \frac{1}{3} e^{-3x} + \frac{16}{3} e^{-6x} \qquad x > 0.$$

Calculate and/or derive
a. $p_1$
b. $\theta$
c. $M_X(r)$
d. expressions for the right-hand sides of (12.6.9) and (12.6.12)
e. an explicit formula for $\psi(u)$.

12.18. Suppose that $\lambda = 1$, $c = 10$, and

$$p(x) = \frac{9x}{25} e^{-3x/5} \quad x > 0.$$

Calculate and/or derive
a. $p_1$
b. $\theta$
c. $M_X(r)$
d. expressions for the right-hand sides of (12.6.9) and (12.6.12)
e. an explicit formula for $\psi(u)$.

12.19. Beekman (1969) and Bowers' discussion thereof suggested the following approximation for the d.f. of $L$:

$$\Pr(L \le u) \cong \xi I(u) + (1 - \xi) G(u:\alpha,\beta)$$

where $I(x)$ is the degenerate d.f. of the constant 0 and $G(x:\alpha,\beta)$ is the gamma distribution with parameters $\alpha$ and $\beta$.
a. Determine $\xi$, $\alpha$ and $\beta$ to match the point mass at the origin and the first two moments of $L$ [see Exercise 12.13(b)].
b. What is the resulting approximation for $\psi(u)$, $u \ge 0$?

*Miscellaneous*

12.20. In the context of formula (12.4.1) let $G_i = U_i - U_{i-1}$ denote the insurer's gain between times $i-1$ and $i$. Suppose that $G_1$, $G_2$, ... are independent, identically distributed random variables. Suppose further that $u(x) = -e^{-\alpha x}$, $\alpha > 0$, is the insurer's utility function. Show that

$$E[u(U_{n+1})|U_n = x] \ge u(x)$$

if and only if $\alpha \le \tilde{R}$, and interpret the result.

12.21. If we change the time units so that the new units are $f$ times the old units (for some $f > 0$), and let $\tilde{c}$, $\tilde{\lambda}$, $\tilde{\psi}(u,t)$ denote parameters of the model in terms of the new units,
a. what are these new parameters in terms of $c$, $\lambda$ and $\psi(u,t)$?
b. For which value of $f$ is $\tilde{\lambda} = 1$? (Some authors refer to these units as **operational time**.)

*Appendix*

12.22. Suppose that all claims are of size 1.
a. State the equation for $\psi(u)$ that corresponds to (12.A.12).
b. Solve the equation if $0 \le u \le 1$.

Chapter 13
## APPLICATIONS OF RISK THEORY

**13**

## 13.1
## Introduction

The collective risk model was developed in Chapters 11 and 12. This model is built on the assumptions that a collection of policies generates a random number of claims in each period and that each claim can be for a random amount. To apply the model, one needs information about the distribution of the number of claims and the distribution of individual claim amounts. The selection of these distributions was discussed in Section 11.3 and only definitional remarks will be added in this chapter for the distribution of the number of claims. Here, the distribution of individual claim amounts will be illustrated in terms of four different lines of insurance, fire, automobile, short-term disability, and hospital.

We will discuss two methods of approximating the individual risk theory model for a portfolio of insurances by a collective model. For short-term situations, this provides the means of substituting collective models for individual models.

The concept of stop-loss reinsurance for a portfolio of policies is explored in general, and in relation to compound Poisson models. For the latter, the recursive method of Section 11.4 for calculating the distribution of aggregate claims provides the means for the calculation of net stop-loss reinsurance premiums. Additionally, we will discuss the interpretation of one form of group insurance dividend formula as a stop-loss insurance.

The effect of reinsurance on the adjustment coefficient, and hence on the probability of ruin, will be examined for various forms of reinsurance.

The main purpose of this chapter is to indicate various ways of applying risk theory to insurance problems.

## 13.2
## Claim Amount
## Distributions

In order to provide an idea of the broad range of applications of risk theory models, four specific but diverse applications will be presented in this section. Here the discussion will be of the individual claim amount distribution. This can then be combined with probabilities of individual claims occurring, to provide an individual risk model, or be compounded with a distribution for number of claims from a collection of insurances, to provide a collective risk model. The applications suggested in this section might be used by an insurance company in managing a line of business or block of similar policies, or by an industrial firm using modeling in its risk management program.

**Fire Insurance:**

In this line of insurance, the claim event is a fire in an insured structure that creates a loss. Because fires may cause heavy damage, adequate probability should be assigned to the higher claim amounts by the d.f. $P(x)$. In actuarial literature, some standard distributions have been suggested. Three of these distributions are listed in Table 13.1.

**Table 13.1**
**Typical Claim Amount Distributions**

| Name | $p(x)$ | Mean | Variance |
|---|---|---|---|
| Lognormal | $(x\,\sigma\sqrt{2\pi})^{-1}\exp\left\{\dfrac{-(\log x - m)^2}{2\sigma^2}\right\},$ $x > 0,\quad \sigma > 0$ | $\exp\,(m + \sigma^2/2)$ | $(e^{\sigma^2} - 1)\exp(2m + \sigma^2)$ |
| Pareto | $\dfrac{\alpha\,x_0^\alpha}{x^{\alpha+1}}$ $x > x_0 > 0,\quad \alpha > 0$ | $\dfrac{\alpha\,x_0}{\alpha - 1}$ $\alpha > 1$ | $\dfrac{\alpha\,x_0^2}{(\alpha - 2)(\alpha - 1)^2}$ $\alpha > 2$ |
| Mixture of Exponentials | $p\,\alpha e^{-\alpha x} + q\,\beta e^{-\beta x}$ $x > 0,\quad 0 < p < 1,\quad q = 1 - p \quad \alpha,\beta > 0$ | $\dfrac{p}{\alpha} + \dfrac{q}{\beta}$ | $\dfrac{p(1+q)}{\alpha^2} + \dfrac{q(1+p)}{\beta^2} - \dfrac{2pq}{\alpha\beta}$ |

An indication of the wide dispersion of probability in the case of the Pareto distribution is given by the fact that the mean does not exist unless $\alpha > 1$ and the variance does not exist unless $\alpha > 2$.

To apply one of these standard distributions, the parameters of the distribution could be estimated from a sample of claim amounts.

### Automobile Physical Damage:

In this line of insurance, a claim event is an incident causing damage to an insured autombile. The claim amount will not have the wide variability found in fire insurance. For this reason, the gamma distribution (11.5.6) has been used on occasion for the claim amount distribution. Again, the parameters of the distribution could be estimated from a sample of claim amounts.

### Short-Term Disability Insurance:

This insurance provides income benefits to disabled lives. Usually there is a defined waiting period, 7 days for example, following the occurrence of disability until benefits commence. There is also an upper limit on the payment period, such as 13 weeks. When issued to a group, the insurance is called *group weekly indemnity insurance.*

The benefit is a fixed amount per day and the amount of claim is directly proportional to the period of time the disability claim has continued beyond the waiting period. Let $Y$ be a random variable representing such period of time. From claim statistics, the distribution of $Y$ can be estimated and tabulated in a form such as in Table 13.2. The reader will note the analogy between the function represented in the second column of Table 13.2 and the survival function discussed for life tables in Chapter 3. As used in this case, the function is referred to as a *continuance function.* It yields probabilities of continuance or survival of a disability claim for the indicated lengths of time. Similar to the way the survival function can be used to express various probabilities of survival and death, the continuance function can be employed to provide various probabilities of continuance and of termination of disability.

# Chapter 13

## APPLICATIONS OF RISK THEORY

In applying a collective risk model for a group disability income insurance of the type illustrated, $\Pr(N = n)$ should be interpreted as the probability that $n$ disabilities, each of which continues at least 7 days, occur during the insurance term among the group of insureds.

**Table 13.2
Illustrative
Distribution of $Y$,
the Length of Claim
Under Group Weekly
Disability Income
Insurance (13-Week
Maximum Benefit,
7-Day Waiting Period)**

| Length of Claim (in Days) $y$ | $\Pr(Y > y)$ | $\Pr(Y = y)$ |
|---|---|---|
| 0 | 1.00000 | — |
| 1 | 0.96500 | 0.03500 |
| 2 | 0.93026 | 0.03474 |
| 3 | 0.89677 | 0.03349 |
| 4 | 0.86359 | 0.03318 |
| 5 | 0.83164 | 0.03195 |
| 6 | 0.80004 | 0.03160 |
| 7 | 0.76964 | 0.03040 |
| 8 | 0.73962 | 0.03002 |
| 9 | 0.71077 | 0.02885 |
| 10 | 0.68376 | 0.02701 |
| 11 | 0.65846 | 0.02530 |
| 12 | 0.63476 | 0.02370 |
| 13 | 0.61254 | 0.02222 |
| 14 | 0.59171 | 0.02083 |
| 15 | 0.57218 | 0.01953 |
| 16 | 0.55387 | 0.01831 |
| 17 | 0.53615 | 0.01772 |
| 18 | 0.51953 | 0.01662 |
| 19 | 0.50342 | 0.01611 |
| 20 | 0.48832 | 0.01510 |
| 21 | 0.47367 | 0.01465 |
| 22 | 0.45993 | 0.01374 |
| 23 | 0.44659 | 0.01334 |
| 24 | 0.43364 | 0.01295 |
| 25 | 0.42150 | 0.01214 |
| 26 | 0.40970 | 0.01180 |
| 27 | 0.39864 | 0.01106 |
| 28 | 0.38788 | 0.01076 |
| 31 | — | 0.06361* |
| 35 | 0.32427 | — |
| 38 | — | 0.04832 |
| 42 | 0.27595 | — |
| 45 | — | 0.03753 |
| 49 | 0.23842 | — |
| 52 | — | 0.02980 |
| 56 | 0.20862 | — |
| 59 | — | 0.02399 |
| 63 | 0.18463 | — |
| 66 | — | 0.01939 |
| 70 | 0.16524 | — |
| 73 | — | 0.01586 |
| 77 | 0.14938 | — |
| 80 | — | 0.01300 |
| 84 | 0.13638 | — |
| 87 | — | 0.01077 |
| 91 | 0.00000 | 0.12561 |
|  |  | 1.00000 |

*For convenience, claim terminations of a week from here on have been considered as terminations at the end of the third day of the week.

# APPLICATIONS OF RISK THEORY

If the income benefit is an amount $c$ per day, the claim amount distribution is given by

$$p(x) = \Pr\left(Y = \frac{x}{c}\right) \qquad x = c, 2c, 3c, \ldots, 28c, 31c, \ldots, 87c, 91c.$$

Here, for this short-term insurance, interest is not considered.

**Hospital Insurance:**

Here we consider hospital insurance that provides a flat daily benefit during hospitalization. A hospitalization continuance table can be used to produce a p.f. for length of stay in a hospital for each hospitalization. A graph of a hospitalization continuance function is given in Figure 13.1.

In applying a collective risk model to a hospital insurance of this type issued to a group of lives, $\Pr(N = n)$ should be interpreted as the probability that $n$ hospitalizations, which meet the definition contained in the policy, occur during the period to members of the covered group. If the benefit amount is $c$ per day, the p.f. of the claim amount is given by

$$p(x) = \Pr\left(Y = \frac{x}{c}\right) \qquad x = c, 2c, \ldots, mc$$

where the random variable $Y$ represents the length of hospitalization in days and $m$ is the maximum number of days for which benefits are paid.

The use of risk models in these applications permits the required total pure premium to be estimated. In addition, this estimate may be supplemented with statements about variability of losses.

**Figure 13.1
Continuance Function
for Hospital Insurance**

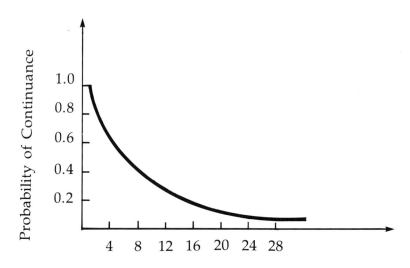

Duration of Confinement (Days)

# Chapter 13
## APPLICATIONS OF RISK THEORY

### 13.3 Approximating the Individual Model

The individual and collective risk models are alternative constructions designed to capture key aspects of insurance systems. Each model leads to the development of a distribution of total claims for the insurance system being modeled. In this section we shall develop two methods by which the compound Poisson distribution, usually associated with the collective risk model, can be used to approximate the distribution of total claims in the individual model.

We consider the individual model developed in Chapter 2 for application to a group of $n$ policies. The total claims in a policy period for the group is $S = X_1 + X_2 + \cdots + X_n$ where $X_j$ is the claim that results from policy $j$ ($j = 1,2,\ldots,n$). We distinguish between the occurrence of a claim and its amount, and we write

$$X_j = I_j B_j. \tag{13.3.1}$$

Here $I_j$ is 1 if policy $j$ leads to a claim and 0 otherwise; $B_j$ is the amount of such a claim, given that it occurs. On the assumption that $I_j$, $B_j$, $j = 1,2,\ldots,n$, are mutually independent, it follows that

$$E[S] = \sum_{j=1}^{n} q_j \mu_j \tag{13.3.2}$$

and

$$\text{Var}[S] = \sum_{j=1}^{n} q_j(1 - q_j)\mu_j^2 + \sum_{j=1}^{n} q_j \sigma_j^2, \tag{13.3.3}$$

[see (2.2.25) and (2.2.26)] where $q_j$ denotes the probability that policy $j$ leads to a claim and $\mu_j = E[B_j]$, $\sigma_j^2 = \text{Var}[B_j]$.

We shall denote the d.f. of $B_j$ by $P_j(x)$. If a claim occurs, the probability that it comes from policy $j$ is, by Bayes Theorem, approximately $q_j/(q_1 + q_2 + \cdots + q_n)$. Then by the law of total probability, the d.f. of the amount of a given claim is approximately

$$\sum_{j=1}^{n} \frac{q_j P_j(x)}{q_1 + \cdots + q_n}. \tag{13.3.4}$$

We shall consider two methods of approximating the distribution of $S$ by a compound Poisson distribution.

The first method uses the compound Poisson distribution with Poisson parameter

$$\lambda = q_1 + q_2 + \cdots + q_n \tag{13.3.5}$$

and d.f. of individual claim amounts

$$P(x) = \sum_{j=1}^{n} \frac{q_j}{\lambda} P_j(x). \tag{13.3.6}$$

The interpretation of (13.3.5) is that the expected number of claims in the compound Poisson model is the same as in the original individual risk model. Similarly, (13.3.6) means that the distribution of a claim, given that it has occurred, is the same in the two models, as can be seen from (13.3.4).

The compound Poisson distribution specified by (13.3.5) and (13.3.6) can also be explained as follows: In the individual model, the number of claims produced by policy $j$ is a Bernoulli random variable. Now we approximate its distribution by the Poisson distribution with parameter $q_j$. Correspondingly, the distribution of $X_j$ is approximated by the compound Poisson distribution given by $q_j$ and $P_j(x)$. Then we use Theorem 11.1 to approximate the distribution of $S$ by the compound Poisson distribution given by (13.3.5) and (13.3.6).

From (13.3.6), it follows that

$$p_k = \sum_{j=1}^{n} \frac{q_j}{\lambda} E[B_j^k] \qquad k = 1, 2, \dots. \tag{13.3.7}$$

In particular,

$$p_1 = \sum_{j=1}^{n} \frac{q_j}{\lambda} \mu_j$$

and

$$p_2 = \sum_{j=1}^{n} \frac{q_j}{\lambda} (\mu_j^2 + \sigma_j^2).$$

Thus, the mean of the approximating compound Poisson distribution, $\lambda p_1$, coincides with the mean of the total claims in the original individual model [see (13.3.2)]. On the other hand, the variance of the approximating compound Poisson distribution, $\lambda p_2$, is

$$\sum_{j=1}^{n} q_j (\mu_j^2 + \sigma_j^2) \tag{13.3.8}$$

and exceeds the variance of total claims in the individual model [see (13.3.3)]. However, if the $q_j$'s are small, the two variances are approximately the same.

Let us consider the special case where the claim amount for each policy is constant, $B_j = b_j$, so that $\mu_j = b_j$ and $\sigma_j = 0$. Then the p.f. of individual claim amounts according to (13.3.6) is

$$p(x) = \sum_{b_j = x} \frac{q_j}{\lambda} \tag{13.3.9}$$

where the sum is taken over the policies for which $b_j = x$. Furthermore, the ratio of the variance of total claims in the individual model [see (13.3.3)] to the variance of the approximating compound Poisson distribution [see (13.3.8)] is

$$\frac{\sum_{j=1}^{n} q_j b_j^2 (1 - q_j)}{\sum_{j=1}^{n} q_j b_j^2}. \tag{13.3.10}$$

# APPLICATIONS OF RISK THEORY

This ratio can be interpreted as a weighted average of the probabilities of no claims, $1 - q_j$.

**Example 13.1:**

In Example 2.3 we considered a portfolio of 1800 policies. Approximate the distribution of aggregate claims by a compound Poisson distribution, and discuss the resulting approximation for the variance of aggregate claims.

**Solution:**

According to (13.3.5),

$$\lambda = 500\,(0.02) + 500\,(0.02) + 300\,(0.1) + 500\,(0.1) = 100.$$

According to (13.3.9)

$$p(1) = \frac{500\,(0.02) + 300\,(0.1)}{100} = 0.4$$

$$p(2) = \frac{500\,(0.02) + 500\,(0.1)}{100} = 0.6.$$

Then $p_2 = p(1) + 4\,p(2) = 2.8$, and the variance of the compound Poisson approximation is $\lambda\,p_2 = 280$. As expected, this exceeds the variance of aggregate claims in the individual model, which was found to be 256 in Example 2.3. ▼

The second method uses the compound Poisson distribution with Poisson parameter

$$\tilde{\lambda} = \tilde{\lambda}_1 + \tilde{\lambda}_2 + \cdots + \tilde{\lambda}_n \qquad (13.3.11)$$

where $\tilde{\lambda}_j = -\log\,(1 - q_j)$, and d.f. of individual claim amounts

$$\tilde{P}(x) = \sum_{j=1}^{n} \frac{\tilde{\lambda}_j}{\tilde{\lambda}} P_j(x). \qquad (13.3.12)$$

The motivation for (13.3.11) and (13.3.12) is similar to that for (13.3.5) and (13.3.6). The key difference is that in (13.3.5) the expected numbers of claims in the two models are matched while (13.3.11) implies

$$e^{-\tilde{\lambda}} = \prod_{j=1}^{n} (1 - q_j);$$

that is, the probabilities of no claims are the same in the two models.

**Example 13.2:**

For the portfolio of 1800 policies studied in Examples 2.3 and 13.1, calculate the compound Poisson approximation to the distribution of aggregate claims by the second method.

**Solution:**

$$\tilde{\lambda} = -500\log\,(0.98) - 500\log\,(0.98) - 300\log\,(0.9)$$

$$-500\log\,(0.9) = 104.5$$

$$\bar{p}(1) = \frac{-500 \log (0.98) - 300 \log (0.9)}{104.5} = 0.399$$

$$\bar{p}(2) = \frac{-500 \log (0.98) - 500 \log (0.9)}{104.5} = 0.601.$$  ▼

In this section we have presented two methods for approximating the distribution of aggregate claims in the individual model by a compound Poisson distribution. If all the $q_j$'s for the individual model are small (which could well be the case in connection with life insurance policies), the two methods produce very similar results since, in that case,

$$\tilde{\lambda}_j = -\log (1 - q_j) = q_j + \frac{1}{2} q_j^2 + \cdots \cong q_j.$$

**13.4
Stop-Loss
Reinsurance**

The concept of an insurance with a deductible was discussed in Section 1.5. A definition was given in (1.5.1) and a property of optimality was established in Theorem 1.1. When such a coverage is written for a collection of insurance risks it is called stop-loss reinsurance, which is the topic of this section. In a given application, $S$ may denote the total claims in a given period for an insurance company, or for a block of business of a company, or for a life or health group insurance contract.

For a stop-loss contract with deductible $d$, the amount paid by the reinsurer to the ceding insurer is

$$I_d = \begin{cases} 0 & S \le d \\ S - d & S > d. \end{cases} \tag{13.4.1}$$

Note that $I_d$, as a function of the aggregate claims $S$, is also a random variable. The amount of claims retained by the ceding insurer is

$$S - I_d = \begin{cases} S & S \le d \\ d & S > d. \end{cases} \tag{13.4.2}$$

Thus, the amount retained is bounded by $d$, which explains the name stop-loss contract.

We shall discuss methods to calculate $E[I_d]$, the net stop-loss (reinsurance) premium when the deductible is $d$. We denote the d.f. of $S$ by $F(x)$, and first assume that $S$ has a p.d.f. $f(x)$. Then

$$E[I_d] = \int_d^\infty (x - d) f(x) \, dx. \tag{13.4.3}$$

Usually, $S$ cannot assume any negative values. Then we can extend the integral to $(0,\infty)$ and subtract the integral over $(0,d)$ to see that

$$E[I_d] = E[S] - d + \int_0^d (d - x) f(x) \, dx. \tag{13.4.4}$$

# Chapter 13

## APPLICATIONS OF RISK THEORY

If we set

$$f(x) = -\frac{d}{dx}[1 - F(x)]$$

in (13.4.3), and integrate by parts, we get

$$E[I_d] = \int_d^\infty [1 - F(x)]\,dx. \tag{13.4.5}$$

Similarly, we obtain

$$E[I_d] = E[S] - \int_0^d [1 - F(x)]\,dx \tag{13.4.6}$$

from (13.4.4).

Each of these four expressions for $E[I_d]$ has its own merit. If $E[S]$ is available, formulas (13.4.4) and (13.4.6) are preferable where numerical integration is required, since the range of integration is finite. This reduces the possibilities of inaccurate approximation of $f(x)$ for large $x$. Formulas (13.4.5) and (13.4.6) hold for general distributions, including those of discrete or of mixed type. If the distribution of $S$ is given in analytical form, for example, if it is a normal or gamma distribution, (13.4.3) might be the most tractable formula.

**Example 13.3:**
If $S$ has a gamma distribution, that is, if $F(x) = G(x:\alpha,\beta)$ [see (11.5.6)], show that

$$E[I_d] = \frac{\alpha}{\beta}[1 - G(d:\alpha + 1, \beta)] - d\,[1 - G(d:\alpha,\beta)].$$

**Solution:**
From (13.4.3), we obtain

$$E[I_d] = \int_d^\infty x f(x)\,dx - d\,[1 - F(d)]$$

$$= \int_d^\infty \frac{\beta^\alpha}{\Gamma(\alpha)} x^\alpha e^{-\beta x}\,dx - d\,[1 - G(d:\alpha,\beta)].$$

Since $\alpha\,\Gamma(\alpha) = \Gamma(\alpha + 1)$, the integrand is $\alpha/\beta$ times the gamma p.d.f. with parameters $\alpha + 1$ and $\beta$. Hence the given formula follows. ▼

**Example 13.4:**
Suppose that $a,b$ are numbers with $\Pr(a < S < b) = 0$. Show that, for $a < d < b$, $E[I_d]$ can be obtained from $E[I_a]$ and $E[I_b]$ by linear interpolation.

**Solution:**
From the assumption, it follows that $F(x) = F(a)$ for $a \le x < b$. We use this in (13.4.6) to see that

$$E[I_d] = E[I_a] - (d - a)\,[1 - F(a)],$$

that is, $E[I_d]$ is a linear function of $d$ in the interval $[a,b]$. ▼

We shall now consider the case where the possible values of $S$ are nonnegative integers and denote by $f(x)$ the p.f. of $S$ ($x = 0,1,2,\ldots$). In the following, it is assumed that the deductible $d$ is an integer. According to the preceding example, the net stop-loss premium for noninteger deductibles can be obtained by linear interpolation.

The formulas

$$E[I_d] = \sum_{x=d+1}^{\infty} (x - d) f(x) \qquad (13.4.7)$$

and

$$E[I_d] = E[S] - d + \sum_{x=0}^{d-1} (d - x) f(x) \qquad (13.4.8)$$

are the counterparts of (13.4.3) and (13.4.4). The integrals in formulas (13.4.5) and (13.4.6) can be written as sums, since $F(x)$ is piecewise constant. We obtain

$$E[I_d] = \sum_{x=d}^{\infty} [1 - F(x)] \qquad (13.4.9)$$

and

$$E[I_d] = E[S] - \sum_{x=0}^{d-1} [1 - F(x)]. \qquad (13.4.10)$$

**Example 13.5:**  For the aggregate claims distribution in Example 11.2 calculate, by two methods, the net stop-loss premium when the deductible is 7.

> **Solution:**
> According to (13.4.7),
>
> $$E[I_7] = f(8) + 2 f(9) = 0.0028.$$
>
> Alternatively, according to (13.4.9),
>
> $$E[I_7] = [1 - F(7)] + [1 - F(8)] = 0.0028. \qquad \blacktriangledown$$

**Example 13.6:**  Calculate $E[I_6]$ for the compound Poisson distribution used in Example 11.6.

> **Solution:**
> Since the compound Poisson distribution has an infinite range, the use of (13.4.8) and (13.4.10) is more practical here. For example, using (13.4.8) we obtain
>
> $$E[I_6] = E[S] - 6 + \sum_{x=0}^{5} (6 - x) f(x)$$
>
> $$= 1.7 - 6 + 4.3547 = 0.0547. \qquad \blacktriangledown$$

In general, from (13.4.9), we obtain a recursive formula

$$E[I_{d+1}] = E[I_d] - [1 - F(d)] \qquad d = 0,1,2,\ldots. \qquad (13.4.11)$$

Thus $E[I_d]$ can be obtained recursively with starting value $E[I_0] = E[S]$.

# Chapter 13

# APPLICATIONS OF RISK THEORY

This recursive approach is particularly convenient if $S$ has a compound Poisson distribution with Poisson parameter $\lambda$ and a p.f. $p(x)$, $x = 1,2,\ldots$, of individual claim amounts. In this case, $f(x)$ also can be calculated recursively [see (11.4.15)]. Thus, starting with

$$f(0) = F(0) = e^{-\lambda}$$

and

$$E[I_0] = \lambda\, p_1,$$

we use the recursive formulas

$$f(x) = \frac{\lambda}{x} \sum_{j=1}^{\infty} j\, p(j)\, f(x - j)$$

$$F(x) = F(x - 1) + f(x)$$

$$E[I_x] = E[I_{x-1}] - [1 - F(x - 1)]$$

successively for $x = 1,2,3,\ldots$.

**Example 13.7:**

Assume that $S$ has a compound Poisson distribution with $\lambda = 1.5$, $p(1) = 2/3$, $p(2) = 1/3$. Calculate values of $f(x)$, $F(x)$, $E[I_x]$ for $x = 0,1,2,\ldots,6$.

**Solution:**
First,

$$f(0) = F(0) = e^{-1.5} = 0.223$$

and

$$E[I_0] = \lambda\, p_1 = 1.5\,\frac{4}{3} = 2.$$

Then, since $\lambda\, j\, p(j) = 1$ for $j = 1,2$,

$$f(x) = \frac{1}{x}[f(x - 1) + f(x - 2)] \qquad x = 1,2,\ldots,6.$$

Note that $f(1) = f(0)$.

The remaining steps and the results are displayed below.

| $x$ | $f(x) = \frac{1}{x}[f(x-1) + f(x-2)]$ | $F(x) = F(x-1) + f(x)$ | $E[I_x] = E[I_{x-1}] + F(x-1) - 1$ |
|---|---|---|---|
| 0 | 0.223 | 0.223 | 2.000 |
| 1 | 0.223 | 0.446 | 1.223 |
| 2 | 0.223 | 0.669 | 0.669 |
| 3 | 0.149 | 0.818 | 0.338 |
| 4 | 0.093 | 0.911 | 0.156 |
| 5 | 0.048 | 0.959 | 0.067 |
| 6 | 0.024 | 0.983 | 0.026 |

▼

Our discussion has focused on the calculation of $E[I_d]$, the net stop-loss premium. Typically, this is merely a lower bound for an actual stop-loss premium. The actual premium will contain a loading that reflects the variability of the reinsurer's payment, $I_d$. One measure of this variability is

$$\text{Var}[I_d] = E[I_d^2] - E[I_d]^2.$$

In the discrete case, it is possible to compute $E[I_d^2]$ recursively (see Exercise 13.8).

We now turn to a dividend formula of group insurance because it is identical in concept to a stop-loss reinsurance. You will recall that group insurance is the name used when an insurance covering many individuals is purchased in the form of a single contract by a sponsor such as an employer. An example was given in the short-term disability illustration in Section 13.2. In this section we shall discuss one type of dividend formula that can be used in relation to group insurance.

We shall assume that for a gross premium of $G$ the insurer will provide full coverage for the total claims $S$ in a given period. With the policyholder's knowledge, the premium contains a substantial loading $G - E[S] > 0$. Consequently, the policyholder anticipates a dividend $D$, at the end of the period, which will be a function of $S$. Specifically, we assume that the dividend is of the form

$$D = \begin{cases} kG - S & S < kG \\ 0 & S \geq kG \end{cases} \tag{13.4.12}$$

where $0 < k < 1$. Thus the policyholder pays $G$ and in return receives $S$ and $D$.

We now consider the expected value of $D$. For notational convenience, we assume that the distribution of $S$ is continuous and denote the p.d.f. of $S$ by $f(x)$; the discrete case is very similar, as will be seen in Example 13.8. From (13.4.12), we have

$$E[D] = \int_0^{kG} (kG - x) f(x)\,dx. \tag{13.4.13}$$

Presumably, the insurer will set $k$ small enough so that $E[S] + E[D] < G$.

**Example 13.8:**

For a premium of 5 the insurer covers total claims $S$, having the compound Poisson distribution considered in Example 13.7. The insurer agrees to pay a dividend equal to the excess of 80% of the premium over the claims. Calculate $G - E[S] - E[D]$ (this is the expected value of the amount available to cover expenses, security loading, and so on).

**Solution:**
The dividend is of the form (13.4.12) with $k = 0.8$. Thus

$$E[D] = 4 f(0) + 3 f(1) + 2 f(2) + f(3) = 2.156.$$

Chapter 13

# APPLICATIONS OF RISK THEORY

Then

$$G - E[S] - E[D] = 5 - 2 - 2.156 = 0.844. \qquad \blacktriangledown$$

If we extend the integral in (13.4.13) to $\infty$, we obtain

$$E[D] = \int_0^\infty (kG - x) f(x)\, dx + \int_{kG}^\infty (x - kG) f(x)\, dx.$$

Thus

$$E[D] = kG - E[S] + E[I_{kG}] \qquad (13.4.14)$$

where $I_{kG}$ is the payment under a stop-loss contract with deductible $kG$. If the net stop-loss premium $E[I_d]$ has been calculated already for various deductibles, this is a convenient formula to obtain $E[D]$.

**Example 13.9:**    Use (13.4.14) to obtain $E[D]$ in Example 13.8.

**Solution:**
Since $E[I_4] = 0.156$,

$$E[D] = 4 - 2 + 0.156 = 2.156. \qquad \blacktriangledown$$

There are more facets to the connection between a dividend formula of the type (13.4.12) and a stop-loss contract. We start with the identity

$$S + D = kG + I_{kG}. \qquad (13.4.15)$$

This can be verified by distinguishing the cases: $S \leq kG$ where both sides equal $kG$; $S > kG$ where both sides equal $S$. Subtracting $G$ from both sides, we obtain

$$S + D - G = I_{kG} - (1 - k)G \qquad (13.4.16)$$

having the following interpretation: The balance of the claim payments and dividends received over the premium paid is the same as the corresponding balance for a stop-loss contract with deductible $kG$ and stop-loss premium $(1 - k)G$.

This interpretation suggests that the insurer can regard the premium as split into two components,

$$G = kG + (1 - k)G. \qquad (13.4.17)$$

Claims are first paid from $kG$, and any remaining balance $kG - S$ (for $S < kG$) is paid as a dividend in accordance with (13.4.12). The second component, $(1 - k)G$, is used to provide a stop-loss reinsurance with deductible $kG$.

Formula (13.4.15) rearranged as

$$D = kG - S + I_{kG}$$

yields (13.4.14) again when expectations are taken on each side.

## 13.5
## The Effect of Reinsurance on the Probability of Ruin

Questions about type and amount of reinsurance to purchase can be answered in various ways. One approach is provided by the insurer adopting a utility function. Then, from all available reinsurance arrangements, the insurer selects the one yielding the highest expected utility. This ideal approach, which is very simple in concept, is not commonly used in practice.

In preparation for a second approach, we observe that in Chapter 12 we considered the insurer's premium rate $c$ to have a relative security loading $\theta$ such that $c = (1 + \theta)\lambda p_1$ [see (12.3.1)]. Here $\theta$ did not include any loading for expenses, and all of $c$ was available for the risk process. For our further discussion of reinsurance, it is useful to define a reinsurance loading $\xi$ by the formula

(reinsurance premium rate)

$$= (1 + \xi)(\text{expected rate of reinsurance payment}). \quad (13.5.1)$$

Here the reinsurance premium rate, as determined by the reinsurer, will provide for reinsurance payments, expenses, security and profit. The insurer can express the reinsurance premium rate in the format of the right-hand side of (13.5.1) to determine $\xi$. In particular, for the net stop-loss premium rate $E[I_d]$, given by (13.4.3), the loading $\xi$ is 0.

The second approach recognizes that the purchase of reinsurance is necessarily a compromise between expected gain and security. Because of the loading contained in the reinsurance premium, the purchase of reinsurance will reduce the insurer's expected gain; on the other hand, a reasonable reinsurance arrangement will increase security in some sense. For this approach, a required standard of security is first defined. Then only reinsurance arrangements satisfying this standard are considered. From this set of admissible arrangements, the insurer selects the one that allows for the highest expected gain.

We will consider one particular measure of security, the probability of ruin. One might require, for instance, that the probability of ruin not be more than 1%. Since explicit formulas for the probability of ruin are available only in special cases, we will restrict our discussion to the effects that various reinsurance arrangements have on the adjustment coefficient. Statements about the adjustment coefficient can always be used to obtain information about the probability of ruin [see (12.3.5), (12.3.7) or (12.4.8)].

At this point the name adjustment coefficient reveals its meaning: If a certain reinsurance arrangement produces a value of $R$ (or $\bar{R}$) that is not large enough, the arrangement needs to be adjusted.

**Example 13.10:**

An insurer has a portfolio producing annual aggregate claims that are independent and identically distributed; their common distribution is compound Poisson with $\lambda = 1.5$, $p(1) = 2/3$, $p(2) = 1/3$ (see Example 13.7). The annual premiums received are $c = 2.5$.

# APPLICATIONS OF RISK THEORY

a. Calculate the adjustment coefficient that results from this portfolio.
b. Stop-loss coverage can be obtained for a reinsurance loading charge of 100%. Calculate the adjustment coefficient if a stop-loss contract is purchased with a deductible of

$$(i)\ 3 \quad (ii)\ 4 \quad (iii)\ 5.$$

Also, compare these alternatives from the point of view of expected gain.

**Solution:**
a. In this case, $R = \tilde{R}$ and we can obtain $R$ from (12.4.6) or (12.3.2). The latter condition is that

$$1.5 + 2.5\,r = e^r + (0.5)\,e^{2r}.$$

We obtain $R = \tilde{R} = 0.28$.

b. We consider case (i), $d = 3$, in detail. In Example 13.7 we computed $E[I_3] = 0.338$. The actual stop-loss premium is twice this amount, or 0.676. Thus the insurer's retained premium in year $i$ is $2.5 - 0.676 = 1.824$ and retained claims are

$$\hat{W}_i = \begin{cases} W_i & W_i = 0,1,2,3 \\ 3 & W_i > 3 \end{cases}$$

where $W_i$ denotes the aggregate claims of year $i$. According to (12.4.5), $\tilde{R}$ is the positive solution of the equation

$$e^{-1.824r}\left[\sum_{x=0}^{2} f(x)\,e^{xr} + [1 - F(2)]\,e^{3r}\right] = 1$$

(see Example 13.7). We calculate $\tilde{R} = 0.25$. The expected gain per year is

(the expected gain in the absence of reinsurance, $c - E[S_i] = 2.5 - 2 = 0.5$)

− (the expected return of the reinsurer, which, because the reinsurer charges at rate $2\,E[I_3]$, is $E[I_3] = 0.338$)

= 0.162.

The calculations for cases (ii) and (iii) are similar. The results are displayed below where $d = \infty$ represents the case of no reinsurance.

| Stop-loss Deductible, $d$ | Adjustment Coefficient, $\tilde{R}$ | Expected Gain |
|---|---|---|
| 3 | 0.25 | 0.162 |
| 4 | 0.35 | 0.344 |
| 5 | 0.34 | 0.433 |
| $\infty$ | 0.28 | 0.500 |

With respect to security (as measured by the adjustment coefficient), a deductible of 4 is better than one of 5, which in turn is better than no reinsurance. With respect to expected gain, this order is reversed. Further, it can be observed that selecting a deductible of 3 would be an irrational decision. It is worse than no reinsurance with respect to both security and expected gain. ▼

In the following we shall consider reinsurance arrangements where the reinsurer's payments depend on the individual claim amounts. In general, such a coverage is defined in terms of a function $h(x)$ with $0 \le h(x) \le x$ for all $x$. The interpretation is that $h(x)$ is the amount payable (by the reinsurer to the insurer) if a claim is of size $x$. A special case is **proportional reinsurance** where

$$h(x) = \alpha x \qquad 0 \le \alpha \le 1, \tag{13.5.2}$$

that is, where the reinsurer reimburses a constant percentage of the claim. A second case is **excess-of-loss reinsurance** where

$$h(x) = \begin{cases} 0 & x \le \beta \\ x - \beta & x > \beta \end{cases} \tag{13.5.3}$$

with $\beta \ge 0$ playing the role of a deductible. An excess-of-loss coverage is reminiscent of a stop-loss coverage [see (13.4.1)]. However, the former is applied to individual claims, while the latter is applied to aggregate claims.

We shall assume the continuous time compound Poisson model of Chapter 12 and its notation. Correspondingly, we assume that reinsurance premiums are payable continuously at a rate, say, of $c_h$. Then the adjustment coefficient, $R_h$, is the nontrivial solution of the equation

$$\lambda + (c - c_h)r = \lambda \int_0^\infty e^{r[x - h(x)]} p(x)\, dx. \tag{13.5.4}$$

This follows from (12.3.1) since the insurer now receives income at a net rate of $c - c_h$ and pays $x - h(x)$ for a claim of size $x$.

**Example 13.11:**

Suppose that claims for a compound Poisson process are given by $\lambda = 1$ and $p(x) = 1$, for $0 < x < 1$, and that premiums are received at a rate of $c = 1$. Calculate the adjustment coefficient if proportional reinsurance is purchased with $\alpha = 0, 0.1, 0.2, \ldots, 1$ and if the reinsurance loading, $\theta$, is

a. 100%
b. 140%.

**Solution:**

$$c_h = (1 + \theta)\lambda \int_0^1 h(x) p(x)\, dx$$

$$= (1 + \theta)\lambda \int_0^1 (\alpha x)(1)\, dx$$

$$= \frac{(1 + \theta)\lambda \alpha}{2}$$

Chapter 13

# APPLICATIONS OF RISK THEORY

a. Here $\theta = 1$ so that (13.5.4) is

$$1 + (1 - \alpha)r = \int_0^1 e^{r(1-\alpha)x}\,dx = \frac{e^{r(1-\alpha)} - 1}{r(1-\alpha)}. \qquad (13.5.5)$$

In the absence of reinsurance ($\alpha = 0$), the nontrivial solution of this equation is $R = 1.793$. It follows that for $\alpha \neq 0$, $1.793/(1-\alpha)$ is the nontrivial solution of (13.5.5).

b. Now we have $\theta = 1.4$, hence (13.5.4) is now

$$1 + (1 - 1.2\,\alpha)r = \frac{e^{r(1-\alpha)} - 1}{r(1-\alpha)}. \qquad (13.5.6)$$

The numerical solutions of this equation and of (13.5.5) are compared below. In part (a), the reinsurance loading coincides with the insurer's relative security loading since $c = 2\lambda p_1 = 1$ and $R$ is an increasing function of $\alpha$. In part (b), the reinsurance loading exceeds the insurer's security loading. With increasing $\alpha$, $R$ increases gradually and then decreases sharply. If the net rate of income equals the expected net claims paid by the insurer per unit time, that is, if $1 - 1.2\,\alpha = (1 - \alpha)/2$, or $\alpha = 5/7$, then the relative security loading after reinsurance is 0. This implies that there is not a positive root to (12.3.1) and that ruin is certain. For $\alpha > 5/7$, this loading is negative and ruin again is certain.

|  | Adjustment Coefficient with Proportional Reinsurance when Reinsurance Loading is: | |
|---|---|---|
| $\alpha$ | 100% | 140% |
| 0.0 | 1.793 | 1.793 |
| 0.1 | 1.993 | 1.936 |
| 0.2 | 2.242 | 2.095 |
| 0.3 | 2.562 | 2.268 |
| 0.4 | 2.989 | 2.436 |
| 0.5 | 3.587 | 2.538 |
| 0.6 | 4.483 | 2.335 |
| 0.7 | 5.978 | 0.635 |
| 0.8 | 8.966 | — |
| 0.9 | 17.933 | — |
| 1.0 | $\infty$ | — |

▼

**Example 13.12:**

Assume that the insurer in Example 13.11 can buy excess-of-loss coverage with $\beta = 0, 0.1, 0.2, \ldots, 1$. Calculate the adjustment coefficient if the reinsurance loading is

a. 100%

b. 140%.

**Solution:**

a. $c_h = 2\lambda \int_0^1 h(x) p(x) dx$

$\qquad = 2 \int_\beta^1 (x - \beta) dx = (1 - \beta)^2$

From (13.5.4) we obtain the condition for $R$:

$$1 + [1 - (1 - \beta)^2] r = \int_0^\beta e^{rx} dx + \int_\beta^1 e^{r\beta} dx$$

$$= \frac{e^{r\beta} - 1}{r} + (1 - \beta) e^{r\beta}. \qquad (13.5.7)$$

b. Reinsurance premiums are now paid at a rate of $1.2(1 - \beta)^2$. Hence the equation for $R$ becomes

$$1 + [1 - 1.2(1 - \beta)^2] r = \frac{e^{r\beta} - 1}{r} + (1 - \beta) e^{r\beta}. \qquad (13.5.8)$$

The solutions of (13.5.7) and (13.5.8) are compared below.

| Deductible $\beta$ | Adjustment Coefficient with Excess-of-Loss Reinsurance when Reinsurance Loading is: | |
|---|---|---|
| | 100% | 140% |
| 1.0 | 1.793 | 1.793 |
| 0.9 | 1.833 | 1.828 |
| 0.8 | 1.940 | 1.920 |
| 0.7 | 2.116 | 2.062 |
| 0.6 | 2.378 | 2.259 |
| 0.5 | 2.768 | 2.518 |
| 0.4 | 3.373 | 2.840 |
| 0.3 | 4.400 | 3.138 |
| 0.2 | 6.478 | 2.525 |
| 0.1 | 12.746 | — |
| 0.0 | $\infty$ | — |

We observe the same phenomena as in the case of proportional coverage: If the reinsurance loading equals the insurer's security loading, the adjustment coefficient increases with the degree of reinsurance. If, however, the reinsurance loading exceeds the insurer's loading, the adjustment coefficient will increase up to a certain point and then decrease rapidly. ▼

**Example 13.13:** Compare the results of Examples 13.11 and 13.12 for pairs of $\alpha$ and $\beta$ such that the reinsurer's expected payments are the same, that is, if $\alpha/2 = (1 - \beta)^2/2$.

Chapter 13

# APPLICATIONS OF RISK THEORY

**Solution:**
For such pairs of $\alpha$ and $\beta$, the corresponding values of the adjustment coefficient are given below.

| | | Adjustment Coefficients, with Equal Payments Expected from Reinsurer, when Reinsurance Loading is: | | | |
|---|---|---|---|---|---|
| | | 100% | | 140% | |
| $\alpha$ | $\beta$ | Proportional | Excess-of-Loss | Proportional | Excess-of-Loss |
| 0.00 | 1.0 | 1.793 | 1.793 | 1.793 | 1.793 |
| 0.01 | 0.9 | 1.811 | 1.833 | 1.807 | 1.828 |
| 0.04 | 0.8 | 1.868 | 1.940 | 1.848 | 1.920 |
| 0.09 | 0.7 | 1.971 | 2.116 | 1.921 | 2.062 |
| 0.16 | 0.6 | 2.135 | 2.378 | 2.030 | 2.259 |
| 0.25 | 0.5 | 2.391 | 2.768 | 2.181 | 2.518 |
| 0.36 | 0.4 | 2.802 | 3.373 | 2.372 | 2.840 |
| 0.49 | 0.3 | 3.516 | 4.400 | 2.535 | 3.138 |
| 0.64 | 0.2 | 4.981 | 6.478 | 1.992 | 2.525 |
| 0.81 | 0.1 | 9.438 | 12.746 | — | — |
| 1.00 | 0.0 | $\infty$ | $\infty$ | — | — |

For a given reinsurance loading, the excess-of-loss coverage consistently leads to a higher adjustment coefficient than that provided by the corresponding proportional coverage. In the following, we shall see that this is not a coincidence. ▼

Somewhat similar to Theorem 1.1 is another theorem giving an optimality feature of excess-of-loss reinsurance. The proof of Theorem 13.1 is in the Appendix to this chapter.

**Theorem 13.1:**

Let an arbitrary reinsurance be defined by $h(x)$, $0 \le h(x) \le x$, and by $c_h$ its premium rate. Similarly, let an excess-of-loss reinsurance with deductible $\beta$ be defined by $h_\beta(x)$ and $c_\beta$ (simplified notation for $c_{h_\beta}$). Furthermore, let $R_h$, $R_\beta$ denote the resulting adjustment coefficients, respectively. If $E[h(X)] = E[h_\beta(X)]$ and $c_h = c_\beta$, then $R_h \le R_\beta$.

Since $c_h = (1 + \xi_h)\lambda E[h(X)]$ and $c_\beta = (1 + \xi_\beta)\lambda E[h_\beta(X)]$ where $\xi_h$ and $\xi_\beta$ are the reinsurance loadings for the respective reinsurances, the conditions of the theorem imply $\xi_h = \xi_\beta$. This limits the application of the theorem as it may not be possible to secure excess-of-loss reinsurance with the same reinsurance loading as for other reinsurances.

To illustrate this point, assume that proportional reinsurance with reinsurance loading of 100% can be obtained as an alternative to excess-of-loss reinsurance with loading of 140%. From Examples 13.11–13.13, we can see that proportional reinsurance with $\alpha = 0.49$, $\xi_h = 1$ would have a premium rate $c_h = 2(\alpha/2) = 0.49$, which is less than the rate for excess-of-loss reinsurance with $\beta = 0.3$, $\xi_\beta = 1.4$, namely, $c_\beta = 2.4(0.7)^2/2 = 0.588$. Then not only would the proportional reinsurance have a lower premium rate, but we note from Example 13.13 its resulting adjustment coefficient, 3.516, is larger than the adjustment coefficient of 3.138 resulting from the excess-of-loss reinsurance.

**13.6
Notes and
References**

A monograph by Hogg and Klugman (1984) demonstrates the use of claim statistics for selecting a claim amount distribution and estimating the parameters. Other references for this can be found in Seal (1969). The claim amount distribution for group weekly indemnity insurance was taken from papers by Miller (1951) and Bartlett (1965). The hospitalization continuance curve was derived from data in a paper by Gingery (1952).

The two methods for approximating the individual model by a collective model were suggested by Mereu (1972) and Wooddy (1973).

Calculating stop-loss premiums has been the subject of many papers. Bohman and Esscher (1963–64) reported on an extensive study of alternative methods of approximating the distribution of total claims and expected stop-loss claims. Bartlett (1965) discussed the use of the gamma distribution for the calculation of expected stop-loss claims. Bowers (1969) presented an upper bound, in terms of the mean and variance of aggregate claims, for the net stop-loss premium. This result has been generalized by Taylor (1977) and by Goovaerts and DeVylder (1980). In recent years several papers have developed methods for use with discrete claim distributions. These include Halmstad (1972), Mereu (1972), Gerber and Jones (1976), Panjer (1980).

The effect of reinsurance on the probability of ruin is discussed by Gerber (1980).

**Appendix**

**Proof of Theorem 13.1:**
We know that $R_h$ is the positive root of

$$\lambda + (c - c_h)r = \lambda M_{X-h(X)}(r)$$

and $R_\beta$ is the positive root of

$$\lambda + (c - c_\beta)r = \lambda M_{X-h_\beta(X)}(r).$$

**Figure 13.2
Proof of Theorem
13.1**

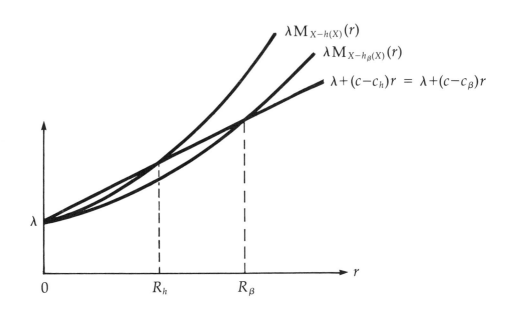

# APPLICATIONS OF RISK THEORY

Since $c_h = c_\beta$, we can see from Figure 13.2 that

$$M_{X-h(X)}(r) \geq M_{X-h_\beta(X)}(r) \qquad r > 0 \tag{13.A.1}$$

implies $R_h \leq R_\beta$.

To establish (13.A.1), we first use the convexity of the exponential function to show that

$$\exp\{r\,[x - h(x)]\} \geq \exp\{r\,[x - h_\beta(x)]\}$$
$$+ r\exp\{r\,[x - h_\beta(x)]\}\,[h_\beta(x) - h(x)].$$

Since $x - h_\beta(x) \leq \beta$ and $x - h_\beta(x) = \beta$ whenever $h_\beta(x) - h(x) > 0$, it follows that

$$\exp\{r\,[x - h(x)]\} \geq \exp\{r\,[x - h_\beta(x)]\} + r\exp\{r\beta\}\,[h_\beta(x) - h(x)].$$

Then

$$E[\exp\{r\,[X - h(X)]\}] \geq E[\exp\{r\,[X - h_\beta(X)]\}]$$
$$+ r\exp\{r\beta\}\,E[h_\beta(X) - h(X)].$$

By the hypothesis of the theorem the last expectation is 0. This yields (13.A.1), from which the theorem follows. ∎

**Exercises**

*Section 13.1*

13.1.  A term insurance provides the amount $b$ if a claim occurs. The probability of a claim occurring is $q$.
   a.  Consider the following loss random variable,

$$L = \begin{cases} b - bq & \text{with probability } q \\ 0 - bq & \text{with probability } p = 1 - q. \end{cases}$$

   Verify that $E[L] = 0$.
   b.  Calculate $\mathrm{Var}[L]$.
   c.  The security-loaded premium is taken as $bq + s\sqrt{\mathrm{Var}[L]}$. If 100 identical policies of this type are sold and the loss random variables, as defined in part (a), for these policies are mutually independent, calculate the loading factor $s$ such that the probability that the sum of these loss random variables exceeds the total security loading is less than 0.01.

*Section 13.2*

13.2.  Verify the mean and variance entries in Table 13.1.

13.3.  a.  Calculate the mean of the distribution described in Table 13.2.
   b.  By how much would the average benefit per case of disability be reduced in the short-term disability insurance illustration if the 13-week maximum were replaced by a 10-week maximum?

13.4.  Given that a disability has occurred, evaluate, on the basis of Table 13.2,

# APPLICATIONS OF RISK THEORY

a. $\Pr(3 \le Y \le 6)$
b. $\Pr(10 \le Y \le 13)$
c. $\Pr(20 \le Y \le 23)$.

*Section 13.3*

13.5. Consider a portfolio of 100 policies, each of which is for a 1-year term life insurance.

|  |  | Amount Insured | |
|---|---|---|---|
|  |  | 1 | 4 |
| **1-year** | **0.01** | 10 | 20 |
| **Mortality Rate** | **0.02** | 30 | 40 |

The matrix entries give the number of policies in the portfolio for the indicated combination of amount insured and mortality rate.
a. If $S$ represents the aggregate claims, calculate $E[S]$ and $\mathrm{Var}[S]$.
b. What compound Poisson distribution would be used for approximating the individual model by the first method? What would be the resulting approximation for $\mathrm{Var}[S]$?

13.6. Suppose that $B_j = b_j > 0$ for $j = 1,2,\ldots,n$.
a. Write expressions for the mean and variance of the compound Poisson distribution chosen according to the second method.
b. Show that the values in (a) are higher than the corresponding values obtained by the first method. [Hint: First show that $\bar{\lambda}_j > q_j$, $j = 1,2,\ldots,n$.]
c. Compute the mean and variance of the compound Poisson distribution in Example 13.2.

13.7. Calculate the probability that two claims that occur in the individual model are from policies $i$ and $j$ $(i \ne j)$.

*Section 13.4*

13.8. Suppose that the possible claims are integers. Show that
$$E[I_d^2] = E[I_{d-1}^2] - 2\,E[I_{d-1}] + 1 - F(d-1).$$

13.9. Calculate $E[I_d]$ if $S$ has the normal distribution with parameters $\mu$ and $\sigma$.

13.10. Suppose that the possible claims are integers. Calculate
a. $\Delta E[I_x]$         b. $\Delta^2 E[I_x]$.

13.11. It is known that $E[I_d] = 1 - d - (1 - d^3)/3$ for $0 \le d \le 1$ and is equal to 0 for $d > 1$. Derive the p.d.f. of the underlying distribution of aggregate claims.

13.12. If $S$ has a compound Poisson distribution given by $\lambda = 3$, $p(1) = 5/6$, $p(2) = 1/6$, calculate $f(x)$, $F(x)$, $E[I_x]$ for $x = 0,1,2$.

13.13. A dividend of the form (13.4.12) is to be used in Examples 13.8 and 13.9.
a. Calculate $G - E[S] - E[D]$ if $k = 0.9$.
b. Determine $k$ such that $G - E[S] - E[D] = 0$.

# Chapter 13

## APPLICATIONS OF RISK THEORY

13.14. A reinsurer will pay 80% of the excess of $S$ over a deductible $d$, subject to a maximum payment of $m$. Express the net premium for this coverage in terms of net stop-loss premiums.

13.15. In Example 13.7 determine $d$ such that $E[I_d] = 0.2$.

*Section 13.5*

13.16. The claims of a certain insurance portfolio form a compound Poisson process with $\lambda = 1$ and $p(x) = e^{-x}$, $x > 0$. The premiums received contain a relative security loading of $\theta > 0$.
   a. Calculate the adjustment coefficient if a proportional reinsurance of the form (13.5.2) is purchased and if the reinsurance loading is $\xi > 0$.
   b. Calculate the insurer's relative security loading after reinsuring as in (a).
   c. What restrictions are needed on $\alpha$?

13.17. In the preceding exercise, assume that excess-of-loss coverage, with deductible $\beta$ and reinsurance loading $\xi$, is available.
   a. Determine the equation from which the adjustment coefficient can be obtained.
   b. Calculate the insurer's relative security loading after reinsuring by means of the excess-of-loss coverage.

13.18. The annual claims, $W_i$, $i = 1,2,\ldots$, for an insurance company are mutually independent and identically distributed, $N(10, 4)$. The company collects a relative security loading of 25%. A reinsurer is willing to accept the risk on any part, $\alpha$, of the portfolio on a proportional basis for a reinsurance premium equal to 140% of the expected value of the claims reinsured.
   a. Express the adjustment coefficient, $\tilde{R}$, for the portfolio with proportional reinsurance as a function of $\alpha$.
   b. Determine the value of $\alpha$ that maximizes the security of the insurance company by giving the largest value of $\tilde{R}$.

*Miscellaneous*

13.19. A reinsurer with wealth $w$ and utility function $u(w)$ sets the stop-loss premium $H_d$ corresponding to a deductible $d$ so that $u(w) = E[u(w + H_d - I_d)]$ [see (1.3.5)]. Calculate $H_d$ if $u(w) = -\alpha e^{-\alpha w}$ ($\alpha > 0$) and if $S$ has the normal distribution with parameters $\mu$ and $\sigma$.

# Chapter 14
## INSURANCE MODELS INCLUDING EXPENSES

**14**

## 14.1 Introduction

The principle of equivalence was introduced in Chapter 6 as a means for determining insurance premiums. In that chapter, the principle imposed the condition that the actuarial present values of benefits and of net premiums be equal at the time the insurance is issued. In Chapter 7 this principle was applied to time periods beyond the initial date of contract. Reserves were expressed as the actuarial present value of the difference between future benefit payments and future net premium income.

The foregoing chapters were devoted, in large part, to building a comprehensive model for insurance systems based on the equivalence principle. However, this model did not incorporate several aspects of insurance practice and economic reality. For example, an insurer has cash outflows other than claim payments. Expenditures of this general type include those for taxes and licenses as well as those for selling and servicing insurance policies. These expenses must be met from premium and investment income. In this chapter we will incorporate expenses into the model for premiums and reserves.

## 14.2 General Expenses

The main ideas needed to incorporate expenses will first be examined in an extended illustration. Tables 14.1.A and B specify the salient features, selected for convenience and ease of calculation rather than for realism.

**Table 14.1.A Specifications of Illustration: Description**

| | |
|---|---|
| 1. Plan of insurance: | 3-year annual premium endowment insurance, issued to $(x)$ |
| 2. Payment basis: | Fully discrete |
| 3. Mortality: | $q_x = 0.1$, $q_{x+1} = 0.1111$, $q_{x+2} = 0.5$ |
| 4. Interest: | Annual effective rate of $i = 0.15$ |
| 5. Amount of insurance: | 1000 |
| 6. Expenses: | |
|    a. Timing: | Paid at the beginning of each policy year |
|    b. Amount: | (as given in Table 14.1.B) |

**Table 14.1.B Specifications of Illustration: Amount of Expenses**

| | Time | | | |
|---|---|---|---|---|
| | First Year | | Renewal | |
| Type of Expense | Percentage of Premium | Constant | Percentage of Premium | Constant |
| Sales commission | 10% | — | 2% | — |
| General expense | 4% | 3 | — | 1 |
| Taxes, licenses and fees | 2% | — | 2% | — |
| Policy maintenance | 2% | 1 | 2% | 1 |
| Issue and classification | 2% | 4 | — | — |
| Total | 20% | 8 | 6% | 2 |

## 14.2.1 Premium and Reserves

Descriptive specifications 1 through 5 from Table 14.1.A can be used with the equivalence principle to determine the net annual premium for this insurance, $1000 P_{x:\overline{3}|} = 288.41$. Table 14.2 provides the details of the calculation of net premium reserves.

# INSURANCE MODELS INCLUDING EXPENSES

**Table 14.2**
**Reserve Calculations**

| (1) Outcome | (2) Loss | (3) Probability | (4) (2) × (3) |
|---|---|---|---|
| \multicolumn{4}{c}{At issue ($_0L$)} | | | |
| $k = 0$ | 581.16 | 0.1 | 58.12 |
| $k = 1$ | 216.94 | 0.1 | 21.69 |
| $k \geq 2$ | $-99.76$ | 0.8 | $-79.81$ |
| | | $1000 \, _0V_{x:\overline{3}|} = E[_0L] =$ | 0.00 |
| | | $\sigma(_0L) =$ | 215.51 |
| \multicolumn{4}{c}{1 year after issue ($_1L$)} | | | |
| $k = 0$ | 581.16 | 0.1111 | 64.57 |
| $k \geq 1$ | 216.94 | 0.8889 | 192.84 |
| | | $1000 \, _1V_{x:\overline{3}|} = E[_1L] =$ | 257.41 |
| | | $\sigma(_1L) =$ | 114.46 |
| \multicolumn{4}{c}{2 years after issue ($_2L$)} | | | |
| $k \geq 0$ | 581.16 | 1 | 581.16 |
| | | $1000 \, _2V_{x:\overline{3}|} = E[_2L] =$ | 581.16 |
| | | $\sigma(_2L) =$ | 0 |

As a final confirmation we can verify that $_3V_{x:\overline{3}|} = 1$:

$$1000 \, (_2V_{x:\overline{3}|} + P_{x:\overline{3}|}) \, (1 + i) = 1000$$

$$(581.16 + 288.41)(1.15) = 1000$$

The expenses, as provided by Table 14.1.B, will be incorporated by modifying the loss variables. The present value of benefits will be increased by the present value of expenses. This new total will then be offset by the present value of expense-loaded premiums, denoted by $G$. Table 14.3 is constructed using information from Table 14.1.B.

**Table 14.3**
**Expense Augmented**
**Loss Variable ($_0L_e$)**

| Outcome | Benefits + | Expenses | − Premium | Probability |
|---|---|---|---|---|
| $k = 0$ | $1000 v$ | $+ (0.20\,G + 8)$ | $- G\,\ddot{a}_{\overline{1}|}$ | 0.1 |
| $k = 1$ | $1000 v^2$ | $+ (0.20\,G + 8) + (0.06\,G + 2) a_{\overline{1}|}$ | $- G\,\ddot{a}_{\overline{2}|}$ | 0.1 |
| $k \geq 2$ | $1000 v^3$ | $+ (0.20\,G + 8) + (0.06\,G + 2) a_{\overline{2}|}$ | $- G\,\ddot{a}_{\overline{3}|}$ | 0.8 |

The expense-loaded premium will be determined by the equivalence principle; that is, the expected value of the expense-augmented loss variable shall be 0. This yields

$$G = 1000 P_{x:\overline{3}|} + \text{expense loading } (e) = 288.41 + 43.94 = 332.35.$$

Table 14.4 exhibits the calculations of the expected values and standard deviations of the expense-augmented loss variables at policy issue and at 1 and 2 years after issue. The total reserve is broken into benefit and expense components. In each year, expected income from net level insurance premium payments does not match expected benefit payments. This mismatching creates a nonnegative benefit reserve. Likewise in each year, expected income from level expense loadings does not match expected payments for expenses. This mismatching creates a nonpositive expense reserve.

# Chapter 14

## INSURANCE MODELS INCLUDING EXPENSES

**Table 14.4**
**Expected Values of Expense Augmented Loss Variables**

| Outcome | (Present value of benefits | $- 1000\,P_{x:\overline{3}|}\,\ddot{a}_{\overline{k+1}|}$) | + | (Present value of expenses | $- e\,\ddot{a}_{\overline{k+1}|}$) | Probability |
|---|---|---|---|---|---|---|
| | | At issue $(_0L_e)$ | | | | |
| $k = 0$ | (869.57 | $-$ 288.41) | + | (74.47 | $-$ 43.94) | 0.1 |
| $k = 1$ | (756.14 | $-$ 539.20) | + | (93.55 | $-$ 82.15) | 0.1 |
| $k \geq 2$ | (657.52 | $-$ 757.28) | + | (110.14 | $-$ 115.37) | 0.8 |

Expected Values:   Benefit reserve + Expense reserve = Total reserve
$$\phantom{Expected Values:}\quad 0 \qquad + \qquad 0 \qquad = \qquad 0$$
$$\sigma(_0L_e) = 226.82$$

| | | 1 year after issue $(_1L_e)$ | | | | |
|---|---|---|---|---|---|---|
| $k = 0$ | (869.57 | $-$ 288.41) | + | (21.94 | $-$ 43.94) | 0.1111 |
| $k \geq 1$ | (756.14 | $-$ 539.20) | + | (41.02 | $-$ 82.15) | 0.8889 |

Expected Values:   Benefit reserve + Expense reserve = Total reserve
$$\phantom{Expected Values:}\quad 257.41 \qquad - \qquad 39.00 \qquad = \qquad 218.41$$
$$\sigma(_1L_e) = \qquad 120.47$$

| | | 2 years after issue $(_2L_e)$ | | | | |
|---|---|---|---|---|---|---|
| $k \geq 0$ | (869.57 | $-$ 288.41) | + | (21.94 | $-$ 43.94) | 1.0 |

Expected Values:   Benefit reserve + Expense reserve = Total reserve
$$\phantom{Expected Values:}\quad 581.16 \qquad - \qquad 22.00 \qquad = \qquad 559.16$$
$$\sigma(_2L_e) = 0$$

As a confirmation, the terminal total reserve (at the end of 3 years) is:

[total reserve + loaded premium − expenses] $(1 + i)$
$$= [\quad 559.16 \quad + \quad 332.35 \quad - \quad 21.94 \quad](1.15) = 1000$$

The following identify some of the key ideas in the illustration.

**Observation:**

1. Loss variables, as originally introduced, measure the present value of benefits less the present value of net premiums at the various times when benefits might be paid. These variables can be augmented to incorporate expenses and expense-loaded premiums.

2. The equivalence principle can be used to determine expense-loaded premiums and the associated total reserves (benefit reserves plus expense reserves).

3. The expense reserve is often negative in early policy years. This is a consequence of matching a decreasing stream of expense payments with a level stream of expense loadings.

4. Analysis and projection of expenses precede the determination of expense-loaded premiums.

5. The standard deviation of the expense-augmented loss variable can be used to determine a contingency fund. This fund guards against inadequate matching of premium and investment income

with benefit and expense payments. Such a situation is possible due to the random nature of the time benefits are paid. Methods for this were illustrated in Chapter 7.

## 14.2.2 Accounting

In manufacturing enterprises, a product is usually built before it is sold. In most businesses providing services, the service is performed before payment is received. An insurance operation is unusual in that premium income is received before the service of risk assumption is performed.

Accounting is directed, in part, to matching the cost of providing a product or service with the revenue derived from selling it. The objective is to measure the gain or loss from engaging in these activities. Accounting in life insurance and annuity operations differs from that in many enterprises because income is received before costs are known. The reserve systems, net level premium and expense-loaded premium, illustrated earlier, can be used to achieve an improved matching between premium income and associated expenditures.

The illustration is continued in Tables 14.5 and 14.6. In these, it is assumed that the annual gross premium for each policy is the expense-loaded premium of 332.35 plus an arbitrary amount of 10 for profit and contingencies. The accounting statements are derived using a deterministic survivorship group, initially consisting of 10 insureds. Each accounting entry can be divided by 10 to produce entries that can be interpreted as expected amounts for each initial insured. Expenses are paid and investment income is earned exactly as specified in Tables 14.1.A and B. This hypothetical insurance operation starts with an initial fund of 1000. In one of the accounting statements only benefit (net level premium) reserves are recognized as liabilities. In a second set of statements benefit plus expense reserves are recognized as liabilities.

**Table 14.5**
**Income Statements**
**(10 initial insureds)**

| (1) Recognizing Net Level Premium Reserves as Liabilities | | (2) Recognizing Benefit Plus Expense Reserves as Liabilities |
|---|---|---|
| | During first year | |
| | *Income* | |
| 3 423.50 | Premium (10) | 3 423.50 |
| 548.82 | Investment (15%) | 548.82 |
| 3 972.32 | | 3 972.32 |
| | *Charges to income* | |
| | Expenses | |
| 684.70 | Percentage (20%) | 684.70 |
| 80.00 | Constant (8) | 80.00 |
| 1 000.00 | Claims (1) | 1 000.00 |
| 2 316.69 | Increase in reserves | 1 965.69 |
| 4 081.39 | | 3 730.39 |
| −109.07 | Net Income | 241.93 |

# INSURANCE MODELS INCLUDING EXPENSES

**Table 14.5 (cont.)
Income Statements
(10 initial insureds)**

| | | (1) Recognizing Net Level Premium Reserves as Liabilities | | (2) Recognizing Benefit Plus Expense Reserves as Liabilities |
|---|---|---|---|---|

**During second year**
*Income*

| (1) | | (2) |
|---|---|---|
| 3 081.15 | Premium (9) | 3 081.15 |
| 912.88 | Investment (15%) | 912.88 |
| 3 994.03 | | 3 994.03 |

*Charges to income*
Expenses

| (1) | | (2) |
|---|---|---|
| 184.87 | Percentage (6%) | 184.87 |
| 18.00 | Constant (2) | 18.00 |
| 1 000.00 | Claims (1) | 1 000.00 |
| 2 332.59 | Increase in reserves | 2 507.59 |
| 3 535.46 | | 3 710.46 |
| 458.57 | Net Income | 283.57 |

**During third year**
*Income*

| (1) | | (2) |
|---|---|---|
| 2 738.80 | Premium (8) | 2 738.80 |
| 1 283.59 | Investment (15%) | 1 283.59 |
| 4 022.39 | | 4 022.39 |

*Charges to income*
Expenses

| (1) | | (2) |
|---|---|---|
| 164.33 | Percentage (6%) | 164.33 |
| 16.00 | Constant (2) | 16.00 |
| 8 000.00 | Claims and maturities (8) | 8 000.00 |
| −4 649.28 | Increase in reserves | −4 473.28 |
| 3 531.05 | | 3 707.05 |
| 491.34 | Net Income | 315.34 |

1. investment income = [assets at end of prior year + premium income − expenses] (0.15)
2. total net income = −109.07 + 458.57 + 491.34     Col. (1)
   = 241.93 + 283.57 + 315.34     Col. (2)
   = 840.84
3. Alternative calculation (review specifications in Table 14.1.B):
   total net income = [interest income on initial funds] + [accumulated value of net profit loadings]
   $$= 1000[(1.15)^3 - 1] + 10[(10)(0.8)(1.15)^3 + 9(0.94)(1.15)^2 + (8)(0.94)(1.15)]$$
   = 840.91
   The difference between these two calculations is attributed to rounding errors.

The following indicate some additional key points in the accounting illustration.

**Observation:**

6. The amounts recognized as net income in the accounting statements are less variable when benefit plus expense reserves are reported as liabilities than in the situation where net premium

**Table 14.6**
**Balance Sheets**
**(10 Initial Insureds)**

| | (1) Recognizing Net Level Premium Reserves as Liabilities | | (2) Recognizing Benefit Plus Expense Reserves as Liabilities |
|---|---|---|---|
| | | **At end of first year** | |
| 3 207.62 | | Assets | 3 207.62 |
| 2 316.69 | | Liabilities (Reserves) | 1 965.69 |
| 890.93 | | Surplus | 1 241.93 |
| 3 207.62 | | | 3 207.62 |
| | | **At end of second year** | |
| 5 998.78 | | Assets | 5 998.78 |
| 4 649.28 | | Liabilities (Reserves) | 4 473.28 |
| 1 349.50 | | Surplus | 1 525.50 |
| 5 998.78 | | | 5 998.78 |
| | | **At end of third year** | |
| 1 840.84 | | Assets | 1 840.84 |
| 0 | | Liabilities (Reserves) | 0 |
| 1 840.84 | | Surplus | 1 840.84 |
| 1 840.84 | | | 1 840.84 |

1. increase in surplus = total gains (see footnote 2 to table 14.5). 1840.84 − 1000 = 840.84
2. surplus = [surplus at end of previous year + net income]
3. assets = [assets at end of previous year + (net income + increase in reserves)]
   = [assets at end of previous year + (premiums + investment income − claims − expenses)]

reserves are used. Also, net income can be related to interest on surplus and the net profit loadings accumulated with interest.

7. Total gain over the 3-year period is not affected by the method selected for recognizing liabilities.

8. In actual practice, expected results are not realized with the degree of certainty assumed in the illustration.

**14.3 Types of Expenses**

The accounting system of an insurance enterprise is designed to record, classify and summarize financial transactions. The same system, though, will furnish data on activity levels: the number and amount of sales, the number of claims paid, the number of premiums billed and so on. After collecting this information, analysis can be performed with the goal of relating major expense items to the activities they support. These allocations will guide the determination of expense loading on premiums for insurance policies sold in the future. If the equivalence principle is applied, the actuarial present value of expense loadings will equal the actuarial present value of expenses charged to the policy.

Classification and allocation of the expenses of an insurance organization are perplexing tasks. An example is given in Table 14.7. Here a tentative classification system is adopted and the results traced.

Chapter 14

# INSURANCE MODELS INCLUDING EXPENSES

**Table 14.7
Possible
Classification Scheme
for the Expenses of
an Insurance
Organization**

| Expense Classification | Components |
|---|---|
| Investment | (a) analysis |
| | (b) costs of buying, selling and servicing |
| Insurance | |
| 1. Acquisition | (a) selling expense, including agents' commissions and advertising |
| | (b) risk classification, including health examinations |
| | (c) preparing new policies and records |
| 2. Maintenance | (a) premium collection and accounting |
| | (b) beneficiary change and settlement option preparation |
| | (c) policyholder correspondence |
| 3. General | (a) research |
| | (b) actuarial and general legal services |
| | (c) general accounting |
| | (d) taxes, licenses and fees |
| 4. Settlement | (a) claim investigation and legal defense |
| | (b) costs of disbursing benefit payments |

In the determination of expense-loaded premiums, attention is concentrated on the insurance expenses. On the other hand, investment expenses are typically viewed as an offset to investment income and reflected in premiums through a reduction in the assumed interest rate.

In some instances practice indicates a natural relationship between expense items and activity levels. For example, it is common to compensate sales agents by a commission structure of percentages applied to first-year and renewal premiums. In Section 14.2 the commission paid was 10% of the premium in the first year and 2% in the second and third years. Taxes on insurance organizations, especially those levied by the states, are typically a percentage of the premium collected within the taxing jurisdiction. In Section 14.2, 2% of premiums were allocated to taxes, licenses and fees.

The allocation of other items of expense is less clear cut. A combination of statistical analysis and judgment is often used. It is common practice to allocate acquisition expenses to the first policy year in premium loading formulas. This is because marketing and classification expenses are incurred for the purpose of generating and selling new insurance business. Some of these acquisition expenses vary with the size of the premium, commissions for instance. Some vary with the amount of insurance, risk classification expense for example. Some expenses are incurred for each policy issued, independently of the size of the policy or premium, the creation of records for example.

The classification and allocation of expenses is an important management tool for controlling the operation of an insurance system. However, in the determination of premiums, the view of expenses

# INSURANCE MODELS INCLUDING EXPENSES

is prospective rather than retrospective. The goal is to match future expenses with future premium loadings. Therefore, expense trends with expectations of inflation or deflation are built into expense loadings.

Table 14.8 provides an illustration of the classification system in Table 14.7 for insurance expenses and associated loading factors.

**Table 14.8**
**Illustration of the Allocation of Future Insurance Expenses**

| Classification | First Year Per Policy | First Year Per 1000 Insurance | First Year Percent Premium | Renewal Per Policy | Renewal Per 1000 Insurance | Percent Premium by Policy Year 2–9 | Percent Premium by Policy Year 10–15 | Percent Premium by Policy Year 16 over |
|---|---|---|---|---|---|---|---|---|
| 1. Acquisition | | | | | | | | |
| a. Sales expenses | | | | | | | | |
| Commission | — | — | 60% | — | — | 7.0% | 5.0% | 3% |
| Sales offices | — | — | 25% | — | — | 2.5% | 1.5% | 1% |
| Other sales related | 12.50 | 4.00 | — | — | — | — | — | — |
| b. Classification | 18.00 | 0.50 | — | — | — | — | — | — |
| c. Issue and records | 4.00 | — | — | — | — | — | — | — |
| 2. Maintenance | 2.00 | 0.25 | — | 2.00 | 0.25 | — | — | — |
| 3. General | | | | | | | | |
| a, b, c | 4.00 | 0.25 | — | 4.00 | 0.25 | — | — | — |
| d. Taxes | — | — | 2% | — | — | 2.0% | 2.0% | 2% |
| Total (1, 2, 3) | 40.50 | 5.00 | 87% | 6.00 | 0.50 | 11.5% | 8.5% | 6% |
| 4. Settlement | 18.00 per policy plus 0.10 per 1000 insurance | | | | | | | |

**Example 14.1:**

Using the equivalence principle, develop a formula for the expense-loaded annual premium on a whole life policy, semicontinuous basis, issued to (x) for an amount of 20,000. The expenses are those listed in Table 14.8.

**Solution:**
Let G denote the expense-loaded premium:

(actuarial present value of expense-loaded premium)

= (actuarial present value of claim and claim settlement expense plus other expenses)

$$G\ddot{a}_{[x]} = 20{,}020\,\bar{A}_{[x]} + [(40.50 + 100.00 + 0.87\,G) + 6\,a_{[x]} + 10\,a_{[x]}$$

$$+ (0.115\,a_{[x]:\overline{8}|} + 0.085\ _{9|}\ddot{a}_{[x]:\overline{6}|} + 0.06\ _{15|}\ddot{a}_{[x]})\,G]$$

$$G = \frac{20{,}020\,\bar{A}_{[x]} + 140.50 + 16\,a_{[x]}}{0.94\,\ddot{a}_{[x]} - 0.755 - 0.03\,\ddot{a}_{[x]:\overline{9}|} - 0.025\,\ddot{a}_{[x]:\overline{15}|}}.$$

▼

# Chapter 14

## INSURANCE MODELS INCLUDING EXPENSES

In Example 14.1, the expense-loaded premium for a policy with a sum insured of 20,000 was required. In practice, premiums are usually stated as a rate per unit of insurance. For life insurance, these rates have typically been per 1000 of initial death benefit. For life annuities, the rates have typically been per unit of monthly income. When premiums are stated as rates, a problem is created in the allocation of per-policy expenses for policies of different amounts. This is the subject of Section 14.4.

## 14.4 Per Policy Expenses

Let $G(b)$ denote the expense-loaded premium for a policy of amount $b$. Also let

$$G(b)(1-f) = ab + c \qquad (14.4.1)$$

where $a$, $c$ and $f$ are nonnegative constants and $f < 1$. The constant $a$ captures those components of insurance cost that vary directly with the amount of insurance; the net premium for a unit of insurance is the largest. The constant $c$ may be interpreted as the per policy expenses. The constant $f$ is the portion of the premium used to match the expenses that vary with the amount of the premium.

Formula (14.4.1) may be rewritten as

$$G(b) = b\frac{a + c/b}{1 - f} \qquad (14.4.2)$$
$$= bR(b)$$

where

$$R(b) = \frac{a + c/b}{1 - f}.$$

The function $R(b)$ is the premium rate for a policy of amount $b$. The formula for $R(b)$ can be simplified to

$$R(b) = a' + \frac{c'}{b}$$

where $a' = a/(1-f)$ and $c' = c/(1-f)$. However, it is frequently convenient to use the form where the three elements of the premium are explicitly represented.

A typical graph of the premium rate function $R(b)$ is displayed in Figure 14.1. The number $m$ indicates the minimum policy size and $\bar{b}$ denotes the average policy size. Also indicated are three methods of recognizing the per policy expenses:

1. Charge a **policy fee** of amount $c/(1-f) = c'$, to be added to the quantity $b[a/(1-f)] = ba'$ to produce the expense-loaded premium (14.4.2). Under this approach, the premium rate actually charged would be $R(b)$.

# INSURANCE MODELS INCLUDING EXPENSES

**Figure 14.1
Premium Rate as a
Function of Amount
of Insurance**

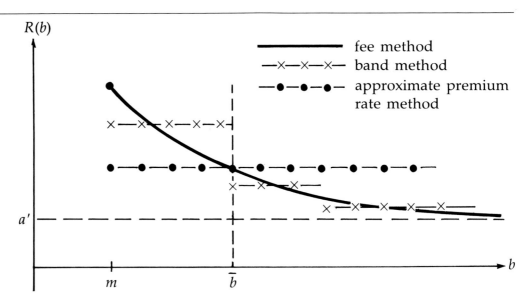

2. Approximate the function $R(b)$ by a set of straight lines. This approach is called the **band method** since the same premium rate is charged for amounts of insurance falling in a particular band.

3. Approximate the premium rate with $R(\bar{b})$.

Method 2, the band method, also has been called the **quantity discount approach** because, by increasing the amount of insurance, the insured can achieve a significant decrease in the premium rate. Under Method 3, the actuarial present value of expense loadings will be less than the actuarial present value of expenses for policies of amount $b < \bar{b}$. Note that if we view the amount of insurance as a random variable, denoted by $B$, and evaluate the expected premium on a policy we have

$$E[B\,R(\bar{b})] = \frac{\bar{b}\,[a + c/\bar{b}]}{1-f} = \frac{a\bar{b}+c}{1-f}.$$

That is, if the realized distribution of insurance amounts corresponds to that used in establishing the premium rate, $R(\bar{b})$, there will be a balance between the actuarial present values of premium loadings and charged expenses.

**Example 14.2:**     A type of single premium life insurance policy has the following premium components.

# INSURANCE MODELS INCLUDING EXPENSES

| Net Premium | $\bar{A}_x = 0.20$ |
|---|---|
| Expenses | |
| Sales Commissions | 7.5% of premium |
| Taxes, licenses and fees | 3.0% of premium |
| Per policy expenses: | |
| First year | 23.00 |
| Renewal | 2.50 |
| Claims settlement per policy | 12.00 |

Calculate $R(b)$ for this type of policy. The amount of insurance is measured in units of 1000 and $i = 0.06$.

**Solution:**
Substituting the given amounts into (14.4.1), and using

$$a_x = \frac{1 - A_x}{d} - 1 = \frac{1 - (\delta/i)\bar{A}_x}{d} - 1 = 13.2353,$$

we have

$$(1 - 0.105)\,G(b) = [1000\,b + 12]\,(0.2) + 23 + 2.50\,a_x$$

$$0.895\,G(b) = 200\,b + 2.4 + 23 + 2.50\,[13.2353]$$

$$G(b) = 223.46\,b + 65.35$$

and

$$R(b) = 223.46 + \frac{65.35}{b}. \qquad \blacktriangledown$$

**Example 14.3:** A type of whole life policy, issued on a semicontinuous basis, has the following expense allocations.

| | Percent of Premium | Per 1000 Insurance | Per Policy |
|---|---|---|---|
| First year | 30% | 3.00 | 10.00 |
| Renewal | 5% | 0.50 | 2.50 |

a. Write formulas for the expense-loaded first-year and renewal net premiums assuming that per policy expenses are matched separately by first-year and renewal policy fees.

b. Write the formula for a single policy fee to be paid in each year.

**Solution:**
a. Let $k(b)$ denote the loaded premium without provision for per policy expenses ($b$ is measured in thousands):

(actuarial present value of expense-loaded premium)

= (actuarial present value of benefits and expenses excluding per policy expenses)

$$k(b)\ddot{a}_x = b[1000\,\bar{A}_x + 3 + 0.50\,a_x] + 0.30\,k(b) + 0.05\,k(b)\,a_x$$

$$k(b) = b\left[\frac{1000\,\bar{A}_x + 0.5\,\ddot{a}_x + 2.50}{0.95\,\ddot{a}_x - 0.25}\right] = b\,a'.$$

When the policy fee is added to the premium, the percent-of-premium expenses are applied to the policy fee as well. Thus, we have

First year:

$$k(b) + \frac{10}{0.70} = k(b) + 14.29$$

$$= b\,a' + 14.29$$

$$= b\left(a' + \frac{14.29}{b}\right)$$

Renewal years:

$$k(b) + \frac{2.50}{0.95} = k(b) + 2.63$$

$$= b\left(a' + \frac{2.63}{b}\right).$$

b. Let $g$ denote the policy fee to be collected with each premium. The component $g$ is determined from the equation

$$10 + 2.5\,a_x + 0.3\,g + 0.05\,g\,a_x = g\,\ddot{a}_x,$$

and the premium becomes

$$k(b) + g = b\left(a' + \frac{g}{b}\right). \qquad \blacktriangledown$$

## 14.5 Algebraic Foundations of Accounting

In this section many of the ideas illustrated in Section 14.2.2 will be made more precise. Frequent reference to Tables 14.5 and 14.6 may help the reader to follow the arguments.

One of the objectives of financial accounting is the determination, at periodic intervals, of the elements of the balance sheet equation

$$A(h) = L(h) + U(h). \qquad (14.5.1)$$

In (14.5.1), $A(h)$ denotes the amount of assets, $L(h)$ the amount of liabilities and $U(h)$ the amount of owner's equity (surplus in the terminology of insurance accounting) at the end of accounting period $h$. Changes in surplus can be represented by

$$\Delta U(h) = \Delta A(h) - \Delta L(h)$$

$$= \text{net income in period } h + 1. \qquad (14.5.2)$$

We will illustrate this basic model using an algebraic development under idealized conditions as stated in Table 14.9.

# INSURANCE MODELS INCLUDING EXPENSES

**Table 14.9**
**Specifications of**
**Accounting**
**Illustration**

| | |
|---|---|
| 1. Plan of insurance: | Whole life, unit amount |
| 2. Payment basis: | Fully discrete |
| 3. Age and time of issue: | Issued to $(x)$ at the beginning of the first accounting period |
| 4. Expenses: | No expenses or expense loadings |
| 5. Experience: | Investment experience conforms to that assumed |
| | Accounting entries will be in terms of expected values at policy issue for each initial insured. |

The illustration will build on the reserve recursion formula (7.8.2) with $b_h = 1$, $\pi_{h-1} = P_x$, $_hV = {}_hV_x$ and multiplied by $_{h-1}p_x (1 + i)$:

$$_{h-1}p_x \left( {}_{h-1}V_x + P_x \right) (1 + i) - {}_{h-1}p_x \, q_{x+h-1} = {}_hp_x \, {}_hV_x \qquad h = 1,2,\ldots. \quad (14.5.3)$$

Accordingly, at the end of the first accounting period the expected balance sheet equation for each initial insured is

$$A(1) = L(1)$$

or

$$p_x \, {}_1V_x = p_x \, {}_1V_x. \qquad (14.5.4)$$

Formula (14.5.4) can be established by the following argument: During the first accounting period the expected assets per initial insured would change as follows:

| | | |
|---|---|---|
| Increase | Premium income | $= P_x$ |
| | Interest income | $= P_x \, i$ |
| Decrease | Death claims | $= q_x$ |

$$A(1) = A(0) + [A(1) - A(0)] = 0 + [P_x(1 + i) - q_x]$$
$$= p_x \, {}_1V_x$$
$$= L(1).$$

In this illustration, $A(1) - L(1) = U(1) = 0$.

Formula (14.5.3) can also be used to study the progress of accounting statements in a recursive fashion. Suppose that at the end of accounting period $h$

$$A(h) = L(h)$$

and that we start the process during accounting period $h + 1$:

$$\Delta A(h) = \left\{ \begin{array}{l} \text{premium income} \\ + \text{ interest income} \\ - \text{ death claims} \end{array} \right\} = \left\{ \begin{array}{l} {}_hp_x \, P_x \\ + {}_hp_x \, ({}_hV_x + P_x)\, i \\ - {}_hp_x \, q_{x+h} \end{array} \right\}.$$

Then

$$A(h + 1) = A(h) + \Delta A(h)$$

$$= {}_hp_x \, {}_hV_x + \{{}_hp_x \, [P_x + ({}_hV_x + P_x)\,i] - {}_hp_x \, q_{x+h}\}$$

$$= {}_hp_x \, [(P_x + {}_hV_x)(1 + i)] - {}_hp_x \, q_{x+h}$$

$$= {}_{h+1}p_x \, {}_{h+1}V_x = L(h + 1).$$

In this illustration, with no initial funds, profit or contingency loadings, tracing expected results yields $A(h) - L(h) = U(h) = 0$, $h = 0,1,2,3,\ldots.$

We now modify the assumptions of Table 14.9 by assuming that the net premium is loaded by the positive constant $c$ and that the expenses for each surviving policy, paid at the beginning of accounting period $h$, are $e_{h-1}$. The loading constant may contain a component for profit. That is, the actuarial present value of the loadings $c$ may be greater than the actuarial present value of the set of $e_{h-1}$, $h = 1,2,\ldots.$

The augmented version of (14.5.3), incorporating loaded premiums and expenses, is

$$_{h-1}p_x \, \{[_{h-1}V_x + u(h - 1)] + (P_x + c) - e_{h-1}\} \, (1 + i) - {}_{h-1}p_x \, q_{x+h-1}$$

$$= {}_hp_x \, [_hV_x + u(h)] \quad h = 1,2,3,\ldots. \tag{14.5.5}$$

In (14.5.5), $u(h)$ denotes the target surplus for each surviving insured at the end of accounting period $h$.

Subtracting the unloaded version, (14.5.3), from (14.5.5) yields

$$_{h-1}p_x \, [u(h - 1) + (c - e_{h-1})] \, (1 + i) = {}_hp_x \, u(h) \quad h = 1,2,3,\ldots. \tag{14.5.6}$$

Multiplying difference equation (14.5.6) by $v^h$ and rearranging terms yields

$$\Delta[v^{h-1} \, {}_{h-1}p_x \, u(h - 1)] = v^{h-1} \, {}_{h-1}p_x \, (c - e_{h-1}). \tag{14.5.7}$$

Imposing the initial condition $u(0) = 0$, we obtain from (14.5.7)

$$\sum_{j=1}^{h} \Delta[v^{j-1} \, {}_{j-1}p_x \, u(j - 1)] = \sum_{j=1}^{h} v^{j-1} \, {}_{j-1}p_x \, (c - e_{j-1})$$

$$v^h \, {}_hp_x \, u(h) = \sum_{j=1}^{h} v^{j-1} \, {}_{j-1}p_x \, (c - e_{j-1})$$

$$_hp_x \, u(h) = \sum_{j=1}^{h} (1 + i)^{h-j+1} \, {}_{j-1}p_x \, (c - e_{j-1}). \tag{14.5.8}$$

That is, the expected surplus at the end of $h$ accounting periods for each initial insured is the accumulated value of the expected contributions to surplus in each earlier accounting period. This result should be compared with Table 14.5, Footnote 3.

If net premium reserves (benefit reserves) are recognized as the measure of liabilities, the expected entries for each initial insured in the

# Chapter 14

## INSURANCE MODELS INCLUDING EXPENSES

accounting statements of our idealized insurance system at the end of the accounting period $h$ are as follows.

### Balance Sheet
(At end of accounting period $h$)

$$A(h) = L(h) + U(h)$$

$$= {}_hp_x \, {}_hV_x + {}_hp_x \, u(h)$$

$$= {}_hp_x \, {}_hV_x + \sum_{1}^{h} (1 + i)^{h-j+1} \, {}_{j-1}p_x \, (c - e_{j-1})$$

### Income Statement
($h$th accounting period)

Income:

| | |
|---|---|
| Premium Income | ${}_{h-1}p_x \, (P_x + c)$ |
| Investment Income | ${}_{h-1}p_x \, [{}_{h-1}V_x + u(h - 1) + P_x + c - e_{h-1}] \, i$ |
| Total | ${}_{h-1}p_x \, [(P_x + c) \, (1 + i) + ({}_{h-1}V_x + u(h - 1) - e_{h-1}) \, i]$ |

### Charges to Income

| | |
|---|---|
| Death claims | ${}_{h-1}p_x \, q_{x+h-1}$ |
| Expenses | ${}_{h-1}p_x \, e_{h-1}$ |
| Changes in reserve liability | ${}_hp_x \, {}_hV_x - {}_{h-1}p_x \, {}_{h-1}V_x$ |
| Total | ${}_hp_x \, {}_hV_x - {}_{h-1}p_x \, ({}_{h-1}V_x - e_{h-1}) + {}_{h-1}p_x \, q_{x+h-1}$ |
| Net income (Change in surplus) | ${}_{h-1}p_x \, [u(h - 1) \, i + (c - e_{h-1}) \, (1 + i)]$      (14.5.9) |

In completing the accounting statements we have made use of (14.5.8) and (14.5.3). The left-hand columns of Tables 14.5 and 14.6 provide numerical illustrations of this display. The tables are in terms of a deterministic survivorship group rather than expected entries for each initial insured.

Thus the expected surplus at the end of $h$ accounting periods for each initial insured is

$$
{}_hp_x \, u(h) = {}_{h-1}p_x \, u(h - 1) + {}_{h-1}p_x \, [u(h - 1) \, i
$$
$$
+ \, (c - e_{h-1}) \, (1 + i)]. \qquad (14.5.10)
$$

Formula (14.5.10) is identical to (14.5.6); however, it was derived from an accounting viewpoint. Multiplying by $v^h$ yields

$$\Delta[v^{h-1} \, {}_{h-1}p_x \, u(h - 1)] = v^{h-1} \, {}_{h-1}p_x \, (c - e_{h-1}),$$

which is (14.5.7) rederived with accounting interpretations.

Earlier in this chapter the point was made that, in practice, expenses tend to decrease as duration increases. Thus the expected surplus,

$$_hp_x \, u(h) = \sum_{j=1}^{h} (1 + i)^{h-j+1} \,_{j-1}p_x \, (c - e_{j-1}),$$

will typically be negative for small values of $h$ and positive for larger values. This observation is made with respect to an accounting model in which net premium reserves are recognized as the measure of liabilities, loadings are level and expenses decrease with time following policy issue.

To avoid the situation in which assets are less than liabilities, in the early durations, several actions are possible:

- The insurance organization may obtain additional capital for the initial surplus, $u(0)$, to keep

$$u(0) \, (1 + i)^h + \sum_{j=1}^{h} (1 + i)^{h-j+1} \,_{j-1}p_x \, (c - e_{j-1})$$

  positive for $h = 0,1,2,3,\ldots$.
- Loadings may depend on duration so that $c_{h-1} - e_{h-1} \geq 0$, $h = 1,2,3,\ldots$.
- The liabilities of the insurance organization could be based on a modified reserve principle that would reduce recognized liabilities in early policy years. The reserve system of benefit plus expense reserves used in Column (2) of Tables 14.5 and 14.6 is an example of such a system. (This last alternative will be the subject of the remainder of this chapter.)

## 14.6 Modified Reserve Methods

A modified reserve method is one that does not use the actuarial present value of a set of level net premiums as a deduction from the actuarial present value of future benefits in defining reserves. Instead a system of **step premiums** is defined. Usually no more than three different levels are involved, although the theory would permit more steps in the path. The three premium levels are denoted by: $\alpha$, the first-year net premium; $\beta$, the net premium for the next $j-1$ years; and $P$, the net level premium assumed payable beyond the first $j$ policy years. This set of premiums is constrained to have the same actuarial present value as the set of net level premiums in order that

$$\alpha + \beta \, a_{x:\overline{j-1}|} + P \,_{j|}\ddot{a}_{x:\overline{h-j}|} = P \, \ddot{a}_{x:\overline{h}|}$$
$$\alpha + \beta \, a_{x:\overline{j-1}|} = P \, \ddot{a}_{x:\overline{j}|} \tag{14.6.1}$$

where $h$ is the length of the premium paying period.

In the notation of Section 14.5, for net level premium reserves, amount $c$ is expected to be available in the first policy year. This comes from a loaded premium of $P + c$ to offset first-year expenses. If $\alpha < P$, then $P + c - \alpha > c$ will be expected to be available, within the modified reserve accounting method, to match first-year expenses. If $\alpha < P$, a consequence is that $\beta > P$. This can be seen by rewriting (14.6.1) as

Chapter 14

# INSURANCE MODELS INCLUDING EXPENSES

**Figure 14.2
Premiums in a
Modified Reserve
Method**

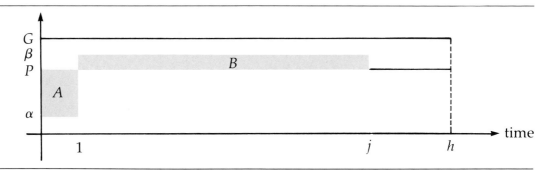

$$\alpha + \beta a_{x:\overline{j-1}|} = P(a_{x:\overline{j-1}|} + 1)$$

$$\beta = P + \frac{P - \alpha}{a_{x:\overline{j-1}|}}. \tag{14.6.2}$$

A second useful expression can be obtained from (14.6.1) as follows:

$$\beta(\ddot{a}_{x:\overline{j}|} - 1) = P\ddot{a}_{x:\overline{j}|} - \alpha$$

$$\beta = P + \frac{\beta - \alpha}{\ddot{a}_{x:\overline{j}|}}. \tag{14.6.3}$$

Thus a modified reserve method can be defined by specifying the length of the modification period $j$ and one of the first-year premium $\alpha$, the renewal premium $\beta$, or the difference $\beta - \alpha$. Figure 14.2 provides a schematic diagram summarizing the relationship among the premiums making up a modified reserve method. The actuarial present value of the premium components depicted by the shaded areas $A$ and $B$ are equal as can be seen from (14.6.1) rearranged as $P - \alpha = (\beta - P)a_{x:\overline{j-1}|}$.

In (14.6.1) and (14.6.2) we have used the symbols $\alpha$ and $\beta$ to denote, respectively, the first-year and renewal net premiums for a $j$-year modified reserve method and $P$ to denote the general symbol for the net level premium. In a similar fashion we shall use the symbol $V^{Mod}$ to denote a terminal reserve computed by a modified method.

The following formula is used to calculate terminal reserves in the general case of an $h$-payment, $n$-year endowment insurance under a modified reserve method with a $j$-year modification period. During the modification period, $k < j$,

$$\begin{aligned}
{}_{k}^{h}V_{x:\overline{n}|}^{Mod} &= A_{x+k:\overline{n-k}|} - \beta\,\ddot{a}_{x+k:\overline{j-k}|} - {}_{h}P_{x:\overline{n}|}\,{}_{j-k|}\ddot{a}_{x+k:\overline{h-j}|} \\
&= A_{x+k:\overline{n-k}|} - {}_{h}P_{x:\overline{n}|}\,\ddot{a}_{x+k:\overline{h-k}|} - (\beta - {}_{h}P_{x:\overline{n}|})\,\ddot{a}_{x+k:\overline{j-k}|} \\
&= {}_{k}^{h}V_{x:\overline{n}|} - (\beta - {}_{h}P_{x:\overline{n}|})\,\ddot{a}_{x+k:\overline{j-k}|}.
\end{aligned}$$

# INSURANCE MODELS INCLUDING EXPENSES

After duration $j$, reserves under the modified reserve method are equal to those under the net-level method.

**Example 14.4:** Whole life insurances, on a fully continuous basis, are to have reserves determined by a modified reserve method. Under this method, the first-year and renewal net annual premium rates are $\bar{\alpha}_x$ and $\bar{\beta}_x$, $\bar{\alpha}_x < \bar{P}(\bar{A}_x)$; the modification period is the entire policy period. Define the future loss variable and write equations that may be used to evaluate reserves.

**Solution:**

$$_tL^{Mod} = \begin{cases} v^U - \bar{\alpha}_x\,\bar{a}_{\overline{U}|} & 0 \le U < 1 - t, \\ v^U - \bar{\alpha}_x\,\bar{a}_{\overline{1-t}|} - \bar{\beta}_{x\ 1-t|}\bar{a}_{\overline{U-(1-t)}|} & U \ge 1 - t, \\ v^U - \bar{\beta}_x\,\bar{a}_{\overline{U}|} & t \ge 1 \end{cases} \quad \left. \begin{array}{c} \\ \\ \end{array} \right\} 0 \le t < 1$$

By analogy with (7.2.2), the reserve is

$$_t\bar{V}(\bar{A}_x)^{Mod} = \begin{cases} \bar{A}_{x+t} - \bar{\alpha}_x\,\bar{a}_{x+t:\overline{1-t}|} - \bar{\beta}_{x\ 1-t|}\bar{a}_{x+t} & 0 \le t < 1 \\ \bar{A}_{x+t} - \bar{\beta}_x\,\bar{a}_{x+t} & t \ge 1. \end{cases}$$

In addition,

$$_t\bar{V}(\bar{A}_x) - {}_t\bar{V}(\bar{A}_x)^{Mod} = [\bar{\beta}_x - \bar{P}(\bar{A}_x)]\,\bar{a}_{x+t} \quad t \ge 1.$$

Since we require that

$$\bar{\alpha}_x\,\bar{a}_{x:\overline{1}|} + \bar{\beta}_{x\ 1|}\bar{a}_x = \bar{P}(\bar{A}_x)\,(\bar{a}_{x:\overline{1}|} + {}_{1|}\bar{a}_x), \tag{14.6.4}$$

we have, similar to (14.6.2),

$$\bar{\beta}_x = \bar{P}(\bar{A}_x) + \frac{[\bar{P}(\bar{A}_x) - \bar{\alpha}_x]\,\bar{a}_{x:\overline{1}|}}{{}_{1|}\bar{a}_x},$$

and

$$\bar{\beta}_x > \bar{P}(\bar{A}_x).$$

Therefore,

$$_t\bar{V}(\bar{A}_x) - {}_t\bar{V}(\bar{A}_x)^{Mod} \ge 0 \quad t \ge 1. \qquad \blacktriangledown$$

**Example 14.5:** Using the information given in Example 14.4, derive a retrospective formula for $_t\bar{V}(\bar{A}_x)^{Mod}$.

**Solution:**
Consider the case where $0 \le t < 1$ and recall that

$$\bar{A}_x = \bar{\alpha}_x\,\bar{a}_{x:\overline{1}|} + \bar{\beta}_{x\ 1|}\bar{a}_x$$

$$= \bar{\alpha}_x\,(\bar{a}_{x:\overline{1}|} + \bar{a}_{x+t:\overline{1-t}|}\,{}_tE_x) + \bar{\beta}_x\,({}_{1-t|}\bar{a}_{x+t}\,{}_tE_x).$$

Then, using notation from Section 7.3, we have

$$_t\bar{V}(\bar{A}_x)^{Mod} = \bar{A}_{x+t} - \bar{\alpha}_x\,\bar{a}_{x+t:\overline{1-t}|} - \bar{\beta}_{x\ 1-t|}\bar{a}_{x+t}$$

# INSURANCE MODELS INCLUDING
# EXPENSES

$$= \bar{A}_{x+t} - \frac{\bar{A}_x - \bar{\alpha}_x \, \bar{a}_{x:\bar{t}|}}{{}_tE_x} \qquad 0 \le t < 1$$

$$= \bar{\alpha}_x \, \bar{s}_{x:\bar{t}|} - {}_tk_x.$$

In addition

$$_t\bar{V}(\bar{A}_x) - {}_t\bar{V}(\bar{A}_x)^{Mod} = [\bar{P}(\bar{A}_x) - \bar{\alpha}_x] \, \bar{s}_{x:\bar{t}|} \qquad 0 \le t < 1.$$

In the case $t \ge 1$, we recall that

$$\bar{A}_x = \bar{\alpha}_x \, \bar{a}_{x:\bar{1}|} + \bar{\beta}_x \, ({}_{1|}\bar{a}_{x:\overline{t-1}|} + \bar{a}_{x+t} \, {}_tE_x).$$

Then

$$_t\bar{V}(\bar{A}_x)^{Mod} = \bar{A}_{x+t} - \bar{\beta}_x \, \bar{a}_{x+t}$$

$$= \bar{A}_{x+t} - \frac{\bar{A}_x - \bar{\alpha}_x \, \bar{a}_{x:\bar{1}|} - \bar{\beta}_x \, {}_{1|}\bar{a}_{x:\overline{t-1}|}}{{}_tE_x}$$

$$= \frac{\bar{\alpha}_x \, \bar{a}_{x:\bar{1}|}}{{}_tE_x} + \bar{\beta}_x \, \bar{s}_{x+1:\overline{t-1}|} - {}_tk_x. \qquad \blacktriangledown$$

## 14.7
## Full Preliminary
## Term

In order to develop a reserve method that increases the effective expense loading, $G - \alpha$, in the first policy year to better match the large first-year expenses, $\alpha$ is usually constrained to be less than $P$. However, in accordance with certain regulatory principles, there is a practical lower bound on the value of $\alpha$.

This lower bound is derived from the recognition that negative reserve liabilities are effectively accounting assets. Since the collection of future expense-loaded premiums is uncertain, regulatory agencies have not permitted such negative reserves to be included in the balance sheet in statutory assessment of insurance company solvency. Thus a practical objective of the reserve method is to avoid a negative reserve at the end of the first policy year. This means that, for a level benefit policy, the smallest feasible value of $\alpha$ will be $A^1_{x:\bar{1}|}$ on the fully discrete basis. This result may be seen as follows:

$$_1V \ge 0,$$

$$\alpha \, \ddot{s}_{x:\bar{1}|} - {}_1k_x \ge 0, \qquad (14.7.1)$$

$$\alpha \ge A^1_{x:\bar{1}|}.$$

If $\alpha$ is set at the minimum level and the modification period, $j$, is the entire premium paying period, the resulting method is called the **full preliminary term** (*FPT*) method. Under the *FPT* method, the reserve at the end of the first policy year is 0.

For this fully discrete basis, the renewal valuation premium $\beta$ may be obtained from (14.6.1) by substituting for a general $h$-payment level premium insurance with net single premium denoted by $A$. That is, let $A(1)$ denote the net single premium for an insurance issued at age

# INSURANCE MODELS INCLUDING EXPENSES

$x + 1$ for the benefits remaining thereafter. Then

$$A^1_{x:\overline{1}|} + \beta \;_{1|}\ddot{a}_{x:\overline{h-1}|} = P \, \ddot{a}_{x:\overline{h}|}$$

$$= A$$

$$= A^1_{x:\overline{1}|} + \;_1E_x \, A(1) \qquad (14.7.2)$$

or

$$\beta = \frac{_1E_x \, A(1)}{_{1|}\ddot{a}_{x:\overline{h-1}|}} = \frac{A(1)}{\ddot{a}_{x+1:\overline{h-1}|}}.$$

In words, $\beta$ is the net annual premium for a similar insurance issued at an age 1 year older, with premiums paid for 1 less year in the case of a limited premium paying period, and maturing at the same age as the original insurance.

For a fully continuous basis, the smallest feasible value for the first-year premium rate, $\bar{\alpha}$, is $\bar{A}^1_{x:\overline{1}|}/\bar{a}_{x:\overline{1}|}$, again based on avoiding a negative terminal reserve at time 1. That is,

$$_1\bar{V}(\bar{A}_x) \geq 0$$

$$\frac{\bar{\alpha} \, \bar{a}_{x:\overline{1}|}}{_1E_x} - \;_1\bar{k}_x \geq 0 \qquad (14.7.3)$$

$$\bar{\alpha} \geq \frac{\bar{A}^1_{x:\overline{1}|}}{\bar{a}_{x:\overline{1}|}}.$$

The development for the renewal premium rate, $\bar{\beta}$, corresponds closely with the development of (14.7.2) above.

$$\bar{A}^1_{x:\overline{1}|} + \bar{\beta} \;_{1|}\bar{a}_{x:\overline{h-1}|} = \bar{P}(\bar{A}) \, \bar{a}_{x:\overline{h}|} \qquad (14.7.4)$$

$$= \bar{A}$$

$$= \bar{A}^1_{x:\overline{1}|} + \;_1E_x \, \bar{A}(1)$$

or

$$\bar{\beta} = \frac{_1E_x \, \bar{A}(1)}{_{1|}\bar{a}_{x:\overline{h-1}|}}.$$

The effect of the *FPT* method on accounting statements can be demonstrated by modifying (14.5.5). We note that expense-loaded premiums under *FPT* are given by

$$P_x + c = A^1_{x:\overline{1}|} + c_0 = \beta_x + c_1$$

where $c_0$ is the loading in the first year and $c_1$ the loading in renewal premiums. The analogue of (14.5.5) where, as before, $u(k)$ denotes the target surplus for each expected surviving insured at end of accounting period $k$ is, for $u(0) = 0$,

$$[(A^1_{x:\overline{1}|} + c_0) - e_0](1 + i) - q_x = p_x u(1)$$

$$(c_0 - e_0)(1 + i) = p_x u(1) \qquad k = 0 \qquad (14.7.5A)$$

Chapter 14

# INSURANCE MODELS INCLUDING EXPENSES

$$ {}_kp_x \{[{}_kV_x^{FPT} + u(k)] + (\beta_x + c_1) - e_k\} (1 + i) - {}_kp_x\, q_{x+k} $$
$$ = {}_{k+1}p_x \,[{}_{k+1}V_x^{FPT} + u(k + 1)] \quad k = 1,2,\ldots. \tag{14.7.5B} $$

Therefore, if

$$ c_0 - e_0 = (P_x + c - A^1_{x:\overline{1}|} - e_0) > 0, $$

the first-year surplus in our idealized accounting illustration will be positive. In realistic situations,

$$ c_0 = P_x + c - A^1_{x:\overline{1}|} > c $$

and $p_x\, u(1)$ will be greater than when liabilities are measured by net level premium reserves.

The recursion formulas, analogous to (7.8.2), are

$$ A^1_{x:\overline{1}|}(1 + i) - q_x = 0 \tag{14.7.6A} $$

and

$$ {}_kp_x \,({}_kV_x^{FPT} + \beta_x) (1 + i) - {}_kp_x\, q_{x+k} = {}_{k+1}p_x \,{}_{k+1}V_x^{FPT}. \tag{14.7.6B} $$

Subtracting (14.7.6B) from (14.7.5B) we obtain

$$ {}_kp_x \,[u(k) + c_1 - e_k] (1 + i) = {}_{k+1}p_x \,u(k + 1) \quad k = 1,2,3,\ldots. \tag{14.7.7} $$

Multiply (14.7.5A) and (14.7.7) by $v^{k+1}$, let $c'_k = c_0$ when $k = 0$ and $c'_k = c_1$ when $k = 1,2,\ldots$, and we have

$$ \Delta[v^k \,{}_kp_x \,u(k)] = v^k \,{}_kp_x \,(c'_k - e_k). \tag{14.7.8} $$

With $u(0) = 0$, difference equation (14.7.8) yields

$$ \sum_{j=0}^{k-1} \Delta[v^j \,{}_jp_x \,u(j)] = \sum_{j=0}^{k-1} v^j \,{}_jp_x \,(c'_j - e_j) \tag{14.7.9} $$

$$ {}_kp_x \,u(k) = \sum_{j=0}^{k-1} (1 + i)^{k-j} \,{}_jp_x \,(c'_j - e_j). \tag{14.7.10} $$

As in (14.5.8), the expected surplus for each initial insured in our idealized model is the accumulated value of the excess of loadings over expenses in each earlier year. The following comparisons of the annual expected contributions to surplus for each surviving insured in the cases of *FPT* reserves and of net level premium *NLP* reserves may be developed using (14.5.7) and (14.7.8).

| *FPT* | *NLP* | |
|---|---|---|
| $c_0 - e_0 >$ | $c - e_0$ | (14.7.11) |
| $c_1 - e_k <$ | $c - e_k \quad k = 1,2,\ldots$ | |

The inequalities, displayed in (14.7.11), for the expected contributions to surplus are valid when $\alpha < P$ and $\beta > P$.

## 14.8 Modified Full Preliminary Term

If one adopts the principle that negative reserve liabilities are inappropriate on the balance sheet of an insurance enterprise, the $FPT$ reserve method provides a minimum first-year terminal reserve and minimum first-year net premiums. According to (14.7.11), the annual surplus contribution in the first year under $FPT$ and $NLP$ is

$$\overset{FPT}{P + c - A^1_{x:\overline{1}|} - e_0} = \overset{NLP}{c_0 - e_0} > c - e_0.$$

A difficulty arises in that the magnitude of $P - A^1_{x:\overline{1}|}$ depends on the plan of insurance. Since $P_{x:\overline{n}|}$ is normally much greater than $P^1_{x:\overline{n}|}$, the expense margin to be used to offset first-year expenses will also be much greater for an $n$-year endowment insurance than for an $n$-year term insurance. One school of thought holds that if $P - A^1_{x:\overline{1}|}$ provides an acceptable expense margin for low-premium policies, it provides an excessive margin for high-premium policies. Under this line of reasoning, low-premium policies may be valued satisfactorily under the $FPT$ method, but high-premium policies should use a modified reserve method that will produce a positive first-year terminal reserve.

A modified preliminary term standard requires a decision rule by which policies are separated into low- and high-premium classes; the $FPT$ method is permitted for low-premium policies, and one of $\beta$, $\beta - \alpha$ or $\alpha > A^1_{x:\overline{1}|}$, along with the length of the modification period, must be specified for high-premium policies to define a valuation method to complete the standard.

An objective of government regulation is to reduce the threat to insureds that an insurance company cannot meet its obligations. In accordance with this objective, insurance laws and regulations often limit the choice of valuation methods and assumptions. In some jurisdictions, these valuation laws and regulations have defined various modified reserve standards. Only one such standard remains of direct interest to actuaries practicing in the United States. The Standard Valuation Law defines the Commissioners valuation standard for life insurance. The elements of this standard are that

- high-premium policies are defined as those for which $\beta^{FPT} > {}_{19}P_{x+1}$, the $FPT$ renewal net premium for a 20-payment life;
- the $FPT$ method is required as a minimum for low-premium policies;
- a specific Commissioners reserve valuation method ($Com$) be used for high-premium policies. In this, the premium payment period is the modification period,

$$\beta^{Com} - \alpha^{Com} = {}_{19}P_{x+1} - A^1_{x:\overline{1}|}.$$

An application of (14.6.3) yields

$$\beta^{Com} = P + \frac{{}_{19}P_{x+1} - A^1_{x:\overline{1}|}}{\ddot{a}_{x:\overline{h}|}} \tag{14.8.1}$$

where $h$ is the length of the premium paying period.

# Chapter 14
## INSURANCE MODELS INCLUDING EXPENSES

A problem in the application of modified preliminary term valuation standards is in extending them to policies with nonlevel premiums and nonlevel benefits. In Section 7.4 a general insurance, using a fully discrete basis, was discussed. This general insurance will be used to illustrate the problem. Recall that, under the insurance, a death benefit $b_{j+1}$ is paid at the end of policy year $j + 1$ if death has occurred in that year. Annual premiums are payable, contingent on survival, at the beginning of each policy year during the premium period. The gross premium $G_j$ is paid at time $j$, the beginning of policy year $j + 1$.

We will describe the several rules, as interpreted by Menge (1946), for applying the Commissioners reserve standard to this general insurance. Formulas are given for a term insurance with a description of the modifications for an endowment insurance. Calculations for an endowment insurance are illustrated in Example 14.6.

The first task is to determine the criterion for using *FPT*. As a first step, we calculate an equivalent level renewal amount (*ELRA*). For this insurance we have

$$ELRA = \frac{\sum_{j=0}^{n-2} b_{j+2}\, v^{j+1}\, {}_jp_{x+1}\, q_{x+1+j}}{A^{1}_{x+1:\overline{n-1}|}}. \tag{14.8.2}$$

The *ELRA* for an endowment insurance is calculated on the basis of the death benefits only and is thus also given by (14.8.2).

In addition, the average ratio of renewal net premiums to renewal gross premiums is denoted by $r_F$ and is determined by

$$r_F = \frac{\sum_{j=0}^{n-2} b_{j+2}\, v^{j+1}\, {}_jp_{x+1}\, q_{x+1+j}}{\sum_{j=0}^{h-2} G_{j+1}\, v^{j}\, {}_jp_{x+1}}. \tag{14.8.3}$$

For endowment insurances, pure endowment benefits are included in the numerator for $r_F$.

Under the Menge interpretation, *FPT* is allowed if

$$r_F\, G_0 \le ELRA\ {}_{19}P_{x+1}. \tag{14.8.4}$$

If this condition is satisfied, *FPT* is interpreted as involving net premiums $\pi_0 = v b_1 q_x$ and $\pi_j = r_F G_j$, $j = 1, 2, \ldots, h - 1$, where $h$ is the length of the premium paying period. The modified reserve, for $k \ge 1$, is given by

$$_kV^{Mod} = \sum_{j=0}^{n-k-1} b_{k+j+1}\, v^{j+1}\, {}_jp_{x+k}\, q_{x+k+j} - r_F \sum_{j=0}^{h-k-1} G_{k+j}\, v^{j}\, {}_jp_{x+k}. \tag{14.8.5}$$

In cases where (14.8.4) is not satisfied, the excess first-year expense allowance, comparable to $\beta - \alpha$, is given by

$$ELRA\ {}_{19}P_{x+1} - b_1\, A^{1}_{x:\overline{1}|}.$$

A modified average ratio of net premiums to gross premiums, denoted by $r_C$, is determined as

$$r_C = \frac{\sum_{j=0}^{n-1} b_{j+1}\, v^{j+1}\,{}_j p_x\, q_{x+j} + [ELRA\, {}_{19}P_{x+1} - b_1\, A^1_{x:\overline{1}|}]}{\sum_{j=0}^{h-1} G_j\, v^j\, {}_j p_x}. \qquad (14.8.6)$$

The modified reserve in this high-premium case is given by

$$_kV^{Mod} = \sum_{j=0}^{n-k-1} b_{k+j+1}\, v^{j+1}\, {}_j p_{x+k}\, q_{x+k+j} - r_C \sum_{j=0}^{h-k-1} G_{k+j}\, v^j\, {}_j p_{x+k}. \qquad (14.8.7)$$

For endowment insurances, the numerator of $r_C$ and the right-hand sides of (14.8.5) and (14.8.7) are adjusted to include pure endowment benefits.

**Example 14.6:** Calculate the net annual premiums under the Commissioners standard for a special 30-year endowment policy issued at age 35. The benefit is 150,000 for the first 20 years and 100,000 thereafter with a maturity benefit of 100,000. The gross premium is a level 2500 for 10 years and thereafter is 1250. Use the Illustrative Life Table with $i = 0.06$.

**Solution:**
The *ELRA* is based on the death benefit and is calculated as

$$ELRA = 50,000\,\frac{3M_{36} - M_{55} - 2M_{65}}{M_{36} - M_{65}}$$

$$= 130,153.30.$$

The $r_F$ factor is given by

$$r_F = \frac{50,000\,(3M_{36} - M_{55} - 2M_{65} + 2D_{65})}{1250\,(2N_{36} - N_{45} - N_{65})}$$

$$= 0.91014604$$

and

$$_{19}P_{36} = 0.0116543.$$

For *FPT* to apply, (14.8.4) must be satisfied. However, since

$$r_F\, G_0 = (0.91014604)(2500) = 2275.37 > 1516.85 = ELRA\, {}_{19}P_{36},$$

*FPT* is not allowed. The excess first-year expense allowance, corresponding to $\beta - \alpha$, is given by

$$ELRA\, {}_{19}P_{x+1} - b_1\, A^1_{x:\overline{1}|} = 1516.8456 - 284.9395 = 1231.9061$$

and

$$r_C = \frac{50,000\,(3M_{35} - M_{55} - 2M_{65} + 2D_{65}) + 1231.9061\,D_{35}}{1250\,(2N_{35} - N_{45} - N_{65})}$$

$$= 0.88223578.$$

# INSURANCE MODELS INCLUDING EXPENSES

Thus the net renewal premiums are

$$r_C(2500) = 2205.59 \quad \text{years } 2,3,\ldots,10$$

$$r_C(1250) = 1102.79 \quad \text{years } 11,12,\ldots,30,$$

and the first-year net premium $= r_C(2500) - 1231.9061 = 973.68.$ ▼

**14.9
Canadian
Standard**

The Canadian Insurance Act prescribes a modified reserve method (*CAN*) that permits the valuation actuary wide discretion in the choice of assumptions. Mathematically, there are equivalent ways of defining a modified reserve method. The definition of the Canadian modified reserve method will be given in alternative ways in order to gain insight.

First, let $E^{Can}$ be the extra first-year expense allowance measured with respect to the net level premium. That is,

$$\alpha^{Can} = P - E^{Can}, \tag{14.9.1}$$

and using (14.6.2), where the modification period is the premium paying period, we have

$$\beta^{Can} = P + \frac{E^{Can}}{a_{x:\overline{h-1}|}} \tag{14.9.2}$$

where

$$E^{Can} = \min\left[(a),\,(b),\,(c)\right]$$

where

(a) = 150% of net level premium.

(b) = actual acquisition expenses.

(c) = the actuarial present value of expenses recoverable in the second and later years, while still providing for administrative expenses and policyholder dividends.

Multiplying (14.9.2) by $a_{x:\overline{h-1}|}$ and adding the result to (14.9.1) yields

$$\alpha^{Can} + \beta^{Can}\, a_{x:\overline{h-1}|} = A.$$

Reserves follow,

$$_0V^{Can} + \alpha^{Can} = P - E^{Can} \tag{14.9.3A}$$

$$_kV^{Can} = A(k) - \beta^{Can}\, \ddot{a}_{x+k:\overline{h-k}|} \tag{14.9.3B}$$

$$= {}_k^hV - \frac{E^{Can}\, \ddot{a}_{x+k:\overline{h-k}|}}{a_{x:\overline{h-1}|}}, \tag{14.9.3C}$$

where $A(k)$ denotes the actuarial present value of future benefits at duration $k$ and (14.9.3C) follows by substituting (14.9.2).

An equivalent approach was considered in discussions preliminary to the adoption of the Canadian modified reserve method. Under that approach, the terminal reserve at time 0 is defined to be $-E^{Can}$, the first-year premium is $P$ and $\beta^{Can}$ is defined as in (14.9.2). In each of these approaches, the initial reserve at time 0 is $P - E^{Can}$ and subsequent terminal reserves are given by (14.9.3B).

## 14.10 Notes and References

In this chapter we have used the clumsy term "expense-loaded premiums" for what some would call gross premiums. The use of the longer term is intended as a warning that the subject of premiums contains many topics other than the net premiums discussed in previous chapters and the expense loadings introduced here. These topics include competitive considerations, profit loadings in nonparticipating insurance, expected dividends in participating insurance, risk factors and the impact of withdrawal benefits. Guertin (1965) discusses many of these topics.

Fassel (1956) discusses the issues involved in estimating and allocating per policy expenses. Until the time of Fassel's paper, most per policy expenses were included in the loading for expenses that vary with the amount of insurance (assuming an average size policy). In fact the use of either policy fees or the band system was viewed for many years as an inequitable allocation of expense charges.

Noback (1969) has written a treatise on life insurance accounting. Horn (1971) studied the impact of various reserve systems on the time incidence of reported net income.

Full preliminary term reserves are also called Zillmerized reserves for the Swiss actuary who developed the method. The Commissioners method and related recommendations were developed by two National Association of Insurance Commissioners (NAIC) committees with almost identical membership: The Committee to Study the Need for a New Mortality Table and Related Topics (1939) and the Committee to Study Nonforfeiture Benefits and Related Matters (1941). In recognition of their common chairman, these committees were popularly known as the Guertin Committees. Menge (1946) wrote a comprehensive paper on technical aspects of the Commissioners method.

## Exercises

*Section 14.2*

14.1. a. A gambling enterprise collects 0.55 from each of 1000 customers on July 1 of year $A$. It immediately invests the funds in a savings account earning 3% interest each 6 months. On July 1 of year $A + 1$, 1000 coins will be tossed, each assigned to a specific customer. If the customer's coin comes up heads, the customer receives a prize of 1. If the coin comes up tails, the prize is 0. Supply the figures for the balance sheet and income statement for the gambling enterprise on December 31 of year $A$. Use actuarial present values for liabilities.

# Chapter 14

## INSURANCE MODELS INCLUDING EXPENSES

---

Balance Sheet

| Assets | Liabilities |
|---|---|
| Savings Account | Reserves |
| | Surplus |

Income Statement

Premium Income

Interest Income

Increase in reserves

---

b. The random variable $Y$ is the amount of the payments made on July 1 of year $A + 1$ and has a binomial distribution. Using a normal approximation, evaluate

$$\Pr[Y(1.03)^{-1} - A > 0]$$

where $A$ represents the assets as of December 31 of year $A$.

c. If the enterprise had only one customer, the scale of the operation would be 0.001 of that in part (a). Show that the probability displayed in (b) is equal to 1/2 for the reduced enterprise.

14.2. An expense-augmented loss variable for use with a whole life policy, fully continuous model, is given by

$$L_e = L + X$$

where

$$L = v^T - \bar{P}(\bar{A}_x)\,\bar{a}_{\overline{T}|}$$

and

$$X = c_0 + (g - e)\,\bar{a}_{\overline{T}|}.$$

In these expressions, $L$ is interpreted as the loss variable associated with the benefit portion of the policy and $X$ with the expenses. The symbol $c_0$ denotes nonrandom initial expenses, $g$ the rate of continuous maintenance expense, and $e$ the expense loading in the premium. The equivalence principle has been adopted and $E[L] = E[X] = 0$. Show that
a. $X = c_0 L$
b. $\text{Var}[L_e] = (1 + c_0)^2 \,\text{Var}[L]$.

*Section 14.3*

14.3. The expense-loaded annual premium for a 1000 endowment at age 65 life insurance with annual premiums issued at age 40 is calculated using the following assumptions:
- selling commission is 40% of the expense-loaded premium in the first year;
- renewal commissions are 5% of the expense-loaded premium for policy years 2 through 10;
- premium tax is 2% of the expense-loaded premium each year;

- maintenance expense is 12.50 per 1000 of insurance in the first year and 4.00 per 1000 of insurance thereafter;
- the net premium is to provide for the immediate payment of death claims with no premium adjustment on death;
- a 15-year select-and-ultimate mortality table is to be used.

Write an expression for the expense-loaded premium.

14.4. The expense-loaded premium for a single premium $n$-year endowment insurance is determined using the following assumptions:
- taxes are $2\frac{1}{2}\%$ of the expense-loaded premium;
- commission is 4% of the expense-loaded premium;
- other expenses are 5 in the first year, and 2.50 in each renewal year, per 1000 of insurance.

Claims are paid immediately and expenses are incurred at the start of each policy year. Develop a formula for the expense-loaded premium issued to $(x)$ for a 1000 benefit insurance policy.

14.5. For a whole life policy of amount 1 on a fully discrete payment basis, the expense-loaded annual premium is based on the following schedule of expenses:
- an initial expense of $e_0$;
- each policy year, including the first, an expense of $e_1 + e_2 P_x$;
- the cost of claims settlement, paid along with the claim, of $e_3$ per unit of insurance.

If $G = a P_x + c$, determine $a$ and $c$.

*Section 14.4*

14.6. Let

$$G(b) = \frac{b(a + c/b)}{1 - f}$$

and

$$R(b) = \frac{a}{1 - f} + \frac{c}{b - bf}.$$

Given that $a/(1-f) = 25$, $c/(1-f) = 7.50$ and $m$ (the minimum amount of insurance measured in thousands) $= 2$, plot a graph of $R(b)$.

14.7. Using the facts stated in Exercise 14.6, let $t = 5$ and show that
a. $R(t) = 26.50$
b. $R(b) = R(t) + Z(b)$
   where $Z(b) = c/(1-f)b - c/(1-f)t$.
c. Plot $Z(b)$.
In this problem $t$ is called a **pivot** with $Z(b) > 0$ when $b < t$, and $Z(b) < 0$ when $b > t$.

14.8. The p.d.f. of the amount of insurance issued on an individual policy for a particular plan of insurance is given by
$$f(b) = k b^{-3} \qquad b > 10$$

# Chapter 14

## INSURANCE MODELS INCLUDING EXPENSES

where $b$ is measured in thousands. Calculate
a. the normalizing constant $k$
b. the expected policy amount
c. the median of the distribution of amounts of insurance
d. $R(\bar{b})$ if $a = 25$, $f = 0.15$ and $c = 12$.

*Section 14.5*

14.9. The continuous analogue of (14.5.5) is the differential equation

$$\frac{d}{dt} \, {}_tp_x \, [{}_t\bar{V}(\bar{A}_x) + \bar{u}(t)] = {}_tp_x \, [\bar{P}(\bar{A}_x) + \delta \, {}_t\bar{V}(\bar{A}_x)$$

$$+ \, \bar{c} - \bar{e}(t) + \delta \bar{u}(t) - \mu_{x+t}].$$

Using this equation, and (7.11.5) rearranged to express

$$\frac{d}{dt} \, [{}_tp_x \, {}_t\bar{V}(\bar{A}_x)],$$

show that

$$ {}_tp_x \, \bar{u}(t) = \int_0^t e^{\delta(t-y)} \, {}_yp_x \, [\bar{c} - \bar{e}(y)] \, dy.$$

*Section 14.6*

14.10. For a modified reserve method the period of modification is equal to the premium paying period. Show that

$$ {}_kV_{x:\overline{n}|}^{Mod} = 1 - (\beta + d) \, \ddot{a}_{x+k:\overline{n-k}|}.$$

14.11. A modified reserve method for a whole life insurance, fully continuous basis, is defined by

$$\bar{\alpha}(t) = \frac{t}{m} \, \bar{\beta} \qquad 0 \le t < m$$

where $\bar{\beta}$ is the level premium for $t \ge m$.
a. Write a formula for $\bar{\beta}$.
b. Write a prospective formula for ${}_t\bar{V}(\bar{A}_x)^{Mod}$, $t < m$.

14.12. Calculate $\alpha_x^{Mod}$ and $\beta_x^{Mod}$ in a modified reserve method for a fully discrete whole life insurance where ${}_1V_x^{Mod} = K$. The modification period is the premium paying period.

14.13. Under a modified reserve method for a fully discrete whole life insurance policy, the net annual premiums, $P_x$, are replaced (for reserve purposes) by annual premiums of $\alpha_x^{Mod}$ for the first $n$ years and $\beta_x^{Mod}$ thereafter. Show that

$$\frac{\beta_x^{Mod} - P_x}{P_x - \alpha_x^{Mod}} = \frac{\ddot{a}_x}{{}_{n|}\ddot{a}_x} - 1.$$

14.14. Show that

$$ {}_kV - {}_kV^{Mod} = \left( \frac{\beta - \alpha}{\ddot{a}_{x:\overline{j}|}} \right) \ddot{a}_{x+k:\overline{j-k}|}$$

# INSURANCE MODELS INCLUDING EXPENSES

where $j$ is the length of the modification period. Note that this difference can be interpreted as the unamortized portion of the extra first-year expense allowance.

*Section 14.7*

14.15. Show that

$$_kV^{FPT}_{x:\overline{n}|} = 1 - \frac{\ddot{a}_{x+k:\overline{n-k}|}}{\ddot{a}_{x+1:\overline{n-1}|}} \qquad k = 1,2,\ldots,n.$$

14.16. A **2-year preliminary term reserve method** is defined with three valuation net premiums:

First year: $\qquad\qquad A^1_{x:\overline{1}|}$

Second year: $\qquad\quad A^{\phantom{1}1}_{x+1:\overline{1}|}$

Thereafter: $\qquad\qquad$ Net level premium for age $x+2$, no change in benefits or premium paying period.

Show that, for this method, the reserve on a whole life policy to $(x)$ is given by

$$_1V^{Mod} = {}_2V^{Mod} = 0$$

$$_kV^{Mod} = {}_kV_x - (P_{x+2} - P_x)\,\ddot{a}_{x+k} \qquad k = 3,4,5,\ldots.$$

(This type of reserve system is common in health insurance.)

14.17. A proposed reserve valuation method has a first-year net premium $\alpha$ and a renewal net premium $\beta$ applicable in all renewal years. The first-year premium is constrained to be at least equal to $A^1_{x:\overline{1}|}$. This provision allows the use of *FPT* for some policies and some ages. The excess of $\beta$ over $\alpha$ cannot exceed 0.05. Assume that on a particular valuation basis $d = 0.03$, $\ddot{a}_x = 17$, $\ddot{a}_{x:\overline{12}|} = 9$, $A_{x:\overline{12}|} = 2/3$ and $A^1_{x:\overline{1}|} = 0.01$.

   a. Calculate $\beta$ for a whole life policy issued to $(x)$.
   b. Calculate $_{12}V^{Mod}_x$ for this method.
   c. Assuming $\alpha = A^1_{x:\overline{1}|} = 0.01$, calculate a test value for $\beta$ for a 12-year endowment insurance on $(x)$. Confirm that this value for $\beta$ is inadmissible since $\beta - \alpha > 0.05$.
   d. Using the result in (c), calculate $\beta$ for a 12-year endowment insurance on $(x)$.
   e. Calculate $_1V^{Mod}_{x:\overline{12}|}$.

*Section 14.8*

14.18. Write formulas for the first-year and renewal premiums under the Commissioners reserve method for a 15 payment, 15-year endowment issued to $(x)$ on a fully discrete payment basis.

14.19. A modified preliminary term reserve standard is described as follows:

   • Policies are divided into two classes: Class I, if the *FPT* net renewal premium is greater than $_{19}P_{x+1}$; Class II, if the policy does not belong to Class I.

# INSURANCE MODELS INCLUDING EXPENSES

- For policies in Class I, the first-year net premium is the same as that defined by the Commissioners reserve method. The net renewal premium is such that the net level premium reserve is reached at the end of the premium period or 15 years, whichever comes first.
- For policies in Class II, the $FPT$ method is prescribed.

For a fully discrete payment basis, 20-payment, 20-year endowment issued to $(x)$, write an expression for $\alpha$ and $\beta$ under this standard.

14.20. If $\beta^{FPT} > {}_{19}P_{x+1}$, the $k$th terminal reserve by the Commissioners method on a fully discrete basis life insurance issued to $(x)$ and paying level benefits may be written as

$$_{k}V^{Com} = \frac{A^{1}_{x:\overline{1}|}}{{}_{k}E_{x}} + {}_{19}P_{x+1}\,\ddot{s}_{x+1:\overline{k-1}|} + T\,\ddot{s}_{x:\overline{k}|} - \frac{A^{1}_{x:\overline{k}|}}{{}_{k}E_{x}}.$$

Derive an expression for $T$.

14.21. Assume $\beta^{FPT} > {}_{19}P_{x+1}$ and

$$b_{j+1} = 1 \quad j = 0,1,\ldots,n-1,$$

$$G_{j} = P(1 + \lambda) \quad j = 0,1,\ldots,h-1.$$

Show that (14.8.7) reduces to the formula for the $k$th reserve by the Commissioners standard.

*Section 14.9*

14.22. Before the adoption of the Canadian modified reserve method, the Canadian standard was defined in Canadian law. High-premium policies were defined as those satisfying $P > P_{x}$. For such a policy, the modification period and the premium paying period coincide and $P - \alpha = P_{x} - A^{1}_{x:\overline{1}|}$. $FPT$ was permitted for other policies. Show that for an $n$-year endowment insurance

$$\beta = P_{x:\overline{n}|} + \frac{P_{x} - A^{1}_{x:\overline{1}|}}{a_{x:\overline{n-1}|}}.$$

*Miscellaneous*

14.23. a. Calculate alternatives to the net incomes in Column (2) of Table 14.5 by means of the equation

net income = (interest income on surplus)

+ (net profit loadings plus interest).

b. Compare the net income expression in part (a) with the corresponding expression (14.5.9), and comment on the difference in viewpoints.

# Chapter 15
## NONFORFEITURE BENEFITS AND DIVIDENDS

## 15.1 Introduction

A single decrement model for individual life insurance net annual premiums and reserves was built in Chapters 6 and 7. In this model the timing and, perhaps, the amount of benefit payments are determined by the time of death of the insured, and premiums are paid until death or the end of the premium period as specified in the policy. In practice, there is no way to prevent the cessation of premium payments before death or the end of the premium period. In this situation an issue arises about how to reconcile the interests of the parties to the policy. A model derived from multiple decrement theory is appropriate for examining this issue. Public policy considerations that should guide the reconciliation of the interests of the insurance system and the terminating insured have been subject to discussion since the earliest days of insurance.

Before premiums and reserves can be determined, a guiding principle must be adopted. Likewise in the determination of *nonforfeiture benefits*, those benefits that will not be lost because of the premature cessation of premium payments, a guiding principle is required. In this section we shall adopt a simple operational principle, one that is, in effect, close to that adopted in United States insurance regulation. The principle is that the withdrawing insured shall receive a value such that the benefit, premium and reserve structure, built using the single decrement model, remains appropriate in the multiple decrement context.

This principle is motivated by a particular concept of equity about the treatment of the two classes of policyholders, those who terminate before the basic insurance contract is fulfilled and those who continue. Clearly several concepts of what constitutes equity are possible, ranging from the view that terminating policyholders have not fulfilled the contract, and are therefore not entitled to nonforfeiture benefits, to the view that a terminating policyholder should be returned to his original position by the return of the accumulated value of all premiums, perhaps less an insurance charge. The concept of equity, which is the foundation of the principle adopted in the United States, is an intermediate one. That is, withdrawing life insurance policyholders are entitled to nonforfeiture benefits, but these benefits should not force a change in the price-benefit structure for continuing policyholders.

To illustrate some of the implications of this principle, we will develop a model for a whole life policy on a fully continuous payment basis with death and withdrawal benefits. The introduction of withdrawals into the model will be assumed not to change the force of mortality, labeled for this development $\mu_{x+t}^{(1)}$ in both the single and double decrement models. The force of withdrawal is denoted by $\mu_{x+t}^{(2)}$ with

$$\mu_{x+t}^{(\tau)} = \mu_{x+t}^{(1)} + \mu_{x+t}^{(2)}.$$

For multiple decrement models, it is required that

$$\int_0^\infty \mu_{x+t}^{(\tau)} \, dt = \infty,$$

so that

$$\lim_{t \to \infty} {}_t p_x^{(\tau)} = 0,$$

but it is not necessary for $\mu_{x+t}^{(2)}$ to have this property.

We start our model by specializing (7.11.3) to the case of a whole life insurance with single decrement premiums and reserves,

$$\frac{d}{dt} {}_t\bar{V}(\bar{A}_x) = \bar{P}(\bar{A}_x) + \delta \, {}_t\bar{V}(\bar{A}_x) - \mu_{x+t}^{(1)} \, [1 - {}_t\bar{V}(\bar{A}_x)]. \quad (15.1.1)$$

Recalling from Section 9.2 that

$$\frac{d}{dt} {}_t p_x^{(\tau)} = -{}_t p_x^{(\tau)} \, (\mu_{x+t}^{(1)} + \mu_{x+t}^{(2)}),$$

we can express the following derivative as

$$\frac{d}{dt} [v^t \, {}_t p_x^{(\tau)} \, {}_t\bar{V}(\bar{A}_x)] = v^t \, {}_t p_x^{(\tau)} \, [\bar{P}(\bar{A}_x) + \delta \, {}_t\bar{V}(\bar{A}_x) - \mu_{x+t}^{(1)} \, (1 - {}_t\bar{V}(\bar{A}_x))]$$

$$- v^t \, {}_t p_x^{(\tau)} \, {}_t\bar{V}(\bar{A}_x) \, [\delta + \mu_{x+t}^{(1)} + \mu_{x+t}^{(2)}] \quad (15.1.2)$$

$$= v^t \, {}_t p_x^{(\tau)} \, [\bar{P}(\bar{A}_x) - \mu_{x+t}^{(1)} - \mu_{x+t}^{(2)} \, {}_t\bar{V}(\bar{A}_x)].$$

The progress of the reserves for a whole life insurance which includes withdrawal benefit ${}_t\bar{V}(\bar{A}_x)$, using premiums and reserves derived from a double decrement model, is analogous to (15.1.1) and is shown below in (15.1.3). In this expression, the superscript $\underline{2}$ denotes premiums and reserves based on the double decrement model:

$$\frac{d}{dt} ({}_t\bar{V}(\bar{A}_x)^{\underline{2}}) = \bar{P}(\bar{A}_x)^{\underline{2}} + \delta \, {}_t\bar{V}(\bar{A}_x)^{\underline{2}} - \mu_{x+t}^{(1)} \, [1 - {}_t\bar{V}(\bar{A}_x)^{\underline{2}}]$$

$$- \mu_{x+t}^{(2)} \, ({}_t\bar{V}(\bar{A}_x) - {}_t\bar{V}(\bar{A}_x)^{\underline{2}}). \quad (15.1.3)$$

The last term in (15.1.3) is the net cost of withdrawal when the reserve ${}_t\bar{V}(\bar{A}_x)^{\underline{2}}$ is treated as a savings fund available to offset benefits [see (7.11.5)]. Thus,

$$\frac{d}{dt} [v^t \, {}_t p_x^{(\tau)} \, {}_t\bar{V}(\bar{A}_x)^{\underline{2}}] = v^t \, {}_t p_x^{(\tau)} \, \{\bar{P}(\bar{A}_x)^{\underline{2}} + \delta \, {}_t\bar{V}(\bar{A}_x)^{\underline{2}}$$

$$- \mu_{x+t}^{(1)} \, [1 - {}_t\bar{V}(\bar{A}_x)^{\underline{2}}] - \mu_{x+t}^{(2)} \, [{}_t\bar{V}(\bar{A}_x) - {}_t\bar{V}(\bar{A}_x)^{\underline{2}}]\}$$

$$- v^t \, {}_t p_x^{(\tau)} \, {}_t\bar{V}(\bar{A}_x)^{\underline{2}} \, [\delta + \mu_{x+t}^{(1)} + \mu_{x+t}^{(2)}] \quad (15.1.4)$$

$$= v^t \, {}_t p_x^{(\tau)} \, [\bar{P}(\bar{A}_x)^{\underline{2}} - \mu_{x+t}^{(1)} - \mu_{x+t}^{(2)} \, {}_t\bar{V}(\bar{A}_x)].$$

Combining (15.1.2) and (15.1.4) we obtain

# NONFORFEITURE BENEFITS AND DIVIDENDS

$$\frac{d}{dt}[v^t \, _tp_x^{(\tau)} \, (_t\bar{V}(\bar{A}_x)^2 - \, _t\bar{V}(\bar{A}_x))] = v^t \, _tp_x^{(\tau)} \, [\bar{P}(\bar{A}_x)^2 - \bar{P}(\bar{A}_x)]. \quad (15.1.5)$$

We now integrate (15.1.5) from $t = 0$ to $t = \omega - x$ to obtain

$$0 = \bar{a}_x^{(\tau)} \, [\bar{P}(\bar{A}_x)^2 - \bar{P}(\bar{A}_x)], \quad (15.1.6)$$

implying that

$$\bar{P}(\bar{A}_x)^2 = \bar{P}(\bar{A}_x).$$

Thus (15.1.5) reduces to

$$\frac{d}{dt}\{v^t \, _tp_x^{(\tau)} \, [_t\bar{V}(\bar{A}_x)^2 - \, _t\bar{V}(\bar{A}_x)]\} = 0,$$

which implies that

$$_s\bar{V}(\bar{A}_x)^2 = \, _s\bar{V}(\bar{A}_x) \quad s \geq 0. \quad (15.1.7)$$

Therefore, if the withdrawal benefit in a double decrement model whole life insurance, fully continuous payment basis, is the reserve under the single decrement model, the premium and reserves under the double decrement model are equal to the premium and reserves under the single decrement model. This result will not be directly applied to the practical problem of defining nonforfeiture benefits. However, it does suggest the basic idea of how to minimize the impact of withdrawal, or nonforfeiture, benefits on premiums and reserves (determined under a single decrement model) and will permeate the discussions in the remainder of this chapter.

## 15.2 Cash Values

The development in Section 15.1 did not include consideration of expenses and corresponding premium loadings. Therefore, if the general principle stated in that section is adopted for determining the value, at the time of premium default, of nonforfeiture benefits, some allowance needs to be made for these missing factors. An approximate method for adjusting net level premium reserves for initial expenses not yet recovered from premium loadings, and for the risk of withdrawal at a financially inopportune time for the insurer, is to define

$$_kCV = \, _kV - \, _kSC. \quad (15.2.1)$$

In (15.2.1), $_kCV$ is the **cash value** of nonforfeiture benefits at time $k = 1,2,3,\ldots$ following policy issue, $_kV$ is the terminal reserve and $_kSC$ is the **surrender charge.**

The quantity $_kSC$ received its name in early insurance regulation and practice. For many years the laws of some states specified a maximum value for $_kSC$, such as 0.025 for each unit of insurance. In practice, negative values of $_kCV$ cannot be collected from withdrawing policyholders. Therefore, the values of (15.2.1), per unit of insurance, are positive or 0.

A continuing theme in the regulation of the cash value of nonforfeiture benefits has been the need for direct recognition of the amount and incidence of expenses. One idea, in accord with this theme, is to define a minimum cash value for a unit insurance as

$$
\begin{aligned}
{}_kCV &= A(k) - P^a\,\ddot{a}(k)\\
&= {}_kV - (P^a - P)\,\ddot{a}(k)
\end{aligned}
\tag{15.2.2}
$$

where $A(k)$ and $\ddot{a}(k)$ are, respectively, general net single premium insurance and annuity symbols appropriate for time $k$, $k = 1,2,3,\ldots$ following policy issue, ${}_kV$ denotes a terminal reserve at the same time, $P$ is a net annual premium and $P^a$ is called an *adjusted premium.* (The symbols $A(0)$, $\ddot{a}(0)$ will be abbreviated to $A$ and $\ddot{a}$, respectively.) The regulatory problem becomes that of defining adjusted premiums.

The 1975 report of the Society of Actuaries committee studying nonforfeiture benefits and related matters contained consideration of two types of expenses in defining adjusted premiums. First is a level amount per unit of insurance, denoted by $E$, incurred each year throughout the premium paying period. Second is an additional expense allowance for the first year of amount $E_1$. The gross premium rate $G$ is assumed to be composed of an adjusted premium and the level annual expense component $E$. The first-year expense component $E_1$ is assumed to be provided by the adjusted premium. That is,

$$
G = P^a + E
\tag{15.2.3A}
$$

$$
G\,\ddot{a} = (P^a + E)\,\ddot{a} = A + E_1 + E\,\ddot{a}.
\tag{15.2.3B}
$$

From (15.2.3B) we obtain

$$
P^a = \frac{A + E_1}{\ddot{a}}.
\tag{15.2.4}
$$

Formula (15.2.4) can be rewritten, by substituting $\ddot{a} = a + 1$, as

$$
P^a - E_1 + P^a\,a = A.
\tag{15.2.5}
$$

Formula (15.2.5) is to be compared with (14.6.1), showing that $P^a - E_1$ can be viewed as a first-year premium, $\alpha$, and $P^a$ as the renewal premium, $\beta$, in a modified reserve method. An adjusted premium is determined as soon as $E_1$, the provision for first-year expenses per unit of insurance, is defined.

The 1941 NAIC Standard Nonforfeiture Law for Life Insurance specified $E_1$ and then defined minimum cash values per unit of insurance using (15.2.2). In its 1975 Report, the Society of Actuaries committee recommended retention of (15.2.2) as the basic means for regulating cash values, but also recommended some changes and

# Chapter 15

## NONFORFEITURE BENEFITS AND DIVIDENDS

simplifications in the definition of $E_1$. These recommendations were incorporated into the 1980 NAIC Standard Nonforfeiture Law.

**Table 15.1
Definition of $E_1$,
First-Year Expense
Allowance Per Unit
of Insurance**

| 1941 | $0.4 \min (P^a,\ 0.04) + 0.25 \min (P^a,\ P_x^a,\ 0.04) + 0.02$ |
|---|---|
| 1980 | $1.25 \min (P,\ 0.04) + 0.01$ |

Note that

- $P^a$ denotes the adjusted premium rate for this policy.
- $P$ denotes the net premium rate for this policy.
- $P_x^a$ denotes the adjusted premium rate for a whole life policy on $(x)$.

In implementing the 1941 NAIC rules, one must first compute $P_x^a$. We have

$$P_x^a = \frac{A_x + E_1}{\ddot{a}_x},$$

where

$$E_1 = \begin{cases} 0.40\,P_x^a + 0.25\,P_x^a + 0.02 = 0.65\,P_x^a + 0.02 & P_x^a < 0.04, \\ 0.016 + 0.010 + 0.020 = 0.046 & P_x^a \geq 0.04. \end{cases}$$

These results lead to

$$P_x^a = \begin{cases} \dfrac{A_x + 0.02}{\ddot{a}_x - 0.65} & P_x^a < 0.04 \\[2mm] \dfrac{A_x + 0.046}{\ddot{a}_x} & P_x^a \geq 0.04. \end{cases}$$

One of the objectives of the 1980 law is to achieve simplification by removing the circularity in the 1941 definitions. This is accomplished by using percentage expense allowances on net premiums rather than on adjusted premiums.

Table 15.2, adapted from a table in the 1941 report, illustrates the range of possibilities for adjusted premiums according to the model legislation developed from the report. It is important to keep in mind that these adjusted premiums are used to define the legal minimum cash value per unit of insurance. Higher cash values are permitted.

**Example 15.1:**

For each row in Tables 15.2 and 15.3, calculate the corresponding first-year expense provision $E_1$.

# NONFORFEITURE BENEFITS AND DIVIDENDS

**Table 15.2
Adjusted Premiums,
1941 Report**

| Plan of Insurance | Range of Adjusted Premium For | | Formula for Adjusted Premium Per Unit of Insurance |
| | Whole Life | Plan of Insurance | |
|---|---|---|---|
| 1. Whole life | $<0.04$ | $<0.04$ | $\dfrac{A_x + 0.02}{\ddot{a}_x - 0.65}$ |
| 2. Whole life | $\geq0.04$ | $\geq0.04$ | $\dfrac{A_x + 0.046}{\ddot{a}_x}$ |
| 3. Other plans | $<0.04$ | $<0.04$ and $\leq P_x^a$ | $\dfrac{A + 0.02}{\ddot{a} - 0.65}$ |
| 4. Other plans | $<0.04$ | $<0.04$ but $> P_x^a$ | $\dfrac{A + 0.02 + 0.25\,P_x^a}{\ddot{a} - 0.4}$ |
| 5. Other plans | $\geq0.04$ | $<0.04$ | $\dfrac{A + 0.02}{\ddot{a} - 0.65}$ |
| 6. Other plans | $<0.04$ | $\geq0.04$ | $\dfrac{A + 0.036 + 0.25\,P_x^a}{\ddot{a}}$ |
| 7. Other plans | $\geq0.04$ | $\geq0.04$ | $\dfrac{A + 0.046}{\ddot{a}}$ |

**Table 15.3
Adjusted Premiums,
1980 Law**

| Plan of Insurance | Range of Net Premium | Formula for Adjusted Premium |
|---|---|---|
| 1. Any plan | $<0.04$ | $\dfrac{A + 1.25\,P + 0.01}{\ddot{a}}$ |
| 2. Any plan | $\geq0.04$ | $\dfrac{A + 0.06}{\ddot{a}}$ |

**Solution:**
Rewriting (15.2.4) yields $E_1 = P^a\,\ddot{a} - A$ or $E_1 = (P^a - P)\,\ddot{a}$.

| Table 15.2 | $E_1$ |
|---|---|
| Line | |
| 1. | $\left[\dfrac{0.65\,P_x + 0.02}{\ddot{a}_x - 0.65}\right]\ddot{a}_x$ |
| 2. | $0.046$ |
| 3. | $\left[\dfrac{0.65\,P + 0.02}{\ddot{a} - 0.65}\right]\ddot{a}$ |
| 4. | $\left[\dfrac{0.4\,P + 0.25\,P_x^a + 0.02}{\ddot{a} - 0.40}\right]\ddot{a}$ |

5. $\left[\dfrac{0.65\,P + 0.02}{\ddot{a} - 0.65}\right]\ddot{a}$

6. $0.25\,P_x^a + 0.036$

7. $0.046$

| Table 15.3 | $\underline{E_1}$ |
|---|---|
| Line | |
| 1. | $1.25\,P + 0.01$ |
| 2. | $0.06$ ▼ |

**Example 15.2:** Develop formulas, using the 1941 report and the 1980 law, for the adjusted premium on a 10-payment, 15-year endowment insurance issued to (20), under the realistic assumptions that $P_{20}^a < 0.04$ and $_{10}P_{20:\overline{15}|} \geq 0.04$.

**Solution:**
Table 15.2 line 6 yields

$$_{10}P_{20:\overline{15}|}^a = \frac{A_{20:\overline{15}|} + 0.036 + 0.25\,P_{20}^a}{\ddot{a}_{20:\overline{10}|}},$$

while Table 15.3 line 2 yields

$$_{10}P_{20:\overline{15}|}^a = \frac{A_{20:\overline{15}|} + 0.06}{\ddot{a}_{20:\overline{10}|}}. \qquad ▼$$

In Section 14.8, some of the problems in applying modified reserve standards to policies with nonlevel gross premiums and nonlevel benefit amounts were discussed. The issues that arise with nonforfeiture benefits for such policies are similar, but there are differences. The 1980 law refers to an *average amount of insurance* (*AAI*) and indicates that this amount is based on benefit amounts at the beginnings of the first 10 policy years. Thus, in the notation of the general insurance of Section 7.4,

$$AAI = \frac{\displaystyle\sum_{j=0}^{9} b_{j+1}}{10}$$

when $n \geq 10$. Also, a net level premium is

$$P = \frac{\displaystyle\sum_{j=0}^{n-1} b_{j+1}\, v^{j+1}\, _jp_x\, q_{x+j}}{\ddot{a}_{x:\overline{h}|}}. \qquad (15.2.6)$$

An additional term is included in the numerator of (15.2.6) if pure endowment benefits are included. The formula for the first-year expense allowance depends on $P$ and $AAI$, and is defined as follows:

$$E_1 = \begin{cases} 1.25\,P + 0.01\,AAI & P < 0.04\,AAI \\ 0.06\,AAI & P \geq 0.04\,AAI. \end{cases} \quad (15.2.7)$$

The adjusted premium for any policy year is a multiple, $r_N$, of the corresponding gross premium for that policy year where

$$r_N = \frac{E_1 + \sum_{j=0}^{n-1} b_{j+1}\, v^{j+1}\, {}_jp_x\, q_{x+j}}{\sum_{j=0}^{h-1} G_j\, v^j\, {}_jp_x}. \quad (15.2.8)$$

The minimum cash value is given as

$${}_kCV = \sum_{j=0}^{n-k-1} b_{k+j+1}\, v^{j+1}\, {}_jp_{x+k}\, q_{x+k+j} - r_N \sum_{j=0}^{h-k-1} G_{k+j}\, v^j\, {}_jp_{x+k}. \quad (15.2.9)$$

Again, both (15.2.8) and (15.2.9) must be modified if pure endowment benefits are provided.

**Example 15.3:**    Calculate the minimum cash values at durations 1, 2, 10 and 20 for the special 30-year endowment policy described in Example 14.6. Use (15.2.7) and (15.2.8) with the Illustrative Life Table and 6% interest.

**Solution:**
The death benefit is 150,000 for the first 20 years and 100,000 thereafter. However, since the $AAI$ is based on the first 10 policy years, $AAI = 150,000$. The net level premium for this policy is, at issue age 35,

$$P = \frac{50,000\,(3\,M_{35} - M_{55} - 2\,M_{65} + 2\,D_{65})}{N_{35} - N_{65}}$$

$$= 1622.9358.$$

Since

$$P = 1622.94 \leq 6000 = 0.04\,AAI,$$

then, according to (15.2.7),

$$E_1 = 1.25\,P + 0.01\,AAI$$

$$= 3528.6698.$$

The gross premiums are 2500 annually for 10 years and 1250 annually for the remaining 20 years. The adjusted premium multiple, $r_N$, is

$$r_N = \frac{E_1\,D_{35} + 50,000\,[3\,M_{35} - M_{55} - 2\,M_{65} + 2\,D_{65}]}{1250\,(2\,N_{35} - N_{45} - N_{65})}$$

$$= 0.9667466.$$

Formula (15.2.9) was used to obtain the following cash values for this contract.

| $k$ | $_kCV$ |
|---|---|
| 1 | 0.00 |
| 2 | 669.73 |
| 10 | 22 519.81 |
| 20 | 48 776.92 |

Formula (15.2.9) gave $-1483.53$ for $_1CV$, however, negative values of $CV$ cannot be collected from withdrawing policyholders. ▼

In this section we have discussed the framework for defining minimum cash values. Important components are the interest rate and the life table that are specified. In the history of nonforfeiture value regulation, changes in the general framework have been infrequent. Legislative changes to update the interest and mortality bases of minimum cash values have occurred more frequently. The 1980 law provides for revisions of the maximum interest rate according to a formula based, in part, on an index of average interest rates prevailing during a period of time before policy issue.

The nonforfeiture values developed in this section are typically available in cash or as insurance benefits with the same actuarial present value. In Section 15.3 these insurance options will be discussed. In addition, cash values form the basis of another important policy provision, the policy loan clause. This provision provides that the insurer will grant, on the security of the policy's cash value, a loan not greater than the cash value. The interest rate on such loans is usually stated in the policy. However, in response to volatile interest rates in the 1970s there has been a move to link policy loan interest rates to some market interest rate appropriate to the time the loan is made. Upon settlement of the policy on death, maturity, or surrender for cash, the outstanding indebtedness is subtracted from the proceeds.

## 15.3 Insurance Options

Section 15.2 was devoted to defining the value of nonforfeiture benefits, guided by the principle stated in Section 15.1. These cash values are available as a lump sum or as a benefit of equal actuarial present value. Three common insurance benefits are discussed in the following.

## 15.3.1 Paid-Up Insurance

The equivalence principle is used to determine the reduced amount of paid-up insurance according to the benefit provision in the policy. The general equation for the amount of paid-up insurance, denoted by $b_k$, is

$$_kCV = b_k A(k)$$

$$b_k = \frac{_kCV}{A(k)},$$

(15.3.1)

where $_kCV$ is the cash value available at the time of premium default and $A(k)$ is the net single premium for a unit of insurance for future benefits under the policy at time $k$, measured from policy issue. Various elaborations on the symbol $A(k)$ indicate, if appropriate, that

# NONFORFEITURE BENEFITS AND DIVIDENDS

continuous payment of claims and various term and endowment benefits are required in practice.

For a unit of insurance and in the special case when $_kCV = {}_kV$, where $_kV$ is a net level premium reserve, (15.3.1) may be rewritten to provide insights. Some of these ideas were developed in connection with (7.3.2) and (7.4.7). In this special case, the symbol $_kW = b_k = {}_kV/A(k)$ is used to denote the amount of paid-up insurance. In Table 15.4 some of the relationships between $_kW$ and other actuarial quantities are listed. Additional relationships of this type are called for in Exercises 15.9 and 15.10.

**Table 15.4
Amounts of Reduced
Paid-up Insurance**

**Special case $b_k = {}_kW = {}_kV/A(k)$**

| Fully Continuous Basis | Fully Discrete |
|---|---|

### Whole Life

$$_k\bar{W}(\bar{A}_x) = \frac{\bar{A}_{x+k} - \bar{P}(\bar{A})_x\, \bar{a}_{x+k}}{\bar{A}_{x+k}}$$

$$_kW_x = \frac{A_{x+k} - P_x\, \ddot{a}_{x+k}}{A_{x+k}}$$

$$= 1 - \frac{\bar{P}(\bar{A}_x)}{\bar{P}(\bar{A}_{x+k})}$$

$$= 1 - \frac{P_x}{P_{x+k}}$$

### $n$-Payment Life ($k < n$)

$$_k^n\bar{W}(\bar{A}_x) = \frac{\bar{A}_{x+k} - {}_n\bar{P}(\bar{A}_x)\, \bar{a}_{x+k:\overline{n-k}|}}{\bar{A}_{x+k}}$$

$$_k^nW_x = \frac{A_{x+k} - {}_nP_x\, \ddot{a}_{x+k:\overline{n-k}|}}{A_{x+k}}$$

$$= 1 - \frac{{}_n\bar{P}(\bar{A}_x)}{{}_{n-k}\bar{P}(\bar{A}_{x+k})}$$

$$= 1 - \frac{{}_nP_x}{{}_{n-k}P_{x+k}}$$

### $n$-Year Endowment ($k < n$)

$$_k\bar{W}(\bar{A}_{x:\overline{n}|}) = \frac{\bar{A}_{x+k:\overline{n-k}|} - \bar{P}(\bar{A}_{x:\overline{n}|})\, \bar{a}_{x+k:\overline{n-k}|}}{\bar{A}_{x+k:\overline{n-k}|}}$$

$$_kW_{x:\overline{n}|} = \frac{A_{x+k:\overline{n-k}|} - P_{x:\overline{n}|}\, \ddot{a}_{x+k:\overline{n-k}|}}{A_{x+k:\overline{n-k}|}}$$

$$= 1 - \frac{\bar{P}(\bar{A}_{x:\overline{n}|})}{\bar{P}(\bar{A}_{x+k:\overline{n-k}|})}$$

$$= 1 - \frac{P_{x:\overline{n}|}}{P_{x+k:\overline{n-k}|}}$$

There is a general reasoning argument that leads to the results in Table 15.4. At age $x + k$ the net annual premium for a whole life insurance of 1 is $P_{x+k}$. Thus an annual premium of $P_x$, payable commencing at age $x + k$, would be sufficient to provide insurance of only $P_x/P_{x+k}$. Since $P_x$ is the net premium actually being paid for a unit of insurance, the difference at time $k$, $1 - P_x/P_{x+k}$, must be provided by the reserve. This reasoning can be applied to the other insurances.

**15.3.2
Extended Term**

The equivalence principle is used to determine the length of a paid-up term insurance for the full amount of the policy. The equation to be solved for $s$, in connection with an insurance with unit amount, is

$$_kCV = \bar{A}^{\,1}_{x+k:\overline{s}|}.$$

(15.3.2)

Chapter 15

# NONFORFEITURE BENEFITS
# AND DIVIDENDS

In practice $s$ in days is determined by linear interpolation to the nearest day.

In the case of an endowment insurance, it may happen that $s > n - k$, the remaining time to maturity. In that case the amount of cash value not used to purchase paid-up term insurance is used to buy a pure endowment of amount

$$\frac{{}_kCV - \bar{A}_{\overline{x+k:\overline{n-k}|}}^{\,1}}{A_{x+k:\overline{n-k}|}^{\,1}}. \tag{15.3.3}$$

If a policy of amount $b$ is subject to an outstanding policy loan of amount $L$ at the time of premium default, life insurance policies usually provide that the extended term insurance will be for amount $b - L$. Without this provision a policyholder with a policy loan of amount $L$ and current death benefit of $b - L$ could, by the act of premium default, increase the amount of insurance to $b$. In the case of a policy loan of amount $L$, (15.3.2) is modified to

$$b \, {}_kCV - L = (b - L) \, \bar{A}_{\overline{x+k:s|}}^{\,1}.$$

## 15.3.3
## Automatic
## Premium Loan

Some people would not classify the automatic premium loan provision, which appears in some life insurance policies, as a nonforfeiture benefit. This provision keeps the policy in full force, if premium default occurs, for as long as the cash value is greater than the balance of the policy loan, which will be increasing because of interest and unpaid premiums added to the balance. For default at time $k$, on a policy with a continuous payment basis for unit amount, the maximum length of the premium loan period would be determined by solving

$$G\,\bar{s}_{\overline{t}|i} = {}_{k+t}CV \tag{15.3.4}$$

for $t$. In (15.3.4),
- $G$ is the gross premium per unit of insurance,
- ${}_{k+t}CV$ is the cash value per unit of insurance and
- $i$ is the policy loan interest rate.

In practice, $t$ is sometimes taken as an integer such that

$$G\,\ddot{s}_{\overline{t}|i} \leq {}_{k+t}CV$$

and

$$G\ddot{s}_{\overline{t+1}|i} > {}_{k+t+1}CV.$$

The remaining cash value, ${}_{k+t}CV - G\,\ddot{s}_{\overline{t}|i}$, is used to buy extended term insurance.

**Example 15.4:**

A fully continuous whole life insurance for unit amount issued to $(x)$ is changed to a nonforfeiture benefit at the end of $k$ years.

a. If ${}_kCV = {}_k\bar{V}(\bar{A}_x)$, express the ratio of the variance of the future loss associated with the changed insurance, immediately after the

# NONFORFEITURE BENEFITS AND DIVIDENDS

change, to the variance of the future loss at duration $k$ on the original insurance if the nonforfeiture benefit is
 (i) paid-up insurance
 (ii) extended-term insurance.
b. If $x = 35$ and $k = 10$, calculate the ratios in parts [a.(i)] and [a.(ii)] on the basis of the Illustrative Life Table with interest at 6%. (See Exercise 6.7 and Exercise 7.13.)

**Solution:**

a.(i) By (7.2.4), the variance before the change is

$$\left(1 + \frac{\bar{P}(\bar{A}_x)}{\delta}\right)^2 [^2\bar{A}_{x+k} - (\bar{A}_{x+k})^2] = \frac{^2\bar{A}_{x+k} - (\bar{A}_{x+k})^2}{(1 - \bar{A}_x)^2}.$$

For the paid-up insurance, we recall the definition of $U$ in Section 7.2 and consider the loss

$$_k\bar{W}(\bar{A}_x)\, v^U - {}_k\bar{V}(\bar{A}_x),$$

which has variance

$$[_k\bar{W}(\bar{A}_x)]^2\, [^2\bar{A}_{x+k} - (\bar{A}_{x+k})^2].$$

The ratio of this to the variance before the change is

$$[_k\bar{W}(\bar{A}_x)]^2\, (1 - \bar{A}_x)^2,$$

which is less than 1.

(ii) In the case of extended-term insurance, we have from (15.3.2) and (4.2.5) that the variance after the change is

$$^2\bar{A}^{\,1}_{x+k:\overline{s}|} - (\bar{A}^{\,1}_{x+k:\overline{s}|})^2.$$

Now the ratio of the variances is

$$\frac{[^2\bar{A}^{\,1}_{x+k:\overline{s}|} - (\bar{A}^{\,1}_{x+k:\overline{s}|})^2]\,(1 - \bar{A}_x)^2}{^2\bar{A}_{x+k} - (\bar{A}_{x+k})^2}.$$

b.(i) $_{10}\bar{W}(\bar{A}_{35}) = {}_{10}\bar{V}(\bar{A}_{35})/\bar{A}_{45} = 0.08604/0.20718 = 0.41529$

$\bar{A}_{35} = 0.13254$

$[0.41529\,(1 - 0.13254)]^2 = 0.13$
That is, the variance of the loss on the paid-up insurance is 13% of the variance of the loss at duration 10 on the original insurance.

(ii) $_{10}\bar{V}(\bar{A}_{35}) = 0.08604 = \dfrac{(i/\delta)(M_{45} - M_{45+s})}{D_{45}}$

yields a value of $s$ between 19 and 20. With $s = 19$,

$$\frac{^2\bar{A}^{\,1}_{45:\overline{19}|} - (\bar{A}^{\,1}_{45:\overline{19}|})^2}{^2\bar{A}_{45} - (\bar{A}_{45})^2}\,(1 - \bar{A}_{35})^2 = \frac{0.04308}{0.02922}\,(0.86746)^2 = 1.11.$$

Since $s$ is between 19 and 20, the variance has increased to approximately 111% of what it was before. ▼

## Chapter 15

## NONFORFEITURE BENEFITS
## AND DIVIDENDS

**15.4**
**Asset Shares**

A life insurance policy is a long-term contract involving income to the insurer from premiums and investments and outgo as a result of death and withdrawal benefit payments and expenses. Gross premiums actually charged for a unit of insurance are influenced by competition, and nonforfeiture values are influenced by law and competition. There is need for a calculation of the balance, in the sense of actuarial present values, between the various elements of the price-benefit structure. The asset share calculation, outlined in this section, is designed to fill this need. It is not a historic summary of past results, but is a prospective calculation of some complexity attempting to capture most elements influencing the expected financial progress of a group of policies.

We will start with an elaboration of (14.5.5) for a unit of insurance,

$$_{k+1}AS \, p^{(\tau)}_{x+k} = [_kAS + G(1 - c_k) - e_k](1 + i)$$
$$- q^{(1)}_{x+k} - q^{(2)}_{x+k} \, _{k+1}CV \qquad k = 0,1,2,3,\ldots \qquad (15.4.1)$$

where

$_kAS$    denotes the expected asset share $k$ years following policy issue, immediately before the start of policy year $k+1$,

$G$    denotes the gross premium,

$c_k$    denotes the fraction of the gross premium paid at time $k$ for expenses,

$e_k$    denotes the amount of per policy expenses paid at time $k$,

$q^{(1)}_{x+k}$    denotes the probability of decrement by death, before the attainment of age $x+k+1$, for an insured now age $x+k$,

$q^{(2)}_{x+k}$    denotes the probability of decrement by withdrawal, before the attainment of age $x+k+1$, for an insured now age $x+k$.

Formula (15.4.1) is based on the assumptions of a fully discrete payment basis, unit death claims paid at the end of the year of death, and cash values of $_kCV$ paid at the end of the year of withdrawal.

Formula (15.4.1) is an obvious generalization of the recursion relationship connecting successive terminal reserves. It will be rewritten in several ways that are reminiscent of similar manipulations with reserve equations. Multiplying (15.4.1) by $v^{k+1} l^{(\tau)}_{x+k}$ yields

$$\Delta[l^{(\tau)}_{x+k} v^k \, _kAS] = [G(1 - c_k) - e_k] l^{(\tau)}_{x+k} v^k$$
$$- [d^{(1)}_{x+k} + d^{(2)}_{x+k} \, _{k+1}CV] v^{k+1}. \qquad (15.4.2)$$

Then,

$$l^{(\tau)}_{x+k} v^k \, _kAS \Big|^n_0 = \sum_{k=0}^{n-1} \{[G(1 - c_k) - e_k] l^{(\tau)}_{x+k} v^k$$
$$- [d^{(1)}_{x+k} + d^{(2)}_{x+k} \, _{k+1}CV] v^{k+1}\}, \qquad (15.4.3)$$

# NONFORFEITURE BENEFITS AND DIVIDENDS

and, if $_0AS = 0$, we have $_nAS$ equal to

$$\sum_{k=0}^{n-1} \frac{[G(1 - c_k) - e_k]\, l_{x+k}^{(\tau)} (1 + i)^{n-k} - [d_{x+k}^{(1)} + d_{x+k}^{(2)}\, _{k+1}CV] (1 + i)^{n-k-1}}{l_{x+n}^{(\tau)}}.$$

(15.4.4)

Also, setting $n = \omega - x$ in (15.4.3) and rearranging yields

$$G\ddot{a}_x^{(\tau)} = A_x^{(1)} + \sum_{k=0}^{\omega-x-1} [G c_k + e_k]\, v^k\, _kp_x^{(\tau)} + \sum_{k=0}^{\omega-x-1} {_kp_x^{(\tau)}}\, q_{x+k}^{(2)}\, v^{k+1}\, _{k+1}CV.$$

(15.4.5)

Formula (15.4.5) can be interpreted as a general formula for an expense-loaded premium using the equivalence principle. Appropriate modifications can alter the formula from a whole life to an endowment or term policy.

Making the substitution

$$p_{x+k}^{(\tau)} = 1 - q_{x+k}^{(1)} - q_{x+k}^{(2)}$$

enables us to rewrite (15.4.1) as

$$_{k+1}AS = [_kAS + G(1 - c_k) - e_k](1 + i) - q_{x+k}^{(1)}(1 - {_{k+1}AS})$$

$$- q_{x+k}^{(2)}({_{k+1}CV} - {_{k+1}AS}).$$

(15.4.6)

This form emphasizes the importance of the difference, $_{k+1}CV - {_{k+1}AS}$, on the progression of asset shares.

Asset share calculations can be viewed as tracing the expected progress of the assets, per surviving policy, of a block of similar policies. The calculations for fixed gross premiums, expense commitments and cash values can be made to check the balance between the various components of the price-benefit structure. The objective of the calculations might be to determine if $_kAS \geq {_kV}$, for all but the very early policy years.

An alternative application of asset share calculations would be to determine $G$. In this application, an asset share goal, $K > {_{20}V}$ for instance, might be established. If expense commitments and cash values are already fixed, (15.4.4) can be used to determine $G$. Let a trial value of the gross premium, denoted by $H$, be selected arbitrarily. Let $_{20}AS_1$ be the result of using (15.4.4) with this $H$ and with $n = 20$; let $K$ be the result using the desired premium $G$ and $n = 20$. Then

$$K - {_{20}AS_1} = \sum_{k=0}^{19} \frac{(G - H)(1 - c_k)\, l_{x+k}^{(\tau)} (1 + i)^{20-k}}{l_{x+20}^{(\tau)}},$$

and the desired gross premium $G$ is found by

$$G = H + \frac{(K - {_{20}AS_1})\, _{20}p_x^{(\tau)}\, v^{20}}{\sum_{k=0}^{19} (1 - c_k)\, _kp_x^{(\tau)}\, v^k}.$$

(15.4.7)

# NONFORFEITURE BENEFITS AND DIVIDENDS

The effect of the second term in (15.4.7) is to produce a correction to the premium $H$, which will cause the asset share goal, $K$, to be reached.

Asset share calculations may be much more refined than indicated in this section. For example, if death claims are paid at the moment of death, the term $q_{x+k}^{(1)}$ in (15.4.1) could be multiplied by $i/\delta$. Adjustments for the payment of premiums at other than annual intervals could also be made.

**Example 15.5:**

Compare asset shares for the illustration of Section 14.2, assuming $_kCV = 1000\,_kV_{x:\overline{3|}} - 10$, $k = 1,2$, $_3CV = 1000$ and the following double decrement table.

| $k$ | $p_{x+k}^{(\tau)}$ | $q_{x+k}^{(\tau)}$ | $q_{x+k}^{(1)}$ | $q_{x+k}^{(2)}$ |
|---|---|---|---|---|
| 0 | 0.54 | 0.46 | 0.08 | 0.38 |
| 1 | 0.62 | 0.38 | 0.09 | 0.29 |
| 2 | 0.50 | 0.50 | 0.50 | 0.00 |

**Solution:**
We use (15.4.1) as our model.

| $k$ | $\{[_kAS + G(1-c_k) - e_k](1+i) - 1000q_{x+k}^{(1)} - {}_{k+1}CV\,q_{x+k}^{(2)}\}/p_{x+k}^{(\tau)} = {}_{k+1}AS$ |
|---|---|
| 0 | $\{[\ 0.00 + 332.35(0.80) - 8](1.15) - 80 - (247.41)(0.38)\}/0.54 = 226.94$ |
| 1 | $\{[226.94 + 332.35(0.94) - 2](1.15) - 90 - (571.16)(0.29)\}/0.62 = 584.38$ |
| 2 | $\{[584.38 + 332.35(0.94) - 2](1.15) - 500 - (1000.00)(0.00)\}/0.50 = 1058.01$ |

In this example the final asset share, 1058.01, is greater than the final terminal reserve of 1000. ▼

## 15.5 Experience Adjustments

The set of asset shares as computed using (15.4.1), before a block of policies is issued, will almost certainly not equal the assets per surviving insured developed by experience. Nevertheless, the formulas of Section 15.4 can be used to gain insights into sources of financial gain or loss, measured with respect to expected results. Suppose that we trace the progress of $_kAS$ to $_{k+1}\widehat{AS}$ where the hat (circumflex) indicates that the $k+1$st asset share is derived from the expected $k$th asset share using experience cost factors. A cost factor based on experience will have a hat added. More particularly, $\hat{i}_{k+1}$ is the experience interest rate earned over the $k+1$st policy year. The experience asset share will be given by

$$_{k+1}\widehat{AS} = [_kAS + G(1-\hat{c}_k) - \hat{e}_k](1+\hat{i}_{k+1}) - \hat{q}_{x+k}^{(1)}(1 - {}_{k+1}\widehat{AS})$$

$$- \hat{q}_{x+k}^{(2)}(_{k+1}CV - {}_{k+1}\widehat{AS}). \tag{15.5.1}$$

Subtracting (15.4.6), which traced the expected progress of the asset share, from (15.5.1) yields

a. $_{k+1}\widehat{AS} - {}_{k+1}AS = ({}_kAS + G)(\hat{i}_{k+1} - i)$

b. $\qquad\qquad + [(Gc_k + e_k)(1 + i) - (G\hat{c}_k + \hat{e}_k)(1 + \hat{i}_{k+1})]$

(15.5.2)

c. $\qquad\qquad + [q^{(1)}_{x+k}(1 - {}_{k+1}AS) - \hat{q}^{(1)}_{x+k}(1 - {}_{k+1}\widehat{AS})]$

d. $\qquad\qquad + [q^{(2)}_{x+k}({}_{k+1}CV - {}_{k+1}AS) - \hat{q}^{(2)}_{x+k}({}_{k+1}CV - {}_{k+1}\widehat{AS})].$

In (15.5.2) the total deviation between the experience asset share and the expected asset share has been broken up into four components. Component (a) is associated with the deviation between the experience and the assumed interest rates. Component (b) is the difference between experience expenses and expected expenses, with an interest adjustment. Component (c) is the difference between assumed and experience mortality costs and component (d) is the difference between assumed and experience withdrawal costs.

Participating life insurance is based on the principle that premiums are set at a level such that the probability is very low that premiums and associated investment income will be insufficient to fulfill the benefit and expense commitments implicit in the issuance of a block of policies. Under this principle, which can be viewed as an alternative to the equivalence principle, the expected value of a loss variable should be negative to generate financial margins to provide for deviations in experience unfavorable to the insurance system. As the uncertainty about experience is removed by the passage of time, the margins for adverse deviations built into the original price-benefit structure can be released and returned to the policyholders who, through higher premiums, carried the risks. These returns of funds not needed to match future risks are called *dividends.* A simplified version of (15.5.2) is used frequently in the analysis that leads to the determination of dividends.

We start with a modification of (15.4.6). In this development $_kF$ will take the place of $_kAS$. The new symbol denotes a fund share that is no longer a consequence of the expected operation of the insurance system. Instead, the values of $_kF$ are amounts, set in advance, such that, with future premium and investment income, the block of policies under consideration has a high probability of meeting its benefit and expense obligations. Thus,

$$_{k+1}F = [{}_kF + G(1 - c_k) - e_k](1 + i) - q^{(1)}_{x+k}(1 - {}_{k+1}F)$$
$$- q^{(2)}_{x+k}({}_{k+1}CV - {}_{k+1}F).$$

(15.5.3)

In (15.5.3), $c_k$, $e_k$, $q^{(1)}_{x+k}$ and $q^{(2)}_{x+k}$ are typically set at levels somewhat higher than expected, and $i$ is set at a level somewhat lower than expected in order to provide margins to cover adverse deviations. These margins result in a small probability of a need for outside funds.

Formula (15.5.4) describes the progress of fund share for a unit of insurance where experience cost factors are denoted with hats. That is,

# NONFORFEITURE BENEFITS AND DIVIDENDS

$$_{k+1}F + {}_{k+1}D = [{}_kF + G(1 - \hat{c}_k) - \hat{e}_k](1 + \hat{i}_{k+1})$$
$$- \hat{q}^{(1)}_{x+k}(1 - {}_{k+1}F - {}_{k+1}D) \qquad (15.5.4)$$
$$- \hat{q}^{(2)}_{x+k}({}_{k+1}CV - {}_{k+1}F - {}_{k+1}D).$$

In (15.5.4) the dividend is denoted by $_{k+1}D$ and is the difference between the predetermined goal of $_{k+1}F$ and the fund share generated by experience. Subtracting (15.5.3) from (15.5.4) yields

a.  $_{k+1}D = ({}_kF + G)(\hat{i}_{k+1} - i)$

b.  $\qquad + [(Gc_k + e_k)(1 + i) - (G\hat{c}_k + \hat{e}_k)(1 + \hat{i}_{k+1})]$

c.  $\qquad + (1 - {}_{k+1}F)(q^{(1)}_{x+k} - \hat{q}^{(1)}_{x+k}) \qquad (15.5.5)$

d.  $\qquad + ({}_{k+1}CV - {}_{k+1}F)(q^{(2)}_{x+k} - \hat{q}^{(2)}_{x+k})$

e.  $\qquad + {}_{k+1}D(\hat{q}^{(1)}_{x+k} + \hat{q}^{(2)}_{x+k}).$

The components of (15.5.5) may be identified with experience factors that determine their size. Thus, (a) is associated with interest, (b) with expenses, (c) with mortality, (d) with voluntary terminations and (e) with the payment of dividends only to survivors. If $_{k+1}CV = {}_{k+1}F$ and dividends are paid to insureds who die or withdraw, and if $Gc_k + e_k$ is denoted by $E_k$ while $G\hat{c}_k + \hat{e}_k$ is denoted by $\hat{E}_k$, then (15.5.5) can be written in a three-term form,

$$_{k+1}D = ({}_kF + G)(\hat{i}_{k+1} - i)$$
$$+ [E_k(1 + i) - \hat{E}_k(1 + \hat{i}_{k+1})] \qquad (15.5.6)$$
$$+ (1 - {}_{k+1}F)(q^{(1)}_{x+k} - \hat{q}^{(1)}_{x+k}).$$

## 15.6 Assumptions and Reserves

In previous chapters, we have discussed variation in expected results as a consequence of the inclusion of random variables in the models. In Section 15.5, a second kind of variation, namely, that between actual experience and expected experience for a fund share, was analyzed to identify each component source of deviation. The process was illustrated by somewhat different models in (15.5.2), (15.5.5) and (15.5.6). In the present section, a closely related type of analysis is performed with the recursion equations relating successive reserves under two different sets of actuarial assumptions. Thereby, we shall observe a third kind of variation, namely, the variation in expected results as a consequence of different assumptions. The goal of the analysis in this section is to gain insight into the influence of the actuarial assumptions on the relative size of reserves.

We shall present the theory of this analysis in terms of an $n$-year insurance with

* sum insured 1 payable at the end of the year of death,
* level premiums $P$ at the beginning of each year while the insured, $(x)$, survives, and
* the reserve, on whatever basis used, to be equal to $W$ at the end of $m$ years, $m \leq n$. In most cases, $m$ can be taken equal to $n$, but sometimes the case $m = n$ must be an exception.

Let $P$ and $_hV$ denote the net level premium and the terminal reserve at the end of $h$ years on one basis with interest rate $i$ and mortality rates $q_h$ (short for $q_{x+h}$). Also, let $P'$ and $_hV'$ denote the corresponding net premium and reserve on a second basis with interest rate $i'$ and mortality rates $q_h'$. By (7.8.5) we can write, in regard to policy year $h+1$, that

$$(_hV + P)(1 + i) = {}_{h+1}V + q_h(1 - {}_{h+1}V) \qquad (15.6.1)$$

and

$$(_hV' + P')(1 + i') = {}_{h+1}V' + q_h'(1 - {}_{h+1}V'). \qquad (15.6.2)$$

We set $_hV' = {}_hV + R_h$ and rearrange (15.6.2) as

$$(_hV + P + R_h + P' - P)(1 + i') = {}_{h+1}V + R_{h+1}$$
$$+ q_h'(1 - {}_{h+1}V - R_{h+1}). \qquad (15.6.3)$$

After subtracting (15.6.1) from (15.6.3), and gathering terms involving the function $R_h$ on the right-hand side, we obtain

$$(_hV + P)(i' - i) + (P' - P)(1 + i')$$
$$- (q_h' - q_h)(1 - {}_{h+1}V) = p_h' R_{h+1} - R_h(1 + i'). \qquad (15.6.4)$$

These steps are similar to those followed in subtracting (15.5.3) from (15.5.4) to obtain the deviation between a fund objective and the fund achieved as a result of experience.

The left-hand side of equation (15.6.4) will be denoted by $S_h$, and the expression $[(_hV + P)(i' - i) - (q_h' - q_h)(1 - {}_{h+1}V)]$ by $c_h$. The term $[(P' - P)(1 + i')]$ is independent of $h$, but $c_h$, called the **critical function**, may vary with $h$. If $i' > i$ and $q_h' > q_h$, then the critical function consists of excess interest on the initial reserve, $_hV + P$, less excess mortality cost based on the net amount at risk, $1 - {}_{h+1}V$, where in both instances reserves are in respect to the first basis with interest rate $i$ and mortality rates $q_h$. In this notation, (15.6.4) becomes

$$S_h = p_h' R_{h+1} - R_h(1 + i'), \qquad (15.6.5)$$

which is a linear difference equation for the reserve difference function, $R_h = {}_hV' - {}_hV$. Further, we have $R_0 = {}_0V' - {}_0V = 0$ and $R_m = W - W = 0$. If we multiply (15.6.5) through by $D_h'$ ($D_{x+h}$ based on rates $i'$ and $q'$), we obtain

$$D_h' S_h = (1 + i')[D_{h+1}' R_{h+1} - D_h' R_h]. \qquad (15.6.6)$$

Then

$$\sum_{h=0}^{k-1} D_h' S_h = (1 + i') D_k' R_k$$

so that

$$R_k = v' \frac{\displaystyle\sum_{h=0}^{k-1} D_h' S_h}{D_k'} \qquad (15.6.7)$$

## NONFORFEITURE BENEFITS AND DIVIDENDS

and

$$R_m = 0 = v' \, \frac{\sum\limits_{h=0}^{m-1} D'_h \, S_h}{D'_m}. \tag{15.6.8}$$

If $S_h$ is a constant $S$, then from (15.6.8) $S = 0$. It then follows from (15.6.7) that $R_k = 0$; that is, $_kV' = {}_kV$, $k = 0,1,2,\ldots,m$. In this case,

$$S_h = 0 = [(_hV + P)(i' - i) - (q'_h - q_h)(1 - {}_{h+1}V)]$$
$$+ (P' - P)(1 + i') \tag{15.6.9}$$
$$= c_h + (P' - P)(1 + i')$$

is known as the **equation of equilibrium** for reserves on the two bases. Here the critical function $c_h$ is constant and equals $[(P - P')(1 + i')]$, the premium difference accumulated for a year at rate of interest $i'$. In other words, each year the excess interest less the excess mortality cost is balanced by the constant premium difference, and reserves remain the same on the two bases.

In all cases, equation (15.6.7) exhibits the reserve difference $R_k$ as the actuarial accumulated value of the year-by-year $S_h$, $h = 0,1,2,\ldots,k-1$, times $v'$. If some information is available about $S_h$ (usually from examination of the critical function $c_h$), then one may be able to make statements about the reserve difference $R_k$.

If $S_h$ decreases as $h$ increases (denoted by $S_h \downarrow$), then graphs (continuous rather than discrete) of $S_h$ and $R_k$ are of the form depicted in Figure 15.1.

**Figure 15.1**
**Graphs of $S_h \downarrow$ and $R_k$**

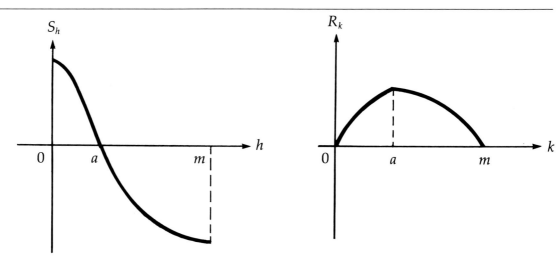

Here $S_h$ must start off positive and decrease to negative values if (15.6.8) is to be satisfied. Actually, we do not need $S_h$ to be strictly decreasing, it is sufficient if $S_h$ starts off positive and later becomes and remains negative. While $S_h$ is positive, $R_k$ will increase; but when $S_h$ becomes negative, $R_k$ will decrease as indicated in Figure 15.1. However, $R_k$ cannot become negative at any point because with $S_h\downarrow$, $R_k$ could not recover to produce $R_m = 0$. Thus $R_k > 0$, and $_kV'$ exceeds $_kV$ for $k = 1,2,\ldots,m-1$.

If, to the contrary, $S_h$ increases as $h$ increases (denoted by $S_h\uparrow$), then graphs of $S_h$ and $R_k$ are of the form depicted in Figure 15.2.

**Figure 15.2**
**Graphs of $S_h\uparrow$**
**and $R_k$**

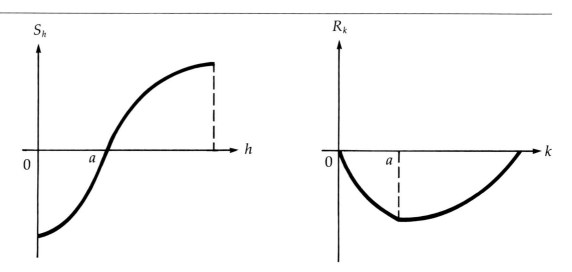

Here $S_h$ must start off negative and later become and remain positive. Then $R_k < 0$ and $_kV'$ is less than $_kV$ for $k = 1,2,\ldots,m-1$.

For applications, it is convenient to replace the conditions $S_h\downarrow$ and $S_h\uparrow$ by the equivalent conditions $c_h\downarrow$ and $c_h\uparrow$. The foregoing results are summarized in the following.

**Theorem 15.1:**   For an $n$-year insurance with sum insured 1 payable at the end of the year of death, with level annual premiums payable throughout the $n$ years and with reserve $W$ at the end of $m$ years, $m \leq n$, let
- $P$ and $_hV$ denote the net level premium and terminal reserve at the end of $h$ years on one basis with interest rate $i$ and mortality rates $q_h$ and
- $P'$ and $_hV'$ denote the corresponding net premium and reserve on a second basis with interest rate $i'$ and mortality rates $q_h'$.

Let

$$c_h = (_hV + P)(i' - i) - (q_h' - q_h)(1 - _{h+1}V) \qquad 0 \leq h < m$$

# Chapter 15

## NONFORFEITURE BENEFITS AND DIVIDENDS

denote the critical function. Then if $c_h$ decreases (increases) as $h$ increases, the reserves $_kV'$ exceed (are less than) the reserves $_kV$ for integral $k$, $0 < k < m$. If $c_h$ is constant, the reserves $_kV'$ equal the reserves $_kV$ for integral $k$, $0 \le k \le m$.

If the second basis differs from the first only in regard to the interest rate assumption, for example, $i' = i + e$, $e$ a constant $> 0$, and if $_hV \uparrow$, then $c_h \uparrow$ since here

$$c_h = (_hV + P)e.$$

This gives the following result.

**Corollary 15.1:**  Provided reserves increase with duration, a constant increase in the rate of interest produces a decrease in reserves at durations $k$, $0 < k < n$, for the insurance described in Theorem 15.1 (with $m = n$).

If the second basis has the same rate of interest as the first basis, but $q'_h = q_h + e$, with $e > 0$, then

$$c_h = -e(1 - {}_{h+1}V).$$

Here, if $_hV \uparrow$, then $c_h \uparrow$ and application of Theorem 15.1 gives the next result.

**Corollary 15.2:**  Provided reserves increase with duration, a constant increase in the rates of mortality produces decreases in reserves at durations $k$, $0 < k < n$, for the insurance described in Theorem 15.1 (with $m = n$).

To consider the effect of a constant decrease in the rate of interest, or in the rates of mortality, one can simply interchange the roles of $_hV$ and $_hV'$.

We next consider, if $i' = i$, the relationship between $q'_h$ and $q_h$ so that $_kV' = {}_kV$, $0 \le k \le m$. We require that

$$S_h = (P' - P)(1 + i) - (q'_h - q_h)(1 - {}_{h+1}V) = 0, 0 \le h < m. \quad (15.6.10)$$

In the case of unit endowment insurances, if $_{n-1}V' = {}_{n-1}V$, then

$$_{n-1}V' + P' = v = {}_{n-1}V + P$$

implies $P' = P$. To avoid this trivial case, we shall assume $m \le n - 2$, and from (15.6.10) we can state the following.

**Corollary 15.3:**  If $i' = i$, then a necessary condition for $_kV' = {}_kV$, $0 \le k \le m$, for the insurance described in Theorem 15.1 (with $m \le n - 2$) is

$$q'_h = q_h + \frac{P' - P}{v(1 - {}_{h+1}V)} \quad 0 \le h < m. \quad (15.6.11)$$

Conversely, we have the next result.

# NONFORFEITURE BENEFITS AND DIVIDENDS

**Corollary 15.4:**

If $i' = i$, and if for a constant $\Delta$

$$q'_h = q_h + \frac{\Delta}{v(1 - {}_{h+1}V)} \qquad 0 \le h < m, \ m \le n - 2, \qquad (15.6.12)$$

then $P + \Delta$ is the net annual premium (based on the mortality rates $q'_h$), which, for the first $m$ policy years, provides the benefits of the insurance of Theorem 15.1 and maintains reserves equal to ${}_kV$, $0 \le k \le m$.

**Proof:**
Writing (15.6.12) in the form

$$q'_h = q_h + \frac{P + \Delta - P}{v(1 - {}_{h+1}V)}$$

and rearranging, we obtain

$$P + \Delta - vq'_h(1 - {}_{h+1}V) = P - vq_h(1 - {}_{h+1}V) = v\,{}_{h+1}V - {}_hV$$

by (7.8.6). Then

$$P + \Delta = vq'_h(1 - {}_{h+1}V) + v\,{}_{h+1}V - {}_hV. \qquad (15.6.13)$$

That is, $P + \Delta$ is the level annual amount that, on the basis of mortality rates $q'_h$, will provide 1-year term insurance for the net amount at risk (if reserves are maintained as ${}_kV$) and the annual deposits required to build up reserves ${}_kV$ on a savings fund basis. In year $h + 1$, the net amount at risk $1 - {}_{h+1}V$ plus the reserve ${}_{h+1}V$ provides for the full unit sum insured. Thus, $P + \Delta$ provides the benefits of the insurance of Theorem 15.1 and maintains reserves equal to ${}_kV$, $0 \le k \le m$, which proves the statement of Corollary 15.4. ∎

Corollaries 15.3 and 15.4 apply to whole life insurances provided $m \le \omega - x - 2$.

In some cases, the theory can be useful for the comparison of net level premiums on the two bases. This is illustrated in the following example.

**Example 15.6:**

If $q'_h = q_h$, but $i' < i$, show that for an $n$-year endowment insurance

$$P + d - d' > P' > P\frac{v'}{v}.$$

**Solution:**
Here

$$S_h = ({}_hV + P)(i' - i) + (P' - P)(1 + i'),$$

so that $S_h \downarrow$, and hence $S_0 > 0$. This gives

$$P(i' - i) + (P' - P)(1 + i') > 0$$

$$P'(1 + i') > P(1 + i)$$

or

$$P' > P\frac{v'}{v}.$$

From $S_{n-1} < 0$, and noting that $_{n-1}V + P = v$, we get

$$v(i' - i) + (P' - P)(1 + i') < 0$$

or

$$P' < P + (i - i')vv' = P + d - d'.$$

This last inequality could have been obtained directly by noting that

$$P' = \frac{1}{\ddot{a}'_{x:\overline{n}|}} - d'$$

$$P = \frac{1}{\ddot{a}_{x:\overline{n}|}} - d$$

$$\ddot{a}'_{x:\overline{n}|} > \ddot{a}_{x:\overline{n}|}. \qquad \blacktriangledown$$

**15.7
Notes and
References**

The result stated in Section 15.1, concerning the neutral impact on premiums and reserves when a withdrawal benefit equal to the reserve on the death benefit is introduced, does not hold for fully discrete insurances. This was pointed out by Nesbitt (1964) reporting on work by Schuette. The problem results from the fact that, in the discrete model, the probability of withdrawal,

$$q_x^{(2)} = \int_0^1 \exp\left[-\int_x^{x+t} \mu_y^{(\tau)} \, dy\right] \mu_{x+t}^{(2)} \, dt,$$

depends on the force of mortality.

Cummins (1973) outlines the history of insurance surrender values in the United States with emphasis on the pioneering work of Elizur Wright. Developments in other nations followed different paths. The 1941 NAIC report on nonforfeiture benefits provides a historical summary of United States regulation, a brief review of practices in other countries, discussion of the philosophic considerations regarding equity for withdrawing policyholders, and a development of the adjusted premium approach for defining minimum cash values. The 1975 Society of Actuaries committee report on nonforfeiture requirements is especially interesting for its discussions of problems in connection with policies that provide for variation in benefits after issue. Richardson (1977) supplemented this later report with an expense investigation for the purpose of defining the loading factors in adjusted premiums.

In two papers, one covering asset shares and nonforfeiture values, (1939), and one covering gross premiums, (1929), Hoskins developed many of the ideas in Section 15.4. Huffman (1978) discusses refinements in asset share calculations.

Dividends are discussed in detail by Jackson (1959) and by Maclean and Marshall (1937) in a monograph that also traces the history of surplus distribution.

Theorem 15.1 is known in actuarial literature as Lidstone's Theorem in recognition of G. J. Lidstone who presented the concepts to the Institute of Actuaries in a 1905 paper. Baillie (1951) discussed various extensions, in particular, to limited payment policies. Promislow (1981) has given still further extensions to cases involving critical functions with more complex patterns of change and considers these for general insurances with benefits, interest rates and premiums varying freely by duration. The relationship between Lidstone's Theorem and dividends was known to Lidstone and was discussed by Ziock (1978) and by Kabele (1981).

## Exercises

*Section 15.2*

15.1. Given the following information, $A_x = 0.3208$, $\ddot{a}_x = 12$, $A_{x:\overline{n}|} = 0.5472$, $\ddot{a}_{x:\overline{n}|} = 8$, calculate the adjusted premium $P^a_{x:\overline{n}|}$ (1941 report).

15.2. Given that $P^a_x > 0.04$ and $i = 0.06$, express $P^a_x$ in terms of $P_x$ under both the 1941 report and the 1980 law.

*Section 15.3*

15.3. A company is planning to adopt a new life table. Indicate how you would determine the ages at policy issue, and times since issue, for which the reduced paid-up life insurance nonforfeiture benefits under whole life policies will be increased and for which they will be decreased. Use only a table of the net annual premiums for whole life policies computed on the bases of both the old and the new mortality tables. Assume that the cash values are calculated by applying the same percentage of the net premium reserve under the new table as was used under the old table.

15.4. An $n$-year, $n$-payment endowment insurance on a fully discrete payment basis, with unit amount of insurance, is issued to $(x)$. In the event of default of premium payments, the insured has the option of
• reduced paid-up whole life insurance or
• an extended term insurance, to the end of the endowment period, with a reduced pure endowment paid at age $x + n$. The cash value at time $t$ is ${}_tV_{x:\overline{n}|}$ and is sufficient to purchase paid-up whole life insurance of amount $b$ or to purchase extended term insurance of 1 together with a pure endowment at age $x + n$ of amount $f$. If $A_{x+t:\overline{n-t}|} = 2A_{x+t}$, express $f$ in terms of $b$, $A^{1}_{x+t:\overline{n-t}|}$ and ${}_{n-t}E_{x+t}$.

15.5. A 20-year endowment of unit amount on a fully continuous payment basis issued to (30) is lapsed at the end of 10 years

# NONFORFEITURE BENEFITS AND DIVIDENDS

when there is an indebtedness of amount $L$ outstanding against the cash value $_{10}CV$. Express, in terms of net single premiums,
a. the amount of pure endowment, $E$, at the regular maturity date if extended term insurance for the amount of the policy less indebtedness, $1 - L$, can be continued to the maturity date
b. the amount of the reserve on the extended term insurance and the pure endowment 5 years after the date of lapse.

15.6. It has been suggested that the amount of reduced paid-up insurance should be in proportion to the number of annual premiums paid to the total number of premiums payable under the terms of the policy. Compare the amount of paid-up insurance under this suggested rule with $_{10}^{20}W_{40}$ and $_{10}W_{40:\overline{20}|}$ using the Illustrative Life Table and 6% interest.

15.7. Show that

$$\frac{d}{dt}[_{t}\bar{W}(\bar{A}_{x:\overline{n}|})] = \frac{\bar{P}(\bar{A}_{x:\overline{n}|}) - \mu_{x+t}\,[1 - {}_{t}\bar{W}(\bar{A}_{x:\overline{n}|})]}{\bar{A}_{x+t:\overline{n-t}|}},$$

and interpret the equation. [Hint: Use (7.11.3) to write the derivatives of $_{t}\bar{V}(\bar{A}_{x:\overline{n}|})$ and $\bar{A}_{x+t:\overline{n-t}|}$.]

15.8. In the early years of life insurance, one company defined its cash values as

$$_{k}CV = h\,(G_{x+k} - G_{x})\,\ddot{a}(k) \qquad k = 1,2,\dots$$

where the symbol $G$ denotes a gross premium at the indicated age, and $\ddot{a}(k)$ denotes a life annuity due commencing at age $x + k$, continuing on survival to the end of the premium paying period. In practice $h$ was set at 2/3. If, by the 1980 law, the gross premiums for a whole life policy are taken as adjusted premiums, and if it is given that $P_{x}$ and $P_{x+k}$ are each less than 0.04 and $h = 0.9$, show that

$$_{k}CV = (0.909 + 1.125\,P_{x})\,_{k}V_{x} + 1.125\,(P_{x+k} - P_{x}).$$

15.9. Let $_{k}\hat{W} = {}_{k}CV/A(k)$ where $_{k}CV = A(k) - P^{a}\,\ddot{a}(k)$, as in (15.2.2), and $P^{a}$ is an adjusted premium. Construct a table for the three policies shown in Table 15.4, under a fully discrete model, relating $_{k}\hat{W}$ to adjusted and net level premiums.

15.10. If $_{k}W^{Mod} = {}_{k}V^{Mod}/A(k)$, where $_{k}V^{Mod}$ is the reserve at the end of the $k$th policy year under the Commissioners standard, construct a table for the three policies shown in Table 15.4, under a fully discrete model, relating $_{k}W^{Mod}$ to renewal and net level premiums. Assume the premium payment period in the limited payment plans is less than 20 years.

15.11. If $_{k+t}CV = {}_{k+t}\bar{V}(\bar{A}_{x})$,
a. show that equation (15.3.4) for the length of the automatic premium loan period can be written as $H(t) = 0$ where $H(t) = \bar{a}_{x}\,G\,\bar{s}_{\overline{t}|i} + \bar{a}_{x+k+t} - \bar{a}_{x}$

# NONFORFEITURE BENEFITS
# AND DIVIDENDS

---

    b. confirm that $H(0) < 0$ for survival functions where the force of mortality is increasing and, that as $t \to \infty$, $H(t)$ becomes positive and unbounded

    c. calculate $H'(t)$.

*Section 15.4*

15.12. If, in relation to (15.4.6), $_{10}AS_1$ is the asset share at the end of 10 years based on $G_1$ and $_{10}AS_2$ is the corresponding quantity based on $G_2$, write a formula for $_{10}AS_2 - {}_{10}AS_1$.

*Section 15.5*

15.13. Suppose that there is an experience premium, denoted by $\hat{G}$, based on realistic mortality and expense assumptions such that

$$\hat{G} = v\,{}_{k+1}F - {}_kF + \hat{g} + v\,\hat{q}^{(1)}_{x+k}\,(1 - {}_{k+1}F)$$

where $\hat{g} = G\hat{c}_k + \hat{e}_k$, $k = 0,1,2,\ldots$. In addition, assume $_{k+1}CV = {}_{k+1}F$ for $k = 0,1,2,3,\ldots$. Show that under these assumptions

    a. $_{k+1}F = ({}_kF + \hat{G} - \hat{g})(1 + i) - \hat{q}^{(1)}_{x+k}(1 - {}_{k+1}F)$

    b. if dividends are paid to insureds who die or withdraw, (15.5.4) can be written as

$$_{k+1}F + {}_{k+1}D = [{}_kF + G - \hat{g}](1 + \hat{i}_{k+1}) - \hat{q}^{(1)}_{x+k}(1 - {}_{k+1}F) \quad \text{and}$$

$$_{k+1}D = (G - \hat{G})(1 + \hat{i}_{k+1}) + ({}_kF + \hat{G} - \hat{g})(\hat{i}_{k+1} - i).$$

This exercise outlines the ***experience premium method*** of dividend calculation.

15.14. The recursion relation between successive life annuity values is given by

$$(\ddot{a}_{x+h} - 1)(1 + i) = p_{x+h}\,\ddot{a}_{x+h+1} \quad h = 0,1,2,\ldots.$$

    a. If the actual experience interest rate is $\hat{i}_{h+1}$ and the experience survival probability is $\hat{p}_{x+h}$, the fund progress will be described by

$$(\ddot{a}_{x+h} - 1)(1 + \hat{i}_{h+1}) = \hat{p}_{x+h}(\ddot{a}_{x+h+1} + \Delta_{h+1})$$

where $\Delta_{h+1}$ is the survivor's share of deviations. Show that

$$\Delta_{h+1} = \frac{(\hat{i}_{h+1} - i)(\ddot{a}_{x+h} - 1) + (p_{x+h} - \hat{p}_{x+h})\,\ddot{a}_{x+h+1}}{\hat{p}_{x+h}},$$

and interpret the result. [This formula is the basis of the two-factor contribution formula for annuity dividends.]

    b. If the annuity income at the end of the year is adjusted to be $r_{h+1}$ times the income as of the beginning of the year where

$$(\ddot{a}_{x+h} - 1)(1 + \hat{i}_{h+1}) = \hat{p}_{x+h}(r_{h+1})\,\ddot{a}_{x+h+1},$$

express $r_{h+1}$ in terms of $i$, $\hat{i}_{h+1}$, $p_{x+h}$ and $\hat{p}_{x+h}$.

*Section 15.6*

15.15. Determine the effect on reserves for an insurance as described in Theorem 15.1 (with $m = n$), assuming that

# Chapter 15

## NONFORFEITURE BENEFITS AND DIVIDENDS

- reserves increase with duration and
- $p_x$ decreases with age when each $p_x$ is multiplied by $(1 + k)$, $k > 0$.

15.16. Show that, for the general insurance of Section 7.4 (providing a benefit of $b_{h+1}$ at the end of the policy year $h + 1$, if death occurs in that year, and paid for by net annual premiums $\pi_h$, $h = 0,1,\ldots$, payable at the beginning of policy years), the function $S_h$ in (15.6.4) generalizes to

$$(\pi_h' - \pi_h)(1 + i') + (_hV + \pi_h)(i' - i) - (q_h' - q_h)(b_{h+1} - {}_{h+1}V).$$

15.17. a. Show that for a whole life insurance with unit benefit payable at the end of the year of death, (15.6.12) becomes

$$q_y' = q_y + \frac{c}{v\,\ddot{a}_{y+1}} \qquad x \le y < x + m$$

where $y = x + h$ and $c = \ddot{a}_x\,\Delta$.

b. On the basis of the mortality rates $q_y'$ of part (a) and interest at rate $i$, what net annual premium, payable from age $x$ up to $x + m$, will provide the same death benefits and maintain the same reserves $_kV_x$, $0 \le k \le m$, as for the whole life insurance with net annual premium $P_x$, based on the mortality rates $q_y$ and interest at rate $i$?

# Chapter 16
## SPECIAL ANNUITIES AND INSURANCES

**16**

## 16.1
## Introduction

In this chapter we study a wide variety of policies providing special annuity and insurance benefits, with the aim of determining actuarial present values, net and gross premiums, and net premium reserves. In Section 16.2 we examine a number of annuity contracts for a single life where the period during which payments are made may be longer than the future lifetime of the annuitant, or where there are benefits payable upon death. These contracts can arise from a settlement option under a life insurance policy, from the provisions of a pension plan or from those of an individual annuity policy. Section 16.3 covers the closely related matter of the family income policy. In Section 16.4 a type of policy providing a paid-up annuity at maturity and a death benefit prior to maturity equal to the face amount, or reserve if greater, is considered. Variable products, where benefit levels and reserves depend on investment results, are the subject of Section 16.5. These products become important when price inflation erodes the value of benefits stated in terms of fixed monetary units. In Section 16.6 new types of policies providing wide flexibility for changing benefit amounts and premium levels are examined. In Section 16.7 we describe various forms of disability insurance. Included is a discussion of a widely used single decrement approximation for calculating net premiums and net premium reserves for disability insurances.

## 16.2
## Special Types of Annuity Benefits

In this section we shall concentrate on calculating the actuarial present values of special forms of annuity benefits. Two of the payment patterns depend on the gross premium collected, and in these cases we shall determine the gross premium. We emphasize continuous payment annuities and justify the corresponding results for *m*thly-payment annuities by analogy.

We start with an analysis of an ***n-year certain and life annuity.*** This is a life annuity with a guarantee of payments for at least *n* years. If the time of death of the annuitant is denoted by $T$, then the present value of payments under such an annuity of 1 per year, payable on a continuous basis, is given by

$$Z = \begin{cases} \bar{a}_{\overline{n}|} & T \leq n \\ \bar{a}_{\overline{T}|} & T > n. \end{cases} \tag{16.2.1}$$

For an annuity issued to $(x)$, the actuarial present value, in aggregate payment form, is given by

$$\int_0^n \bar{a}_{\overline{n}|} \; {}_tp_x \; \mu_{x+t} \; dt + \int_n^\infty \bar{a}_{\overline{T}|} \; {}_tp_x \; \mu_{x+t} \; dt. \tag{16.2.2}$$

Integration by parts can be used to obtain the equivalent formula,

$$\bar{a}_{\overline{n}|} + \int_n^\infty v^t \; {}_tp_x \; dt. \tag{16.2.3}$$

This is the current payment form of the actuarial present value, since at times 0 to $n$ payment is certain to be made while for times $t$ greater than $n$ payment is made only if $(x)$ is then alive.

Two other expressions can be derived from the integral in (16.2.3). First, the integral can be written as

$$\int_0^\infty v^t \, {}_tp_x \, dt - \int_0^n v^t \, {}_tp_x \, dt,$$

and the actuarial present value (16.2.3) becomes

$$\bar{a}_{\overline{n}|} + \bar{a}_x - \bar{a}_{x:\overline{n}|}. \tag{16.2.4}$$

This bears a strong resemblance to the type of expression found in Chapter 8 in regard to the last-survivor status. It suggests the notation $\bar{a}_{\overline{x:\overline{n}|}}$ for the actuarial present value. This is appropriate since the annuity is payable until both the statuses, $(x)$ and $(\overline{n}|)$, have failed.

Second, a change of variable, replacing $t$ by $s + n$, in the integral of (16.2.3) gives us

$$\bar{a}_{\overline{x:\overline{n}|}} = \bar{a}_{\overline{n}|} + {}_nE_x \, \bar{a}_{x+n}. \tag{16.2.5}$$

For discrete versions of this annuity we have, analogous to (16.2.4) and (16.2.5),

$$a^{(m)}_{\overline{x:\overline{n}|}} = a^{(m)}_{\overline{n}|} + a^{(m)}_x - a^{(m)}_{x:\overline{n}|} \tag{16.2.6}$$

$$= a^{(m)}_{\overline{n}|} + {}_nE_x \, a^{(m)}_{x+n}. \tag{16.2.7}$$

A special form of this annuity is the ***installment refund annuity.*** A sufficient number of payments is guaranteed so that the annuitant receives at least as much as the gross premium that was paid. Thus, for such a continuous annuity with gross premium $G$, the actuarial present value of benefits is

$$\bar{a}_{\overline{G}|} + {}_GE_x \, \bar{a}_{x+G}.$$

If the gross premium is to contain a loading of $r$ times the gross premium, the equivalence principle requires that $G$ satisfy

$$G(1 - r) = \bar{a}_{\overline{G}|} + {}_GE_x \, \bar{a}_{x+G}. \tag{16.2.8}$$

The difference between the left- and right-hand sides of the above expressions could be evaluated for integer values of $G$. Then, a value of $G$ that equates the two sides is found by linear interpolation. Similar expressions hold for discrete versions, and $G$ could be found for those in a similar manner.

A related annuity containing some insurance features is the ***cash refund annuity.*** A death benefit is defined as the excess, if any, of the gross premiums paid over the annuity payments received. If $G$ is the gross single premium and $T$ is the time of death, the present value of benefits on a continuous basis is

$$Z = \begin{cases} \bar{a}_{\overline{T}|} + (G - T)v^T & T \leq G \\ \bar{a}_{\overline{T}|} & T > G. \end{cases} \tag{16.2.9}$$

The actuarial present value of these benefits is given by

$$\int_0^\infty \bar{a}_{\overline{t}|} \, {}_tp_x \, \mu_{x+t} \, dt + \int_0^G (G - t) \, v^t \, {}_tp_x \, \mu_{x+t} \, dt$$

$$= \bar{a}_x + G \, \bar{A}^1_{x:\overline{G}|} - (\bar{I}\bar{A})^1_{x:\overline{G}|}. \qquad (16.2.10)$$

As for the installment refund annuity, the principle of equivalence is used to determine $G$. If the loading is $r$ times the gross premium,

$$G(1 - r) = \bar{a}_x + G \, \bar{A}^1_{x:\overline{G}|} - (\bar{I}\bar{A})^1_{x:\overline{G}|}. \qquad (16.2.11)$$

Linear interpolation can be used to approximate $G$ after the difference between the left- and right-hand sides of (16.2.11) is evaluated for integer values of $G$.

We conclude this section with an example of a variation of the $n$-year certain and life annuity.

**Example 16.1:**

Calculate the actuarial present value of a continuous annuity providing payments until $n$ years after the death of an annuitant $(x)$.

**Solution:**
Let $T$ be the time of death of $(x)$. Then, the present value of benefits is

$$Z = \bar{a}_{\overline{T+n}|},$$

and the actuarial present value of the annuity is

$$\int_0^\infty \bar{a}_{\overline{T+n}|} \, {}_tp_x \, \mu_{x+t} \, dt.$$

Integration by parts gives us an alternative integral,

$$\bar{a}_{\overline{n}|} + \int_0^\infty v^{t+n} \, {}_tp_x \, dt = \bar{a}_{\overline{n}|} + v^n \, \bar{a}_x.$$

If we make the change of variable $t + n = s$, the actuarial present value can be written as

$$\bar{a}_{\overline{n}|} + \int_n^\infty v^s \, {}_{s-n}p_x \, ds.$$

This current payment formulation recognizes that payments are made before time $n$ with certainty and after time $n$ only if $(x)$ was alive $n$ years previously. ▼

## 16.3 Family Income Insurances

An *n-year family income insurance* provides an income from the date of death of the insured, continuing until $n$ years have elapsed from the date of issue of the policy. It is typically paid for by premiums over the $n$-year period, or some period shorter than $n$ years, to keep terminal reserves positive. Again, we start with a continuous annuity. If $T$ is the time of death of the insured, the present value of benefits is

$$Z = \begin{cases} v^T \, \bar{a}_{\overline{n-T}|} & T \le n \\ 0 & t > n. \end{cases} \qquad (16.3.1)$$

Usually, the interest rate involved in the annuity factor, $\bar{a}_{\overline{n-T}|}$, is the same as that in the present value factor, $v^T$. A variation of this type of contract is the **mortgage protection policy** where the annuity factor in the benefit function represents the outstanding balance on a mortgage. The mortgage interest rate used in evaluating $\bar{a}_{\overline{n-T}|}$ may then be different from that used for evaluating $v^T$.

The actuarial present value for the family income benefit is given by

$$\int_0^n v^t \, \bar{a}_{\overline{n-t}|} \, {}_tp_x \, \mu_{x+t} \, dt. \qquad (16.3.2)$$

This aggregate payment integral can be converted to a current payment integral by integration by parts,

$$\bar{a}_{\overline{n}|} - \int_0^n v^t \, {}_tp_x \, dt = \bar{a}_{\overline{n}|} - \bar{a}_{x:\overline{n}|} = \int_0^n v^t (1 - {}_tp_x) \, dt. \qquad (16.3.3)$$

The interpretation here is that the annuity is payable at time $t$ for $t < n$ only if $(x)$ is dead at that time, the probability of that being $1 - {}_tp_x$.

There are two possible variations when we consider the discrete analog of the continuous family income policy. First, the annuity payments could be paid at the end of each $m$th of the year after the death of the insured with time measured from the date of the policy issue. The actuarial present value for such an annuity would be given by

$$a_{\overline{n}|}^{(m)} - a_{x:\overline{n}|}^{(m)}. \qquad (16.3.4)$$

The alternative benefit has the $m$thly annuity starting at the date of death and continuing to time $n$ with a fractional final payment. The actuarial present value for this benefit is

$$\int_0^n v^t \, \ddot{a}_{\overline{n-t}|}^{(m)} \, {}_tp_x \, \mu_{x+t} \, dt = \frac{\delta}{d^{(m)}} \int_0^n v^t \, \bar{a}_{\overline{n-t}|} \, {}_tp_x \, \mu_{x+t} \, dt$$

$$= \frac{\delta}{d^{(m)}} (\bar{a}_{\overline{n}|} - \bar{a}_{x:\overline{n}|}). \qquad (16.3.5)$$

Let us now determine the size of the final fractional payment that is consistent with (16.3.5). We define $k$ to be the number of full years of benefit and $j$ the number of full $m$thly payments in the last year. Thus, $k = [n - t]$ and $j = [m(n - k - t)]$ where the brackets refer to the greatest integer function and $t$ is the time of death. For instance, if $n = 30$, $m = 12$ and $t = 18.8$, then $k = 11$ and $j = 2$. Writing $n - t$ as $k + (j/m) + s$, we have

$$\ddot{a}_{\overline{n-t}|}^{(12)} = \ddot{a}_{\overline{k+(j/m)+s}|}^{(12)} = \ddot{a}_{\overline{k+j/m}|}^{(12)} + v^{k+j/m} \frac{1 - v^s}{d^{(12)}}.$$

# SPECIAL ANNUITIES AND INSURANCES

Thus the size of the final fractional payment is $(1-v^s)/d^{(12)}$. This is very close to $s$, which is the amount typically paid. In our numerical example, with

$$s = n - t - k - \frac{j}{m} = \frac{1}{30},$$

$$\frac{1 - v^s}{d^{(12)}} = 0.033382$$

for $i = 0.06$, which differs from $1/30$ by $0.00005$.

We conclude this section with an example combining aspects of a family income policy and a retirement annuity with a term certain.

**Example 16.2:** Calculate the actuarial present value of the benefits under a policy issued at age 40 providing the following annuity benefits payable continuously at a rate of 1 per year:
- in the event of death prior to age 65, a family income benefit ceasing at age 65 or 10 years after death, if later, and
- in the event of survival to age 65, a life annuity with 10 years certain.

**Solution:**
We prepare to write a current payment integral. The following table gives the conditions required for payments at time $t$ and the corresponding probabilities.

| Time | Condition | Probability |
|------|-----------|-------------|
| $0 < t \le 25$ | (40) is dead | $1 - {}_t p_{40}$ |
| $25 < t \le 35$ | (40) was alive at $t - 10$ | ${}_{t-10} p_{40}$ |
| $t > 35$ | (40) is alive | ${}_t p_{40}$ |

The actuarial present value is

$$\int_0^{25} v^t (1 - {}_t p_{40}) \, dt + \int_{25}^{35} v^t {}_{t-10} p_{40} \, dt + \int_{35}^{\infty} v^t {}_t p_{40} \, dt.$$

If we replace $t - 10$ by $s$ in the middle integral, we obtain

$$\int_{15}^{25} v^{s+10} {}_s p_{40} \, ds = v^{10} (\bar{a}_{40:\overline{25}|} - \bar{a}_{40:\overline{15}|}).$$

Thus the actuarial present value of the benefit can be written as

$$\bar{a}_{\overline{25}|} - \bar{a}_{40:\overline{25}|} + v^{10} (\bar{a}_{40:\overline{25}|} - \bar{a}_{40:\overline{15}|}) + \bar{a}_{40} - \bar{a}_{40:\overline{35}|}. \qquad \blacktriangledown$$

## 16.4 Retirement Income Policies

A *retirement income policy* is an endowment policy characterized by having a maturity amount greater than the face amount. The maturity amount is typically chosen to provide a particular level of annuity income. Since the reserve must approach the maturity amount, there is a time after which the reserve exceeds the face amount. When the reserve exceeds the face amount, the death benefit is set equal to the reserve.

# SPECIAL ANNUITIES AND INSURANCES

We begin our analysis with a fully continuous model. Let $\bar{P}$ be the annual rate of premium payment and let $1 + k$ be the maturity amount at time $n$ for a policy with unit face amount. Let $a$ be the time at which the reserve equals 1. Then the benefit amount $b_t$ is given as

$$b_t = \begin{cases} 1 & t \le a \\ {}_t\bar{V} & a < t \le n. \end{cases}$$

The reserve at time $a$, known to be 1, can be expressed retrospectively as

$$1 = {}_a\bar{V} = \bar{P}\bar{s}_{x:\overline{a}|} - {}_a\bar{k}_x = \frac{\bar{P}\bar{a}_{x:\overline{a}|} - \bar{A}^1_{x:\overline{a}|}}{{}_aE_x}. \tag{16.4.1}$$

The differential equation for the reserve is given by (7.11.3) as

$$\frac{d}{dt}{}_t\bar{V} = \bar{P} + \delta\,{}_t\bar{V} - \mu_{x+t}(b_t - {}_t\bar{V}).$$

For times $t \ge a$ where $b_t = {}_t\bar{V}$, the term involving $\mu_{x+t}$ vanishes, so the differential equation involves only the force of interest. Thus, compound interest theory can be applied to yield

$${}_a\bar{V} = v^{n-a}\,{}_n\bar{V} - \bar{P}\,\bar{a}_{\overline{n-a}|}.$$

But ${}_a\bar{V} = 1$ and ${}_n\bar{V} = 1 + k$, so we have

$$1 = (1 + k)v^{n-a} - \bar{P}\,\bar{a}_{\overline{n-a}|}. \tag{16.4.2}$$

Finally, combining (16.4.1) and (16.4.2), we obtain

$$\bar{P} = \frac{\bar{A}^1_{x:\overline{a}|} + {}_aE_x\,v^{n-a}\,(1 + k)}{\bar{a}_{x:\overline{a}|} + {}_aE_x\,\bar{a}_{\overline{n-a}|}}. \tag{16.4.3}$$

Now, from equation (16.4.1), we have

$$\bar{P} = \frac{\bar{A}^1_{x:\overline{a}|} + {}_aE_x}{\bar{a}_{x:\overline{a}|}} = \bar{P}(\bar{A}_{x:\overline{a}|}),$$

therefore

$$\bar{P} = \frac{1}{\bar{a}_{x:\overline{a}|}} - \delta. \tag{16.4.4}$$

Similarly, (16.4.2) gives

$$\bar{P} = \frac{(1 + k)v^{n-a}}{\bar{a}_{\overline{n-a}|}} - \frac{1}{\bar{a}_{\overline{n-a}|}} = \frac{k}{\bar{s}_{\overline{n-a}|}} - \left(\frac{1}{\bar{a}_{\overline{n-a}|}} - \frac{1}{\bar{s}_{\overline{n-a}|}}\right) = \frac{k}{\bar{s}_{\overline{n-a}|}} - \delta.$$

Combining this with (16.4.4) gives us a condition that $a$ must satisfy, namely,

$$\frac{\bar{s}_{\overline{n-a}|}}{\bar{a}_{x:\overline{a}|}} = k. \tag{16.4.5}$$

# Chapter 16
## SPECIAL ANNUITIES AND INSURANCES

The procedure then would be to calculate $a$ by using (16.4.5) and $\bar{P}$ by (16.4.3) or (16.4.4). (See the expression in Exercise 16.14 for $\bar{a}_{x:\overline{a}|}$.)

Reserve formulas are most easily written retrospectively if $t < a$ and prospectively if $t \geq a$. In particular, for $t > a$, compound interest theory applies to give prospectively

$$_t\bar{V} = (1 + k)\,v^{n-t} - \bar{P}\,\bar{a}_{\overline{n-t}|}. \qquad (16.4.6)$$

The fully discrete model is analogous, but $a$ is now the unique integer such that $_aV \leq 1$ and $_{a+1}V > 1$. Exercise 16.12 asks the reader to develop formulas analogous to (16.4.3) and (16.4.5) for this case.

## 16.5
## Variable Products

Here we consider several products where the benefit levels and reserves depend upon the investment results. The investments associated with a product may be of any type. Typically, the particular investments are selected to be in accord with the announced objective of the insurance or annuity product. The original impetus for these products was to participate in the higher expected total returns (dividends, interest and capital gains) available in equity investments, and thus to provide some measure of protection against inflation. A typical contract provides guarantees concerning mortality and expense charges. Thus, the policyholder is not charged for adverse experience, nor does he benefit from favorable experience in these two areas. We examine the mechanisms for change in benefit level on an individual policy basis.

## 16.5.1
## Variable Annuity

We consider here the *variable annuity.* During the premium-paying or *accumulation period,* a fund is accumulated from single contributions, or from periodic deposits, at rates of interest depending upon the investment performance of the fund. Typically, variable annuities make guarantees on maximum sales, administrative and investment expense charges, and on the mortality basis in use. The death benefit during the accumulation period is commonly equal to the share of the accumulation fund, while the withdrawal benefit is often the death benefit less a surrender charge. If withdrawals are ignored, the growth of the fund share is given by

$$[F_k + \pi_k(1 - c_k) - e_k]\,(1 + i'_{k+1}) = F_{k+1} + q_{x+k}(b_{k+1} - F_{k+1}) \quad (16.5.1)$$

[see (15.5.3)]. Here $F_k$ is the fund share at time $k$; $\pi_k$ is the size of the deposit at time $k$; $c_k$ is the fraction of the premium, $\pi_k$, charged for those expenses at time $k$ that are proportional to the premium paid at that time; $e_k$ is the charge at time $k$ for expenses not proportional to the premium; $b_{k+1}$ is the benefit paid at time $k + 1$ for death between times $k$ and $k + 1$; $i'_{k+1}$ is the actual investment return, net of investment expenses, for the year following time $k$. The second term on the right is equal to 0 during the accumulation period, so we have the fund growing with interest only.

At retirement, the existing fund share is used to purchase a paid-up annuity, the purchase rates computed on a predetermined mortality basis and *an assumed investment return* (AIR). If the AIR is low, then the initial annuity payment will be low relative to the fund share, but the contract can, as we shall see, provide an increasing payment pattern that offsets some of the effects of inflation. Let the AIR be denoted by $i$ and, again, let the net actual investment return in the year following time $k$ be $i'_{k+1}$. If the annuity benefit is paid only to those living at the beginning of each year, with the annuity payment level at time $k$ equal to $b_k$, the reserve just before the payment is $b_k \ddot{a}_{x+k}$, with $x$ the retirement age. The equation for the progress of the fund share would be

$$(b_k \ddot{a}_{x+k} - b_k)(1 + i'_{k+1}) = b_{k+1} p_{x+k} \ddot{a}_{x+k+1}. \qquad (16.5.2)$$

But from (5.8.4), we have

$$(\ddot{a}_{x+k} - 1)(1 + i) = p_{x+k} \ddot{a}_{x+k+1}. \qquad (16.5.3)$$

Dividing the last two equations gives

$$b_{k+1} = b_k \frac{1 + i'_{k+1}}{1 + i}. \qquad (16.5.4)$$

Thus, if $i'_{k+1} > i$, the benefit level will increase. Note that a high AIR can lead to a situation where the benefit amounts are frequently decreased.

The result, (16.5.4), holds for other pay-out options. This is indicated for the $n$-year certain and life annuity in Exercise 16.15. It also holds for $m$thly pay-outs in slightly modified forms. First, let us consider adjusting the pay-out amount monthly. The formula connecting the annuity values for the first and second months of a contract year is

$$\left( \ddot{a}^{(12)}_{x+k} - \frac{1}{12} \right)\left( 1 + \frac{i^{(12)}}{12} \right) = {}_{1/12} p_{x+k} \, \ddot{a}^{(12)}_{x+k+1/12},$$

while the progress of the fund share would be expressed by

$$\left( b_k \ddot{a}^{(12)}_{x+k} - \frac{b_k}{12} \right)\left( 1 + \frac{i'^{(12)}_{k+1}}{12} \right) = {}_{1/12} p_{x+k} \, b_{k+1/12} \, \ddot{a}^{(12)}_{x+k+1/12}.$$

Division yields

$$b_{k+1/12} = \frac{b_k \left( 1 + i'^{(12)}_{k+1}/12 \right)}{1 + i^{(12)}/12}. \qquad (16.5.5)$$

Alternatively, we could adjust the payment size on an annual basis even though the pay-out is monthly. First, the formula for successive annual reserves for a monthly annuity is

$$(\ddot{a}^{(12)}_{x+k} - \ddot{a}^{(12)}_{x+k:\overline{1|}})(1 + i) = p_{x+k} \ddot{a}^{(12)}_{x+k+1}.$$

[see (5.8.1)]. The equation for the growth of the fund share would be

$$(b_k \ddot{a}^{(12)}_{x+k} - b_k \ddot{a}^{(12)}_{x+k:\overline{1|}})(1 + i'_{k+1}) = p_{x+k} b_{k+1} \ddot{a}^{(12)}_{x+k+1}.$$

# SPECIAL ANNUITIES AND INSURANCES

Thus we make a charge, $b_k \, \ddot{a}^{(12)}_{x+k:\overline{1}|}$, for the present year's annuity payments. Dividing the last two expressions gives (16.5.4) again,

$$b_{k+1} = b_k \frac{1 + i'_{k+1}}{1 + i}.$$

There are a large number of possible designs for **variable life insurance.** We shall examine three distinct designs, all based on a whole life insurance. Each of these designs is easily adapted to limited payment life insurances or to endowment insurances. Each will be based on annual premiums with immediate payment of claims. Benefit amounts are changed at the beginning of each year.

## 16.5.2
## Fully Variable Life Insurance

The first design is what we shall call **fully variable life insurance.** Benefit amounts change with investment results and premiums are kept proportional to benefit amounts. We start with a unit benefit amount and net premium $P(\bar{A}_x)$. The terminal reserve at time $k$ is equal to the product of $_kV(\bar{A}_x)$ and $b_k$, the benefit amount to be paid in the year following time $k$. The net premium payable at time $k$ is $b_k \, P(\bar{A}_x)$. Upon receipt of the net premium, term insurance for the benefit for the year is purchased, the cost being $b_k \, \bar{A}^{1}_{x+k:\overline{1}|}$. The equation connecting the fund size at the beginning and end of the year, and used to define the benefit for the subsequent year, is

$$[b_k \,_kV(\bar{A}_x) + b_k \, P(\bar{A}_x) - b_k \, \bar{A}^{1}_{x+k:\overline{1}|}] (1 + i'_{k+1}) = p_{x+k} \, b_{k+1} \,_{k+1}V(\bar{A}_x).$$

$$(16.5.6)$$

But we know

$$[_kV(\bar{A}_x) + P(\bar{A}_x) - \bar{A}^{1}_{x+k:\overline{1}|}] (1 + i) = p_{x+k} \,_{k+1}V(\bar{A}_x). \qquad (16.5.7)$$

Dividing (16.5.6) by (16.5.7), we obtain

$$b_{k+1} = b_k \frac{1 + i'_{k+1}}{1 + i}. \qquad (16.5.8)$$

This is the same relationship that holds during the pay-out phase of a variable annuity, namely, (16.5.4).

## 16.5.3
## Fixed Premium Variable Life Insurance

We next examine a **fixed premium variable life insurance.** The main difference from the fully variable design, as the name suggests, is that the net premium remains constant. Again we start with a unit benefit amount and write the equation connecting fund sizes,

$$[b_k \,_kV(\bar{A}_x) + P(\bar{A}_x) - b_k \, \bar{A}^{1}_{x+k:\overline{1}|}] (1 + i'_{k+1}) = p_{x+k} \, b_{k+1} \,_{k+1}V(\bar{A}_x). \qquad (16.5.9)$$

Combining this with (16.5.7) gives us

$$b_{k+1} = b_k \left[ \frac{_kV(\bar{A}_x) + P(\bar{A}_x)/b_k - \bar{A}^{1}_{x+k:\overline{1}|}}{_kV(\bar{A}_x) + P(\bar{A}_x) - \bar{A}^{1}_{x+k:\overline{1}|}} \right] \frac{1 + i'_{k+1}}{1 + i}. \qquad (16.5.10)$$

The first factor on the left-hand side of (16.5.9) can be written as

$$(b_k - 1) \,_kV(\bar{A}_x) + \,_kV(\bar{A}_x) + P(\bar{A}_x) - b_k \, \bar{A}^{1}_{x+k:\overline{1}|}.$$

This shows that the fixed net premium supports both the initial face amount of 1 and the additional benefit, $b_k - 1$, generated by the actual investment returns. Thus the changes in the benefit amount are, under this design, premium paying.

## 16.5.4 Paid-up Insurance Increments

Here we consider an alternative used for the third design. We consider the changes in the benefit amount as paid-up and use the premium to support only the original benefit level. The equation connecting fund shares becomes

$$[(b_k - 1)\,\bar{A}_{x+k} + {_kV}(\bar{A}_x) + P(\bar{A}_x) - b_k\,\bar{A}_{\overline{x+k:\overline{1}|}}]\,(1 + i'_{k+1})$$
$$= p_{x+k}\,[(b_{k+1} - 1)\,\bar{A}_{x+k+1} + {_{k+1}V}(\bar{A}_x)]. \qquad (16.5.11)$$

The left-hand side of (16.5.11) can be transformed as follows:

$$\left(b_k\,(\bar{A}_{x+k} - \bar{A}_{\overline{x+k:\overline{1}|}}) - [\bar{A}_{x+k} - {_kV}(\bar{A}_x) - P(\bar{A}_x)]\right)\,(1 + i'_{k+1})$$
$$= [b_k\,{_1E_{x+k}}\,\bar{A}_{x+k+1} - P(\bar{A}_x)\,(\ddot{a}_{x+k} - 1)]\,(1 + i'_{k+1})$$
$$= [b_k\,{_1E_{x+k}}\,\bar{A}_{x+k+1} - P(\bar{A}_x)\,({_1E_{x+k}}\,\ddot{a}_{x+k+1})]\,(1 + i'_{k+1})$$
$$= p_{x+k}\,\bar{A}_{x+k+1}\left[b_k - \frac{P(\bar{A}_x)}{P(\bar{A}_{x+k+1})}\right]\frac{1 + i'_{k+1}}{1 + i}.$$

The right-hand side of (16.5.11) is most easily transformed by using the paid-up insurance formula for the reserve. It becomes

$$p_{x+k}\left[(b_{x+1} - 1)\,\bar{A}_{x+k+1} + \bar{A}_{x+k+1}\left(1 - \frac{P(\bar{A}_x)}{P(\bar{A}_{x+k+1})}\right)\right]$$
$$= p_{x+k}\,\bar{A}_{x+k+1}\left[b_{k+1} - \frac{P(\bar{A}_x)}{P(\bar{A}_{x+k+1})}\right].$$

Thus, the recursion formula for the benefit amount is

$$b_{k+1} - \frac{P(\bar{A}_x)}{P(\bar{A}_{x+k+1})} = \left[b_k - \frac{P(\bar{A}_x)}{P(\bar{A}_{x+k+1})}\right]\frac{1 + i'_{k+1}}{1 + i}. \qquad (16.5.12)$$

This third design has the advantage that if, after a period of years with favorable investment returns resulting in $b_k > 1$, the investment returns level off at the AIR, then the benefit amounts will remain fixed. This is not true for the second design that led to (16.5.10).

## 16.6 Flexible Plan Products

In the early 1970s insurance companies began to offer several types of policies intended to provide the policyholder a broad range of options for changing benefit amounts, premiums and plan of insurance. The companies typically allowed small increases in benefit amounts without new evidence of insurability, but larger increases required such evidence. The insurance plans usually included all types of level premium, level benefit term plans, which as a limiting case include whole life. The more expensive plans offered were either all limited payment life plans or all endowment plans. Both participat-

# SPECIAL ANNUITIES AND INSURANCES

ing and nonparticipating versions were made available. A special dividend option was devised to allow the dividend to be added at net rates directly related to the cash value. This larger cash value was then used to extend the expiry date on term plans or to increase the benefit amounts on permanent plans. We refer to such products as *flexible plans* and illustrate a particularly simple version that shows some of the inherent complexities. We conclude the section by describing a second design that has less emphasis on the plan of insurance and some features in common with variable life plans, as described in the previous section.

## 16.6.1 Flexible Plan Illustration

Basic to the design of the type of flexible plan considered here is a formula used in reserve calculations relating the gross premium to the net premium. We shall use the following very simple relationship applied to both term and limited payment life plans, the latter being our choice for permanent coverage,

$$0.8\,G = P. \tag{16.6.1}$$

Here $G$ is the gross premium and $P$ is the net premium.

Another basic decision is to determine the form of the total expense charge and the related question of the adjustment of the reserves at times of plan change. We shall use full preliminary term reserves and nonforfeiture values in our illustration. It should be noted that the nonforfeiture and valuation laws may require higher minimum values, particularly for limited payment life plans. We define $_0V = -E$, where $E$ is the excess first-year expense allowance. Then, from our adoption of full preliminary term reserves, we have $_1V = 0$ and, assuming a fully discrete basis,

$$_0V + P = v\,q_x\,b,$$

thus

$$E = -_0V = P - v\,q_x\,b. \tag{16.6.2}$$

The equation connecting initial benefit amount, $b$, initial net premium, $P$, and initial plan of insurance with $h$, denoting the premium payment term, is

$$_0V + P\,\ddot{a}_{x:\overline{h}|} = b\,A^1_{x:\overline{j}|}. \tag{16.6.3}$$

Here $j$ equals either $h$ (in case of a term plan) or $\omega - x$ (in case of limited payment life). Reserves are most easily determined by retrospective formulas since, as we shall see, minor adjustments in benefits in the final year of a policy are usually required. Thus

$$_kV = \frac{_0V + P\,\ddot{a}_{x:\overline{k}|} - b\,A^1_{x:\overline{k}|}}{_kE_x}. \tag{16.6.4}$$

We illustrate the applications of these formulas with the following example.

**Example 16.3:** Consider a policy issued at age 35 with an initial gross premium of 1000 and an initial benefit amount of 120,000. Use the Illustrative Life

# SPECIAL ANNUITIES AND INSURANCES

Table with 6% interest to determine the excess first-year expense allowance, the fifth year reserve, and the plan of insurance.

**Solution:**
From (16.6.1), we have $P = 800$. Therefore, the excess first-year expense allowance is

$$-{}_0V = P - 120,000\, v\, q_{35} = 572.05,$$

and the fifth year reserve is given by

$$_5V = \frac{-572.05 + 800\, \ddot{a}_{35:\overline{5}|} - 120,000\, A^1_{35:\overline{5}|}}{_5E_{35}}$$

$$= 2491.24.$$

The renewal net premium for 120,000 of whole life insurance at age 35 on a full preliminary basis is $120,000\, P_{36} = 1057.37$. Since our net premium is only 800, the plan of insurance is one of the term plans. It can be verified that, by using retrospective formulas,

$$_{39}V = 3375.72$$

and

$$_{40}V = -1313.14.$$

Thus the plan of insurance is Term to Age 74. The reserve remaining at time 39 would typically be used to provide term insurance for a fraction of the following year. In our example, the number of days is given by

$$\frac{_{39}V}{120,000\, A^1_{74:\overline{1}|}}\, 365 = 230.$$ ▼

At the time of change of benefit amount or premium, a new net premium is calculated along with any change in the reserve that might result from, for instance, a change in the assumed excess first-year expense allowance. For our simplified plan, the net premiums are a constant percentage of the gross premiums and we shall assume that the revised reserve at the time of change, $_kV'$, is equal to the full preliminary term reserve on hand. The relationship between the revised reserve, new net premium, $P'$, and new benefit amount, $b'$, is of the same form as (16.6.3), namely,

$$_kV' + P'\, \ddot{a}_{x+k:\overline{h}|} = b'\, A^1_{x+k:\overline{j}|}. \tag{16.6.5}$$

Here $j$ and $h$ would, in general, change with the new relationship between premium and benefit amounts. Again, $j$ equals either $h$ or $\omega - x - k$, and it is most convenient to evaluate reserves by a retrospective formula. Thus, for $g = 1,2,3,\ldots$, we have

$$_{k+g}V' = \frac{_kV' + P'\, \ddot{a}_{x+k:\overline{g}|} - b'\, A^1_{x+k:\overline{g}|}}{_gE_{x+k}}. \tag{16.6.6}$$

We continue with three examples that are continuations of Example

# SPECIAL ANNUITIES AND INSURANCES

16.3. These illustrate different types of changes and show some characteristic calculations.

**Example 16.4:**

The policyholder in Example 16.3 wishes, 5 years after issue, to change the gross premium of the policy to 2000 and the benefit amount to 150,000. Determine the reserve 10 years after original issue and the new plan of insurance.

**Solution:**
$P' = 1600$ and $_5V' = 2491.24$ ($_5V' = {_5}V$ in Example 16.3). Thus, by (16.6.6),

$$_{10}V' = \frac{2491.24 + 1600\,\ddot{a}_{40:\overline{5}|} - 150,000\,A^1_{40:\overline{5}|}}{_5E_{40}}$$

$$= 10,319.89.$$

We know the plan of insurance is one of the limited payment life plans since $2491.24 + 1600\,\ddot{a}_{40}$ exceeds $150,000\,A_{40}$. It can be determined that the reserve at age 69 is the first one exceeding the actuarial present value of 150,000 of whole life insurance at the same age. Thus,

$$_{34}V' = \frac{2491.24 + 1600\,\ddot{a}_{40:\overline{29}|} - 150,000\,A^1_{40:\overline{29}|}}{_{29}E_{40}}$$

$$= 75,597.32,$$

while $150,000\,A_{69} = 74,954.44$. When the policyholder attains age 69, the policy will probably be changed to a paid-up life policy with face amount

$$\frac{75,597.32}{A_{69}} = 151,287. \qquad \blacktriangledown$$

**Example 16.5:**

The policyholder in Example 16.3 wishes to change the policy after 5 years to Life Paid-up at Age 60 with a gross premium of 2000. Determine the benefit level that results from these changes.

**Solution:**
$P = 0.8(2000) = 1600$, thus (16.6.5) gives us

$$2491.24 + 1600\,\ddot{a}_{40:\overline{20}|} = b'\,A_{40}.$$

Solving for $b'$ gives us $b' = 132,090.$ $\qquad \blacktriangledown$

**Example 16.6:**

After 5 years, the policyholder in Example 16.3 wishes to change his policy to Term to Age 65 with a coverage of 150,000. Determine the gross premium appropriate after the change.

**Solution:**
$P = 0.8\,G$; thus (16.6.5) gives us

$$2491.24 + 0.8\,G\,\ddot{a}_{40:\overline{25}|} = 150,000\,A^1_{40:\overline{25}|}.$$

The solution of this equation is $G = 895.00.$ $\qquad \blacktriangledown$

## 16.6.2
## An Alternative
## Design

A second design combines aspects of variable life insurance with the preceding design of a flexible plan policy. The emphasis on the plan of insurance is not as strong in this design as it was in the first. Further, the emphasis is on the *risk amount* (previously referred to as the net amount at risk), rather than on the benefit amount. The risk amount may be determined at the beginning of policy year $k+1$ and a fund growth equation written in terms of this factor, which we denote by $r_k$. Our analysis will be in terms of an annual model but, in practice, a monthly or even more frequent calculation is more common. The basic growth equation for the fund share, the analogue of (15.5.3) without allowance for withdrawals, is

$$(_kF + G - E - r_k\, \bar{A}^{\,1}_{x+k:\overline{1}|})\,(1 + i'_{k+1}) = {}_{k+1}F. \qquad (16.6.7)$$

Note that accumulation is under interest only, and, in case of death, the policyholder receives both the fund share, that is, the fund at the beginning of the year, $_kF + G - E - r_k\,\bar{A}^{\,1}_{x+k:\overline{1}|}$, and the risk amount adjusted for interest to the date of death. The risk amount might be selected to maintain an approximate level total benefit amount. The policyholder is given considerable flexibility in the choice of $G$, the gross premium, and $r_k$, the risk amount. The insurer typically makes a number of guarantees. Usually, $i'_{k+1}$ is an investment return that must be at least equal to some minimum rate $i$. The risk charge is typically guaranteed to be no more than $r_k\,\bar{A}^{\,1}_{x+k:\overline{1}|}$, where the 1-year term insurance single premium is calculated on the basis of interest rate $i$ and a mortality table used in statutory reserve calculations.

Expense charges, $E$ in (16.6.7), currently used are of several forms including
- a constant percentage charge against all gross premiums,
- surrender charges such as a large but declining (with duration) percentage of the first-year premium or a transaction charge such as 25 for each withdrawal,
- a flat amount per policy either in the first year only or a smaller amount for each policy year, and
- a first-year charge expressed as an amount per 1000 of benefit.

The charges most subject to regulation are the excess first-year expense charges and the risk charges. Expenses are covered by the insurer, in addition to the stated formula charges, by a number of devices. Some of these are
- reduced interest credits, limited to the guaranteed rate, for an initial corridor of policy cash values, for example, the first 1000 of cash values,
- an interest rate spread of 1 to $1\frac{1}{2}\%$ between the net investment yield and the rate applied to the cash values, and
- recognizing that part of the risk charge actually contains some provision for expenses, just as do regular term insurance premiums.

As stated above, the emphasis on plan of insurance is not strong.

At any time, a calculation parallel to that used in Examples 16.3 and 16.4 could be performed to determine the plan that is implicit in any specific pattern of premiums and benefits, current risk charges, expense charges, interest rates and reserve.

## 16.7 Disability Benefits for Individual Life Insurance

In Section 10.5 we discussed disability benefits included in pension plans. We now turn to disability benefits commonly found in conjunction with individual life insurance. Provision may be made for the waiver of life insurance premiums during periods of disability. Alternatively, policies may contain provision for a monthly income of 5 or 10 per 1000 of face amount if disability occurs.

The usual disability clause provides a benefit for total disability. Total disability may require a disability severe enough to prevent engaging in any gainful occupation, or it may require only the inability to engage in one's own occupation. Total disability that has been continuous for a period of time specified in the policy, called the *waiting period,* qualifies the policyholder to receive benefit payments. The waiting period may be 3, 4, 6 or 12 months. In policies with waiver of premium, it is common to make the benefits *retroactive,* that is, to refund any premiums paid by the insured during the waiting period. Coverage for the disability contingency may expire prior to the maturity date of the life insurance policy. The disability benefit expiry ages are typically 60 or 65; however, benefits in the form of an annuity, either as disability income or as waiver of premiums, will often cease at a higher age, typically, at the maturity date or paid-up date of the life insurance policy.

## 16.7.1 Disability Income Benefits

Let us start by expressing the actuarial present value of a disability income benefit of 1000 per month issued to $(x)$ under a coverage expiring at age $y$ and with income running to age $u$. We assume that the waiting period is $m$ months. Using notations from Chapters 9 and 10, we can express the actuarial present value as

$$12,000 \sum_{k=0}^{y-x-1} v^k \, {}_kp_x^{(\tau)} \, v^{1/2} \, q_{x+k}^{(i)} \, v^{m/12} \, {}_{m/12}p_{[x+k+1/2]}^i \, \ddot{a}_{[x+k+1/2]+m/12:\overline{u-x-k-(1/2)-m/12}|}^{(12)i} .$$

(16.7.1)

In life insurance, $x + k + 1/2$ relates to the *age at disablement,* while $x + k + (1/2) + m/12$ represents the age at which qualification for benefits occurs.

Several simplifications of the above formula have been used in practice. First, the decrement $i$ (for disability) is assumed to occur only if the person who is disabled survives to the end of the waiting period of $m$ months; if death occurs during that period, the decrement is regarded as death. This means that the survivorship factor, ${}_{m/12}p_{[x+k+1/2]}^i$, is unnecessary as it has been taken into account in the definition of $q_{x+k}^{(i)}$.

A second simplification is to use continuous annuities for disabled lives, by means of the approximation

$$\bar{a}^i_{[x+k+1/2]+m/12:\overline{u-x-k-(1/2)-m/12|}} + \frac{1}{24} \tag{16.7.2}$$

for the value of the monthly temporary annuity for the disabled life in (16.7.1). In practice, the total rate of decrement for newly disabled lives is composed of a high but declining rate of mortality and a substantial recovery rate that may peak and then decline. Under these circumstances, it may be best to justify (16.7.2) by noting that, relative to the monthly annuity, the continuous annuity loses approximately 1/2 month's interest on each monthly payment of size 1/12. Also in case of termination by death or recovery there is a partial loss of payment. In case of survival to age $u$, this partial loss does not occur. Therefore, an adjustment of the continuous annuity by 1/2 of a monthly payment is convenient and perhaps conservative.

The third simplification is to use a standard single decrement life table for the survivorship of active lives instead of a double decrement table with mortality and disability. This has the effect of increasing the actuarial present value of benefits. The same simplification is used in evaluating active life annuity values for the purpose of determining net annual premiums and reserves. An approximation is also used for the factor $q^{(i)}_{x+k}$. We start with

$$q^{(i)}_{x+k} = \int_0^1 {}_tp^{(\tau)}_{x+k}\, \mu^{(i)}_{x+k+t}\, dt$$

$$= \int_0^1 {}_tp'^{(d)}_{x+k}\, {}_tp'^{(i)}_{x+k}\, \mu^{(i)}_{x+k+t}\, dt.$$

Now we replace ${}_tp'^{(d)}_{x+k}$ by its value at $t = 1/2$ and write this single decrement function as ${}_{1/2}p_{x+k}$. Thus

$$q^{(i)}_{x+k} = {}_{1/2}p_{x+k} \int_0^1 {}_tp'^{(i)}_{x+k}\, \mu^{(i)}_{x+k+t}\, dt$$

$$= {}_{1/2}p_{x+k}\, q'^{(i)}_{x+k}. \tag{16.7.3}$$

These simplifications, known as the *Phillips approximation,* produce only a slight distortion in net premiums and net premium reserves.

Making all these simplifications allows us to write (16.7.1) as

$$12,000 \sum_{k=0}^{y-x-1} v^{k+1/2}\, {}_kp_x\, {}_{1/2}p_{x+k}\, q'^{(i)}_{x+k}\, v^{m/12} \left( \bar{a}^i_{[x+k+1/2]+m/12:\overline{u-x-k-(1/2)-m/12|}} + \frac{1}{24} \right).$$

$$\tag{16.7.4}$$

There remains the problem of calculating the values of the continuous annuities for the disabled lives. The references cited in Section 16.8 provide sources of information on this.

Commutation functions similar to those introduced in Chapter 10 can be defined. Let $l_x$ be a value from a single decrement life table. Then, with $D_x = v^x \, l_x$, we define

$$\bar{C}^i_x = v^{1/2} \,_{1/2}p_x \, q'^{(i)}_x \, D_x \tag{16.7.5}$$

$$^u\bar{C}^i_x = \bar{C}^i_x \, v^{m/12} \, \bar{a}^i_{[x+1/2]+m/12:\overline{u-x-(1/2)-m/12}|}. \tag{16.7.6}$$

If the income is to be continued for the remainder of life, $u$ is replaced in the notation by $\omega$. We define

$$_y\bar{M}^i_x = \sum_{z=x}^{y-1} \bar{C}^i_z \tag{16.7.7}$$

$$^u_y\bar{M}^i_x = \sum_{z=x}^{y-1} {}^u\bar{C}^i_z. \tag{16.7.8}$$

In this notation, if coverage continues up to age $u$, so that $y = u$, the subscript $y$ in the notation is suppressed in (16.7.8).

We can now write the actuarial present value for the disability income benefit in (16.7.4) as

$$\frac{12{,}000 \, {}^u_y\bar{M}^i_x + 500 \, v^{m/12} \, _y\bar{M}^i_x}{D_x}. \tag{16.7.9}$$

## 16.7.2
## Waiver of
## Premium Benefit

Let us go through the same process for a general waiver of premium benefit. We assume the premium, $P$, to be waived is payable $g$ times per year for life. We assume, further, that the benefit is retroactive so that premiums paid during the waiting period are refunded at the end of the waiting period. The primary difference between this and the disability income benefit is that the waiver benefit is a $g$thly payment annuity starting at the first premium due date after the end of the waiting period. If we assume that disablements occur uniformly throughout the year, there will be an average period of $1/(2g)$ between the end of the waiting period and the first subsequent premium due date. Therefore, the annuity value to be used in the actuarial present value formula is

$$_{1/(2g)|}\ddot{a}^{(g)i}_{[x+k+1/2]+m/12}.$$

But this is reasonably approximated by

$$\bar{a}^i_{[x+k+1/2]+m/12}, \tag{16.7.10}$$

which has the advantage of being independent of the frequency, $g$, of premium payments per year.

The retroactive benefit amount can be seen to average $(m/12)P$, which is clearly the case if premiums are payable continuously or if $m$ is an integer multiple of $g$. To see what happens in other cases, consider semiannual premiums and a 4-month waiting period. If the waiting period ended within 2 months of the next premium payment, no premium was paid during the waiting period. Otherwise,

$(1/2)P$ was paid within the waiting period. If we assume a uniform distribution of disablements in the year, then we arrive at

$$\left[\frac{2}{6}(0) + \left(\frac{4}{6}\right)\frac{1}{2}\right]P = \frac{4}{12}P$$

as the mean retroactive benefit amount.

Making use of the several simplifications discussed here and in the previous subsection on disability income benefits, we now express the actuarial present value of the waiver benefit as

$$P\sum_{k=0}^{y-x-1} v^{k+1/2} {}_{k}p_x {}_{1/2}p_{x+k} q'^{(i)}_{x+k} v^{(m/12)} \left(\bar{a}^i_{[x+k+1/2]+m/12} + \frac{m}{12}\right). \quad (16.7.11)$$

In terms of the commutation functions defined in (16.7.5)–(16.7.8), this actuarial present value can be written as

$$\frac{P({}^{\omega}_{y}\bar{M}^i_x + (m/12)\,v^{m/12}\,{}_{y}\bar{M}^i_x)}{D_x}. \quad (16.7.12)$$

### 16.7.3
### Net Annual Premiums and Reserves

Net annual premiums for these benefits are found by the equivalence principle, by equating the actuarial present value of benefits to the actuarial present value of net premiums. For a waiver benefit on a Life Paid-up at Age 75 policy with premiums and coverage on the waiver benefit continuing to age 65, the net annual premium, ${}_{65-x}\pi_x$, would be given by

$$_{65-x}\pi_x\,\ddot{a}_{x:\overline{65-x}|} = \frac{P({}^{75}_{65}\bar{M}^i_x + (m/12)\,v^{(m/12)}\,{}_{65}\bar{M}^i_x)}{D_x}$$

or by

$$_{65-x}\pi_x = \frac{P({}^{75}_{65}\bar{M}^i_x + (m/12)\,v^{(m/12)}\,{}_{65}\bar{M}^i_x)}{N_x - N_{65}} \quad (16.7.13)$$

where $P$ denotes the premium to be waived.

Active life terminal reserves are most conveniently expressed by a premium-difference formula,

$$_kV = ({}_{65-x-k}\pi_{x+k} - {}_{65-x}\pi_x)\,\ddot{a}_{x+k:\overline{65-x-k}|}. \quad (16.7.14)$$

The terminal reserve for a disabled life is the actuarial present value of future disability benefits, calculated on the assumption that the insured has incurred a qualifying disability. The amount of premium waived, or disability income rate, is multiplied by the actuarial present value of an appropriate disabled life annuity. This value takes into account the age at disablement, the duration since disablement, and the terminal age for benefits.

### 16.8
### Notes and References

Individual retirement income policies have been used in funding employee benefits, life insurance and retirement income. These policies have been the subject of many actuarial papers. Fassel (1930) provides an important early paper. Smith (1961) uses a continuous model.

# Chapter 16

## SPECIAL ANNUITIES AND INSURANCES

The foundations for variable annuities were built in a paper by Duncan (1952). Since 1969 there has been a flurry of activity on variable life insurance. The paper by Fraser, Miller and Sternhell (1969), and its extensive discussion, is the basic reference. Miller (1971) provides a less formal introduction and some numerical illustrations. Papers by Biggs (1969) and Macarchuk (1969), and discussions of those, provide additional information on variable annuities.

It is difficult to discuss flexible plans of insurance in a book devoted to basic actuarial models. Issues related to these plans are primarily regulatory and administrative. The type of policy described in Subsection 16.6.1 is studied by Chapin (1976). The type of policy in Subsection 16.6.2 is the subject of a paper by Chalke and Davlin (1983).

The subject of disability benefits issued in connection with individual life insurance is covered in a monograph by Hunter and Phillips (1932) and in the textbook, *Individual Health Insurance*, by O'Grady (1987). Cueto (1954) reviews the notation and numerical processes and gives monetary values for these benefits. See also the Society of Actuaries publication "Monetary Tables for Disability Benefits based on 1952 Disability Study—Period 2 combined with the 1958 CSO Mortality Table (1962)."

## Exercises

*Section 16.2*

16.1. Use the results of Chapter 5, concerning uniform distribution of deaths in each year of age, to express the actuarial present value in (16.2.6) as

$$\frac{i}{i^{(m)}}\left[ a_{\overline{n}|} + v^n \,_n p_x \, a_{x+n} + \left(\frac{1}{d} - \frac{1}{d^{(m)}}\right) v^n \,_n p_x \, A_{x+n}\right].$$

[Hint: Refer to Exercise 5.17.]

16.2. Show that $Z$ as defined in (16.2.1) has the same variance as the present-value random variable $Y$ for an $n$-year deferred continuous life annuity of 1 per year, and hence $\text{Var}[Z]$ is given by (5.3.20) or by the equivalent expression in Exercise 5.40.

16.3. Consider a partial cash refund annuity with the present-value random variable defined as

$$Z^* = \begin{cases} \bar{a}_{\overline{T}|} + (\rho G - T)v^T & T < \rho G,\ 0 < \rho < 1 \\ \bar{a}_{\overline{T}|} & T \geq \rho G. \end{cases}$$

a. Show that (16.2.11) may be rewritten for a partial cash refund annuity as

$$G(1 - r) = \bar{a}_x + \rho G \bar{A}^1_{x:\overline{\rho G}|} - (\bar{I}\bar{A})^1_{x:\overline{\rho G}|}.$$

b. Form $H(G) = G(1 - r) - \bar{a}_x - \rho G \bar{A}^1_{x:\overline{\rho G}|} + (\bar{I}\bar{A})^1_{x:\overline{\rho G}|}$ for the purpose of determining $G$ such that $H(G) = 0$.
   (i) Display $H'(G)$ and $H''(G)$.
   (ii) Discuss the sign of $H'(G)$ and $H''(G)$ in the neighborhood of a root.

16.4. Show that, for $Z$ given in Example 16.1,

$$\text{Var}[Z] = \frac{v^{2n}[^2\bar{A}_x - \bar{A}_x^2]}{\delta^2}.$$

*Section 16.3*

16.5. Use the results of Chapter 5, concerning uniform distribution of deaths in each year of age, to express the actuarial present value in (16.3.4) as

$$\frac{i}{i^{(m)}}\left[a_{\overline{n}|} - a_{x:\overline{n}|} - \left(\frac{1}{d} - \frac{1}{d^{(m)}}\right)A^1_{x:\overline{n}|}\right].$$

[Hint: Refer to Exercise 5.17.]

16.6. If $Z$ is defined as in (16.3.1), show that

$$\text{Var}[Z] = \frac{^2\bar{A}_{x:\overline{n}|} - \bar{A}_{x:\overline{n}|}^2}{\delta^2}.$$

16.7. Prove that the actuarial present value of an $n$-year continuous family income insurance with the annuity value calculated at a force of interest $\delta'$ is

$$\frac{\bar{A}^1_{x:\overline{n}|} - e^{-\delta'n}\,''\bar{A}^1_{x:\overline{n}|}}{\delta'}$$

where $''\bar{A}^1_{x:\overline{n}|}$ is evaluated at a force of interest $\delta'' = \delta - \delta'$.

16.8. A policy provides a continuous annuity-certain of 1 per annum beginning at the date of death of $(x)$. If death occurs within 15 years of policy issue, the annuity is payable to the end of 20 years from policy issue. If death occurs between 15 and 20 years from policy issue, the annuity is payable for 5 years certain. Coverage ceases 20 years from policy issue. Write an exact expression for the net single premium.

16.9. A contract provides for the payment of 1000 at the end of 20 years if the insured is then living or an income of 10 a month in the event of death before the 20th anniversary of the policy. The first income payment is due at the end of the policy month of death, but no payments are made after 20 years from the date of policy issue. Write the formula for the net annual premium at age $x$.

16.10. Show that

$$\bar{a}_{\overline{n}|} - \bar{a}_{x:\overline{n}|} = \frac{\bar{A}^1_{x:\overline{n}|} - v^n\,_nq_x}{\delta}.$$

16.11. a. In relation to Example 16.2, construct the present value of benefits as a function of the time-until-death.
b. Express the actuarial present value of benefits by the aggregate payment technique.
c. Verify that integration by parts in the answer for (b) yields the expression obtained in Example 16.2.

*Section 16.4*

16.12. For a fully discrete retirement income policy, we define $a$ as the unique integer such that $_aV \leq 1$ and $_{a+1}V > 1$. Complete the analysis for the fully discrete retirement income policy as follows:

a. Determine $_aV$ retrospectively in terms of $P$, the net annual premium.

b. Determine $_aV$ prospectively in terms of $P$ by using compound interest theory.

c. Solve for $P$ by equating the two expressions for $_aV$.

d. From the foregoing, and the inequalities $_aV \leq 1$, $P \leq P_{x:\overline{a}|}$, $_{a+1}V > 1$ and $P > P_{x:\overline{a+1}|}$, show that $a$ is the greatest integer such that

$$\frac{\ddot{s}_{\overline{n-a}|}}{\ddot{a}_{x:\overline{a}|}} \geq k.$$

16.13. An extended version of the Hattendorf theorem for a general, fully continuous insurance is

$$\int_0^n (v^t\, b_t - \bar{P}\, \bar{a}_{\overline{t}|})^2\, {}_tp_x\, \mu_{x+t}\, dt + (v^n\, b_n - \bar{P}\, \bar{a}_{\overline{n}|})^2\, {}_np_x$$

$$= \int_0^n v^{2t}\, (b_t - {}_t\bar{V})^2\, {}_tp_x\, \mu_{x+t}\, dt$$

where $n$ is the premium payment period and also the insurance term, $b_t$ is the death benefit in case of death at time $t$, and $b_n$ is the maturity benefit (see Exercise 7.45). By means of the above, show that for a retirement income insurance, on a fully continuous basis, the variance of the loss variable is equal to the variance of the loss variable for an $a$-year endowment insurance for a unit amount, and hence equals

$$\frac{{}^2\bar{A}_{x:\overline{a}|} - \bar{A}_{x:\overline{a}|}{}^2}{(\delta\, \bar{a}_{x:\overline{a}|})^2}.$$

16.14. Show that if, for a retirement income policy, $a = h + r$ where $h = [a]$ and $0 < r < 1$, then under the assumption of a uniform distribution of deaths in policy year $h + 1$

$$\bar{a}_{x:\overline{a}|} = \bar{a}_{x:\overline{h}|} + {}_hE_x\, \frac{(\delta - q_{x+h})\, \bar{a}_{\overline{r}|} + v^r\, r\, q_{x+h}}{\delta}.$$

*Section 16.5*

16.15. a. Verify that

$$(\ddot{a}_{x:\overline{n}|} - 1)\,(1 + i) = p_x\, \ddot{a}_{x+1:\overline{n-1}|} + q_x\, \ddot{a}_{\overline{n-1}|}.$$

b. Verify that (16.5.4) holds for a variable annuity with the pay-out made on an *n*-year certain and life basis.

16.16.  a.  Rearrange (16.5.10) to the following equivalent form

$$b_{k+1} = \left[ b_k - \frac{(b_k - 1)\, P(\bar{A}_x)}{_1E_{x+k\ k+1}V(\bar{A}_x)} \right] \frac{1 + i'_{k+1}}{1 + i}.$$

b.  If for the formula in part (a), $i'_{k+1} = i$, $k = 0,1,2,\dots$, and $b_0 = 1$, show that $b_{k+1} = 1$, $k = 0,1,2,\dots$.

c.  If for the formula in part (a) $i'_{k+h} = i$ for some $k > 0$ and $h = 1,2,\dots$, show that the $b_{k+h}$ will be constrained toward 1.

16.17.  Rework Exercise 15.14(b) assuming $p'_{x+h} = p_{x+h}$ and show that $r_{h+1} = b_{h+1}/b_h$ as given in (16.5.4).

16.18.  A fixed premium variable whole life insurance, discrete model, has death benefit $b_{k+1}$ in year $k+1$ equal to $F_{k+1} + (1 - {}_{k+1}V_x)$ $= 1 + (F_{k+1} - {}_{k+1}V_x)$, where the fund share $F_k$ satisfies the recursion equation

$$(F_k + P_x)(1 + i'_{k+1}) = q_{x+k}\, b_{k+1} + p_{x+k}\, F_{k+1}.$$

Here $i'_{k+1}$ is the interest rate earned on the matching investments in year $k+1$, and the premium $P_x$ and reserve ${}_kV_x$ are based on the interest rate $i$.

a.  Show that the recursion equation can be rearranged as

$$(F_k + P_x)(1 + i'_{k+1}) - q_{x+k}(1 - {}_{k+1}V_x) = F_{k+1}$$

and interpret this equation.

b.  If $i'_{k+1} = i$, $k = 0,1,2,\dots$, show that $F_{k+1} = {}_{k+1}V_x$ so that $b_{k+1}$ is constant at 1.

c.  Show that

$$b_{k+1} = b_k + (F_k + P_x)\, i'_{k+1} - ({}_kV_x + P_x)\, i.$$

[Note that in this design the death benefit for year $k+1$ is $b_{k+1}$ rather than $b_k$, as in (16.5.9). Further, the 1-year term insurance cost, as of the beginning of year $k+1$, is here $b_{k+1}\, q_{x+k}/(1 + i'_{k+1})$ rather than $b_k\, q_{x+k}/(1+i)$, as in (16.5.9).]

*Section 16.6*

16.19.  The policyholder in Example 16.3 wishes to change the policy after 5 years to Endowment Insurance to Age 65 with a gross annual premium of 5000. Determine the benefit level that results from these changes.

16.20.  a.  The policyholder in Exercise 16.19 decides to elect only 160,000 of Endowment Insurance to Age 65, but will still pay a gross annual premium of 5000 until a final, fractional premium is payable 1 year after the date of the last full premium. At what age is this fractional premium payable?

b.  For the policy in part (a), what would be the reserve at the end of 10 years after the change to the endowment form?

*Section 16.7*

16.21.  a.  Express, in terms of commutation functions, the net annual premium, payable to age 60, for a disability income insurance issued to (35) of 1000 per month payable to age

65 in case (35) becomes disabled before age 60 and survives a waiting period of 6 months.

b. Write a formula for the active life terminal reserve at the end of 10 years for the insurance in part (a).

16.22. A disability rider, attached at issue to a whole life policy on $(x)$, provides the following benefits if $(x)$ becomes totally disabled before age $y$ and remains disabled during a waiting period of 6 months:

• a monthly income commencing at the end of the waiting period and payable for life during continued disability and

• waiver of the life insurance premiums falling due on or after the initial date of disability and during continued disability.

Determine the amount of the monthly income and the amount of the annual premium to be waived (assumed payable continuously) if the net annual premium for the disability rider is

$$\frac{1720 \, {}^{\omega}_{y}\bar{M}^{i}_{x} + 200 \, v^{1/2} \, {}_{y}\bar{M}^{i}_{x}}{N_x - N_y}.$$

Chapter 17

# ADVANCED MULTIPLE LIFE THEORY

**17**

## 17.1
## Introduction

In Chapter 8 we defined the joint-life and last-survivor statuses, expressing their time-until-failure random variables in terms of those for the individual lives. For this the concepts of Chapters 3–5 were extended to obtain actuarial functions for statuses of just two lives. On the assumption that the future lifetimes of the two lives were independent, the multiple-life actuarial functions were expressed in terms of the single-life functions, making it possible to calculate them using readily available life tables for single lives. Probabilities, annuities and insurances, contingent on the order of the deaths of the two lives, were also discussed in Chapter 8.

In this chapter we extend these ideas to more than two lives. In fact, with more than two lives, the idea of a surviving status can be generalized. (See Sections 17.2 and 17.3.) With the ultimate goal of numerical evaluation of these functions, Theorem 17.1 is used to express the survival functions of these statuses in terms of only joint-life survival functions. Again, under the independent lifetimes assumptions, these joint-life survival functions are evaluated as products of individual life survival probabilities. Theorem 17.1 is a form of a general theorem of probability theory used in the so-called inclusion-exclusion method. A statement and proof of this more general theorem is in the Appendix to this chapter.

Contingent probabilities and functions are also generalized to cover more than two lives. In addition, reversionary annuities, which may be offered as post-retirement death benefits in retirement plans, are discussed in Section 17.6.

The annual premium models of Chapters 6 and 7 are developed for the multiple-life statuses in Section 17.7.

## 17.2
## More General
## Statuses

For $m$ lives, $(x_1),(x_2),\ldots,(x_m)$, the ***k-survivor status,*** denoted by

$$\left(\frac{k}{x_1 x_2 \cdots x_m}\right),$$

exists as long as at least $k$ of the $m$ lives survive and fails upon the $m-k+1$st death among the $m$ lives. The previously defined joint-life status and the last-survivor status are, respectively, the $m$-survivor status and the 1-survivor status. When referring to either of these statuses, we will use its special symbol rather than the general $k$-survivor form. The future lifetime of the $k$-survivor status is the $k$th largest of the set of $m$ lifetimes $T(x_1),T(x_2),\ldots,T(x_m)$. Like the future lifetimes in Chapters 3 and 8, this one for the $k$-survivor status is the period of existence from a fixed initial time to a random termination time. With only a change in notation to display the status

$$\left(\frac{k}{x_1 x_2 \cdots x_m}\right),$$

the probability distribution and life table functions of Chapter 3 are applicable to the future lifetime of this status.

Annuity and insurance benefits are defined in terms of the future lifetime of a $k$-survivor status just as they were in Chapters 4 and 5 for $(x)$. For a continuous annuity of 1 payable annually as long as at least $k$ of the $m$ lives survive, we have from (5.3.2B) that the actuarial present value is

$$\bar{a}_{\overline{x_1 x_2 \cdots x_m}}^{\ k} = \int_0^\infty v^t \ {}_t p_{\overline{x_1 x_2 \cdots x_m}}^{\ k} \ dt. \tag{17.2.1}$$

The insurance paying a unit on the $m - k + 1$st death among the $m$ lives would have the net single premium given by (4.2.6), that is,

$$\bar{A}_{\overline{x_1 x_2 \cdots x_m}}^{\ k} = \int_0^\infty v^t \ {}_t p_{\overline{x_1 x_2 \cdots x_m}}^{\ k} \ \mu_{\overline{x_1 x_2 \cdots x_m}}^{\ k}(t) \ dt. \tag{17.2.2}$$

For the analysis and evaluation of probabilities and actuarial present values for these benefits (and other combinations of benefits) we will define a new type of status. For the $m$ lives $(x_1),(x_2),\ldots,(x_m)$, the **[k]-deferred survivor status** exists while exactly $k$ of the $m$ lives survive; that is, it comes into existence upon the $m - k$th death and remains in existence until the next death. The notation for this status will be

$$\left( \frac{[k]}{x_1 x_2 \cdots x_m} \right).$$

For $k = m$, the [m]-deferred survivor status coincides with the $m$-survivor status. For $k = 0$, the [0]-deferred survivor status exists forever following the $m$th death.

The deferral of the existence of

$$\left( \frac{[k]}{x_1 x_2 \cdots x_m} \right)$$

makes it different from the general status, $(u)$, of Chapter 8. For instance, for $k < m$, ${}_t p_{\frac{[k]}{x_1 x_2 \cdots x_m}}$, which is the probability that exactly $k$ of the $m$ lives are surviving at time $t$, does not equal 1 at $t = 0$ and thus does not meet the requirements of a survival function as given in Table 3.1. For $k = 0$ as $t \to \infty$, ${}_t p_{\frac{[0]}{x_1 x_2 \cdots x_m}}$ goes to 1, which also violates those requirements. Moreover, for a [k]-deferred survivor status, the period of existence and the period from the initial time to the time of failure are not equal, as they are for the general status. This means that annuity benefits must be carefully defined for this new status. The annuity with actuarial present value $\bar{a}_{\frac{[k]}{x_1 x_2 \cdots x_m}}$ is defined to be payable during the future lifetime of the [k]-deferred survivor status, hence it is a deferred annuity with a random deferment period. Since the time of failure of the [k]-deferred survivor status is equal to the time of failure of the $k$-survivor status, insurance benefits payable upon failure of the deferred status are essentially applications of the $k$-survivor status.

**Example 17.1:**     A continuous annuity is payable as long as any of $(w)$, $(x)$, $(y)$ and $(z)$ are alive. At each death the annual rate of payment is reduced

# ADVANCED MULTIPLE LIFE THEORY

by 50%. Express the actuarial present value of such an annuity in terms of $\bar{a}_{\overline{wxyz}}^{[k]}$, $k = 1,2,3,4$. Assume a unit initial benefit rate.

**Solution:**
The actuarial present value is

$$\bar{a}_{\overline{wxyz}}^{[4]} + \frac{1}{2}\bar{a}_{\overline{wxyz}}^{[3]} + \frac{1}{4}\bar{a}_{\overline{wxyz}}^{[2]} + \frac{1}{8}\bar{a}_{\overline{wxyz}}^{[1]}.$$

The discussion of this annuity is continued (after Theorem 17.1) in Example 17.2. ▼

In Chapter 8, we expressed last-survivor probabilities and related actuarial present values in terms of those for single- and joint-life statuses. We shall use the following theorem to aid in obtaining the same results for the general $k$-survivor statuses. A more general statement of the theorem for arbitrary events, as well as its proof, is given in the Appendix to this chapter.

**Theorem 17.1:**

Let ${}_tp_{\overline{x_1 x_2 \cdots x_m}}^{[j]}$ be the probability that exactly $j$ of the $m$ lives will be surviving at time $t$. Let

$$ {}_tB_j = \sum {}_tp_{x_{(1)}x_{(2)}\cdots x_{(j)}} $$

where the sum is over all combinations of $j$ out of the $m$ lives. Then, for arbitrary numbers, $c_0, c_1, \ldots, c_m$,

$$ \sum_{j=0}^{m} c_j \, {}_tp_{\overline{x_1 x_2 \cdots x_m}}^{[j]} = c_0 + \sum_{j=1}^{m} \Delta^j c_0 \, {}_tB_j. \qquad (17.2.3) $$

Theorem 17.1 is applicable for lives with dependent future-lifetime random variables. However, in applications we will assume mutually independent future lifetimes and calculate the terms of the ${}_tB_j'$s as products of individual survival probabilities.

**Example 17.2:**

Express the actuarial present value of the annuity described in Example 17.1 in terms of actuarial present values for annuities on single- and joint-life statuses.

**Solution:**
The actuarial present value is

$$ \int_0^\infty v^t \left( \sum_{j=1}^{4} \left(\frac{1}{2}\right)^{4-j} {}_tp_{\overline{wxyz}}^{[j]} \right) dt. $$

The coefficients and their differences are given below.

| $j$ | $c_j$ | $\Delta c_j$ | $\Delta^2 c_j$ | $\Delta^3 c_j$ | $\Delta^4 c_j$ |
|---|---|---|---|---|---|
| 0 | 0 | 1/8 | 0 | 1/8 | 0 |
| 1 | 1/8 | 1/8 | 1/8 | 1/8 | — |
| 2 | 1/4 | 1/4 | 1/4 | — | — |
| 3 | 1/2 | 1/2 | — | — | — |
| 4 | 1 | — | — | — | — |

Thus, the integral is equal to

$$\int_0^\infty v^t \left( \frac{1}{8}\, _tB_1 + \frac{1}{8}\, _tB_3 \right) dt$$

$$= \frac{1}{8} (\bar{a}_w + \bar{a}_x + \bar{a}_y + \bar{a}_z) + \frac{1}{8} (\bar{a}_{wxy} + \bar{a}_{wxz} + \bar{a}_{wyz} + \bar{a}_{xyz}).$$

Such expressions can be examined for reasonableness by interpreting the final form in terms of a collection of annuities for which, at any outcome, the total of their rates of payment equals the rate of payment of the original annuity. For example, in this particular case the original annuity commences payment at rate 1, while the final form relates to a collection of four single-life and four joint-life annuities all paying at the rate 1/8. At a time between the first and second deaths, the original annuity's rate would be 1/2, while three of the single-life annuities and one of the joint-life annuities would still be in payment status, each with rate 1/8. The rates at other times can be compared in a similar way. ▼

We have an expression for $_tp_{\overline{x_1 x_2 \cdots x_m}}^{[k]}$ as a special case of Theorem 17.1.

**Corollary 17.1:**

$$_tp_{\overline{x_1 x_2 \cdots x_m}}^{[k]} = \sum_{j=k}^{m} (-1)^{j-k} \binom{j}{k}\, _tB_j \qquad (17.2.4)$$

**Proof:**
In Theorem 17.1, set $c_k = 1$ and $c_j = 0$ for $j \neq k$. For these $c_j$'s, $\Delta^j c_0 = (E - 1)^j\, c_0 = (-1)^{j-k} \binom{j}{k}$, $j = k, k+1, \ldots, m$. ■

**Example 17.3:**

Express the actuarial present value of a continuous annuity of 1 per annum while exactly three of five lives survive, in terms of actuarial present values of joint-life annuities.

**Solution:**
Using (5.3.2B) and then (17.2.4), we have

$$\bar{a}_{\overline{x_1 x_2 x_3 x_4 x_5}}^{[3]} = \int_0^\infty v^t\, _tp_{\overline{x_1 x_2 x_3 x_4 x_5}}^{[3]}\, dt$$

$$= \int_0^\infty v^t \left( _tB_3 - 4\, _tB_4 + 10\, _tB_5 \right) dt$$

$$= \bar{a}_{x_1 x_2 x_3} + \bar{a}_{x_1 x_2 x_4} + 8 \text{ more joint three-life annuity values}$$

$$- 4 \left( a_{x_1 x_2 x_3 x_4} + \bar{a}_{x_1 x_2 x_3 x_5} + 3 \text{ more joint four-life annuity values} \right)$$

$$+ 10\, \bar{a}_{x_1 x_2 x_3 x_4 x_5}. \qquad ▼$$

From the relationship

$$_tp_{\overline{x_1 x_2 \cdots x_m}}^{\overline{h}} = \sum_{j=h}^{m} {}_tp_{\overline{x_1 x_2 \cdots x_m}}^{[j]}, \qquad (17.2.5)$$

we have the following corollary to Theorem 17.1.

Chapter 17

## ADVANCED MULTIPLE LIFE THEORY

**Corollary 17.2:**

For arbitrary numbers $d_0, d_1, ,d_m, \ldots, d_m,$

$$\sum_{j=0}^{m} d_j \, {}_tp_{\overline{x_1 x_2 \cdots x_m}^{\,j}} = d_0 + \sum_{j=1}^{m} \Delta^{j-1} d_1 \, {}_tB_j. \tag{17.2.6}$$

**Proof:**
Using (17.2.5) we start with

$$\sum_{h=0}^{m} d_h \, {}_tp_{\overline{x_1 x_2 \cdots x_m}^{\,h}} = \sum_{h=0}^{m} \sum_{j=h}^{m} d_h \, {}_tp_{\overline{x_1 x_2 \cdots x_m}^{\,[j]}}.$$

Interchanging the summations, we can write

$$\sum_{j=0}^{m} d_j \, {}_tp_{\overline{x_1 x_2 \cdots x_m}^{\,j}} = \sum_{j=0}^{m} \left( \sum_{h=0}^{j} d_h \right) {}_tp_{\overline{x_1 x_2 \cdots x_m}^{\,[j]}},$$

which, by defining $c_j = \Sigma_{h=0}^{j} d_h$ for $j = 0,1,\ldots,m$, is in the form of (17.2.3). For these $c$'s, $c_0 = d_0$ and $\Delta c_j = d_{j+1}$ for $j = 0,1,\ldots,m-1$, thus $\Delta^j c_0 = \Delta^{j-1}(\Delta c_0) = \Delta^{j-1} d_1$ for $j = 1,2,\ldots,m$. Then we have, from the right-hand side of (17.2.3),

$$\sum_{j=0}^{m} d_j \, {}_tp_{\overline{x_1 x_2 \cdots x_m}^{\,j}} = d_0 + \sum_{j=1}^{m} \Delta^{j-1} d_1 \, {}_tB_j. \qquad \blacksquare$$

Corollary 17.2 can be used to express the survival function of the $k$-survivor status in terms of joint- and single-life survival functions.

**Corollary 17.3:**

$$_tp_{\overline{x_1 x_2 \cdots x_m}^{\,k}} = \sum_{j=k}^{m} [(-1)^{j-k} \binom{j-1}{k-1}] \, {}_tB_j \tag{17.2.7}$$

**Proof:**
In Corollary 17.2, set $d_k = 1$ and $d_j = 0$, for $j \neq k$. For these $d$'s, $\Delta^{j-1} d_1 = (E-1)^{j-1} d_1 = (-1)^{j-k} \binom{j-1}{k-1}$, $j = k,k+1,\ldots,m$. $\blacksquare$

From the expression for its survival function in (17.2.7) we can obtain, by differentiation, a parallel expression for the p.d.f. of the future lifetime of the $k$-survivor status, $T$, as

$$f_T(t) = \frac{d}{dt}(1 - {}_tp_{\overline{x_1 x_2 \cdots x_m}^{\,k}})$$

$$= \sum_{j=k}^{m} (-1)^{j-k} \binom{j-1}{k-1} (-{}_tB_j'). \tag{17.2.8}$$

The actuarial present value and other characteristics of the probability distribution of the present value of a set of payments that depend on $T$ can be determined using (17.2.7) or (17.2.8). In such determinations we shall use the fact that $- {}_tB_j'$ is the sum of the p.d.f.'s of the future lifetimes of the $\binom{m}{j}$ joint $j$-life statuses of the $m$ lives.

**Example 17.4:**

Let $T$ denote the future lifetime of the last-survivor status of three lives. Exhibit in terms of joint- and single-life functions

    a. the survival function
    b. $E[v^T]$
    c. $E[\bar{a}_{\overline{T|}}]$.

# ADVANCED MULTIPLE LIFE THEORY

**Solution:**
a. By (17.2.7),

$$_tp_{\overline{x_1x_2x_3}} = \sum_{j=1}^{3} (-1)^{j-1} \binom{j-1}{0} {}_tB_j$$

$$= {}_tB_1 + (-1) {}_tB_2 + {}_tB_3$$

where

$$_tB_1 = {}_tp_{x_1} + {}_tp_{x_2} + {}_tp_{x_3}$$

$$_tB_2 = {}_tp_{x_1x_2} + {}_tp_{x_1x_3} + {}_tp_{x_2x_3}$$

$$_tB_3 = {}_tp_{x_1x_2x_3}.$$

b. We denote $E[v^T]$ by $\bar{A}_{\overline{x_1x_2x_3}}$ and use (17.2.8) to obtain

$$\bar{A}_{\overline{x_1x_2x_3}} = \int_0^\infty v^t(-1)({}_tB_1' - {}_tB_2' + {}_tB_3')\,dt$$

$$= \bar{A}_{x_1} + \bar{A}_{x_2} + \bar{A}_{x_3} - (\bar{A}_{x_1x_2} + \bar{A}_{x_1x_3} + \bar{A}_{x_2x_3}) + \bar{A}_{x_1x_2x_3}.$$

c. Replacing $v^T$ by $\bar{a}_{\overline{T}|}$ in part (b) and denoting $E[\bar{a}_{\overline{T}|}]$ by $\bar{a}_{\overline{x_1x_2x_3}}$ we have

$$\bar{a}_{\overline{x_1x_2x_3}} = \bar{a}_{x_1} + \bar{a}_{x_2} + \bar{a}_{x_3} - (\bar{a}_{x_1x_2} + \bar{a}_{x_1x_3} + \bar{a}_{x_2x_3}) + \bar{a}_{x_1x_2x_3}.$$

For any general status, $v^T + \delta\bar{a}_{\overline{T}|} = 1$, so we can calculate either of the expected values from the other using $\bar{A}_{\overline{x_1x_2x_3}} + \delta\bar{a}_{\overline{x_1x_2x_3}} = 1$. ▼

By differentiating both sides of (17.2.6), we can extend the relationship to the corresponding p.d.f.'s. This can be used for insurances paying an amount upon each death among the $m$ lives.

**Example 17.5:**

Consider an insurance on $(x)$, $(y)$ and $(z)$ paying 1 on the first death, 2 on the second death and 3 on the third death. Express the net single premium for the insurance in terms of net single premiums for unit amount insurances on single- and joint-life statuses.

**Solution:**
Let $f_j(t)$ be the p.d.f. for the future lifetime of the $j$-survivor status. The net single premium is

$$\int_0^\infty v^t [1f_3(t) + 2f_2(t) + 3f_1(t)]\,dt.$$

In the notation of (17.2.6) we have the following.

| $j$ | $d_j$ | $\Delta d_j$ | $\Delta^2 d_j$ | $\Delta^3 d_j$ |
|---|---|---|---|---|
| 0 | 0 | 3 | $-4$ | 4 |
| 1 | 3 | $-1$ | 0 | — |
| 2 | 2 | $-1$ | — | — |
| 3 | 1 | — | — | — |

# Chapter 17

# ADVANCED MULTIPLE LIFE THEORY

Hence the net single premium is

$$\int_0^\infty v^t\,(-1)\,(3\,_tB_1' - \,_tB_2')\,dt = 3\,(\bar{A}_x + \bar{A}_y + \bar{A}_z) - (\bar{A}_{xy} + \bar{A}_{xz} + \bar{A}_{yz}).\qquad\blacktriangledown$$

## 17.3 Compound Statuses

In the previous section we defined statuses for several lives by means of the general $k$-survivor status. Others statuses can be defined by compounding. A **compound status** is said to exist if the status is based on a combination of statuses, at least one of which is itself a status involving more than one life. We examine some possibilities in Example 17.6.

**Example 17.6:**

Describe the conditions of payment for the annuities and insurances corresponding to the following actuarial present value and net single premium symbols.

a. $\bar{a}_{\overline{wx}:\overline{yz}}$      b. $\bar{a}_{\overline{\overline{wx}}:(yz)}$      c. $\bar{a}_{(x:\overline{n}):(yz:\overline{m})}$

d. $\bar{A}_{\overline{wx}:yz}$      e. $\bar{A}_{\overline{(wx):(yz)}}$      f. $\bar{A}_{\overline{(wx):y:z}}$

**Solution:**

a. The annuity is payable continuously at the rate of 1 per year while at least one of $(w)$ and $(x)$ and at least one of $(y)$ and $(z)$ survive. Thus the annuity is payable while three or four of the lives survive and while two survive if one is from the pair $(w)$, $(x)$ and the other from the pair $(y)$,$(z)$.

b. The annuity is payable continuously at the rate of 1 per year while at least two of the four lives survive and also while only one survives if that survivor is either $(w)$ or $(x)$.

c. The annuity is payable continuously at the rate of 1 per year while either $(x)$ is alive and an $n$-year period has not elapsed or while both $(y)$ and $(z)$ are alive and an $m$-year period has not elapsed.

d. A unit amount is payable at the moment of the first death if $(y)$ or $(z)$ dies first and otherwise on the second death.

e. A unit amount is payable at the moment of the second death if two deaths consist of one from the $(w)$,$(x)$ group and the other from the $(y)$,$(z)$ group. If not, the payment is made at the time of the third death.

f. A unit amount is payable only after $(y)$,$(z)$, and one of $(w)$ and $(x)$ have died. In other words, it is payable at the moment of the third death if $(w)$ or $(x)$ remains alive, but otherwise at the moment of the fourth death.      $\blacktriangledown$

In applications, a numerical value for any one of these actuarial present values or net single premiums would most likely be obtained by first expressing it in terms of those for single- and joint-life statuses. The relationships in (8.3.5) among $T(xy)$, $T(\overline{xy})$, $T(x)$ and $T(y)$, and in (8.5.6) and (8.5.7) among $K(xy)$, $K(\overline{xy})$, $K(x)$ and $K(y)$, hold for general statuses $(u)$,$(v)$. For example,

$$v^{T(uv)} + v^{T(\overline{uv})} = v^{T(u)} + v^{T(v)}.\qquad(17.3.1)$$

Employing parts of Example 17.6, we will illustrate the process of

# ADVANCED MULTIPLE LIFE THEORY

using (17.3.1) and similar identities. First, we consider part (e).

$$\bar{A}_{\overline{(wx):(yz)}} = \bar{A}_{wx} + \bar{A}_{yz} - \bar{A}_{wxyz}.$$

Here, $(u) = (wx)$ and $(v) = (yz)$. To write $\bar{A}_{\overline{(wx):(yz)}}$ as $\bar{A}_{wxyz}$ we have used

$$\min\{\min[T(w), T(x)], \min[T(y), T(z)]\}$$
$$= \min[T(w), T(x), T(y), T(z)]. \qquad (17.3.2)$$

For part (c) of Example 17.6, we have

$$\bar{a}_{\overline{(x:\overline{n}|)(yz:\overline{m}|)}} = \bar{a}_{x:\overline{n}|} + \bar{a}_{yz:\overline{m}|} - \bar{a}_{xyz:\overline{n}|}$$

where the last term is obtained from

$$\min[T(x), T(y), T(z), T(\overline{n}|), T(\overline{m}|)] = \min[T(x), T(y), T(z), T(\overline{n}|)]$$

for the case $n \le m$.

Other arrangements, as in parts (a), (b), (d) and (f) of Example 17.6, require the use of other relationships. For part (a), we want

$$\bar{a}_{\overline{\overline{wx}:\overline{yz}}} = \mathrm{E}[\bar{a}_{\overline{T}|}] \qquad (17.3.3)$$

where

$$T = \min[T(\overline{wx}), T(\overline{yz})]$$
$$= \min\{\max[T(w), T(x)], \max[T(y), T(z)]\}.$$

A simple answer, like (17.3.2), is not available for this random variable. To proceed, let us first assume that $T(\overline{wx})$ and $T(\overline{yz})$ are independent and look at the survival function of $T$, $s(t)$. Thus

$$s(t) = \Pr[T > t] = \Pr\{\min[T(\overline{wx}), T(\overline{yz})] > t\}$$
$$= \Pr\{T(\overline{wx}) > t, T(\overline{yz}) > t\}$$
$$= \Pr\{T(\overline{wx}) > t\}\Pr\{T(\overline{yz}) > t\}$$
$$= {}_t p_{\overline{wx}} \, {}_t p_{\overline{yz}} \qquad (17.3.4)$$
$$= ({}_t p_w + {}_t p_x - {}_t p_{wx})({}_t p_y + {}_t p_z - {}_t p_{yz})$$
$$= {}_t p_{wy} + {}_t p_{wz} + {}_t p_{xy} + {}_t p_{xz} - {}_t p_{wyz} - {}_t p_{xyx}$$
$$\quad - {}_t p_{wxy} - {}_t p_{wxz} + {}_t p_{wxyz}$$

for the independent case. Now using (17.3.4) we obtain

$$\bar{a}_{\overline{\overline{wx}:\overline{yz}}} = \int_0^\infty v^t s(t)\, dt \qquad (17.3.5)$$
$$= \bar{a}_{wy} + \bar{a}_{wz} + \bar{a}_{xy} + \bar{a}_{xz} - \bar{a}_{wyz} - \bar{a}_{xyz} - \bar{a}_{wxy} - \bar{a}_{wxz} + \bar{a}_{wxyz}.$$

Let's return to (17.3.4) and show that a parallel relationship for the random variables holds and then that (17.3.4) is true without the independence assumption. We start with the assertion that for all possible outcomes,

$$T(\overline{wx}:\overline{yz}) = T(wy) + T(wz) + T(xy) + T(xz)$$
$$- T(wyz) - T(xyz) - T(wxy) - T(wxz) \quad (17.3.6)$$
$$+ T(wxyz).$$

The outcomes can be collected into 24 mutually exclusive events according to the order of $T(w)$, $T(x)$, $T(y)$ and $T(z)$. Since the given assertion is symmetric in $w$ and $x$ and symmetric in $y$ and $z$, only 6 different outcomes require verification. As an example, consider $T(w) < T(x) < T(y) < T(z)$ for which the left-hand side of (17.3.6) is $T(\overline{wx}:\overline{yz}) = T(x)$ and the right-hand side is, on a term-by-term basis,

$$T(w) + T(w) + T(x) + T(x) - T(w) - T(x) - T(w) - T(w) + T(w) = T(x)$$

as required. The other cases can be verified in the same way.

An expression in annuities that is parallel to (17.3.6) can be established by similar reasoning. Thus,

$$\bar{a}_{\overline{T(\overline{wx}:\overline{yz})}|} = \bar{a}_{\overline{T(wy)}|} + \bar{a}_{\overline{T(wz)}|} + \bar{a}_{\overline{T(xy)}|} + \bar{a}_{\overline{T(xz)}|} \quad (17.3.7)$$
$$- \bar{a}_{\overline{T(wyz)}|} - \bar{a}_{\overline{T(xyz)}|} - \bar{a}_{\overline{T(wxy)}|} - \bar{a}_{\overline{T(wxz)}|} + \bar{a}_{\overline{T(wxyz)}|}.$$

Taking expectations of both sides of this expression we have (17.3.5).

We emphasize two aspects of the independence assumption for this case. It would not be used to establish (17.3.7), nor is it required in the expectation calculation used to obtain (17.3.5) from (17.3.7). However, again, to obtain joint-life status functions from single-life life tables, we do, for convenience, assume that individual future lifetimes are independent.

## 17.4 Contingent Probabilities and Insurances

In this section we extend the notion of contingent functions (Section 8.8) to more than two lives. We start with an integral expression for the required probability, or net single premium, which can then be rewritten in terms of probabilities or net single premiums defined on the first death. It is then possible to use some of the techniques of Section 8.9 to complete the evaluation. In any case, numerical integration methods can be used.

To obtain an integral expression for a probability, we use

$$\Pr(A) = \int_{-\infty}^{\infty} \Pr(A|T = t) f_T(t) \, dt \quad (17.4.1)$$

where $T$ will usually mean the time of death of an individual life.

**Example 17.7:** Express $_n q_{wx\overset{2}{y}z}$ in terms of functions contingent on the first death.

**Solution:**
Here $A$ is the event that $(y)$ is the second life among $(w)$, $(x)$, $(y)$ and $(z)$ to die and does so within $n$ years. Since $A$ is defined by $T(y)$, we use $T(y)$ as $T$ in (17.4.1) to obtain

$$_n q^2_{wxyz} = \int_0^n \Pr(A|T(y) = t)\,_t p_y\,\mu_{y+t}\,dt.$$

The integral's limits follow from

$$f_{T(y)}(t) = 0 \qquad\qquad t < 0$$

and

$$\Pr(A|T(y) = t) = 0 \quad t > n.$$

Now $(y)$ will be the second to die if and only if there are exactly two of $(w)$, $(x)$ and $(z)$ surviving at that time. If we assume that $T(y)$ is independent of $T(w)$, $T(x)$ and $T(z)$, then

$$\Pr(A|T(y) = t) = \,_t p^{[2]}_{\overline{wxz}} \quad t < n$$

and

$$\begin{aligned}
_n q^2_{wxyz} &= \int_0^n {}_t p^{[2]}_{\overline{wxz}}\, {}_t p_y\, \mu_{y+t}\, dt \\
&= \int_0^n ({}_t B_2 - 3\,{}_t B_3)\, {}_t p_y\, \mu_{y+t}\, dt \\
&= {}_n q^1_{wxy} + {}_n q^1_{wyz} + {}_n q^1_{xyz} - 3\,{}_n q^1_{wxyz}.
\end{aligned}$$

(The second integral comes from applying Theorem 17.1.)      ▼

The similarity of the final expression of Example 17.7 to previous results that did not require independence suggests the assumed independence was not necessary. Alternative derivations in Exercises 17.18 and 17.40 will verify that this is the case.

A contingent insurance can be analyzed by a similar procedure based on

$$E[Z] = \int_{-\infty}^{\infty} E[Z|T = t] f_T(t)\, dt. \qquad (17.4.2)$$

**Example 17.8:**    Express $\bar{A}^2_{wxy}$ in terms of net single premiums for insurances contingent on the first death only.

**Solution:**
Let $Z$ be the random variable representing the present value at issue of the insurance benefit. Since the insurance is payable on the death of $(y)$, we choose $T(y)$ to play the role of $T$ in the conditional expectation of (17.4.2):

$$\bar{A}^2_{wxy} = E[Z] = \int_0^{\infty} E[Z|T(y) = t]\, {}_t p_y\, \mu_{y+t}\, dt.$$

If, at the death of $(y)$ at duration $t$, there is exactly one of $(w)$ and $(x)$ surviving, the unit benefit will be paid; otherwise no benefit will be paid. Thus, we have

## ADVANCED MULTIPLE LIFE THEORY

$$E[Z|T(y) = t] = v^t \, {}_tp_{\overline{wx}}^{[1]}$$

and

$$\bar{A}_{wxy}^{\,2} = \int_0^\infty v^t \, {}_tp_{\overline{wx}}^{[1]} \, {}_tp_y \, \mu_{y+t} \, dt$$

$$= \int_0^\infty v^t ({}_tB_1 - 2\,{}_tB_2) \, {}_tp_y \, \mu_{y+t} \, dt$$

$$= \bar{A}_{xy}^{\,1} + \bar{A}_{wy}^{\,1} - 2\,\bar{A}_{wxy}^{\,1}.$$

The Var $[Z]$ can be obtained by the principle of Theorem 4.1.  ▼

**17.5
Compound
Contingent
Functions**

The functions in this section are distinguished from those in the previous section by specifications on the order of deaths prior to the death when the benefits are paid, or the event is defined. These specifications on the prior deaths are indicated by numbers placed below the symbols for the lives involved. We examine two such symbols and note the distinctions possible in the notation.

The symbols ${}_nq_{\substack{x\,yz \\ 1}}^{\,2}$ and ${}_nq_{\substack{x\,yz \\ 1}}^{\,3}$ both refer to events in which $T(x) <$ $T(y) < T(z)$. They differ though in that the second death must occur before time $n$ in the first event, while the third death must precede time $n$ in the second event.

It is not always possible to express compound contingent functions completely in terms of functions depending only on the first death. On the other hand, the function can always be expressed as one or more multiple integrals of the joint p.d.f. of the future-lifetime random variables of the lives involved. The example of this general procedure (Example 17.9) is more complex than others in this section.

**Example 17.9:**

Derive an expression for the probability that $(w)$, $(x)$, $(y)$ and $(z)$ die in that order with less than 10 years between the deaths of $(w)$ and $(z)$ and less than 5 years between the deaths of $(x)$ and $(y)$.

**Solution:**
We first define the event $A$ for use in a multivariate version of (17.4.1):

$$A = \left\{ \begin{array}{c} T(w) < T(x) < T(y) < T(z) \\ T(z) - T(w) < 10 \\ T(y) - T(x) < 5 \end{array} \right\}. \qquad (17.5.1)$$

We choose to condition on $T(w)$ and $T(x)$ because these are involved in both the upper and lower bounds for $T(y)$ and $T(z)$. That is,

$$\Pr(A) = \int_0^\infty \int_0^\infty \Pr[A|(T(w) = r) \cap (T(x) = s)] \, g(r,s) \, ds \, dr \qquad (17.5.2)$$

where $g(r,s)$ is the p.d.f. of $T(w)$ and $T(x)$. Now $\Pr[A|(T(w) = r) \cap$

$(T(x) = s)]$ is equal to $\Pr(A^*)$ where

$$A^* = \left\{ \begin{array}{c} r < s < T(y) < T(z) < r + 10 \\ T(y) < s + 5 \end{array} \right\},$$

and the probability is calculated by the conditional distribution of $T(y)$ and $T(z)$, given $T(x) = s$ and $T(w) = r$. Thus $\Pr(A^*)$ can be set up in the sample space of the random variables $T(y)$ and $T(z)$. Two cases are displayed in Figure 17.1.

Thus, letting $h(t,u)$ denote the conditional p.d.f. of $T(y)$ and $T(z)$ given $T(w) = r$ and $T(x) = s$, we have

$$\Pr(A^*) = \begin{cases} \displaystyle\int_s^{s+5} \int_t^{r+10} h(t,u)\,du\,dt & r < s < r + 5 \\[4mm] \displaystyle\int_s^{r+10} \int_t^{r+10} h(t,u)\,du\,dt & r + 5 < s < r + 10 \\[4mm] 0 & s > r + 10 \text{ or } s < r. \end{cases}$$

Substituting into (17.5.2), we have

$$\Pr(A) = \int_0^\infty \int_r^{r+5} \int_s^{s+5} \int_t^{r+10} h(t,u)\,g(r,s)\,du\,dt\,ds\,dr$$

$$+ \int_0^\infty \int_{r+5}^{r+10} \int_s^{r+10} \int_t^{r+10} h(t,u)\,g(r,s)\,du\,dt\,ds\,dr.$$

**Figure 17.1**
**Cases (A), $s < r + 5$,**
**and (B), $r + 5 < s < r + 10$**

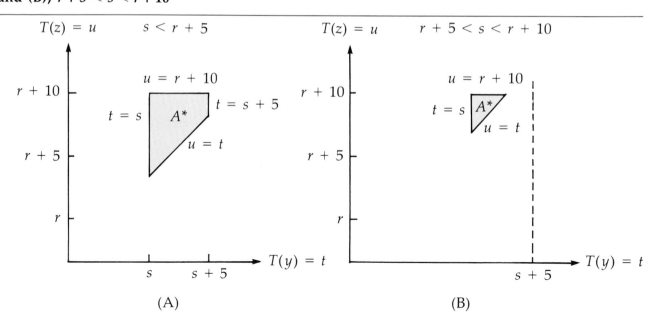

# ADVANCED MULTIPLE LIFE THEORY

Under the assumption of mutually independent future lifetimes, the integrand can be replaced by

$$_r p_w \, \mu_{w+r} \, _s p_x \, \mu_{x+s} \, _t p_y \, \mu_{y+t} \, _u p_z \, \mu_{z+u}. \qquad \blacktriangledown$$

We now examine some compound contingent probabilities that can be written in terms of single integrals. We will first obtain equivalent forms for a probability by applying (17.4.1).

**Example 17.10:** Write three different integrals for $_n q_{\substack{xyz \\ 1}}^{\;3}$ and reduce one of them to probability functions dependent on only the first death.

**Solution:**
Here $A = \{T(x) < T(y) < T(z) < n\}$. We set three integrals by conditioning on each of the future lifetimes:

$$_n q_{\substack{xyz \\ 1}}^{\;3} = \int_0^\infty \Pr[A|T(x) = t] \, _t p_x \, \mu_{x+t} \, dt$$

and

$$\Pr[A|T(x) = t] = \begin{cases} 0 & t > n \\ _t p_{yz} \; _{n-t} q_{\substack{y+t:z \\ 1}}^{\;2} & t \le n, \end{cases}$$

thus

$$_n q_{\substack{xyz \\ 1}}^{\;3} = \int_0^n \; _t p_{yz} \; _{n-t} q_{\substack{y+t:z \\ 1}}^{\;2} \; _t p_x \, \mu_{x+t} \, dt.$$

Similarly,

$$_n q_{\substack{xyz \\ 1}}^{\;3} = \int_0^\infty \Pr[A|T(y) = t] \, _t p_y \, \mu_{y+t} \, dt$$

$$= \int_0^n \; _t q_x \; _t p_z \; _{n-t} q_{z+t} \; _t p_y \, \mu_{y+t} \, dt$$

and

$$_n q_{\substack{xyz \\ 1}}^{\;3} = \int_0^\infty \Pr[A|T(z) = t] \, _t p_z \, \mu_{z+t} \, dt$$

$$= \int_0^n \; _t q_{\substack{xy \\ 1}}^{\;2} \; _t p_z \, \mu_{z+t} \, dt.$$

The second of these integrals can be expressed in terms of first-death probabilities as follows:

$$_n q_{\substack{xyz \\ 1}}^{\;3} = \int_0^n (1 - _t p_x) \, (_t p_z - _n p_z) \, _t p_y \, \mu_{y+t} \, dt$$

$$= \; _n q_{yz}^1 - \; _n q_{\substack{xyz \\ 1}}^1 - \; _n p_z \left( _n q_y - \; _n q_{\substack{xy \\ 1}}^1 \right). \qquad \blacktriangledown$$

# ADVANCED MULTIPLE LIFE THEORY

**Example 17.11:**    Use (17.4.1) to write four different integral expressions for $_nq^{\;\;\;3}_{wx\underset{1\,2}{y}z}$.

**Solution:**
Here $A = \{T(w) < T(x) < T(y) < T(z) \text{ and } T(y) < n\}$. Then

$$_nq^{\;\;\;3}_{wx\underset{1\,2}{y}z} = \int_0^n {}_tp_{xyz}\; {}_{n-t}q_{x+t:y}\;{}^2_{\underset{1}{}t:z+t}\; {}_tp_w\, \mu_{w+t}\, dt$$

$$= \int_0^n {}_tq_w\; {}_tp_{yz}\; {}_{n-t}q^{\;\;\;1}_{y+t:z+t}\; {}_tp_x\, \mu_{x+t}\, dt \qquad (17.5.3)$$

$$= \int_0^n {}_tq^{\;\;2}_{wx}\; {}_tp_z\; {}_tp_y\, \mu_{y+t}\, dt$$

$$= \int_0^n {}_tq^{\;\;\;3}_{wx\underset{1}{y}}\; {}_tp_z\, \mu_{z+t}\, dt + {}_nq^{\;\;\;3}_{wx\underset{1}{y}}\; {}_np_z.$$

The last line, obtained by conditioning on $T(z)$, requires an expression for $T(z) < n$ and another for $T(z) > n$.    ▼

In the application of (17.4.1) to the examples of this section we have used the assumption of independent future lifetimes in writing the $\Pr[A|T = t]$ factors of the integrands. We now consider the numerical evaluation of these probabilities when a single Gompertz mortality law is used for each life involved.

**Example 17.12:**    Under a Gompertz law, show that

$$_\infty q^{\;\;\;3}_{wx\underset{1\,2}{y}z} = {}_\infty q^{\;\;1}_{wxyz}\; {}_\infty q^{\;1}_{xyz}\; {}_\infty q^{\;1}_{yz}.$$

**Solution:**
Letting $n \to \infty$ in (17.5.3) we have

$$_\infty q^{\;\;\;3}_{wx\underset{1\,2}{y}z} = \int_0^\infty {}_tq_w\; {}_tp_{yz}\; {}_\infty q^{\;\;\;1}_{y+t:z+t}\; {}_tp_x\, \mu_{x+t}\, dt. \qquad (17.5.4)$$

In Example 8.8(b) it was shown that, under the Gompertz mortality law,

$$_nq^{\;1}_{xy} = \frac{c^x}{c^w}\; {}_nq_w \qquad (17.5.5)$$

where $c^w = c^x + c^y$. Adapting this and substituting it for $_\infty q^{\;\;\;1}_{y+t:z+t}$ in the integrand of (17.5.4), we obtain

$$_\infty q^{\;\;\;3}_{wx\underset{1\,2}{y}z} = \int_0^\infty \frac{c^{y+t}}{c^{y+t}+c^{z+t}}\; {}_tq_w\; {}_tp_{yz}\; {}_tp_x\, \mu_{x+t}\, dt$$

$$= \frac{c^y}{c^y + c^z}\left({}_\infty q^{\;1}_{xyz} - {}_\infty q^{\;1}_{wxyz}\right).$$

Formula (17.5.5) can be extended to more than two lives and then

# ADVANCED MULTIPLE LIFE THEORY

used in this expression; therefore,

$$_{\infty}q^{\;\;3}_{wx\overset{y}{z}} = \frac{c^y}{c^y + c^z}\left(\frac{c^x}{c^x + c^y + c^z} - \frac{c^x}{c^w + c^x + c^y + c^z}\right)$$

$$= \left(\frac{c^w}{c^w + c^x + c^y + c^z}\right)\left(\frac{c^x}{c^x + c^y + c^z}\right)\left(\frac{c^y}{c^y + c^z}\right)$$

$$= {}_{\infty}q^1_{wxyz}\;{}_{\infty}q^1_{xyz}\;{}_{\infty}q^1_{yz}. \qquad\qquad \blacktriangledown$$

## 17.6 Reversionary Annuities

A *reversionary annuity* is payable during the existence of a status $(u)$, but only after the failure of a second status $(v)$. Such an annuity is used as a post-retirement death benefit in some pension plans. The basic notation for the actuarial present value of this annuity is $a_{v|u}$ with adornments to indicate frequency and timing of the payments. If $(v)$ is a term certain, the reversionary annuity reduces to a deferred life annuity to $(u)$. If $(u)$ is a term certain, the reversionary annuity is a family income insurance.

We start with an annuity of 1 per year payable continuously to $(y)$ after the death of $(x)$. The present value at time 0, denoted by Z, is

$$Z = \begin{cases} {}_{T(x)|}\bar{a}_{\overline{T(y)\,-\,T(x)}|} & T(x) \le T(y) \\ 0 & T(x) > T(y). \end{cases} \qquad (17.6.1)$$

Then, for independent future lifetimes, the actuarial present value of this annuity is

$$\bar{a}_{x|y} = \mathrm{E}[Z] = \int_0^\infty \int_t^\infty {}_{t|}\bar{a}_{\overline{s-t}|}\; {}_sp_y\, \mu_{y+s}\, {}_tp_x\, \mu_{x+t}\, ds\, dt$$

$$= \int_0^\infty v^t\, {}_tp_y \left[\int_t^\infty \bar{a}_{\overline{s-t}|}\; {}_{s-t}p_{y+t}\, \mu_{y+s}\, ds\right] {}_tp_x\, \mu_{x+t}\, dt \qquad (17.6.2)$$

$$= \int_0^\infty v^t\, {}_tp_y\, \bar{a}_{y+t}\, {}_tp_x\, \mu_{x+t}\, dt.$$

This last expression is in the form of (17.4.2) with conditioning on $T(x)$.

Formula (17.6.1) can be rewritten as

$$Z = \begin{cases} \bar{a}_{\overline{T(y)}|} - \bar{a}_{\overline{T(x)}|} & T(x) \le T(y) \\ 0 & T(x) > T(y) \end{cases}$$

or as

$$Z = \begin{cases} \bar{a}_{\overline{T(y)}|} - \bar{a}_{\overline{T(x)}|} & T(x) \le T(y) \\ \bar{a}_{\overline{T(y)}|} - \bar{a}_{\overline{T(y)}|} & T(x) > T(y), \end{cases}$$

which implies

$$Z = \bar{a}_{\overline{T(y)}|} - \bar{a}_{\overline{T(xy)}|}. \qquad (17.6.3)$$

From (17.6.3),

$$\bar{a}_{x|y} = \mathrm{E}[Z] = \mathrm{E}[\bar{a}_{\overline{T(y)|}}] - \mathrm{E}[\bar{a}_{\overline{T(xy)|}}] = \bar{a}_y - \bar{a}_{xy}. \tag{17.6.4}$$

If (17.6.4) is expressed in the form of (5.3.2B), we have

$$\bar{a}_{x|y} = \bar{a}_y - \bar{a}_{xy} = \int_0^\infty v^t {}_tp_y \, dt - \int_0^\infty v^t {}_tp_{xy} \, dt = \int_0^\infty v^t {}_tp_y \, (1 - {}_tp_x) \, dt,$$

which shows that, at any time $t$ when a payment is made, $(y)$ must be alive and $(x)$ must be dead.

Formulas (17.6.3) and (17.6.4) hold for arbitrary statuses $(u)$ and $(v)$. For example,

$$\bar{a}_{x:\overline{n}|y} = \bar{a}_y - \bar{a}_{xy:\overline{n}|}$$

$$\bar{a}_{x|y:\overline{n}|} = \bar{a}_{y:\overline{n}|} - \bar{a}_{xy:\overline{n}|}$$

$$\bar{a}_{\overline{xy}|z} = \bar{a}_z - a_{\overline{xy}:z} = \bar{a}_z - \bar{a}_{xz} - \bar{a}_{yz} + \bar{a}_{xyz}.$$

In the above examples, the term certain is measured from time 0. For a reversionary annuity paying an $n$-year temporary annuity to $(y)$ after the death of $(x)$, the term certain is a deferred status so we go back to first principles. The present value at policy issue, $Z$, is

$$Z = \begin{cases} 0 & T(y) \le T(x) \\ v^{T(x)} \bar{a}_{\overline{T(y) - T(x)|}} & T(x) < T(y) \le T(x) + n \\ v^{T(x)} \, \bar{a}_{\overline{n}|} & T(y) > T(x) + n. \end{cases}$$

Using (17.4.2) with conditioning on $T(x) = t$, we can write the actuarial present value as

$$\mathrm{E}[Z] = \int_0^\infty \mathrm{E}[Z|T(x) = t] \, {}_tp_x \, \mu_{x+t} \, dt$$

$$= \int_0^\infty {}_tp_y \, v^t \, \bar{a}_{y+t:\overline{n}|} \, {}_tp_x \, \mu_{x+t} \, dt. \tag{17.6.5}$$

By substituting

$$\bar{a}_{y+t:\overline{n}|} = \int_t^{t+n} v^{s-t} \, {}_{s-t}p_{y+t} \, ds$$

into (17.6.5) we obtain

$$\mathrm{E}[Z] = \int_0^\infty \int_t^{t+n} v^s \, {}_sp_y \, {}_tp_x \, \mu_{x+t} \, ds \, dt.$$

Next we invert the order of integration so that

# ADVANCED MULTIPLE LIFE THEORY

$$E[Z] = \int_0^n \int_0^s v^s \, {}_sp_y \, {}_tp_x \, \mu_{x+t} \, dt \, ds + \int_n^\infty \int_{s-n}^s v^s \, {}_sp_y \, {}_tp_x \, \mu_{x+t} \, dt \, ds$$

$$= \int_0^n v^s \, {}_sp_y \, (1 - {}_sp_x) \, ds + \int_n^\infty v^s \, {}_sp_y \, ({}_{s-n}p_x - {}_sp_x) \, ds \qquad (17.6.6)$$

$$= \bar{a}_{y:\overline{n}|} - \bar{a}_{xy:\overline{n}|} + v^n \, {}_np_y \, \bar{a}_{x:y+n} - v^n \, {}_np_{xy} \, \bar{a}_{x+n:y+n}.$$

Formula (17.6.6) is a current payment form for this actuarial present value.

In practice annuities are paid on a discrete basis so a distinction must be made between contracts in which payment periods are based on the date of death and contracts in which payment periods are based on the contract issue date. A circumflex is placed above the annuity symbol to indicate a contract with payment periods based on the date of death. (See Appendix 4.) We now seek expressions that can be used in the numerical evaluation of these discrete basis annuities.

For two statuses $(u)$ and $(v)$, (17.6.3) and (17.6.4) can be modified for the different payment frequency to obtain

$$\ddot{a}_{v|u}^{(m)} = \ddot{a}_u^{(m)} - \ddot{a}_{uv}^{(m)}. \qquad (17.6.7)$$

Evaluation of these annuity values was covered in Chapters 5 and 8. By using relationships from those chapters, this reversionary annuity value can be related to the annually paid reversionary annuity. If the failure times of $(u)$ and $(uv)$ are uniformly distributed over the year of duration, we have

$$\ddot{a}_{v|u}^{(m)} = [\alpha(m)\ddot{a}_u - \beta(m)] - [\alpha(m)\ddot{a}_{uv} - \beta(m)] = \alpha(m)\ddot{a}_{v|u}. \qquad (17.6.8)$$

**Example 17.13:**     Express

a. $\ddot{a}_{x|y}^{(12)}$

b. $\ddot{a}_{x:\overline{n}||y}^{(12)}$

in terms of $\ddot{a}_{x|y}$ and $\ddot{a}_{x:\overline{n}||y}$ respectively.

**Solution:**
a. Assuming $T(y)$ is uniformly distributed over the year of age and $T(xy)$ is approximately uniformly distributed over the year of duration in the sense of (8.7.9), we will use (17.6.8) to write

$$\ddot{a}_{x|y}^{(12)} = \alpha(12)\ddot{a}_{x|y}.$$

b. Since the time-until-failure of $(yx:\overline{n}|)$ is not uniformly distributed over the $n$th year, we can not use (17.6.8) for the second annuity. Thus, we reconsider the argument of (17.6.8) for this case,

$$\ddot{a}_{x:\overline{n}||y}^{(12)} = \ddot{a}_y^{(12)} - \ddot{a}_{yx:\overline{n}|}^{(12)}$$

$$= [\alpha(12)\ddot{a}_y - \beta(12)] - [\alpha(12)\ddot{a}_{yx:\overline{n}|} - \beta(12)(1 - {}_nE_{xy})]$$

$$= \alpha(12)\ddot{a}_{x:\overline{n}||y} - \beta(12)\, {}_nE_{xy}. \qquad \blacktriangledown$$

# ADVANCED MULTIPLE LIFE THEORY

For reversionary annuities with payment periods based on the date of death, we must return to first principles. If $Z$ denotes the present-value random variable for the $m$thly paid annuity-due to $(y)$ commencing on the date of death of $(x)$, we have

$$\hat{\ddot{a}}_{x|y}^{(m)} = E[Z] = \int_0^\infty E[Z|T(x) = t] \; _tp_x \, \mu_{x+t} \, dt$$

$$= \int_0^\infty v^t \; _tp_y \, \ddot{a}_{y+t}^{(m)} \; _tp_x \, \mu_{x+t} \, dt.$$

Using (5.5.9) we can write

$$\ddot{a}_{y+t}^{(m)} = \frac{\alpha(m)}{\alpha(\infty)} \bar{a}_{y+t} + \frac{\alpha(m)}{\alpha(\infty)} \beta(\infty) - \beta(m)$$

and then, letting

$$\varepsilon(m) = \frac{\alpha(m)}{\alpha(\infty)} \beta(\infty) - \beta(m) = \frac{i^{(m)} - \delta}{i^{(m)} d^{(m)}}, \qquad (17.6.9)$$

we have

$$\hat{\ddot{a}}_{x|y}^{(m)} = \frac{\alpha(m)}{\alpha(\infty)} \int_0^\infty v^t \; _tp_y \, \bar{a}_{y+t} \; _tp_x \, \mu_{x+t} \, dt + \varepsilon(m) \int_0^\infty v^t \; _tp_y \; _tp_x \, \mu_{x+t} \, dt$$

$$= \frac{\alpha(m)}{\alpha(\infty)} (\bar{a}_y - \bar{a}_{xy}) + \varepsilon(m) \bar{A}_{xy}^1 \qquad (17.6.10)$$

$$= \alpha(m) \ddot{a}_{x|y} + \varepsilon(m) \bar{A}_{xy}^1.$$

## 17.7
## Net Premiums and Reserves

Here we examine net premiums and net premium reserves for the insurances of this chapter. As in Chapter 6, the net premium will be defined by the equivalence principle. The net premium reserve will be defined prospectively as the conditional expectation of the future loss, given survival to the duration of the reserve.

The premium payment period must end no later than the time of claim payment and, in the case of contingent insurances, when it is clear that no claim payment can be made. The period can always be shorter.

In the case of insurances payable on the first death, the premiums are payable only while all lives survive. Using the equivalence principle we have the following:

$$P_{xy} \, \ddot{a}_{xy} = A_{xy}$$

$$_{10}P^{\{4\}}(\bar{A} \, _{\overline{xy}:\overline{20|}}^1) \, \ddot{a}_{xy:\overline{10|}}^{\{4\}} = \bar{A} \, _{\overline{xy}:\overline{20|}}^1$$

and

$$P(\bar{A}_{xyz}^1) \, \ddot{a}_{xyz} = \bar{A}_{xyz}^1.$$

# Chapter 17
## ADVANCED MULTIPLE LIFE THEORY

Insurances payable on the second or a later death give rise to more than one natural premium payment period. To minimize the net premium that can be charged for a particular insurance benefit, we use the longest period. The following example illustrates the process for a number of cases.

**Example 17.14:** Using the equivalence principle, write the equation for the following net premiums.

a. $P_{\overline{xy}}$  
b. $P(\bar{A}_{\overline{xyz}}^{\,2})$  
c. $P(\bar{A}_{\overline{wx}:yz})$  
d. $P(\bar{A}_{xyz}^{\,2})$  
e. $P(\bar{A}_{\underset{1}{xyz}}^{\,2})$.

**Solution:**

a. $P_{\overline{xy}}\,\ddot{a}_{\overline{xy}} = A_{\overline{xy}}$

b. $P(\bar{A}_{\overline{xyz}}^{\,2})\,\ddot{a}_{\overline{xyz}}^{\,2} = \bar{A}_{\overline{xyz}}^{\,2}$

c. $P(\bar{A}_{\overline{wx}:yz})\,\ddot{a}_{\overline{wx}:yz} = \bar{A}_{\overline{wx}:yz}$

d. As long as $(y)$ and at least one of $(x)$ and $(z)$ are alive, payment of the benefit is still possible. Therefore

$$P(\bar{A}_{xyz}^{\,2})\,\ddot{a}_{y:\overline{xz}} = \bar{A}_{xyz}^{\,2}.$$

e. In this case payment of the benefit is still possible if all are alive or if only $(y)$ and $(z)$ are alive. Thus the appropriate premium payment period is the lifetime of $(yz)$, and

$$P(\bar{A}_{\underset{1}{xyz}}^{\,2})\,\ddot{a}_{yz} = \bar{A}_{\underset{1}{xyz}}^{\,2}. \qquad \blacktriangledown$$

As the conditional expectation of the future loss, the net premium reserve will depend on the condition of the status used in the calculation. The reserve is unique for an insurance payable on the first death because all lives must survive until termination of the insurance. We illustrate reserve formulas for two of these insurances:

$$_5V_{\overline{xy}:\overline{10}|}^{\,1} = A_{\overline{x+5:y+5}:\overline{5}|}^{\quad\quad 1} - P_{\overline{xy}:\overline{10}|}^{\,1}\,\ddot{a}_{x+5:y+5:\overline{5}|}$$

where

$$P_{\overline{xy}:\overline{10}|}^{\,1}\,\ddot{a}_{xy:\overline{10}|} = A_{\overline{xy}:\overline{10}|}^{\quad 1}$$

and

$$_5V_{xyz}^{\,1} = A_{x+5:y+5:z+5}^{\quad\quad\quad 1} - P_{xyz}^{\,1}\,\ddot{a}_{x+5:y+5:z+5}.$$

For an insurance payable on the second or a later death, the net premium reserve can be calculated with the given condition of the expectation being either which lives are surviving or that the insurance has not terminated. Consider the simple case of a unit payable upon the failure of $(\overline{xy})$ and let $_tL$ be the future loss at $t$. Conditioning on which lives are surviving, we would have

$$E[_tL\,|\,T(x) > t \text{ and } T(y) > t] = \bar{A}_{\overline{x+t:y+t}} - \bar{P}(\bar{A}_{\overline{xy}})\,\ddot{a}_{\overline{x+t:y+t}}, \quad (17.7.1)$$

$$E[_tL\,|\,T(x) > t \text{ and } T(y) \le t] = \bar{A}_{x+t} - \bar{P}(\bar{A}_{\overline{xy}})\,\ddot{a}_{x+t} \quad (17.7.2)$$

and the similar expression for $(y)$ surviving alone.

# ADVANCED MULTIPLE LIFE THEORY

Under the condition that the insurance has not terminated, we want $E[_tL|T(\overline{xy}) > t]$, which we can calculate as the sum

$$E[_tL|T(x) > t, T(y) \le t] \Pr[T(x) > t, T(y) \le t|T(\overline{xy}) > t]$$

$$+E[_tL|T(x) \le t, T(y) > t] \Pr[T(x) \le t, T(y) > t|T(\overline{xy}) > t]$$

$$+E[_tL|T(x) > t, T(y) > t] \Pr[T(x) > t, T(y) > t|T(\overline{xy}) > t].$$

In this expression the conditional expectations are given by (17.7.1) and (17.7.2). On the assumption of independent $T(x)$ and $T(y)$, the probabilities are of the form

$$\Pr[T(x) > t, T(y) \le t|T(\overline{xy}) > t] = \frac{_tp_x (1 - {}_tp_y)}{_tp_x (1 - {}_tp_y) + {}_tp_y (1 - {}_tp_x) + {}_tp_x\,{}_tp_y}.$$

Combining these we have

$$_tV(\bar{A}_{\overline{xy}}) = \frac{1}{_tp_x (1 - {}_tp_y) + {}_tp_y (1 - {}_tp_x) + {}_tp_x\,{}_tp_y} \big\{ _tp_x (1 - {}_tp_y) [\bar{A}_{x+t}$$

$$- \bar{P}(\bar{A}_{\overline{xy}})\,\bar{a}_{x+t}] + {}_tp_y (1 - {}_tp_x)[\bar{A}_{y+t} - \bar{P}(\bar{A}_{\overline{xy}})\,\bar{a}_{y+t}]$$

$$+ {}_tp_x\,{}_tp_y [\bar{A}_{\overline{x+t:y+t}} - \bar{P}(\bar{A}_{\overline{xy}})\,\bar{a}_{\overline{x+t:y+t}}]\big\}.$$

## 17.8
## Notes and
## References

The practical applications of the ideas of this chapter have not been as numerous as those in some of the others. Nevertheless, extensive actuarial literature exists on various topics in multiple-life theory. Parts of Chapters 10, 11, 12 and 13 in Jordan (1967), and parts of Chapters 7 and 8 in Neill (1977), contain material on these topics.

Theorem 17.2 is a basic theorem of probability. It combines many of the ideas in Chapter 4 of Feller (1968). The technique used in proving results of this type is often called the *method of inclusion and exclusion*. The main results in the field are summarized, and an extensive reference list provided, by Takács (1967). Credit for the application of these algebraic methods in calculating life annuity values has been given to Waring. Earlier actuarial textbooks gave the results of Corollaries 17.1 and 17.3 by the so-called *Z method*. This was an algebraic mnemonic based on the observation that the coefficients of $_tB_j$ in $_tp\frac{[k]}{\overline{x_1\cdots x_m}}$ and in $_tp\frac{k}{\overline{x_1\cdots x_m}}$ are, respectively, those in the expansions of $Z^k/(1 + Z)^{k+1}$ and $Z^k/(1 + Z)^k$.

An earlier version of Theorem 17.2 is contained in a discussion by Schuette and Nesbitt of a paper by White and Greville (1959). The use of these methods to determine the actuarial present value of a share in a share-and-share-alike last-survivor annuity is the subject of Exercise 17.38 and a paper by Rasor and Myers (1952).

Some of the issues regarding premiums and reserves on last-survivor insurances were discussed by Frasier in *The Actuary* (1978).

# Chapter 17

# ADVANCED MULTIPLE LIFE THEORY

## Appendix

**Theorem 17.2:**

Let $A_1, A_2, \ldots, A_n$ represent the events of interest, and let $P_{[j]}$ denote the probability that exactly $j$ of the $n$ events take place. Further, let $B_j$ be the sum, for all combinations of $j$ events out of the $n$, of the probabilities that $j$ specified events will occur, irrespective of the occurrence of the other $n - j$ events. Then, for any choice of numbers $c_0, c_1, \ldots, c_n$,

$$c_0 P_{[0]} + c_1 P_{[1]} + c_2 P_{[2]} + \cdots + c_n P_{[n]}$$
$$= c_0 + B_1 \Delta c_0 + B_2 \Delta^2 c_0 + \cdots + B_n \Delta^n c_0.$$

**Proof:**
Let $X_i$ denote the indicator for the event $A_i$, that is, $X_i = 1$ for sample points in $A_i$ and $X_i = 0$ for sample points not in $A_i$. Let $Y_j$ be the indicator such that $Y_j = 1$ for sample points in exactly $j$ of the $n$ events $A_1, A_2, \ldots, A_n$ and $Y_j = 0$ for the other sample points. We note that the expectation of $Y_j = P_{[j]}$. Finally, we define an operator, $\phi(E)$, a function of the shift operator, $E = 1 + \Delta$, by

$$\phi(E) = (X_1 E + 1 - X_1)(X_2 E + 1 - X_2) \cdots (X_n E + 1 - X_n).$$

We note that any factor equals $E$ if the corresponding $X_i = 1$ and equals 1 if $X_i = 0$. After multiplying, we have for any single point

$$\phi(E) = Y_0 + Y_1 E + Y_2 E^2 + \cdots + Y_n E^n$$

since, in the expansion of the product, the power of $E$ is equal to the number of the $X_i$ equaling 1. Thus the exponent of $E$ is equal to the number of the events $A_1, A_2, A_3, \ldots A_n$ containing the sample point.

Since a power of the shift operator, $E^j$, applied to $c_0$ yields $c_j$, we obtain

$$\phi(E) c_0 = c_0 Y_0 + c_1 Y_1 + \cdots + c_n Y_n,$$

and then the expectation of $\phi(E) c_0$ is

$$c_0 P_{[0]} + c_1 P_{[1]} + \cdots + c_n P_{[n]}.$$

Since $E = 1 + \Delta$, we can also write $\phi(E)$ as

$$\phi(E) = (1 + X_1 \Delta)(1 + X_2 \Delta) \cdots (1 + X_n \Delta)$$

$$= 1 + \sum_{j=1}^{n} \left( \sum_{i_1, i_2, \ldots, i_j} X_{i_1} X_{i_2} \cdots X_{i_j} \right) \Delta^j,$$

which displays the coefficient of $\Delta^j$ as the sum of all possible products, $\binom{n}{j}$ in number, of the $X_i$ taken $j$ at a time. Since $X_{i_1} X_{i_2} \cdots X_{i_j} = 1$ only if the sample point is in $A_{i_1} A_{i_2} \ldots A_{i_j}$, the expectation of $X_{i_1} X_{i_2} \cdots X_{i_j}$ is $\Pr[A_{i_1} A_{i_2} \cdots A_{i_j}]$ and the expectation of

$$\sum_{i_1, i_2, \ldots, i_j} X_{i_1} X_{i_2} \cdots X_{i_j}$$

is $B_j$. Hence the expectation of $\phi(E)c_0$ can also be written as

$$c_0 + B_1 \Delta c_0 + B_2 \Delta^2 c_0 + \cdots + B_n \Delta^n c_0.$$

Equating the two forms for the expectation of $\phi(E)c_0$ completes the proof of the theorem. ■

The familiar In-and-Out theorem of probability provides an example of applying Theorem 17.2. For $n = 4$,

$$\Pr(A_1 \cup A_2 \cup A_3 \cup A_4) = P_{[1]} + P_{[2]} + P_{[3]} + P_{[4]}.$$

Here $c_0 = 0$, and $c_1 = c_2 = c_3 = c_4 = 1$ in the first form of the expectation of $\phi(E)c_0$. From the table

| $i$ | $c_i$ | $\Delta c_i$ | $\Delta^2 c_i$ | $\Delta^3 c_i$ | $\Delta^4 c_i$ |
|---|---|---|---|---|---|
| 0 | 0 | 1 | $-1$ | 1 | $-1$ |
| 1 | 1 | 0 | 0 | 0 | — |
| 2 | 1 | 0 | 0 | — | — |
| 3 | 1 | 0 | — | — | — |
| 4 | 1 | — | — | — | — |

we see that the second form of the expectation is

$$\Pr(A_1 \cup A_2 \cup A_3 \cup A_4) = B_1 - B_2 + B_3 - B_4$$

$$= \sum_{i=1}^{4} \Pr(A_i) - \sum_{\substack{\text{all combinations} \\ \text{of two of} \\ 1,2,3,4}} \Pr(A_i A_j)$$

$$+ \sum_{\substack{\text{all combinations} \\ \text{of three of} \\ 1,2,3,4}} \Pr(A_i A_j A_k) - \Pr(A_1 A_2 A_3 A_4).$$

## Exercises

Unless otherwise indicated, all lives are subject to the same table of mortality rates and their time-until-death random variables are independent.

*Section 17.2*

17.1. Describe the events having probabilities given by the following expressions

a. $_t p_{wx} + {}_t p_{wy} + {}_t p_{wz} + {}_t p_{xy} + {}_t p_{xz} + {}_t p_{yz}$
$- 3\left( {}_t p_{wxy} + {}_t p_{wxz} + {}_t p_{wyz} + {}_t p_{xyz} \right) + 7 {}_t p_{wxyz}$

b. $_t p_w + {}_t p_x + {}_t p_y + {}_t p_z - 2\left( {}_t p_{wx} + {}_t p_{wy} + {}_t p_{wz} + {}_t p_{xy} + {}_t p_{xz} \right.$
$\left. + {}_t p_{yz} \right) + 4\left( {}_t p_{wxy} + {}_t p_{wxz} + {}_t p_{wyz} + {}_t p_{xyz} \right) - 8 {}_t p_{wxyz}.$

17.2. Use the corollaries of Section 17.2 to verify that $_t p_{\overline{x_1 x_2 \cdots x_m}}^{[0]}$

$= 1 - {}_t p_{\overline{x_1 x_{2_1} \cdots x_m}}^{\phantom{1}}.$

17.3. An extract from a table of joint-life annuities valued at $3\tfrac{1}{2}\%$ interest reads as follows.

# Chapter 17
## ADVANCED MULTIPLE LIFE THEORY

| Joint-Life Status | Actuarial Present Value of Joint-Life Annuity-Immediate |
|---|---|
| 20:26:28 | 14.4 |
| 20:26:29 | 14.3 |
| 20:28:29 | 14.0 |
| 26:28:29 | 13.8 |
| 20:26:28:29 | 12.5 |

    a. Calculate the actuarial present value of an annuity payable at the end of each year while exactly three of (20), (26), (28) and (29) are alive.

    b. Calculate the net single premium for an insurance of 10,000 payable at the end of the year of death of the second life to fail out of (20), (26), (28) and (29).

17.4. Express $_tp_{\overline{wxyz}}^{\;2} - {_tp_{\overline{wxyz}}^{\;[2]}}$ in terms of $_tB_j$, $j = 1,2,3,4$.

17.5. Express, in terms of annuity symbols, the actuarial present value of an annuity of 1 per year payable at the end of each year while $(w)$ and at most one of $(x)$, $(y)$ and $(z)$ are alive.

17.6. If $\mu_{40+t} = 0.002$, $0 \le t \le 10$, and $\delta = 0.05$, calculate the value of $\bar{A}_{40:40:40:40:40:\overline{10}|}$.

17.7. A trust is set up to provide income to $(x)$, $(y)$, and $(z)$. The fund is to provide a continuous income at the rate of 8 per year to each while all three are alive, at a rate of 10 per year to each while two are alive, and at a rate of 15 per year to a sole survivor. Calculate the actuarial present values of
    a. all the payments to be made
    b. all the payments to be made to $(x)$.

17.8. An insurance policy provides a death benefit of 4 payable immediately upon the first death among four lives aged $x$, a benefit of 3 payable upon the second death, a benefit of 2 payable upon the third death, and a benefit of 1 payable upon the last death. If $\bar{A}_x = 0.4$ and $\bar{A}_{xx} = 0.5$, evaluate the net single premium for this policy.

*Section 17.3*

17.9. Develop an expression in terms of single- and joint-life annuity symbols for the actuarial present value of an annuity-immediate of 1000 per month payable
    a. while exactly one of (40) and (35) is surviving during the next 25 years
    b. while at least one of (40) and (35) survives at an age less than age 65.

17.10. Express the following in terms of symbols for annuities-certain and single- and joint-life annuities.
    a. $\bar{a}_{\overline{x:y:\overline{n}|}}$
    b. $\bar{a}_{\overline{(\overline{25:40|}):\overline{30}|}}$

*Section 17.4*

17.11. If at each duration the force of mortality for $(x)$ is $1/2$ that for $(y)$ while the force of mortality for $(z)$ is twice that for $(y)$, what is the probability that of the three lives $(x)$ will die
a. first
b. second
c. third.

17.12. Which of the following statements are true? Correct the others as necessary.

I. $\bar{A}^{\quad 1}_{\overline{wxyz}} = \bar{A}^1_{wxyz} + \bar{A}_{w\,xyz}^{\quad1} + \bar{A}_{wx\,yz}^{\quad1} + \bar{A}_{wxy\,z}^{\quad1}$

II. $\bar{A}^{\quad 3}_{\overline{wxyz}} = \bar{A}^2_{wxyz} + \bar{A}_{w\,xyz}^{\quad2} + \bar{A}_{wx\,yz}^{\quad2} + \bar{A}_{wxy\,z}^{\quad2}$

III. $\bar{A}_{wxyz}^{\quad3} = \bar{A}_{wz}^{\;1} + \bar{A}_{xz}^{\;1} + \bar{A}_{yz}^{\;1} - (\bar{A}_{wxz}^{\;\;1} + \bar{A}_{wyz}^{\;\;1} + \bar{A}_{xyz}^{\;\;1}) + \bar{A}_{wxyz}^{\quad1}$

17.13. Write, as a definite integral, the net single premium for an insurance to be paid at the moment of death of $(x)$ if $(x)$ survives $(y)$. The benefit amount is equal to the time elapsed between the issue of the policy and the date of death of $(y)$.

17.14. If Gompertz's law applies with $\mu_{40} = 0.003$ and $\mu_{56} = 0.012$, calculate
a. $_{\infty}q^{\,2:3}_{40:48:56}$          b. $_{\infty}q^{\,2}_{40:48:56}$.
[Note: In part (a) the notation 2:3 indicates the event that (48) dies second or third among the lines involved.]

17.15. An insurance of 1 issued on the lives $(x)$, $(y)$ and $(z)$ is payable at the moment of death of $(z)$ only if $(x)$ has been dead at least 10 years and $(y)$ has been dead less than 10 years. Express the net single premium for this insurance in terms of net single premiums for insurances and pure endowments.

17.16. Develop an expression that does not involve integrals for the net single premium for an insurance of 1 payable 10 years after the death of $(x)$, provided that either or both of $(y)$ and $(z)$ survive $(x)$ and both are dead before the end of the 10-year period.

17.17. Obtain a formula for the gross single premium for a special contingent, unit insurance payable if (30) dies before (60), or within 5 years after the death of the latter, with return of the single premium, without interest, 5 years after the death of (60) if no claim under the insurance arises by the death of (30). Assume the loading is $7^1/_2\%$ of the net premium.

*Section 17.5*

17.18. Without using the independence assumption, establish relations such as

$$_{n}q_{wxy}^{\;\;1} = \,_{n}q_{wxyz}^{\;\;1} + \,_{n}q_{wxyz}^{\;\;2},$$

and use them to obtain the result of Example 17.7.

17.19. Without using the independence assumption, establish the relations

# Chapter 17

## ADVANCED MULTIPLE LIFE THEORY

$$\bar{A}^{1}_{xy} = \bar{A}^{1}_{xyz} + \bar{A}^{2}_{\substack{xyz\\1}}$$

$$\bar{A}^{1}_{yz} = \bar{A}^{1}_{xyz} + \bar{A}^{2}_{\substack{xyz\\1}},$$

and use them to obtain the result of Example 17.8.

17.20. Express $_{\infty}q^{2}_{\substack{wxyz\\1}}$

    a. as a definite integral
    b. in terms of simple contingent probabilities.

17.21. Assuming Gompertz's law applies, show that

    a. $_{t}q^{2}_{xy} = {}_{t}q_{y} - \dfrac{c^{y}}{c^{x} + c^{y}} \, {}_{t}q_{xy}$

    b. $\bar{A}^{3}_{\substack{xyz\\1}} = \dfrac{c^{x}}{c^{x} + c^{y}} \bar{A}_{z} - \dfrac{c^{z}}{c^{y} + c^{z}} \bar{A}_{yz} + \dfrac{c^{y}}{c^{x} + c^{y}} \dfrac{c^{z}}{c^{x} + c^{y} + c^{z}} \bar{A}_{xyz}.$

17.22. If $\mu_{x} = 1/(100 - x)$ for $0 < x < 100$ applies for (20), (40) and (60), evaluate

    a. $_{\infty}q^{2}_{\substack{20:40:60\\1}}$      b. $_{\infty}q^{1}_{20:40:60}$      c. $_{\infty}q^{1}_{20:40}.$

    This illustrates that $_{\infty}q^{2}_{\substack{xyz\\1}} = {}_{\infty}q^{1}_{xyz} \, {}_{\infty}q^{1}_{yz}$, which holds on the basis of Gompertz's law, does not hold in general.

17.23. On the basis of a mortality table following Gompertz's law (with $c^{8} = 2$), $\bar{A}_{54} = 0.3$, $\bar{A}_{62} = 0.4$ and $\bar{A}_{70} = 0.52$. Determine $\bar{A}^{2}_{\substack{54:54:62\\1}}.$

17.24. Given   $\bar{A}_{w} = 0.6$,   $\bar{A}^{1}_{wx} = 0.3$, $\bar{A}^{1}_{wxx} = 0.2$   and   $\bar{A}^{1}_{wxxx} = 0.1$, evaluate

    a. $\bar{A}^{2}_{wxxx}$      b. $\bar{A}^{4}_{wxxx}$      c. $\bar{A}^{4}_{\substack{wxxx\\1 2 3}}.$

17.25. Express in integral form the probability that $(x)$, $(y)$, and $(z)$ will die in that order within the next 25 years with at least 10 years separating the times of any pair of deaths.

17.26. Express in integral form the probability that (10), (20), and (30) will all die before attaining age 60 with (20) being the second to die.

17.27. Given $_{\infty}q^{1}_{xy} = 0.5537$, $_{\infty}q^{1}_{xz} = 0.6484$, $_{\infty}q^{1}_{xyz} = 0.5325$ and $_{\infty}q^{2}_{xyz} = {}_{\infty}q^{3}_{xyz}$, calculate $q^{2}_{\substack{xyz\\1}}.$

17.28. According to a certain mortality table, the probability that three lives aged 70, 55 and 40 will die in that order at intervals of not less than 15 years is 0.048, and the probability that at least one of two lives now aged 70 will be alive 15 years before the death of a life now aged 55 is 0.8. Calculate the probability that neither of two lives now aged 40 will survive to age 70.

17.29. Which of the following statements are true? Correct the others as necessary.

# ADVANCED MULTIPLE LIFE THEORY

I. $\bar{A}_{\underset{12}{wxyz}}^{\;\;3} = \int_0^\infty v^t \, {}_tq_w \, {}_tp_{xyz} \, \mu_{x+t} \, \bar{A}_{y+t} \, dt$

II. $\int_0^{10} (1 - {}_{t+10}p_{50}) \, {}_tp_{60} \, \mu_{60+t} \, dt$

$+ \int_{10}^\infty ({}_{t-10}p_{50} - {}_{t+10}p_{50}) \, {}_tp_{60} \, \mu_{60+t} \, dt$

$= \int_0^{10} (1 - {}_{t+10}p_{60}) \, {}_tp_{50} \, \mu_{50+t} \, dt$

$+ \int_{10}^\infty ({}_{t-10}p_{60} - {}_{t+10}p_{60}) \, {}_tp_{60} \, \mu_{50+t} \, dt$

III. ${}_{30}q_{40:50:60}^1 + {}_{30}q_{40:50:60}^2 = {}_{30}q_{40:\overline{50:60}}^1$

*Section 17.6*

17.30. Show that
  a. $\bar{A}_{xy}^2 = \bar{A}_{xy}^1 - \delta \bar{a}_{y|x}$

  b. $\dfrac{\partial}{\partial x} \bar{a}_{y|x} = \mu_x \, \bar{a}_{y|x} - \bar{A}_{xy}^2.$

17.31. Express $\ddot{a}_{x|y:\overline{10|}}^{(12)}$ in terms of $\ddot{a}_{x|y:\overline{10|}}$.

17.32. Write an expression, free of integrals, for the actuarial present value of a continuous annuity payable at a rate of 1 per year
  a. during the lifetime of $(y)$ and for 10 years following the death of $(y)$ with no payments to be made while $(x)$ is alive
  b. during the lifetime of $(y)$ and for 10 years following the death of $(y)$ with no payments to be made while $(x)$ is alive or if $(y)$ dies before $(x)$.

17.33. Express in terms of annuity and insurance symbols, the gross single premium to provide the following benefits with a loading of 8% of the gross premium:
  A last-survivor annuity of 1 per annum on $(x)$ and $(y)$ deferred $n$ years and reducing by 1/3 on the first death: If the death of $(x)$ occurs before the death of $(y)$ and during the deferred period, the annuity on the reduced basis is commenced on the next anniversary. If the death of $(x)$ occurs after the death of $(y)$ and during the deferred period, the single premium is to be refunded at the end of the year of death.

17.34. In Section 17.6, the reversionary annuities commenced payment if a status $(u)$ was surviving upon the failure of a status $(v)$. This idea can be extended to annuities with payment commencing upon the occurrence of two or more deaths in a prescribed order.

a. Show that

$$a^2_{\overline{xy}|z} = a_{y|z} - a^1_{\overline{xy}|z}.$$

b. On the basis of a Gompertz mortality table, prove that

$$a^2_{\overline{xy}|z} = \frac{c^x}{c^x + c^y} a_z - a_{yz} + \frac{c^y}{c^x + c^y} a_{xyz}.$$

*Section 17.7*

17.35. Develop an expression for the net annual premium for a contingent pure endowment of 1 payable if $(x)$ is alive $n$ years after the death of $(y)$.

17.36. What annuity actuarial present value should be used to obtain the net annual premium corresponding to the net single premium $A^2_{\underset{1}{wxyz}}$?

*Miscellaneous*

17.37. An insurance on the event that $(x)$ dies before age $x + n$ and $(y)$ dies before age $y + m$, with $m < n$, pays 1 at the end of the year in which the second death occurs.
a. Show that the net single premium can be expressed as

$$A^1_{\overline{xy}:\overline{m}|} + v^m\, {}_mp_x\, (1 - {}_mp_y)\, A^1_{\overline{x+m}:\overline{n-m}|}.$$

b. What is the appropriate annuity actuarial present value to be used to obtain the net annual premium?

17.38. A collection of $m$ lives are to share-and-share-alike in the income from a last-survivor annuity of 1 per annum payable continuously. The actuarial present value of $(x_1)$'s share is

$$\sum_{j=0}^{m-1} \frac{1}{j+1} \bar{a}_{x_1:\overline{x_2x_3\cdots x_m}}^{[j]}.$$

Show that this actuarial present value can be expressed as

$$\bar{a}_{x_1} - \frac{1}{2}(\bar{a}_{x_1x_2} + \cdots + \bar{a}_{x_1x_m})$$

$$+ \frac{1}{3}(\bar{a}_{x_1x_2x_3} + \cdots + \bar{a}_{x_1x_{m-1}x_m}) - \cdots (-1)^{m-1}\frac{1}{m}\bar{a}_{x_1x_2\cdots x_m}.$$

$$\left[ \text{Hint: Use Theorem 17.1 on} \right.$$

$$\left. \sum_{j=0}^{m-1} \frac{1}{j+1}\, {}_tp_{\overline{x_2\cdots x_m}}^{[j]} \cdot \right]$$

17.39. State in words what is represented by

$$\int_0^\infty v^t\, {}_tq_x\, {}_tp_{yz}\, \mu_{y+t}\, \bar{A}^1_{z+t:\overline{10}|}\, dt.$$

17.40. In the notation of Theorem 17.2, let

$$A_1 = \{T(y) < \min[n, T(x), T(z)]\}$$

$$A_2 = \{T(y) < \min[n, T(x), T(w)]\}$$

$$A_3 = \{T(y) < \min[n, T(w), T(z)]\}.$$

Show that the event $A$ of Example 17.7 is the same as the event that occurs when exactly one of $A_1$, $A_2$ and $A_3$ occurs. Hence use Theorem 17.2 to establish the result of Example 17.7 without use of the independence assumption. [Hint: Argue that $\Pr(A_1) = {}_nq^1_{x\overline{yz}}$, $\Pr(A_1 A_2) = \Pr(A_1 A_3) = \Pr(A_2 A_3) = \Pr(A_1 A_2 A_3) = {}_nq^1_{wx\overline{yz}}$, and $\Pr[A_1 \,(\text{not } A_2)\,(\text{not } A_3)] = {}_nq^2_{wx\overline{yz}}.]$

# Chapter 18
## POPULATION THEORY

**18**

## 18.1
## Introduction

Many of the ideas in Chapter 3 are building blocks in the construction of a mathematical theory of populations. For example, the survival function used to define the distribution of the random variable time-until-death, and to trace the progress of a survivorship group, also plays a role in constructing models for populations.

The models developed in this chapter are general. They may be applied, with appropriate modifications, to the population of a political unit, a population of workers or a wildlife population.

We are particularly interested in certain actuarial applications of population theory. In Section 18.5 a population model will be used to study the progress of a system providing life insurance benefits to a population. In Chapter 19 a population model will be used as a component of a model for studying the progress of a system providing retirement income benefits to a population.

## 18.2
## The Lexis
## Diagram

In this section we will introduce a convenient method of picturing the progress of a population. For example, the history of a work-force's participation can be represented by parallel line segments in a two-dimensional diagram called a *Lexis diagram.* (See Figure 18.1.) The pictured point of entry of an individual into the work-force population (with coordinates time of entry and age at entry) represents one end point of the line segment associated with that individual. The line segment then follows a diagonal path to the terminal end point representing exit from the work-force population (with coordinates time of exit and age at exit).

Figure 18.1 illustrates, for the population of workers depicted, that at time $-25$ measured from the present ($t = 0$) there are 3 active

**Figure 18.1**
**A Lexis Diagram**

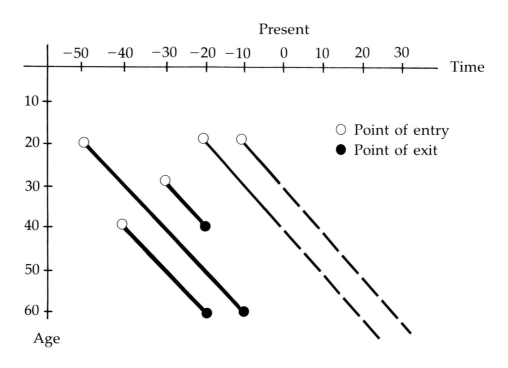

workers. At the present time there are 2 active workers. One might be interested in making statements about their future working lifetimes. The dashed line segments in Figure 18.1 denote the prospective working lifetimes of the 2 currently active workers.

The following comments summarize features of a Lexis diagram.

**Observation:**

1. A fixed point in time is represented by a vertical line. The number of members of a population at that time is given by the number of parallel lines segments (each representing an individual) intersecting the vertical line.

2. A fixed age is represented by a horizontal line. If a line segment associated with an individual intersects a horizontal line at age $x_0$, then that individual attained age $x_0$ while a member of the population.

3. If a member attains age $x$ at time $t$, the member's time of birth is $u = t - x$. While $x$ and $t$ are used as coordinates in a Lexis diagram, we will frequently use the variables $x$ and $u$ in our developments. One of the reasons for this is that while $u$ is constant for each member of a population, it is not constant over the population.

There are many extensions of these ideas. For example, Lexis diagrams are used to picture the progress of cohorts of lives rather than of individuals. A cohort is a collection of individuals with a common birth period. In a model for a population of workers, several modes of exit may be recognized and entries can occur at different ages. These possibilities were discussed in Chapters 9 and 10.

The demographic models developed in the next two sections will utilize only one mode of exit, interpreted as death. Likewise, only birth will be considered as a mode of entry. A deterministic approach will be taken.

## 18.3 A Continuous Model

For the remainder of this chapter we will use a continuous model for populations rather than a discrete set of parallel line segments (each corresponding to a member) as was used for the illustration in Figure 18.1. This shift will permit us to use calculus as well as many of the tools developed in earlier chapters. A parallel development based on a discrete model, and using tools from linear algebra, could have been used.

Again, we will assume all entries are by birth and all exits are by death. Migration is excluded from the model. Births occur continuously and $b(u)$ denotes the ***density function of births*** at time $u$. That is, $b(u)\,du$ is the number of births between times $u$ and $u + du$. We denote by $s(x,u)$ the survival function of those born at time $u$. This is called a ***generation survival function.*** We define

$$l(x,u) = b(u)\,s(x,u). \tag{18.3.1}$$

# Chapter 18

## POPULATION THEORY

The function denoted by $l(x,u)$ is called a ***population density function.***

The interpretation of the function $l(x,u)$ is facilitated by reference to a continuous version of a Lexis diagram. (See Figure 18.2.) This figure and the remaining Figures 18.3, 18.4, 18.5 and 18.6 of this section are two dimensional. They are designed to aid in the interpretation of differential terms or to illustrate regions of integration. In each case, a three-dimensional figure, illustrating the function defined on the time-age plane, could have been drawn.

**Figure 18.2**
**Interpretation**
**of $l(x,u)$**

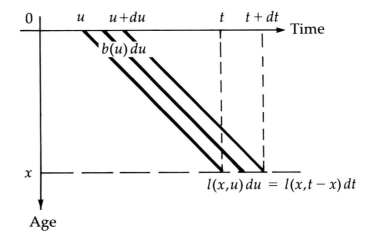

Of the $l(0,u)\,du = b(u)\,du$ births between times $u$ and $u+du$, $l(x,u)\,du$ survive to age $x$. Let $t = x + u$, then $dt = du$ and this expression can be restated as

$$l(x,t-x)\,dt = \text{(number attaining age } x \text{ between}$$
$$\text{times } t \text{ and } t + dt). \qquad (18.3.2)$$

From this it follows that the number attaining age $x$ between times $t_0$ and $t_1$ is

$$\int_{t_0}^{t_1} l(x,t-x)\,dt. \qquad (18.3.3)$$

Now we consider a different question. Let $x_0 < x_1$ be two ages and $t_0$ a given time. The question is: How many lives are there between ages $x_0$ and $x_1$ at time $t_0$? In posing this question the word lives has been attached to the values of an integral of the function $l(x,u)$ and, as in Chapter 3, no longer denotes a variable that must take on only integer values.

These lives would have attained age $x_0$ between times $t_0 - (x_1 - x_0)$ and $t_0$ and then survived to time $t_0$, as indicated in Figure 18.3. The diagonal dashed line traces a typical cohort of lives that will be between ages $x_0$ and $x_1$ at time $t_0$.

**Figure 18.3**
**Number of Lives**
**Between Ages $x_0$ and**
**$x_1$ at Time $t_0$**

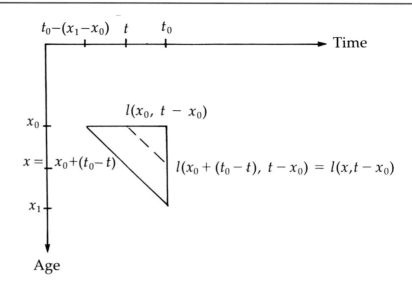

Thus the number we seek is

$$\int_{t_0-(x_1-x_0)}^{t_0} l(x_0,t-x_0)\frac{s(x_0+t_0-t,t-x_0)}{s(x_0,t-x_0)}\,dt. \qquad (18.3.4)$$

In evaluating (18.3.4) we make use of (18.3.1) to write the integrand as $b(t-x_0)s(x_0+t_0-t,t-x_0) = l(x_0+t_0-t,t-x_0)$. If we let $x = x_0 + (t_0-t)$, we can transform (18.3.4) into

$$-\int_{x_1}^{x_0} l(x,t_0-x)\,dx = \int_{x_0}^{x_1} l(x,t_0-x)\,dx. \qquad (18.3.5)$$

From (18.3.5) we can make the following statement,

$$l(x,t_0-x)\,dx = \text{(number of lives between ages}$$
$$x \text{ and } x+dx \text{ at time } t_0). \qquad (18.3.6)$$

Therefore, the population density function has two interpretations. The first is given by (18.3.2) and (18.3.3) and relates to the number of lives attaining age $x$ between times $t$ and $t+dt$. The second is given by (18.3.5) and (18.3.6) and relates to the number of lives between ages $x$ and $x+dx$ at time $t$. The two interpretations correspond to slicing a Lexis diagram for the population with the lines $t$ and $t+dt$ in the first interpretation, and slicing the diagram with lines $x$ and $x+dx$ in the second interpretation.

In order to incorporate deaths into our model we let

$$\mu(x,u) = -\frac{1}{s(x,u)}\frac{\partial}{\partial x}s(x,u) = -\frac{1}{l(x,u)}\frac{\partial}{\partial x}l(x,u) \qquad (18.3.7)$$

denote the **generation force of mortality** at age $x$ for those born at time $u$. Figure 18.4 provides three interpretations following from this definition. These can be verified by making the indicated linear transformation to the bivariate population density function times the

# Chapter 18
## POPULATION THEORY

generation force of mortality and confirming that the Jacobian of the transformation is 1.

The total number of deaths in a given region of the time-age plane, as depicted in a Lexis diagram, is obtained by integrating one of the expressions in Figure 18.4 over the given region. The solution requires the calculation of a double integral.

There is an alternative method called the **in-and-out method,** which often provides an easy way of obtaining the required number of deaths. This alternative method involves determining the numbers of lives entering and leaving the region. The difference between these two numbers is the number of deaths. In most situations, the in-and-out method requires evaluation of only two single integrals.

**Figure 18.4
Interpretations of
Population Density
times Generation
Force of Mortality**

A.  $l(t - u,u)\,\mu(t - u,u)\,du\,dt$ = number of deaths between time $t$ and $t + dt$ among those born between $u$ and $u + du$.

B.  Substitute $u = t - x$, and we have $l(x,t - x)\,\mu(x,t - x)\,dt\,dx$ = number of deaths between ages $x$ and $x + dx$ at times between $t$ and $t + dt$.

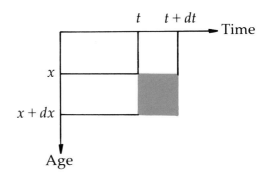

C.  Substitute $x = t - u$, and we have $l(x,u)\,\mu(x,u)\,du\,dx$ = number of deaths between ages $x$ and $x + dx$ of those born between $u$ and $u + du$.

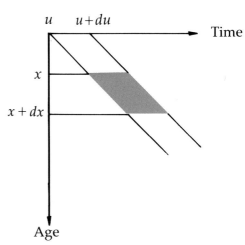

**Figure 18.5
Region Where Deaths
are Counted,
Example 18.1**

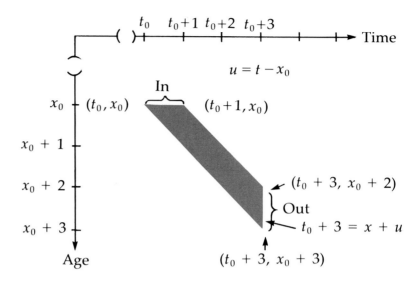

**Example 18.1:**

How many lives will attain age $x_0$ between times $t_0$ and $t_0+1$ and die before time $t_0+3$?

**Solution:**

We must derive an expression for the number of deaths in the trapezoid illustrated in Figure 18.5.

Double integral method: Using the interpretation of Figure 18.4C, we have for the required number of deaths

$$\int_{t_0-x_0}^{t_0+1-x_0} \int_{x_0}^{t_0+3-u} l(x,u)\,\mu(x,u)\,dx\,du.$$

Using (18.3.7), we have for the number of deaths

$$\int_{t_0-x_0}^{t_0+1-x_0} \int_{x_0}^{t_0+3-u} \left[-\frac{\partial l(x,u)}{\partial x}\right] dx\,du$$

$$= \int_{t_0-x_0}^{t_0+1-x_0} [l(x_0,u) - l(t_0+3-u,u)]\,du$$

$$= \int_{t_0-x_0}^{t_0+1-x_0} l(x_0,u)\,du - \int_{t_0-x_0}^{t_0+1-x_0} l(t_0+3-u,u)\,du.$$

We let $y = u + x_0$ in the first integral and $w = t_0 + 3 - u$ in the second to obtain for the number of deaths

$$\int_{t_0}^{t_0+1} l(x_0, y-x_0)\,dy - \int_{x_0+2}^{x_0+3} l(w, t_0+3-w)\,dw.$$

In-and-out method: To obtain the required number of deaths we take the difference between the number of ins who attain age $x_0$ between times $t_0$ and $t_0+1$ and the number of outs who die between ages $x_0+2$ and $x_0+3$ at time $t_0+3$.

## POPULATION THEORY

Using (18.3.3) and (18.3.5), we have

$$\int_{t_0}^{t_0+1} l(x_0, y - x_0)\, dy - \int_{x_0+2}^{x_0+3} l(w, t_0 + 3 - w)\, dw,$$

which agrees with the result obtained using double integration.

▼

**Example 18.2:**  Determine the number of those between ages 20 and 40 at time $t_0$ who will die before reaching age 70.

**Solution:**
We are asked to derive an expression for the number of deaths in the trapezoid illustrated in Figure 18.6.

Double integral method: Using the interpretation in Figure 18.4C, the required number of deaths is given by

$$\int_{t_0-40}^{t_0-20} \int_{t_0-u}^{70} l(x,u)\, \mu(x,u)\, dx\, du$$

$$= \int_{t_0-40}^{t_0-20} \int_{t_0-u}^{70} \left[ -\frac{\partial l(x,u)}{\partial x} \right] dx\, du$$

**Figure 18.6**
**Region Where Deaths are Counted in Example 18.2**

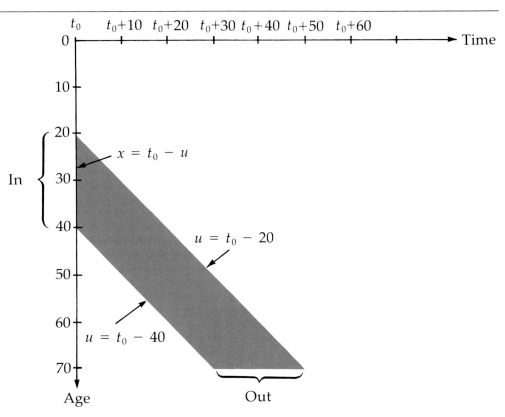

$$= \int_{t_0-40}^{t_0-20} [l(t_0 - u,u) - l(70,u)] \, du$$

$$= \int_{t_0-40}^{t_0-20} l(t_0 - u,u) \, du - \int_{t_0-40}^{t_0-20} l(70,u) \, du.$$

We let $y = t_0 - u$ in the first integral and $w = u + 70$ in the second integral to obtain the required number of deaths

$$\int_{20}^{40} l(y,t_0 - y) \, dy - \int_{t_0+30}^{t_0+50} l(70,w - 70) \, dw.$$

In-and-out method: We use (18.3.5) for the ins and (18.3.3) for the outs to obtain

$$\int_{20}^{40} l(x,t_0 - x) \, dx - \int_{t_0+30}^{t_0+50} l(70,t - 70) \, dt,$$

which agrees with the result using double integrals.     ▼

## 18.4
## Stationary and
## Stable
## Populations

Here we study two important special cases of the model described in Section 18.3. If $l(x,u)$ is independent of $u$, we call the result a *stationary population.* For a stationary population (18.3.1) becomes

$$l(x,u) = b \, s(x) \tag{18.4.1}$$

where $b$ is the constant density of births and $s(x)$ is a survival function that does not depend on the time of birth. For human populations $b$ is typically expressed as a number of births per year and the age variable is measured in years. In accord with (3.3.1), we rewrite (18.4.1) as

$$l(x,u) = b \, s(x) = l_x \tag{18.4.2}$$

where $b$ plays the role of the radix $l_0$.

For a stationary population we can write (18.3.5) as

$$\int_{x_0}^{x_1} l_x \, dx = T_{x_0} - T_{x_1}$$

and obtain the number of lives in the stationary population between ages $x_0$ and $x_1$ at any time $t$, expressed in terms of the function $T_x$ introduced in (3.5.10) in connection with the analysis of a survivorship group. In addition, the interpretation of $l_x \mu_x$ given by Figure 18.4B leads to

$$\int_{x_0}^{x_1} l_x \mu_x \, dx = l_{x_0} - l_{x_1}$$

as the density of deaths between ages $x_0$ and $x_1$ at any time $t$. In particular, the density of deaths at age $x_0$ and greater equals the density of the number of lives attaining age $x_0$ at any time $t$, the

# Chapter 18
## POPULATION THEORY

interpretation provided by (18.3.2). These facts illustrate the aptness of the name stationary population.

If the population density function is of the form

$$l(x,u) = e^{Ru} b s(x) = e^{Ru} l_x \qquad (18.4.3)$$

where $b > 0$ and $R$ are constant and $s(x)$ is a survival function that is independent of the time of birth, the resulting population is called a **stable population.** The density of births at time $u$ in a stable population is $e^{Ru} b = e^{Ru} l_0$. If $R = 0$, a stable population is a stationary population.

Using (18.3.5) we see that the total population at time $t$, denoted by $N(t)$, for a stable population is given by

$$N(t) = \int_0^\infty l(x,t-x)\,dx = e^{Rt} \int_0^\infty e^{-Rx} l_x\,dx. \qquad (18.4.4)$$

Therefore, if $R > 0$, the population is growing exponentially, and if $R < 0$, the population is decreasing exponentially.

Using (18.3.5) we see that the fraction of the total stable population that lies between ages $x_0$ and $x_1$ at time $t$ is

$$\frac{\displaystyle\int_{x_0}^{x_1} l(x,t-x)\,dx}{\displaystyle\int_0^\infty l(x,t-x)\,dx} = \frac{\displaystyle\int_{x_0}^{x_1} e^{-Rx} l_x\,dx}{\displaystyle\int_0^\infty e^{-Rx} l_x\,dx}, \qquad (18.4.5)$$

which is independent of $t$. Thus, while the size of a stable population may change over time, its relative age distribution is constant.

For a stable population, we can express the number of members between ages $x_0$ and $x_1$, using (18.3.5), as

$$\int_{x_0}^{x_1} l(x,t-x)\,dx = \int_{x_0}^{x_1} e^{R(t-x)} l_x\,dx$$

$$= e^{Rt}(\bar{N}'_{x_0} - \bar{N}'_{x_1}). \qquad (18.4.6)$$

The commutation function $\bar{N}_x$ was introduced in Chapter 5. In this chapter, a prime will be added to commutation functions and net single premiums to denote that they are valued using a force of interest equal to the rate, $R$, of stable population change. In accordance with this convention, the number of members alive above age $x_0$ at time $t$ in a stable population may be written as $e^{Rt} \bar{N}'_{x_0}$.

For a stable population, the force of mortality as given by (18.3.7) becomes, by reference to (18.4.3),

$$\mu(x,u) = -\frac{1}{l(x,u)} \frac{\partial}{\partial x} l(x,u) = \mu_x.$$

We can express the density of deaths at time $t$ for a stable population between ages $x_0$ and $x_1$ as

$$\int_{x_0}^{x_1} e^{R(t-x)} l_x \mu_x \, dx = e^{Rt} (\bar{M}'_{x_0} - \bar{M}'_{x_1}),$$  (18.4.7)

and the density of deaths at time $t$ above age $x_0$ is $e^{Rt} \bar{M}'_{x_0}$. The commutation function $\bar{M}_x$ was introduced in Chapter 4 and here the prime indicates evaluation at force of interest $R$.

These facts about stable populations can be used, in connection with an identity from Chapter 5, to confirm a property of stable populations:

[rate of population
change at time $t$
above age $x_0$]

$$= \frac{\begin{matrix} [\text{density of those} & [\text{density of deaths} \\ \text{reaching age } x_0 & - \text{ above age } x_0 \\ \text{at time } t] & \text{at time } t] \end{matrix}}{\begin{matrix} [\text{number above} \\ \text{age } x_0 \text{ at time } t] \end{matrix}}$$

$$= \frac{e^{Rt} [D'_{x_0} - \bar{M}'_{x_0}]}{e^{Rt} \bar{N}'_{x_0}} = R.$$

The final step follows because

$$\bar{A}'_{x_0} + R \bar{a}'_{x_0} = 1,$$

which yields

$$\bar{M}'_{x_0} + R \bar{N}'_{x_0} = D'_{x_0},$$

and the result follows.

**Example 18.3:**  For a stationary population the complete life expectancy at age 0, derived from the survival function, can be obtained by dividing the number in the population at time $t$ by the birth density. That is,

$$\overset{\circ}{e}_0 = \int_0^\infty s(x) \, dx = \int_0^\infty \frac{l_x}{l_0} \, dx = T_0 / l_0.$$

What is the result of performing a similar calculation with a stable population?

**Solution:**

$$\frac{N(t)}{e^{Rt} l_0} = \frac{\displaystyle\int_0^\infty l(x, t-x) \, dx}{e^{Rt} l_0} = \frac{\displaystyle\int_0^\infty e^{R(t-x)} l_x \, dx}{e^{Rt} l_0} = \bar{a}'_0.$$

If $R > 0$, $\bar{a}'_0 < \overset{\circ}{e}_0$, and if $R < 0$, $\bar{a}'_0 > \overset{\circ}{e}_0$, and if $R = 0$, the stationary

# POPULATION THEORY

population result is obtained. This example demonstrates how the life expectancies cannot be observed directly from stable populations unless $R = 0$. ▼

## 18.5
## Actuarial
## Applications

The conditions for a stable or stationary population are seldom realized because of changes in either the survival function or the density of births. However, these models are useful in studying alternative plans for funding life insurance or retirement income systems. By a funding plan we mean a budgeting plan for accumulating the funds necessary to provide the insurance or annuity benefits.

In this section and in Chapter 19 we will depart from the models developed in Chapters 4 through 10, 14 and 15. These models were built by starting with a consideration of the operation of a single policy. In this section we will study aggregate models for life insurance. In Chapter 19 similar models for pension systems will be examined. The models considered will be especially relevant to social and group insurance systems providing benefits on death or retirement to broad groups or populations.

**Example 18.4:**

Assume a population density function $l(x,u) = b(u)s(x)$ where the survival function is independent of $u$. Further, assume that in this population each member above age $a$ is insured for a unit benefit under a fully continuous, whole life insurance with annual premiums payable from age $a$. The premium paid by each member is based on force of interest $\delta$ and survival function $s(x)$. Prove that

$$\bar{P}(\bar{A}_a) \int_a^\infty l(x,t-x)\,dx + \delta \int_a^\infty l(x,t-x)\,_{x-a}\bar{V}(\bar{A}_a)\,dx$$

$$= \int_a^\infty l(x,t-x)\,\mu_x\,dx + \frac{d}{dt}\int_a^\infty l(x,t-x)\,_{x-a}\bar{V}(\bar{A}_a)\,dx. \tag{18.5.1}$$

**Solution:**
General reasoning solution: Stated in words (18.5.1) asserts:

[rate of premium income at time $t$]

+ [rate of investment income at time $t$]

= [rate of benefit outgo at time $t$]

+ [rate of change in aggregate reserve at time $t$].

That is, (18.5.1) can be interpreted as an income allocation equation for a life insurance system covering a population aged $a$ or greater. The left-hand side of (18.5.1) displays the sources of income, premiums and interest, and the right-hand side displays the allocation of income to death benefits and changes in aggregate reserve fund.

Analytic solution: We start with (7.11.5), implying for the present case,

$$\frac{d}{dx}\,_{x-a}\bar{V}(\bar{A}_a) - \mu_x\,_{x-a}\bar{V}(\bar{A}_a) + \mu_x = \bar{P}(\bar{A}_a) + \delta\,_{x-a}\bar{V}(\bar{A}_a). \quad (18.5.2)$$

We multiply (18.5.2) by $l(x,t-x)$ and integrate between $a$ and the upper limit of survival. These operations yield

$$\int_a^\infty l(x,t-x)\,d[_{x-a}\bar{V}(\bar{A}_a)] - \int_a^\infty l(x,t-x)\,\mu_x\,_{x-a}\bar{V}(\bar{A}_a)\,dx$$

$$+ \int_a^\infty l(x,t-x)\,\mu_x\,dx \qquad (18.5.3)$$

$$= \bar{P}(\bar{A}_a)\int_a^\infty l(x,t-x)\,dx$$

$$+ \delta \int_a^\infty l(x,t-x)\,_{x-a}\bar{V}(\bar{A}_a)\,dx.$$

The first integral on the left-hand side of (18.5.3) is evaluated using integration by parts. We obtain

$$l(x,t-x)\,_{x-a}\bar{V}(\bar{A}_a)\,\Big|_a^\infty + \int_a^\infty [b'(t-x)s(x) + l(x,t-x)\,\mu_x]\,_{x-a}\bar{V}(\bar{A}_a)\,dx.$$

$$(18.5.4)$$

In completing the integration by parts it is important to recall that

$$\frac{d}{dx}l(x,t-x) = \frac{d}{dx}b(t-x)s(x) = -b'(t-x)s(x) - b(t-x)s(x)\mu_x.$$

Substituting (18.5.4) into (18.5.3) and rearranging yields (18.5.1).

▼

**Example 18.5:**

For the population life insurance system described in Example 18.4 assume that funding is on an assessment plan rather than on a whole life plan. That is, the annual assessment rate, denoted by $\pi_t$, per member at time $t$ is equal to the rate of outgo per member at time $t$. Determine $\pi_t$.

**Solution:**
The assessment rate can be determined from

$$\pi_t \int_a^\infty l(x,t-x)\,dx = \int_a^\infty l(x,t-x)\,\mu_x\,dx$$

or from

$$\pi_t = \frac{\displaystyle\int_a^\infty l(x,t-x)\,\mu_x\,dx}{\displaystyle\int_a^\infty l(x,t-x)\,dx}. \tag{18.5.5}$$

▼

**Example 18.6:**      Assume a stable population and rework

a. Example 18.4
b. Example 18.5.

**Solution:**

a. We start with (18.5.1), which has been established already for the more general population density function $l(x,u) = b(u)\,s(x)$. For this example, $l(x,u) = e^{Ru}\,b\,s(x)$ and the income allocation equation becomes

$$\bar{P}(\bar{A}_a)\int_a^\infty e^{R(t-x)}l_x\,dx + \delta\int_a^\infty e^{R(t-x)}l_{x\;x-a}\bar{V}(\bar{A}_a)\,dx$$

$$= \int_a^\infty e^{R(t-x)}l_x\,\mu_x\,dx + R\int_a^\infty e^{R(t-x)}l_{x\;x-a}\bar{V}(\bar{A}_a)\,dx. \tag{18.5.6}$$

The factor $e^{Rt}$ can be canceled from each term of (18.5.6). By an interpretation of (18.5.6) developed in the general reasoning solution of Example 18.4, the ratio of the rate of premium income to the rate of benefit outgo is

$$\frac{\bar{P}(\bar{A}_a)\displaystyle\int_a^\infty e^{-Rx}l_x\,dx}{\displaystyle\int_a^\infty e^{-Rx}l_x\,\mu_x\,dx} = \frac{\bar{P}(\bar{A}_a)}{\bar{P}'(\bar{A}'_a)}. \tag{18.5.7}$$

If $R = 0$, the population is stationary and the income allocation equation (18.5.6) becomes

$$\bar{P}(\bar{A}_a)\,T_a + \delta\int_a^\infty l_{x\;x-a}\bar{V}(\bar{A}_a)\,dx = l_a, \tag{18.5.8}$$

while the ratio of the rate of premium income to the rate of benefit outgo, (18.5.7), becomes $\bar{P}(\bar{A}_a)\,\mathring{e}_a$.

b. In the stable population, the assessment rate determined in (18.5.5) becomes

$$\pi_t = \frac{\displaystyle\int_a^\infty e^{-Rx} l_x \mu_x\, dx}{\displaystyle\int_a^\infty e^{-Rx} l_x\, dx} = \bar{P}'(\bar{A}_a'), \qquad (18.5.9)$$

which is independent of $t$. If $R = 0$, that is, the population is stationary, $\pi_t = 1/\overset{\circ}{e}_a$. ▼

**Remark:**

One aspect of Example 18.6 deserves special comment. The rate of premium payment required of each member of the stable population above age $a$ under the whole life and assessment funding methods are, respectively, $\bar{P}(\bar{A}_a)$ and $\bar{P}(\bar{A}_a')$. In Exercise 18.21 it is demonstrated that if the force of mortality is increasing, then

$$\bar{P}(\bar{A}_a) > \bar{P}(\bar{A}_a') \text{ if } \delta < R$$
$$\bar{P}(\bar{A}_a) = \bar{P}(\bar{A}_a') \text{ if } \delta = R$$
$$\bar{P}(\bar{A}_a) < \bar{P}(\bar{A}_a') \text{ if } \delta > R.$$

That is, if the force of interest is less than the population growth rate, the required premium rate under the assessment funding method is less than under the whole life funding method. If the force of interest is greater than the population growth rate, the whole life funding method results in a smaller premium rate than does the assessment funding method.

**Example 18.7:**

Provide a general reasoning interpretation of the stationary population income allocation equation (18.5.8) rearranged as

$$\int_a^\infty l_x \,_{x-a}\bar{V}(\bar{A}_a)\, dx = \frac{l_a - \bar{P}(\bar{A}_a)\, T_a}{\delta}.$$

**Solution:**

This rearranged form indicates that the aggregate reserve can be interpreted as the difference between the present values of two perpetuities:

$$\frac{l_a}{\delta} = \begin{array}{l}\text{(the present value of a}\\ \text{continuous perpetuity paying}\\ \text{death benefits at an annual}\\ \text{rate of } l_a)\end{array}$$

$$= \text{(the present value of death}\\ \text{benefits to current members)}$$

$$+ \text{(the present value of death}\\ \text{benefits to future members)}.$$

$$\frac{\bar{P}(\bar{A}_a)\,T_a}{\delta} = \begin{array}{l}\text{(the present value of a}\\ \text{continuous perpetuity paying}\\ \text{premiums at an annual rate of}\\ \bar{P}(\bar{A}_a)\,T_a)\end{array}$$

$$= \text{(the present value of premiums}$$
$$\quad\text{for current members)}$$

$$+ \text{(the present value of}$$
$$\quad\text{premiums for future members)}.$$

Additional insights are obtained by noting that premiums at rate $\bar{P}(\bar{A}_a)$ will be payable from age $a$ for future members. The present value of their premiums will be equal to the present value of their benefits. Hence, the second component of the interpretations of $l_a/\delta$ and $\bar{P}(\bar{A}_a)\,T_a/\delta$ are offsetting and

$$\frac{l_a}{\delta} - \frac{\bar{P}(\bar{A}_a)\,T_a}{\delta} = \begin{array}{l}\text{(the aggregate reserve for current}\\ \text{members)}\end{array}$$

$$= \text{(the present value of benefits}$$
$$\quad\text{for current members)}$$

$$- \text{(the present value of}$$
$$\quad\text{premiums for current members)}$$

$$= \int_a^\infty l_{x\ x-a}\bar{V}(\bar{A}_a)\,dx.$$ ▼

Examples 18.4, 18.6 and 18.7 treat life insurance funding, or budgeting, methods for which a fund exists. In these examples the characteristics of the funds, after all members of the population above the entry age $a$ are participants and have been since the entry age $a$, were examined. When all eligible members are participating and have participated since the entry age $a$, the system is said to be in a **mature state.** Until that time the total fund is subject to growth by a stream of new entrants. In our examples it will take $\omega - a$ years for the fund to reach a mature state.

## 18.6 Population Dynamics

In this section we return to an examination of the function $b(t)$, the density of births at time $t$. The goal of this examination is to build a foundation under the development of the continuous model of Section 18.3. In addition, the conditions leading to stable or stationary populations, developed in Section 18.4, will be explored.

In developing a mathematical model for the density of births we shall introduce the **force of birth function,** to be denoted by $\beta(x,u)$. Then $\beta(x,t-x)\,dt$ represents the number of female children born between time $t$ and $t + dt$ to a woman age $x$ who was herself born at time $t - x$. The force of birth function is an age and generation specific instantaneous birthrate for female children.

# POPULATION THEORY

The total number of female children born between $t$ and $t + dt$ is

$$b_f(t)\,dt = \left[\int_0^\infty l_f(x,t-x)\,\beta(x,t-x)\,dx\right]dt. \qquad (18.6.1)$$

In (18.6.1) the subscript $f$ denotes that the function relates to female lives. Total births are obtained by multiplying by a constant, (total births)/(female births), which is slightly greater than 2 for most human populations.

If we divide (18.6.1) by $dt$ and substitute for $l_f(x,t-x)$ from (18.3.1), we see that the female birth density function satisfies the integral equation

$$b_f(t) = \int_0^\infty b_f(t-x)\,s_f(x,t-x)\,\beta(x,t-x)\,dx. \qquad (18.6.2)$$

An integral equation is a statement about the relationship between functions where the relationship involves an integral. The problem is to find $b_f(t)$ given the functions $s_f(x,t-x)$ and $\beta(x,t-x)$. In (18.6.3) the function $s_f(x,t-x)\,\beta(x,t-x)$ is called the **net maternity function** and will be denoted by $\phi(x,t-x)$.

For the remainder of this section we will assume that the net maternity function does not depend on the year of birth of the mother. That is, $s_f(x,t-x)\,\beta(x,t-x) = \phi(x)$. With this assumption, the integral equation (18.6.2) becomes

$$b_f(t) = \int_0^\infty b_f(t-x)\,\phi(x)\,dx. \qquad (18.6.3)$$

In this section we will limit ourselves to verifying that a particular solution of (18.6.3) is

$$b_f(t) = b\,e^{Rt} \qquad (18.6.4)$$

where $b$ is a positive constant and $R$ is the unique real solution of the equation

$$H(r) = 1, \qquad (18.6.5)$$

where

$$H(r) = \int_0^\infty e^{-rx}\,\phi(x)\,dx.$$

Direct substitution of (18.6.4) yields

$$b\,e^{Rt} = \int_0^\infty b\,e^{R(t-x)}\,\phi(x)\,dx,$$

and upon the cancellation of constants this becomes

$$1 = \int_0^\infty e^{-Rx}\,\phi(x)\,dx = H(R).$$

# Chapter 18
## POPULATION THEORY

The statement that $H(r) = 1$ yields a unique real solution can be verified by the following.

**Observation:**

1.  $H'(r) = -\displaystyle\int_0^\infty x e^{-rx} \phi(x)\, dx < 0$

2.  $H(0) = \displaystyle\int_0^\infty \phi(x)\, dx > 0$

3.  $\displaystyle\lim_{r\to\infty} H(r) = 0$

4.  $\displaystyle\lim_{r\to-\infty} H(r) = \infty$

These observations are summarized in Figure 18.7 together with the fact that

$$H''(r) = \int_0^\infty x^2 e^{-rx} \phi(x)\, dx > 0.$$

From Figure 18.7 we see that there is a unique real solution $R$ (shown positive, but could be negative) and the verification is complete.

If $b_f(t) = b e^{Rt}$, then $l_f(x, t-x) = b e^{R(t-x)} s_f(x)$ and the population of females is stable. In the special case where $R = 0$, the population of females is stationary.

To check whether $R$ is positive, 0 or negative we examine the number $\beta$ where

$$\beta = H(0) = \int_0^\infty \phi(x)\, dx.$$

**Figure 18.7**
**Typical $H(r)$**
**Function, and**
**Formula (18.6.5)**

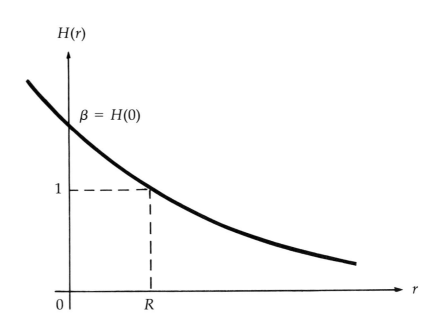

By studying Figure 18.7 we can conclude
- if $\beta > 1$, $R$ is positive and the population is stable and increasing;
- if $\beta = 1$, $R$ is 0, and the population is stationary;
- if $\beta < 1$, $R$ is negative and the population is stable and decreasing.

Since $H(0) = \beta$ can be interpreted as the number of female children produced by each female, it is called the *net reproduction rate*. The parameter $R$ is called the *intrinsic rate of population growth.*

**Remarks:**

All populations are not stable as might be inferred from this section. Several aspects of our model may not be in accord with actual experience. Our basic model, given by (18.6.2), was built on the assumption that the survival function and the force of birth do not change over time. In (18.6.3) we restricted it still further by assuming that the net maternity function depends on the age, but not the birth year of mothers. Public health statistics disclose major changes in survival functions and in the forces of birth over time.

In addition, in solving integral equation (18.6.3), we obtained only the real solution to the equation $H(r) = 1$. Within the complex number field, an infinite number of solutions may be determined in addition to the single real solution. These additional roots of $H(r) = 1$ lead to general solutions of (18.6.3) of the form

$$\sum_j c_j b_f^{(j)}(t)$$

where each $b_f^{(j)}(t)$ is associated with a root of $H(r) = 1$. The complex roots, which occur in conjugate pairs, can serve to put a dampened wave structure into the birth density function.

Population theory is a collection of elegant mathematical ideas. However, there also are some very important statistical problems in estimating its key components, such as the survival function and the force of birth function, from available data. These functions have been observed to shift over time as a reflection of the dynamic nature of human society.

As is true of all models of natural phenomena, the mathematical models of populations capture only a small part of the dynamic forces that shape the size and age distribution of real populations. Even if the stable population model is a satisfactory approximation at one time, it cannot be appropriate for the long term. The constant $R$ cannot be greater than 0 on a finite planet for a long time horizon. In a like manner, if $R$ is negative for too long a period of time, the stable population faces extinction.

**18.7
Notes and
References**

The foundations of population theory were built, in part, by Lokta who had experience answering life insurance questions. The basic theory is developed in a book by Keyfitz (1968) and applications are in another book by Keyfitz (1977). Keyfitz and Beekman (1984) wrote

# Chapter 18
## POPULATION THEORY

a textbook directed toward helping students master demography through a graded set of exercises. Lexis diagrams are named for their originator Wilhelm Lexis (1837–1914), German statistician, demographer and economist. Charles Trowbridge (1952, 1955) promoted the use of stationary population models in the study of the characteristics of pension and life insurance funding methods.

## Exercises

### Section 18.2

18.1. Using the Lexis diagram of Figure 18.1 calculate
  a. the average age of employees at time $-25$
  b. the number of employees who have attained age 50 in the history of this work force
  c. of the employees at time $-25$, the number who have attained or will attain age 50 while in the work force.

### Section 18.3

18.2. Let

$$b(u) = 100\,[1 + \cos(\pi u/200)] \quad -\infty < u < \infty$$

$$s(x,u) = \cos(\pi x/200) \quad 0 < x \le 100.$$

Calculate the number of individuals attaining age 50 between the times 50 and 100.

18.3. Let

$$b(u) = 100\,(1 - e^{-u/100}) \quad u > 0$$

$$s(x) = e^{-x/100} \quad x > 0.$$

Calculate the number of individuals between ages 25 and 50 at time 100.

18.4. Calculate the number of lives who will attain age 25 between times 50 and 51 and die before time 53. Use the functions $b(u)$ and $s(x,u)$ specified in Exercise 18.3. (This is a numerical version of Example 18.1.)

18.5. Rework Example 18.2 assuming $s(x,u) = s(x)$ and $b(u) = l_0$.

18.6. Exhibit integrals for calculating the number of those between ages 20 and 50 at time 0 who will die at an age less than 80 and before time 50.

### Section 18.4

18.7. a. Let $N(t)$ denote the number of members in a stable population at time $t$ and show that $dN(t)/dt = R\,N(t)$.
  b. The birthrate at time $t$ is defined as $b(t)/N(t)$. For a stable population show that the birthrate, denoted by $i(t)$, is

$$i(t) = \left[ \int_0^\infty e^{-Rx} s(x)\,dx \right]^{-1}.$$

18.8. If $\mu_x = ax$, $a > 0$ and $b(u) = be^{Ru}$, express the size of the total population at time $t$ in terms of $\Phi(z)$, the d.f. for a $N(0,1)$ distribution.

18.9. Assume a stable population and derive an expression for the average age of those between ages $a$ and $r$ at time $t$. Restate the expression assuming $R = 0$.

18.10. If $\bar{\mu}_x = \mu_x + 0.05/\mathring{e}_x$, show that $\tilde{p}_x = p_x (T_{x+1}/T_x)^{0.05}$.

18.11. Confirm that $s^*(x) = e^{-Rx} s(x)$, $R \geq 0$, is a survival function. Then
a. exhibit the p.d.f. and d.f. associated with $s^*(x)$
b. show that the complete expectation of life at age $x_0$ associated with the survival function $s^*(x)$ is $\bar{a}'_{x_0}$ and that the variance of the time-until-death is $2\,(\bar{I}\bar{a})'_{x_0} - \bar{a}'^2_{x_0}$.

18.12. The crude death rate at time $t$ is defined by

$$\frac{\displaystyle\int_0^\infty l(x,t-x)\,\mu(x,t-x)\,dx}{\displaystyle\int_0^\infty l(x,t-x)\,dx}.$$

If the population is stable, show that the crude death rate is equal to $i(t) - R$ where $i(t)$ is the birthrate defined in Exercise 18.7(b).

*Section 18.5*

18.13. Assume a stationary population with survival function $s(x)$ and that this same survival function is used in the evaluation of actuarial functions. Verify and interpret the equation

$$l_r \bar{a}_r + \delta \int_r^\infty l_x \bar{a}_x\, dx = T_r.$$

18.14. Assume a stable population with survival function $s(x)$ and that this same survival function is used in the evaluation of actuarial functions. Confirm and interpret the following identities.

a. $l(a,t-a)\,\bar{a}_{a:\overline{r-a}|} + \delta \int_a^r l(x,t-x)\,\bar{a}_{x:\overline{r-x}|}\, dx$

$$= \int_a^r l(x,t-x)\,dx + R \int_a^r l(x,t-x)\,\bar{a}_{x:\overline{r-x}|}\, dx$$

[Hint: Apply (5.3.26).]

b. $l(a,t-a)\,\bar{A}_a + \delta \int_a^\infty l(x,t-x)\,\bar{A}_x\, dx$

$$= \int_a^\infty l(x,t-x)\,\mu_x\, dx + R \int_a^\infty l(x,t-x)\,\bar{A}_x\, dx$$

18.15. If $b(u) = 100\,e^{0.01u}$, age $a = 0$ and $s(x) = e^{-x/50}$, calculate the assessment rate, $\pi_t$, to fund a whole life insurance program as in Example 18.5.

# Chapter 18
## POPULATION THEORY

18.16. The old age dependency ratio for a population at time $t$ is

$$f(t) = \frac{\displaystyle\int_{65}^{\infty} l(x, t - x)\,dx}{\displaystyle\int_{20}^{65} l(x, t - x)\,dx}.$$

For a stable population show that

$$\frac{\partial}{\partial R} \log f(t) = \bar{x}_1 - \bar{x}_2$$

where $\bar{x}_1$ is the average age of those between ages 20 and 65 at time $t$ and $\bar{x}_2$ is the average age of those above age 65 at time $t$.

*Section 18.6*

18.17. Given the net maternity function

$$\phi(x) = x^{\alpha - 1} e^{-\beta x} \qquad \alpha > 0,\ \beta > 0,$$

a. calculate $R$
b. is the population stable or stationary if $\alpha = 2$ and $\beta = 1$?

*Miscellaneous*

18.18. Assume that the number in a population at time $t$ satisfies the differential equation

$$\frac{dN(t)}{dt} = \frac{c}{a} \{N(t)\,[a - N(t)]\} \qquad a > 0.$$

Note that as $N(t)$ approaches $a$, the rate of change in population size approaches 0. Such a model incorporates environmental limits on population growth.
a. Verify that the function $N(t) = a\,[1 + be^{-ct}]^{-1}$, $b > 0$, satisfies the differential equation. This is called the **logistic function.**
b. If $c > 0$, calculate $\lim_{t \to \infty} N(t)$ and sketch the curve of $N(t)$.
c. Determine the abscissa of the point of inflection of $N(t)$.

18.19. If the force of mortality is strictly increasing, show in turn
a. $s(x)s(y) \geq s(x + y)$, $x \geq 0,\ y \geq 0$

b. $s(x) \displaystyle\int_0^{\infty} s(y)\,dy \geq \int_0^{\infty} s(x + y)\,dy$

c. $s(x) \displaystyle\int_0^{\infty} s(y)\,dy \geq \int_x^{\infty} s(w)\,dw$

d. $\displaystyle\int_0^{\infty} s(y)\,dy \geq \int_x^{\infty} \frac{s(w)}{s(x)}\,dw$

e. $\mathring{e}_0 \geq \mathring{e}_x$.

18.20. In Exercise 18.19, multiply by $v^y$ and show that $\bar{a}_0 \geq \bar{a}_x$.

18.21. a. Show that $\bar{P}(\bar{A}_x)$ can be written as the weighted average of the force of mortality $\mu_{x+t}$ where the weight function is

$$w(t,\delta) = \frac{v^t {}_tp_x}{\bar{a}_x}.$$

b. Verify that

(i) $\displaystyle\int_0^\infty w(t,\delta)\,dt = 1$

(ii) $\dfrac{\partial}{\partial t} w(t,\delta) \leq 0$

(iii) $\dfrac{\partial}{\partial \delta} w(t,\delta) = \dfrac{v^t {}_tp_x\,[-t\,\bar{a}_x + (\bar{I}\bar{a})_x]}{(\bar{a}_x)^2}$.

c. If the force of mortality is strictly increasing, use results (b)(ii) and (b)(iii) to demonstrate that an increase in the force of interest increases the weight attached to small values of the force of mortality and decreases the weight attached to large values of the force of mortality. Therefore, if the force of mortality is strictly increasing, an increase in the force of interest will decrease $\bar{P}(\bar{A}_x)$.

Chapter 19
# THEORY OF PENSION FUNDING

## 19.1
## Introduction

In Chapter 10 we studied the actuarial present values of benefits and contributions with respect to a participant in a pension plan. These actuarial present values for individual participants are necessary inputs into the process of determining the aggregate actuarial present values for the plan. These aggregated values together with the current assets are balanced with the aggregate present values of future contributions. The pattern of aggregate contributions required to balance benefit payments is determined by an *actuarial cost* or *funding method.* In this chapter functions useful in summarizing the status of the funding of a pension plan are defined. These functions are then used to define actuarial cost methods and to explore the properties of these methods.

For this we will adopt some of the population theory of Chapter 18. Here the study will be similar to that followed in Examples 18.4, 18.5, 18.6 and 18.7 for alternative funding or budgeting methods in the examination of a life insurance system for a population.

In order to integrate the ideas of this chapter with those developed earlier, the reader should keep in mind some basic limitations on the ideas presented here:

- In order to protect the interests of participants and to limit the amount of income on which taxes are deferred (because it is contributed to a pension plan), governments have chosen to regulate actuarial cost methods. These regulations are important in practice, but will not be discussed here.
- Pension plans frequently provide many types of benefits. In addition to retirement income, death and disability benefits are common and in many jurisdictions withdrawal benefits are required. The determination of the actuarial present value of some of these benefits was covered in Chapter 10. In this chapter, the model used provides only for retirement income benefits. This simplification is adopted so that attention can be focused on the properties of various actuarial cost methods. Although most pension plans provide retirement income at a rate dependent in some way on income levels before retirement, the model used in this chapter specifies an initial pension benefit rate dependent only on the rate of income payment at retirement. Once again this simplification is made to permit concentration on the actuarial cost methods.
- A continuing theme in this work is that actuarial present values require the application of interest factors and probabilities to future contingent payments. In this chapter future payments may depend on a great many uncertain events. However, in accordance with our goal of studying actuarial cost methods, a deterministic view is adopted in this chapter.

## 19.2
## The Model

We assume a population consists of members entering at age $a$, retiring at age $r$ and subject to a survival function, $s(x)$, $x \geq a$ with $s(a) = 1$. For $a \leq x < r$, decrement may occur for mortality or other causes, but for $x \geq r$ mortality will be the only cause of decrement. The density of new entrants at age $a$ at time $u$ will be given by $n(u)$

and the density of those attaining age $x$ at time $t$ by

$$l(x,u) = n(u)\,s(x) \qquad (19.2.1)$$

where $u = t - x + a$ is the time of entry into the plan. Formula (19.2.1) is related to (18.3.1) except that births occur at age $a$ by becoming a plan participant. We assume the survival function does not depend on $u$.

We will also assume that the salary rate for each member aged $x$ at time 0 is $w(x)$, $a \le x < r$. The function $w(x)$ expresses the individual experience and merit components of salary change. Salary rates also change by a year-of-experience factor, $g(t)$, reflecting inflation and changes in the productivity of all participants. This factor does not depend on the age of an individual. Thus the annual salary rate expected at time $t$ by a member aged $x$ is given by the formula

$$w(x)\,g(t) \qquad a \le x < r. \qquad (19.2.2)$$

This should be compared with the simpler model used in (10.2.1) where salary changes that are functions of only attained age are considered.

Comparing with (18.3.5), we recognize that the total salary rate at time $t$ for the $l(x, t - x + a)\,dx$ members between ages $x$ and $x + dx$ is $l(x, t - x + a)\,w(x)\,g(t)\,dx$ and the total annual salary rate at time $t$ is

$$\boldsymbol{W}(t) = \int_a^r l(x, t - x + a)\,w(x)\,g(t)\,dx. \qquad (19.2.3)$$

Formula (19.2.3) incorporates a notational convention used in the remainder of this chapter. A boldface symbol denotes a quantity for all participants. Thus $\boldsymbol{W}(t)$ represents the total payroll payment rate at time $t$.

The model pension plan considered in this chapter provides only retirement annuities payable after attainment of retirement age $r$. The initial annual pension rate is a fraction $f$ of the final salary rate. Thus for a member retiring at time $t$, the projected payment rate is

$$f\,w(r)\,g(t). \qquad (19.2.4)$$

For a retiree aged $x$ at time $t$, the annual rate of pension payment is projected as

$$f\,w(r)\,g(t - x + r)\,h(x) \qquad x \ge r \qquad (19.2.5)$$

where $h(x)$ represents an adjustment factor applied to the initial pension payment rate of $f\,w(r)\,g(t - x + r)$ for those who retired $x - r$ years ago. We note that $h(r) = 1$. As an example, $h(x)$ may be the exponential function $\exp[\beta\,(x - r)]$ where $\beta$ is a constant rate of increase (possibly related to the expected inflation rate).

The model plan that will be at the center of our discussion of actuarial cost methods is a **defined benefit plan.** The plan defines the

# THEORY OF PENSION FUNDING

benefits to be received by retiring participants, and we will concentrate on describing actuarial cost methods that will produce a stream of contributions and investment income to balance the benefit payments. In **defined contribution plans** the starting point shifts. The contribution made on behalf of each participant is stated, perhaps as a constant or as a fraction of salary. The actuarial problem is then to calculate the benefit level that will produce an actuarial present value equal to the actuarial present value of the contributions. This may be determined at time of retirement by using the accumulated contributions to provide an equivalent retirement annuity, or on a year-by-year basis whereby a deferred retirement annuity is purchased by the contribution of each year.

**19.3
Terminal Funding**

Under the *terminal funding method* pensions are not funded by contributions during active membership. Instead single contributions are made to the fund at the time of retirement. The required contribution rate, or *normal cost rate,* under the terminal funding method at time $t$, denoted by $^{T}P(t)$, is the rate at which the actuarial present value of future pensions for members reaching age $r$ is incurred at time $t$. To determine $^{T}P(t)$ for the model plan, we assume interest is earned at an annual force of $\delta$ and we denote by $\bar{a}_r^h$ the actuarial present value of a life annuity payable continuously to a life aged $r$ with income rate $h(x)$ per year when $(r)$ attains age $x$. Therefore,

$$\bar{a}_r^h = \int_r^{\infty} e^{-\delta(x-r)}\, h(x)\, \frac{s(x)}{s(r)} dx. \qquad (19.3.1)$$

From (18.3.2), we have $l(r, t-r+a)\,dt$ members attaining age $r$ between times $t$ and $t + dt$, and by (19.2.4) they will collect pensions at an average initial rate of $f\, w(r)\, g(t)$. Therefore,

$$^{T}P(t) = f\, w(r)\, g(t)\, l(r, t - r + a)\, \bar{a}_r^h. \qquad (19.3.2)$$

We will see that $^{T}P(t)$ is a basic building block for the various functions used to describe the funding operations for the model plan.

To illustrate the theory, we shall often refer to the *exponential case* having the following characteristics:
- $n(u) = n e^{Ru}$, $n > 0$. Since we have assumed that the survival function is independent of time, we see from (18.4.3) and the form of $n(u)$ that the size of the population is changing exponentially at rate $R$, but with a stable age distribution within the population.
- $g(t) = e^{\tau t}$; that is, salaries are changing exponentially at a rate $\tau$.
- $h(x) = e^{\beta(x-r)}$; that is, pensions are adjusted at a constant annual rate of $\beta$.

Before exploring the exponential case we should understand its limitations. It is clear that conditions for exponential growth or decay cannot exist indefinitely. When the exponential case is approximately realized, the three key economic rates, interest $\delta$, wages $\tau$ and pension adjustment $\beta$ are interrelated. For example, if $\beta$ is related to inflation, it is conventional to assume that $\delta > \beta$ even though there have been periods of unexpected inflation where the reverse holds. (If $\beta > \tau$, the consequence would be an improvement in the economic position of retired lives relative to active lives, and therefore $\beta \leq \tau$ is usually assumed.)

**Example 19.1:**

In the exponential case, show that $^{T}P(t + u) = e^{\rho u}\,^{T}P(t)$ where $\rho = \tau + R$.

**Solution:**
From (19.2.1) we have

$$l(r, t + u - r + a) = n\, s(r)\, e^{R(t + u - r + a)}$$

and from (19.3.1)

$$\bar{a}_r^h = \int_r^\infty e^{-(\delta - \beta)(x - r)}\, \frac{s(x)}{s(r)}\, dx = \bar{a}_r'$$

where $\bar{a}_r'$ is valued at force of interest $\delta - \beta$. Then using (19.3.2) we obtain

$$^{T}P(t + u) = f\, w(r)\, e^{\tau(t + u)}\, n\, s(r)\, e^{R(t + u - r + a)}\, \bar{a}_r'$$

$$= e^{(\tau + R)u}\, f\, w(r)\, e^{\tau t}\, n\, s(r)\, e^{R(t - r + a)}\, \bar{a}_r' = e^{\rho u}\,^{T}P(t).$$

Several terms in this development can be interpreted independently. The rate $\rho = \tau + R$ can be interpreted as a total economic growth or decay rate. The term $n\,s(r)$ may be interpreted as $l_r$, the number of survivors at age $r$ of $n$ members in a survivorship group at age $a$ governed by the multiple decrement survival function $s(x)$, $a \leq x \leq r$. ▼

**19.4
Accrual of
Actuarial Liability**

Actuarial cost methods differ by the rate at which prospective pension obligations are recognized during the participants' working lifetimes. The terminal cost method described in Section 19.3 does not recognize the liability until the attainment of retirement age $r$. To express the accrual of actuarial liability for a pension commencing at age $r$, we define for a cost method an *accrual function* $M(x)$. Here $M(x)$ represents that fraction of the actuarial value of future pensions accrued as an actuarial liability at age $x$ under the actuarial cost method. The function $M(x)$ is a nondecreasing, right-continuous function of the age variable with $0 \leq M(x) \leq 1$ for all $x \geq a$. Under *initial funding* all the liability for the future pension is recognized when the participant enters at age $a$, thus $M(x) = 0$ for $x < a$ and $M(x) = 1$ for $x \geq a$. For other actuarial cost methods it will be assumed that $M(a) = 0$. For funding methods requiring accrual or recognition of the total liability by age $r$, $M(x) = 1$ for $x \geq r$.

The function $M(x)$ can also be defined in terms of a *pension accrual density function* denoted by $m(x)$ such that

$$M(x) = \int_a^x m(y)\, dy \qquad x \geq a. \tag{19.4.1}$$

# Chapter 19
## THEORY OF PENSION FUNDING

Note the analogy between $M(x)$ and $m(x)$ and the d.f., $F(x)$, and a p.d.f., $f(x)$. In general it will be assumed that $m(x)$ is continuous for $a < x < r$, right continuous at $a$ and left continuous at $r$, and that $m(x) = 0$ for $x > r$. In this continuous case it follows from (19.4.1) that

$$m(x) = M'(x) \quad a < x < r. \tag{19.4.2}$$

At points of discontinuity of $M'(x)$, the density $m(x)$ is not defined and we can assign an arbitrary value to it, for example, the limit from the left or from the right.

The advantage of introducing the accrual function is that one can develop pension theory simultaneously for a whole family of actuarial cost methods rather than separately for each method.

**Example 19.2:**

For $M(x) = \bar{a}_{a:\overline{x-a}}/\bar{a}_{a:\overline{r-a}}$, $a \le x \le r$, verify that
a. $M(x)$ has the properties of an accrual function
b. $M(x) \,_{r-x|}\bar{a}_x$ is equal to the reserve at age $x$ on a continuous annual premium deferred life annuity issued at age $a$ and paying a continuous annuity of 1 per year commencing at age $r$.

**Solution:**

a.
$$M(x) = \frac{\displaystyle\int_a^x e^{-\delta(y-a)} s(y)\,dy}{\displaystyle\int_a^r e^{-\delta(y-a)} s(y)\,dy},$$

thus

$$M'(x) = m(x) = \frac{e^{-\delta(x-a)} s(x)}{\displaystyle\int_a^r e^{-\delta(y-a)} s(y)\,dy} > 0. \tag{19.4.3}$$

$M(a) = 0$ and $M(r) = 1$ confirm that $M(x)$ has the properties of an accrual function.

b. A retrospective formula gives the reserve at age $x$ as

$$\bar{P}(_{r-a|}\bar{a}_a)\, \bar{s}_{a:\overline{x-a}} = \frac{_{r-a|}\bar{a}_a}{\bar{a}_{a:\overline{r-a}}}\, \bar{s}_{a:\overline{x-a}}$$

$$= \frac{_{x-a}E_a \;_{r-x|}\bar{a}_x\, \bar{a}_{a:\overline{x-a}}}{\bar{a}_{a:\overline{r-a}} \;_{x-a}E_a}$$

$$= {}_{r-x|}\bar{a}_x\, M(x). \qquad \blacktriangledown$$

## 19.5
## Basic Functions for Active Members

In this section we define a number of basic functions related to the funding of pension benefits in the model plan. The functions will relate to the active group and will be denoted in the symbols with a prefixed $a$.

## 19.5.1
## Actuarial Present Value at Time $t$ of Future Pensions for the Active Group, $(aA)(t)$

The $l(x, t-x+a)\,dx$ members between ages $x$ and $x+dx$ at time $t$ will, at the end of $r-x$ years, incur the terminal funding cost of $^TP(t+r-x)dx$. Hence

$$(aA)(t) = \int_a^r e^{-\delta(r-x)}\, {}^TP(t+r-x)\,dx. \tag{19.5.1}$$

**Example 19.3:**

Show that

$$\frac{d}{dt}(aA)(t) = e^{-\delta(r-a)}\,{}^TP(t+r-a) - {}^TP(t) + \delta\,(aA)(t) \tag{19.5.2}$$

and interpret the equation.

**Solution:**
We note that

$$\frac{\partial}{\partial t}\,{}^TP(t+r-x) = -\frac{\partial}{\partial x}\,{}^TP(t+r-x). \tag{19.5.3}$$

Thus

$$\frac{d}{dt}(aA)(t) = \int_a^r e^{-\delta(r-x)}\frac{\partial}{\partial t}\,{}^TP(t+r-x)\,dx$$

$$= -\int_a^r e^{-\delta(r-x)}\frac{\partial}{\partial x}\,{}^TP(t+r-x)\,dx$$

$$= -e^{-\delta(r-x)}\,{}^TP(t+r-x)\Big|_{x=a}^{x=r} + \delta\int_a^r {}^TP(t+r-x)\,e^{-\delta(r-x)}\,dx$$

$$= e^{-\delta(r-a)}\,{}^TP(t+r-a) - {}^TP(t) + \delta\,(aA)(t).$$

The rate of change in the actuarial present value of future pensions equals the present value of the future terminal funding rate for new entrants (who will retire $r-a$ years later) less the terminal funding rate for active members retiring now plus the rate of interest income on the actuarial present value at time $t$. ▼

## 19.5.2
## Normal Cost Rate, $P(t)$

We assume that an actuarial cost method with accrual function $M(t)$ has been selected. We seek to express the normal cost rate for the model plan, that is, to display the function that, for our continuous model, allocates the actuarial present value of future pension benefits to the various times of valuation in a participant's active life.

As in (19.5.1) the future terminal funding cost for members between ages $x$ and $x+dx$ at time $t$ is $^TP(t+r-x)dx$. In the normal cost function this liability is being recognized at an accrual rate $m(x)$. We have

$$P(t) = \int_a^r e^{-\delta(r-x)}\,{}^TP(t+r-x)\,m(x)\,dx. \tag{19.5.4}$$

One can visualize how the normal cost rate, $P(t)$, $u \le t \le u+r-a$, completely funds the pension benefit of a member who enters at age $a$ at time $u$ and retires $r - a$ years later. Consider the participants who enter between $u$ and $u + du$. Their ultimate terminal funding cost rate will be $^TP(u + r - a)$. At time $t$, $u \leq t \leq u + r - a$, the density of contributions of this group to the integral defining $P(t)$ is

$$e^{-\delta(r-x)} \, ^TP(t + r - x) \, m(x)$$

where $x = a + t - u$. In the $r - x$ years until retirement this will increase, because of interest earned, to

$$^TP(t + r - x) \, m(x), \qquad (19.5.5)$$

and this density in terms of $u$ is $^TP(u + r - a) \, m(a + t - u)$. Integrating these interest-accumulated contributions we obtain

$$\int_u^{u+r-a} {}^TP(u + r - a) \, m(a + t - u) \, dt = {}^TP(u + r - a),$$

the required terminal funding cost rate.

**Example 19.4:**   a. Show that in the exponential case

$$P(t) = \exp\{-\delta[r - X(\theta)]\} \, ^TP[t + r - X(\theta)] \qquad (19.5.6)$$

where

$$\theta = \delta - \rho = \delta - \tau - R$$

and

$$e^{\theta X(\theta)} = \int_a^r m(x) \, e^{\theta x} \, dx. \qquad (19.5.7)$$

b. Interpret (19.5.6).

**Solution:**
a. From (19.5.4) and the solution to Example 19.1 we have

$$P(t) = \int_a^r e^{-\delta(r-x)} \, ^TP(t + r - x) \, m(x) \, dx$$

$$= \int_a^r e^{-\delta(r-x)} \, ^TP\{t + [X(\theta) - x] + r - X(\theta)\} \, m(x) \, dx$$

$$= \int_a^r e^{-\delta(r-x)} \, e^{\rho[X(\theta)-x]} \, ^TP[t + r - X(\theta)] \, m(x) \, dx$$

$$= e^{[-\delta r + \rho X(\theta)]} \, ^TP[t + r - X(\theta)] \int_a^r e^{(\delta-\rho)x} \, m(x) \, dx.$$

Now substitute $\delta - \theta$ for $\rho$ and, using (19.5.7), we have

$$P(t) = e^{[-\delta r + (\delta - \theta)X(\theta)]} \, ^TP[t + r - X(\theta)] \, e^{\theta X(\theta)},$$

which reduces to (19.5.6).

b. The annual normal cost rate at time $t$ is sufficient with interest to provide the terminal funding cost $r - X(\theta)$ years later. The number $X(\theta)$ has its existence assured by the mean value theorem for integrals and may be interpreted as an average age of normal cost payment associated with the accrual density function $m(x)$ in the exponential case with $\theta = \delta - \tau - R$. Hence $X(\theta)$ depends on the interest rate and on the salary and population change rates. ▼

**19.5.3**
**Actuarial Accrued**
**Liability, $(aV)(t)$**

We shall assume as in Section 19.5.2 that an actuarial cost method with accrual function $M(x)$ has been chosen. By analogy with (19.5.4) we have that the actuarial accrued liability for active lives at time $t$ is given by

$$(aV)(t) = \int_a^r e^{-\delta(r-x)} \, {}^T\!P(t + r - x) \, M(x) \, dx. \qquad (19.5.8)$$

In the integral we are applying the concept that a fraction $M(x)$ of the actuarial present value of the future pension has accrued as an actuarial liability by age $x$.

If we rewrite (19.5.4) in the form

$$P(t) = \int_a^r e^{-\delta(r-x)} \, {}^T\!P(t + r - x) \, dM(x)$$

and integrate by parts, we obtain, by use of (19.5.3),

$$P(t) = e^{-\delta(r-x)} \, {}^T\!P(t + r - x) \, M(x) \, \Big|_{x=a}^{x=r}$$

$$- \delta \int_a^r M(x) \, e^{-\delta(r-x)} \, {}^T\!P(t + r - x) \, dx \qquad (19.5.9)$$

$$+ \int_a^r M(x) \, e^{-\delta(r-x)} \, \frac{\partial}{\partial t} \, {}^T\!P(t + r - x) \, dx$$

$$= {}^T\!P(t) - \delta(aV)(t) + \frac{d}{dt}(aV)(t),$$

or

$$P(t) + \delta(aV)(t) = {}^T\!P(t) + \frac{d}{dt}(aV)(t). \qquad (19.5.10)$$

Equation (19.5.10) can be interpreted from the viewpoint of compound interest theory. We consider the actuarial accrued liability, $(aV)(t)$, as a fund into which normal costs, at rate $P(t)$, are paid and from which terminal funding costs, at rate ${}^T\!P(t)$, are transferred when active members retire. The left-hand side of (19.5.10) is the income rate to the fund from normal costs and interest. The right-hand side represents the allocation of this income rate to the terminal funding rate and rate of change in the fund size.

# Chapter 19
## THEORY OF PENSION FUNDING

**Example 19.5:**

Show that in the exponential case

a. $P(t + u) = e^{\rho u} P(t)$, $\rho = \tau + R$                               (19.5.11)

b. $(aV)(t + u) = e^{\rho u} (aV)(t)$                                     (19.5.12)

c. $P(t) + \theta(aV)(t) = {}^{T}P(t)$, $\theta = \delta - \rho$                     (19.5.13)

d. $P(t) < {}^{T}P(t)$    if    $\theta > 0$

     $P(t) = {}^{T}P(t)$    if    $\theta = 0$                                (19.5.14)

     $P(t) > {}^{T}P(t)$    if    $\theta < 0$.

**Solution:**

a. In Example 19.2 we saw that ${}^{T}P(t + u) = e^{\rho u} {}^{T}P(t)$. Then substituting into (19.5.4) we obtain

$$P(t + u) = \int_{a}^{r} e^{-\delta(r-x)} {}^{T}P(t + u + r - x) \, m(x) \, dx$$

$$= e^{\rho u} \int_{a}^{r} e^{-\delta(r-x)} {}^{T}P(t + r - x) \, m(x) \, dx$$

$$= e^{\rho u} P(t).$$

b. The solution starts with the definition of $(aV)(t)$ in (19.5.8) and follows the same steps as used in part (a).

c. Rewriting (19.5.12) as

$$\frac{(aV)(t + u) - (aV)(t)}{u} = \frac{e^{\rho u} - 1}{u} (aV)(t)$$

and letting $u \to 0$, we obtain

$$\frac{d}{dt} (aV)(t) = \rho (aV)(t). \qquad (19.5.15)$$

Now substituting (19.5.15) into (19.5.10) yields (19.5.13).

d. The inequalities follow from (19.5.13). This example reveals the critical role that $\theta = \delta - \tau - R$ plays in the exponential case. ▼

## 19.5.4
## Actuarial Present Value of Future Normal Costs, $(Pa)(t)$

In Section 19.5.1 we noted that $l(x, t + x - a) \, dx$ members between ages $x$ and $x + dx$ at time $t$ will have a terminal funding cost of ${}^{T}P(t + r - x) \, dx$ when they retire $r - x$ years later. As these members pass from age $y$ to $y + dy$, $x \le y < r$, the normal cost $e^{-\delta(r-y)} {}^{T}P(t + r - x) \, dx \, m(y) \, dy$ will be payable. The present value of this normal cost is

$$e^{-\delta(r-x)} {}^{T}P(t + r - x) \, dx \, m(y) \, dy, \qquad (19.5.16)$$

and the present value of future normal costs, denoted by $(Pa)(t)$, for all active members is

$$(Pa)(t) = \int_{a}^{r} e^{-\delta(r-x)} {}^{T}P(t + r - x) \int_{x}^{r} m(y) \, dy \, dx \qquad (19.5.17)$$

or

$$(Pa)(t) = \int_a^r e^{-\delta(r-x)} \, {}^T\!P(t + r - x) \, [1 - M(x)] \, dx.$$

**Figure 19.1
Formulation of
$(Pa)(t)$**

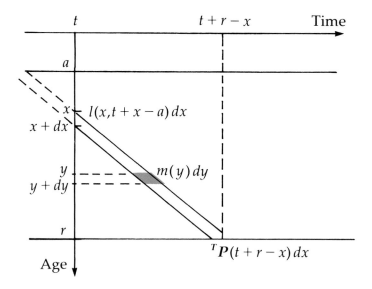

Figure 19.1 illustrates the ideas in the development of $(Pa)(t)$. Expression (19.5.16) represents the present value at time $t$ of the cost element in the shaded area. In (19.15.17), the inside integral represents the addition of elements along the diagonal and the outer integral the present value of future normal costs at time $t$ for all ages.

It follows from (19.5.17), (19.5.1) and (19.5.8) that

$$(Pa)(t) = (aA)(t) - (aV)(t) \tag{19.5.18}$$

or

$$(aV)(t) = (aA)(t) - (Pa)(t). \tag{19.5.19}$$

Formula (19.5.19) expresses the same concept as the prospective reserve formulas of Chapter 7 and is frequently used to define $(aV)(t)$. That is,

$$\begin{aligned}
&\text{(the actuarial liability at} \\
&\quad \text{time } t \text{ for active members)} \\[4pt]
=\; &\text{(the actuarial present value of} \\
&\quad \text{future pensions for active members)} \\[4pt]
-\; &\text{(the actuarial present value} \\
&\quad \text{of future normal costs).}
\end{aligned}$$

By analogy with concepts from Chapter 7, $V = A - Pa$ or $A = V + Pa$, one can argue that the actuarial present value of future pensions for active lives is balanced by the actuarial accrued liability for active lives and the actuarial present value of future normal costs. That is,

$$(aA)(t) = (aV)(t) + (Pa)(t). \qquad (19.5.20)$$

The split between the two terms on the right-hand side of (19.5.20) is determined by the actuarial cost method selected as reflected in the accrual function $M(x)$.

**Example 19.6:**

a. Consider two accrual density functions, $M_I(x)$ and $M_{II}(x)$. Show that if $D(x) = M_I(x) - M_{II}(x)$ is such that $D'(a) > 0$ and $D'(x) = 0$ has exactly one solution, $a < x < r$, then $(aV)_I(t) > (aV)_{II}(t)$.

b. If

$$M_I(x) = \frac{\bar{a}_{a:\overline{x-a}|}}{\bar{a}_{a:\overline{r-a}|}}$$

and

$$M_{II}(x) = \frac{x - a}{r - a},$$

show that

$$(aV)_I(t) > (aV)_{II}(t).$$

**Solution:**

a. By properties of the accrual function, $D(a) = D(r) = 0$. We are given that $D'(a) > 0$ and $D'(x) = 0$ for exactly one value of $x$, $a < x < r$, hence, $D(x) > 0$ for $a < x < r$. Thus

$$(aV)_I(t) - (aV)_{II}(t) = \int_a^r e^{-\delta(r-x)} \, {}^TP(t + r - x) \, D(x) \, dx$$

is greater than 0 and the inequality follows.

b. We have

$$D'(x) = \frac{e^{-\delta(x-a)} s(x)}{\displaystyle\int_a^r e^{-\delta(y-a)} s(y) \, dy} - \frac{1}{r - a}.$$

Further, if $\delta > 0$, $e^{-\delta(y-a)} s(y)$ is less than 1 and thus

$$\int_a^r e^{-\delta(y-a)} s(y) \, dy < \int_a^r dy = r - a.$$

Therefore

$$D'(a) = \frac{1}{\displaystyle\int_a^r e^{-\delta(y-a)} s(y) \, dy} - \frac{1}{r - a} > 0.$$

By a similar argument, $D'(r) > 0$. Since both $e^{-\delta(x-a)}$ and $s(x)$ are decreasing but positive functions of $x$, $D''(x) < 0$ and thus $D'(x) = 0$ for exactly one value of $x$, $a < x < r$. Then $(aV)_I(t) > (aV)_{II}(t)$ follows from part (a).

In addition by (19.5.20), we have

$$(aA)(t) = (aV)_{\mathrm{I}}(t) + (Pa)_{\mathrm{I}}(t) = (aV)_{\mathrm{II}}(t) + (Pa)_{\mathrm{II}}(t)$$

so that

$$(Pa)_{\mathrm{II}}(t) > (Pa)_{\mathrm{I}}(t). \qquad \blacktriangledown$$

**19.6
Individual
Actuarial Cost
Methods**

The generalized actuarial cost method defined by the accrual function $M(x)$ or its derivative, the accrual density function, is an individual cost method in the sense that $m(x)$ and $M(x)$ can be applied to yield the normal cost rate and the actuarial accrued liability for each participant. The total normal cost rate and actuarial accrued liability for active lives in the plan may be determined by adding the components attributed to each participant.

The individual pension funding functions, for an annuity starting at age $r$ with a unit initial benefit rate for an active life aged $x$, $a \leq x < r$, are defined as follows:

The actuarial present value of the benefit is given by

$$(aA)(x) = e^{-\delta(r-x)} \frac{s(r)}{s(x)} \bar{a}_r^h. \qquad (19.6.1)$$

The normal cost rate is given by

$$P(x) = (aA)(x)\, m(x). \qquad (19.6.2)$$

The accrued actuarial liability is given by

$$(aV)(x) = (aA)(x)\, M(x). \qquad (19.6.3)$$

The actuarial present value of future normal costs are defined by

$$(Pa)(x) = (aA)(x) - (aV)(x) = (aA)(x)\,[1 - M(x)]. \qquad (19.6.4)$$

Note that these are functions for a unit benefit for $(x)$, instead of aggregate plan functions as of time $t$. Exercise 19.15 develops the details of the relations between these functions and the basic functions relating to the entire group studied in Section 19.5.

In *accrued benefit cost methods* $M(x)$ is directly related to the accrued benefit a participant has acquired at age $x$ under provisions of the plan. We look at three possibilities. If the projected benefit accrues uniformly during active service,

$$m(x) = \frac{1}{r - a}. \qquad (19.6.5)$$

If the accrual of the benefit is in proportion to total salary where there is no time trend affecting all salaries,

$$m(x) = \frac{w(x)}{\displaystyle\int_a^r w(y)\,dy}. \qquad (19.6.6)$$

Finally, if the accrual of benefits is in proportion to total salary with an exponential time trend in salary,

$$m(x) = \frac{w(x)\,e^{\tau x}}{\displaystyle\int_a^r w(y)\,e^{\tau y}\,dy}. \tag{19.6.7}$$

For *entry-age actuarial cost methods,* the projected benefit is funded by a contribution that is either a level amount or a level percentage of salary from entry age to retirement. Again we look at three possibilities. The case with a level amount of contribution was examined in Example 19.2. Formula (19.4.3) shows that

$$m(x) = \frac{e^{-\delta x}\,s(x)}{\displaystyle\int_a^r e^{-\delta y}\,s(y)\,dy}. \tag{19.6.8}$$

If the contribution rate is a level fraction, $\pi$, of the salary where there is no time trend affecting all salaries, we have by equating the actuarial present value of contributions to the actuarial present value of a unit benefit, $(aA)(a)$,

$$\pi \int_a^r e^{-\delta(y-a)}\,s(y)\,w(y)\,dy = e^{-\delta(r-a)}\,s(r)\,\bar{a}_r^h. \tag{19.6.9}$$

The actuarial accrued liability for an individual age $x$, that is, the difference between the actuarial present values of benefits and of future contributions, is

$$(aV)(x) = e^{-\delta(r-x)}\frac{s(r)}{s(x)}\bar{a}_r^h - \pi\int_x^r e^{-\delta(y-x)}\frac{s(y)}{s(x)}w(y)\,dy$$

$$= e^{-\delta(r-x)}\frac{s(r)}{s(x)}\bar{a}_r^h\left[1 - \frac{\displaystyle\int_x^r e^{-\delta y}\,s(y)\,w(y)\,dy}{\displaystyle\int_a^r e^{-\delta y}\,s(y)\,w(y)\,dy}\right]$$

$$= (aA)(x)\,M(x).$$

Thus

$$m(x) = \frac{e^{-\delta x}\,s(x)\,w(x)}{\displaystyle\int_a^r e^{-\delta y}\,s(y)\,w(y)\,dy}. \tag{19.6.10}$$

By a similar process it can be shown that if an exponential trend in salaries by time is assumed, the pension accrual density function is

$$m(x) = \frac{e^{-\delta x} s(x) e^{\tau x} w(x)}{\displaystyle\int_a^r e^{-\delta y} s(y) e^{\tau y} w(y) \, dy}. \qquad (19.6.11)$$

It is important to note that the fraction of projected benefits accrued as an actuarial liability in entry-age actuarial cost methods differs from the definition of the accrued benefits in most plans. A definition of accrued benefits is required for regulatory purposes and to communicate to participants about the benefits they are accruing. The distinction here is similar to the distinction between the reserve and the nonforfeiture benefit in ordinary insurance.

It also should be noted that the contribution rate, paid by a plan sponsor who is following an individual actuarial cost method, will usually differ from the total normal cost rate specified by that method. There are two general reasons for this. First, at the inception of a plan, or at times when a plan is amended, actuarial accrued liabilities for prior service may be changed. Second, the actuarial assumptions will not be realized exactly, thereby generating funding gains or losses. The decisions on how to adjust the contribution rate to fund these changes in the actuarial accrued liability, or to adjust for gains or losses, are important ones that are the subject of regulation. The particular adjustments chosen are not compelled by the choice of individual actuarial cost method.

## 19.7 Aggregate Cost Methods

In this section we shall consider aggregate or group actuarial cost methods for which contributions are determined on a collective basis and not as a sum of contributions for individual participants. For the purpose of defining aggregate actuarial cost methods, we need three additional functions:

1. $(aF)(t)$, the fund allocated to active members at time $t$,
2. $(aC)(t)$, the annual contribution rate at time $t$ with respect to active participants,
3. $(aU)(t)$, the unfunded actuarial accrued liability with respect to active participants at time $t$.

Thus,

$$(aU)(t) = (aV)(t) - (aF)(t). \qquad (19.7.1)$$

The fund for active members at time $t$ can be described by the differential equation

$$\frac{d}{dt}(aF)(t) = (aC)(t) + \delta (aF)(t) - {}^T P(t) \qquad (19.7.2)$$

with the initial value $(aF)(0)$. The right-hand member of (19.7.2) indicates the two sources of income to the fund and the one source of outgo, that is, the transfer of the terminal funding cost to a fund for retired members.

In relation to an actuarial cost method, as determined by an accrual function, which implies a normal cost rate $P(t)$ [see (19.5.4)] and the unfunded accrued liability of active members $(aU)(t)$ [see (19.5.8) and (19.7.1)], a natural form of contribution rate is

$$(aC)(t) = P(t) + \lambda(t)(aU)(t). \tag{19.7.3}$$

In (19.7.3) $\lambda(t)$ defines the process for amortizing $(aU)(t)$.

Equation (19.7.3) points out a characteristic of aggregate actuarial cost methods not heretofore stated. These methods define a contribution rate, $(aC)(t)$, that depends on the level of funding, that is, on the magnitude of $(aU)(t)$. Here the adjustments required by plan changes or by gains and losses can be made automatically by following the actuarial cost method since the value of $(aU)(t)$ will reflect such changes and gains and losses.

We consider one such amortization process, one in which

$$\lambda(t) = \frac{1}{a(t)} \tag{19.7.4}$$

where

$$a(t) = \frac{(Pa)(t)}{P(t)}.$$

Thus $P(t)\,a(t) = (Pa)(t)$ so $a(t)$ is the value of a unit temporary annuity such that this temporary annuity with a level income rate at the current normal cost rate, $P(t)$, equals the actuarial present value of future normal costs for the current active members, $(Pa)(t)$. In this case the notation has been selected to suggest the motivating idea.

Formula (19.7.3) can be rewritten for this particular choice of $\lambda(t)$ as

$$\begin{aligned}
(aC)(t) &= P(t) + \frac{(aV)(t) - (aF)(t)}{a(t)} \\
&= \frac{(Pa)(t) + (aV)(t) - (aF)(t)}{a(t)} \\
&= \frac{(aA)(t) - (aF)(t)}{a(t)}
\end{aligned} \tag{19.7.5}$$

making use of (19.5.20). Thus with $\lambda(t)$ given by (19.7.4) we have

$$(aC)(t)\,a(t) = (aA)(t) - (aF)(t). \tag{19.7.6}$$

The interpretation of (19.7.6) is that a temporary annuity at the rate of $(aC)(t)$ is equivalent to the actuarial present value of future benefits for active members less the fund for them.

The formula governing the progress of the fund, (19.7.2), becomes, for $\lambda(t)$ given by (19.7.4),

$$\frac{d}{dt}(aF)(t) = P(t) + \frac{(aU)(t)}{a(t)} + \delta(aF)(t) - {}^T P(t). \tag{19.7.7}$$

We can write (19.5.10) as

$$\frac{d}{dt}(aV)(t) = P(t) + \delta(aV)(t) - {}^T\!P(t). \tag{19.7.8}$$

By subtracting (19.7.7) from (19.7.8), we get

$$\frac{d}{dt}(aU)(t) = -\left(\frac{1}{a(t)} - \delta\right)(aU)(t). \tag{19.7.9}$$

The differential equation (19.7.9) may be solved by replacing $t$ by $u$, integrating with respect to $u$ from 0 to $t$, and taking exponentials to obtain

$$(aU)(t) = (aU)(0) \exp\left[-\int_0^t \left[\frac{1}{a(u)} - \delta\right] du\right]. \tag{19.7.10}$$

Upon substituting (19.7.1), we obtain

$$\begin{aligned} (aF)(t) = (aV)(t) \\ - [(aV)(0) - (aF)(0)] \exp\left[-\int_0^t \left(\frac{1}{a(u)} - \delta\right) du\right]. \end{aligned} \tag{19.7.11}$$

Provided that $a(u)$ is smaller than $\bar{a}_{\overline{\infty}|} = 1/\delta$ so that

$$\frac{1}{a(u)} - \delta \geq \epsilon > 0,$$

$$\exp\left[-\int_0^t \left(\frac{1}{a(u)} - \delta\right) du\right] \to 0$$

as $t \to \infty$. Therefore $(aF)(t) \to (aV)(t)$.

Here the aggregate cost method with $\lambda(t) = 1/a(t)$ is asymptotically equivalent to the individual cost method defined by the accrual function used to evaluate $(aV)(t)$ and $P(t)$. There may be many accrual functions that produce functions such that $(Pa)(u)/P(u)$ is sufficiently small to assure the convergence of $(aF)(t)$ to $(aV)(t)$. Each of these accrual functions could produce a different pattern of contributions and a different ultimate fund. For completeness, when referring to an aggregate actuarial cost method one should always specify the accrual function used. The aggregate cost method with entry-age accrual has been particularly important in practice.

Clearly there are many possible choices for the function $\lambda(t)$ in determining the rate of amortization of $(aU)(0)$. If the goal is the completion of amortization by the end of $n$ years from some initial time 0, one choice for $\lambda(t)$ is

$$\lambda(t) = \frac{1}{\bar{a}_{\overline{n-t}|}} \qquad 0 < t < n. \tag{19.7.12}$$

Then corresponding to (19.7.10) we obtain

$$(aU)(t) = (aU)(0) \exp\left[-\int_0^t \left(\frac{1}{\bar{a}_{\overline{n-u}|}} - \delta\right) du\right]$$

$$= (aU)(0) \exp\left[-\int_0^t \frac{1}{\bar{s}_{\overline{n-u}|}} du\right]. \qquad (19.7.13)$$

It can be shown (Exercise 19.17) that

$$-\int_0^t \frac{1}{\bar{s}_{\overline{n-u}|}} du = \log \frac{\bar{s}_{\overline{n}|} - \bar{s}_{\overline{t}|}}{\bar{s}_{\overline{n}|}}.$$

Therefore (19.7.13) becomes

$$(aU)(t) = (aU)(0) \frac{\bar{s}_{\overline{n}|} - \bar{s}_{\overline{t}|}}{\bar{s}_{\overline{n}|}} \qquad 0 \le t \le n,$$

and it can be shown that

$$(aC)(t) = P(t) + \frac{(aU)(0)}{\bar{a}_{\overline{n}|}} \qquad 0 \le t \le n.$$

At time $n$, the funding goal will be achieved with $(aU)(n) = 0$ and $(aC)(t)$ will drop to $P(t)$.

**Example 19.7:** Assume a stationary plan, that is, $n(a) = l_a$, $g(t) = 1$ and $h(x) = 1$, with the accrual function associated with the level amount entry-age actuarial cost method, $M(x) = \bar{a}_{a:\overline{x-a}|}/\bar{a}_{a:\overline{r-a}|}$ (see Example 19.2).
a. Display $\lambda$.
b. Calculate $(aC)(0)$ if $(aF)(0) = 0$.

**Solution:**
a. Formula (19.3.2) gives, for the stationary case,

$$^TP(t) = f \, w(r) \, l_r \, \bar{a}_r$$

for all $t$. Thus from (19.5.17)

$$(Pa)(t) = \int_a^r e^{-\delta(r-x)} f \, w(r) \, l_r \, \bar{a}_r \left(1 - \frac{\bar{a}_{a:\overline{x-a}|}}{\bar{a}_{a:\overline{r-a}|}}\right) dx.$$

Now $M'(x) = m(x) = {}_{x-a}E_a/\bar{a}_{a:\overline{r-a}|}$, so by (19.5.4)

$$P(t) = \int_a^r e^{-\delta(r-x)} f \, w(r) \, l_r \, \bar{a}_r \frac{{}_{x-a}E_a}{\bar{a}_{a:\overline{r-a}|}} dx.$$

Thus, (19.7.4) gives

$$a(t) = \frac{(Pa)(t)}{P(t)} = \frac{\displaystyle\int_a^r e^{\delta x}\,_{x-a}E_a\,\bar{a}_{x:\overline{r-x}|}\,dx}{\displaystyle\int_a^r e^{\delta x}\,_{x-a}E_a\,dx}$$

$$= \frac{\displaystyle\int_a^r l_x\,\bar{a}_{x:\overline{r-x}|}\,dx}{\displaystyle\int_a^r l_x\,dx}$$

and $\lambda = 1/a$.

b. Substituting into (19.7.5) from (19.5.1)

$$(aC)(0) = \frac{\displaystyle\int_a^r e^{-\delta(r-x)}\,f\,w(r)\,l_r\,\bar{a}_r\,dx}{a}$$

$$= \frac{f\,w(r)\,l_r\,\bar{a}_r\,\bar{a}_{\overline{r-a}|}\displaystyle\int_a^r l_x\,dx}{\displaystyle\int_a^r l_x\,\bar{a}_{x:\overline{r-x}|}\,dx}.$$

▼

## 19.8
## Basic Functions for Retired Members

In this section we will discuss a number of basic functions defining several main concepts of pension funding as related to the retired group. A prefixed $r$ will be used in the notation to indicate the retired group.

## 19.8.1
## Actuarial Present Value of Future Benefits, $(rA)(t)$

The $l(x,\,t-x+a)\,dx$ members between ages $x$ and $x+dx$ at time $t$ retired $x-r$ years ago with pensions at an initial annual rate of $f\,w(r)\,g(t-x+r)$. For each unit of initial pension of a surviving retiree, there remains the actuarial present value

$$\bar{a}_x^h = \int_x^\infty e^{-\delta(y-x)}\,h(y)\,\frac{s(y)}{s(x)}\,dy \qquad y \geq r \tag{19.8.1}$$

where $s(y)$ is a single decrement survival function based only on mortality. Therefore,

$$(rA)(t) = \int_r^\infty l(x,\,t-x+a)\,f\,w(r)\,g(t-x+r)\,\bar{a}_x^h\,dx. \tag{19.8.2}$$

Since by (19.2.1) $l(x,\,t-x+a) = n(t-x+a)\,s(x)$, we can, on substituting from (19.8.1), write a double integral form for $(rA)(t)$; that is,

$$(rA)(t) = \int_r^\infty n(t - x + a)\, f\, w(r)\, g(t - x + r)\left[\int_x^\infty e^{-\delta(y-x)}\, h(y)\, s(y)\, dy\right] dx.$$

(19.8.3)

In line with our assumption that $M(x) = 1$ for $x \geq r$, there is no future normal cost in respect to the closed group of retirees at time $t$. Therefore, the actuarial accrued liability, $(rV)(t)$, for retired members equals the actuarial present value of their future pensions. That is,

$$(rV)(t) = (rA)(t).$$

(19.8.4)

This is in contrast to the situation for active members indicated in (19.5.19).

**19.8.2
Benefit Payment
Rate, $B(t)$**

For the retired members there is a new function to consider, $B(t)$, the rate of benefit outgo at time $t$. In developing (19.8.2) for the actuarial present value of future benefits for retired lives, we saw that pensions for retirees now between ages $x$ and $x + dx$ were paid at the initial rate of $l(x, t - x + a)\, f\, w(r)\, g(t - x + r)\, dx$. By age $x$, this rate has been adjusted by the factor $h(x)$. Hence

$$B(t) = \int_r^\infty l(x, t - x + a)\, f\, w(r)\, g(t - x + r)\, h(x)\, dx.$$

(19.8.5)

The alternative formulation, using (19.2.1), for $B(t)$ is

$$B(t) = \int_r^\infty n(t - x + a)\, g(t - x + r)\, f\, w(r)\, s(x)\, h(x)\, dx.$$

(19.8.6)

Differentiation of $B(t)$, as given in (19.8.6), leads to

$$\frac{d}{dt} B(t) = \int_r^\infty f\, w(r)\, s(x)\, h(x)\, \frac{\partial}{\partial t}\, [n(t - x + a)\, g(t - x + r)]\, dx$$

$$= -\int_r^\infty f\, w(r)\, s(x)\, h(x)\, \frac{\partial}{\partial x}\, [n(t - x + a)\, g(t - x + r)]\, dx$$

$$= -f\, w(r)\, s(x)\, h(x)\, n(t - x + a)\, g(t - x + r)\, \Big|_{x=r}^{x=\infty}$$

$$+ \int_r^\infty f\, w(r)\, n(t - x + a)\, g(t - x + r)\, [s'(x)\, h(x) + s(x)\, h'(x)]\, dx$$

$$= \left[ f\, w(r)\, l(r, t - r + a)\, g(t) \right.$$

$$\left. - \int_r^\infty f\, w(r)\, l(x, t - x + a)\, g(t - x + r)\, h(x)\, \mu_x\, dx \right]$$

$$+ \int_r^\infty f\, w(r)\, l(x, t - x + a)\, g(t - x + r)\, h'(x)\, dx.$$

(19.8.7)

The terms within the brackets on the right-hand side of (19.8.7) measure the **replacement effect.** The first term is the rate at which the initial pensions for the newly retired members is increasing the benefit payment rate. The second term is the rate at which the benefit payment rate is being reduced by deaths at time $t$. The term outside the brackets is known as the **adjustment effect.** It measures the amount by which the benefit payment rate is being adjusted at time $t$.

**19.8.3
The Allocation
Equation**

We are now in a position to state the formula for retired lives that is analogous to (19.5.10) for active lives,

$$^TP(t) + \delta(rV)(t) = B(t) + \frac{d}{dt}(rV)(t). \tag{19.8.8}$$

This equation can be argued from compound interest theory by considering $(rV)(t)$ as a fund into which terminal funding costs and interest are paid and from which pensions are paid. The difference between the total rate of income and the rate of outgo determines the rate of change of the size of the fund.

The verification of (19.8.8) can be accomplished by differentiating $(rA)(t) = (rV)(t)$, as given by (19.8.3). We have

$$\frac{d}{dt}(rV)(t)$$

$$= \int_r^\infty f\,w(r)\frac{\partial}{\partial t}[n(t-x+a)\,g(t-x+r)]\left[\int_x^\infty e^{-\delta(y-x)}s(y)h(y)\,dy\right]dx$$

$$= -f\,w(r)\int_r^\infty \left[\int_x^\infty e^{-\delta(y-x)}s(y)h(y)\,dy\right]\frac{\partial}{\partial x}[n(t-x+a)\,g(t-x+r)]dx$$

$$= -f\,w(r)\left\{n(t-x+a)\,g(t-x+r)\int_x^\infty e^{-\delta(y-x)}s(y)h(y)\,dy\,\bigg|_{x=r}^{x=\infty}\right.$$

$$\left.-\int_r^\infty\left[\delta\int_x^\infty e^{-\delta(y-x)}s(y)h(y)\,dy - s(x)h(x)\right]n(t-x+a)\,g(t-x+r)\,dx\right\}$$

$$= {}^TP(t) + \delta(rV)(t) - B(t)$$

where (19.8.6) is used to identify the $B(t)$ term.

**Example 19.8:**

Show that for the exponential case

a. $B(t+u) = e^{\rho u}B(t)$, $\rho = \tau + R$ \hfill (19.8.9)

b. $(rV)(t+u) = e^{\rho u}(rV)(t)$ \hfill (19.8.10)

c. $^TP(t) + \theta(rV)(t) = B(t)$, $\theta = \delta - \rho$ \hfill (19.8.11)

d. $^TP(t) < B(t)$ if $\theta > 0$

$^TP(t) = B(t)$ if $\theta = 0$ \hfill (19.8.12)

$^TP(t) > B(t)$ if $\theta < 0$.

**Solution:**

a. From (19.8.6)

$$B(t + u) = \int_r^\infty n\, e^{R(t+u-x+a)}\, e^{\tau(t+u-x+r)}\, f\, w(r)\, s(x)\, e^{\beta(x-r)}\, dx$$

$$= e^{(R+\tau)u} \int_r^\infty n\, e^{R(t-x+a)}\, e^{\tau(t-x+r)}\, f\, w(r)\, s(x)\, e^{\beta(x-r)}\, dx$$

$$= e^{\rho u}\, B(t).$$

b. Substituting into (19.8.2) and following the pattern of the so-lution of part (a) yields the result.

c. Rewriting (19.8.10) as

$$\frac{(rV)(t + u) - (rV)(t)}{u} = \frac{e^{\rho u} - 1}{u}\, (rV)(t)$$

and letting $u \to 0$, we obtain

$$\frac{d}{dt}\, (rV)(t) = \rho\, (rV)(t). \tag{19.8.13}$$

Then substituting (19.8.13) into (19.8.8) yields the result for part (c).

d. The inequalities follow from (19.8.11). Again we see the critical role played by $\theta = \delta - \tau - R$ in the exponential case. ▼

**Example 19.9:**

If the model plan is operating in a stationary population with fixed salaries and level pensions, develop and interpret the formula

$$(rV)(t) = f\, w(r)\, \frac{T_r - l_r\, \bar{a}_r}{\delta}. \tag{19.8.14}$$

**Solution:**
Here $h(x) = g(t) = 1$, $\theta = \delta$, $B(t) = f\, w(r)\, T_r$, $^TP(t) = f\, w(r)\, l_r\, \bar{a}_r$ and (19.8.14) follows by substituting into (19.8.11). To interpret this re-sult, we note that pensions of $f\, w(r)$ per year are payable contin-uously to all persons aged $r$ or older in the stationary population. This includes pensions for future new retirees who become eligible at the rate of $l_r$ per year. These future pension payments form a perpetuity with present value equal to $f\, w(r)\, l_r\, \bar{a}_r/\delta$. The difference in the present values of these two perpetuities is the present value of the future pensions to the closed group of participants now aged $r$ years or older, $(rV)(t)$. ▼

**19.9
Basic Functions
for Active and
Retired Members**

In Sections 19.5 and 19.8 we developed separate basic functions for active and retired members. This is a useful division for many pur-poses. The administrative system, the actuarial valuation problems and even the investment policy may be different for the two groups. However, for other purposes it is useful to consider basic functions for the combined group of active and retired members.

The basic actuarial functions for the combined group are the sums of those for the active members given in Section 19.5 and those for the retired members given in Section 19.8. These are summarized in Table 19.1.

**Table 19.1**
**Actuarial Functions for the Active, Retired, and Combined Member Groups of a Pension Plan**

| Function | Actives | Retireds | Combined |
|---|---|---|---|
| Actuarial Present Value at time $t$ of Future Pensions[1,2] | $(aA)(t)$ | $(rA)(t)$ | $A(t) = (aA)(t) + (rA)(t)$ |
| Normal Cost Rate[3] | $P(t)$ | $0$ | $P(t)$ |
| Actuarial Accrued Liability[4,5] | $(aV)(t)$ | $(rV)(t)$ | $V(t) = (aV)(t) + (rV)(t)$ |
| Actuarial Present Values of Future Normal Costs[6] | $(Pa)(t)$ | $0$ | $(Pa)(t)$ |

1. $(aA)(t)$ is given in (19.5.1).
2. $(rA)(t)$ is given in (19.8.2).
3. $P(t)$ is given in (19.5.4).
4. $(aV)(t)$ is given in (19.5.8).
5. $(rV)(t)$ is given in (19.8.4).
6. $(Pa)(t)$ is given in (19.5.17).

We can use the income allocation equations for active members (19.5.10) and for retired members (19.8.8) to obtain such an equation for the combined group. Thus,

$$\frac{d}{dt} V(t) = P(t) + \delta V(t) - B(t) \qquad (19.9.1)$$

or

$$P(t) + \delta V(t) = B(t) + \frac{d}{dt} V(t).$$

In this equation normal cost and interest income into the fund are allocated to pension benefit payments and change in the actuarial accrued liability.

To obtain formulas for the combined group under aggregate funding we will assume that pensions for retired members are fully funded so that $(rV)(t) = (rF)(t)$. Then (19.7.1) may be rewritten as the unfunded actuarial liability for all members as

$$U(t) = V(t) - F(t)$$
$$= (aV)(t) + (rV)(t) - (aF)(t) - (rF)(t)$$
$$= (aU)(t). \qquad (19.9.2)$$

Further, since no contribution is required for the retired members, the contribution rate $C(t)$ for all members equals $(aC)(t)$, the contribution rate for active members. In this case (19.7.3) may be rewritten as

$$C(t) = P(t) + \lambda(t) U(t). \qquad (19.9.3)$$

If $\lambda(t) = 1/a(t)$, the contribution rate becomes

$$C(t) = \frac{P(t)\,a(t) + V(t) - F(t)}{a(t)}$$

$$= \frac{A(t) - F(t)}{a(t)}. \tag{19.9.4}$$

Thus when $(rF)(t) = (rV)(t)$, the results of the aggregate cost method defined for active members at $t$ by (19.7.5) are equivalent to the results defined for all members by (19.9.4).

**19.10
Notes and
References**

Many of the rudiments of the theory of pension funding appeared in a government publication known as the Bulletin on 23P. Charles Trowbridge (1952, 1963) did much to create a mathematical theory of pension funding. The more elaborate model used in this chapter was developed for a series of papers by Bowers, Hickman and Nesbitt (1976, 1979). The stress on separate functions for active and retired lives is due to Kischuk (1976).

Several authors have studied the problems created for pension funding by inflationary influences on salaries, interest rates and benefits. Papers by Allison and Winklevoss (1975) and Myers (1960) are in this class. John Trowbridge (1977) provides many observations on changes in pension funding in different nations in response to inflation.

**Exercises**

*Section 19.2*

19.1. In a stationary population with level salaries at rate $w$, what is the payroll function $W(t)$?

*Section 19.3*

19.2. In the exponential case, what is the payroll function $W(t)$?

19.3. Assume that the initial annual rate of retirement income for a life retiring at time $t$ is given by

$$\frac{f}{b} \int_{t-b}^{t} w(r - t + y)\,g(y)\,dy \qquad 0 < b < r - a.$$

Other aspects of the model plan remain unchanged. For this benefit definition, based on a final average formula,
a. show that the initial benefit rate at time $t$ is given by

$$\frac{f}{b} \int_{0}^{b} w(r - z)\,g(t - z)\,dz$$

b. display a formula for the terminal funding cost rate at time $t$
c. rework Example 19.1.

19.4. The initial annual rate of retirement income for a life retiring at time $t$ is given by $c(r - a)\,w\,e^{\tau t}$. Other aspects of the model plan remain unchanged. For this initial benefit rate, based on the product of years of service and final salary level,

a. display a formula for the terminal funding cost rate at time $t$

b. rework Example 19.1.

19.5. If $s(x) = e^{-\mu(x-a)}, a \leq x \leq r$, display $^T P(t)$ in the exponential case.

*Section 19.4*

19.6. What is $M(x)$ in the case of terminal funding?

*Section 19.5*

19.7. Using the assumptions of Exercise 19.5 with $m(x) = 1/(r-a)$, determine $P(t)$.

19.8. a. Show that

$$(aA)(t) = \int_t^{t+r-a} e^{-\delta(y-t)}\, {}^T P(y)\, dy.$$

b. Differentiate the expression in part (a) to obtain an alternative solution to Example 19.3.

19.9. If

$$e^{\theta X(\theta)} = \int_a^r e^{\theta x}\, m(x)\, dx$$

and

$$\mu = \int_a^r x\, m(x)\, dx,$$

show that

a. $X(\theta) > \mu$ if $\theta > 0$

b. $X(\theta) < \mu$ if $\theta < 0$.

[Hint: Use Jensen's inequality (1.3.2).]

19.10. In the exponential case, show that

a. $P(t) = {}^T P(t)\, \exp\{-\theta[r - X(\theta)]\}$

b. $(aV)(t) = {}^T P(t)\, \bar{a}_{\overline{r-X(\theta)}|\theta} = P(t)\, \bar{s}_{\overline{r-X(\theta)}|\theta}$.

19.11. a. What do the formulas in Exercise 19.10 become if the model plan operates in a stationary population with $g(t) = 1$?

b. What do the formulas in Exercise 19.10 become if $\theta = \delta - \rho = 0$?

19.12. a. Derive a normal cost rate $\pi(u)$ to be applied to all salaries of those who enter at time $u$. Other aspects of the model plan are unchanged.

b. Using the result in (a), display the corresponding function $m(x,u)$.

19.13. a. For the model plan show that

$$P(t) = f\, w(r)\, s(r)\, \bar{a}_r^h \int_a^r e^{-\delta(r-x)}\, g(t + r - x)\, n(t - x + a)\, m(x)\, dx.$$

b. If $g(t) = 1$, $n(t) = l_a$, show that

$$P(t) = f\,w(r)\int_a^r l_{x\,r-x}E_x\,\bar{a}_r^h\,m(x)\,dx$$

where $_{r-x}E_x$ is based on the survival function $s(x)$ and force of interest $\delta$.

19.14. If $g(t) = e^{\tau t}$, $n(t) = l_a$ and

$$m(x) = \frac{w(x)\,e^{\tau x}}{\displaystyle\int_a^r w(y)\,e^{\tau y}\,dy},$$

show that

$$P(t+u) = e^{\tau u}\,P(t).$$

*Section 19.6*

19.15. Assume the projected initial benefit rate at retirement for a life aged $x$ at time $t$ is $f\,w(r)\,g(t+r-x)$ and the number of lives age $x$ to $x+dx$ at time $t$ is $n(t-x+a)\,s(x)\,dx$.

a. Verify that $(aA)(t)$ as given by (19.5.1) is equal to

$$\int_a^r f\,w(r)\,g(t+r-x)\,n(t-x+a)\,s(x)\,(aA)(x)\,dx.$$

b. Verify that $P(t)$ as given by (19.5.4) is equal to

$$\int_a^r f\,w(r)\,g(t+r-x)\,n(t-x+a)\,s(x)\,P(x)\,dx.$$

c. Verify that $(aV)(t)$ as given by (19.5.8) is equal to

$$\int_a^r f\,w(r)\,g(t+r-x)\,n(t-x+a)\,s(x)\,(aV)(x)\,dx.$$

d. Verify that $(Pa)(t)$ as given by (19.5.17) is equal to

$$\int_a^r f\,w(r)\,g(t+r-x)\,n(t-x+a)\,s(x)\,(Pa)(x)\,dx.$$

19.16. Verify formula (19.6.11).

*Section 19.7*

19.17. Verify that

a. $$-\int_0^t \frac{1}{\bar{s}_{\overline{n-y}|}}\,dy = \log\frac{\bar{s}_{\overline{n}|} - \bar{s}_{\overline{t}|}}{\bar{s}_{\overline{n}|}}$$

b. $$-\int_0^t \frac{1}{\bar{a}_{\overline{n-y}|}}\,dy = \log\frac{\bar{a}_{\overline{n}|} - \bar{a}_{\overline{t}|}}{\bar{a}_{\overline{n}|}}.$$

19.18. a. Obtain a simplified formula for $a(t)$ in the exponential case.

b. What does $a(t)$ become in the exponential case if $\theta = \delta - \rho = 0$?

*Section 19.8*

19.19. In the exponential case, show that $B(t) = {}^TP(t)\,(\bar{a}\,'^h_r / \bar{a}^h_r)$ where

$$\bar{a}\,'^h_r = \int_r^\infty e^{-(\rho - \beta)(x - r)}\,\frac{s(x)}{s(r)}\,dx.$$

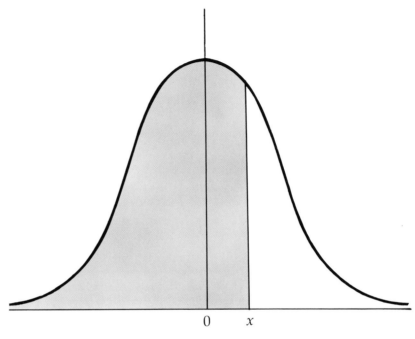

Normal Distribution

The table below gives the value of $\Phi(x) = \dfrac{1}{\sqrt{2\pi}} \displaystyle\int_{-\infty}^{x} e^{-w^2/2}\, dw$ for certain values of $x$. The integer of $x$ is given in the left column, and the first decimal place of $x$ is given in the top row. Since the density function of $x$ is symmetric, the value of the cumulative distribution function for negative $x$ can be obtained by subtracting from unity the value of the cumulative distribution function for $x$.

| $x$ | 0.0 | 0.1 | 0.2 | 0.3 | 0.4 | 0.5 | 0.6 | 0.7 | 0.8 | 0.9 |
|---|---|---|---|---|---|---|---|---|---|---|
| 0 | 0.5000 | 0.5398 | 0.5793 | 0.6179 | 0.6554 | 0.6915 | 0.7257 | 0.7580 | 0.7881 | 0.8159 |
| 1 | 0.8413 | 0.8643 | 0.8849 | 0.9032 | 0.9192 | 0.9332 | 0.9452 | 0.9554 | 0.9641 | 0.9713 |
| 2 | 0.9772 | 0.9821 | 0.9861 | 0.9893 | 0.9918 | 0.9938 | 0.9953 | 0.9965 | 0.9974 | 0.9981 |
| 3 | 0.9987 | 0.9990 | 0.9993 | 0.9995 | 0.9997 | 0.9998 | 0.9998 | 0.9999 | 0.9999 | 1.0000 |

## Selected Points of the Normal Distribution

| $\Phi(x)$ | 0.800 | 0.850 | 0.900 | 0.950 | 0.975 | 0.990 | 0.995 |
|---|---|---|---|---|---|---|---|
| $x$ | 0.842 | 1.036 | 1.282 | 1.645 | 1.960 | 2.326 | 2.576 |

**Illustrative Life Table: Basic Functions**

| Age | $l_x$ | $d_x$ | $1000\,q_x$ |
|-----|-------|-------|-------------|
| 0 | 100 000.00 | 2 042.1700 | 20.4217 |
| 1 | 97 957.83 | 131.5672 | 1.3431 |
| 2 | 97 826.26 | 119.7100 | 1.2237 |
| 3 | 97 706.55 | 109.8124 | 1.1239 |
| 4 | 97 596.74 | 101.7056 | 1.0421 |
| 5 | 97 495.03 | 95.2526 | 0.9770 |
| 6 | 97 399.78 | 90.2799 | 0.9269 |
| 7 | 97 309.50 | 86.6444 | 0.8904 |
| 8 | 97 222.86 | 84.1950 | 0.8660 |
| 9 | 97 138.66 | 82.7816 | 0.8522 |
| 10 | 97 055.88 | 82.2549 | 0.8475 |
| 11 | 96 973.63 | 82.4664 | 0.8504 |
| 12 | 96 891.16 | 83.2842 | 0.8594 |
| 13 | 96 807.88 | 84.5180 | 0.8730 |
| 14 | 96 723.36 | 86.0611 | 0.8898 |
| 15 | 96 637.30 | 87.7559 | 0.9081 |
| 16 | 96 549.54 | 89.6167 | 0.9282 |
| 17 | 96 459.92 | 91.6592 | 0.9502 |
| 18 | 96 368.27 | 93.9005 | 0.9744 |
| 19 | 96 274.36 | 96.3596 | 1.0009 |
| 20 | 96 178.01 | 99.0569 | 1.0299 |
| 21 | 96 078.95 | 102.0149 | 1.0618 |
| 22 | 95 976.93 | 105.2582 | 1.0967 |
| 23 | 95 871.68 | 108.8135 | 1.1350 |
| 24 | 95 762.86 | 112.7102 | 1.1770 |
| 25 | 95 650.15 | 116.9802 | 1.2330 |
| 26 | 95 533.17 | 121.6585 | 1.2735 |
| 27 | 95 411.51 | 126.7830 | 1.3288 |
| 28 | 95 284.73 | 132.3953 | 1.3895 |
| 29 | 95 152.33 | 138.5406 | 1.4560 |
| 30 | 95 013.79 | 145.2682 | 1.5289 |
| 31 | 94 868.53 | 152.6317 | 1.6089 |
| 32 | 94 715.89 | 160.6896 | 1.6965 |
| 33 | 94 555.20 | 169.5052 | 1.7927 |
| 34 | 94 385.70 | 179.1475 | 1.8980 |
| 35 | 94 206.55 | 189.6914 | 2.0136 |
| 36 | 94 016.86 | 201.2179 | 2.1402 |
| 37 | 93 815.64 | 213.8149 | 2.2791 |
| 38 | 93 601.83 | 227.5775 | 2.4313 |
| 39 | 93 374.25 | 242.6085 | 2.5982 |
| 40 | 93 131.64 | 259.0186 | 2.7812 |
| 41 | 92 872.62 | 276.9271 | 2.9818 |
| 42 | 92 595.70 | 296.4623 | 3.2017 |
| 43 | 92 299.23 | 317.7619 | 3.4427 |
| 44 | 91 981.47 | 340.9730 | 3.7070 |
| 45 | 91 640.50 | 366.2529 | 3.9966 |
| 46 | 91 274.25 | 393.7687 | 4.3141 |
| 47 | 90 880.48 | 423.6978 | 4.6621 |
| 48 | 90 456.78 | 456.2274 | 5.0436 |
| 49 | 90 000.55 | 491.5543 | 5.4617 |
| 50 | 89 509.00 | 529.8844 | 5.9199 |
| 51 | 88 979.11 | 571.4316 | 6.4221 |
| 52 | 88 407.68 | 616.4165 | 6.9724 |
| 53 | 87 791.26 | 665.0646 | 7.5755 |
| 54 | 87 126.20 | 717.6041 | 8.2364 |
| 55 | 86 408.60 | 774.2626 | 8.9605 |

| Age | $l_x$ | $d_x$ | $1000\,q_x$ |
|---|---|---|---|
| 56 | 85 634.33 | 835.2636 | 9.7538 |
| 57 | 84 799.07 | 900.8215 | 10.6230 |
| 58 | 83 898.25 | 971.1358 | 11.5752 |
| 59 | 82 927.11 | 1 046.3843 | 12.6181 |
| 60 | 81 880.73 | 1 126.7146 | 13.7604 |
| 61 | 80 754.01 | 1 212.2343 | 15.0114 |
| 62 | 79 541.78 | 1 302.9994 | 16.3813 |
| 63 | 78 238.78 | 1 399.0010 | 17.8812 |
| 64 | 76 839.78 | 1 500.1504 | 19.5231 |
| 65 | 75 339.63 | 1 606.2618 | 21.3203 |
| 66 | 73 733.37 | 1 717.0334 | 23.2871 |
| 67 | 72 016.33 | 1 832.0273 | 25.4391 |
| 68 | 70 184.31 | 1 950.6476 | 27.7932 |
| 69 | 68 233.66 | 2 072.1177 | 30.3680 |
| 70 | 66 161.54 | 2 195.4578 | 33.1833 |
| 71 | 63 966.08 | 2 319.4639 | 36.2608 |
| 72 | 61 646.62 | 2 442.6884 | 39.6240 |
| 73 | 59 203.93 | 2 563.4258 | 43.2982 |
| 74 | 56 640.51 | 2 679.7050 | 47.3108 |
| 75 | 53 960.80 | 2 789.2905 | 51.6911 |
| 76 | 51 171.51 | 2 889.6965 | 56.4708 |
| 77 | 48 281.81 | 2 978.2164 | 61.6840 |
| 78 | 45 303.60 | 3 051.9717 | 67.3671 |
| 79 | 42 251.62 | 3 107.9833 | 73.5589 |
| 80 | 39 143.64 | 3 143.2679 | 80.3009 |
| 81 | 36 000.37 | 3 154.9603 | 87.6369 |
| 82 | 32 845.41 | 3 140.4624 | 95.6134 |
| 83 | 29 704.95 | 3 097.6146 | 104.2794 |
| 84 | 26 607.34 | 3 024.8830 | 113.6860 |
| 85 | 23 582.45 | 2 921.5530 | 123.8867 |
| 86 | 20 660.90 | 2 787.9129 | 134.9367 |
| 87 | 17 872.99 | 2 625.4088 | 146.8926 |
| 88 | 15 247.58 | 2 436.7474 | 159.8121 |
| 89 | 12 810.83 | 2 225.9244 | 173.7533 |
| 90 | 10 584.91 | 1 998.1533 | 188.7738 |
| 91 | 8 586.75 | 1 759.6818 | 204.9298 |
| 92 | 6 827.07 | 1 517.4869 | 222.2749 |
| 93 | 5 309.58 | 1 278.8606 | 240.8589 |
| 94 | 4 030.72 | 1 050.9136 | 260.7257 |
| 95 | 2 979.81 | 840.0452 | 281.9122 |
| 96 | 2 139.77 | 651.4422 | 304.4456 |
| 97 | 1 488.32 | 488.6776 | 328.3410 |
| 98 | 999.65 | 353.4741 | 353.5993 |
| 99 | 646.17 | 245.6772 | 380.2041 |
| 100 | 400.49 | 163.4494 | 408.1188 |
| 101 | 237.05 | 103.6560 | 437.2837 |
| 102 | 133.39 | 62.3746 | 467.6133 |
| 103 | 71.01 | 35.4358 | 498.9935 |
| 104 | 35.58 | 18.9023 | 531.2793 |
| 105 | 16.68 | 9.4105 | 564.2937 |
| 106 | 7.27 | 4.3438 | 597.8266 |
| 107 | 2.92 | 1.8458 | 631.6360 |
| 108 | 1.08 | 0.7163 | 665.4495 |
| 109 | 0.36 | 0.2517 | 698.9685 |
| 110 | 0.11 | 0.0793 | 731.8742 |

**Illustrative Life Table: Commutation Functions, $D_x$, $N_x$, $S_x$, $i = 0.06$**

| Age | $D_x$ | $N_x$ | $S_x$ |
|---|---|---|---|
| 0 | 100 000.00 | 1 680 095.45 | 27 526 802.72 |
| 1 | 92 413.05 | 1 580 095.45 | 25 846 707.27 |
| 2 | 87 065.03 | 1 487 682.41 | 24 266 611.82 |
| 3 | 82 036.31 | 1 400 617.38 | 22 778 929.41 |
| 4 | 77 305.76 | 1 318 581.07 | 21 378 312.03 |
| 5 | 72 853.96 | 1 241 275.31 | 20 059 730.96 |
| 6 | 68 663.00 | 1 168 421.35 | 18 818 455.64 |
| 7 | 64 716.38 | 1 099 758.35 | 17 650 034.29 |
| 8 | 60 998.82 | 1 035 041.97 | 16 550 275.94 |
| 9 | 57 496.23 | 974 043.15 | 15 515 233.97 |
| 10 | 54 195.50 | 916 546.92 | 14 541 190.82 |
| 11 | 51 084.50 | 862 351.43 | 13 624 643.89 |
| 12 | 48 151.94 | 811 266.93 | 12 762 292.47 |
| 13 | 45 387.31 | 763 114.99 | 11 951 025.54 |
| 14 | 42 780.83 | 717 727.68 | 11 187 910.54 |
| 15 | 40 323.37 | 674 946.85 | 10 470 182.86 |
| 16 | 38 006.37 | 634 623.48 | 9 795 236.01 |
| 17 | 35 821.78 | 596 617.11 | 9 160 612.54 |
| 18 | 33 762.02 | 560 795.33 | 8 563 995.42 |
| 19 | 31 819.93 | 527 033.30 | 8 003 200.10 |
| 20 | 29 988.76 | 495 213.37 | 7 476 166.79 |
| 21 | 28 262.14 | 465 224.62 | 6 980 953.42 |
| 22 | 26 634.09 | 436 962.48 | 6 515 728.80 |
| 23 | 25 098.94 | 410 328.39 | 6 078 766.32 |
| 24 | 23 651.37 | 385 229.45 | 5 668 437.93 |
| 25 | 22 286.35 | 361 578.07 | 5 283 208.49 |
| 26 | 20 999.15 | 339 291.72 | 4 921 630.41 |
| 27 | 19 785.29 | 318 292.57 | 4 582 338.70 |
| 28 | 18 640.57 | 298 507.28 | 4 264 046.13 |
| 29 | 17 561.00 | 279 866.71 | 3 965 538.85 |
| 30 | 16 542.86 | 262 305.71 | 3 685 672.13 |
| 31 | 15 582.61 | 245 762.85 | 3 423 366.42 |
| 32 | 14 676.93 | 230 180.23 | 3 177 603.57 |
| 33 | 13 822.67 | 215 503.30 | 2 947 423.34 |
| 34 | 13 016.88 | 201 680.64 | 2 731 920.04 |
| 35 | 12 256.76 | 188 663.76 | 2 530 239.40 |
| 36 | 11 539.70 | 176 406.99 | 2 341 575.65 |
| 37 | 10 863.21 | 164 867.29 | 2 165 168.65 |
| 38 | 10 224.96 | 154 004.08 | 2 000 301.36 |
| 39 | 9 622.73 | 143 779.13 | 1 846 297.28 |
| 40 | 9 054.46 | 134 156.39 | 1 702 518.15 |
| 41 | 8 518.19 | 125 101.93 | 1 568 361.76 |
| 42 | 8 012.06 | 116 583.74 | 1 443 259.83 |
| 43 | 7 534.35 | 108 571.68 | 1 326 676.08 |
| 44 | 7 083.41 | 101 037.33 | 1 218 104.41 |
| 45 | 6 657.69 | 93 953.92 | 1 117 067.08 |
| 46 | 6 255.74 | 87 296.23 | 1 023 113.16 |
| 47 | 5 876.18 | 81 040.49 | 935 816.93 |
| 48 | 5 517.72 | 75 164.31 | 854 776.44 |
| 49 | 5 179.14 | 69 646.60 | 779 612.12 |
| 50 | 4 859.30 | 64 467.45 | 709 965.53 |
| 51 | 4 557.10 | 59 608.16 | 645 498.07 |
| 52 | 4 271.55 | 55 051.05 | 585 889.92 |
| 53 | 4 001.66 | 50 779.51 | 530 838.86 |
| 54 | 3 746.55 | 46 777.85 | 480 059.36 |
| 55 | 3 505.37 | 43 031.29 | 433 281.51 |

| Age | $D_x$ | $N_x$ | $S_x$ |
|---|---|---|---|
| 56 | 3 277.32 | 39 525.92 | 390 250.22 |
| 57 | 3 061.66 | 36 248.59 | 350 724.30 |
| 58 | 2 857.67 | 33 186.93 | 314 475.71 |
| 59 | 2 664.71 | 30 329.26 | 281 288.77 |
| 60 | 2 482.16 | 27 664.55 | 250 959.22 |
| 61 | 2 309.44 | 25 182.39 | 223 294.97 |
| 62 | 2 146.01 | 22 872.95 | 198 112.58 |
| 63 | 1 991.37 | 20 726.94 | 175 239.63 |
| 64 | 1 845.06 | 18 735.57 | 154 512.70 |
| 65 | 1 706.64 | 16 890.50 | 135 777.13 |
| 66 | 1 575.71 | 15 183.86 | 118 886.62 |
| 67 | 1 451.90 | 13 608.15 | 103 702.76 |
| 68 | 1 334.88 | 12 156.25 | 90 094.61 |
| 69 | 1 224.32 | 10 821.37 | 77 938.36 |
| 70 | 1 119.94 | 9 597.05 | 67 116.99 |
| 71 | 1 021.49 | 8 477.11 | 57 519.94 |
| 72 | 928.72 | 7 455.62 | 49 042.83 |
| 73 | 841.44 | 6 526.90 | 41 587.20 |
| 74 | 759.44 | 5 685.46 | 35 060.31 |
| 75 | 682.56 | 4 926.02 | 29 374.84 |
| 76 | 610.64 | 4 243.47 | 24 448.82 |
| 77 | 543.54 | 3 632.83 | 20 205.36 |
| 78 | 481.14 | 3 089.29 | 16 572.53 |
| 79 | 423.33 | 2 608.14 | 13 483.24 |
| 80 | 369.99 | 2 184.81 | 10 875.10 |
| 81 | 321.02 | 1 814.82 | 8 690.28 |
| 82 | 276.31 | 1 493.80 | 6 875.46 |
| 83 | 235.74 | 1 217.49 | 5 381.66 |
| 84 | 199.21 | 981.75 | 4 164.17 |
| 85 | 166.57 | 782.54 | 3 182.42 |
| 86 | 137.67 | 615.97 | 2 399.88 |
| 87 | 112.35 | 478.30 | 1 783.90 |
| 88 | 90.42 | 365.95 | 1 305.60 |
| 89 | 71.67 | 275.52 | 939.66 |
| 90 | 55.87 | 203.85 | 664.13 |
| 91 | 42.76 | 147.98 | 460.28 |
| 92 | 32.07 | 105.23 | 312.30 |
| 93 | 23.53 | 73.16 | 207.08 |
| 94 | 16.85 | 49.63 | 133.92 |
| 95 | 11.75 | 32.78 | 84.29 |
| 96 | 7.96 | 21.02 | 51.52 |
| 97 | 5.22 | 13.06 | 30.49 |
| 98 | 3.31 | 7.84 | 17.43 |
| 99 | 2.02 | 4.53 | 9.59 |
| 100 | 1.18 | 2.51 | 5.07 |
| 101 | 0.66 | 1.33 | 2.56 |
| 102 | 0.35 | 0.67 | 1.23 |
| 103 | 0.18 | 0.32 | 0.56 |
| 104 | 0.08 | 0.14 | 0.24 |
| 105 | 0.04 | 0.06 | 0.10 |
| 106 | 0.02 | 0.02 | 0.04 |
| 107 | 0.01 | 0.01 | 0.01 |
| 108 | 0.00 | 0.00 | 0.00 |
| 109 | 0.00 | 0.00 | 0.00 |
| 110 | 0.00 | 0.00 | 0.00 |

**Illustrative Life Table: Commutation Functions,** $C_x$, $M_x$, $R_x$, $i = 0.06$

| Age | $C_x$ | $M_x$ | $R_x$ |
|---|---|---|---|
| 0 | 1 926.5755 | 4 900.2574 | 121 974.5442 |
| 1 | 117.0943 | 2 973.6819 | 117 074.2868 |
| 2 | 100.5108 | 2 856.5876 | 114 100.6049 |
| 3 | 86.9817 | 2 756.0768 | 111 244.0173 |
| 4 | 76.0003 | 2 669.0951 | 108 487.9406 |
| 5 | 67.1494 | 2 593.0948 | 105 818.8455 |
| 6 | 60.0413 | 2 525.9454 | 103 225.7507 |
| 7 | 54.3618 | 2 465.9041 | 100 699.8053 |
| 8 | 49.8349 | 2 411.5424 | 98 233.9012 |
| 9 | 46.2248 | 2 361.7075 | 95 822.3588 |
| 10 | 43.3308 | 2 315.4827 | 93 460.6513 |
| 11 | 40.9833 | 2 272.1519 | 91 145.1686 |
| 12 | 39.0469 | 2 231.1686 | 88 873.0168 |
| 13 | 37.3824 | 2 192.1217 | 86 641.8482 |
| 14 | 35.9013 | 2 154.7393 | 84 449.7264 |
| 15 | 34.5448 | 2 118.8290 | 82 294.9871 |
| 16 | 33.2804 | 2 084.2842 | 80 176.1581 |
| 17 | 32.1122 | 2 051.0038 | 78 091.8738 |
| 18 | 31.0353 | 2 018.8916 | 76 040.8700 |
| 19 | 30.0454 | 1 987.8562 | 74 021.9784 |
| 20 | 29.1381 | 1 957.8109 | 72 034.1222 |
| 21 | 28.3097 | 1 928.6728 | 70 076.3113 |
| 22 | 27.5563 | 1 900.3631 | 68 147.6386 |
| 23 | 26.8746 | 1 872.8068 | 66 247.2755 |
| 24 | 26.2613 | 1 845.9322 | 64 374.4687 |
| 25 | 25.7134 | 1 819.6709 | 62 528.5365 |
| 26 | 25.2281 | 1 793.9575 | 60 708.8656 |
| 27 | 24.8026 | 1 768.7294 | 58 914.9081 |
| 28 | 24.4344 | 1 743.9268 | 57 146.1787 |
| 29 | 24.1213 | 1 719.4924 | 55 402.2519 |
| 30 | 23.8610 | 1 695.3711 | 53 682.7595 |
| 31 | 23.6514 | 1 671.5101 | 51 987.3885 |
| 32 | 23.4906 | 1 647.8586 | 50 315.8784 |
| 33 | 23.3767 | 1 624.3680 | 48 668.0198 |
| 34 | 23.3080 | 1 600.9913 | 47 043.6517 |
| 35 | 23.2829 | 1 577.6833 | 45 442.6604 |
| 36 | 23.2997 | 1 554.4004 | 43 864.9771 |
| 37 | 23.3569 | 1 531.1008 | 42 310.5767 |
| 38 | 23.4531 | 1 507.7439 | 40 779.4760 |
| 39 | 23.5869 | 1 484.2907 | 39 271.7321 |
| 40 | 23.7569 | 1 460.7038 | 37 787.4414 |
| 41 | 23.9618 | 1 436.9469 | 36 326.7375 |
| 42 | 24.2001 | 1 412.9851 | 34 889.7907 |
| 43 | 24.4705 | 1 388.7850 | 33 476.8056 |
| 44 | 24.7717 | 1 364.3144 | 32 088.0206 |
| 45 | 25.1022 | 1 339.5427 | 30 723.7061 |
| 46 | 25.4604 | 1 314.4406 | 29 384.1634 |
| 47 | 25.8449 | 1 288.9801 | 28 069.7229 |
| 48 | 26.2539 | 1 263.1352 | 26 780.7427 |
| 49 | 26.6857 | 1 236.8813 | 25 517.6075 |
| 50 | 27.1383 | 1 210.1957 | 24 280.7261 |
| 51 | 27.6095 | 1 183.0574 | 23 070.5305 |
| 52 | 28.0972 | 1 155.4478 | 21 887.4731 |
| 53 | 28.5988 | 1 127.3506 | 20 732.0252 |
| 54 | 29.1113 | 1 098.7519 | 19 604.6746 |
| 55 | 29.6319 | 1 069.6405 | 18 505.9227 |

| Age | $C_x$ | $M_x$ | $R_x$ |
|-----|-------|-------|-------|
| 56 | 30.1571 | 1 040.0086 | 17 436.2822 |
| 57 | 30.6831 | 1 009.8515 | 16 396.2736 |
| 58 | 31.2057 | 979.1685 | 15 386.4221 |
| 59 | 31.7204 | 947.9628 | 14 407.2536 |
| 60 | 32.2223 | 916.2423 | 13 459.2908 |
| 61 | 32.7057 | 884.0201 | 12 543.0485 |
| 62 | 33.1646 | 851.3144 | 11 659.0284 |
| 63 | 33.5925 | 818.1498 | 10 807.7140 |
| 64 | 33.9824 | 784.5573 | 9 989.5642 |
| 65 | 34.3265 | 750.5749 | 9 205.0070 |
| 66 | 34.6167 | 716.2484 | 8 454.4320 |
| 67 | 34.8444 | 681.6317 | 7 738.1836 |
| 68 | 35.0005 | 646.7873 | 7 056.5519 |
| 69 | 35.0755 | 611.7868 | 6 409.7645 |
| 70 | 35.0597 | 576.7113 | 5 797.9777 |
| 71 | 34.9434 | 541.6516 | 5 221.2663 |
| 72 | 34.7168 | 506.7082 | 4 679.6147 |
| 73 | 34.3706 | 471.9914 | 4 172.9066 |
| 74 | 33.8959 | 437.6208 | 3 700.9152 |
| 75 | 33.2850 | 403.7249 | 3 263.2944 |
| 76 | 32.5312 | 370.4400 | 2 859.5695 |
| 77 | 31.6300 | 337.9087 | 2 489.1295 |
| 78 | 30.5786 | 306.2787 | 2 151.2208 |
| 79 | 29.3771 | 275.7002 | 1 844.9421 |
| 80 | 28.0289 | 246.3230 | 1 569.2419 |
| 81 | 26.5407 | 218.2941 | 1 322.9189 |
| 82 | 24.9234 | 191.7534 | 1 104.6247 |
| 83 | 23.1918 | 166.8300 | 912.8714 |
| 84 | 21.3654 | 143.6382 | 746.0413 |
| 85 | 19.4675 | 122.2729 | 602.4031 |
| 86 | 17.5254 | 102.8054 | 480.1303 |
| 87 | 15.5697 | 85.2799 | 377.3249 |
| 88 | 13.6329 | 69.7102 | 292.0449 |
| 89 | 11.7485 | 56.0773 | 222.3347 |
| 90 | 9.9494 | 44.3288 | 166.2574 |
| 91 | 8.2660 | 34.3795 | 121.9286 |
| 92 | 6.7248 | 26.1135 | 87.5491 |
| 93 | 5.3465 | 19.3887 | 61.4356 |
| 94 | 4.1449 | 14.0421 | 42.0470 |
| 95 | 3.1256 | 9.8973 | 28.0048 |
| 96 | 2.2867 | 6.7716 | 18.1075 |
| 97 | 1.6183 | 4.4850 | 11.3359 |
| 98 | 1.1043 | 2.8667 | 6.8509 |
| 99 | 0.7241 | 1.7624 | 3.9842 |
| 100 | 0.4545 | 1.0384 | 2.2218 |
| 101 | 0.2719 | 0.5839 | 1.1834 |
| 102 | 0.1543 | 0.3120 | 0.5995 |
| 103 | 0.0827 | 0.1577 | 0.2875 |
| 104 | 0.0416 | 0.0749 | 0.1299 |
| 105 | 0.0196 | 0.0333 | 0.0549 |
| 106 | 0.0085 | 0.0138 | 0.0216 |
| 107 | 0.0034 | 0.0052 | 0.0079 |
| 108 | 0.0012 | 0.0018 | 0.0026 |
| 109 | 0.0004 | 0.0006 | 0.0008 |
| 110 | 0.0001 | 0.0002 | 0.0002 |

**Illustrative Life Table:**
**Net Single Premiums,**
$i = 0.06$

| Age | $\ddot{a}_x$ | $1000\,A_x$ | $1000\,(^2A_x)$ |
|---|---|---|---|
| 0 | 16.80096 | 49.0025 | 25.9210 |
| 1 | 17.09819 | 32.1781 | 8.8845 |
| 2 | 17.08703 | 32.8097 | 8.6512 |
| 3 | 17.07314 | 33.5957 | 8.5072 |
| 4 | 17.05670 | 34.5264 | 8.4443 |
| 5 | 17.03786 | 35.5930 | 8.4547 |
| 6 | 17.01675 | 36.7875 | 8.5310 |
| 7 | 16.99351 | 38.1031 | 8.6666 |
| 8 | 16.96823 | 39.5341 | 8.8553 |
| 9 | 16.94100 | 41.0757 | 9.0917 |
| 10 | 16.91187 | 42.7245 | 9.3712 |
| 11 | 16.88089 | 44.4782 | 9.6902 |
| 12 | 16.84807 | 46.3359 | 10.0460 |
| 13 | 16.81340 | 48.2981 | 10.4373 |
| 14 | 16.77685 | 50.3669 | 10.8638 |
| 15 | 16.73836 | 52.5459 | 11.3268 |
| 16 | 16.69782 | 54.8404 | 11.8295 |
| 17 | 16.65515 | 57.2558 | 12.3749 |
| 18 | 16.61024 | 59.7977 | 12.9665 |
| 19 | 16.56299 | 62.4720 | 13.6080 |
| 20 | 16.51330 | 65.2848 | 14.3034 |
| 21 | 16.46105 | 68.2423 | 15.0569 |
| 22 | 16.40614 | 71.3508 | 15.8730 |
| 23 | 16.34843 | 74.6170 | 16.7566 |
| 24 | 16.28783 | 78.0476 | 17.7128 |
| 25 | 16.22419 | 81.6496 | 18.7472 |
| 26 | 16.15740 | 85.4300 | 19.8657 |
| 27 | 16.08733 | 89.3962 | 21.0744 |
| 28 | 16.01385 | 93.5555 | 22.3802 |
| 29 | 15.93683 | 97.9154 | 23.7900 |
| 30 | 15.85612 | 102.4835 | 25.3113 |
| 31 | 15.77161 | 107.2676 | 26.9520 |
| 32 | 15.68313 | 112.2754 | 28.7206 |
| 33 | 15.59057 | 117.5148 | 30.6259 |
| 34 | 15.49378 | 122.9935 | 32.6772 |
| 35 | 15.39262 | 128.7194 | 34.8843 |
| 36 | 15.28696 | 134.7002 | 37.2574 |
| 37 | 15.17666 | 140.9437 | 39.8074 |
| 38 | 15.06159 | 147.4572 | 42.5455 |
| 39 | 14.94161 | 154.2484 | 45.4833 |
| 40 | 14.81661 | 161.3242 | 48.6332 |
| 41 | 14.68645 | 168.6916 | 52.0077 |
| 42 | 14.55102 | 176.3572 | 55.6199 |
| 43 | 14.41022 | 184.3271 | 59.4833 |
| 44 | 14.26394 | 192.6071 | 63.6117 |
| 45 | 14.11209 | 201.2024 | 68.0193 |
| 46 | 13.95459 | 210.1176 | 72.7205 |
| 47 | 13.79136 | 219.3569 | 77.7299 |
| 48 | 13.62235 | 228.9234 | 83.0624 |
| 49 | 13.44752 | 238.8198 | 88.7329 |
| 50 | 13.26683 | 249.0475 | 94.7561 |
| 51 | 13.08027 | 259.6073 | 101.1469 |
| 52 | 12.88785 | 270.4988 | 107.9196 |
| 53 | 12.68960 | 281.7206 | 115.0885 |
| 54 | 12.48556 | 293.2700 | 122.6672 |
| 55 | 12.27581 | 305.1431 | 130.6687 |

| Age | $\ddot{a}_x$ | $1000\,A_x$ | $1000\,(^2A_x)$ |
|-----|--------------|-------------|------------------|
| 56 | 12.06042 | 317.3346 | 139.1053 |
| 57 | 11.83953 | 329.8381 | 147.9883 |
| 58 | 11.61327 | 342.6452 | 157.3280 |
| 59 | 11.38181 | 355.7466 | 167.1332 |
| 60 | 11.14535 | 369.1310 | 177.4113 |
| 61 | 10.90412 | 382.7858 | 188.1682 |
| 62 | 10.65836 | 396.6965 | 199.4077 |
| 63 | 10.40837 | 410.8471 | 211.1318 |
| 64 | 10.15444 | 425.2202 | 223.3401 |
| 65 | 9.89693 | 439.7965 | 236.0299 |
| 66 | 9.63619 | 454.5553 | 249.1958 |
| 67 | 9.37262 | 469.4742 | 262.8299 |
| 68 | 9.10664 | 484.5296 | 276.9212 |
| 69 | 8.83870 | 499.6963 | 291.4559 |
| 70 | 8.56925 | 514.9481 | 306.4172 |
| 71 | 8.29879 | 530.2574 | 321.7850 |
| 72 | 8.02781 | 545.5957 | 337.5361 |
| 73 | 7.75683 | 560.9339 | 353.6443 |
| 74 | 7.48639 | 576.2419 | 370.0803 |
| 75 | 7.21702 | 591.4895 | 386.8119 |
| 76 | 6.94925 | 606.6460 | 403.8038 |
| 77 | 6.68364 | 621.6808 | 421.0184 |
| 78 | 6.42071 | 636.5634 | 438.4155 |
| 79 | 6.16101 | 651.2639 | 455.9527 |
| 80 | 5.90503 | 665.7528 | 473.5861 |
| 81 | 5.65330 | 680.0019 | 491.2698 |
| 82 | 5.40629 | 693.9837 | 508.9574 |
| 83 | 5.16446 | 707.6723 | 526.6012 |
| 84 | 4.92824 | 721.0431 | 544.1537 |
| 85 | 4.69803 | 734.0736 | 561.5675 |
| 86 | 4.47421 | 746.7428 | 578.7956 |
| 87 | 4.25710 | 759.0320 | 595.7923 |
| 88 | 4.04700 | 770.9244 | 612.5133 |
| 89 | 3.84417 | 782.4056 | 628.9163 |
| 90 | 3.64881 | 793.4636 | 644.9611 |
| 91 | 3.46110 | 804.0884 | 660.6105 |
| 92 | 3.28118 | 814.2726 | 675.8298 |
| 93 | 3.10914 | 824.0111 | 690.5878 |
| 94 | 2.94502 | 833.3007 | 704.8565 |
| 95 | 2.78885 | 842.1408 | 718.6115 |
| 96 | 2.64059 | 850.5325 | 731.8321 |
| 97 | 2.50020 | 858.4791 | 744.5010 |
| 98 | 2.36759 | 865.9853 | 756.6047 |
| 99 | 2.24265 | 873.0577 | 768.1330 |
| 100 | 2.12522 | 879.7043 | 779.0793 |
| 101 | 2.01517 | 885.9341 | 789.4400 |
| 102 | 1.91229 | 891.7573 | 799.2147 |
| 103 | 1.81639 | 897.1852 | 808.4054 |
| 104 | 1.72728 | 902.2295 | 817.0170 |
| 105 | 1.64472 | 906.9025 | 825.0563 |
| 106 | 1.56850 | 911.2170 | 832.5324 |
| 107 | 1.49838 | 915.1860 | 839.4558 |
| 108 | 1.43414 | 918.8224 | 845.8386 |
| 109 | 1.37553 | 922.1396 | 851.6944 |
| 110 | 1.32234 | 925.1507 | 857.0377 |

**Illustrative Life Table: Net Single Premiums, $i = 0.06$**

| Age | $\ddot{a}_{xx}$ | $1000\,A_{xx}$ | $1000\,(^2A_{xx})$ | $\ddot{a}_{x:x+10}$ | $1000\,A_{x:x+10}$ | $1000\,(^2A_{x:x+10})$ |
|---|---|---|---|---|---|---|
| 0 | 16.13448 | 86.7274 | 50.8875 | 16.28443 | 78.2400 | 34.7076 |
| 1 | 16.71842 | 53.6745 | 17.4565 | 16.55328 | 63.0218 | 18.1309 |
| 2 | 16.70637 | 54.3565 | 16.9753 | 16.52270 | 64.7527 | 18.2195 |
| 3 | 16.68957 | 55.3072 | 16.6683 | 16.48839 | 66.6947 | 18.4277 |
| 4 | 16.66839 | 56.5060 | 16.5191 | 16.45053 | 68.8378 | 18.7468 |
| 5 | 16.64317 | 57.9339 | 16.5121 | 16.40925 | 71.1745 | 19.1700 |
| 6 | 16.61421 | 59.5733 | 16.6324 | 16.36464 | 73.6996 | 19.6923 |
| 7 | 16.58178 | 61.4085 | 16.8664 | 16.31677 | 76.4091 | 20.3096 |
| 8 | 16.54614 | 63.4258 | 17.2017 | 16.26571 | 79.2997 | 21.0188 |
| 9 | 16.50749 | 65.6137 | 17.6271 | 16.21147 | 82.3696 | 21.8172 |
| 10 | 16.46599 | 67.9626 | 18.1330 | 16.15408 | 85.6181 | 22.7036 |
| 11 | 16.42178 | 70.4655 | 18.7116 | 16.09353 | 89.0457 | 23.6776 |
| 12 | 16.37492 | 73.1176 | 19.3572 | 16.02977 | 92.6543 | 24.7402 |
| 13 | 16.32547 | 75.9170 | 20.0661 | 15.96277 | 96.4469 | 25.8935 |
| 14 | 16.27340 | 78.8643 | 20.8373 | 15.89244 | 100.4282 | 27.1413 |
| 15 | 16.21865 | 81.9632 | 21.6726 | 15.81866 | 104.6042 | 28.4891 |
| 16 | 16.16111 | 85.2203 | 22.5769 | 15.74131 | 108.9826 | 29.9441 |
| 17 | 16.10065 | 88.6424 | 23.5556 | 15.66025 | 113.5710 | 31.5141 |
| 18 | 16.03715 | 92.2366 | 24.6142 | 15.57534 | 118.3771 | 33.2071 |
| 19 | 15.97049 | 96.0099 | 25.7588 | 15.48645 | 123.4087 | 35.0317 |
| 20 | 15.90053 | 99.9697 | 26.9958 | 15.39343 | 128.6737 | 36.9970 |
| 21 | 15.82715 | 104.1234 | 28.3320 | 15.29615 | 134.1800 | 39.1126 |
| 22 | 15.75021 | 108.4786 | 29.7746 | 15.19448 | 139.9353 | 41.3884 |
| 23 | 15.66958 | 113.0429 | 31.3311 | 15.08826 | 145.9474 | 43.8349 |
| 24 | 15.58511 | 117.8241 | 33.0098 | 14.97738 | 152.2240 | 46.4632 |
| 25 | 15.49667 | 122.8299 | 34.8192 | 14.86169 | 158.7725 | 49.2847 |
| 26 | 15.40413 | 128.0682 | 36.7681 | 14.74106 | 165.6003 | 52.3114 |
| 27 | 15.30734 | 133.5468 | 38.8662 | 14.61538 | 172.7144 | 55.5555 |
| 28 | 15.20617 | 139.2737 | 41.1234 | 14.48452 | 180.1217 | 59.0301 |
| 29 | 15.10047 | 145.2564 | 43.5502 | 14.34836 | 187.8286 | 62.7483 |
| 30 | 14.99012 | 151.5028 | 46.1574 | 14.20681 | 195.8411 | 66.7238 |
| 31 | 14.87498 | 158.0203 | 48.9566 | 14.05976 | 204.1648 | 70.9706 |
| 32 | 14.75491 | 164.8162 | 51.9595 | 13.90712 | 212.8047 | 75.5028 |
| 33 | 14.62981 | 171.8977 | 55.1785 | 13.74882 | 221.7652 | 80.3352 |
| 34 | 14.49953 | 179.2716 | 58.6264 | 13.58478 | 231.0501 | 85.4824 |
| 35 | 14.36398 | 186.9444 | 62.3164 | 13.41497 | 240.6623 | 90.9593 |
| 36 | 14.22304 | 194.9221 | 66.2622 | 13.23933 | 250.6040 | 96.7805 |
| 37 | 14.07662 | 203.2104 | 70.4777 | 13.05785 | 260.8765 | 102.9610 |
| 38 | 13.92461 | 211.8144 | 74.9770 | 12.87052 | 271.4799 | 109.5154 |
| 39 | 13.76695 | 220.7386 | 79.7749 | 12.67736 | 282.4136 | 116.4579 |
| 40 | 13.60357 | 229.9867 | 84.8858 | 12.47840 | 293.6755 | 123.8024 |
| 41 | 13.43441 | 239.5619 | 90.3247 | 12.27370 | 305.2625 | 131.5623 |
| 42 | 13.25943 | 249.4664 | 96.1064 | 12.06333 | 317.1700 | 139.7502 |
| 43 | 13.07861 | 259.7015 | 102.2457 | 11.84740 | 329.3924 | 148.3778 |
| 44 | 12.89194 | 270.2677 | 108.7571 | 11.62604 | 341.9222 | 157.4559 |
| 45 | 12.69943 | 281.1642 | 115.6552 | 11.39940 | 354.7507 | 166.9939 |
| 46 | 12.50112 | 292.3892 | 122.9537 | 11.16767 | 367.8678 | 177.0001 |
| 47 | 12.29706 | 303.9398 | 130.6661 | 10.93105 | 381.2615 | 187.4810 |
| 48 | 12.08733 | 315.8114 | 138.8051 | 10.68978 | 394.9184 | 198.4414 |
| 49 | 11.87202 | 327.9986 | 147.3826 | 10.44412 | 408.8233 | 209.8841 |
| 50 | 11.65127 | 340.4941 | 156.4093 | 10.19438 | 422.9597 | 221.8099 |
| 51 | 11.42522 | 353.2895 | 165.8951 | 9.94087 | 437.3092 | 234.2171 |
| 52 | 11.19405 | 366.3746 | 175.8482 | 9.68395 | 451.8518 | 247.1016 |
| 53 | 10.95797 | 379.7377 | 186.2752 | 9.42400 | 466.5661 | 260.4567 |
| 54 | 10.71721 | 393.3656 | 197.1814 | 9.16142 | 481.4292 | 274.2728 |

| Age | $\ddot{a}_{xx}$ | $1000\,A_{xx}$ | $1000\,(^2A_{xx})$ | $\ddot{a}_{x:x+10}$ | $1000\,A_{x:x+10}$ | $1000\,(^2A_{x:x+10})$ |
|---|---|---|---|---|---|---|
| 55 | 10.47203 | 407.2435 | 208.5696 | 8.89664 | 496.4168 | 288.5375 |
| 56 | 10.22273 | 421.3546 | 220.4410 | 8.63011 | 511.5030 | 303.2353 |
| 57 | 9.96964 | 435.6810 | 232.7940 | 8.36232 | 526.6612 | 318.3475 |
| 58 | 9.71308 | 450.2029 | 245.6250 | 8.09375 | 541.8633 | 333.8526 |
| 59 | 9.45345 | 464.8990 | 258.9275 | 7.82491 | 557.0805 | 349.7258 |
| 60 | 9.19114 | 479.7465 | 272.6922 | 7.55633 | 572.2833 | 365.9390 |
| 61 | 8.92659 | 494.7213 | 286.9070 | 7.28853 | 587.4417 | 382.4614 |
| 62 | 8.66024 | 509.7977 | 301.5568 | 7.02206 | 602.5251 | 399.2593 |
| 63 | 8.39257 | 524.9491 | 316.6234 | 6.75745 | 617.5030 | 416.2961 |
| 64 | 8.12406 | 540.1477 | 332.0853 | 6.49524 | 632.3449 | 433.5327 |
| 65 | 7.85522 | 555.3647 | 347.9183 | 6.23597 | 647.0206 | 450.9279 |
| 66 | 7.58658 | 570.5707 | 364.0947 | 5.98016 | 661.5006 | 468.4383 |
| 67 | 7.31867 | 585.7356 | 380.5839 | 5.72831 | 675.7560 | 486.0192 |
| 68 | 7.05202 | 600.8289 | 397.3525 | 5.48092 | 689.7590 | 503.6243 |
| 69 | 6.78718 | 615.8203 | 414.3642 | 5.23847 | 703.4830 | 521.2065 |
| 70 | 6.52467 | 630.6790 | 431.5803 | 5.00138 | 716.9030 | 538.7185 |
| 71 | 6.26504 | 645.3750 | 448.9598 | 4.77008 | 729.9954 | 556.1128 |
| 72 | 6.00881 | 659.8785 | 466.4595 | 4.54495 | 742.7386 | 573.3422 |
| 73 | 5.75650 | 674.1606 | 484.0346 | 4.32634 | 755.1127 | 590.3606 |
| 74 | 5.50858 | 688.1934 | 501.6393 | 4.11456 | 767.1002 | 607.1233 |
| 75 | 5.26555 | 701.9503 | 519.2266 | 3.90989 | 778.6857 | 623.5869 |
| 76 | 5.02783 | 715.4057 | 536.7489 | 3.71254 | 789.8559 | 639.7107 |
| 77 | 4.79586 | 728.5362 | 554.1588 | 3.52273 | 800.6001 | 655.4561 |
| 78 | 4.57002 | 741.3197 | 571.4091 | 3.34060 | 810.9096 | 670.7874 |
| 79 | 4.35066 | 753.7364 | 588.4536 | 3.16625 | 820.7782 | 685.6720 |
| 80 | 4.13809 | 765.7683 | 605.2473 | 2.99977 | 830.2020 | 700.0806 |
| 81 | 3.93260 | 777.3999 | 621.7467 | 2.84117 | 839.1791 | 713.9874 |
| 82 | 3.73442 | 788.6175 | 637.9108 | 2.69046 | 847.7098 | 727.3701 |
| 83 | 3.54375 | 799.4102 | 653.7007 | 2.54760 | 855.7965 | 740.2101 |
| 84 | 3.36075 | 809.7690 | 669.0804 | 2.41251 | 863.4431 | 752.4921 |
| 85 | 3.18552 | 819.6876 | 684.0169 | 2.28509 | 870.6554 | 764.2049 |
| 86 | 3.01814 | 829.1617 | 698.4806 | 2.16521 | 877.4407 | 775.3401 |
| 87 | 2.85866 | 838.1892 | 712.4451 | 2.05273 | 883.8075 | 785.8931 |
| 88 | 2.70706 | 846.7701 | 725.8879 | 1.94748 | 889.7655 | 795.8619 |
| 89 | 2.56332 | 854.9067 | 738.7899 | 1.84925 | 895.3253 | 805.2478 |
| 90 | 2.42735 | 862.6027 | 751.1355 | 1.75786 | 900.4984 | 814.0543 |
| 91 | 2.29908 | 869.8636 | 762.9129 | 1.67309 | 905.2969 | 822.2875 |
| 92 | 2.17836 | 876.6967 | 774.1136 | 1.59471 | 909.7331 | 829.9554 |
| 93 | 2.06505 | 883.1102 | 784.7323 | 1.52251 | 913.8199 | 837.0680 |
| 94 | 1.95899 | 889.1137 | 794.7670 | 1.45626 | 917.5703 | 843.6367 |
| 95 | 1.85998 | 894.7179 | 804.2185 | 1.39571 | 920.9973 | 849.6744 |
| 96 | 1.76783 | 899.9341 | 813.0901 | 1.34065 | 924.1140 | 855.1951 |
| 97 | 1.68232 | 904.7742 | 821.3876 | 1.29084 | 926.9335 | 860.2140 |
| 98 | 1.60324 | 909.2506 | 829.1188 | 1.24605 | 929.4689 | 864.7475 |
| 99 | 1.53035 | 913.3762 | 836.2934 | 1.20604 | 931.7333 | 868.8126 |
| 100 | 1.46344 | 917.1638 | 842.9228 | 1.17060 | 933.7399 | 872.4279 |
| 101 | 1.40226 | 920.6266 | 849.0197 | 1.13946 | 935.5020 | 875.6129 |
| 102 | 1.34659 | 923.7777 | 854.5980 | 1.11241 | 937.0336 | 878.3888 |
| 103 | 1.29620 | 926.6301 | 859.6727 | 1.08917 | 938.3489 | 880.7785 |
| 104 | 1.25086 | 929.1969 | 864.2600 | 1.06949 | 939.4630 | 882.8066 |
| 105 | 1.21032 | 931.4911 | 868.3771 | 1.05308 | 940.3917 | 884.5002 |
| 106 | 1.17437 | 933.5261 | 872.0421 | 1.03965 | 941.1518 | 885.8881 |
| 107 | 1.14277 | 935.3151 | 875.2746 | 1.02889 | 941.7609 | 887.0017 |
| 108 | 1.11526 | 936.8720 | 878.0956 | 1.02047 | 942.2374 | 887.8735 |
| 109 | 1.09161 | 938.2110 | 880.5276 | 1.01406 | 942.6001 | 888.5376 |
| 110 | 1.07154 | 939.3470 | 882.5952 | 1.00934 | 942.8678 | 889.0280 |

**Illustrative
Service Table**

| Age x | $l_x^{(\tau)}$ | $d_x^{(d)}$ | $d_x^{(w)}$ | $d_x^{(i)}$ | $d_x^{(r)}$ | $S_x$ |
|---|---|---|---|---|---|---|
| 30 | 100 000 | 100 | 19 990 | — | — | 1.00 |
| 31 | 79 910 | 80 | 14 376 | — | — | 1.06 |
| 32 | 65 454 | 72 | 9 858 | — | — | 1.13 |
| 33 | 55 524 | 61 | 5 702 | — | — | 1.20 |
| 34 | 49 761 | 60 | 3 971 | — | — | 1.28 |
| 35 | 45 730 | 64 | 2 693 | 46 | — | 1.36 |
| 36 | 42 927 | 64 | 1 927 | 43 | — | 1.44 |
| 37 | 40 893 | 65 | 1 431 | 45 | — | 1.54 |
| 38 | 39 352 | 71 | 1 181 | 47 | — | 1.63 |
| 39 | 38 053 | 72 | 989 | 49 | — | 1.74 |
| 40 | 36 943 | 78 | 813 | 52 | — | 1.85 |
| 41 | 36 000 | 83 | 720 | 54 | — | 1.96 |
| 42 | 35 143 | 91 | 633 | 56 | — | 2.09 |
| 43 | 34 363 | 96 | 550 | 58 | — | 2.22 |
| 44 | 33 659 | 104 | 505 | 61 | — | 2.36 |
| 45 | 32 989 | 112 | 462 | 66 | — | 2.51 |
| 46 | 32 349 | 123 | 421 | 71 | — | 2.67 |
| 47 | 31 734 | 133 | 413 | 79 | — | 2.84 |
| 48 | 31 109 | 143 | 373 | 87 | — | 3.02 |
| 49 | 30 506 | 156 | 336 | 95 | — | 3.21 |
| 50 | 29 919 | 168 | 299 | 102 | — | 3.41 |
| 51 | 29 350 | 182 | 293 | 112 | — | 3.63 |
| 52 | 28 763 | 198 | 259 | 121 | — | 3.86 |
| 53 | 28 185 | 209 | 251 | 132 | — | 4.10 |
| 54 | 27 593 | 226 | 218 | 143 | — | 4.35 |
| 55 | 27 006 | 240 | 213 | 157 | — | 4.62 |
| 56 | 26 396 | 259 | 182 | 169 | — | 4.91 |
| 57 | 25 786 | 276 | 178 | 183 | — | 5.21 |
| 58 | 25 149 | 297 | 148 | 199 | — | 5.53 |
| 59 | 24 505 | 316 | 120 | 213 | — | 5.86 |
| 60 | 23 856 | 313 | — | — | 3 552 | 6.21 |
| 61 | 19 991 | 298 | — | — | 1 587 | 6.56 |
| 62 | 18 106 | 284 | — | — | 2 692 | 6.93 |
| 63 | 15 130 | 271 | — | — | 1 350 | 7.31 |
| 64 | 13 509 | 257 | — | — | 2 006 | 7.70 |
| 65 | 11 246 | 204 | — | — | 4 448 | 8.08 |
| 66 | 6 594 | 147 | — | — | 1 302 | 8.48 |
| 67 | 5 145 | 119 | — | — | 1 522 | 8.91 |
| 68 | 3 504 | 83 | — | — | 1 381 | 9.35 |
| 69 | 2 040 | 49 | — | — | 1 004 | 9.82 |
| 70 | 987 | 17 | — | — | 970 | 10.31 |

**Symbol Index**

| Symbol | Page | Symbol | Page |
|---|---|---|---|
| $a$ | 533 | $(\boldsymbol{a}\boldsymbol{U})(t)$ | 546 |
| $\boldsymbol{a}(t)$ | 547 | $(aV)(x)$ | 544 |
| $a(x)$ | 66 | $(\boldsymbol{a}\boldsymbol{V})(t)$ | 540 |
| $a_x$ | 133 | $A(h)$ | 410 |
| $\bar{a}_{\overline{n}|}$ | 123 | $\boldsymbol{A}(t)$ | 554 |
| $\bar{a}_{\overline{T}|}$ | 123 | $A_x$ | 99 |
| $\bar{a}_x$ | 123 | $\bar{A}_x$ | 86 |
| $\ddot{a}_x$ | 130 | $A_x^{(m)}$ | 116 |
| $\bar{a}_r^h$ | 535 | $\bar{A}_x^{PR}$ | 179 |
| $\bar{a}_{x+t}^i$ | 294 | $A_{x:\overline{n}|}$ | 101 |
| $\bar{a}_{x+t}^r$ | 294 | $\bar{A}_{x:\overline{n}|}$ | 91 |
| $\ddot{a}_x^{(m)}$ | 136 | $A_{x:\frac{1}{n}|}$ | 90 |
| $\mathring{a}_x^{(m)}$ | 146 | $\bar{A}_{x:\overline{n}|}^1$ | 85 |
| $\ddot{a}_x^{\{m\}}$ | 148 | $\tilde{A}_{x:\overline{n}|}^1$ | 183 |
| $a_{x:\overline{n}|}$ | 134 | $^2A_{x:\frac{1}{n}|}$ | 90 |
| $\bar{a}_{x:\overline{n}|}$ | 126 | $^2\bar{A}_{x:\overline{n}|}^1$ | 86 |
| $\ddot{a}_{x:\overline{n}|}$ | 132 | $_{m|}\bar{A}_x$ | 92 |
| $\ddot{a}_{x:\overline{n}|}^{(m)}$ | 139 | $_{m|n}\bar{A}_x$ | 98 |
| $\mathring{a}_{x:\overline{n}|}^{(m)}$ | 148 | $A_{xy}$ | 232 |
| $\ddot{a}_{x:\overline{n}|}^{\{m\}}$ | 148 | $A_{\overline{xy}}$ | 238 |
| $\bar{a}_{\overline{x:\overline{n}|}}$ | 460 | $A_{xy}^{(m)}$ | 247 |
| $a_{\overline{x:\overline{n}|}}^{(m)}$ | 460 | $\bar{A}_{xy}^{\ 2}$ | 249 |
| $^2\bar{a}_{x:\overline{n}|}$ | 127 | $\bar{A}_{xy}^1$ | 252 |
| $_{n|}a_x$ | 134 | $A_{xy:\overline{n}|}$ | 239 |
| $_{n|}\bar{a}_x$ | 127 | $\bar{A}_{\overline{xy}:\overline{n}|}^1$ | 241 |
| $_{n|}\ddot{a}_x$ | 132 | $^2A_{xy:\overline{n}|}$ | 239 |
| $_{n|}\ddot{a}_x^{(m)}$ | 139 | $\bar{A}_{wxy}^{\ \ 2}$ | 492 |
| $_{m|n}\bar{a}_x$ | 128 | $\bar{A}_{\overline{x_1 x_2 x_3}}$ | 488 |
| $\ddot{a}_{xy}^{(m)}$ | 247 | $_kAS$ | 443 |
| $\ddot{a}_{xy:\overline{n}|}$ | 239 | $_k\widehat{AS}$ | 445 |
| $^2\ddot{a}_{xy:\overline{n}|}$ | 239 | $(AS)_{x+h}$ | 294 |
| $\bar{a}_{x|y}$ | 497 | $(AAI)$ | 437 |
| $\ddot{a}_{v|u}^{(m)}$ | 499 | $(ATPC)_{x+h}$ | 307 |
| $\hat{\ddot{a}}_{x|y}^{(m)}$ | 500 | | |
| $\bar{a}_{\overline{x_1 x_2 x_3}}$ | 488 | $b(u)$ | 512 |
| $(aA)(x)$ | 544 | $b_t$ | 83 |
| $(\boldsymbol{a}A)(t)$ | 538 | $b_f(t)$ | 526 |
| $(\boldsymbol{a}C)(t)$ | 546 | $\boldsymbol{B}(t)$ | 551 |
| $(\boldsymbol{a}F)(t)$ | 546 | $\hat{B}_{x+k}$ | 283 |

| Symbol | Page | Symbol | Page |
|---|---|---|---|
| $B_{x+t}^{(j)}$ | 281 | $\hat{e}_k$ | 445 |
| $B(x,h,t)$ | 307 | $\overset{\circ}{e}_{x:\overline{n}\rceil}$ | 78 |
| $_tB_j$ | 485 | $e_{xy}$ | 237 |
| | | $e_{\overline{xy}}$ | 237 |
| $c$ | 345 | $\overset{\circ}{e}_{xy}$ | 236 |
| $c_k$ | 443 | $\overset{\circ}{e}_{\overline{xy}}$ | 236 |
| $\hat{c}_k$ | 445 | $\mathbf{E}$ | 5, 584 |
| $C_x$ | 112 | $E$ | 434 |
| $\bar{C}_x$ | 113 | $E_1$ | 434 |
| $\bar{C}_y^h$ | 308 | $E^{Can}$ | 423 |
| $\bar{C}_x^i$ | 475 | $_nE_x$ | 120 |
| $^a\bar{C}_y^h$ | 309 | $(ES)_{x+h+t}$ | 295 |
| $^a\bar{C}_y^i$ | 311, 475 | $ELRA$ | 421 |
| $^a\bar{C}_{x+h+k}^r$ | 310 | | |
| $^{Sa}\bar{C}_y^h$ | 309 | $f$ | 534 |
| $^{Za}\bar{C}_y^h$ | 309 | $f_S(s)$ | 32 |
| $^{Za}\bar{C}_y^r$ | 309 | $F(x)$ | 28 |
| $^{Sa'}\bar{C}_y^w$ | 311 | $\boldsymbol{F}(t)$ | 554 |
| $_kCV$ | 433 | $F^{(k)}$ | 34 |
| | | $F_S(s)$ | 32 |
| | | $_kF$ | 446 |
| $_nd_x$ | 52 | | |
| $_nd_x^{(j)}$ | 267 | $g(t)$ | 534 |
| $_nd_x^{(\tau)}$ | 267 | $G$ | 4, 386, 406, 434 |
| $D_x$ | 112 | $G(b)$ | 407 |
| $D_x^{(\tau)}$ | 308 | $G(x:\alpha,\beta)$ | 336 |
| $\bar{D}_y^{(\tau)}$ | 308 | | |
| $\tilde{D}_y^{(m)}$ | 144 | $h(x)$ | 390, 534 |
| $_{k+1}D$ | 447 | $H(r)$ | 526 |
| $^S\bar{D}_y^{(\tau)}$ | 308 | $H(x:\alpha,\beta,x_0)$ | 336 |
| $(D\ddot{a})_{x:\overline{n}\rceil}^{(m)}$ | 154 | | |
| $(DA)_{x:\overline{n}\rceil}^1$ | 102 | $\hat{\imath}_{k+1}$ | 445 |
| $(D\bar{A})_{x:\overline{n}\rceil}^1$ | 97 | $I_d$ | 382 |
| $(\bar{D}\bar{s})_{\overline{1}\rceil}$ | 108 | $I_d(x)$ | 17 |
| $_n\mathcal{D}_x$ | 52 | $(\bar{I}\bar{a})_x$ | 155 |
| $_n\mathcal{D}_x^{(j)}$ | 267 | $(I\ddot{a})_{x:\overline{n}\rceil}^{(m)}$ | 154 |
| $_n\mathcal{D}_x^{(\tau)}$ | 267 | $(I_{\overline{n}\rceil}\ddot{a})_x^{(m)}$ | 155 |
| | | $(IA)_x$ | 101 |
| $e_x$ | 65, 443 | $(I\bar{A})_x$ | 95 |
| $\overset{\circ}{e}_x$ | 62 | $(\bar{I}\bar{A})_x$ | 96 |
| | | $(I^{(m)}\bar{A})_x$ | 95 |
| | | $(IA)_{x:\overline{n}\rceil}^1$ | 103 |

| Symbol | Page | Symbol | Page |
|---|---|---|---|
| $J$ | 260 | $N_x^{(m)}$ | 141 |
| | | $\bar{N}_x^{(\tau)}$ | 308 |
| $_t\bar{k}_x$ | 197 | | |
| $K$ | 64 | $p(x)$ | 320 |
| $K(\overline{xy})$ | 235 | $p_k$ | 318 |
| | | $p_{[x]+r}$ | 75 |
| | | $p^{*n}(x)$ | 320 |
| $l_x$ | 52, 518 | $_tp_x$ | 47 |
| $l_{[x]+k}$ | 75 | $_tp_x^{(\tau)}$ | 262 |
| $l_x^{(\tau)}$ | 267 | $_tp_x'^{(j)}$ | 271 |
| $l(x,u)$ | 513 | | |
| $l_f(x,u)$ | 526 | $_tp_{xy}$ | 232 |
| $L$ | 162, 361 | $_tp_{\overline{xy}}$ | 234 |
| $L_1$ | 359 | $_tp_{\overline{x_1 x_2 \overline{x_3}}}^{\frac{k}{}}$ | 484 |
| $L_x$ | 65 | $P(x)$ | 318, 544 |
| $L(h)$ | 410 | $\boldsymbol{P}(t)$ | 538 |
| $_tL$ | 193 | $^T\boldsymbol{P}(t)$ | 535 |
| $\mathscr{L}(x)$ | 52 | $P^a$ | 434 |
| $\mathscr{L}_x^{(\tau)}$ | 267 | $P_x$ | 167 |
| | | $P_x^a$ | 435 |
| $m(x)$ | 63, 536 | $P_{x:\overline{n}|}$ | 170 |
| $m_x$ | 65 | $P_{x:\overline{n}|}^1$ | 170 |
| $m_x^{(j)}$ | 273 | $P_{x:\overline{n}|}^{\ 1}$ | 170 |
| $m_x^{(\tau)}$ | 273 | $\tilde{P}_{x:\overline{n}|}^1$ | 183 |
| $m_x'^{(j)}$ | 273 | $P^{*n}(x)$ | 320 |
| $M_x(t)$ | 11 | $_hP_x$ | 170 |
| $M(x)$ | 536 | $_hP_{x:\overline{n}|}$ | 170 |
| $M_x$ | 112 | $(Pa)(x)$ | 544 |
| $\bar{M}_x$ | 113 | $(\boldsymbol{Pa})(t)$ | 541 |
| $_yM_x^i$ | 475 | $P(_{n|}\ddot{a}_x)$ | 170 |
| $_y^u\bar{M}_x^i$ | 475 | $\bar{P}(_{n|}\bar{a}_x)$ | 165 |
| $^{Za}\bar{M}_x^h$ | 309 | $\bar{P}(\bar{A}_x)$ | 163 |
| $^{Za}\bar{M}_y^r$ | 309 | $P^{(m)}(\bar{A}_x)$ | 176 |
| $^{Sa'}\bar{M}_y^w$ | 311 | $P^{\{m\}}(\bar{A}_x)$ | 178 |
| | | $P(\bar{A}_x^{PR})$ | 179 |
| $n(u)$ | 533 | $\bar{P}(\bar{A}_{x:\overline{n}|})$ | 165 |
| $N$ | 317 | $\bar{P}(\bar{A}_{x:\overline{n}|}^1)$ | 165 |
| $N(t)$ | 346, 519 | $\bar{P}(A_{x:\overline{n}|}^{\ 1})$ | 165 |
| $N_x$ | 140 | $P^{(m)}(\bar{A}_{x:\overline{n}|})$ | 176 |
| $\bar{N}_x$ | 142 | $P^{(m)}(\bar{A}_{x:\overline{n}|}^1)$ | 176 |

| Symbol | Page | Symbol | Page |
|---|---|---|---|
| $\rho$ | 536 | $\psi(u)$ | 346 |
|  |  | $\bar{\psi}(u)$ | 354 |
| $\tau$ | 262, 535 | $\psi(u,t)$ | 346 |
|  |  | $\psi(u;w)$ | 370 |
| $\phi(x)$ | 526 | $\bar{\psi}(u,w)$ | 357 |
| $\phi(x,u)$ | 526 |  |  |
| $X(\theta)$ | 539 | $\omega$ | 53 |

## General Rules for Symbols of Actuarial Functions

An actuarial function is represented by a principal symbol and a combination of auxiliary symbols such as letters, numerals, double dots, circles, hats, horizontal and vertical bars. The principal symbol expresses the general definition of the function; choice and placement of the auxiliary symbols at the top and corners give precise meaning. We will review the rules for selecting and placing the symbols, showing one or more functional forms in common application areas.

This notation is based upon the system of International Actuarial Notation (IAN) that was originally adopted by the Second International Congress of Actuaries in London in 1898 and is modified periodically under the guidance of the Permanent Committee of Actuarial Notations of the International Actuarial Association. IAN is a basic system of principles which does not cover all areas of actuarial applications. In this text these principles have been followed, and sometimes extended, to construct consistent notation where needed.

This Appendix is meant to provide the student with an overview of basic patterns for expressing the symbols appearing in this textbook. While it is a good introduction to IAN, it is not exhaustive. Authoritative sources for further reference are:

Actuarial Society of America, "International Actuarial Notation," *Transactions*, XLVIII, 1947: 166–176.

Faculty of Actuaries, *Transactions*, XIX, 1950: 89.

*Journal of the Institute of Actuaries*, LXXV, 1949: 121.

An actuarial symbol can be viewed as illustrated below. Box I represents the principal symbol, the others subscripts or superscripts. The roman numerals in the boxes correspond to the section designations of this Appendix.

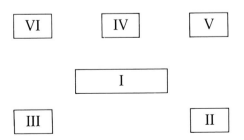

## Section I
## Center

| Principal Symbol | Description | Topic |
|---|---|---|
| $i$ | Effective rate of interest for a time period, usually one year, or with a superscript in Position V, a nominal rate. | Interest |
| $v$ | Present value of 1 due at the end of the effective interest period, usually one year. | |
| $\delta$ | Force of interest, usually stated as an annual rate. | |
| $d$ | Effective rate of interest-in-advance, or discount rate, for a time period of usually one year, or with a superscript in Position V, a nominal rate. This symbol never has a subscript in Position II. | |
| $l$ | Expected number, or number, of survivors at a given age. | Life Tables |
| $d$ | Expected number, or number, of those dying within a given time period. This symbol always has a subscript in Position II. | |
| $p$ | Probability of surviving for a given period of time. | |
| $q$ | Probability of dying within a given time period. | |
| $\mu$ | Force of mortality, usually stated on an annual basis. | |
| $m$ | Central death rate for a given time period. | |
| $L$ | Expected number, or number, of years lived within a time period by the survivors at the beginning of the period. | |
| $T$ | Expected total, or total, future lifetime of the survivors at a given age. | |
| | (The above are survivorship group definitions of the life table functions denoted by $l$, $d$, $L$ and $T$. For the alternative stationary population definitions, see Chapter 18.) | |
| $A$ | Actuarial present value (net single premium) of an insurance or pure endowment of 1. | Life Insurance and Pure Endowments |
| $(IA)$ | Actuarial present value (net single premium) of an insurance with a benefit amount of 1 at the end of the first year, increasing linearly at a rate of 1 per year. | |

| Principal Symbol | Description | Topic |
|---|---|---|
| $(DA)$ | Actuarial present value (net single premium) of a term insurance with an initial benefit amount equal to the term and decreasing linearly at the rate of 1 per year. | |
| $E$ | Actuarial present value of a pure endowment of 1. | |
| $a$ | Actuarial present value of an annuity of 1 per time period, usually one year. | Annuities |
| $s$ | Actuarial accumulated value of an annuity of 1 per time period, usually one year. | |
| $(Ia)$ | Actuarial present value of an annuity payable at the rate of 1 per year at the end of the first year and increasing linearly at a rate of 1 per year. | |
| $(Da)$ | Actuarial present value of a temporary annuity with an initial payment rate equal to the term and decreasing linearly at a rate of 1 per period. | |
| $P$ | Level annual premium to cover only benefits. | Premiums |
| $V$ | Reserve to cover future benefits in excess of future benefit premiums. | Reserves |
| $W$ | Face amount of a paid-up policy purchased with a cash value equal to the reserve. | |
| | (Principal symbols for benefit premiums, reserves, and amounts of reduced paid-up insurance, $P$, $V$, and $W$, are combined with benefit symbols unless the benefit is a level unit insurance payable at the end of the year of death.) | (Examples: $\bar{P}_x$, $P(\bar{A}_x)$ $_{10}V^{(4)}(\bar{A}_{x:\overline{n}\mid})$ $P^{(12)}(_{30\mid}\ddot{a}^{(12)}_{35}))$ |
| $D$ | Actuarial present value at age 0 of a unit payment to each of the survivors at a given age. | Commutation Functions |
| $C$ | Actuarial present value at age 0 of a unit death benefit in regard to those dying in a specified year of age. | |
| $N$ | Sum of the values of the $D$ function from a specified age to the greatest age listed in the table. | |
| $M$ | Sum of the values of the $C$ function from a specified age to the greatest age listed in the table. | |

| Principal Symbol | Description | Topic |
|---|---|---|
| $S$ | Sum of the values of the $N$ function from a specified age to the greatest age listed in the table. (Not to be confused with the pension salary scale function.) | |
| $R$ | Sum of the values of the $M$ function from a specified age to the greatest age listed in the table. | |
| $s$ | Salary scale function used to project salaries. (Not to be confused with the commutation function $S$.) | Pensions |
| $z$ | Average of a given number of salary scale function values, usually at unit intervals in the independent variable. | |
| | (In pension applications, complex auxiliary symbols are used with commutation function symbols to represent the many complicated benefits. These are discussed in Section 10.7.) | *(Example* $^{za}\bar{M}^r_x$*)* |

### Section II
### Lower Space to the Right

| Auxiliary Symbol | Description | Examples |
|---|---|---|
| $x$; $10$ | A single letter or numeral is the individual's age at the commencement of the overall time period implied by the principal symbol. | $a_x$; $\bar{a}_{10}$<br>$q_x$; $_5q_{10}$<br>$\bar{A}_x$; $A_{10}$ |
| $\overline{n}$; $\overline{10}$ | A term certain is indicated by a single letter or numeral under an angle. | $A_{x:\overline{n}}$; $\ddot{a}_{\overline{10}}$ |
| $[x]$; $[35]$<br><br>$[x]+t$; $[35-n]+n$ | Alphanumeric expressions enclosed by brackets indicate the age at which the life was selected. A term, representing duration since selection, may be added to the bracketed expression to express the attained age of the life. | $l_{[x]}$; $l_{[x]+10}$<br><br>$A_{[35]}$; $\ddot{a}^i_{[35-n]+n}$ |
| $xyz$ or $x{:}y{:}z$<br><br>$25{:}\overline{10}$ | Two or more alphanumeric characters indicate a joint status that survives until the first death or expiration of the indicated lives and term certains. | $l_{xyz}$; $A_{x:y:z}$<br><br>$\ddot{a}_{25:\overline{10}}$; $P_{25:\overline{10}}$ |
| $\frown$ | This symbol emphasizes the joint status when ambiguity is possible. | $A^1_{\overline{xy}:z}$ |

| Auxiliary Symbol | Description | Examples |
|---|---|---|
| $\overset{1}{x}:\overline{10\vert}$; $\overset{2}{xyz}\atop\underset{1}{}$ | Numerals can be placed above or below the individual statuses of a collection of alphanumeric characters to show the order in which the units are to fail for an (insurable) event to occur. Benefits are payable upon the failure of the status with a numeral above it. | $\bar{A}^1_{x:\overline{n\vert}}$; $_x q^3_{\underset{12}{xyz}}$ |
| $\overline{xyz}$; $\overline{65:60:\overline{10\vert}}$ | A horizontal bar over a collection of alphanumeric characters defines a status that survives until the last survivor of the individual statuses fails. | $a_{\overline{xyz}}$; $\bar{A}_{\overline{xy:\overline{n\vert}}}$ |
| $\overset{r}{\overline{xyz}}$; $\overset{[r]}{\overline{x:y:10}}$ | A single alphanumeric character, say $r$, above the right end of the bar over the set of alphanumeric characters defines a status that survives as long as at least $r$ of the individual statuses survive. If the $r$ is enclosed in brackets, the status exists only while exactly $r$ of the individual statuses survive. | $\bar{a}^{[2]}_{\overline{xyz}}$; $\bar{A}^2_{\overline{xyz}}$ |
| $y\vert x$; $60\vert 55$; $\overset{1}{yz}\vert x$ | A vertical bar separating the alphanumeric characters indicates that the income or coverage of the principal symbol commences upon the failure, as specified, of the status before the bar and continues until the failure of the status following the bar, providing the statuses fail in that order. | $a_{y\vert x}$ $a_{\underset{1}{\overset{3}{wyz}}\vert x}$ |

## Section III
## Lower Space to the Left

| Auxiliary Symbol | Description | Examples |
|---|---|---|
| $n$; 15 | A single alphanumeric character shows the time for which the principal symbol is evaluated. For an annual premium, $P$, this position shows the maximum number of years for which the premiums are paid if this is less than the period of coverage of an insurance or the period of deferral for a deferred annuity. | $_n p_x$; $_{15}E_{30}$ $_{20}P_{25}$; $_{20}V_{40:\overline{30\vert}}$ |
| $n\vert m$; $n\vert$ | An alphanumeric pair separated by a vertical bar indicates a period of deferment (left of the bar) and a period following deferment (right of the bar). In some cases, when either is equal to 1 or infinity, it can be omitted. | $_{n\vert m}q_x$; $_{n\vert}\bar{a}_x$ |

## Section IV
## Top Center

| Auxiliary Symbol | Description | Examples |
|---|---|---|
| .. | The double dot (dieresis) on an annuity symbol indicates that the payments are at the beginning of the periods, that is, an annuity-due. Without the dieresis, the annuity is an annuity-immediate with payments at the ends of the periods. | $\ddot{a}_x$; $\ddot{s}_{\overline{40|}}$ |
| ‾ | A horizontal bar indicates that the frequency of events is infinite. For annuities the payments are considered to be made continuously and for insurances the benefit is paid at the moment of failure. | $\bar{a}_x$; $\bar{A}_x$ $_3\bar{V}_x$; $\bar{P}(\bar{A}_x)$ |
| ∘ | A circle (degree sign) means that the benefit or lifetime is complete, that is, credited up to the time of death. | $\mathring{a}_x$; $\mathring{e}_x$ |
| ^ | A hat (circumflex) indicates that payment periods are measured from the time of the random event (usually a death) that defines the deferral period. | $\hat{a}_{y|x}$ |

## Section V
## Upper Space to the Right

| Auxiliary Symbol | Description | Examples |
|---|---|---|
| (m); (12) | An alphanumeric character in parentheses shows the number of annuity payments in an interest period, usually a year. For an insurance it is the number of periods in a year at the end of which the death benefit can be paid. On multiple decrement symbols it indicates the cause of decrement to be used or that the total of all decrements is to be used. | $s_{\overline{10|}}^{(12)}$; $A_x^{(m)}$ $q_x^{(2)}$; $_t p_x^{(\tau)}$ |
| {m}; {12} | An alphanumeric character in braces shows the number of apportionable annuity-due payments in a time period, usually a year. On a principal symbol of a premium or a reserve, it shows that premiums are paid on this basis. | $\ddot{a}_{30:\overline{20|}}^{\{12\}}$; $P_{30}^{\{1\}}$ $_t V^{\{2\}}(\bar{A}_x)$ |
| r; i | An alphabetic character indicates the special basis used for the actuarial present value. | $\ddot{a}_{65}^r$; $\ddot{a}_{[x]}^i$ |

## Section VI
## Upper Space to the Left

| Auxiliary Symbol | Description | Examples |
|---|---|---|
| $h$; 2 | Alphanumeric character indicating the number of years during which premiums are paid if this is less than the coverage period of the insurance or the deferral period of the deferred annuity. This is used only on the principal symbols $V$ or $W$ where position III is used for the time for which the function is evaluated. | ${}_{5}^{h}V_{30}$ |
| | In this text a new use for this position is to show that the actuarial present value of an annuity or an insurance is calculated at a multiple of the assumed force of interest. | ${}^{2}\bar{A}_{x}$; ${}^{2}\ddot{a}_{20:\overline{10}|}$ |

## Some Mathematical Formulas Useful in Actuarial Mathematics

The purpose here is not to recall familiar standard formulas and techniques, but to indicate some that may be less familiar to actuarial students.

### Calculus

If

$$F(t) = \int_{\alpha(t)}^{\beta(t)} f(x,t)\, dx,$$

then

$$\frac{dF(t)}{dt} = \int_{\alpha(t)}^{\beta(t)} \frac{\partial}{\partial t} f(x,t)\, dx + f(\beta(t),\, t) \frac{d}{dt}\beta(t)$$

$$- f(\alpha(t),\, t) \frac{d}{dt}\alpha(t).$$

### Calculus of Finite Differences

*Operators*

a. Shift:

$$E[f(x)] = f(x + 1)$$

b. Difference:

$$\Delta f(x) = f(x + 1) - f(x) = (E - 1)f(x)$$

c. Repeated differences:

$$\Delta^n f(x) = \Delta[\Delta^{n-1}f(x)]$$
$$= (E - 1)^n f(x)$$
$$= \sum_{k=0}^{n} \binom{n}{k}(-1)^{n-k}f(x + k)$$

d. Difference of a product:

$$\Delta[f(x)\, g(x)] = f(x + 1)\, \Delta g(x) + g(x)\, \Delta f(x)$$

e. Antidifference:
   If

$$\Delta f(x) = g(x),$$

then

$$\Delta^{-1}g(x) = f(x) + w(x)$$

where

$$w(x) = w(x + 1).$$

*Applications*

a. Representation of a polynomial (Newton's formula):
Let $p_n(x)$ be a polynomial of degree $n$, then

$$p_n(x) = \sum_{k=0}^{n} \binom{x-a}{k} \Delta^k p_n(a).$$

b. Summation of series:
If

$$\Delta F(x) = f(x),$$

then

$$f(1) = F(2) - F(1)$$
$$f(2) = F(3) - F(2)$$
$$\vdots$$
$$f(n) = F(n+1) - F(n)$$

$$\sum_{x=1}^{n} f(x) = F(n+1) - F(1) = \Delta^{-1} f(x) \Big|_{1}^{n+1}.$$

c. Summation by parts:

$$\sum_{x=1}^{n} g(x) \, \Delta f(x) = f(x) \, g(x) \Big|_{1}^{n+1} - \Delta^{-1}[f(x+1) \, \Delta g(x)] \Big|_{1}^{n+1}$$

[Proof: Sum each side of the equation for $\Delta(f(x) \, g(x))$ from $x = 1$ to $x = n$.]

## Probability Distributions

| Discrete Distributions | p.f. | Restrictions on Parameters | Moment Generating Function, M(s) | Moments Mean | Moments Variance |
|---|---|---|---|---|---|
| Binomial | $\binom{n}{x}p^x q^{n-x}$; $x = 0,1,\ldots n$ | $0 < p < 1$ $q = 1 - p$ | $(pe^s + q)^n$ | $np$ | $npq$ |
| Bernoulli | Special case $n = 1$ | | | | |
| Negative Binomial | $\binom{r+x-1}{x}p^r q^x$; $x = 0,1,2,\ldots$ | $0 < p < 1$ $q = 1 - p$ $r > 0$ | $\left(\dfrac{p}{1 - qe^s}\right)^r$; $qe^s < 1$ | $\dfrac{rq}{p}$ | $\dfrac{rq}{p^2}$ |
| Geometric | Special case $r = 1$ | | | | |
| Poisson | $\dfrac{e^{-\lambda}\lambda^x}{x!}$; $x = 0,1,2,\ldots$ | $\lambda > 0$ | $e^{\lambda(e^s-1)}$ | $\lambda$ | $\lambda$ |
| Uniform | $\dfrac{1}{n}$; $x = 1,\ldots,n$ | $n$, a positive integer | $\dfrac{e^s(1 - e^{sn})}{n(1 - e^s)}$; $s \neq 0$ $1$; $s = 0$ | $\dfrac{n+1}{2}$ | $\dfrac{n^2 - 1}{12}$ |

| Continuous Distributions | p.d.f. | Restrictions on Parameters | Moment Generating Function, M(s) | Moments Mean | Moments Variance |
|---|---|---|---|---|---|
| Uniform | $\dfrac{1}{b - a}$; $a < x < b$ | — | $\dfrac{e^{bs} - e^{as}}{(b - a)s}$; $s \neq 0$ $1$; $s = 0$ | $\dfrac{b + a}{2}$ | $\dfrac{(b - a)^2}{12}$ |
| Normal | $\dfrac{1}{\sigma\sqrt{2\pi}}\exp\{-(x - \mu)^2/2\sigma^2\}$; $-\infty < x < \infty$ | $\sigma > 0$ | $\exp\{\mu s + \sigma^2 s^2/2\}$ | $\mu$ | $\sigma^2$ |
| Gamma | $\dfrac{\beta^\alpha}{\Gamma(\alpha)}x^{\alpha-1}e^{-\beta x}$; $x > 0$ | $\alpha > 0$, $\beta > 0$ | $\left(\dfrac{\beta}{\beta - s}\right)^\alpha$; $s < \beta$ | $\dfrac{\alpha}{\beta}$ | $\dfrac{\alpha}{\beta^2}$ |
| Exponential | Special case $\alpha = 1$ | | | | |
| Chi-square | Special case $\alpha = \dfrac{k}{2}$; $\beta = \dfrac{1}{2}$ | $k$, a positive integer | | | |

| | | | | Moments Mean | Moments Variance |
|---|---|---|---|---|---|
| Pareto | $\alpha x_0^\alpha/x^{\alpha+1}$; $x > x_0$ | $x_0 > 0$, $\alpha > 0$ | | $\dfrac{\alpha x_0}{\alpha - 1}$ $\alpha > 1$ | $\dfrac{\alpha x_0^2}{(\alpha - 2)(\alpha - 1)^2}$ $\alpha > 2$ |
| Lognormal | $\dfrac{1}{x\sigma\sqrt{2\pi}}\exp\{-(\log x - m)^2/2\sigma^2\}$, $x > 0$ | $-\infty < m < \infty$ $\sigma > 0$ | | $e^{m+\sigma^2/2}$ | $(e^{\sigma^2} - 1)e^{2m+\sigma^2}$ |

**Selected References**

Actuarial Society of America. "International Actuarial Notation." *Transactions* of the Actuarial Society of America, XLVIII, (1947):166–176.

Allen, J. M. "On the Relation Between the Theories of Compound Interest and Life Contingencies." *Journal of the Institute of Actuaries,* XLI, (1907):305–337.

Allison, G. D. and Winklevoss, H. E. "The Interrelationship Among Inflation Rates, Interest Rates, and Pension Costs," *Transactions* of the Society of Actuaries, XXVII, (1975):197–210.

Arrow, K. J. "Uncertainty and the Welfare of Medical Care." *The American Economic Review,* LIII, (1963):941–973.

Baillie, D. C. "Actuarial Note: The Equation of Equilibrium." *Transactions* of the Society of Actuaries, III, (1951):74–81.

Bartlett, D. K. "Excess Ratio Distributions in Risk Theory." *Transactions* of the Society of Actuaries, XVII, (1965):435–463.

Batten, R. W. 1978. *Mortality Table Construction.* Englewood Cliffs, New Jersey: Prentice Hall, Inc.

Beard, R. E., Pentikäinen, T., and Pesonen, E. 1977. *Risk Theory; The Stochastic Basis of Insurance* (2nd ed.). London: Methuen.

Becker, D., Bojrab, I., and Buchele, L. "Letters to the Editor." *The Actuary,* XI, (1977):7.

Beekman, J. A. "A Ruin Function Approximation." *Transactions* of the Society of Actuaries, XXI, (1969):41–48, with discussion by N. L. Bowers, 275–277.

1974. *Two Stochastic Processes.* New York: Halsted Press.

Beekman, J. A., and Bowers, N. L. "An Approximation to the Finite Time Ruin Function." *Skandinavisk Aktuarietidskrift,* LV, (1972):41–56 and 128–137.

Bellhouse, D. R. and Panjer, H. H. "Stochastic Modelling of Interest Rates with Applications to Life Contingencies." *Journal of Risk and Insurance,* XLVII, (1980):91–110.

Bellman, R. E., Kalaba, R. E., and Lockett, J. 1966. *Numerical Inversion of the Laplace Transform: Applications to Biology, Economics, Engineering, and Physics.* New York: American Elsevier Publishing Company.

Bicknell, W. S. and Nesbitt, C. J. "Premiums and Reserves in Multiple Decrement Theory." *Transactions* of the Society of Actuaries, VIII, (1956):344–377.

Biggs, J. H. "Alternatives in Variable Annuity Benefit Design." *Transactions* of the Society of Actuaries, XXI, (1969):495–517.

Boermeester, J. M. "Frequency Distribution of Mortality Costs." *Transactions* of the Society of Actuaries, VIII, (1956):1–9.

Bohman, H., and Esscher F. "Studies in Risk Theory with Numerical Illustrations Concerning Distribution Functions and Stop-Loss Premiums." *Skandinavisk Aktuarietidskrift,* XLVI, (1963):173–225, and XLVII, (1964):1–40.

Borch, K. "An Attempt to Determine the Optimum Amount of Stop-Loss Reinsurance." *Transactions of the 16th International Congress of Actuaries,* I, (1960):597–610.

1974. *The Mathematical Theory of Insurance.* Lexington, Massachusetts: Lexington Books.

Bowers, N. L. "Expansions of Probability Density Functions as a Sum of Gamma Densities with Applications in Risk Theory." *Transactions* of the Society of Actuaries, XVIII, (1966):125–137.

"An Approximation to the Distribution of Annuity Costs." *Transactions* of the Society of Actuaries, XIX, (1967):295–309.

"An Upper Bound for the Net Stop-Loss Premium." *Transactions* of the Society of Actuaries, XXI, (1969):211–218.

Bowers, N. L., Jr., Hickman, J. C., and Nesbitt, C. J. "Introduction to the Dynamics of Pension Funding." *Transactions* of the Society of Actuaries, XXVIII, (1976):177–203.

"The Dynamics of Pension Funding: Contribution Theory." *Transactions* of the Society of Actuaries, XXXI, (1979):93–119.

Brillinger, D. R. "A Justification of Some Common Laws of Mortality." *Transactions* of the Society of Actuaries, XIII, (1961):116–119.

Bühlmann, H. 1970. *Mathematical Methods in Risk Theory.* New York: Springer.

Chalke, S. A. and Davlin, M. F. "Universal Life Valuation and Nonforfeiture: A Generalized Model." *Transactions* of the Society of Actuaries, XXXV, (1983):249–298.

Chamberlin, G. "The Proficient Instrument—a New Appraisal of the Commutation Function in the Context of Pension Fund Work." *Journal of the Institute of Actuaries Students' Society,* XXV, (1982):1–46.

Chapin, W. L. "Toward Adjustable Individual Life Policies." *Transactions* of the Society of Actuaries, XXVIII, (1976):237–269.

Chiang, C. L. 1968. *Introduction to Stochastic Processes in Biostatistics.* New York: John Wiley and Sons.

Cramér, H. 1930. *On the Mathematical Theory of Risk.* Stockholm: Centraltryckeriet.

Cueto, M. R. "Monetary Values for Ordinary Disability Benefits, Based on Period 2 of the 1952 Intercompany Study of the Society's Committee, with $2\frac{1}{2}\%$ Interest." *Transactions* of the Society of Actuaries, VI, (1954):108–177.

Cummins, J. D. 1973. *Development of Life Insurance Surrender Values in the United States*. Homewood, Illinois: Richard D. Irwin.

DeGroot, M. H. 1970. *Optimal Statistical Decisions*. New York: McGraw Hill.

1986. *Probability and Statistics*. Second Edition. Reading, Massachusetts: Addison-Wesley.

DeVylder, F. "Martingales and Ruin in a Dynamic Risk Process." *Scandinavian Actuarial Journal*. (1978):217–225.

Dropkin, L. B. "Some Considerations on Automobile Rating Systems Utilizing Individual Driving Records." *Proceedings of the Casualty Actuarial Society*, XLVI, (1959):165–176.

Dubourdieu, J. 1952. *Théorie Mathématique Des Assurances*. Paris: Gauthier Villars.

Duncan, R. M. "A Retirement System Granting Unit Annuities and Investing in Equities." *Transactions* of the Society of Actuaries, IV, (1952):317–344.

Edelstein, Hermann. "How Accurate are Approximations?" *The Actuary*, XI, (1977):2.

Elandt-Johnson, R. C. and Johnson, N. L. 1980. *Survival Models and Data Analysis*. New York: John Wiley and Sons.

Fassel, E. G. "Insurance for Face Amount or Reserve if Greater." *Record of the American Institute of Actuaries*, XIX, (1930):233–246.

"Premium Rates Varying by Policy Size." *Transactions* of the Society of Actuaries, VIII, (1956):390–419.

Feller, W. 1966. *An Introduction to Probability Theory and Its Applications, Vol. II*. New York: John Wiley and Sons.

1968. *An Introduction to Probability Theory and Its Applications, Vol. I* (3rd ed.). New York: John Wiley and Sons.

Fraser, J. C., Miller, W. N., and Sternhell, C. M. "Analysis of Basic Actuarial Theory for Fixed Premium Variable Benefit Life Insurance." *Transactions* of the Society of Actuaries, XXI, (1969):343–378, and discussions 379–457.

Frasier, W. M. "Second to Die Joint Life Cash Values and Reserves." *The Actuary*, XII, (1978):3.

Fretwell, R. L. and Hickman, J. C. "Approximate Probability Statements about Life Annuity Costs." *Transactions* of the Society of Actuaries, XVI, (1964):55–60.

Friedman, Milton and Savage. "The Utility Analysis of Choices Involving Risk." *Journal of Political Economy*, LVI, (1948):279–304.

Gerber, H. U. "Martingales in Risk Theory." *Mitteilungen der Vereinigung Schweizerischer Versicherungsmathematiker*, LXXIII, (1973):205–216.

"The Dilemma between Dividends and Safety and a Generalization of the Lundberg-Cramér Formulas." *Scandinavian Actuarial Journal*, LXXIV, (1974):46–57.

"A Probabilistic Model for (Life) Contingencies and a Delta-free Approach to Contingency Reserves." *Transactions* of the Society of Actuaries, XXVIII, (1976):127–141.

1979. *An Introduction to Mathematical Risk Theory*. Huebner Foundation Monograph 8, distributed by Richard D. Irwin (Homewood, Ill.).

"Principles of Premium Calculation and Reinsurance." *Transactions of the 21st International Congress of Actuaries*, I, (1980):137–142.

Gerber, H. U., and Jones, D. A. "Some Practical Considerations in Connection with the Calculation of Stop-Loss Premiums." *Transactions* of the Society of Actuaries, XXVIII, (1976):215–232.

Gingery, S. W. "Special Investigation of Group Hospital Expense Insurance Experience." *Transactions* of the Society of Actuaries, IV, (1952):44–112.

Goovaerts, M. J., and DeVylder, F. "Upper Bounds on Stop-Loss Premiums under Constraints on Claim Size Distributions as Derived from Representation Theorems for Distribution Functions." *Scandinavian Actuarial Journal*, LXXX, (1980):141–148.

Greenwood, M., and Yule, G. U. "An Inquiry into the Nature of Frequency Distributions Representative of Multiple Happenings with Particular Reference to the Occurrence of Multiple Attacks of Disease or Repeated Accidents." *Journal of the Royal Statistical Society*, LXXXIII, (1920):255–279.

Greville, T. N. E. "Mortality Tables Analyzed by Cause of Death." *Record of the American Institute of Actuaries*, XXXVII, (1948):283–294. (Discussion in XXXVIII, (1949):77–79)

"Laws of Mortality which Satisfy a Uniform Seniority Principle." *Journal of the Institute of Actuaries*, LXXXII, (1956):114–122.

Guertin, A. N. "Life Insurance Premiums." *Journal of Risk and Insurance*, 32, (1965):23–50.

Halmstad, D. G. "Underwriting the Catastrophe Accident Hazard." *Transactions* of the Society of Actuaries, XXIV, (1972):D408–D418.

"Exact Numerical Procedures in Discrete Risk Theory." *Transactions of the 20th International Congress of Actuaries*, III, (1976):557–562.

Hattendorf. *Rundschau der Versicherungen*, XVIII, (1868).

Hickman, J. C. "A Statistical Approach to Premiums and Reserves in Multiple Decrement Theory." *Transactions* of the Society of Actuaries, XVI, (1964):1–16.

Hogg, R. V. and Klugman, S. A. 1984. *Loss Distributions*. New York: John Wiley and Sons.

Hooker, P. F. and Longley-Cook, L. H. 1953. *Life and Other Contingencies, Vol. I*. Cambridge: Cambridge University Press.

1957. *Life and Other Contingencies, Vol. II*. Cambridge: Cambridge University Press.

Horn, R. G. "Life Insurance Earnings and the Release from Risk Policy Reserve." *Transactions* of the Society of Actuaries, XXIII, (1971):391–399.

Hoskins, J. E. "A New Method of Computing Non-Participating Premiums." *Transactions* of the Actuarial Society of America, XXX, (1929):140–166.

"Asset Shares and Their Relation to Nonforfeiture Values." *Transactions* of the Actuarial Society of America, XL, (1939):379–393.

Huffman, P. J. "Asset Share Mathematics." *Transactions* of the Society of Actuaries, XXX, (1978):277–296.

Hunter, A. and Phillips, J. T. 1932. *Disability Benefits in Life Insurance Policies*, The Actuarial Society of America, New York.

Institute of Actuaries, Faculty of Actuaries, "The A1967–70 Tables for Assured Lives." Institute of Actuaries, Staple Inn Hall, High Holborn, London WCIV7QJ, U.K.; Faculty of Actuaries, 23 St. Andrew Square, Edinburgh EH21AQ, U.K.

Jackson, R. T. "Some Observations on Ordinary Dividends." *Transactions* of the Society of Actuaries, XI, (1959):764–796.

Jenkins, W. A. "An Analysis of Self-Selection, among Annuitants, Including Comparisons with Selection among Insured Lives." *Transactions* of the Actuarial Society of America, XLIV, (1943):227–239.

Jordan, C. W. 1952 1st ed., 1967 2nd ed. *Life Contingencies*. Chicago: Society of Actuaries.

Kabele, T. G. Discussions of "Expanded Structure for Ordinary Dividends" and "Extensions of Lidstone's Theorem." *Transactions* of the Society of Actuaries, XXXVI, (1981):360, 403.

Kahn, P. M. "Some Remarks on a Recent Paper by Borch." *ASTIN Bulletin*, I, (1961):265–272.

"An Introduction to Collective Risk Theory and Its Application to

Stop-Loss Reinsurance." *Transactions* of the Society of Actuaries, XIV, (1962):400–425.

Kellison, S. G. 1975. *Fundamentals of Numerical Analysis,* Homewood, Illinois: Richard D. Irwin.

Kendall, M. and Stuart, A. 1977. *The Advanced Theory of Statistics, Vol. I.* New York: MacMillan Publishing Co., Inc.

Keyfitz, N. 1968. *Introduction to the Mathematics of Population.* Reading, Massachusetts: Addison-Wesley.

1977. *Applied Mathematical Demography.* New York: John Wiley and Sons.

Keyfitz, N. and Beekman, J. 1984. *Demography Through Problems.* New York: Springer-Verlag.

King, G. 1887 1st ed., 1902 2nd ed., *Institute of Actuaries' Textbook, Part II.* London: Charles and Edwin Layton.

Kischuk, R. K. Discussion of "Fundamentals of Pension Funding" by Bowers, Hickman and Nesbitt. *Transactions* of the Society of Actuaries, XXVIII, (1976):205–211.

Lauer, J. A. 1967. "Apportionable Basis for Net Premiums and Reserves." *Transactions* of the Society of Actuaries, XIX, (1967):13–23.

Lidstone, G. L. "Changes in Pure Premium Policy Values Consequent upon Variations in the Rate of Interest or Rate of Mortality." *Journal of the Institute of Actuaries,* 39, (1905):209–252.

Linton, M. A. "Analysis of the Endowment Premium." *Transactions* of the Actuarial Society of America, XX, (1919):430–439.

Lukacs, E. "On the Mathematical Theory of Risk." *Journal of the Institute of Actuaries Students' Society,* VIII, (1948):20–37.

Lundberg, O. 1940. *On Random Processes and Their Application to Sickness and Accident Statistics.* Uppsala: Almqvist and Wiksells.

Macarchuk, J. "Some Observations on the Actuarial Aspects of the Insured Variable Annuity." *Transactions* of the Society of Actuaries, XXI, (1969):529–538.

Maclean, J. B. and Marshall, E. W. 1937. *Distribution of Surplus.* Chicago: Society of Actuaries.

Makeham, W. M. "On the Application of the Theory of the Composition of Decremental Forces." *Journal of the Institute of Actuaries,* XVIII, (1874):317–322.

Menge, W. O. "Forces of Decrement in a Multiple-Decrement Table." *Record of the American Institute of Actuaries,* XXI, (1932):41–46.

"Commissioners Reserve Valuation Method," *Record of the American Institute of Actuaries,* XXXV, (1946):258–300.

Mereu, J. A. "Some Observations on Actuarial Approximations." *Transactions* of the Society of Actuaries, XIII, (1961):87–102.

"Annuity Values Directly from Makeham Constants." *Transactions* of the Society of Actuaries, XIV, (1962):269–286.

"An Algorithm for Computing Expected Stop-Loss Claims under a Group Life Contract." *Transactions* of the Society of Actuaries, XXIV, (1972):311–320.

"Letters to the Editor." *The Actuary*, XI, (1977):8.

Miller, M. D. "Group Weekly Indemnity Continuation Table Study." *Transactions* of the Society of Actuaries, III, (1951):31–67.

Miller, W. N. "Variable Life Insurance Product Design." *Journal of the Risk and Insurance Association*, Vol. 38, (1971):527–542.

Mood, A. M., Graybill, F. A. and Boes, D. C. (1974). *Introduction to the Theory of Statistics*, New York: McGraw Hill.

Myers, R. J. "Actuarial Analysis of Pension Plans under Inflationary Conditions." *Transactions-16th International Congress of Actuaries*, 1, (1960):301–315.

National Association of Insurance Commissioners. 1939. "Report of the Committee to Study the Need for a New Mortality Table and Related Topics." Kansas City: National Association of Insurance Commissioners.

1941. "Report and Statements on Nonforfeiture Benefits and Related Matters." Kansas City: National Association of Insurance Commissioners.

Neill, A. 1977. *Life Contingencies*. London: Heinemann.

Nesbitt, C. J. Discussion of "A Statistical Approach to Premiums and Reserves in Multiple Decrement Theory." *Transactions* of the Society of Actuaries, XVI, (1964):149–153.

Nesbitt, C. J. and Van Eenam, M. L. "Rate Functions and Their Role in Actuarial Mathematics." *The Record of the American Institute of Actuaries*, XXXVII, (1948):202–222.

Noback, J. C. 1969. *Life Insurance Accounting: A Study of the Financial Statements of Life Insurance Companies in the United States*. Homewood, Illinois: Richard D. Irwin.

O'Grady, F. T. 1987. *Individual Health Insurance*. Itasca, Illinois: Society of Actuaries.

Panjer, H. H. "The Aggregate Claims Distribution and Stop-Loss Reinsurance." *Transactions* of the Society of Actuaries, XXXII, (1980):523–535.

Pesonen, E. "On the Calculation of the Generalized Poisson Function." *ASTIN Bulletin*, IV, (1967):120–128.

Pratt, J. W. "Risk Aversion in the Small and in the Large." *Econometrica*, XXXII, (1964):122–136.

Preston, S. H., Keyfitz, N. and Schoen, R. "Cause-of-Death Life Tables: Application of a New Technique to Worldwide Data." *Transactions* of the Society of Actuaries, XXV, (1973):83–109.

Promislow, S. D. "Extensions of Lidstone's Theorem." *Transactions* of the Society of Actuaries, XXXIII, (1981):367–401.

Rasor, E. A. and Greville, T. N. E. "Complete Annuities." *Transactions* of the Society of Actuaries, IV, (1952):574–582.

Rasor, E. A. and Myers, R. J. "Actuarial Note: Valuation of the Shares in a Share-and-Share-Alike Last Survivor Annuity." *Transactions* of the Society of Actuaries, IV, (1952):128-130.

Renyi, A. 1962. *Wahrscheinlichkeitsrechnung.* Berlin: Deutscher Verlag der Wissenschaften.

Richardson, C. F. B. "Expense Formulas for Minimum Nonforfeiture Values." *Transactions* of the Society of Actuaries, XXIX, (1977):209–229.

Scher, E. "Relationships among the Fully Continuous, the Discounted Continuous, and the Semicontinuous Reserve Bases for Ordinary Life Insurance." *Transactions* of the Society of Actuaries, XXVI, (1974):597–606.

Seal, H. L. 1969. *Stochastic Theory of a Risk Business.* New York: John Wiley and Sons.

"Studies in the History of Probability and Statistics. Multiple Decrements or Competing Risks." *Biometrika*, LXIV, (1977):429–439.

"From Aggregate Claims Distribution to Probability of Ruin." *ASTIN Bulletin*, X, (1978):47–53.

1978. *Survival Probabilities—The Goal of Risk Theory.* New York: John Wiley and Sons.

Simon, L. J. "The Negative Binomial and the Poisson Distributions Compared." *Proceedings of the Casualty Actuarial Society*, XLVII, (1960):20–24.

Smith, F. C. "The Use of Continuous Functions with the Retirement Endowment Plan—Actuarial Note." *Transactions* of the Society of Actuaries, XIII, (1961):364–367.

Society of Actuaries. 1962. "Monetary Tables for Disability Benefits based on 1952 Disability Study—Period 2 combined with the 1958 CSO Mortality Table, $2\frac{1}{2}$% Interest." Chicago: Society of Actuaries.

"1965–70 Basic Tables." *Transactions* of the Society of Actuaries, 1973 Reports: 199–223.

1976. "Report on Actuarial Principles and Practical Problems with regard to Nonforfeiture Requirements." Chicago: Society of Actuaries.

Spurgeon, E. F. 1922 1st ed., 1929 2nd ed., 1932 3rd ed. *Life Contingencies*. Cambridge: Cambridge University Press.

Steffensen, J. F. "On Hattendorf's Theorem in the Theory of Risk." *Skandinavisk Aktuarietidskrift*, XII, (1929):1–17.

Takács, L. 1967. *Combinatorial Methods in the Theory of Stochastic Processes*. New York: John Wiley & Sons.

Taylor, R. H. "The Probability Distribution of Life Annuity Reserves and Its Application to a Pension System." *The Proceedings of the Conference of Actuaries in Public Practice*, II, (1952):100–150.

Taylor, G. C. "Upper Bounds on Stop-Loss Premiums under Constraints on Claim Size Distributions." *Scandinavian Actuarial Journal*, LXXVII, (1977):94–105.

Tenenbein, A. and Vanderhoof, I. T. "New Mathematical Laws of Select and Ultimate Mortality." *Transactions* of the Society of Actuaries, XXXII, (1980):119–158.

Thompson, J. S. "Select and Ultimate Mortality." *Transactions of the 10th International Congress of Actuaries*, II, (1934):252–263.

Trowbridge, C. L. "Fundamentals of Pension-Funding." *Transactions*, Society of Actuaries, IV, (1952):17–43.

"Funding of Group Life Insurance." *Transactions*, Society of Actuaries, VII, (1955):270–285.

"The Unfunded Present Value Family of Pension Funding Methods." *Transactions* of the Society of Actuaries, XV, (1963):151–169.

Trowbridge, J. R. "Assessmentism—An Alternative to Pensions Funding?" *Journal of the Institute of Actuaries*, 104, (1977):173–204.

U.S. Department of Health and Welfare. Public Health Service. 1985. *United States Life Tables: 1979–81*. Washington D.C.: Government Printing Office.

White, R. P. and Greville, T. N. E. 1959. "On Computing the Probability that Exactly $k$ of $n$ Independent Events will Occur." *Transactions* of the Society of Actuaries, XI, (1959):88–95.

Willett, A. H. 1951. *The Economic Theory of Risk and Insurance*. Philadelphia: University of Pennsylvania Press.

Williamson, W. R. "Selection." *Transactions* of the Actuarial Society of America, XLIII, (1942):33–43.

Wooddy, J. 1973. *Study Notes for Risk Theory*. Chicago: Society of Actuaries.

Woolhouse, W. S. B. "On the Construction of Tables of Mortality." *Journal of the Institute of Actuaries*, XIII, (1867):75–102.

Ziock, R. W. "A Proof of Lidstone's Theorem." *Actuarial Research Clearing House*, 1978.2, (1978):273–274.

*Chapter 1*

1.1. a. and b.

| $w$ | $u(w)$ | $u(w_1,w_2)$ | $u(w_1,w_2,w_3)$ |
|---|---|---|---|
| 0 | $-1.00$ | $125 \times 10^{-6}$ | $-48 \times 10^{-10}$ |
| 4 000 | $-0.500$ | $93 \times 10^{-6}$ | $-34 \times 10^{-10}$ |
| 6 700 | $-0.250$ | $78 \times 10^{-6}$ | $-14 \times 10^{-10}$ |
| 8 300 | $-0.125$ | $74 \times 10^{-6}$ | — |
| 10 000 | $0.000$ | — | — |

1.2. b. 2, 2   d. $2\log 2$

1.3. c. $\mathrm{Var}[X]$

1.7. a. Yes, for all $w$   b. $(90 < w < 100) \cup (w > 110)$

1.11. $-\dfrac{n}{2\alpha}\log(1-2\alpha)$

1.12. a. $G = 400\log\dfrac{13}{12} = 32.02$   b. $G = 150\log\dfrac{3}{2} = 60.82$

1.13. a. 30   b. 26

1.15. a. $-[1-F(d)]$

1.17. a. 10,   100

1.18. a. 50, $\dfrac{2500}{3}$   b. $k = 0.25$, $d = 50$

c. $\mathrm{Var}[X - I_1(X)] = 468.75$; $\mathrm{Var}[X - I_2(X)] = 260.42$

*Chapter 2*

2.1. 1/2, 19/4

2.2. 1/2, 77/12

2.3. 35/4, 1085/48

2.4. 7/4, 77/48

2.5. 49/4, 735/16

2.6. $a/100$ and $a^2(197/30,000)$

2.7.

| $x$ | $F_S(x)$ |
|---|---|
| 0 | 0.2268 |
| 1 | 0.2916 |
| 2 | 0.4374 |
| 3 | 0.6210 |
| 4 | 0.7434 |
| 5 | 0.8586 |
| 6 | 0.9018 |
| 7 | 0.9582 |
| 8 | 0.9762 |
| 9 | 0.9918 |
| 10 | 0.9948 |
| 11 | 0.9988 |
| 12 | 0.9996 |
| 13 | 1.0000 |

2.8.  c.  1/48, 1/6, 1/2

2.9.  $f_S(x) = \dfrac{1}{2}e^{-x} - 2e^{-x/2} + \dfrac{3}{2}e^{-x/3}$

2.10.  $E[X] = 1$, $Var[X] = 1/3$; $E[Y] = 3/2$, $Var[Y] = 3/4$;
$Pr(X + Y > 4) \cong 0.0748$; $Pr(X + Y > 4) = 0.0833$

2.11.  a.  $b = -1$, $c = 1$, $d = a$ or $b = 1$, $c = 0$, $d = -a$
b.  0.0228, 0.1587, 0.5000

2.12.  a.  18, 36    b.  27.8713, 31.9607

2.13.  a.  0.0041    b.  0.0045

2.14.  3.56; that is, 35,600

2.15.  a.  6.4, 6.144    b.  $7(10^4)$, $17.072(10^8)$    c.  1.37341

2.16.  0.0062

*Chapter 3*

3.1.

| $s(x)$ | $F(x)$ | $f(x)$ | $\mu_x$ |
|---|---|---|---|
| $\cos x$ | $1 - \cos x$ | $\sin x$ | — |
| — | $1 - e^{-x}$ | $e^{-x}$ | 1 |
| $\dfrac{1}{1+x}$ | — | $\dfrac{1}{(1+x)^2}$ | $\dfrac{1}{1+x}$ |

3.2.  a.  $\exp\left\{-\dfrac{B}{\log c}(c^x - 1)\right\}$    b.  $\exp\{-u x^{n+1}\}$, $u = \dfrac{k}{n+1}$

c.  $\left(1 + \dfrac{x}{b}\right)^{-a}$

3.3.  $\mu_x = \dfrac{x^2}{4}$, $f(x) = \dfrac{x^2}{4}e^{-x^3/12}$, $F(x) = 1 - e^{-x^3/12}$

3.4.  a.  $\displaystyle\int_0^{\infty} \mu_x \, dx < \infty$

b.  $s'(x) > 0$ for some $x$, including $x = 1,2$

c.  $\displaystyle\int_0^{\infty} f(x)\, dx \neq 1$

3.5.  a.  $\dfrac{1}{(100 - x)}$    b.  $\dfrac{x}{100}$    c.  $\dfrac{1}{100}$    d.  $\dfrac{3}{10}$

3.7.  0.0020

3.8.  $f(x) = \binom{10}{x}(0.77107)^x(0.22893)^{10-x}$, $x = 0,1,2,\ldots,10$
$E[\mathscr{L}(65)] = 7.7107$; $Var[\mathscr{L}(65)] = 1.7652$

3.9.  a.  $\dfrac{9}{4}$ for each    b.  $\dfrac{27}{16}$ for each    c.  $-\dfrac{1}{3}$ for each

3.10. a. $_5q_0 = 0.01505$ is more than 10 times $_5q_5 = 0.00150$   b. 0.15673

3.13. 1436.19

3.15. a. $\dfrac{1}{c}$   b. $\dfrac{1}{c^2}$   c. $\dfrac{(\log 2)}{c}$

3.16. a. $te^{-t^2/2}$   b. $\sqrt{\dfrac{\pi}{2}}$

3.17. a. $(100 - x)/2$   b. $(100 - x)^2/12$   c. $(100 - x)/2$

3.19. a. $\dfrac{8}{9}$   b. $\dfrac{1}{8}$   c. $\dfrac{1}{8}$   d. $\dfrac{1}{128}$   e. $\dfrac{128}{3}$

3.23. Uniform distribution:  0.98971
　　　Constant force:　　　0.98966
　　　Balducci:　　　　　　0.98960

3.24. a. 77.59   b. 29.11

3.25. a. 0.0440   b. 0.0442

3.26.

| | Uniform distribution | Constant force | Balducci |
|---|---|---|---|
| a. | 0.01270 | 0.01262 | 0.01254 |
| b. | 0.01368 | 0.01377 | 0.01387 |
| c. | 0.01377 | 0.01377 | 0.01377 |

3.30. a. $\alpha/(\omega - x)$   b. $(\omega - x)/(\alpha + 1)$

3.31. a. 0.00142   b. 0.99867

3.32. 0.317, 0.140

3.33. 0.979

3.34. $\log\left(1 - \dfrac{1}{2}q_x\right) - \log(1 - q_x)$

3.35. $q_x' < 2q_x$

3.37. a. $\left(\dfrac{1 + Bc^x}{1 + B}\right)^{-A/(B \log c)}$

3.38. a. $\dfrac{5^7}{4^{10}} = 0.07451$   b. 77.21

3.39. b. $-\log(1 - q_x)$   c. $\dfrac{-q_x^2}{[(1 - q_x)\log(1 - q_x)]}$   d. $\dfrac{1}{45}$

*Chapter 4*

4.5. b. $\bar{A}^1_{x:\overline{n}|} = \dfrac{\mu_{x+n}}{\delta + \mu_{x+n}} A_{x:\overline{n}|}^{\,1}$   c. $-\dfrac{\mu_{x+n}}{\delta + \mu_{x+n}}(A_{x:\overline{n}|}^{\,1})^2$, where $n$ satisfies (b).

　　　d. $n = \dfrac{\log 2}{\mu + \delta}$, $\min \text{Cov}[Z_1, Z_2] = -\dfrac{\mu}{4(\mu + \delta)}$

4.6. a. 0.237832   b. 0.416667

4.7.  a.  0.092099   b.  0.055321

4.8.  a.  $\dfrac{20}{3\,(100-x)}\left[1-\left(\dfrac{20}{120-x}\right)^{3}\right]$;

$\dfrac{20}{7\,(100-x)}\left[1-\left(\dfrac{20}{120-x}\right)^{7}\right]$

$-\left\{\dfrac{20}{3\,(100-x)}\left[1-\left(\dfrac{20}{120-x}\right)^{3}\right]\right\}^{2}$

b.  $\dfrac{20}{3\,(100-x)}\left[10-10\left(\dfrac{20}{120-x}\right)^{2}-(100-x)\left(\dfrac{20}{120-x}\right)^{3}\right]$

4.10.  a.  $\mu/(\mu+\delta)^{2}$   b.  $\mu[2/(\mu+2\,\delta)^{3}-\mu/(\mu+\delta)^{4}]$

4.11.  a.  0.407159   b.  5.554541

4.13.  a.  0.5   b.  0.05

4.14.  b.  $(IA)_{x:\overline{m}|}=(IA)^{1}_{x:\overline{m}|}+mA_{x:\frac{1}{m}|}$

4.15.  a.  $v^{(k+(j+1)/m)}$   b.  $A_{x}^{(m)}=\displaystyle\sum_{k=0}^{\infty}v^{k+1}\,{}_{k}p_{x}\sum_{j=0}^{m-1}{}_{j/m|1/m}q_{x+k}\,(1+i)^{(1-(j+1)/m)}$

4.22.  $\dfrac{1}{D_{x}}(2\,M_{x}-M_{65})$

4.23.  $\dfrac{1000}{D_{0}}(\bar{R}_{0}+\bar{R}_{2}-2\,\bar{R}_{6}+40\,\bar{M}_{21})$

4.24.  a.  $\dfrac{1}{D_{30}}\left[\dfrac{i}{\delta}(R_{30}-R_{65}-35\,M_{65})+35\,D_{65}\right]$

b.  $\dfrac{1}{D_{30}}\left[\dfrac{i}{\delta}(R_{30}-R_{65}-35\,M_{65})-\dfrac{i}{\delta}\left(\dfrac{1}{d}-\dfrac{1}{\delta}\right)(M_{30}-M_{65})+35\,D_{65}\right]$

c.  $\dfrac{1}{D_{30}}\left[\dfrac{i}{\delta}(R_{30}-R_{40}-10\,M_{65})-\dfrac{i}{\delta}\left(\dfrac{1}{d}-\dfrac{1}{\delta}\right)(M_{30}-M_{40})+10\,D_{65}\right]$

4.26.  a.  $9100/(14-k)$

b.  $1{,}000{,}000\,[^{2}A_{x:\overline{n}|}^{1}-(A_{x:\overline{n}|}^{1})^{2}]+(k\,\pi)^{2}\,[^{2}\bar{A}_{x:\overline{n}|}^{1}-(\bar{A}_{x:\overline{n}|}^{1})^{2}]$

$-2000\,k\,\pi\,\bar{A}_{x:\overline{n}|}^{1}A_{x:\overline{n}|}^{1}$ where $\pi$ is the net single premium in (a)

4.27.  a.  0.307215

4.28.  b.  0.001493   c.  0.001493

*Chapter 5*

5.1.  230.47

5.2.  4338.89

5.4.  a.  16.008, 12.761, 5.397   b.  3.137, 10.230, 9.523

5.5.  a.  0.111, 0.251, 0.572   b.  0.0251

5.7. $-\text{Var}\,[v^T] = -(^2\bar{A}_x - \bar{A}_x^2)$

5.9. $\displaystyle\sum_{k=m}^{m+n-1} v^k\,{}_kp_x;\ \ddot{a}_{x:\overline{m+n|}} - \ddot{a}_{x:\overline{m|}};\ \dfrac{A_{x:\overline{m|}} - A_{x:\overline{m+n|}}}{d};\ {}_mE_x\,\ddot{a}_{x+m:\overline{n|}}$

5.13. $1 = i\,a_{x:\overline{n|}} + i\,A^1_{x:\overline{n|}} + A_{x:\overline{n|}}$

5.16. $\ddot{a}_{x:\overline{n|}} - \dfrac{m-1}{2m}(1 - {}_nE_x),\ \ \ {}_{n|}\ddot{a}_x - \dfrac{m-1}{2m}\,{}_nE_x$

5.22. a. $\alpha(m)\,\ddot{s}_{25:\overline{40|}} - \beta(m)\left(\dfrac{1}{{}_{40}E_{25}} - 1\right)$    b. (i) 15.038    (ii) 196.380

5.23. a. $N_x/D_x$   b. $N_{x+1}/D_x$   c. $(N_x - N_{x+n})/D_x$
d. $(N_{x+1} - N_{x+n+1})/D_x$   e. $N_{x+n}/D_x$
f. $N_{x+n+1}/D_x$   g. $[N_x^{(m)} - N_{x+n}^{(m)}]/D_x$   h. $N_{x+n}^{(m)}/D_x$

5.24. a. $\tilde{N}_{60}^{(12)}/D_{60}$   b. $(\tilde{N}_{40}^{(12)} - \tilde{N}_{65}^{(12)})/D_{40}$   c. $\tilde{N}_{70}^{(12)}/D_{40}$

5.31. b. $(^2\bar{A}_x - \bar{A}_x^2)/i^2$

5.34. a. $\ddot{a}_x + 0.03\,(Ia)_x = (N_x + 0.03\,S_{x+1})/D_x$

b. $\displaystyle\sum_{k=0}^{\infty} (1.03)^k v^k\,{}_kp_x = \ddot{a}'_x$ evaluated at interest rate $i' = \dfrac{i - 0.03}{1.03}$

5.35. $\displaystyle\int_0^n (n - t)\,v^t\,{}_tp_x\,dt$

5.36. $1200\,[\tilde{N}_{30}^{(12)} + \tilde{N}_{40}^{(12)} + 3\,\tilde{N}_{50}^{(12)} + 5\,\tilde{N}_{60}^{(12)} - 10\,\tilde{N}_{70}^{(12)}]/D_{70}$

5.37. $\bar{a}_{35:\overline{25|}} - {}_{25}p_{35}\,\bar{a}_{\overline{25|}}$

5.38. $\ddot{a}_{x:\overline{m|}} - {}_np_x\,\ddot{a}_{\overline{m|}}$

5.39. $\dfrac{1}{12}\,\ddot{a}_{x:\overline{25|}} - \dfrac{25}{12}\,{}_{25}E_x$

5.41. $v^{2n}\,{}_np_x\,(1 - {}_np_x)\,\ddot{a}^2_{x+n} + v^{2n}\,{}_np_x\,\dfrac{{}^2A_{x+n} - A^2_{x+n}}{d^2}$

5.44. a. $\alpha(m) = 1 + \dfrac{m^2 - 1}{12\,m^2}\,\delta^2 + \dfrac{2\,m^4 - 5\,m^2 + 3}{720\,m^4}\,\delta^4 + \cdots$

$\beta(m) = \dfrac{m-1}{2m}\left[1 + \dfrac{m+1}{3m}\,\delta + \dfrac{m(m+1)}{12\,m^2}\,\delta^2\right.$

$\left. + \dfrac{(m+1)(6\,m^2 - 4)}{360\,m^3}\,\delta^3 + \cdots\right]$

b. $\alpha(\infty) = 1 + \dfrac{1}{12}\,\delta^2 + \dfrac{1}{360}\,\delta^4 + \cdots$

$\beta(\infty) = \dfrac{1}{2}\left[1 + \dfrac{1}{3}\,\delta + \dfrac{1}{12}\,\delta^2 + \dfrac{1}{60}\,\delta^3 + \cdots\right]$

5.46. $\dfrac{I}{\delta} + \left(J - \dfrac{I}{\delta}\right) v^T; \quad \dfrac{I}{\delta} + \left(J - \dfrac{I}{\delta}\right) \bar{A}_x; \quad \left(J - \dfrac{I}{\delta}\right)^2 ({}^2\bar{A}_x - \bar{A}_x^2)$

5.47. a. 14.353   b. 13.350   c. 1.002

5.51. a. 14,624   b. 15,422

5.54. a. 488.23   b. 700.48   c. 531.77

*Chapter 6*

6.1. 0, 0.1779

6.3. $\dfrac{\mu}{\mu + 2\,\delta} = {}^2\bar{A}_x$

6.7.

| Insurance | Annual Premiums for (35) | | |
| | Fully Continuous | Semicontinuous | Fully Discrete |
| --- | --- | --- | --- |
| 10-Year Endowment | 0.075128 | 0.072885 | 0.072810 |
| 30-Year Endowment | 0.015371 | 0.014894 | 0.014751 |
| 60-Year Endowment | 0.008913 | 0.008621 | 0.008374 |
| Whole Life | 0.008903 | 0.008611 | 0.008362 |
| 30-Year Term | 0.005117 | 0.004958 | 0.004815 |
| 10-Year Term | 0.002669 | 0.002589 | 0.002514 |

6.9. $A_x = (1 - r)/(1 + i - r); \quad P_x = (1 - r)/(1 + i);$
$\ddot{a}_x = (1 + i)/(1 + i - r);$
$({}^2A_x - A_x^2)/(d\,\ddot{a}_x)^2 = (1 - r)\,r/(1 + 2\,i + i^2 - r)$

6.10. 0.019139

6.12. 0.032868

6.13. 0.0413

6.14. With the common $(\bar{A}_{40:\overline{25}|})$ omitted from the premium symbols,
$$P \le P^{(2)} \le P^{\{4\}} \le P^{\{12\}} \le \bar{P}.$$

6.15. 100/99

6.16. 740.93

6.18. a. $(\bar{M}_x - \bar{M}_{x+30} + D_{x+30})/(N_x^{(12)} - N_{x+20}^{(12)})$
b. $(\bar{M}_x - \bar{M}_{x+30} + D_{x+30})/(\bar{N}_x - \bar{N}_{x+20})$
c. $(d^{(4)}/\delta)(b)$   d. $N_{65}/(N_{25} - N_{45})$

6.19. $5000\,(d/\delta)\,[40\,\bar{M}_{30} - (\bar{R}_{31} - \bar{R}_{71})]/(\bar{N}_{30} - \bar{N}_{50})$

6.20. $P(A'^{1}_{45:\overline{20}|})$ where $A'^{1}_{45:\overline{20}|}$ is the net single premium for a 20-year term insurance on (45) under which $b_{k+1} = \ddot{s}_{\overline{k+1}|}$

6.21. a. 11.5451, 20.4106   b. 6.3099, 25.6458

6.23. $_{25}P_{60}$

6.24. b. $P^{(12)}(A^{(12)}_{1 \atop 65:\overline{10}|}) + d^{(12)}$

6.25. $100,000/[1.1\,\ddot{s}_{\overline{30|}} - 0.1\,\ddot{s}_{35:\overline{30|}}]$

6.26. $0.008$

6.27. $[11,000\,M_x + 25\,(N_x - N_{x+20})]/[N_x - N_{x+20} - 1.1\,(R_x - R_{x+20})]$

6.28. $(M_{25} + M_{35})/(N_{25} + N_{35} - 2\,N_{65})$

6.29. $P^{(m)}(\bar{A}_x) = \bar{M}_x/N_x^{(m)};\ P^{(m)}(\bar{A}^1_{x:\overline{n|}}) = [\bar{M}_x - \bar{M}_{x+n}]/[N_x^{(m)} - N_{x+n}^{(m)}];$
$P^{(m)}(\bar{A}_{x:\overline{n|}}) = [\bar{M}_x - \bar{M}_{x+n} + D_{x+n}]/[N_x^{(m)} - N_{x+n}^{(m)}];$
$_hP^{(m)}(\bar{A}_x) = \bar{M}_x/[N_x^{(m)} - N_{x+h}^{(m)}];$
$_hP^{(m)}(\bar{A}_{x:\overline{n|}}) = [\bar{M}_x - \bar{M}_{x+n} + D_{x+n}]/[N_x^{(m)} - N_{x+h}^{(m)}]$

6.30. $L_1 = v^T - \bar{P}(\bar{A}_x)\,\bar{a}_{\overline{T|}} \equiv 1 - (1/\bar{a}_x)\,\bar{a}_{\overline{T|}} = L_2$

6.31. a. $-0.08$   b. $0.1296$   c. $0.1587$

*Chapter 7*

7.1. $_tL = \begin{cases} v^U - \bar{P}(\bar{A}_{x:\overline{n|}})\,\bar{a}_{\overline{U|}} & U < n - t \\ v^{n-t} - \bar{P}(\bar{A}_{x:\overline{n|}})\,\bar{a}_{\overline{n-t|}} & U \geq n - t \end{cases}$

7.2. $\mathrm{E}[_tL] = \bar{a}_{x+t:\overline{n-t|}};\ \mathrm{Var}[_tL] = (^2\bar{A}_{x+t:\overline{n-t|}} - \bar{A}^2_{x+t:\overline{n-t|}})/\delta^2$

7.3. a. $\bar{A}_{45:\overline{20|}} - {}_{20}\bar{P}(\bar{A}_{35:\overline{30|}})\,\bar{a}_{45:\overline{10|}}$   b. $\bar{A}^1_{50:\overline{5|}}$

7.4. $\bar{A}_{50} - {}_{20}\bar{P}(\bar{A}_{40})\,\bar{a}_{50:\overline{10|}};\ [{}_{10}\bar{P}(\bar{A}_{50}) - {}_{20}\bar{P}(\bar{A}_{40})]\,\bar{a}_{50:\overline{10|}};$
$\left[1 - \dfrac{{}_{20}\bar{P}(\bar{A}_{40})}{{}_{10}\bar{P}(\bar{A}_{50})}\right]\bar{A}_{50};\ {}_{20}\bar{P}(\bar{A}_{40})\,\bar{s}_{40:\overline{10|}} - {}_{10}\bar{k}_{40}$

7.5. $\bar{A}_{50:\overline{10|}} - \bar{P}(\bar{A}_{40:\overline{20|}})\,\bar{a}_{50:\overline{10|}};\ [\bar{P}(\bar{A}_{50:\overline{10|}}) - \bar{P}(\bar{A}_{40:\overline{20|}})]\,\bar{a}_{50:\overline{10|}}$
$\left[1 - \dfrac{\bar{P}(\bar{A}_{40:\overline{20|}})}{\bar{P}(\bar{A}_{50:\overline{10|}})}\right]\bar{A}_{50:\overline{10|}};\ \bar{P}(\bar{A}_{40:\overline{20|}})\,\bar{s}_{40:\overline{10|}} - {}_{10}\bar{k}_{40}$
$1 - \dfrac{\bar{a}_{50:\overline{10|}}}{\bar{a}_{40:\overline{20|}}};\ \dfrac{\bar{P}(\bar{A}_{50:\overline{10|}}) - \bar{P}(\bar{A}_{40:\overline{20|}})}{\bar{P}(\bar{A}_{50:\overline{10|}}) + \delta};\ \dfrac{\bar{A}_{50:\overline{10|}} - \bar{A}_{40:\overline{20|}}}{1 - \bar{A}_{40:\overline{20|}}}$

7.6. $\bar{P}({}_{30|}\bar{a}_{35})\,\bar{s}_{35:\overline{20|}}$

7.8. (7.3.3)

7.9. $A_{50} - {}_{20}P_{40}\,\ddot{a}_{50:\overline{10|}};\ [{}_{10}P_{50} - {}_{20}P_{40}]\,\ddot{a}_{50:\overline{10|}};\ \left[1 - \dfrac{{}_{20}P_{40}}{{}_{10}P_{50}}\right]A_{50};$
${}_{20}P_{40}\,\ddot{s}_{40:\overline{10|}} - {}_{10}k_{40}$

7.10. $A_{50:\overline{10|}} - P_{40:\overline{20|}}\,\ddot{a}_{50:\overline{10|}};\ [P_{50:\overline{10|}} - P_{40:\overline{20|}}]\,\ddot{a}_{50:\overline{10|}};$
$\left[1 - \dfrac{P_{40:\overline{20|}}}{P_{50:\overline{10|}}}\right]A_{50:\overline{10|}};\ P_{40:\overline{20|}}\,\ddot{s}_{40:\overline{10|}} - {}_{10}k_{40};$
$1 - \dfrac{\ddot{a}_{50:\overline{10|}}}{\ddot{a}_{40:\overline{20|}}};\ \dfrac{P_{50:\overline{10|}} - P_{40:\overline{20|}}}{P_{50:\overline{10|}} + d};\ \dfrac{A_{50:\overline{10|}} - A_{40:\overline{20|}}}{1 - A_{40:\overline{20|}}}$

7.12. $1/5$

7.13.

| Insurance | Fully Continuous | Semicontinuous | Fully Discrete |
|---|---|---|---|
| 30-Year Endowment | 0.17530 | 0.17504 | 0.17407 |
| Whole Life | 0.08604 | 0.08566 | 0.08319 |
| 30-Year Term | 0.03379 | 0.03370 | 0.03273 |

7.14. (b) and (c)

7.16. All but (d)

7.17. All

7.25. $(\bar{A}_{x:\overline{40}|})$ is omitted from the reserve and premium symbols.

a. $\frac{1}{2}\,_{20}V + \frac{1}{2}\,_{21}V + \frac{1}{2}\,P$   b. $\frac{1}{2}\,_{20}\bar{V} + \frac{1}{2}\,_{21}\bar{V}$

c. $\frac{1}{2}\,_{20}V^{(2)} + \frac{1}{2}\,_{21}V^{(2)}$   d. $\frac{1}{3}\,_{20}V^{(2)} + \frac{2}{3}\,_{21}V^{(2)} + \frac{1}{3}\,P^{(2)}$

e. Same as (b)   f. $\frac{1}{3}\,_{20}\bar{V} + \frac{2}{3}\,_{21}\bar{V} + \frac{1}{3}\,P^{\{2\}}$

7.26. 0.05448

7.30. b. $\mathrm{Var}\,[L] = 0.076090$

7.31. a. 0.0067994   b. 0.1858077   c. 0.2012024
      d. 0.0275369   e. 0.0255406

7.34. $-{}_t p_x\,[\,\delta\,_t\bar{V}(\bar{A}_x) + \bar{P}(\bar{A}_x)]$

7.35. a. $\{10{,}000\,[10\,\bar{M}_{30} - \bar{M}_{50} - \bar{M}_{55} - 2\,\bar{M}_{60} - 6\,\bar{M}_{65}]/(\bar{N}_{30} - \bar{N}_{65})\}\,2\,\bar{a}_{\overline{1/2}|}$
      b. $60{,}000\,(\bar{M}_{60} - \bar{M}_{65})/D_{60} - P\,(\bar{N}_{60} - \bar{N}_{65})/D_{60}$
      where $P$ is the fully continuous premium between the braces in (a)

7.36. a. $100{,}000\,D_{65}/(D_{35} - M_{35} + M_{65})$
      b. $[100{,}000\,D_{65} + S\,(M_{35+k} - M_{65})]/D_{35+k}$
      c. $S\,[D_{35} - (M_{35} - M_{35+k})]/D_{35+k}$

7.37. a. $[(\bar{M}_{40} - \bar{M}_{65} + D_{65}) - P\,(N_{40}^{(12)} - N_{50}^{(12)})]/D_{40}$;
      $[P\,(N_{30}^{(12)} - N_{40}^{(12)}) - (\bar{M}_{30} - \bar{M}_{40})]/D_{40}$
      b. $(\bar{M}_{55} - \bar{M}_{65} + D_{65})/D_{55}$;   $[P\,(N_{30}^{(12)} - N_{50}^{(12)}) - (\bar{M}_{30} - \bar{M}_{55})]/D_{55}$

7.38. 0.008

7.39. 0.240

7.40. a. $P_{25}\,N_{35}/(N_{35} - N_{65})$
      b. $P_{25}\,(N_{25} - N_{35})/D_{35} - (M_{25} - M_{35})/D_{35} = {}_{10}V_{25}$
      c. $1 - P_{25}\,N_{65}/M_{35}$
      d. $_{20}V_{25} + (1 - B)\,(M_{35} - M_{45})/D_{45}$

7.41. a. $_t p_x\,(\pi_t + \delta\,_t\bar{V} - b_t\,\mu_{x+t})$
      b. $v^t\,(\pi_t + \mu_{x+t}\,_t\bar{V} - b_t\,\mu_{x+t})$
      c. $v^t\,_t p_x\,[\pi_t - b_t\,\mu_{x+t}]$

7.43. a. 0.0241821   b. 0.0189660

7.47. a. and b. 1491.03   c. 343.84   d. 0

7.48. a. 1,490,915
 b. 6,450,962; 1,495,093, which is 1.00280 times the reserve
 c. 5,311,375; supplement is 3,791, which is 0.00254 times the reserve
 d. For b.: 645,096,250; 149,133,281, which is 1.00028 times the reserve
 For c.: 531,137,500; supplement is 37,911, which is 0.00025 times the reserve

7.49. a. 1,104,260 is the reserve for these policies
 b. 6,450,962; 1,108,438, which is 1.00378 times the reserve
 c. 5,311,375; supplement is 3,791, which is 0.00343 times the reserve
 d. For b.: 645,096,250; 110,467,781, which is 1.00038 times the reserve
 For c.: 531,137,500; supplement is 37,911, which is 0.00034 times the reserve

7.50. a. Replace ${}_{k}^{h}V(\bar{A}_{x:\overline{n}|})$, ${}_{h}P(\bar{A}_{x:\overline{n}|})$ by ${}_{k}^{h}\bar{V}(\bar{A}_{x:\overline{n}|})$, ${}_{h}\bar{P}(\bar{A}_{x:\overline{n}|})$ and add bars over the $N$ symbols.
 b. Replace ${}_{k}^{h}V(\bar{A}_{x:\overline{n}|})$, ${}_{h}P(\bar{A}_{x:\overline{n}|})$ by ${}_{k}^{h}V_{x:\overline{n}|}$, ${}_{h}P_{x:\overline{n}|}$ and delete the bars over the $M$ symbols.

7.51. $5000\left[{}_{10}\bar{V}(\bar{A}_{30}) + P^{\{1\}}(\bar{A}_{30}) + {}_{11}\bar{V}(\bar{A}_{30})\right]$

7.52. a. 0.2   b. 0.25   c. 0.7584   d. 0.27

*Chapter 8*

8.1. a. ${}_{n}p_{x}\,{}_{n}p_{y}$
 b. ${}_{n}p_{x} + {}_{n}p_{y} - 2\,{}_{n}p_{x}\,{}_{n}p_{y}$
 c. ${}_{n}p_{x} + {}_{n}p_{y} - {}_{n}p_{x}\,{}_{n}p_{y}$
 d. $1 - {}_{n}p_{x}\,{}_{n}p_{y}$
 e. Same as for (d)
 f. $(1 - {}_{n}p_{x})(1 - {}_{n}p_{y}) = 1 - {}_{n}p_{x} - {}_{n}p_{y} + {}_{n}p_{x}\,{}_{n}p_{y}$

8.3. ${}_{n}q_{xx}$

8.5. ${}_{n|}q_{x} + {}_{n|}q_{y} - {}_{n|}q_{x}\,{}_{n|}q_{y}$
 No, since for ${}_{n|}q_{\overline{xy}}$ the second death must occur in year $n+1$ and this is not the case for the requested probability.

8.6. 2/9

8.7. a. 2/3   b. 29/30   c. 18.06   d. 36.94   e. 160.11   f. 182.33
 g. 82.95   h. 0.49

8.8. $\mu_{xx}\,\overset{\circ}{e}_{xx} - 1$

8.11. 531/2000

8.12. An annuity of 1 payable at the end of each year for $n$ years and for as long thereafter as $(xy)$ exists.

8.13. An insurance of 1 payable on the death of $(x)$, or at the end of $n$ years, whichever is later.

8.15. $\bar{a}_{25:\overline{25}|} + \bar{a}_{30:\overline{20}|} - \bar{a}_{25:30:\overline{20}|}$

8.16. ${}_{20|}a_{30} + {}_{25|}a_{25} - {}_{25|}a_{25:30}$

8.17. $\dfrac{1}{6}\ddot{a}_{xy:\overline{n}|} + \dfrac{1}{2}\ddot{a}_{y:\overline{n}|} + \dfrac{1}{3}\ddot{a}_{x:\overline{n}|}$

8.18. $a_{x:\overline{n}|} + v^n \, {}_np_x \, a_{x+n:y:\overline{m-n}|}$

8.19. $_{5|}\bar{a}_{55} + _{20|}\bar{a}_{40} - _{5|10}\bar{a}_{40:55} - _{20|}\bar{a}_{40:55}$

8.20. a. $[\ddot{a}_x^{(m)} + p\,(\ddot{a}_y^{(m)} - \ddot{a}_{xy}^{(m)})]$ b. $\ddot{a}_x^{(m)}/[\ddot{a}_x^{(m)} + p\,(\ddot{a}_y^{(m)} - \ddot{a}_{xy}^{(m)})]$

8.22. a. 7.0753 b. 7.0756

8.25. $w = \dfrac{3}{5}x + \dfrac{2}{5}y$

8.26. 1/3

8.30. $_\infty q_{xy}^1 = {}_\infty q_{xy}^2$

8.33. $\bar{A}_{50} - \bar{A}_{50:20:\overline{20}|}^1$

8.34. $\bar{A}_{x:\overline{n}|}^1 - \bar{A}_{xy}^1 + {}_nE_x \, \bar{A}_{\overline{x+n}:y}^1$

8.35. 1/12

8.36. a. 0.2755 b. $\dfrac{1}{4}\bar{A}_{40:50} + 0.0015\,\bar{a}_{40:50}$

8.37. 1/3, 52.68

8.38. a. $\bar{a}_x + \bar{a}_{\overline{n}|} - \bar{a}_{x:\overline{n}|}$ b. $v^n \, {}_nq_x$

8.40. $\mu_x \, \overset{\circ}{e}_{xy} - {}_\infty q_{xy}^1$

*Chapter 9*

9.1. a. $e^{-t\mu_x^{(\tau)}}\mu_x^{(j)}$ b. $\mu_x^{(j)}/\mu_x^{(\tau)}$ c. $e^{-t\mu_x^{(\tau)}}\mu_x^{(\tau)}$

9.2. a. $j(50-t)^2/50^3$ b. $3(50-t)^2/50^3$ c. $j/3$ d. $j/3$

9.3. $_3p_{65}^{(\tau)} = 0.75321$; $_{3|}q_{65}^{(1)} = 0.03766$; $_3q_{65}^{(2)} = 0.16504$

9.4. a. 302.4 and 210.95 b. 231.0 and 177.64

9.5. a. $h(1) = 0.231$; $h(2) = 0.4666$; $h(3) = 0.3024$
b. $h(1|k=2) = 0.25$; $h(2|k=2) = 0.75$; $h(3|k=2) = 0$

9.6. $l_x^{(\tau)} = (a-x)e^{-x}$; $d_x^{(1)} = e^{-x}(1-e^{-1})$;
$d_x^{(2)} = (a-x-1)e^{-x} - (a-x-2)e^{-x-1}$

9.7. $1000\left[\dfrac{a-x^2}{a}\right]e^{-cx}$

9.8. a. $_tp_x^{(\tau)}[\mu_{x+t}^{(\tau)} - \mu_x^{(\tau)}]$ b. $_tp_x^{(\tau)}\mu_{x+t}^{(j)} + {}_tq_x^{(j)}\mu_x^{(\tau)} - \mu_x^{(j)}$ c. $_tp_x^{(\tau)}\mu_{x+t}^{(j)}$

9.9.

| $k$ | $q_k'^{(1)} = 1 - (p_k^{(\tau)})^{q_k^{(1)}/q_k^{(\tau)}}$ | $q_k'^{(2)} = 1 - (p_k^{(\tau)})^{q_k^{(2)}/q_k^{(\tau)}}$ |
|---|---|---|
| 0 | 0.17433 | 0.27332 |
| 1 | 0.11210 | 0.21163 |
| 2 | 0.05426 | 0.15410 |
| 3 | 0.00000 | 0.10000 |

9.10. a. $1 - e^{-c}$ b. $c$ c. $c\displaystyle\int_0^1 {}_tp_x^{(\tau)}\,dt$

9.12. $m_x'^{(j)} \geq q_x'^{(j)} \geq q_x^{(j)}$

9.13. 0.0592

9.14. a. 0.0909   b. 0.0906

9.15.

| $k$ | $m_k^{(1)}$ | $m_k^{(2)}$ |
|---|---|---|
| 0 | 0.18750 | 0.31250 |
| 1 | 0.11765 | 0.23529 |
| 2 | 0.05556 | 0.16667 |
| 3 | 0.00000 | 0.10526 |

9.16.

| $x$ | $p_x^{(\tau)}$ | $q_x^{(1)}$ | $q_x^{(2)}$ | $q_x^{(3)}$ |
|---|---|---|---|---|
| 62 | 0.76048 | 0.01767 | 0.02665 | 0.19520 |
| 63 | 0.85027 | 0.02054 | 0.03193 | 0.09726 |
| 64 | 0.82115 | 0.02578 | 0.03705 | 0.11603 |

9.17.

| $x$ | $m_x^{(1)} = m_x'^{(1)}$ | $m_x^{(2)} = m_x'^{(2)}$ | $m_x^{(3)} = m_x'^{(3)}$ | $m_x^{(\tau)}$ | $q_x^{(1)}$ | $q_x^{(2)}$ | $q_x^{(3)}$ |
|---|---|---|---|---|---|---|---|
| 62 | 0.02020 | 0.03046 | 0.22222 | 0.27288 | 0.01777 | 0.02680 | 0.19554 |
| 63 | 0.02224 | 0.03459 | 0.10526 | 0.16209 | 0.02057 | 0.03200 | 0.09737 |
| 64 | 0.02840 | 0.04082 | 0.12766 | 0.19688 | 0.02585 | 0.03716 | 0.11622 |

9.19.

| $x$ | $m_x^{(1)}$ | $m_x^{(2)}$ | $m_x'^{(1)}$ | $m_x'^{(2)}$ |
|---|---|---|---|---|
| 65 | 0.02073 | 0.05181 | 0.02073 | 0.05183 |
| 66 | 0.03141 | 0.06283 | 0.03144 | 0.06286 |
| 67 | 0.04233 | 0.07407 | 0.04237 | 0.07412 |
| 68 | 0.05348 | 0.08556 | 0.05355 | 0.08565 |
| 69 | 0.06486 | 0.09730 | 0.06499 | 0.09744 |

9.20. Revise (a) to $m_x^{(j)} \bigg/ \left(1 + \dfrac{1}{2} m_x^{(\tau)}\right)$.

9.22.

| $k$ | $q_k'^{(1)}$ | $q_x'^{(2)}$ |
|---|---|---|
| 0 | 0.17143 | 0.27027 |
| 1 | 0.11111 | 0.21053 |
| 2 | 0.05405 | 0.15385 |
| 3 | 0.00000 | 0.10000 |

9.24. a. From $q_x^{(3)} = q_x'^{(3)} \left[ 1 - \dfrac{1}{2}(q_x'^{(1)} + q_x'^{(2)}) + \dfrac{1}{3} q_x'^{(1)} q_x'^{(2)} \right]$, obtain $q_x'^{(3)}$, then use (9.6.3).

b. Obtain $q_x^{(1)}$ from a relation derived in Exercise 9.18,

$$q_x^{(1)} \cong q_x'^{(1)} \left[ 1 - \frac{1}{2}(q_x^{(2)} + q_x^{(3)}) \right].$$

9.25. $q_{69}^{(3)} = 0.94434$

9.26. $q'^{(1)}_{50} = 0.015$

9.27. If 1 denotes death and 2 withdrawal for any other reason, the actuarial present value is

$$20,000 \int_0^{40} v^t \,_t p^{(\tau)}_{30} \, \mu^{(1)}_{30+t} \, dt + 300 \int_0^{40} v^t \,_t p^{(\tau)}_{30} \, \mu^{(2)}_{30+t} \, t \,_{40-t|}\bar{a}_{30+t} \, dt$$

$$+ 12,000 \, v^{40} \,_{40} p^{(\tau)}_{30} \, \bar{a}_{70}.$$

9.28. $1 - \sum_{k=0}^{44} d^{(2)}_{20+k}/l^{(\tau)}_{20} = 1 - [l^{(2)}_{20} - l^{(2)}_{65}]/l^{(\tau)}_{20}$

9.29. a. Approximate $m^{(1)}_x$, $m^{(2)}_x$ from $q'^{(1)}_x$, $q'^{(2)}_x$, or approximate $q'^{(3)}_x$, $q'^{(4)}_x$ from $m^{(3)}_x$, $m^{(4)}_x$.

   b. $1 - \sum_{k=0}^{\infty} d^{(4)}_{y+k}/l^{(\tau)}_y = 1 - l^{(4)}_y/l^{(\tau)}_y$

9.30.   (The probability of decrement due to cause $j$ when all causes are operating)

   = (the absolute rate of decrement due to cause $j$)

   − (the probability that decrement will occur due to causes $k$, $k \neq j$, and thereafter the event associated with $j$ will occur prior to $(x)$ attaining age $x + 1$.)

9.32. a. $f(t,j) = \dfrac{\theta \beta^\alpha}{\Gamma(\alpha)} t^{\alpha-1} e^{-\beta t} \quad j = 1, t \geq 0$

   $= \dfrac{(1 - \theta) \beta^\alpha t^{\alpha-1} e^{-\beta t}}{\Gamma(\alpha)} \quad j = 2, t \geq 0,$

   $h(j) = \begin{cases} \theta & j = 1 \\ 1 - \theta & j = 2, \end{cases}$

   $g(t) = \dfrac{\beta^\alpha t^{\alpha-1} e^{-\beta t}}{\Gamma(\alpha)}$

   b. $E[T] = \dfrac{\alpha}{\beta}$; $\mathrm{Var}[T] = \dfrac{\alpha}{\beta^2}$

   c.   (i) $L = \begin{cases} vT - \bar{A} & J = 1, \quad T \geq 0 \\ -\bar{A} & J = 2, \quad T \geq 0 \end{cases}$

   (ii) $\bar{A} = \theta(1 + \delta/\beta)^{-\alpha}$

   (iii) $\mathrm{Var}[L] = \theta(1 + 2\delta/\beta)^{-\alpha} - \theta^2(1 + \delta/\beta)^{-2\alpha}$

*Chapter 10*

10.1. a. Take $S_{30} = 1$. Then

$$S_{30+k} = \begin{cases} (1.05)^k & 0 \le k < 10 \\ (1.1)(1.05)^k & 10 \le k < 20 \\ (1.1)^2(1.05)^k & 20 \le k < 30 \\ (1.1)^3(1.05)^k & k \ge 30. \end{cases}$$

b. $1200 \displaystyle\sum_{k=0}^{\omega-31} v^{k+1/2} \,_{k+1/2}p_{30}^{(\tau)} \, S_{30+k}$

10.2. $0.1 \displaystyle\sum_{k=0}^{\omega-36} v^{k+1/2} \,_{k+1/2}p_{35}^{(\tau)} \, [25{,}000\,(S_{35+k}/S_{35}) - 10{,}000\,(1.05)^k]$

10.3. $5940 \, v^{23} \,_{23}p_{40}^{(\tau)} \, \bar{a}_{63}^r$; $3960 \, v^{23} \,_{23}p_{40}^{(\tau)} \, \bar{a}_{63:\overline{2|}}^r$

10.4. Assume $12{,}000\,(_3Z_{25+k}/S_{25}) < 15{,}000\,(1.04)^k$ for $k \le a$, then

$$R(25,0,k) = 120\,k\,(_3Z_{25+k}/S_{25}) \qquad k \le a$$

$$R(25,0,k) = k\,[180\,(_3Z_{25+k}/S_{25}) - 75\,(1.04)^k] \qquad k > a.$$

10.5. a. $R(40,0,25) = 15{,}000\,(_3\tilde{Z}_{65}/S_{40}) - 0.50\,I_{65}$,

where $_3\tilde{Z}_{65} = \dfrac{1}{3}(S_{62} + S_{63} + S_{64})$

b. $R(40,0,28\,{}^1/_2) = 17{,}100\,(_3Z_{68}/S_{40}) - 0.50\,I_{68{}^1/_2}$

10.6. Here $\alpha = 55$, $\omega = 68$

$$\sum_{k=5}^{17} v^{k+1/2} \,_{k}p_{50}^{(\tau)} \, q_{50+k}^{(r)} \, (20 + k + 1/2)\,(_3Z_{50+k}/S_{50})\,480\,\bar{a}_{50+k+1/2}^r$$

$$+ \sum_{k=5}^{14} v^{k+1/2} \,_{k}p_{50}^{(\tau)} \, q_{50+k}^{(r)} \, (20 + k + 1/2)\,(_3Z_{50+k}/S_{50})\,240\,\bar{a}_{50+k+1/2:\overline{15-k-1/2|}}^r.$$

Since $q_{50+k}^{(r)} = 0$ for $k < 5$, these sums could be extended down to $k = 0$.

10.7. The last three terms in the first sum are changed to

$$\sum_{k=15}^{17} v^{k+1/2} \,_{k}p_{50}^{(\tau)} \, q_{50+k}^{(r)} \, (_3Z_{50+k}/S_{50})\,(16{,}800)\,\bar{a}_{50+k+1/2}^r.$$

10.8. In the answer to Exercise 10.6, replace $(20 + k + 1/2)$ by 20.

10.9. a. $R(30,20,15) = 8000 + 720 \displaystyle\sum_{j=0}^{14} S_{50+j}/S_{50}$

b. $R(30,20,15\,{}^1/_2) = 8000 + 720 \left[ \displaystyle\sum_{j=0}^{14} S_{50+j} + (1/2)\,S_{65} \right] \Big/ S_{50}$

c. $8000 \displaystyle\sum_{k=8}^{17} v^{k+1/2} \,_{k}p_{50}^{(\tau)} \, q_{50+k}^{(r)} \, \bar{a}_{50+k+1/2}^r$

d. $\displaystyle\sum_{k=0}^{17} v^{k+1/2}\ {}_kp_{50}^{(\tau)}\ q_{50+k}^{(r)}\ 720\left[\left(\sum_{j=0}^{k-1} S_{50+j} + (1/2)\,S_{50+k}\right)\Big/ S_{50}\right]\bar{a}_{50+k+1/2}^r,$

which equals the sum with $k = 8$ to $17$, or

$$\frac{720}{S_{50}}\left[\sum_{j=0}^{17} S_{50+j}\left(\frac{1}{2}v^{j+1/2}\ {}_jp_{50}^{(\tau)}\ q_{50+j}^{(r)}\ \bar{a}_{50+j+1/2}^r + \sum_{k=j+1}^{17} v^{k+1/2}\ {}_kp_{50}^{(\tau)}\ q_{50+k}^{(r)}\ \bar{a}_{50+k+1/2}^r\right)\right]$$

10.10. $[0.7\,(25{,}000) - 8000]\,\bar{a}_{50^{1/2}}^i = 9500\,\bar{a}_{50^{1/2}}^i$

10.11. $5000\displaystyle\sum_{k=0}^{4} v^{k+1/2}\ {}_kp_{35}^{(\tau)}\ q_{35+k}^{(w)}\ (1.06)^{k+1/2}$

10.12. a. $0.01c\,(AS)_{x+h}\displaystyle\int_0^1 v^t\ {}_tp_{x+h}^{(\tau)}\ \mu_{x+h+t}^{(w)}\int_0^t (1+j)^{t-s}\,ds\,dt$

b. $0.01c\,(AS)_{x+h}\,q_{x+h}^{(w)}\dfrac{1}{\log(1+j)}\left[\dfrac{1-((1+j)/(1+i))}{\log(1+i)-\log(1+j)}\right.$

$\left.-\dfrac{1-(1/(1+i))}{\log(1+i)}\right]$

c. $0.4856429;\ 0.4873039;$ both multiplied by $0.01c\,(AS)_{x+h}\,q_{x+h}^{(w)}$

10.13. a. $1200\,[{}^SN_{30}^{(\tau)}/{}^SD_{30}^{(\tau)}]$

b. $2500\,[{}^S\bar{N}_{35}^{(\tau)}/{}^SD_{35}^{(\tau)}] - [1000\,(1.05)^{-1/2}\,\bar{N}_{35}'^{(\tau)}]/D_{35}'^{(\tau)}$
where $D_y'^{(\tau)} = v^y\,(1.05)^y\,l_y^{(\tau)}$

c. $5940\,(D_{63}^{(\tau)}/D_{40}^{(\tau)})\,\bar{a}_{63}^r;\ 3960\,(D_{63}^{(\tau)}/D_{40}^{(\tau)})\,\bar{a}_{63:\overline{2}|}^r$

d. $\left\{480\displaystyle\sum_{k=5}^{14}(20+k+1/2)\ {}^{Za}\bar{C}_{50+k}^r\right.$

$+\ 240\displaystyle\sum_{k=5}^{14}(20+k+1/2)\ {}^{Za'}\bar{C}_{50+k+1/2}^r$

$\left.+\ 16{,}800\displaystyle\sum_{k=15}^{17}{}^{Za}\bar{C}_{50+k}^r\right\}\Big/{}^SD_{50}^{(\tau)}$

where ${}^{Za'}\bar{C}_{50+k+1/2}^r = {}_3Z_{50+k}\ \bar{C}_{50+k}^r\ \bar{a}_{50+k+1/2:\overline{15-k-1/2}|}^r$

e. $8000\,({}^a\bar{M}_{50}^r/D_{50}^{(\tau)});\ {}^a\bar{M}_{50}^r = {}^a\bar{M}_{58}^r$

f. $\dfrac{720}{{}^SD_{50}^{(\tau)}}\displaystyle\sum_{k=8}^{17}{}^a\bar{C}_{50+k}^r\left(\sum_{j=0}^{k-1}S_{50+j}+\frac{1}{2}S_{50+k}\right)$ or $\dfrac{720}{{}^SD_{50}^{(\tau)}}\left[\frac{1}{2}{}^{Sa}\bar{M}_{50}^r + {}^{S'a}\bar{R}_{51}^r\right]$

10.14. a. $\dfrac{120}{{}^SD_x^{(\tau)}}\displaystyle\sum_{\alpha-x}^{\omega-x-1}k\ {}^{Za}\bar{C}_{x+k}^r = 120\ {}^{Za}\bar{R}_{x+1}^r/{}^SD_x^{(\tau)}$

b. $120\left[\dfrac{1}{2}\ {}^{Za}\bar{M}_x^r + {}^{Za}\bar{R}_{x+1}^r\right]\Big/{}^SD_x^{(\tau)}$

10.15. If $\alpha - x \geq 10$, then the formula is unchanged.

If $\alpha - x < 10$, the formula becomes

$$120\,[10^{1}/_{2}\ {}^{Za}\bar{M}^{r}_{x+10} + {}^{Za}\bar{R}^{r}_{x+11}]/{}^{S}D^{(\tau)}_{x}.$$

10.16. $\left[\dfrac{1}{2}\ {}^{Za}\bar{M}^{r}_{x} + {}^{Za}\bar{R}^{r}_{x+1}\right]\bigg/{}^{S}\bar{N}^{(\tau)}_{x}$

10.17.  a. $1200\,[\bar{N}^{(\tau)}_{50}/D^{(\tau)}_{50}]$

b. $100\,[12\,\bar{N}^{(\tau)}_{50} + \bar{S}^{(\tau)}_{51}]/D^{(\tau)}_{50}$

c. $1200\,(1.04)^{-1/2}\,[(\bar{N}'^{(\tau)}_{50}/D'^{(\tau)}_{50})]$ where $D'^{(\tau)}_{50}$ and $\bar{N}'^{(\tau)}_{50}$ are calculated at interest rate $i' = 0.02/1.04$

10.18. $1500\,[{}^{S}\bar{N}^{(\tau)}_{50}/{}^{S}D^{(\tau)}_{50}] - 0.05\,[{}^{H}\bar{N}^{(\tau)}_{50}/D^{(\tau)}_{50}]$ where ${}^{H}\bar{D}^{(\tau)}_{50+k} = H_{k}\,\bar{D}^{(\tau)}_{50+k}$

10.19.  a. $\left\{450\,[10^{1}/_{2}\ {}^{Za}\bar{M}^{r}_{40} + {}^{Za}\bar{R}^{r}_{41}] + 18{,}000\ {}_{5}\tilde{Z}_{70}\,D^{(\tau)}_{70}\,\bar{a}^{r}_{70}\right.$

$$\left.+ 150\left[\sum_{k=20}^{24}(10 + k + 1/2)\ {}^{Za'}\bar{C}^{r}_{40+k}\right]\right\}\bigg/{}^{S}D^{(\tau)}_{40}$$

where ${}^{Za'}\bar{C}^{r}_{y}$ incorporates the annuity factor $\bar{a}^{r}_{y+(1/2):\overline{65-y-(1/2)}|}$

b. $4500\left\{{}^{Za}\bar{M}^{r}_{60} + {}_{5}\tilde{Z}_{70}\,D^{(\tau)}_{70}\,\bar{a}^{r}_{70} + \dfrac{1}{3}\sum_{k=20}^{24}{}^{Za'}\bar{C}^{r}_{40+k}\right\}\bigg/{}^{S}D^{(\tau)}_{40}$

10.20. $600\left[\dfrac{1}{2}\,v^{1/2}\,q^{(r)}_{62}\,\bar{a}^{r}_{62^{1}/_{2}} + \sum_{k=1}^{8}v^{k+1/2}\ {}_{k}p^{(\tau)}_{62}\,q^{(r)}_{62+k}\,\bar{a}^{r}_{62+k+1/2}\right]$

10.21. (A)

*Chapter 11*

11.1. $S = X_{1} + X_{2} + \cdots + X_{N}$ where $N$ is the number of cars and $X_{i}$ is the number of passengers in car $i$.

11.2. Let $N$ denote the number of rainfalls and $X_{i}$ the number of inches of rain in rainfall $i$.

11.3.  a. $npp_{1}$   b. $npp_{2} - np^{2}p_{1}^{2}$   c. $(pM_{X}(t) + q)^{n}$

11.4.  a. 1.7   b. 0.81   c. 1.6   d. 0.44   e. 2.72   f. 2.82

11.5.  a. 2.72   b. 5.10

11.6. $e^{-2}$, $0.2e^{-2}$, $0.42e^{-2}$, $0.68133e^{-2}$, $1.00807e^{-2}$

11.8. $r = \dfrac{\lambda}{-\log(1-c)}$, $p = 1 - c$

11.9. $\dfrac{3^{24}e^{-3x}}{23!}\,x^{23}$

11.10. Poisson with parameter $\lambda p$

11.11. Compound Poisson with parameter 8 and $p(1) = 0.05$, $p(2) = 0.15$, $p(3) = 0.425$, $p(4) = 0.375$

11.12. Compound Poisson with parameter 14 and $p(-2) = 1/14$, $p(1) = 4/14$, $p(3) = 9/14$

11.13. $\Pr(N = n + 1) = \dfrac{\lambda}{n + 1} \Pr(N = n)$

11.15. a. 0.425   b. 0.3984   c. 0.184; no:
$\Pr(N_1 = 1, N_2 = 1) \neq \Pr(N_1 = 1)\Pr(N_2 = 1)$

11.20. a. $\beta = \sqrt{\alpha},\ x_0 = -\sqrt{\alpha}$   b. $N(0,1)$

11.21. a. $\Phi(2) = 0.9772$   b. $G\left(\dfrac{44}{3} : \dfrac{256}{9}, \dfrac{8}{3}\right)$

11.22. b. (i) $\dfrac{p_2}{\lambda\,[p_1(1 + \theta)]^2}$   (ii) $\dfrac{p_2 + (q/p)\,p_1^2}{(rq/p)\,[p_1(1 + \theta)]^2}$

*Chapter 12*

12.1. $\dfrac{f(t - s)}{1 - F(t - s)} dt$

12.3. $0;\ \gamma$

12.5. a. 3   b. 1

12.6. $\dfrac{10}{7 \log 2} - 1$

12.8. a. $-1$   b. $e^{-\bar{R}(u+1)}$   c. $\log \dfrac{p}{q}$   d. $\left(\dfrac{q}{p}\right)^{u+1}$

12.12. a. $\left(\dfrac{1}{2}\right)\left(\dfrac{p_2}{p_1}\right)$   b. $\left(\dfrac{1}{3}\right)\left(\dfrac{p_3}{p_1}\right)$   c. $\left(\dfrac{1}{3}\right)\left(\dfrac{p_3}{p_1}\right) - \left(\dfrac{1}{4}\right)\left(\dfrac{p_2}{p_1}\right)^2$

12.13. b. $E[L] = \left(\dfrac{1}{2}\right)\left(\dfrac{p_2}{\theta p_1}\right),\ \mathrm{Var}[L] = \left(\dfrac{1}{3}\right)\left(\dfrac{p_3}{\theta p_1}\right) + \left(\dfrac{1}{4}\right)\left(\dfrac{p_2}{\theta p_1}\right)^2$

12.14. $\dfrac{2\theta r}{1 + (1 + \theta)\,2r - e^{2r}}$

12.15. a. $\dfrac{2}{3}$   b. 2

12.16. $p_1 = \displaystyle\sum_{i=1}^{n} \dfrac{A_i}{B_i}$

12.17. a. $\dfrac{5}{27}$   b. $\dfrac{4}{5}$   c. $\dfrac{-17r + 54}{3\,(3 - r)\,(6 - r)}$

d. $\left(\dfrac{4}{9}\right)\left(\dfrac{10 - 3r}{8 - 6r + r^2}\right) = \left(\dfrac{4}{9}\right)\left(\dfrac{2}{2 - r}\right) + \left(\dfrac{1}{9}\right)\left(\dfrac{4}{4 - r}\right)$

e. $\psi(u) = \dfrac{4}{9}e^{-2u} + \dfrac{1}{9}e^{-4u}$   Check: $\psi(0) = \dfrac{5}{9} = \dfrac{1}{1 + \theta}$

12.18. a. $\dfrac{10}{3}$   b. 2   c. $\dfrac{9}{(3 - 5r)^2}$

d. $\left(\dfrac{2}{3}\right)\left(\dfrac{0.12 - 0.1\,r}{0.24 - 1.1\,r + r^2}\right) = \dfrac{0.4\,(0.3)}{0.3 - r} - \dfrac{0.067\,(0.8)}{0.8 - r}$

e. $\psi(u) = 0.4\,e^{-0.3u} - 0.067\,e^{-0.8u}$

12.19.  a. $\xi = \dfrac{\theta}{1 + \theta};\ E[L] = \left(\dfrac{1}{1 + \theta}\right)\left(\dfrac{\alpha}{\beta}\right);$

$E[L^2] = \dfrac{1}{1 + \theta}\left[\dfrac{\alpha^2}{\beta^2} + \dfrac{\alpha}{\beta^2}\right]$

b. $\psi(u) = \dfrac{1}{1 + \theta}[1 - G(u{:}\alpha,\beta)]$

12.21.  a. $fc,\ f\lambda,\ \psi(u, ft)$   b. $1/\lambda$

12.22.  a. $\psi'(u) = \begin{cases} \dfrac{\lambda}{c}\,\psi(u) - \dfrac{\lambda}{c} & 0 \le u \le 1 \\[2ex] \dfrac{\lambda}{c}\,\psi(u) - \dfrac{\lambda}{c}\,\psi(u - 1) & u > 1 \end{cases}$

b. $\psi(u) = 1 - \left(1 - \dfrac{\lambda}{c}\right)e^{(\lambda/c)u}$     $0 \le u \le 1$

*Chapter 13*

13.1.  b. $b^2 pq$
      c. $s = 0.233$

13.3.  a. 31.35 days   b. $2.99848\,c$

13.4.  a. 0.13022   b. 0.09823   c. 0.05683

13.5.  a. $E[S] = 4.7;\ \mathrm{Var}[S] = 16.40$
      b. $\lambda = 1.7;\ p(1) = 7/17;\ p(4) = 10/17;\ 16.7$

13.6.  a. $\displaystyle\sum_{j=1}^{n} b_j\,\tilde\lambda_j;\ \sum_{j=1}^{n} b_j^2\,\tilde\lambda_j$   c. $167, 293$

13.7.  $\dfrac{q_i\,q_j}{\displaystyle\sum\sum_{k<l} q_k\,q_l}$

13.9.  $\sigma\phi\left(\dfrac{d - \mu}{\sigma}\right) - (d - \mu)\left[1 - \Phi\left(\dfrac{d - \mu}{\sigma}\right)\right]$

13.10.  a. $-[1 - F(x)]$   b. $f(x + 1)$

13.11.  $f(x) = 2x,\ 0 < x < 1$

13.12.

| $x$ | $f(x)$ | $F(x)$ | $E[I_x]$ |
|---|---|---|---|
| 0 | 0.050 | 0.050 | 3.500 |
| 1 | 0.124 | 0.174 | 2.550 |
| 2 | 0.180 | 0.354 | 1.724 |

13.13. a. 0.3885   b. 0.985

13.14. $0.8\,E[I_d] - 0.8\,E[I_l]$ where $l = d + m/0.8$

13.15. 3.758

13.16. a. $R = \dfrac{\theta - \alpha\xi}{(1-\alpha)\,[(1+\theta) - (1+\xi)\,\alpha]}$

b. $\dfrac{\theta - \xi\alpha}{1-\alpha}$   Check: Reduces to $\theta$ if $\xi = \theta$

c. $\alpha < \theta/\xi$ if $\theta < \xi$

13.17. a. $1 + [(1+\theta) - (1+\xi)\,e^{-\beta}]\,r = \dfrac{1 - e^{-(1-r)\beta}}{1-r} + e^{-(1-r)\beta}$

b. $\dfrac{\theta - \xi e^{-\beta}}{1 - e^{-\beta}}$   Check: Reduces to $\theta$ if $\xi = \theta$

13.19. $H_d = \dfrac{1}{\alpha} \log\left\{ \Phi\!\left(\dfrac{d-\mu}{\sigma}\right)\right.$

$\left. + \left[1 - \Phi\!\left(\dfrac{d-\mu}{\sigma} - \alpha\sigma\right)\right] \exp[\alpha\,(\mu - d) + \alpha^2\,\sigma^2/2]\right\}$

Note: The answer of Exercise 13.9 is the limit of $H_d$ when $\alpha \to 0$.

*Chapter 14*

14.1.

| | | | | |
|---|---|---|---|---|
| Savings Account | 566.50 | | Reserves | 485.44 |
| | | | Surplus | 81.06 |
| | 566.50 | | | 566.50 |
| | Premium income | 550.00 | | |
| | Interest income | 16.50 | | |
| | | 566.50 | | |
| | Increase in reserves | 485.44 | | |
| | Net income | 81.06 | | |

14.3. $\dfrac{1000\,\bar{A}_{[40]:\overline{25|}} + 8.50 + 4\,\ddot{a}_{[40]:\overline{25|}}}{0.93\,\ddot{a}_{[40]:\overline{25|}} + 0.05\,_{10}E_{[40]}\,\ddot{a}_{[40]+10:\overline{15|}} - 0.35}$

14.4. $[1000\,\bar{A}_{x:\overline{n|}} + 2.50 + 2.50\,\ddot{a}_{x:\overline{n|}}]/(0.935)$

14.5. $a = (1 + e_0 + e_2 + e_3);\ c = (e_1 + e_0 d)$

14.8. a. $k = 200$   b. $\bar{b} = 20$   c. $m = \sqrt{200}$   d. $R(\bar{b}) = 30.12$

14.11. $\bar{\beta} = \dfrac{\bar{A}_x}{(\bar{I}\bar{a})_{x:\overline{m|}}/m + {}_{m|}\bar{a}_x}$

$_t\bar{V}(\bar{A}_x)^{Mod} = \bar{A}_{x+t} - \bar{\beta}\left[\dfrac{(\bar{I}\bar{a})_{x+t:\overline{m-t|}}}{m} + \dfrac{t}{m}\,\bar{a}_{x+t:\overline{m-t|}} + {}_{m-t|}\bar{a}_{x+t}\right]$

14.12. $\alpha_x^{Mod} = A^1_{x:\overline{1|}} + K\,{}_1E_x;\ \beta_x^{Mod} = P_{x+1} - K/\ddot{a}_{x+1}$

14.17. a. $\beta = 0.03$; $\alpha = 0.01$; $\beta - \alpha < 0.05$   b.  0.28   d.  0.0867
e.  0.0278

14.18. $\beta^{Com}_{x:\overline{15}|} = P_{x:\overline{15}|} + \dfrac{_{19}P_{x+1} - A^1_{x:\overline{1}|}}{\ddot{a}_{x:\overline{15}|}}$; $\alpha^{Com}_{x:\overline{15}|} = \beta_{x:\overline{15}|} - (_{19}P_{x+1} - A^1_{x:\overline{1}|})$

14.19. $\alpha = \beta^{Com}_{x:\overline{20}|} - (_{19}P_{x+1} - A^1_{x:\overline{1}|})$; $\beta = (P_{x:\overline{20}|}\, \ddot{a}_{x:\overline{15}|} - \alpha)/a_{x:\overline{14}|}$

14.20. $T = \beta^{Com} - _{19}P_{x+1}$

*Chapter 15*

15.1.  0.0738

15.2.  $1.046\, P_x + 0.0026$; $1.06\, P_x + 0.0034$

15.3.  $_tW'_x \gtreqless\, _tW_x$ according as $\dfrac{P'_{x+t}}{P_{x+t}} \gtreqless \dfrac{P'_x}{P_x}$

15.4.  $\dfrac{b}{2} + \left(\dfrac{b}{2} - 1\right) \dfrac{A^1_{x+t:\overline{n-t}|}}{_{n-t}E_{x+t}}$

15.5.  a.  $\{_{10}CV - L - (1 - L)\, \bar{A}^1_{40:\overline{10}|}\}/_{10}E_{40}$   b.  $(1 - L)\, \bar{A}^1_{45:\overline{5}|} + E\, _5E_{45}$

15.6.  $_{10}^{20}W_{40} = 0.5829$, $_{10}W_{40:\overline{20}|} = 0.6232$, proportional amount $= 0.5$

15.9.  Whole life: $1 - P^a_x/P_{x+k}$; $n$-Payment Life: $1 - _nP^a_x/_{n-k}P_{x+k}$;
$n$-Year Endowment: $1 - P^a_{x:\overline{n}|}/P_{x+k:\overline{n-k}|}$

15.10.  Whole Life: $1 - P_{x+1}/P_{x+k}$
$n$-Payment Life: $1 - \beta^{Com}/_{n-k}P_{x+k}$ where
$$\beta^{Com} = _nP_x + (_{19}P_{x+1} - A^1_{x:\overline{1}|})/\ddot{a}_{x:\overline{n}|}$$
$n$-Year Endowment: $1 - \beta^{Com}/P_{x+k:\overline{n-k}|}$ where
$$\beta^{Com} = P_{x:\overline{n}|} + (_{19}P_{x+1} - A^1_{x:\overline{1}|})/\ddot{a}_{x:\overline{n}|}$$

15.11.  c.  $\bar{a}_x\, G\, e^{\delta t} + \bar{a}_{x+k+t}\, (\mu_{x+k+t} + \delta) - 1$

15.12.  $(G_2 - G_1) \displaystyle\sum_{k=0}^{9} (1 - c_k)\, l^{(\tau)}_{x+k}\, (1 + i)^{10-k}/l^{(\tau)}_{x+10}$

15.14.  b.  $\left(\dfrac{1 + \hat{\imath}_{h+1}}{1 + i}\right) \left(\dfrac{p_{x+h}}{\hat{p}_{x+h}}\right)$

15.15.  $_hV' > _hV$

15.17.  b.  $P_x + c/\ddot{a}_x$

*Chapter 16*

16.3.  b.  (i) $H'(G) = 1 - r - \rho\, \bar{A}^1_{x:\overline{\rho G}|}$; $H''(G) = -\rho^2\, _{\rho G}p_x\, \mu_{x+\rho G}$

16.8.  $(\bar{A}^1_{x:\overline{15}|} - v^{20}\, _{15}q_x)/\delta + \bar{a}_{\overline{5}|}(\bar{A}^1_{x:\overline{20}|} - \bar{A}^1_{x:\overline{15}|})$, or
$\bar{a}_{\overline{20}|} - \bar{a}_{x:\overline{20}|} + v^{20}\, _{15}p_x\, \bar{a}_{x+15:\overline{5}|} - v^{20}\, _{20}p_x\, \bar{a}_{\overline{5}|}$

16.9.  $[1000\, A^1_{x:\overline{20}|} + 120\,(a^{(12)}_{\overline{20}|} - a^{(12)}_{x:\overline{20}|})]/\ddot{a}_{x:\overline{20}|}$

16.11.  a.
$$Z = \begin{cases} v^T \bar{a}_{\overline{25-T}|} & T \le 15 \\ v^T \bar{a}_{\overline{10}|} & 15 < T \le 25 \\ v^{25} \bar{a}_{\overline{10}|} & 25 < T \le 35 \\ v^{25} \bar{a}_{\overline{T-25}|} & T > 35 \end{cases}$$

b. $\displaystyle \int_0^{15} v^t\, \bar{a}_{\overline{25-t}|}\, {}_tp_{40}\, \mu_{40+t}\, dt + \bar{a}_{\overline{10}|} \int_{15}^{25} v^t\, {}_tp_{40}\, \mu_{40+t}\, dt$

$\displaystyle + v^{25}\, \bar{a}_{\overline{10}|} \int_{25}^{35} {}_tp_{40}\, \mu_{40+t}\, dt + v^{25} \int_{35}^{\infty} \bar{a}_{\overline{t-25}|}\, {}_tp_{40}\, \mu_{40+t}\, dt.$

16.19.  203,421

16.20.  a. 55   b. 53,759.04

16.21.  a. $12{,}000 \left[ {}^{65}_{60}\bar{M}^i_{35} + \dfrac{1}{24} v^{1/2}\, {}_{60}\bar{M}^i_{35} \right] \Big/ (N_{35} - N_{60})$

b. $12{,}000\, [{}^{20}_{15}\pi^i_{45} - {}^{30}_{25}\pi^i_{35}]\, \ddot{a}_{45:\overline{15}|}$ where $12{,}000\, {}^{30}_{25}\pi^i_{35}$, $12{,}000\, {}^{20}_{15}\pi^i_{45}$ are the net annual premiums for the benefit for (35) and (45), respectively

16.22.  120,   280

*Chapter 17*

17.1.  a. An even number of $(w)$, $(x)$, $(y)$, $(z)$ survive to time $t$.
b. An odd number of $(w)$, $(x)$, $(y)$, $(z)$ survive to time $t$.

17.3.  a. 6.5   b. 3,237

17.4.  ${}_tB_3 - 3\, {}_tB_4$ where ${}_tB_3 = {}_tp_{wxy} + {}_tp_{wxz} + {}_tp_{wyz} + {}_tp_{xyz}$ and ${}_tB_4 = {}_tp_{wxyz}$

17.5.  $a_w - (a_{wxy} + a_{wxz} + a_{wyz}) + 2\, a_{wxyz}$

17.6.  0.624

17.7.  a. $15\,(\bar{a}_x + \bar{a}_y + \bar{a}_z) - 10\,(\bar{a}_{xy} + \bar{a}_{xz} + \bar{a}_{yz}) + 9\,\bar{a}_{xyz}$
b. $15\,\bar{a}_x - 5\,(\bar{a}_{xy} + \bar{a}_{xz}) + 3\,\bar{a}_{xyz}$

17.8.  4.6

17.9.  a. $12{,}000\,[a^{(12)}_{40:\overline{25}|} + a^{(12)}_{35:\overline{25}|} - 2\,a^{(12)}_{40:35:\overline{25}|}]$
b. $12{,}000\,[a^{(12)}_{40:\overline{25}|} + a^{(12)}_{35:\overline{30}|} - a^{(12)}_{40:35:\overline{25}|}]$

17.10.  a. $\bar{a}_n + \bar{a}_x + \bar{a}_y - \bar{a}_{x:\overline{m}|} - \bar{a}_{y:\overline{m}|} - \bar{a}_{xy} + \bar{a}_{xy:\overline{m}|}$
b. $\bar{a}_{25:\overline{40}|} + \bar{a}_{\overline{30}|} - \bar{a}_{25:\overline{30}|}$

17.11.  a. $\dfrac{1}{7}$   b. $\dfrac{26}{105}$   c. $\dfrac{64}{105}$

17.12.  I is false. Change right-hand side to $\bar{A}^4_{wxyz} + \bar{A}^4_{wxyz} + \bar{A}^4_{wxyz} + \bar{A}^4_{wxyz}$.
II is true. Each side provides for a unit payable on the second death.

III is false. Correct formula is $\bar{A}_{w\bar{z}}^{1} + \bar{A}_{x\bar{z}}^{1} + \bar{A}_{y\bar{z}}^{1} - 2(\bar{A}_{wx\bar{z}}^{1} + \bar{A}_{wy\bar{z}}^{1} + \bar{A}_{xy\bar{z}}^{1}) + 3\bar{A}_{wxy\bar{z}}^{1}$.

17.13. $\displaystyle\int_{0}^{\infty} v^{t}\ {}_{t}p_{xy}\ \mu_{y+t}\ t\ \bar{A}_{x+t}\ dt$

17.14. a. 5/7   b. 3/7

17.15. $A_{z:\overline{10|}}\ [\bar{A}_{y:\overline{z+10}}^{1} - \bar{A}_{xy:\overline{z+10}}^{1}] - A_{yz:\overline{10|}}\ [\bar{A}_{y+10:\overline{z+10}}^{1} - \bar{A}_{x:y+10:\overline{z+10}}^{1}]$

17.16. $v^{10}[\bar{A}_{xy}^{1} + \bar{A}_{xz}^{1} - \bar{A}_{xyz}^{1}] - A_{y:\overline{10|}}\ \bar{A}_{x:y+10}^{1} - A_{z:\overline{10|}}\ \bar{A}_{x:z+10}^{1}$

   $+ A_{zy:\overline{10|}}\ \bar{A}_{x:y+10:z+10}^{1}$

17.17. $\left(\bar{A}_{30:\overline{5|}}^{1} + A_{30:\overline{5|}}^{1}\ \bar{A}_{35:60}^{1}\right) \Big/ \left(\dfrac{1}{1.075} - A_{30:\overline{5|}}^{1}\ \bar{A}_{35:60}^{1}\right)$

17.20. a. $\displaystyle\int_{0}^{\infty} (1 - {}_{t}p_{w})\ {}_{t}p_{xyz}\ \mu_{x+t}\ dt$   b. $_{\infty}q_{xyz}^{1} - _{\infty}q_{wxyz}^{1}$

17.22. a. 25/72   b. 19/36   c. 5/8

17.23. 0.07

17.24. a. 0.3   b. 0.2   c. 0.03

17.25. $\displaystyle\int_{10}^{15} (1 - {}_{t-10}p_{x})\ {}_{t}p_{y}\ \mu_{y+t}\ ({}_{t+10}p_{z} - {}_{25}p_{z})\ dt$

17.26. $\displaystyle\int_{0}^{30} (1 - {}_{t}p_{10})\ {}_{t}p_{20}\ \mu_{20+t}\ ({}_{t}p_{30} - {}_{30}p_{30})\ dt$

   $+ \displaystyle\int_{0}^{30} (1 - {}_{t}p_{30})\ {}_{t}p_{20}\ \mu_{20+t}\ ({}_{t}p_{10} - {}_{50}p_{10})\ dt$

   $+ \displaystyle\int_{30}^{40} (1 - {}_{30}p_{30})\ {}_{t}p_{20}\ \mu_{20+t}\ ({}_{t}p_{10} - {}_{50}p_{10})\ dt$

17.27. 0.2145

17.28. 0.2704

17.29. I is false. $\bar{A}_{\substack{wxyz \\ 1\ 2}}^{3} = \displaystyle\int_{0}^{\infty} v^{t}\ {}_{t}q_{w}\ {}_{t}p_{xyz}\ \mu_{x+t}\ \bar{A}_{y+t:z+t}^{1}\ dt$

II is true. Both sides give the probability that (50) and (60) will die within 10 years of each other.

III is true. $_{\infty}q_{40:\overline{50:60}}^{1}$ is the probability that (40) dies before the survivor of (50), (60) and hence is the probability that (40) dies first or second.

17.31. $\alpha(12)\ \ddot{a}_{x|y:\overline{10|}} + \beta(12)\ v^{10}\ {}_{10}p_{y}\ {}_{10}q_{x}$

17.32. a. $\bar{a}_{\overline{10|}} - \bar{a}_{x:\overline{10|}} + v^{10}\ \bar{a}_{y} - v^{10}\ {}_{10}p_{x}\ \bar{a}_{x+10:y}$

   b. $\bar{a}_{\overline{10|}}\ \bar{A}_{xy}^{1} + v^{10}\ \bar{a}_{x|y}$

17.33. $G = \left[\left(\dfrac{2}{3}\right)(\ddot{a}_{x|y} + {}_{n|}\ddot{a}_x) + \left(\dfrac{1}{3}\right)({}_{n|}\ddot{a}_{xy})\right]\Big/(0.92 - {}_nA_{xy}^2)$

17.35. $\bar{A}_{x+n:y}^{\;1}/(\ddot{s}_{x:\overline{n}|} + \ddot{a}_{x+n:y})$

17.36. $\ddot{a}_{xyz}$

17.37. b. $\ddot{a}_{\overline{xy}:\overline{m}|} + v^m\,{}_mp_x\,(1 - {}_mp_y)\,\ddot{a}_{x+m:\overline{n-m}|}$

17.39. The net single premium for an insurance of 1 payable on $(z)$'s death, provided $(x)$, $(y)$ and $(z)$ die in that order and $(z)$ dies within 10 years after the death of $(y)$

*Chapter 18*

18.1. a. 45   b. 2   c. 2

18.2. $2500\sqrt{2} + \dfrac{10{,}000}{\pi}$

18.3. $10{,}000\,[e^{-1/4} - e^{-1/2} - (e^{-1}/4)]$

18.4. $100^2\,[e^{-51/100} - e^{-50/100} + e^{-28/100} - e^{-27/100}] + 100\,[e^{-1/4} + e^{-53/100}]$

18.5. $T_{20} - T_{40} - 20\,l_{70}$

18.6. $\displaystyle\int_{20}^{50} l(x,-x)\,dx - \int_{70}^{80} l(x,50-x)\,dx - \int_{30}^{50} l(80,t-80)\,dt$

18.8. $b\,\dfrac{\sqrt{2\,\pi}}{\sqrt{a}}\,[1 - \Phi(R/\sqrt{a})]\,\exp[R\,t + (R^2/2\,a)]$

18.9. $a + \dfrac{(\bar{I}\bar{a})'_{a:\overline{r-a}|}}{\bar{a}'_{a:\overline{r-a}|}};\ \displaystyle\int_a^r x\,l_x\,dx/(T_a - T_r)$

18.11. a. $e^{-Rx}s(x)(R + \mu_x);\ 1 - e^{-Rx}s(x)$

18.15. 0.02

18.17. a. $[\Gamma(\alpha)]^{1/\alpha} - \beta$   b. stationary

18.18. b. $a$   c. $(\log b)/c$

*Chapter 19*

19.1. $W(T_a - T_r)$

19.2. $n\,e^{R(t-a)+\tau t}\displaystyle\int_a^r e^{-Ry}s(y)\,w(y)\,dy$

19.3. b. $l(r,t-r+a)\,\bar{a}_r^h(f/b)\displaystyle\int_0^b w(r-y)\,g(t-y)\,dy$

c. ${}^TP(t+u) = n\,e^{R(t+u-r+a)}s(r)\,\bar{a}_r'\,(f/b)\displaystyle\int_0^b w(r-y)\,e^{\tau(t+u-y)}\,dy$

$= e^{\rho u}\,{}^TP(t).$

19.4.  a.  $c(r-a)\,w(r)\,e^{\tau t}\,l(x,t-r+a)\,\bar{a}_h^r$

b.  ${}^T\!P(t+u) = c(r-a)\,w(r)\,e^{\tau(t+u)}\,n\,e^{R(t-r+a)}\,s(r)\,\bar{a}_r' = e^{\rho u}\,{}^T\!P(t)$

19.5.  $e^{\rho t}\,e^{-(R+\mu)(r-a)}\,f\,w(r)\,\bar{a}_r'$

19.6.  $\mathrm{M}(x) = \begin{cases} 0 & x < r \\ 1 & x \ge r \end{cases}$

19.7.  $f w(r)\,\bar{a}_r'\,e^{-(R+\mu)(r-a)}\,e^{\rho t}\,\dfrac{\bar{a}_{\overline{r-a}|\theta}}{r-a}$  where  $\theta = \delta - \rho$

19.11.  a.  $P(t) = \exp(-\delta[r - X(\delta)])\,{}^T\!P(t);$

$(aV)(t) = {}^T\!P(t)\,\bar{a}_{\overline{r-X(\delta)}|\delta} = P(t)\,\bar{s}_{\overline{r-X(\delta)}|\delta}$

b.  $P(t) = {}^T\!P(t);\ (aV)(t) = {}^T\!P(t)\,(r-\mu)$  where  $\mu = \displaystyle\int_a^r x\,m(x)\,dx$

19.12.  a.  $\dfrac{f\,w(r)\,g(u+r-a)\,e^{-\delta r}\,l(r,u)\,\bar{a}_r^h}{\displaystyle\int_a^r w(y)\,g(u+y-a)\,e^{-\delta y}\,l(y,u)\,dy}$

b.  $\dfrac{e^{-\delta x}\,l(x,u)\,w(x)\,g(u+x-a)}{\displaystyle\int_a^r e^{-\delta y}\,l(y,u)\,w(y)\,g(u+y-a)\,dy}$

19.18.  a.  $\bar{a}_{\overline{X(\theta)-a}|\theta}$   b.  $\mu - a$  where  $\mu = \displaystyle\int_a^r x\,m(x)\,dx$